THE
GREENWOOD GUIDE
TO AMERICAN
POPULAR CULTURE

THE
GREENWOOD GUIDE
TO AMERICAN
POPULAR CULTURE

Volume IV

Edited by M. Thomas Inge and
Dennis Hall

GREENWOOD PRESS
Westport, Connecticut • London

Library of Congress Cataloging-in-Publication Data

The Greenwood Guide to American popular culture / edited by M. Thomas Inge and Dennis Hall.
    p.   cm.
    Includes bibliographical references and index.
    ISBN 0–313–30878–0 (set : alk. paper)—ISBN 0–313–32367–4 (v. 1 : alk. paper)—
    ISBN 0–313–32368–2 (v. 2 : alk. paper)—ISBN 0–313–32369–0 (v. 3 : alk. paper)—
    ISBN 0–313–32370–4 (v. 4 : alk. paper)
    1. Popular culture—United States.   2. Popular culture—United States—History—Sources.
    3. Popular culture—United States—Bibliography.   I. Inge, M. Thomas.   II. Hall, Dennis.
E169.1.H2643   2002
306.4'0973—dc21   2002071291

British Library Cataloguing in Publication Data is available.

Library of Congress Catalog Card Number: 2002071291
ISBN: 0–313–30878–0 (set)
        0–313–32367–4 (v. 1)
        0–313–32368–2 (v. 2)
        0–313–32369–0 (v. 3)
        0–313–32370–4 (v. 4)

First published in 2002

Greenwood Press, 88 Post Road West, Westport, CT 06881
An imprint of Greenwood Publishing Group, Inc.
www.greenwood.com

Printed in the United States of America

The paper used in this book complies with the
Permanent Paper Standard issued by the National
Information Standards Organization (Z39.48–1984).

10 9 8 7 6 5 4 3 2 1

For
Donária Carvalho Inge
and
Susan Hall

They stood by their men.

CONTENTS

Contents

Contents

PULPS AND DIME NOVELS

Bill Blackbeard

HISTORICAL OUTLINE

Until about twenty years ago, the terms *pulp*, *pulp magazine*, and *pulp fiction* were writers' and publishers' trade terms, little known to, or used by, the general public. Readers who bought such magazines as *Dime Detective*, *Argosy*, *Blue Book*, and *Weird Tales* in the 1930s and 1940s did not think of these popular titles as pulps, but just as fiction magazines or, more generically, according to subject matter, as detective story magazines, adventure story magazines, fantasy magazines, and so on. Infrequent and casual articles in such magazines as *Esquire* and *Vanity Fair* dealing with the phenomenon of the popular fiction magazines did, of course, use the term *pulp*, but it did not gain broad usage. From the point of view of general readers, who once absorbed reams of pulp fiction as they do hours of television today, the paper on which their reading matter was printed was simply irrelevant. A western novel serialized in the slick-paper magazine *Saturday Evening Post* could, in their eyes, be quite as entertaining as another printed on pulp paper in *Wild West Weekly*. They read the latter magazine largely because the more eclectic *Post* did not publish enough western fiction to satisfy their specialized cravings over a given period of time.

To the magazine publishers and their potential advertisers, however, the quality of paper used was a vital concern. So-called slick paper, made of rag content stock, afforded a highly desirable surface for the reproduction of advertisements, particularly those involving a lavish use of color. Unfortunately, slick paper was a costly item and was economically feasible only for very large-circulation magazines, such as the *Saturday Evening Post*, *Collier's*, or *Life*, of low newsstand cost supported in large part by their advertising revenue, or for more highly priced "quality" magazines, such as *Esquire*, the *New Yorker*, or *Vanity Fair*, with an "elite" appeal, again substantially supported by their advertisements. Pulp paper, on the other hand, prepared from a wood-fiber base and also called *newsprint*, largely in newspaper publishing circles, was much cheaper than *slick* or coated paper, and its use made it possible for publishers so inclined to reach a mass reading market at low prices without any substantial financial aid from advertisers. (For this reason, "radical" political journals, which tended to alienate advertisers per se, almost always appeared on the cheapest kind of pulp paper stock, generally called *butcher paper* by its left-wing users of the time.)

Many different kinds of magazines with low advertising content utilized pulp paper, such as the early color comic strip magazines (some of which, like *Harper's* and the *Atlantic*, used a high-grade of wood-based paper, called *book paper* in the publishing world); newspaper book review and entertainment supplements; and scholastic, library, and book trade publications. However, only the popular fiction or all-fiction magazine acquired the name *pulp* from its writers and editors in the decades following the turn of the twentieth century, and it is, with this widely circulated, enormously varied body of publications that we are concerned here.

In referring to the pulp fiction magazine in these pages, we are speaking of a specific, readily defined kind of periodical, found only in six sizes and forms, all of which share in common wood-pulp paper and a two-column text. The most frequently encountered form of pulp magazine is a sheaf of several octavo signatures, stapled together at two equidistant points near the spine, enclosed with a slick cover attached with glue over the flat area of the spine, and usually featuring interior illustrations, as well as color printing on the outside of the cover. This basic form of pulp magazine is found in three sizes: the large "flat" of about 8 ½" × 11", usually about ¼" to 1" thick with trimmed page edges and composed of three to four signatures (or, very occasionally, perfect bound, with or without staples); the median, standard size (representing the vast majority of all pulps) of 10" × 7" untrimmed, or about 9" × 6 ½" trimmed, averaging ⅓" to ½" in thickness (some exceptional pulps of this size can go to 2" or more of thickness), made up of six to twelve signatures (or again, in rare instances, dozens of signatures); and the "digest" size, of about 7 ½" to 5", ¼" to ½" thick (with some rare titles reaching an inch or more), almost always trimmed, and involving six to eight signatures (or perfect bound, with or without staples).

A much less frequent form of pulp magazine is the saddle-stitched, single-signature variety. The standard binding (at 9" × 6 ½") for most of the nickel thrillers of the 1880s and later, as well as for virtually all comic books, saddle-stitching (two staples inserted at the signature fold) is most often encountered in pulps in the form of the under-the-counter sex story magazines of the 1920s and 1930s (with marked variations in the 9" × 6 ½" measurements cited for nonpulp formats). Saddle-stitching is also to be seen, although very uncommonly, in some digest science fiction and detective pulps, mostly in the 1950s.

The all-fiction magazine, by its nature, emphasized a basic broad appeal in its writing and narrative content. Here and there, especially in its later closing years, the pulp magazine might chance a "difficult," experimental piece of fiction, because of real editorial enthusiasm and a feeling that one such item in a given issue would not alienate finicky readers provided with a half dozen other standard pieces of fiction. Even in such work some kind of straightforward narrative progress had to be in evidence, so that while as bizarre a writer as H. P. Lovecraft or Joel Townsley Rogers could (and did) appear regularly in pulps, a post-*Dubliners* James Joyce or a contemporary equivalent of John Barth probably would not. Basically,

A mystery dime novel. pulpworld.com

the all-fiction magazines provided a market for genre fiction that, often because of pe-culiar editorial biases as much as any real lack of intrinsic merit, failed to sell to the very limited, but higher-paying, slick-paper magazine markets. While much of the pulp magazine content was, understandably, a mass-produced, stereotyped product seized upon by editors desperate to fill the endless pages of twenty or more titles a month in publishing house after publishing house, virtually all of the fine fiction writtten in America between the turn of the century and the close of the 1940s found print in these magazines if it could not find it in the slicks or literary journals. Much worthwhile material is still being uncovered today and reprinted to critical applause; indeed, in the case of some long-neglected writers, separate publishing houses with a largely academic clientele have been founded essentially to republish the works of such authors complete in successive, highly priced volumes.

It should be kept in mind, however, that the widespread belief that pulp-paper magazines printed popular fiction for vast masses of readers, while slick-paper mag-azines published quality material for more tasteful, elite readers is simply wrong. The reverse, in fact, was true. While such magazines as the *Saturday Evening Post*, *Collier's*, *Ladies' Home Journal*, *Cosmopolitan*, and the *American Magazine* sold in the many millions of issues monthly at generally very low prices, the pulps in general retailed at the higher prices only in the low tens of thousands at best, with such primary titles as *Argosy* or *Blue Book* barely 80,000 or 90,000 copies per issue at peak circulation in the prosperous 1920s. While the nickel slicks were bought by literally everybody—the millions who stare at television today bought the slicks then to marvel at the full-color story illustrations and the endless pages of color ads, without really reading much of the text—the pulps were bought by a small elite of fiction devotees who *really* read what they bought and wanted *much* more of the detective stories, air war stories, westerns, or fantasies that the general-fiction sticks brought them only in small quantities in any given issue. These people, many of them well educated, often academics, often writers themselves, often simply the brightest kids in a given school, numbered at best only a few hundred thousand out of a populace of 100 million or more. Many saved and shelved their pulps over the years, while the multitude of readers of the slicks tossed their magazines out every week or so. Thus, pulp fiction was, in fact, the choice of the bulk of the real reading public of its time, just as today the best genre fiction in paperback is loyally supported by the tiny minority of people who still love to read in a nation inundated by cable television, videocassette recorders (VCRs), and such mass-circulation magazines as *People*, *Today*, and the contemporary *Esquire*.

Today, old pulps sell to highly literate collectors at fancy prices—some select and rare titles can fetch upward of $200 to $300 apiece in fine condition—while the million-issue slicks of the 1950s and earlier can generally be sold only for the appeal of their cover art (Norman Rockwell etc.) or their bountiful color ads for Coca-Cola and the like. The pulps were truly elite fiction, seen as trash only by the "proper" citizenry who read little of anything. (Unfortunately, the great majority of the people who determined public library subscription policy at the time were made of precisely these "proper" types, which is why every library from here to Hoboken still has shelf after shelf laden with unread, dusty volumes of the *Saturday Evening Post* and similar genteel, "decent," large-circulation magazines, while possessing not a single copy of the richly imaginative and pioneering pulp fiction magazines of the same period.)

Although the pulp magazine, as we have been discussing it, was essentially a product of the first half of the twentieth century, the popular, all-fiction magazine as a viable commodity appeared early in the nineteenth century in both England and America and was largely printed on rag-content paper (then much cheaper than it was to become by the 1880s). The American rag-paper "story papers" of the 1850s and, later, weekly publications the size of today's newspapers, holding eight to twelve pages apiece of text and illustration and bearing such excitingly etched logos as *Boys of New York*, *Banner Weekly*, *Young Men of America*, and *New York Weekly*, were crammed cheek to inky jowl with endless columns of sensational fiction by such worthies as Nick Carter, Horatio Alger, and Ned Buntline and sold into the many thousands of copies at five or six cents each (although these papers were primarily designed for home subscription, being too large for full-cover display at most newsstands). Their enormous black-and-white cover illustrations, replete with blood and thunder of a western, detective, or science fiction orientation, were matched by those of the considerably smaller English penny dreadfuls (or penny bloods) of the same period. These were illustrated penny serial parts, published weekly and sold singly or in groups in book stalls, usually eight pages long, 7" × 10", and kept in print so long as the continuing story in each title, often spun out to inordinate length in 200–300 parts, continued to sell profitably. When sales slumped, the stories were brought to a hurried halt, and the authors turned to new titles and characters. Popular titles in these series included *The Boy Detective*, *Varney the Vampire*, *Wild Boys of London*, and *Blue Dwarf*, their notorious authors including Thomas Pecket Prest, Augustus Sala, and Pierce Egan Jr., son of the man whose 1821 comic work, *Life in London*, was the first best-selling English novel-in-parts. Most infamous of all the penny bloods aimed at an adult audience and by far the longest was G.W.M. Reynolds' libidinous *Mysteries of London*, which (with a slight name change midway through) was published weekly at sixteen pages from 1846 to 1852. Many of these English bloods were pirated for U.S. reprint, usually in part issued by the most active of the Yankee cheap fiction buccaneers, Robert M. De Witt of New York. American imitations of the blood thrillers, such as George Lippard's best-selling (60,000 copies in 1844) *Monks of Monk Hall* and George Thompson's horrific *City Crimes* and *New-York Life* (which went far beyond even the loose limits of the English bloods), proliferated in the raucous decades before the Civil War.

A bit later and overlapping the vogue for penny-dreadful part fiction, the English equivalents of the American story papers appeared. Weekly compilations of serials and short stories adorned with sensational cover illustrations like their Yankee kin, the English papers were much smaller in format, generally consisting of sixteen to twenty pages and measuring about 8 ½" × 11". Typical early titles in this immediately popular field were *Lads of the Village*, *Gentleman's Journal*, and *Boy's Herald*. Noticeably more restrained at the outset than their American cousins, the British all-fiction journals speedily plunged into horrific sensationalism as it became evident that what sold the penny-dreadful parts would also sell the boys' journals, and the merry hell with what might upset the odd parent here or there. By the 1880s there were two dozen or more such magazines, such as *Boys of the Empire*, *Comrades*, *Champion*, and *Ching-Ching's Own*, some of them reprinting the texts and illustrations of the new popular boys' periodical form that had largely supplanted the story papers in the States, the so-called dime novel.

The term dime novel was coined to describe the pocket-sized original novels (measuring 6 ¼" × 4") of 100 pages or so published by the New York firm of Beadle and Adams for the reading convenience of Civil War soldiers. Published monthly from the 1860s on and originally intended for adult and young adult readers, with such titles as *The Rival Scouts*, *The Outlaw Brothers*, *The Deer-Hunters*, and *The Dacotah Queen*, the Beadle's Dime Novels line was chiefly concerned with western and frontier adventure until well into the 1870s, when such titles as *The Phantom Hand, or, The Heiress of Fifth Avenue* of 1877 anticipated the urban detective thrillers that would rival the western stories in popularity in the 1880s and after. The ten-cent pocket-novel format continued through the 1870s, with some minor size variations and rival publishers (such as George Munro), but was eventually eclipsed when Beadle and Adams introduced a larger-format dime novel weekly series in 1878, with a gripping cover picture similar to those on the story papers. Measuring 12" × 8 ½" and running to between twenty and forty pages of triple-columned, closely printed text, the new series, called Beadle's New York Dime Library, opened with a detective story, titled *The Spotter Detective, or, The Girls of New York*, switched to a western yarn in the next number, and featured both narrative forms for the remainder of its weekly (and occasionally biweekly) 1,009 novels.

Although the Beadle and Adams dime pocket-sized books and weekly dime magazines were aimed at adults, millions of boys devoured them from the 1860s on. Realizing this and knowing that many boys found a dime very hard to come by, the publishers decided to introduce a nickel publication, to be named Beadle's Half Dime Library, in 1877. Although the stories were about half of the length of those in the dime magazine, running to between sixteen and twenty-four pages, and were intended to attract nickel-bearing boys, there was no perceptible difference in the quality of the stories or their sensational cover art; certainly, there was no great number of boy heroes in the Half Dime Library, and most of the Dime Library authors wrote for the new magazine as well. Opening with a *Deadwood Dick* yarn, the Half Dime Library ran for 1,168 issues, closing down operations (like its companion Dime Library) only with the end of the nineteenth century.

The five-cent price was a sensational success, and other publishers entered this popular fiction field with a flood of new titles of all sorts, all selling for a nickel and all with garish, shocking covers of action and brutality (augmented by full color in the late 1890s). Publishers later to earn fame in the pulp fiction era to follow, such as Street and Smith (who owned story papers in the 1870s), were active in printing what the juvenile readers called nickel (or "nickul") thrillers (although their censorious parents, unconcerned about precise niceties of price, kept on calling them, as they had their predecessors, "dime novels," forcing the term on the entire nickel fiction field to follow). Among the plethora of new titles that flooded the newsstands from the 1880s through the 1910s were such generalized fiction rivals of the Half Dime Library as Wide Awake Library, Morrison's Sensational Series, and the Boys' Star Library and such specialized fiction series (anticipating the variety of narrative emphasis in the pulps to come) as the Red Raven Library (pirate stories), the War Library, Diamond Dick Library (westerns), the New York Detective Library, Old Sleuth Library, Nick Carter Library, and a host of others. By the 1890s, the feature hero series of nickel thrillers was in great vogue (again anticipating a major pulp category), with such detectives and western heroes and outlaws as Nick Carter, Buffalo Bill, Young Wild West, Old Sleuth, Young and Old King Brady, Dick Dobbs (the millionaire detective), Jesse and Frank James, the Youngers, Wild Bill Hickok, and so on, as well as a sports hero, Frank Merriwell, and a pair of science fiction forerunners of Tom Swift: Tom Wright and Frank Reade Jr. (At least two of these characters were later to be featured in their own pulp magazines: Frank Merriwell and Nick Carter, the latter in two different pulps.)

Kids adored these magazines, read them to pieces, collected them, traded them, and generally behaved like the comic book juveniles (adolescent and adult) of today. They were almost universally read by boys in their time, and when their readers in many instances grew up to become men of substance, the old nickel thrillers were ferreted out of attics and basements and the back rooms of second-hand magazine stores and traded and sold again, often for quite high prices, in the 1920s and later. Many of these men ignored the contents of the much better-written pulps of their adult years and gave their spare reading time over to "catching up" on the "dimes" they had missed as kids. Most of these early readers are dead now, and the old nickel thrillers languish long in dealers' hands (when they do still turn up) until an institutional collector picks them up for fifty cents or a dollar apiece. Too antiquated and alien to appeal to even the phony, nostalgia-gripped Yuppies of today (who buy up the more garishly covered pulps avidly), the sensational weeklies of the gaudy era before 1910 are chiefly of interest to popular fiction researchers. Oddly, although virtually all of these magazines were printed on pulp-paper stock (the rag-content story papers also turned to pulp paper to save printing costs in the late 1870s), the term *pulps* is held to apply only to the specific group of magazines that we examine at considerable length shortly, while the *dime novel* misnomer continues to identify the dreadful popular American shockers of the Gilded Age.

In moving from the nickel thrillers of the nineteenth century to the pulps of the twentieth, we are, of course, passing from fiction of minimal literacy aimed almost entirely at juvenile readers or the most naive of uneducated adults, to a narrative prose intended for a mature mass readership not satisfied by the relatively small amount of genre fiction available in quality or general-content magazines or in inexpensive paperback book reprints. Interestingly, the first periodical to establish the profitable existence of such a mature mass readership (initially in England rather than America) was not printed on pulp paper at all, nor was it an all-fiction publication. This was the widely famed, slick-paper magazine of George Newnes, the *Strand*, in which such fictional figures as Sherlock Holmes and Bulldog Drummond appeared in series after series of novelettes and novels, together with sensational adventure and mystery fiction of all kinds, all profusely illustrated, often with color plates in holiday issues. Sandwiched in was a respectable (though peripheral) stock of nonfiction pieces on prominent personalities, exotic places, pets, and patriotism, so that despite its bounty of popular fiction, parlors that had previously accepted only such dull slick-paper periodicals as *Blackwood's*, *Good Words*, and the *Leisure Hour* now received the *Strand*.

Ambitious imitators of the *Strand* appeared almost at once in England, all bounteously illustrated (at the rate of about one cut for every two pages) and replete with thrilling action or detective fiction written by such masters as H. Rider Haggard, R. Austin Freeman, Guy Boothby, E. Phillips Oppenherm, and many others; among these new and sensationally popular magazines were the *Windsor Magazine*, *Pearson's*, *Cassell's*, *Harmworth's* (later, the *London Magazine*), and the *Idler*. Many of these published American editions to protect their copyrights in the United States, and their popular impact was much the same here as in England, although direct American imitations were not at all immediately evident (the earliest, possibly, being *Cosmopolitan* after 1905, when it was purchased by William Randolph Hearst and immediately took an engaging turn toward broadly popular fiction in great and well-illustrated quantity). American publishers of general magazines, dominated by the images of the more serious *Harper's* and *Scribner's* magazines at the close of the century, seemed to eschew the kind of fun-and-games fiction featured in the new group of British publications, and certainly they avoided any broad body of it in their pages at all times. Even the popularly oriented, weekly, slick-paper magazines of wide dimensions, such as *Collier's* and *Saturday Evening Post* of the 1890s and 1900s, in which the Sherlock Holmes and Raffles stories were reprinted for American consumption, ran only one or two pieces of fiction per issue, with but one or two illustrations apiece, and placed their heavier editorial emphasis on journalistic nonfiction and illustrations of various kinds.

The would-be American consumer of quantitatively published popular action fiction was thus frustrated on two fronts: the imported British magazines, such as the *Strand* and *Pearson's*, were too highly priced for the mass trading public's budget even in American reprint form, while the cheaper, popular American magazines, such as *Collier's* and *Saturday Evening Post*, ran about a single evening's worth of engaging fiction per week between them. The stage was thus set in the United States for the emergence of what was to be the single most successful medium for the merchandising of cheap fiction to a mass audience in the history of publishing: the pulps. It was an idea whose time had come, and if one publisher had not developed the concept, another would have done so in short order. As it happened, however, the man who published the first definitive pulp fiction magazine in 1896, the *Argosy*, did so only as one more step to save a foundering magazine, not as a calculated move in opening a new publishing frontier. Frank Andrew Munsey, who first converted his feebly conceived children's weekly of 1882, the *Golden Argosy*, into a boy's adventure story paper called simply the *Argosy* in 1888, then into a general illustrated monthly magazine of the same name in 1894, finally tried making it a monthly all-fiction adult adventure story magazine companion to his previously successful, general, illustrated *Munsey's Magazine* of 1891. By printing his new 1896 version of *Argosy* on pulp paper and omitting all illustrative art, Munsey found that he could provide a fat bundle of reading matter for a dime, well below the quarter charged at the time by slick paper magazines of similar bulk, such as *Harper's* or *Century*. Moreover, a great deal of the normal editorial content of such general magazines was pictorial, while in their fastidious prose, nonfiction usually had a marked edge in pages over fiction. On the average, it would be safe to say that a single monthly issue of *Argosy* of 1896 held more fiction than any six of the leading general monthlies of the time—and it was virtually *all* sensational adventure and mystery fiction of reasonably mature quality—certainly a far cry from the simple, rattletrap prose of the nickel thrillers.

That this kind of magazine was exactly what the mass adult reading public of the 1890s wanted was at once evidenced by the steep increase in *Argosy*'s circulation. From a rock-bottom low of 9,000 in 1894, the new *Argosy*'s sales figures quickly soared to 80,000, gradually ascending to a peak of half a million by 1907, a mere decade from its start. The *Argosy* was not long alone in its pulp paper splendor, but it was some time before its burgeoning imitators equaled or surpassed it in overall story quality. The inspired early editorial work in the post-1895 *Argosy* was not that of Munsey, who was much more involved *Munsey's Magazine* and other projects by that time, but that of Matthew White Jr., who had joined the Munsey staff in 1886 (and who was later closely aided by Robert "Bob" Davis, a Munsey editor hired in 1904). That White's judgment was sound is indicated by the impressive roster of contemporary writers of popular fiction whose early work was printed in *Argosy* between 1896 and 1910: James Branch Cabell, Upton Sinclair, Mary Roberts Rinehart, William Sydney Porter (later O. Henry), Susan Glaspell, George Allen England, Albert Payson Terhune, Joseph Louis Vance, Frank L. Packard, William MacLeod Raine, and Ellis Parker Butler, many of whom became regular contributors to the prestigious *Saturday Evening Post* of the upcoming century.

Among the earliest of *Argosy*'s technical rivals were two other Munsey adventure fiction pulps, *All-Story* of 1905 (later *All-Story Weekly*) and *Cavalier* of 1908. Both monthlies and both essentially duplicates of the *Argosy* with interchangeable authors and cover artists, these two new publications in effect put an over 220-page, all-fiction Munsey magazine on the newsstands three times a month; and when *All-Story* combined with *Cavalier* and went weekly in 1913, there were *five* Munsey adventure pulps for sale every month—and they all sold, voluminously. There seemed to be plenty of people able to devour 1,200 closely printed pages of Munsey fiction per month—and more, if the sales of other publishers' action fiction pulps are added to those of the Munsey magazines. It must be kept in mind that ten cents in the 1900s would buy about what a dollar will buy today, at a time when most actual incomes were smaller in real purchasing power. It can accordingly be assumed that most buyers of the early pulps rarely bought on impulse or just to read one or two stories by favorite authors; they read their money's worth out of every magazine purchased. A persistent point made in letters to the editors at this time and later is that the readers read every story in every issue; many even rated them in terms of enjoyment derived. Contemporary authors can only weep for that once vast reading public, a public that sustained the pulps for fifty years.

Among the early and most substantial imitators of *Argosy* were such other 7" × 10" quarto pulp magazines containing roughly 150 to 200 pages of adventure and action fictions as Street and Smith's *Popular Magazine* of 1904, which reached a quarter million in circulation by 1905; *Gunter's Magazine*, also of 1904, another Street and Smith response to *Argosy* (with a leavening of romantic fiction in an attempt to appeal to some female readers), which became *New Magazine* under another publisher in 1910, then returned to Street and Smith as *New Story Magazine* in 1912; *People's Magazine*, a third Street and Smith undertaking of 1906 with an early emphasis on detective fiction rather than straight adventure; *Top-Notch* of 1910, a final Street and Smith effort in the general action story field issued in an initial dime-novel format, with a bias toward the sports fiction story; *Blue Book* of 1907 (originally titled *Monthly Story Magazine* in its 1905 inauguration), a companion magazine to the women-oriented *Red Book* and the later, theater-slanted *Green Book* of the same period; *Short Stories* of 1910, previously an all-fiction reprint magazine of high price and slick paper; and *Adventure* of 1910, the first issue of which actually appeared on slick paper, apparently for promotional reasons. Some of these newcomers carried a fifteen-cent price, justifying it by a modicum of interior illustrations, while the early *Top-Notch*, the smallest in length of the lot, tried for a nickel, but none ever surpassed the enormous circulation lead attained by *Argosy* or attempted to emulate the weekly publication of *All-Story* (later merged with *Argosy* into a single Munsey pulp adventure fiction weekly in 1920, after *Argosy* itself had been a weekly since 1917), although *Popular*, *Short Stories*, *Adventure*, and *Top-Notch* eventually went to twice-a-month publication for varying periods of time.

It soon became evident to some of these pulp fiction entrepreneurs that the needs of their newly tapped reading public might not be wholly met by action fiction in bulk and that many readers, as indicated by a growing demand in libraries and bookstores, wanted to read rather narrowly along one line of popular fiction, most notably in the 1910s that of detective and mystery narrative, although a spreading interest in western fiction was not far behind. Street and Smith, of course, had earlier noted this phenomenon in their nineteenth-century nickel library series, where tens of thousands of copies of the weekly *Nick Carter* detective and *Buffalo Bill* western thrillers vanished off the newsstands every seven days. Munsey, however, was the first to investigate specialized fiction interests when he launched the *Railroad Man's Magazine* in 1906. A monthly pulp, this publication featured much more nonfiction than the other men's adventure magazines and was actually more of a fraternal journal for railroad and locomotive buffs than anything else; it lasted until 1919 and was revived by Munsey in 1929. More typical of the specialized fiction pulp was a second Munsey effort in this direction, the *Ocean* of 1917. Here, although there was considerable nonfiction, sea stories predominated, with as many as four serials running every month. Munsey's estimate of the public's interest in saltwater narratives was misguided, however (in fact, there was never to be a really successful sea story pulp at any time), and he was forced to fold the venture after only a year.

Street and Smith, experimenting a little later in the game, had much better luck. In 1915, they decided to convert the old *Nick Carter* nickel thriller into a new ten-cent semimonthly pulp magazine of detective fiction, called *Detective Story Magazine*. Nick Carter stories, often serialized, were still featured, but the bulk of the new magazine's contents were purchased from the same freelance authors then supplying the other pulps. Initially only a slim 128 pages, *Detective Story Magazine* quickly fattened to 160 pages, then switched to a weekly schedule at 144 pages with a steadily mounting circulation through the 1920s. Encouraged by their initial success, Street and Smith proceeded in 1919 to alter their successful *Buffalo Bill* weekly nickel thriller into another specialized pulp, this one called *Western Story Magazine*. Like *Detective Story Magazine*, *Western Story Magazine* was launched as a semimonthly, ten-cent publication of 128 pages. By 1920, however, circulation had swelled to such an extent that *Western Story Magazine*, like its predecessor, became a 144-page dime weekly. Then at 300,000 circulation, it later reached a half-million in sales in the mid-1920s, when the extraordinarily popular fiction of the hyperprolific Max Brand (Frederick Faust) began to run in its pages at the rate of two or three serials at a time. A third Street and Smith attempt at a specialized fiction magazine, the fabled *Thrill Book* of 1919, failed because of a lack of courageous editorial direction. Clearly meant to be a magazine emphasizing the weird, bizarre, and fantastic in popular fiction (material that had already proven its wide popularity through its repeated appearance in *Argosy*, where writers famed for fantastic narratives, such as Edgar Rice Burroughs, Abraham Merritt, George Allen England, J. U. Geisy, Francis Stevens, and many others, were acclaimed headliners), *Thrill Book* lacked the nerve to limit its contents to science fiction and fantasy and, by actually taking on the amorphous shape of just another general-action pulp, failed to attract the steadfast band of followers who were later to adhere faithfully to such undiluted exponents of fantastic fiction as the *Weird Tales* of 1923 and *Amazing Stories* of 1926. The *Thrill Book* did run some unusual and memorable fantasy—notably, Francis Stevens' "The Heads of Cerebus"—but not enough to catch the notice of the multitude of readers who were regularly buying *Argosy* and *All-Story* for the same thing.

Street and Smith continued with their pioneering creation of specialized genre fiction pulps in the 1920s and introduced the long-lived and vastly popular *Love Story Magazine* in 1921 as a 144-page, fifteen-cent weekly—and as a cheaper companion to two, older Street and Smith romantic fiction monthlies, *Smith's Magazine* and *Ainslee's Magazine*, once aspiring slicks but now down-at-the-heel twenty-cent pulps. The following year Street and Smith made their own attempt at a salt spray magazine with *Sea Stories* (which had to be abandoned by 1930 and converted to a mystery-adventure pulp called *Excitement*); they also introduced the nation's first magazine of collegiate fiction in *College Stories*, anticipating the later peak success in that field of *College Humor*. *Sport Story* was first published in 1923, as a companion to the sports-oriented *Top-Notch*, while by 1927 another long-established nickel-thriller weekly (actually then selling at seven cents), Harry E. Wolff's *Wild West Weekly*, with its feature novels about Young Wild West, was taken over by Street and Smith as a straight western fiction weekly with the same name.

In the meantime, other publishers had been busy, particularly in the detective and western fiction fields. H. L. Mencken and George Jean Nathan, engaged in developing their famed *Smart Set Magazine*, merrily launched three deliberate potboiler magazines in the 1910s to bring in supportive funds for *Smart Set*. The first two of these "louse" magazines, as Mencken and Nathan called them, were routine, spicy story pulps of the innocent sort prefigured by Street and Smith's *Live Stories* of 1913 or their earlier *Yellow Book* of 1897, the kind of magazine that sold well in wartime; and Mencken and Nathan's *Parisienne* of 1915 and *Saucy Stories* of 1916 were specifically created with the young, war-excited American in mind. Both were immediate hits, with the second giving the leading naughty story magazine of the time, *Snappy Stories*, strong competition for its position. (It might be mentioned at this point that some variety of risqué pulp fiction was always on sale under dozens of different titles from the turn of the century through the 1950s, many published and distributed in legally sub rosa operations. Notable titles in the 1920s and 1930s were *La Paree Stories*, *Bedtime Stories*, *10-Story Book*, *Saucy Movie Stories*, *Vice Squad Detective*, *Spicy Mystery Stories*, and *Hollywood Detective*. There were dozens of other titles, and none ever failed financially; every last one was, in fact, ultimately suppressed only by the authorities.) Mencken and Nathan's third "louse" magazine, however, proved to be quite a different matter from the first two; in fact, its reputation eventually overshadowed that of *Smart Set* itself.

Created several years later in 1920, this new monthly action pulp was titled *Black Mask*, and its initial orientation was toward stories of crime, horror, and the quasi supernatural. Deliberately sensational in title and content, the feisty magazine was intended to attract readers who wanted more fearsome fare than they could find in the relatively sedate *Detective Story Magazine* and *Mystery Magazine* (the latter being a Frank Tousey venture of 1919, a thirty-two-page, 8" × 11" dime publication featuring cheaply acquired fiction by minor writers). A pitch was made for women readers by the early subtitle wording, *A Magazine of Mystery, Romance, and Adventure*, but there was little of the boy–girl romancing that packed the pages of *Ainslee's* or *Love Story Magazine* of the following year; indeed, the cover of the October 1920 issue depicted a young woman cowering from a hot branding iron that has *already* branded her cheek with a livid, smoking image. Although there were a number of generally straightforward detective problem stories in the early issues, these probably reflected the kind of rejects from *Detective Story Magazine* that the editors were initially forced to buy, and the obviously desired theme was powerfully rendered in blood and thunder. There was little hint of the restrained, coldly realistic, well-paced fiction that *Black Mask* was later to personify in the writing of Dashiell Hammett, Raymond Chandler, Paul Cain,

Raoul Whitfield, and others. Indeed, *Black Mask*, for all of its fame as a pioneering, hard-boiled detective story magazine in the 1920s, was in fact a long time in finding its real focus. For most of the 1920s, *Black Mask* was described in its cover subtitle variously as a magazine of air, western, adventure, and he-man fiction, as well as of detective fiction, and its contents reflected that description. Such later noted writers of tough crime fiction as Whitfield and Horace McCoy initially wrote little but air and western stories for *Black Mask*. It was not, in fact, until the public impact and circulation rise of the very late 1920s that accompanied the major Hammett serials, such as *Red Harvest* and *The Maltese Falcon*, that *Black Mask* became wholly a magazine of tough detective fiction. In the meantime, there was little influence exerted on other pulp magazines, and the first out-and-out *Black Mask* imitator, *Black Aces*, did not appear until 1911, while such strong and lasting parallel crime fiction magazines as *Dime Detective* and *Detective Tales* did not reach their peaks of quality until the mid-1930s.

In the 1920s, following the advent of *Black Mask* and the minor curiosity called *Mystery Magazine*, the only notable introductions in detective story magazines were Munsey's first move into the field in 1924 with the weekly *Flynn's* (later, *Flynn's Weekly Detective Fiction* and finally *Flynn's Detective Fiction Weekly*), starting out with 200 pages for a dime; Edwin Baird's somewhat earlier *Detective Tales* of 1923, an oddly old-fashioned magazine that quickly jumped to an 8 ½" × 11" format (the size of the "true" detective and "confession" slicks of the period) but retained its pulp paper as its title changed to a twenty-five-cent *Real Detective Tales & Mystery Stories* in 1924; the Priscilla Company's *Mystery Stories* of 1925, a quality, twenty-five-cent magazine of 160 pages, emphasizing true crime accounts and cruise action fiction; W. M. Clayton's *Clues: A Magazine of Detective Stories* of 1926, which directly paralleled *Detective Story Magazine* and ran twice a month for a while in the late 1920s at fifteen cents; Dell's short-lived *Crime Mysteries* of 1927, a fifteen-cent, 120-page monthly that featured much of the interest in the horrific and grisly that characterized the early *Black Mask*; and Harold Hersey's *Dragnet Magazine* of 1928, a twenty-cent, 128-page monthly that was later (in 1931) to become the famed *Ten Detective Aces*, in which such top pulp writers as Lester Dent and Norvell Page wrote monthly novelettes about continuing feature characters in deliberately fantastic and gruesome adventures. The great bulk of the pulps jamming the newsstands of the 1920s were adventures and westerns, with detectives a slim third and a random spotting of other early genre pulps, such as *Ghost Stories*, *Weird Tales*, *Amazing Stories*, *Secret Service Stories*, *Sky Birds*, and the like. The earlier adventure pulps had been augmented by such 1920s titles as *Danger Trail*, *Complete Stories*, *Five-Novels Monthly*, *Tropical Adventures*, *Thrills*, *Romance*, *Ace-High Magazine*, and so on, while the western fiction deluge inaugurated by *Western Story Magazine* counted among its 1920s arrivals the *Frontier*, *Lariat*, *Cowboy Stories*, *West*, *Rangeland Stories*, *Western Trails*, and many others.

At the close of the 1920s, however, the real torrent of new pulps (and fresh varieties of pulps) took place. Suddenly, by 1929, all sorts of new kinds of pulp magazines were appearing—World War I action fiction, in such titles as *War Stories* (actually dating from 1920), *Submarine Stories*, *Navy Stories*, *Triple-X Magazine*, *War Novels*, *Over the Top*, and a subgenre that quickly outgrew its parent: air war fiction featuring *Airplane Stories*, *Wings*, *Sky Birds*, *Aces*, *Air Stories*, *Eagles of the Air*, *Sky Riders*, *Zeppelin Stories*; gangster fiction, typified by such new titles as *Racketeer Stories*, *Gun Molls*, *Speakeasy Stories*, *Gang World*, *Gangster Stories*, *Gangland Stories*, *Underworld*; and science fiction, reflected by *Amazing Stories*, *Science Wonder Stories*, *Air Wonder Stories*, *Scientific Detective Monthly*, and (just around the corner in 1930) *Astounding Stories of Super-Science*. The quality of pulp fiction had become speedier and breezier, too, with a general dumping of the kind of prolix description and circumlocution that had filled many of those earlier, endless pages in *Argosy* and *Detective Story Magazine* and reflected the general tenor of turn-of-the-century fiction. Those writers who had anticipated the looser, swifter style, such as Edgar Rice Burroughs, Max Brand, Dashiell Hammett, Robert E. Howard, and Erle Stanley Gardner, continued to flourish in the decade ahead, while many others stodgily prominent in the 1910s and 1920s vanished completely from the fast-action pulps of the 1930s, much as certain silent film idols, such as John Gilbert and Ramon Navarro, had essentially slipped from view with the dominance of talkies.

The rising tide of new pulp variations surged into the 1930s, seeing the birth of such minor one-pulp genres as *Prison Stories*, *New York Stories*, *Courtroom Stories*, *Fire Fighters*, *Jungle Stories*, *Northwest Stories*, *Front Page Stories*, and similar titles as well as the introduction of many Federal Bureau of Investigation (FBI) pulps, such as *Federal Agent*, *Public Enemy*, *G-Men*, *G-Men Detective*, *Ace G-Man Stories*, *Feds*; the formal mixing of genre themes and risqué fiction in such mid-1930s magazines as *Spicy Mystery Stories*, *Spicy Detective Stories*, *Spicy Adventure Stories*, *Spicy Western Stories*, *Saucy Detective*, *Saucy Movie Tales*, *Scarlet Adventures*, *Hollywood Detective*; the unleashing of a number of sadistic horror fiction magazines, such as *Dime Mystery Magazine*, *Horror Stories*, *Terror Tales*, *Uncanny Tales*, *Eerie Stories*, *Thrilling Mystery*, *Ace Mystery Magazine*; even more new detective pulp titles—*Popular Detective*, *Thrilling Detective*, *Dime Detective*, *Detective Tales*, *New Detective*, *Crime Busters*, *Private Detective Stories*, *Block Book Detective*, *Double Detective*, *Strange Detective Mysteries*; westerns—*Western Aces*, *Mavericks*, *10-Story Western*, *Popular Western*, *Dime Western Magazine*, *All Western Magazine*, *Nickel Western*, *Thrilling Western*, *Thrilling Ranch Stories*; adventures—*Action Stories*, *Thrilling Adventures*, *All-American Fiction*, *Dynamic Adventures*, *Excitement*, *Northwest Stories*, *Golden Fleece*, *Oriental Stories*, *Magic Carpet*; air war—*Air War*, *Dare-Devil Aces*, *Sky Aces*, *Battle Birds*, *War Birds*, *Sky Fighters*, *Sky Devils*, *George Bruce's Contact*, *George Bruce's Squadron*; and science fiction—*Miracle Science and Fantasy Stories*, *Thrilling Wonder Stories*, *Startling Stories*, *Marvel Science Stories*, *Dynamic Stories*, *Planet Stories*.

Many of the multitude of new magazines were the product of freshly formed pulp chain publishers that carried as many as thirty or more pulp titles apiece; others were the releases of older publishers attracted to the market by the sizable and rising profits in an economic recession (for a nation out of work had little choice but to drink or read, and with bootleg whiskey at a quarter a shot, many chose to read cheap fiction much of the time). Among the major publishers that flooded the newsstands with pulps in the wake of Munsey and Street and Smith were Dell Publishing, Fiction House, the Hersey Magazines, Clayton Magazines, Popular Publications, Thrilling Publications, Culture Publications, Standard Publications (later Better Publications), A. A. Wynn magazines, and others, including spin-offs or front publishers set up by established houses to bring out yet more strings of pulps, such as Fictioneers, backed by Popular publications, or

Trojan Publishing, established by Culture Publications. At the helms of many of the pulps fielded by these publishers, sometimes editing as many as a dozen or more at once, were a number of talented and canny men, such as the much acclaimed Joseph T. "Cap" Shaw of the later *Black Mask*; Harold Brainerd Hersey, of *Thrill Book*, *Ace-High Magazine*, *Danger Trail*, *Clues-Detective*, and *Dragnet*; John W. Campbell Jr., of *Astounding Science Fiction* and *Unknown Worlds*; John L. Nanovic of numerous Street and Smith titles; Ken White of *Dime Detective*; Farnsworth Wright of *Weird Tales* and *Oriental Stories*; Leo Margulies of the Thrilling chain, who shone in his handling of *Thrilling Wonder Stories* and *Startling Stories*; Henry Steeger of Popular, who supervised almost three dozen titles from *Horror Stories* to *Glamorous Love Stories*; Rogers Terrill, direct editor of all Popular titles under Steeger; Hugo Gernsback of *Amazing Stories* and *Wonder Stories*; Daisy Bacon of *Love Story Magazine*; F. Orlin Tremaine of *Top-Notch* and *Astounding Stories*; A. A. Wynn of *Ten Detective Aces*; Donald Kennicott of *Blue Book*; and others of equal capacity and accomplishment.

Probably the most notable and memorable achievement of the large pulp chain publishers and their editors in the 1930s was the fostering of the rebirth of the hero novel, once so central to the prosperity of the nickel thriller magazines of the 1890s. The first of these new monthly pulps was Gilbert Patten's little-known *Swift Story Magazine* of November 1930, which, aside from its twenty-cent price and digest pulp size, itself unusual and innovative for the time, anticipated the content and format of the other hero pulps that followed in every detail: 128-page length, a recurrent hero, in a monthly feature novel dominating the magazine— Derek Dane, Sky Sleuth in this case—several illustrations in the lead novel, a group of short stories in the closing pages, a department for the readers, and a lurid cover featuring the hero. Next, five months later, was Street and Smith's *Shadow Magazine* of April 1931, which introduced the dual-identity outlaw crime fighter to the hero pulps; then came Standard Publications' *Phantom Detective* of February 1933, a Shadow imitation; Street and Smith's *Doc Savage* and *Nick Carter* of March 1933, covering the themes of exotic, fantastic adventure and the private detective, respectively; Standard's *Lone Eagle* of September 1933, featuring a World War I air ace; Popular's *Spider* and *G-8 and His Battle Aces* of October 1933, presenting yet another masked crime fighter (the best of the lot) and a second World War I air ace-cum-spy, respectively; Street and Smith's *Pete Rice* of November 1933, showcasing the first cowpoke sheriff in the hero pulps; Rose Wyn's *Secret Agent "X"* of February 1934, carrying the fourth hidden-identity avenger of crime; Street and Smith's *Bill Barnes*, also of February 1934, a pulp with a contemporary aviation hero like Derek Dane; Popular's *Operator #5* of April 1934, introducing an American master spy facing contemporary enemy operations and foreign invasions; Popular's *Dusty Ayres and His Battle Birds* of July 1934, the first science fiction hero pulp, featuring a future interplanetary war; Popular's *Secret Six* of October 1934, multiplying the dual-identity crime fighter by six; Ranger Publications' *Masked Rider* western of December 1934, starting an imitation of the Lone Ranger of radio; Dell's *Doctor Death* of February 1935, introducing the first criminal lead character, à la Fu Manchu, in a hero pulp; and Fawcett Publications' *Terence X, O'Leary's War Birds* of March 1935, a second science fiction air war hero pulp.

The astonishing average was one new hero pulp every two months between

January 1933 and April 1935, most of which kept going for the remainder of the decade. Nor did the pace slacken; these seventeen stalwart openers of the heroic way were followed by as many more over the next few years: *Wu Fang, Dr. Yen Sin, G-Men, Public Enemy* (later, *Federal Agent*), *Whisperer, Skipper, Captain Stuart, Captain Hazzard, Captain Combat, Captain Danger, Mavericks, Jungle Stories, Ka-Zar, Lone Ranger, Masked Detective, Ghost* (later, *Green Ghost Detective*), *Octopus, Scorpion, Wizard,* and others, including three short-lived newspaper comic strip adaptations: *Flash Gordon, Dan Dunn,* and *Tailspin Tommy.* Only the paper shortages of World War II reduced the tide, but even after the war, in the increasing ebb that ultimately foundered almost all the pulps, a few more hero pulps were expectantly launched, such as *Hopalong Cassidy, Captain Zero,* and *Sheena, Queen of the Jungle,* a comic book adaptation. The last hero pulp to succumb was the third to be created, *Phantom Detective* of 1933, which expired with its 170th quarterly issue in the summer of 1953. In number of issues, however, it was surpassed by *Doc Savage,* with 181 numbers to the summer of 1949, and the twice-a-month *Shadow,* with 325 issues to the same date. The magazine that pioneered the pulp hero concept and format, Burt L. Standish's *Swift Story Magazine* of 1930, curiously, lasted just one issue.

Illustrating the hero pulps, as well as the pulp chain titles in general, was nearly as important for sales by the 1930s as the lurid covers of nickel thrillers had been for their prosperity at the turn of the century. While the earliest pulps (the Munsey titles, *Popular, Short Stories,* etc.) were chary of interior illustrations when they carried them at all and generally garbed themselves in thematic covers featuring adventurous or sporting males in static poses with little or no relation to specific stories within, the number and quality of interior drawings increased sharply through competition in the 1920s, while direct story delineation on covers—initiated by the Munsey magazines in the 1910s—gradually became the norm. While a very few well-budgeted pulps ran virtually an illustration to a page by the mid-1920s and 1930s (notably the stunning *Blue Book Magazine,* which also ran many illustrations in colored ink, *Real Detective Tales,* and the Spicy chain) and a number of others tried to continue with a minimal number of illustrations or none at all (*Best Detective, Great Detective Stories, Scotland Yard, Dragnet,* and *War Stories* were typical), the vast majority carried at least one lead illustration for every story (very short stories were usually excepted) and between two to four for novelettes and novels, plus continuing department heads. Supplying this considerable quantity of artwork was the task of a few dozen well-worked professional ink, watercolor, and oil artists, who varied in quality and reputation from the dreariest kind of scrawlers and daubers who worked for Desperation Row (as the skin-of-their-teeth pulp houses were called) to a number of fine artists of international fame who did occasional or regular pulp magazine illustration for bread-and-butter money. Most, of course, were journeymen artists of reasonable competence and occasional flairs of real genius. Among the renowned artists who did a notable amount of pulp, cover, or interior work were N. C. Wyeth, Rockwell Kent, John Newton Howitt, J. Allen St. John, Gordon Grant, John R. Neill, Jonn Clymer, Austin Briggs, Nick Eggenhoffer, J. C. Leydendecker, and Herbert Morton Stoops; while the most outstanding and popular of the journeymen numbered such memorable talents as Hubert Rogers, Walter M. Baumhofer, Jerome Rozen, Virgil Finlay, Paul Orban, John Fleming Gould, Frederick Blakeslee, Hannes Bok, Elliot Dold,

Edd Cartier, Joseph Doolin, Frank R. Paul, H. W. Wesso, R. G. Harris, Norman Saunders, H. W. Scott, Rudolph Belarski, William Parkhurst, Frank Tinsley, Harold S. DeLay, and Margaret Brundage. Some indifferent comic strip art was introduced experimentally into a few pulps in the 1930s and later, but never with a notable effect on sales or lingering impact, with the possible exception of the classically silly *Sally the Sleuth* in *Spicy Detective Stories*.

The writers, of course—the kids just in from the prairies with their heavy office typewriters in cardboard boxes unloaded on wooden tables in shabby Manhattan furnished rooms, the wealthy top-wordage pulp kings writing from their estates around the world, the 5,000-words-a-day steady producers in their suburban homes on Long Island or in southern California—were the mainstay of the whole pulp operation. Following on the early group of pioneer pulp writers in the old Munsey magazines already mentioned and writing in the 1940s or before were such gifted and entertaining fictioneers as Edgar Rice Burroughs, whose highly contagious visions of Tarzan and Mars first overwhelmed the mass reading public in Munsey's *All-Story* between January and November 1912; Zane Grey, many of whose best-known novels ran in *Popular*, *Argosy*, and *All-Story*; Max Brand, who galloped to fame in virtually every early pulp, from *Argosy* and *Blue Book* through *Black Mask* and *Ace High* to *Western Story* and the *Railroad Man's Magazine*; Frank L. Packard, who introduced the dual-identity outlaw crime fighter to detective fiction in his Jimmie Dale series for *People's Magazine* and later *Detective Fiction Weekly*; Abraham Merritt, who gripped two generations of readers with his splendid fantasy adventures, such as *The Moon Pool* and *The Ship of Ishtar*, in the Munsey titles; Joel Townsley Rogers, one of the most bizarre writers of suspense prose in American fiction, who wrote both aviation and crime fiction for such disparate magazines as *Wings*, *Adventure*, and *New Detective*; George Bruce, the finest author of air war fiction in the pulps, who was the first writer to have a pulp named for his work—and not just one pulp, but three (*George Bruce's Aces*, 1930; *George Bruce's Squadron*, 1933; and *George Bruce's Contact*, 1933); H. P. Lovecraft, the finest American writer of macabre fiction since Poe, whose stories had enormous reader impact in *Weird Tales* and *Astounding Stories* and now constitute the base of a small publishing industry; Lester Dent, who wrote most of the *Doc Savage* hero pulps, of which over 100 were reprinted in top-selling paperback editions in the 1970s; Dashiell Hammett, who introduced his Continental Op, Sam Spade, and other characters in fresh, hard-bitten prose through the pages of *Black Mask*, *Brief Stories*, and *Argosy-All-Story*; Carroll John Daly, who created the lone private-eye concept in *Black Mask* and augmented it through *Done Detective*, *Detective Story*, *Detective Fiction Weekly*, and a dozen other pulps; Robert E. Howard, the freshest writer of adventure prose since Jack London, who wrote for an endless number of pulps from *Weird Tales* to *Argosy* and whose work is being avidly reprinted here and abroad in over 100 hardcover and paperback books; Norvell Page, creator of the *Spider* hero pulp, most powerful and memorable of the hero pulp writers and a regular contributor to many other pulps from *Unknown* to *Dime Mystery Magazine*; Raymond Chandler, who added his own bittersweet cachet to crime fiction in *Black Mask* and *Dime Detective* and even experimented with fantasy in *Unknown*; Ray Bradbury, one of the most noted contemporary American authors, who wrote much of his best fiction for *Weird Tales*, *Startling Stories*, *Detective Tales*, and other pulps; Walter B. Gibson, creator of the *Shadow* hero pulp and

Cover of the August 1927 issue of *Amazing Stories.* ©
Bettmann/CORBIS

the indefatigable author of over 300 novels about his cloaked hero, now in active
reprint, as well as of other pulp hero series for such magazines as *Crime Busters*
and *Mystery Magazine*; and a host of others of almost equal worth and importance:
Robert A. Heinlein, Clark Ashton Smith, Steve Fisher, Frank Gruber, John D.
MacDonald, Frederick C. Davis, Raoul Whitfield, Paul Cain, Henry S. White-
head, Clifford D. Simak, Fritz Leiber, Robert Bloch, Luke Short, H. Bedford
Jones, Victor Rousseau, Malcolm Jameson, C. L. Moore, Henry Kuttner, Ted
Copp, Vincent Starrett, Erle Stanley Gardner, Frederick Nebel, William J. Makin,
Cornell Woolrich, Norbert Davis, Donald Wandrei, Howard Wandrei, Harry
Sinclair Drago, Fred MacIsaac, Theodore Tinsley, Theodore Sturgeon, John W.
Campbell Jr., Emile C. Tepperman, Cyril Kornbluth, Eric Temple Bell, David
H. Keller, Robert J. Hogan, Paul Ernst, J. J. des Ormeaux, Clarence E. Mulford,
Walt Coburn, Paul Chadwick, Huge B. Cave, Jack Kofoed, E. E. Smith, Rex
Stout, A. E. Van Vogt, Isaac Asimov—a heady roster of famous names (and some
no longer so famous) but one that literally cuts away some of the cream of the
pulps' exciting literary fraternity. There are at least fifty more names as well known
or representing as competent a body of work as any on the preceding list. Some—
particularly the writers in the science fiction field and the *Black Mask* school—are

mentioned in other chapters in this volume; others will have to wait for a longer study to be properly cited.

As can be seen from the authors noted, almost every area of popular American literature was blanketed by the pulps, and nearly always the involvement was both intimate and massive, leaving a major and permanent impression behind. There never was a time before or since that more engaging, good prose fiction (with, admittedly, a sizable, perhaps essential admixture of rubbish) has been available as cheaply to so many people. It lasted more than half a century, but when it entered its decline, the end came quickly. Many pulp readers of the time could see it coming, although the bulk of the editors and publishers in those later years did not seem so prescient. Since it was, by and large, their new policies and approaches to the fiction that they were packaging that hastened the ruin of the pulps, this is perhaps not too surprising.

What happened is that the war years of the 1940s led to a reduction in the size of the pulps, their frequency of publication, their abundance of titles, and their very sturdiness (many issues had to be published with only one staple to conserve metal) and to the dismemberment of much of the established editorial staffs as well, with many going into the armed forces or war work. In most cases, these veterans of the great pulp boom of the 1930s, often with little formal schooling and sharing many of the tastes and needs of their readers, were replaced by young, draft-exempt people direct from college with liberal arts degrees in hand, who had rarely had the time or inclination to open a pulp for four or more years previously. Instead of feeling that they were the new, fortunate custodians of a marvelously varied treasure house of ongoing accomplishments and exciting possibilities, most seemed to believe that they had been put in charge of horrendously lowbrow products in antiquated packaging, badly in need of immediate improvement. The improvement that they felt necessary, unfortunately, was the discarding of the lurid, raffish veneer, which attracted the bulk of their readership, and supplanting it with a neat, trimmed, proper, respectable, "distinguished" look that would permit the pulp editors to hold their heads up along Publishers Row in the future. The most extreme steps along this line were taken at what had become the economic mainstay of the shortage-racked pulp chains, Street and Smith, and when the prosperous flagship threw the Jolly Roger and the cutlasses overboard and broke out the doilies and teacups, it was really all over for the pulps. Through the 1940s, they were improved to death; in the 1950s, the corpses were interred.

The tragedy was compounded by the fact that, while the Street and Smith pulp packages were being upgraded to invisibility so far as the public was concerned, and their contents made increasingly unpalatable (the editorship of the classic *Detective Story Magaazine* was taken over in the 1940s by Daisy Bacon, whose whole previous experience and orientation had been derived from her decades with *Love Story Magazine*), the general level of pulp writing elsewhere was improving enormously. A fresh generation of fine young pulp writers, who had cut their creative eyeteeth on the pulps as kids, was entering the field: Frederic Brown, John D. MacDonald, David Goodis, John McPartland, David Karp, Jack Vance, Philip K. Dick, Harlan Ellison, Evan Hunter, James Causey, Robert Turner, Day Keene, Richard S. Prather, Louis L'Amour, and a great many others. Their beautifully written, highly imaginative, and innovative stories filled many of the surviving pulps, notably those of the hardily conservative Popular chain, as well as most of the burgeoning science fiction pulps. It was to no avail; as the sales of the top-selling Street and Smith chain tumbled in the wake of the deadly new garb of neat propriety imposed on its pulps, national magazine distributors grew more nervous and reluctant about carrying any pulps at all. Individual dealers gave over more newsstand space to the proliferating comic books and cut back on that afforded the slower-selling pulps, often stacking them in odd corners rather than giving them cover display. What people did not see, or did not see well, they were less inclined to look for and buy. (It must be kept in mind, too, that the hardcore, devoted purchasers of particular pulp titles were always in a minority among the largely impulsive pulp public. If *Argosy*, say, was prominently displayed, it sold to some extent through familiarity with the title and the look of the cover; hidden from immediate sight, it was not sought out enough to sustain anything like the previous level of sales.) Basically, the public simply wanted light entertainment. If comic books and the exploding new field of paperback fiction (which demanded less space for dealers than pulps) were more visible than the pulps, the public's money was largely spent in these areas. When one of the two major national distributors of magazines refused to carry pulps anymore in the early 1950s, it was all over for publishers. A colorful handful of pulps survived, largely because of strong specialized markets (such as *Ranch Romances'* healthy newsstand pull in the Midwest and Northwest and the tendency of devoted science fiction fans to buy all of the titles in their field as if they were one publication), but almost all had to adopt the digest pulp size to get even a hope of display at the newsstands. One or two, such as *Argosy* and *Blue Book*, gave up their pulp format and contents altogether and began fresh magazines with male appeal.

Although the bulk of their outlets was gone by the mid-1950s, the new writers remained. Those turning out science fiction had no real problem, for most of their old markets kept publishing, often as the only pulp titles left in the reorganized chains, but other writers had to find fresh sources of income. One or two new digest-size pulps were created with some success to carry some of this material in the crime, detective, and western fiction fields, notably, in Flying Eagle's *Manhunt*, *Murder!*, *Alfred Hitchcock's Mystery Magazine*, and *Gunsmoke*, but by and large the more adaptable writers turned to the brand-new markets for original paperback book fiction, such as Fawcett's Gold Medal Books, Atlas News' Lion Books, and similar title lines at Signet and Dell. These markets were almost exclusively for book-length novels but paid very well in contrast to the penny-a-word rate still prevailing with most pulps at their demise. A few old-line pulp writers tried these new outlets, as well as the field of hardcover publishing to which most went. Lester Dent of *Doc Savage* tried both, for example, but generally speaking, it was the postwar group of newcomers, such as Day Keene, John D. MacDonald, and David Goodis, that flourished handsomely in the original paperback field.

Still, the pulps as they had been known in their heyday had irrevocably passed from the land. The sight, feel, and smell of them are no more, apart from the shelves of collectors, rare book dealers, and institutions. Only the living heart of their contents beats healthily in the myriad of briskly selling reprints that continue to be unearthed in great quantity from their yellowing pages both here and abroad where—notably in France and Japan—a youthful cabal of interest has sprung up in recent years. The pulps are dead, but at no time has literary and critical awareness of them been livelier than today.

RESEARCH COLLECTIONS

The State Historical Society of Wisconsin at Madison holds the August Derleth pulp collection, largely comprising fantasy and science fiction pulps, some in incomplete runs, together with many detective and other genre pulps to which the prolific Derleth contributed material; some of these latter items are relatively rare.

The San Francisco Academy of Comic Art contains what has been described as the finest cross-genre collection of pulps and dime novels in any public institution, holding key or first-issue examples of virtually every pulp, as well as many complete runs of titles in all pulp areas. The academy also provides the researcher with the unique opportunity to study pulps in close conjunction with large special collections in all other areas of the popular narrative arts, from comic strips through hardcover and paperback detective, western, adventure, and science fiction, children's books, comic books, films, drama, general fiction, story papers, general periodicals in all areas, extensive bound newspaper runs, Sherlockiana, Dickensiana, and so on, all housed and indexed for efficient cross-reference. The academy can provide a perfect, bound facsimile of any pulp on high-quality paper, including reproductions of the original color covers, for any fellow institution or serious researcher, at about sixty dollars an issue.

Today, much of the academy's collections is shared with Ohio State University's Special Collections division, where formal cataloging is continuing apace under the direction of the curator of the university's Cartoon Research Library, Lucy Caswell. The academy's longer pulp runs, such as science fiction magazines in general, *Argosy*, *The Popular*, *All-Story*, *Black Mask*, *Detective Fiction Weekly*, and *Detective Story Magazine*, are housed at Ohio State, while shorter files of more immediate contemporary research interest, such as certain hero pulps (a complete run of *The Spider*, etc.), detective pulps (*Dime Detective*, *Detective Tales*, *Clues Detective*, *Crime Busters*, etc.), and the penny blood collection, remain at the academy, together with many of its cross-reference popular narrative research files in comic strips, movies, dime novels, hard-cover genre fiction, and so on.

The researcher interested in examining detective, western, science fiction, or other genre pulps in the institutional collections listed here and elsewhere in this volume should bear the following information in mind.

1. No comprehensive pulp collection exists (although that shared by the academy and Ohio State comes closest in breadth of material represented); all suffer frequent and wide gaps in various areas. The researcher may well have to go to a number of widely separated institutions in order to locate a given group of titles and dates, and even then there may be some that can't be found. Science fiction pulp collections tend to be the most complete, however, due to the assiduity of the private collectors whose files have now entered public institutions.

2. Pulp collections are in varying degrees of accessibility. The Library of Congress pulps, once they are ferreted out, can be one or two days in reaching the Main Library from the warehouse where they are stored and often suffer from poor storage handling and aging paper. The pulps in Special Collections at the University of California at Los Angeles are usually brought promptly, but they are kept in a large number of boxes and often filed out of logical genre or title sequence in these boxes, so that the researcher, usually limited to one box at a time,

can spend much time going through successive boxes if he or she wishes to examine any considerable number of pulps. It would be wise, accordingly, to discuss accessibility factors with the institutions prior to visiting them, in order to have a reasonable idea of how much time will have to be expended. It is quite likely to be more than one would spend in looking at an equivalent number of hardcover books from the stacks of most institutions.

3. The readability condition of pulps usually varies greatly within the confines of each collection. Few institutions, unfortunately, have the budgets or the inclination to replace poor copies of pulps received as parts of donated collections with better ones, so that these poor copies steadily deteriorate to the degree that they are used and according to the condition under which they are stored. The researcher and librarian may well find that a pulp vital to the former's concerns is so browned and brittle with age that it literally cannot be further used without falling to pieces, so that the researcher will have to find another copy at some other institution—if he or she can. The librarian, meanwhile, will remove the pulp from the stacks and put it away to await restoration or duplication but will rarely check the collection further to locate similarly aged pulps, which will accordingly continue to stay on the institution's actively accessible list until they also are discovered at the worst possible time. One rarely will be able to learn about the condition of pulps in advance of a visit (many of these collections are not used by anyone for years at a time), so that this is a hazard to be met at any institution.

4. Since study time is understandably limited at most institutions, one will frequently want to leave pulps with stories marked for reproduction by the library. Since reproductive equipment can vary greatly in quality from place to place, it will be wise to sample this by making some few copies of pulp material on the premises, although more and more institutions are acquiring fine reproductive equipment that provides stunning copies.

5. If one hopes to conduct pulp research with the concurrent aid of critical and historical texts, it would be advisable either to bring along copies of these works or to check the institution's general reference stacks prior to arrival. The fact that a library holds a large, donated pulp collection (almost no institution has actually built its own collection from scratch) is no guarantee that it owns many specialized reference books in the field—or, indeed, that any of the institution staff themselves have much knowledge of, or interest in, their pulp holdings.

HISTORY AND CRITICISM

This chapter is concerned with the pulps as a publishing phenomenon, rather than with specific works or even bodies of work that appeared in the pulps. Accordingly, these notes reflect that concern and deal only with those texts that relate in some substantial way to the history of pulps or of some variety of pulps. Texts largely concentrating on single writers who happened to appear in the pulps or on extant popular literary forms that of necessity were represented by pulp genre titles are not discussed, although a number of such works are covered by other chapters in this volume.

Very little of consequence has been written about the pulps as a publishing form in books from the major trade or academic publishers, either in the past or in the present. A good deal more has been done in limited-edition texts, often in paper wrappers, from small publishers, while a small number of relevant and informative pieces do appear from time to time in a few academic and amateur press periodicals devoted to various aspects of the popular arts.

The finest pictorial survey of the pulp field as a whole is Frank Robinson's *sans pareil* volume of 1998, *Pulp Culture*. Here in stunning full-color reproduction are hundreds of major magazine covers from all known pulp genres, with brief, but authoritative, captions for the art and introductory commentary about authors, artists, and publishers for each genre. Included are the most famed and remarkable covers ever published in the pulps, making *Pulp Culture* as close to a definitive survey of pulp cover art as we are likely to see. Unfortunately, in view of the book's title, virtually no interior artwork is included, and little is mentioned in the historical commentary; another book in this area is acutely needed. Very secondary to *Pulp Culture* in breadth of coverage and quality of selections are a few similar works, constituting all that has been done in this field to date (apart from one or two titles limited to science fiction pulp illustrative art). These are, with their editors, *The Pulps* (Tony Goodstone), the earliest pulp cover book, leavened with an introduction by Sam Moscowitz and a broad selection of pulp fiction reprints, with some interior art included; *Pulp Art* (Robert Lesser), a book basically celebrating Lesser's spotty collection of original pulp cover art, with no attempt at inclusivity beyond Lesser's own paintings; and *Danger Is My Business* (Neon McAvey), a pulp history of sorts (with many genres uncovered) illustrated with a desultory lot of covers and some interior art, many selections ruined by creative trimmings and overlapping, with a generally poor selection of art throughout. The best of science fiction cover collections is Vincent Di Fate's *Infinite Worlds*, with fine color reproduction throughout, reflecting a fine knowledge of the pulp art covered.

To turn to largely nonpictorial works dealing with varying aspects of pulp fiction, an odd example of a little-known study of pulps from an unlikely publisher is Random House's lavish edition of an alleged history of Street and Smith (the publishing house that made a fortune from publishing *The Shadow*, *Doc Savage*, *Detective Story Magazine*, and *Astounding Stories*), called *The Fiction Factory: From Pulp Row to Quality Street* and purportedly by Quentin Reynolds, clearly a calculated and well-financed puff job celebrating the publisher's murder of its pulp line in turning to high-fashion, slick-paper magazines. Deadly dull to read, this book is notable only for its color reproductions of several Street and Smith pulp covers and its endless array of historical errors. It does, however, represent the only extant history of any real length covering a major pulp publisher as such, aside from three generally unsatisfactory texts dealing with the Munsey Company.

The first of these is an autobiographical work by Frank Munsey himself, *The Founding of the Munsey Publishing House*, which is colorful and lively with regard to Munsey's vicissitudes and triumphs in the publishing business through 1906 but of little use with regard to the texts and art of the Munsey magazines themselves. The same is largely true of George Britt's posthumous study of Munsey, *Forty Years, Forty Millions*, where references to the Munsey pulps—the book is basically concerned with Munsey's newspaper activity—are primarily for background color and anecdote, rather than celebration or critical concern. Neither book has much to offer in the way of illustrative data on the Munsey pulps. The same is unfortunately true of Frank Luther Mott's account of the Munsey Company in his generally exhaustive, five-volume *A History of American Magazines*. Mott, as in most of his lengthy pieces on major American magazines, is much more concerned with the relatively trivial data of financing and the musical-chair, ins and outs of editors and publishers than with the physical contents from year to year of the magazines that he is discussing. In personal taste, he is not overly interested in fiction and not at all in pulp fiction; accordingly, he slights even those occasional pulp titles published by the slick-paper magazine companies with which his work is primarily concerned. His piece on Munsey in volume 4 of his set represents his work's only coverage of a pulp publisher, and even here his emphasis is on Munsey's one major slick, the relatively feeble *Munsey's Magazine*. The bulk of the data in the piece is derived from the Munsey and Britt works cited, and it, too, is largely valid for reference to the limited extent that it deals with the Munsey pulps at all.

Excellent as anecdotal color relevant to the creative lives and commerce of the pulp writers in the 1930s and 1940s are two fine works: Frank Gruber, *The Pulp Jungle*, and Robert Turner, *Some of My Best Friends Are Writers, But I Wouldn't Want My Daughter to Marry One!* Turner, however, is much more reliable in areas of strict fact than Gruber, wherein anecdotes are often attributed to the wrong writers or editors or to the wrong time and place. There is a good deal of interesting critical commentary on many of the pulps in both books, although Turner is, again, more astute here than Gruber. Neither book, unfortunately, carries an index or illustrations, although Gruber has a nice display of pulp covers on its wraparound jacket. Harold Hersey's *Pulpwood Editor* is rather superficial and a bit confused in its relatively brief attempt to blanket what was obviously a very complex and exciting career in pulp editing that involved over fifty pulps but nevertheless of great value in illustrating the capacity and intelligence necessarily involved in mass pulp editing. (Hersey's later, long article in *Golden Atom* for 1953, "Looking Backward into the Future," which emphasizes his science fiction and fantasy pulp work, is much more precise and interesting than his formal hardcover book.) The book is well indexed, although unillustrated, and has a partial listing of Hersey's pulps. An interesting, but unfortunately latter-day, look at the work of pulp agents (the focus is almost wholly on sales to Gold Medal Books and other paperback replacements of the pulps) is to be found in Donald McCampbell's *Don't Step on It—It Might Be a Writer*. Again, there are no illustrations, but there is a useful index. In a class by itself is the only serious study of a single pulp magazine issued by a major publisher, Philip José Farmer's *Doc Savage: His Apocalyptic Life*. It has no index or illustrations but contains a series of highly informative appendixes.

Among formal instructional texts on pulp and general fiction writing between 1900 and 1930, few provide much worthwhile data on pulps per se, aside from the transient editorial requirements prevailing at the time of the book's publication. (While a study of such requirements can obviously be very informative, they are much better researched in the numerous writers' magazines of the period on a month-to-month basis than by leapfrogging among the various how-to-write texts.) The handful of writing manuals that do contain a good bit of information about the pulp magazines and pulp writers as such are *This Fiction Business*, by H. Bedford Jones; *The Fiction Factory*, by John Milton Edwards (pseudonym for William Wallace Cook); *Love Story Writer*, by Daisy Bacon; and *Science Fiction Handbook*, by L. Sprague de Camp.

Book-length studies of detective fiction or collections of shorter studies rarely mention any pulps other than *Black Mask*, and they are usually misinformed about even that title, thinking it was wholly a detective fiction magazine from the start. A partial exception is David Madden's anthology of articles by various writers, *Tough Guy Writers of the Thirties*, in which *Black Mask* nominally receives a long and separate discussion by Philip Durham. Durham is aware of *Black Mask*'s early multigenre aspect and mentions it but too quickly becomes involved in an exegesis on his King Charles' Heads, Dashiell Hammett, and Raymond Chandler (despite the assignment of special articles—all the studies in the book were written to order—on Hammett and Chandler to other hands) to say much of interest about the magazine itself. (Even in discussing Chandler, Durham seems unaware that the best of Chandler's pulp detective fiction appeared in *Dime Detective*—which he does not mention—rather than in *Black Mask*.) Otherwise, despite the book's assumed focus on the style of writing that prevailed in the detective pulps from 1930 on, there is no other discussion of pulps in any of the articles in the volume; there is not even an entry for "pulps" or "pulp magazines" in the index.

The few books to deal seriously with western fiction neglect the pulps similarly, excepting only John G. Cawelti's *The Six-Gun Mystique*, in which the importance of western pulps is at least acknowledged, and a number of major pulp titles are listed (oddly including *Doc Savage*), but little informative comment about the pulps themselves is made in the text. Similarly, Max Brand's and Zane Grey's pulp sales are duly noted in books on the authors (the two best are *Max Brand: The Big "Westerner,"* by Robert Easton, and *Zane Grey*, by Frank Gruber), but little or nothing is said about the pulps involved, not even such relevant matters as the kind and amount of illustrative art given to major pulp works by the writers discussed. In the area of science fiction, on the other hand, an abundance of talented and scholarly minded "fans," who literally grew up with the pulps of that genre, have seen to it that the central relevance of the pulps to the development of science fiction in the twentieth century has received its just dues in a vast number of amateur, small press, and generally published titles. In fact, there is virtually no text on science fiction as a genre in which the pulps are not discussed in often intimate and highly informative length. (Since a great number of these are analyzed and listed in the chapters on fantasy and science fiction in this volume, I avoid extensive repetition here, mentioning only a few titles in the following passages dealing with small press publications on the pulps.) Aside from texts on detective fiction, western fiction, science fiction, and fantasy, little has appeared from general or academic publishers in book form covering fictional genres prominent in the pulps (e.g., there has been no study of adventure fiction as such or of popular war fiction), so that the relevant pulp facets here remain as unexamined on this level as in detective and western fiction.

Some of the very few texts that touch knowledgeably on the fields of periodical popular fiction and that preceded the pulps might advantageously be mentioned here. These include, certainly, the monumental study of the first dime-novel publishing house, *The House of Beadle and Adams and Its Dime and Nickel Novels*, by Albert Johanssen; *Dime Novels*, by Edmund Pearson; *Books in Black and Red*, by Edmund Pearson; *Villains Galore*, by Mary Noel; *Virgin Land*, by Henry Nash

Smith; *Bang! Bang!*, by George Ade; *Penrod Jashber*, by Booth Tarkington; and (largely for impressionistic humor) *A Plea for Old Cap Collier*, by Irvin S. Cobb.

In the small press area, several works of direct and important relevance to the pulp fiction magazine field have appeared in recent years, while more will apparently continue to appear, thanks to the development over the past decade of a new, concentrated body of interest among bibliophiles in the contents, sequences, and fine points of differentiation to be found in the pulps. This growth of interest has been augmented by the appearance in recent years of several small journals devoted wholly to the pulps, their contents, and collection. Prominent among the small press works that serve this interest is a fine impressionistic study of several pulp genres, with no pretense to formal history, popular fiction writer Ron Goulart's engaging *Cheap Thrills*. Goulart quickly covers most of the major pulp genres with an engaging gloss and includes a number of black-and-white pages of pulp cover and interior art. Some very pertinent information about pulp writing and editing can be found in the several pages of direct quotes obtained by Goulart from surviving pulp writers that close this book. More informative in the sense of its organized emphasis on a single pulp subject is Robert Kenneth Jones' *The Shudder Pulps* from a mail-order book business, Fax Collector's Editions. This data- and quotation-packed text deals wholly with the sex-and-sadism pulps of the 1930s, includes a great many reduced black-and-white pulp cover and interior art cuts, and is meticulously indexed (although, curiously, no checklist of the pulps covered is included). In *The "Weird Tales" Story*, also from Fax, Robert Weinberg similarly focuses on a single pulp subject, the development of the famed fantasy magazine between 1923 and 1973. Although this work lacks the fine index of the Jones title, it includes a large number of black-and-white photos and reproductions of covers and interior art from *Weird Tales*. As with the Goulart book, a number of short, but worthwhile, quotations from writers and artists associated with the magazine are included. Alva Rogers' *A Requiem for "Astounding,"* from Advent Publishers, a mail-order house developed within science fiction fandom in the 1950s, deals engagingly with the history of the central science fiction pulp *Astounding Stories*, through all of its literary and titular permutations, and includes both a detailed index and an excellent selection of cover and interior art in black-and-white reproduction.

The foregoing small press titles are hardcover in the original editions. Among paperback (and generally smaller) texts from this source, one of the most notable works is Lohr McKinstrey and Robert Weinberg's *The Hero Pulp Index*. This painstaking and nearly inclusive compilation by story title and date of all the issues of all of the hero pulps in the 1930s and later has been a vital reference guide to research in this important area of pulp publishing. Included are a number of black-and-white pulp cover reproductions and summaries of the themes of each pulp covered. Some separate (and generally well done) studies of individual hero pulps are *The Man behind Doc Savage* by Robert Weinberg; *America's Secret Service Ace*, by Nick Carr, which deals with *Operater #5*; *Gangland's Doom*, by Frank Eisgruber Jr., covering *The Shadow*; and *The Many Faces of the Whisperer*, by Will Murray. These texts, published by Weinberg, lack indexes, but all are well and appropriately illustrated with black-and-white cuts from the pulps covered and contain full lists of the issues discussed.

Among the small reprint publishers almost wholly devoted to hardcover republication of important works from the pulps (many of which are often reprinted profitably by major paperback houses in several editions) are Arkham House of Wisconsin, founded in 1939 and the forerunner of all such publishers, with nearly 100 titles to its credit, and largely concerned with pulp material from *Weird Tales* and the science fiction and fantasy pulps (particularly the work of H. P. Lovecraft, Clark Ashton Smith, and August Derleth); Donald M. Grant of Rhode Island, who has published over 26 titles to date, which are largely involved with the pulp works of Robert E. Howard and Talbot Mundy; Fax Collector's Editions, which reprints memorable fiction from the broad range of pulps in a myriad of hardcover and paperback volumes; and Carcosa of North Carolina, which specializes in large, definitive anthologies of the pulp work of major writers in all genres. The science fiction field fostered a number of such pulp reprint publishers in the postwar decades, notably, Gnome Press, Fantasy Press, Shasta Publishers, and Hadley Publishing (later Grant-Hadley, now Donald M. Grant); all but the last are now moribund, the large paperback houses having taken over science fiction and fantasy pulp reprinting directly. Popular Press, of Bowling Green State University in Ohio, has emerged in recent years as an important publisher of general pulp studies, bibliographies, and scholarly anthologies in the field, with several new titles appearing annually.

Of important contemporary periodicals concerned in whole or in part with the study of pulps (excluding science fiction fan publications, which are a highly specialized field of their own), it is necessary to mention Nils Hardin's *Xenophile*, Will Murray's *Duende*, Ray B. Browne's *Journal of Popular Culture*, Robert Weinberg's *Weird Tales Collector* and *Pulp*, Allen J. Hubin's *Armchair Detective*, and J. Randolph Cox's *Dime Novel Round-up*. Of these, only the *Journal of Popular Culture*, the *Armchair Detective*, and the *Dime Novel Round-up* are being regularly published now. The two Weinberg titles and *Duende* are now only irregularly issued, with long (years-long) gaps between issues, while *Xenophile*, perhaps the best of the lot, has not published a new issue in many years.

In addition to the works previously discussed, all of which appeared prior to 1978, the subsequent decade saw the publication of a number of excellent volumes by the publishers cited, as well as by some houses new to the field. Remarkable in its ambition and accomplishment is Robert Sampson's six-volume *Yesterday's Faces*, subtitled *A Study of Series Characters in the Early Pulp Magazines*. For Sampson, "early" means largely the pulps printed in the 1920s and before; consequently, he is concerned primarily with the general-content pulps such as *Argosy*, *Blue Book*, and *Adventure*, although some early genre titles such as *Detective Story Magazine* and *Weird Tales* are well covered. The great bulk of Sampson's fascinating subject matter has never been discussed in print before, and his pioneering examination in depth of the exotic creatures that he parades before us in volume after volume is—thanks to the author's lively, humorous style—endlessly absorbing. From Nick Carter to Wu Fang, by way of Semi Dual, Fantomas, and John Carter, Sampson paints a series of garishly arresting portraits; his brisk, witty summation of the kill-and-rescue plots of the Tarzan novels (in volume 2) is the best such recounting that I have ever read. There are two other fact-packed studies by Sampson; one colorfully surveys the 326-novel career of the Shadow, called *The Night Master*, and the other, oddly titled *Spider* (rather than, sensibly, *The Spider*), deals in fascinating detail with the blood-soaked career of Norvell Page's classic crime fighter.

These are the leading works among other informative books celebrating hero pulp figures, such as Tom Johnson and Will Murray's incisive *Secret Agent "X": A History* and Nick Carr's absorbing study of *G-8 and His Battle Aces*, titled *The Flying Spy*.

Excellent biographies of major pulp writers have appeared, notably, Peter Berresford Ellis' account of Talbot Mundy's life, *The Last Adventurer*, and two penned by L. Sprague de Camp: *Lovecraft: A Biography* and (with Catherine Crook de Camp and Jane Whittington Griffin) *Dark Valley Destiny: The Life of Robert E. Howard*. Glenn Lord's *The Last Celt: A Bio-Bibliography of Robert Ervin Howard* deals with both the life and works of Howard in loving detail, much as an earlier work by Darrell C. Richardson, titled *Max Brand: The Man and His Work*, covers the life and work of its subject in roughly equal parts. Notable volumes in still another novel form, which might be termed the biobibliography-anthology, are Douglas G. Greene's engaging *The Door to Doom and Other Detective Stories* by John Dickson Carr (although Carr was only infrequently a writer for the pulps, the emphasis in this text is on this peripheral, periodical work) and Donald M. Grant's *Talbot Mundy: Messenger of Destiny*, which combines articles about Mundy's life and work with an excellent bibliography.

A pair of superficial works derived from (rather than seriously studying) the English parallels of the American dime novel and nickel thriller (called variously penny dreadfuls, penny bloods, and shilling shockers) and chiefly made up of numerous reproductions of the illustrations and color covers of these periodicals have appeared during the past decade. These are Michael Anglo's *Penny Dreadfuls and Other Victorian Horrors* and Peter Haining's *The Art of Horror Stories* (which includes a good deal of American pulp horror fiction art in its later pages). Two other titles in this arcane area by Haining are extremely useful anthologies with all too brief prefatory matter, called *The Penny Dreadful* and *The Shilling Shockers*. A light, but informed, study in some depth of this material is to be found in E. S. Turner's *Boys Will Be Boys*, where the reader will want to consult both the first (1948) and the current (1975) editions, since the two versions contain much dissimilar, but equally informative, matter. Two worthwhile anthologies of dime novel texts are E. F. Bleiler's *Eight Dime Novels* and Gary Hoppenstand's *The Dime Novel Detective*. The Hoppenstand volume includes bibliographies of such long-running dime novel characters as Nick Carter, Old Sleuth, and Secret Service, while the Bleiler book is marvelously informed with the editor's characteristic knowledge of all aspects of nineteenth-century esoterica. Daryl Jones' fine study, *The Dime Novel Western*, is a genuinely gripping and entertaining account in detail of a previously underdiscussed body of bizarre writing.

One of the most outstanding works of scholarship in the pulp and dime novel field is Michael L. Cook's superbly edited and comprehensively encyclopedic *Mystery, Detective, and Espionage Magazines*, in which numerous experts (including Robert Sampson, Nick Carr, and others discussed earlier) have written succinctly definitive entries about virtually every crime suspense dime novel or pulp title published over the past century. Although later findings in pulp research have dated some of the entries in this 1983 book, it remains an indispensable work for the historian or critic. Another book edited by Cook, of *major* use to the researcher in popular fiction history, is *Mystery Fanfare: A Composite Annotated Index to Mystery and Related Fanzines 1963–1981*, in which some seventeen old, current, major, and obscure publications devoted to pulps (as well as another twenty-eight titles about mystery fiction in general, but often touching on pulps) are indexed through some 441 pages and several thousand articles. Even more ambitious and accomplished is a two-volume work coedited by Cook with Stephen T. Miller, which indexes a vast number of single-genre pulps. Titled *Mystery, Detective, and Espionage Fiction: A checklist of Fiction in U.S. Pulp Magazines, 1915–1974*, this indispensable, 1,183-page work was based on many years of national research among private and public pulp collections and is exhaustively indexed by both author and magazine, with the latter index citing the entire fictional contents of each issue of each magazine covered, making it possible for collectors and special collection librarians to determine the contents of issues on their shelves at a glance. A vitally related and more extensive work is Walter Albert's *Detective and Mystery Fiction: An International Bibliography of Secondary Sources*, which lists and discusses (often in considerable detail) all books and many articles in selected general and fan magazines that deal with mystery fiction in hardcover, paperback, pulps, and dime novels in any way at all (although, for space considerations, most Sherlockiana has been excluded). Many long-promised pulp indexes continue in preparation in various places, but two crucial works indexing *Black Mask* and *Dime Detective* have at last been printed. E. R. Hagemann's *A Comprehensive Index to "Black Mask," 1920–1951* is an excellent formal indexing by the author of every story and many articles published in that doyen of detective pulps, although an earlier and more obscure work compiled be E. H. Mundell—*"Black Mask": An Index*—is of much greater use to the collector and institution that has to decide which issues to purchase from dealers who list by date only, since (like the Cook–Miller work) it prints the contents page of every issue from volume 1, number 1, through volume 36, number 2, in simple sequence, exactly as each one appeared in each issue with all titles and authors included, an indexing concept particularly vital at this time in a field with so few complete reference runs of non-science fiction pulps accessible to researchers with the Cook–Miller type of index in hand. James L. Traylor's *Dime Detective Index* wisely combines both forms of indexing in his masterfully accomplished volume, a model for future indexes of single-title magazines.

BIBLIOGRAPHY

Books and Articles

Ade, George. *Bang! Bang!* New York: J. H. Sears, 1928.

Albert, Walter. *Detective and Mystery Fiction: An International Bibliography of Secondary Sources.* Madison, Ind.: Brownstone Books, 1985.

Anglo, Michael. *Penny Dreadfuls and Other Victorian Horrors.* London: Jupiter Books, 1977.

Bacon, Daisy. *Love Story Writer.* New York: Hermitage House, 1954.

Bedford-Jones, Henry. *This Fiction Business.* New York: Covici-Freide, 1929.

Bleiler, E. F., ed. *Eight Dime Novels.* New York: Driver, 1974.

Bleiler, Richard. *The Thrill Book Index.* Mercer, Wash.: Starmont House, 1991.

Britt, George. *Forty Years, Forty Millions: The Career of Frank A. Munsey.* New York: N.p., 1935.

Browne, Ray B., and Gary Hoppenstand, eds. *The Defective Detective in the Pulps.*

Bowling Green, Ohio: Bowling Green State University Popular Press, 1983.

Carr, Nick. *America's Secret Service Ace (Operator #5)*. Oak Lawn, Ill.: Robert Weinberg, 1974.

———. *The Flying Spy (G-8)*. Chicago: Robert Weinberg, 1978.

———. *The Other Detective Pulp Heroes*. Chicago: Tattered Pages Press, 1992.

Cave, Hugh B. *Magazines I Remember*. Chicago: Tattered Pages Press, 1994.

———. *Pulp Man's Odyssey: The Hugh B. Cave Story*. Ed. Audery B. Parente. Mercer Island, Wash.: Starmont House, 1988.

Cawelti, John G. *The Six-Gun Mystique*. Bowling Green, Ohio: Bowling Green State University Popular Press, 1970.

Cobb, Irvin S. *A Plea for Old Cap Collier*. New York: George H. Doran, 1921.

Cook, Michael L. *Mystery, Detective, and Espionage Fiction: A Checklist of Fiction in U.S. Pulp Magazines, 1915–1974*. New York: Garland, 1988.

Cook, Michael L., ed. *Mystery, Detective, and Espionage Magazines*. Westport, Conn.: Greenwood Press, 1983.

———. *Mystery Fanfare: A Composite Annotated Index to Mystery and Related Fanzines, 1963–1981*. Bowling Green, Ohio: Bowling Green State University Popular Press, 1983.

Cook, William Wallace [John Milton Edwards]. *The Fiction Factory*. Ridgewood, N.J.: Editor, 1912.

Day, Donald B. *Index to the Science-Fiction Magazines: 1926–1950*. Portland, Oreg.: Perri Press, 1952.

De Camp, L. Sprague. *Lovecraft: A Biography*. New York: Doubleday, 1975.

———. *Science Fiction Handbook*. New York: Hermitage House, 1953. Rev. ed. Philadelphia: Owlswick Press, 1975.

De Camp, L. Sprague, Catherine Crook de Camp, and Jane Whittington Griffin. *Dark Valley Destiny: The Life of Robert E. Howard*. New York: Bluejay Books, 1983.

Di Fate, Vincent. *Infinite Worlds*. New York: Penguin Putnam, 1997.

Easton, Robert. *Max Brand: The Big "Westerner."* Norman: University of Oklahoma Press, 1970.

Eisgruber, Frank, Jr. *Gangland's Doom: The Shadow of the Pulps*. Oak Lawn, Ill.: Robert Weinberg, 1974.

Ellis, Peter Berresford. *The Last Adventurer: The Life of Talbot Mundy 1879–1940*. West Kingston, R.I.: Donald M. Grant, 1984.

Etulain, Richard W., and Michael T. Marsden, eds. *The Popular Western: Essays toward a Definition*. Bowling Green, Ohio: Bowling Green State University Popular Press, 1974.

Farmer, Philip José. *Doc Savage: His Apocalyptic Life*. Garden City, N.Y.: Doubleday, 1973.

Farsace, Larry. *Golden Atom*. New York: Golden Atom, 1955.

Gibson, Walter B. *The Shadow Scrapbook*. New York: Harcourt Brace Jovanovich, 1979.

Goodstone, Tony, ed. *The Pulps*. New York: Chelsea House, 1970.

Goulart, Ron, *Cheap Thrills: An Informal History of the Pulp Magazines*. New Rochelle, N.Y.: Arlington House, 1972.

Grant, Donald M., ed. *Talbot Mundy: Messenger of Destiny*. West Kingston, R.I.: Donald M. Grant, 1983.

Greene, Douglas G., ed. *The Door to Doom and Other Detections*, by John Dickson Carr. New York: Harper and Row, 1980.

Gruber, Frank. *The Pulp Jungle*. Los Angeles: Sherbourne Press, 1967.

———. *Zane Grey*. Cleveland, Ohio: World, 1970.

Hagemann, E. R. *A Comprehensive Index to "Black Mask," 1920–1951*. Bowling Green, Ohio: Bowling Green State University Popular Press, 1982.

Haining, Peter, ed. *The Art of Horror Stories*. Secaucus, N.J.: Chartwell Books, 1996.

———. *The Art of Mystery and Detective Stories*. Secaucus, N.J.: Chartwell Books, 1986.

———. *The Penny Dreadful*. London: Victor Gollancz, 1975.

———. *The Shilling Shockers*. New York: St. Martin's Press, 1978.

Hamilton, Frank. *The Artist behind Doc Savage*. Oklahoma City: Ron J. Franz, 1977.

Heins, Henry Hardy. *A Golden Anniversary Bibliography of Edgar Rice Burroughs*. West Kingston, R.I.: Donald M. Grant, 1964.

Herron, Don, ed. *The Dark Barbarian: The Writings of Robert E. Howard. A Critical Anthology*. Westport, Conn.: Greenwood Press, 1984.

Hersey, Harold. "Looking Backward into the Future." *Golden Atom* (1953), 45–68.

———. *Pulpwood Editor*. New York: Frederick A. Stokes, 1937.

Hoppenstand, Gary, ed. *The Dime Novel Detective*. Bowling Green, Ohio: Bowling Green State University Popular Press, 1982.

Johanssen, Albert. *The House of Beadle and Adams and Its Dime and Nickel Novels*. Norman: University of Oklahoma Press, 1950. Supplement, 1962.

Johnson, Tom, and Will Murray, *Secret Agent "X": A History*. Oak Lawn, Ill.: Robert Weinberg, 1980.

Jones, Daryl. *The Dime Novel Western*. Bowling Green, Ohio: Bowling Green State University Popular Press, 1978.

Jones, H. Bedford. *This Fiction Business*. New York: Covici-Fried, 1929.

Jones, Robert Kenneth. *The Shudder Pulps: A History of the Weird Menace Magazines of the 1930s*. West Linn, Oreg.: Fax Collector's Editions, 1975.

Lesser, Robert. *Pulp Art*. New York: Random House.

Lord, Glenn. *The Last Celt: A Bio-Bibliography of Robert Ervin Howard*. West Kingston, R.I.: Donald M. Grant, 1976.

Madden, David, ed. *Tough Guy Writers of the Thirties*. Carbondale: Southern Illinois University Press, 1968.

McAvey, Neon. *Danger Is My Business*. San Francisco: Chronicle Books, 1996.

McCampbell, Donald. *Don't Step On It—It Might Be a Writer: Reminiscences of a Literary Agent*. Los Angeles: Sherbourne Press, 1972.

McKinstrey, Lohr, and Robert Weinberg. *The Hero Pulp Index*. Evergreen, Colo.: Opar Press, 1971.

Mott, Frank Luther. *A History of American Magazines*. Vol. 4. Cambridge: Harvard University Press, 1957.

Mundell, E. H. *"Black Mask": An Index*. Portage, Ind.: Mundell, 1969.

Munsey, Frank. *The Founding of the Munsey Publishing House.* New York: Munsey, 1907.

Murray, Will. *Doc Savage: Reflections in Bronze.* Greenwood, Mass.: Odyssey, 1978.

———. *The Many Faces of the Whisperer.* Oak Lawn, Ill.: Robert Weinberg, 1975.

———. *Doc Savage: Supreme Adventure.* Greenwood, Mass.: Odyssey, 1980.

———. *The Duende History of* The Shadow *Magazine.* Addendum insert. Greenwood, Mass.: Odyssey, 1980.

———. *Secrets of Doc Savage.* Greenwood, Mass.: Odyssey, 1981.

Noel, Mary. *Villains Galore: The Heyday of the Popular Story Weekly.* New York: Macmillan, 1954.

Pearson, Edmund. *Books in Black and Red.* New York: Macmillan, 1923.

———. *Dime Novels.* Boston: Little, Brown, 1929.

Porges, Irwin. *Edgar Rice Burroughs: The Man Who Created Tarzan.* Provo, Utah: Brigham Young University Press, 1975.

Reynolds, Quentin. *The Fiction Factory: From Pulp Row to Quality Street.* New York: Random House, 1955.

Richardson, Darrell C. *Max Brand: The Man and His Work.* Los Angeles: Fantasy, 1952.

Roberts, Garyn G. *A Cent a Story! The Best from Ten Detective Aces.* Bowling Green, Ohio: Bowling Green State University Popular Press, 1986.

Robinson, Frank. *Pulp Culture.* Portland, Oreg.: Collectors Press, 1998.

Rogers, Alva. *A Requiem for "Astounding."* Chicago: Advent, 1964.

Sampson, Robert. *Deadly Excitements: Shadows and Phantoms.* Bowling Green, Ohio: Popular Press, 1989.

———. *The Night Master.* Chicago: Pulp Press, 1982.

———. *Spider.* Bowling Green, Ohio: Popular Press, 1987.

———. *Yesterday's Faces: A Study of Series Characters in the Early Pulp Magazines.* 6 vols. Bowling Green, Ohio: Bowling Green State University Popular Press, 1983, 1985, 1986.

Shine, Walter, and Jean Shine. *A Bibliography of the Published Works of John D. MacDonald.* Gainesville: University of Florida, 1980.

Smith, Henry Nash. *Virgin Land: The American West as Symbol and Myth.* Cambridge: Harvard University Press, 1950, 1970.

Tarkington, Booth. *Penrod Jashber.* Garden City, N.Y.: Doubleday, 1929.

Traylor, James L. *Dime Detective Index.* New Carrolton, Md.: Pulp Collector Press, 1986.

Turner, E. S. *Boys Will Be Boys: The Story of Sweeney Todd, Deadwood Dick, Sexton Blake, Billy Bunter, Dick Barton, et al.* London: Michael Joseph, 1975.

Turner, Robert L. *Some of My Best Friends Are Writers, But I Wouldn't Want My Daughter to Marry One!* Los Angeles: Sherbourne Press, 1970.

Van Hise, James. *Edgar Rice Burroughs' Fantastic Worlds.* Yucca Valley, Calif.: James Van Hise, 1996.

———. *The Fantastic Worlds of Robert E. Howard.* Yucca Valley, Calif.: James Van Hise.

———. *Pulp Heroes of the Thirties.* Yucca Valley, Calif.: Midnight Graffiti, 1994.

———. *Pulp Masters.* Yucca Valley, Calif.: Midnight Graffiti, 1996.

Weinberg, Robert. *The Man behind Doc Savage: A Tribute to Lester Dent.* Oak Lawn, Ill.: Robert Weinberg, 1974.

———. *The "Weird Tales" Story*. West Linn, Oreg.: Fax Collector's Editions, 1977.

Periodicals

Armchair Detective. New York, 1967– .
Dime Novel Round-up. Fall River, Mass., 1931– .
Duende. North Quincy, Mass., 1977– .
High Adventure. Silver Spring, Md., 1994– .
Journal of Popular Culture. Bowling Green, Ohio, 1977– .
Weird Tales Collector. Chicago, 1977– .
Xenophile. St. Louis, Mo., 1974– .

RADIO

Erica Scharrer and Thomas Greenfield

Since its earliest days, radio has been widely recognized as a tremendously potent force in American culture. Educators were among the medium's first and most enthusiastic exploiters (see S. E. Frost Jr., *Education's Own Stations: The History of Broadcast Licenses Issued to Educational Institutions*), and the earliest "broadcast pioneers"—Guglielmo Marconi, Lee DeForest, Reginald Fessenden, David Sarnoff—felt strongly that radio would improve the level of American taste by offering every citizen the finest of the world's music, poetry, and drama. In 1910, for instance, DeForest broadcast Caruso and the entire Metropolitan Opera Company as a demonstration of radio's ability to spread Culture (with a capital C) throughout the land. Less than four years after Fessenden had first used a microphone, the medium's artistic potential was being recognized.

Not surprisingly, therefore, the literature of radio is copious and virtually conatal with the medium itself. Even excluding the technical and engineering literature (which dates back to Hertz and other pre-Marconi experimenters), a thorough bibliographer will find newspaper and magazine speculations about "wireless telephony"—even television—scattered here and there throughout the last decade of the nineteenth century. The legal and bureaucratic literature of litigation and regulation dates to Marconi's patent documents in 1896, and by World War I these writings had already assumed huge proportions. Their importance in gauging radio's effect on popular culture cannot be ignored. The United States Navy, for instance, had been allowed to retain full control of radio's development after 1918 (see *History of Communications—Electronics in the United States Navy*, prepared by Captain S. L. Howeth), and at the time it seemed as if there would never be a Herbert Hoover to cooperate with the major broadcasters in the development of commercial program patterns.

In this chapter, however, the concentration is on neither the technical nor the bureaucratic aspects of radio. Rather, the focus is on the programming and the personalities connected with radio's development as an entertainment medium.

Though an occasional nod is bent toward the international setting within which radio has grown, primary attention is given to the American scene, particularly to comedy, drama, music, and variety show broadcasting. Inevitably, some attention is given to news, sports, and "high culture" broadcasting—all of which are at least partially entertainment. Moreover, much of the material reviewed here concerns history, not the contemporary scene. Radio's "golden age," the years of its most obvious and dominating impact on the culture of everyday Americans, came in the 1930s and 1940s.

Even in this comparatively limited field, however, it is not possible to attempt a truly comprehensive bibliography within the confines of this chapter. The first issue of *Radio Broadcast* appeared in 1922, and by 1950 there were literally scores of daily, weekly, monthly, and quarterly publications devoted exclusively or primarily to radio programming. Every newspaper and general-interest magazine of the 1930s and 1940s had regular columnists assigned to cover radio, and the most popular programs generated dozens of spin-off book publications every year— Gertrude Berg's *The Rise of the Goldbergs* and Phillips H. Lord's *Seth Parker's Sunday Evening Meeting: An Entertainment in One Act* are just two examples.

HISTORICAL OUTLINE

It is not easy to summarize the history of radio. In its early days the medium grew so rapidly and in such diverse ways that time still has not fully clarified what things were important and what things were merely interesting. In general, however, radio in America has gone through four developmental stages: the "pioneer period" from the 1890s through the mid-1920s; the "golden age" of network programs in the 1930s and the 1940s; the "television age," which began in the late 1940s and lasted through the 1980s; and the "post-television age," which began in the early 1990s and is still in progress. From the viewpoint of the "old-time radio" fans, this pattern is almost tragic, representing periods of adventurous youth, glorious maturity, pitiable decay, and a static modern existence that bears little resemblance to former glory days. From a less partisan position, however, the pattern looks better. It shows a medium that went through a period of early technological and commercial development and then through a boom period of unstable and rapid growth, achieved a secure place in the structure of American business and culture, and finally regained some of its former vigor through new technologies and specialized programming.

The pioneer years can be traced to Heinrich Hertz and the other pre-Marconi investigators of the nineteenth century. For our purposes, however, radio really began in 1895, when the young Italian inventor Guglielmo Marconi took his wireless telegraph to England. Customs inspectors smashed his prototype (they thought it was a bomb), but he rebuilt it, obtained British patents, and soon had commercial backers. Before the turn of the century, he had used Morse code to broadcast the results of the America's Cup yacht race, and virtually all of the major Western powers were investigating wireless for military and naval communications.

During the next decade, Reginald Fessenden, Lee DeForest, and scores of other inventors and enthusiasts developed technical improvements—the microphone, the vacuum tube, various crystal receivers—that made radio both inexpensive and exciting.

During World War I, the United States Navy took over almost exclusive control of American radio. It severely limited the use of the medium but made rapid technological progress. Then, in 1919, radio stations again became independent, and the mass production of commercial radio equipment became profitable. General Electric formed the Radio Corporation of America (RCA), which took over Marconi's original American company with the idea that the big profits would lie in the production of radio parts. They were not really thinking of broadcasting as anything but a marketing device to help sell radio receivers. The other big electrical companies like Westinghouse and American Telephone and Telegraph had similar ideas. Each of them set up broadcasting stations in order to put interesting things on the air, believing (rightly) that they could sell more receivers that way.

Many other people, however, were also interested in broadcasting. Amateurs broadcast from their garages and basements for the pure joy of contacting people from distant places. Newspapers set up stations to broadcast election results, sporting events, and other notable occurrences because they hoped to sell more newspapers by whetting the public's interest. By the early 1920s, dance bands and Broadway plays were being broadcast live from the cramped, ill-equipped studios of pioneer stations such as WJZ and KDKA, and many stations were beginning to broadcast on regular schedules. Meanwhile, performers were beginning to agitate for payment when they performed on radio.

By 1925, the American Society of Composers, Artists, and Performers (ASCAP) was insisting on pay scales for radio performances. The National Association of Broadcasters had been formed to protect the interests of station owners, and local stations were using telephone lines to achieve multistation broadcasts of major events. In Chicago, Detroit, Pittsburgh, and other areas, not to mention New York, stations had established their own regular programs of drama, comedy, and vaudeville, many of them with commercial sponsors. Broadcasting had become a business of its own.

In 1926, the General Electric Corporation, Westinghouse, and the Radio Corporation of America formed the National Broadcasting Company (NBC). The network system was born. Within a year, the Columbia Broadcasting System (CBS) was also operating. NBC contracted to supply each local station with a certain number of programs, most of which originated in New York. Local stations still had considerable time at their own disposal, but they had to carry the programs that NBC sent them. NBC, in turn, sold airtime to sponsors. The sponsors were to supply the programs; the network simply used its facilities to broadcast whatever program the sponsors wanted. Sponsors, in turn, wanted to use airtime to sell products, and they turned to advertising agencies to produce shows that would sell their wares. The result was that certain advertising agencies became the major employers of actors, singers, directors, writers, and all the other show business professionals. Only Hollywood and Broadway could compete as talent markets. Vaudeville died, but radio grew and grew.

Programming patterns on the networks developed rapidly. At first, comedy-variety shows dominated, and sponsored programs were heard largely at night. In 1929, when Freeman Gosden and Charles Correl took their local Chicago program to New York, *Amos n' Andy* became radio's first nationwide phenomenon.

An ornate radio, ca. 1929. Courtesy of the Library of Congress

Soon, other shows with a continued story line and consistent characters became standard nighttime fare, though the variety show performers like Eddie Cantor, Ed Wynn, and Al Jolson continued to be the biggest crowd pleasers.

In a relatively short time, the *Amos n' Andy* concept was metamorphosed into a form designed for daytime listeners, mainly housewives. The daily, fifteen-minute soap opera was born, and within a few years it became almost the only thing that the networks could carry during the day. There were always sponsors for a soap opera.

During the middle and late 1930s the networks began to discover that they had programming capabilities of their own. They did not have to rely on advertising firms for programs. All of the networks had certain time periods that no sponsor was using, and the networks had to sustain their programming with fillers. So they began using that time for programs, which were showcases for experimentation, such as the *Columbia Workshop*. Archibald MacLeish's verse-drama *The Fall of the City*, for instance, was written for, and performed as part of, sustaining-time programming. Programs stressing new, dynamic approaches to history, current events, and the arts were developed, and in some cases they became hits. In turn, they stimulated sponsors to develop programs; for example, *Time* magazine developed *The March of Time*, which re-created current events through dramatization.

During the late 1930s two more networks formed. The American Broadcasting Company (ABC) was formed when antitrust actions forced RCA to give up NBC, and NBC was forced to become one network rather than two; ABC had formerly been the NBC "blue" network, which supplemented the larger, more popular "red" network. Also, the Mutual Broadcasting System (MBS) was formed as a more or less cooperative venture among stations that wanted more independence than they would be allowed as part of NBC or CBS and yet needed the greater range of programming and services that only a network could provide.

By 1940, the basic programming patterns were set, and they continued through World War II with very little major change. But in the late 1940s, commercial television became a reality. By 1950, television was cutting heavily into radio's market. Network radio tried to respond with some new, creative concepts, such as *Monitor*, a weekend program of interviews, satire, and news features. Basically, the entertainment role that network radio programs had filled for two decades was being thoroughly assumed by television. Radio programming, except for news, reverted primarily to the owners of individual stations. Pioneer stations became "Top-40" stations just to survive.

Radio programming can largely attribute its survival to being basically a local station phenomenon, though today more and more stations find that they must turn to prepackaged models ("soft rock," etc.) to compete for advertising dollars. The networks sponsor a growing number of shows, many in the soft "news you can use" genre (CBS' *Tax Tips* is one example), but radio continues to draw its strength as a local medium. Local weather, traffic, and news reports often supplement down-home DJs and ads from local businesses to give radio its community-centered orientation.

However, four major changes that warrant special mention have occurred since this chapter was first written. First, there has been a revival of the radio network, once thought confined to being an entity of radio's nostalgic past. More and more modern radio stations are once again subscribing to network services and relying increasingly on network-produced programs containing national advertisements. One such example is American Public Radio's (APR) marquis Garrison Keillor program *A Prairie Home Companion*, currently picked up by some 410 APR network affiliates across the country. Commercial radio networks abound as well. Among the standouts in new entries in 1998 were a joint venture from Fox News and Westwood One that provided news programming to thousands of stations worldwide and Radio Voyager Network, a multinational effort poised to offer twenty-four hours of programming to stations in Japan, Italy, the United States, and other locations.

The second major change is the even more marked rise in radio program syndication. Many of those local stations that choose not to participate fully as a network affiliate opt instead to pick up nationally syndicated programs piecemeal. This option allows greater flexibility for the station regarding when to air the program and which programs to choose compared to the more structured and exclusive relationship advanced in network affiliation. Among the more successful syndicated radio programs are the *Howard Stern Show*, *The Rest of the Story* with Paul Harvey, and *Dr. Laura* with psychologist Dr. Laura Schlessinger.

The third substantial development in radio is the rising popularity of nonmusic programming. The twin forces behind this change are the extraordinary growth and power of talk radio and the impressive comeback that has been staged by the AM dial on which these formats are typically found. The call-in commentary, occasionally heated political themes, and controversial figures that constitute talk radio have led in no small part to the revived vitality associated with the medium of radio, particularly with the AM band. The programs are peopled with such charismatic characters as Larry King, Don Imus, and Rush Limbaugh. To varying degrees, these figures have pushed the envelope in their occasionally less-than-subtle tactics and have raised the ire of partisan and nonpartisan audiences alike. What results is a national buzz that has revitalized the AM dial, largely thought to be on its last legs and previously perceived as confined to a limited role as purveyor of scratchy soft-rock music.

Technology has, of course, brought many changes to radio. Perhaps the most important of these, and the fourth and final factor listed here, is automation. Computerized radio systems can now largely run themselves. Disc jockeys' roles are confined to brief sessions in which they enter utterances ("liners") into the computer. The computer then combines the liners with music, ads, and promotional messages, playing the entire sequence back so flawlessly that even the most trained ear may not suspect that it is not live. Other stations use satellite automation in which formats—including music, disc jockey personalities, and national ads—are picked up by the station in their entirety, leaving spaces to be filled by local ads. Automated systems not only are running more smoothly since early bugs have been ironed out and timing has been perfected but are also becoming more affordable and therefore more widespread. It remains a challenge of radio stations to preserve the local flavor and close connection with the community that contributed to their survival over the past decades in the face of automation that could depersonalize the medium.

Radio is no longer the big business that it was in 1940. It is, however, still a vital, important factor in our society. Like its budgets, radio's pretensions and ambitions have become smaller. Yet it continues to be a medium of essential communication, especially at the local level. Its broadcasts of community events, in times of emergency its occasionally heated talk shows featuring local luminaries; and its constant barrage of local advertisements make it an integral part of most people's lives.

REFERENCE WORKS

As of now, there exists no universally accepted definitive bibliography of radio broadcasting materials. However, there are a number of useful bibliographic sources for the study of radio; some of these sources are indispensable. Here and throughout the chapter we emphasize currency but also retain comparatively older resources whose continued usefulness or important place in research history argues for their presence on the list.

Books

A tremendous resource can be found in John Dunning's large, illustrated volume *On the Air: The Encyclopedia of Old-Time Radio*. The book features a carefully cross-referenced alphabetical list of nearly 1,500 radio shows from the golden age with information-packed entries for each. The work updates and expands Dunning's well-known and well-respected *Tune In Yesterday: The Ultimate Encyclopedia of Old Time Radio 1925–1976*, an impressively complete, though concise, volume that focused on nationally prominent drama, comedy, and variety performers and programs from radio's heyday.

Self-described former "Radio Kid" Gerald Nachman's *Raised on Radio* is a fun-to-read story of the programs, actors, writers, and even words and phrases that Americans came to love through the live programming of pretelevision radio. Nachman's chapters feature such topics as "vaudio" (vaudeville-type shows featuring such actors as Abbott and Costello), the "anticomedian" (such as Jack Benny), radio westerns, children's shows, immigrant or ethnically oriented shows (*The Life of Riley*, *Life with Luigi*), cop shows, quiz shows, and famous families (*Father Knows Best*, *Adventures of Ozzie and Harriet*). Overall, the book is a very comprehensive and singular collection of characters and scenes from early radio programming.

Designed to allow for quick and successful searches in American mass communication, *Mass Communications Research Resources: An Annotated Guide*, edited by Christopher H. Sterling and colleagues, organizes its wealth of information by subject. Included are lists of organizations, documents, books, reports, articles, and even on-line information germane to the topic of radio (as well as television, cable, magazines, and newspapers). There is an emphasis on material published after 1980, but significant older resources are provided as well.

Leonard Maltin brings his film review skills and witty writing style to bear on his other, lesser known love, golden age radio programs, in 1997's *The Great American Broadcast: A Celebration of Radio's Golden Age*. Maltin discusses with warm-hearted reverence select soap operas (e.g., *One Man's Family*), comedies (e.g., *Burns and Allen*, *Easy Aces*), and dramatic programs (e.g., *Suspense*, *Escape*), profiling such key figures as Norman Corwin and Orson Welles and examining the forays into radio of the likes of Arthur Miller and Ray Bradbury. The work draws on approximately 100 interviews conducted over ten years with such figures as Elliott Lewis, William Conrad, Arch Oboler, and Jack Lemmon. The result is the amazingly colorful and comprehensive collection of facts and memories that only a fellow Hollywood insider could have gleaned.

The Broadcast Century: A Biography of American Broadcasting by Robert L. Hilliard with Michael C. Keith is an extremely useful and informative explanation of the history of broadcasting in the context of American society. The work includes a running timeline of events occurring in both the world and the broadcast industry that influenced the evolution of broadcasting, forty reminiscences from radio personalities, and 200 rare illustrations.

Often cited by other scholars as an indispensable guide, Frank Buxton, Bill Owen, and Henry Morgan's *The Big Broadcast 1920–1950* is a valuable revision of a work first printed more than twenty-five years ago that has been frustratingly difficult to find since it has been out of print. The book boasts not only interesting essays on important innovations and events that shaped programming (sound effects, network growth, etc.) but also a thorough list of network and syndicated programs of the time, including a complete cast list of characters. The work represents the third manifestation of the truly pioneering achievement that began in

1966 as *Radio's Golden Age: The Programs and the Personalities*, hailed as the first attempt to provide an encyclopedia for radio programming. In previous versions, amount and type of information varied drastically from entry to entry, but the revised edition includes substantial articles that are excellent supplements to some of the earlier, briefer entries.

Radio and sports have long been bosom buddies. John R. Catsis' *Sports Broadcasting* demonstrates the storied history of both radio and television sports programming. The account begins with an introduction by announcer Curt Gowdy and pinpoints the birth of broadcasting and sports with the use of the telegraph to report sports scores to subscribers across the nation. The role of radio was established in 1921, when *Pittsburgh Post* reporter Florent Gibson gave a blow-by-blow description of a prizefight in Motor Square Garden on KDKA, establishing boxing as the first sport carried (followed closely by tennis and then baseball). Catsis' work is filled with information and trivia that will be greedily taken in by fans of broadcasting history and sports alike as well as intriguing details on the creation of such legends as Ted Husing, Harry Caray, and even Ronald Reagan.

Another rich resource is Curt Smith's *Voices of the Game: The First Full-Scale Overview of Baseball Broadcasting, 1921 to the Present*, a book that excels in both breadth and depth. It is an indispensable and, for all its encyclopedic detail, quite readable study. Smith's more recent efforts, 1995's *The Storytellers: From Mel Allen to Bob Costas: Sixty Years of Baseball Tales from the Broadcast Booth* and 1998's *Of Mikes and Men: From Ray Scott to Curt Gowdy: Broadcast Tales from the Pro Football Booth*, are entertaining and educational collections of colorful anecdotes from celebrated sports broadcasters.

A rare attempt to actually list the people, programs, networks, and other topics related to radio in North America from 1920s to present, Ronald W. Lackmann's *Same Time . . . Same Station: An A-Z Guide to Radio from Jack Benny to Howard Stern* includes about 1,000 entries in an ambitious, though at times superficial, effort. It also features photos and helpful, interesting appendixes of radio sponsors, radio show clubs, and other relevant trivia. The guide follows Lackmann's *Remember Radio* which—though intended for the coffee tables of nostalgia buffs rather than the library shelves of scholars—also included useful information. The *World Radio TV Handbook* edited by Andrew G. Sennett, expands radio resources past U.S. borders. It provides an impressive listing of all radio and television stations in the world, sorted by country, their frequencies, the language they broadcast in, and a list of international radio clubs.

The result of over twelve years of research, Jon D. Swartz and Robert C. Reinehr's *Handbook of Old-Time Radio: A Comprehensive Guide to Golden Age Radio Listening and Collecting* takes its place among the most useful reference works on radio. The handbook features an extraordinary compilation of about 4,500 programs organized by type with title, network, and number of episodes available to the researcher; a "descriptive log" of over 2,000 of the more popular programs with data on first and last show, performers involved, length, and story line; and a concise, yet complete, history of broadcasting from 1926 to 1962. The appendix is equally useful in listing public collections, indexes of performers and programs, and a selected, annotated bibliography.

Michael C. Keith and Joseph M. Krause's *The Radio Station* is an account of the challenges and opportunities that face the modern radio station by examining the state of the radio broadcasting industry. Topics and concerns addressed include the arguably diminishing returns of continual audience fragmentation, the higher financial risks involved, and the increased importance of research regarding both descriptions of audience members and the tactics and strategies employed by the station and how each is received.

Sound effects were a crucial element in live radio programming, and their pioneers have long been unsung heroes of that age. They find overdue glory in Robert L. Mott's *Radio Sound Effects: Who Did It, and How, in the Era of Live Broadcasting*. Mott, another author operating with firsthand knowledge from having worked in radio in its heyday, shows how radio became "theater of the mind" largely through sound. He describes machines created for sound (e.g., "wind machines") and other creative ways that sound was produced using naturally occurring substances (e.g., birdseed on wax paper to make the sound of rain) and chronicles the contributions of such old-time sound experts as Arthur and Ora Nichols.

A novel approach in presenting information and opinion of golden age radio programs, Ray E. Barfield and M. Thomas Inge's *Listening to Radio, 1920–1950* is an aggregate of over 150 personal accounts of listeners. Combined with the authors' background and contextual comments, these accounts constitute an unusual and vivid oral history of the reactions and experiences of ordinary people who tuned in to the radio for news and entertainment. The collection is complete in its scope, covering all major categories of programming.

J. Fred MacDonald's edited collection entitled *Richard Durham's Destination Freedom: Scripts from Radio's Black Legacy, 1948–1950* provides an important look at a unique program that aired for two years on WMAQ (Chicago) and that boldly addressed issues of race and championed black leaders during a social climate of racial discrimination and unrest. MacDonald provides an introduction describing Durham's career and the context of *Destination Freedom* within the state of the radio industry and politics at the time. Then he merely lets the scripts speak for themselves with only a brief introduction to the subject matter of each. And speak they do, chronicling such topics as Harriet Tubman and the Underground Railroad, the life of an organizer of a slave rebellion, and the medical contributions of Black doctors. MacDonald succeeds in reminding readers of the dramatic power that live radio once enjoyed.

The Adventures of Amos n' Andy: A Social History of an American Phenomenon by Melvin Patrick Ely examines this show as an opportunity to understand changing racial attitudes in society over the life of the series (1920s–1950s). Ely discusses the history of the program, traces critical reaction as black consciousness developed and objections mounted, and studies the influence that the program exacted on issues of race. It is a successful and significant undertaking that advances knowledge of what is arguably the most important radio program ever produced.

The Portable Radio in American Life by Michael Brian Schiffer documents the cultural reasons for the development and subsequent adoption of the portable radio by Americans beginning in the 1950s. Housewives wanting attractive radio sets to match certain rooms and teenagers wanting radios of their own to take to the beach and elsewhere to play rock and roll music are among the sociocultural conditions that Schiffer argues allowed for the diffusion of portable radios. He also explains how Japanese manufacturers came to dominate the transistor radio market.

Thomas Greenfield's *Radio: A Reference Guide* is a bibliographic collection of both mainstream and obscure research materials. Greenfield gives a concise, yet complete, overview of the history of the medium, including discussions of programming examples and key figures. The work also provides a thorough history of the networks and indexes seventy-six individual station histories. Synopses of the development of radio drama, radio news, music, comedy and variety, sports, and miscellaneous issues such as women in radio, advertising, religious radio, and armed forces radio are included as well.

Due to the broad scope of topics addressed, Peter Fornatale and Joshua E. Mills' *Radio in the Television Age* provides another important and useful reference. Rather than discussing the "golden time" that radio enjoyed before television was introduced, Fornatale and Mills discuss instead the status of radio since television has been on the scene. Among the topics addressed are the impact of television on radio programming, listenership, and ad revenues; recent technological innovations and their impact (such as the transistor, car radios, and clock radios); modern radio pioneers such as Alan Freed and Gordon McLendon; and teen culture and rock and roll. The book also provides important stores of data on when and why people listen, numbers of radios owned and where they're located, listening in times of crisis and when the power is out, and listening at work, outdoors, and at ball games.

Eleanor Blum's *Basic Books in the Mass Media: An Annotated, Selected Booklist Covering General Communications, Book Publishing, Broadcasting, Editorial Journalism, Film, Magazines, Newspapers, Advertising, Indexes and Scholarly and Professional Periodicals* is exactly what it claims to be. The third chapter includes 123 entries on broadcasting, many of them exclusively on radio, and all entries give broad, general treatment to various aspects of the subject. Her annotations are succinct, thorough, and useful. The exact canons governing her selections of material are admittedly vague, and her concern is almost entirely with book-length materials, but for a generalist's overview of the whole field, her selections of histories, handbooks, and bibliographies provide an excellent starting point for somewhat older citations. She includes subject and author-title indexes.

G. Howard Poteet's *Published Radio, Television, and Film Scripts* devotes 125 pages to radio dramas available in printed form. Scripts are cataloged alphabetically by title of the program on which they were aired. He analyzes anthologies and lists their contents by title or program of the individual work. It seems to be a thorough piece of work for published scripts and is an important tool for anyone with an aesthetic or critical eye.

Recordings

Audiocassette tapes themselves can be instrumental resources on the history of radio. Therefore, we have included a selection of collections of radio programming that the researcher can hear in their original form. For example, Paul Brennecke has added a unique contribution to the study of radio's history with the audiocassette tape *America before TV: A Day in Radio, September 21, 1939*. The series of tapes represents a full day of old-time radio programming, including such installments as Arthur Godfrey's *Sunrise* program, news bulletins, an address from President Roosevelt to Congress, a sports competition, and an episode of *Amos n' Andy*.

The Smithsonian Collection of Old Time Radio features programming excerpts from such performers as Dean Martin and Jerry Lewis, Edgar Bergen and Charlie McCarthy, and Ozzie Nelson and Harriet Hilliard as well as entire shows such as *Sergeant Preston of the Yukon* and *Dimension X*. Another series on cassette tape of old-time radio is titled *Nostalgia Radio* and offers such installments as *Thriller* (e.g., *The Haunted Corpse, Three Skeleton Key*), *Sherlock Holmes* (e.g., *The Blackmailer, The Speckled Band*), and *Comedy* (e.g., *Fibber McGee and Molly, The Bickersons*), among others. For a broader overview, *Radio's Golden Years* on one cassette features both comedy and drama with many stars from the 1930s and 1940s.

Golden Age of Radio: Radio's All-Time Greatest Shows is a four-cassette collection of selections from *The Green Hornet, You Bet Your Life, Red Ryder*, and others. The four-cassette collection *Four Decades with Studs Terkel* features forty of the Chicago radio host's most compelling interviews with such luminaries as Woody Allen, Maya Angelou, and Tennessee Williams. *Laughter from the Golden Age of Radio: America before TV*, a four-cassette collection, features excerpts from such favorite shows as *The Jack Benny Program, Burns and Allen, Groucho Marx*, and *Your Hit Parade*. Another four-cassette offering, *Old Time Radio Comedy*, provides original programming snippets starring George Burns and Gracie Allen, Groucho Marx, Spike Jones, Will Rogers, and more. Equally worthy of nostalgic attention are the commercials from radio's heyday, as evident in the cassette *50 Old Time Radio Commercials*, which allows you to revisit the quaint slogans and phrases used to peddle five-cent Pepsi, Ovaltine, and other products.

Other substantial works that continue to be of real utility to those who seek recorded versions of radio programming of the past include Michael R. Pitts' *Radio Soundtracks: A Reference Guide* and Marietta Chicorel's huge three-volume set (Numbers 7, 7a, and 7b of the Chicorel Index series) entitled *Chicorel Index to the Spoken Arts on Discs, Tapes, and Cassettes*. The former is a comprehensive and reasonably thorough treatment of commercially available tapes and records of radio shows from research libraries and other sources. The index is meticulous, and the introduction is clear and informative, both about the book itself and about the legal and technical pitfalls awaiting those who venture into sound tracks. The latter, though focused more broadly on drama and oratory, includes numerous radio programs among the materials and contains several items that are not mentioned by Pitts. This set of interlocking bibliographies is complex and requires a good deal of effort to use, but it is of real value for students of poetry and drama on radio.

Journals, Serials, and Industry Publications

Some of the most valuable bibliographies for radio are available as serials or appendixes to scholarly publications in the area of mass communication. The nearest thing that America has yet produced to a bibliography of the history of broadcasting is the set of references at the end of each volume of Erik Barnouw's three-volume *History of Broadcasting in the United States*. The shortest of them lists over 200 major items, both published and unpublished, and they are a major

Radio shop, 1922. Courtesy of the Library of Congress

starting point for any historical item-hunting that a person might wish to do. Similarly, the bibliography in David Holbrook Culbert's *News for Everyman: Radio and Foreign Affairs in Thirties America* constitutes a major resource for any investigation into the history of news broadcasting.

Barnouw has also contributed the unparalleled resource the *International Encyclopedia of Communications* in four volumes, edited with colleagues George Gerbner, Wilbur Schramm, Tobia Worth, and Larry Gross. This encyclopedia contains entries on the history of each form of the mass media as well as its role in society. Also included are entries on communication processes, major contributors of media research, professional pioneers, and issues and problems in the media industry in the United States and throughout the world.

An extremely useful new academic journal, *Communication Booknotes Quaterly* from Lawrence Erlbaum Associates, is a collection of reviews of books, articles, documents, and electronic reports on a host of subjects related to broadly defined "communication," including radio. Material is drawn from several countries, and issues typically begin with an essay reviewing publications on a particular topic. The last issue of the year provides both an author index and a cumulative index by topic. The journal picks up where *Communication Booknotes* from Christopher H. Sterling left off, which in turn had begun in 1969 as *Broadcast Bibliophile's Booknotes*.

In 1998 the Broadcast Education Association introduced the *Journal of Radio*

Studies, touted as the first and only publication in the world exclusively concerned with research on radio by professionals and academics. Topics addressed in the journal include diversity in the industry, the impact of new technologies, regulation and ownership issues, historical contributions, international radio, and trends, issues, and challenges facing the field. The journal offers a forum for industry professionals and educators, interviews with inductees for the Radio Hall of Fame at the Chicago Museum of Broadcast Communications, and reviews of books and videos as well as a list of dissertations on radio. This journal has made an impressive start and certainly stands to become a preeminent resource on radio research.

For other empirical research and academic essays on radio, the researcher can consult the back pages of other journals in the field to examine their reviews, primarily *Journalism and Mass Communication Quarterly* and *Journal of Communication*. For a comprehensive list of all articles published in these journals and numerous others and organized by topic, *Communication Abstracts* offers complete citations and abstracts in one easy-to-use publication.

In the early 1970s, Kenneth Harwood compiled "World Bibliography of Selected Periodicals on Broadcasting (Revised)," in the Association of Professional Broadcasting Education's official quarterly *Journal of Broadcasting* (now the Broadcast Education Association's *Journal of Broadcasting and Electronic Media*). The article revises the original 1961 "World Bibliography," which listed more than 500 periodicals, and it both updated the listing and made it more useful. *Journal of Broadcasting and Electronic Media* is useful also for its regular inclusion of a "Books Received" feature, which amounts to a bibliographic listing of noteworthy items on broadcasting published during each quarter of the year.

Aside from bibliographies and standard reference works (encyclopedias, biographical dictionaries, etc.), a number of industry publications offer general information on radio programming. *Broadcasting and Cable Yearbook*, for instance, has been published annually since 1935 by *Broadcasting and Cable* (formerly *Broadcasting*). Each issue includes directories of radio stations, both commercial and educational, and brief histories of ownership, licensure, and so on for each station. Virtually an almanac of information about broadcasting companies, organizations, and networks, each issue also includes a bibliography of the year's outstanding books in the field and numerous pieces of statistical information. Feature articles on items of topical interest are included, too. Two other important historical reference publications are *Radio Annual*, put out by Radio Daily of New York from 1938 to 1964, and *Radio Directory*, issued by *Variety* and appearing four times between 1938 and 1941. Both provide data on advertisers, listeners, producers, artists, and stations.

Also in the vein of providing lists of data on radio, James H. Duncan Jr.'s *American Radio: Sixteenth Anniversary Issue, 1976–1992: A Statistical History* is a useful resource. Based on Arbitron ratings, Duncan has calculated national data for leading stations, trends in radio advertising sales, average listening by audience members, FM share of the audience, leading radio groups, station formats, and format audience listening patterns. He also provides sixteen years of data for radio stations in over 150 individual markets.

Sydney Head and Christopher H. Sterling's *Broadcasting in America: A Survey of Electronic Media* is a thorough, carefully researched treatment of the technological, historical, and economic structure of American broadcasting. It pays special attention to the place of radio and television in the total spectrum of the mass media and is especially concerned with the effects of advertising. This is the seventh edition of a survey publication begun by Head in 1956 that is also now available as a brief version in its second edition. A similar work, but with an international focus, is Walter B. Emery's *National and International Systems of Broadcasting: Their History, Operation, and Control*. Organized by continent, then subclassified into regions and, finally, nations, the work surveys the entire world in terms of the history, regulation, and current status of its national broadcast system.

Two works in the H. W. Wilson Reference Shelf series deserve mention in this category. Poyntz Tyler edited *Television and Radio*, and Herbert L. Marx Jr. edited *Television and Radio in American Life*. Each draws from the general-circulation periodicals of its day to anthologize approximately twenty articles on the state of the art of broadcasting. Also along historical lines, Harrison B. Summers' *A Thirty Year History of Programs Carried on National Radio Networks in the United States 1926–1956* is an excellent chronological analysis of every program carried by the four major networks (NBC, CBS, ABC, and MBS), providing title sponsors, seasons on the air, network, length, day and hour, and ratings.

The *Radio Programming Profile* focuses on the 100 top markets in the United States, offering hour-by-hour analyses of stations' programming and identifying their primary audience and policies and practices. A similarly useful publication—and one that has remained up-to-date—is the annual booklet put out by the National Association of Broadcasters, *Dimensions of Radio*. Essentially a statistical handbook, it analyzes station revenues, audience patterns, buying trends, and other information of interest to station owners and operators.

Web Sites

A clear sign of the times is the proliferation of sources on the topic of radio to be found on the Internet. A mere entry of the terms "radio" or "radio history" in any major search engine reveals a vast and varied list of Web pages and sites for the radio researcher or history buff to peruse. For example, a Yahoo! news and media category search of the word "radio" revealed such gems as sites entitled "100 Years of Radio," "Broadcast Archive," "Lives of the Great DJs," and "United States Early Radio History," many of which included audio clips from performers and programs. (This search is easily replicated at home.) We have selected a few of the most extensive and informative Web sites encountered in our search. However, we encourage interested readers to "surf" through the options themselves to obtain the resources most closely related to their concerns. We also caution readers that Internet sources, by and large, are neither juried nor regulated; information on Web sites may be unverified or inaccurate.

The address www.old-time.com gets you to an old-time radio site where you will find links to sites with scholarly articles on the history of broadcasting, a virtual tour of an old NBC station in Chicago, a list of events that happened on any day in radio history, meanings of old-time call letters, and updates on radio personalities of the past. The site also offers links to the Web pages of museums of radio and broadcast history (many of which are included in this chapter), a program guide of where to find old-time radio programs, and chat locations for conversing with fellow enthusiasts.

The site www.asb.com offers a relatively technical and well-researched overview of the history of the technology of radio, including contributions by Fessenden, DeForest, and non-American inventors who are rarely recognized in U.S.-based texts. For an in-depth view of the singular contributions of Guglielmo Marconi, visit www.alpcom.it/hamradio/, an Italian site offering extensive English-language text and a timeline describing major events and innovations.

The address www.comlab.ox.ac.uk/archive/audio.html allows a visit to a "virtual library" on audio resources with a list of on-line radio information sources. Included: World Radio Network, news and public affairs information from stations around the world; Cyberville Radio, which allows the user to listen to music from different formats and use chat rooms; iRADIO, a radio bookstore with recommended texts as well as links to major news organizations; RadioNet Talk Radio, clips from radio talk shows; and RadioTower, where users can listen to live radio from around the world.

For those interested in old-time radio programming, the site located at www.otr.com is an informative and entertaining treasure. This is by far the most impressive collection of facts and original sound that we found on the Internet. The site provides accurate and interesting extended overviews of each program genre followed by an opportunity to hear audio clips from programs typical of the genre. Included are the categories comedy (where you can hear clips from *Fred Allen*, *Vic and Sade*, *The Chase and Sanborn Hour*, and many others), mystery (*Philip Morris Playhouse*, *The Hermit's Cave*, *House of Mystery*, etc.), private eyes (*Dragnet*, *The Adventures of Sam Spade*), science fiction (*Buck Rogers in the Twenty-fifth Century*, *Flash Gordon*), and radio news (Murrow on the McCarthy hearings, Murrow from London just before the invasion of Poland). Similarly, www.dccomics.com provides an opportunity to hear original episodes from the radio series *Superman* but is without the complementary text.

Also providing an extensive list of relevant links is www.mediahistory.com under its entry for radio. The list includes Web sites for museums and institutions with radio resources, resources for general broadcast history, stations and networks, programs and pioneers, technologies, and international radio (the highlights of most are included herein). However, our search revealed that a substantial proportion of the sites listed had either moved or were not found with the addresses listed. Another source of links and lists of on-line resources is found at www.oldradio.com with well-organized connections to archive materials and information on the general history of radio as well as histories of radio hardware, local and network programming, public radio, and individual stations in the United States, Canada, and Mexico. One of the most concise, yet comprehensive, timelines of major events in radio's past is found at www.soundsite.com, a site devoted to the history of sound recording and broadcasting.

The address www.airwaves.com leads the user to a site with connections to the Federal Communications Commission (FCC) database to search a topic, a list of positions available in the field of radio broadcasting, and the *Airwaves Radio Journal* (begun in 1991 as *The Internet Radio Journal*), a professionally oriented forum on broadcast topics.

RESEARCH COLLECTIONS

Radio is blessed with numerous excellent research collections, both public and private. Not surprisingly, these tend to be clustered in California, the northern Midwest, and the section of the eastern seaboard from Boston to Washington, D.C. There are exceptions, of course, as a look at Lee Ash's *Subject Collections: A Guide to Special Book Collections and Subject Emphases as Reported by University, College, Public, and Special Libraries and Museums* reveals. Private collectors and enthusiasts, of course, are to be found throughout the country, and their resources, especially their collections of recorded radio shows, are not to be dismissed lightly. These sources are, however, relatively difficult to track down and not easy to access without actually making a trip to see the materials.

The Washington, D.C., area has several collections of special note. From a bibliographer's point of view the most important of these is the Broadcast Pioneers Library of American Broadcasting, affiliated with the University of Maryland Libraries. The library boasts an extensive collection of program scripts, some 25,000 photographs and slides of broadcast history, over 4,000 historically important pamphlets and government documents, and formerly private collections from such varied sources as composer Philip James and former Dumont and ABC executive Robert L. Coe. The library also boasts audio holdings including nearly 1,000 oral histories, speeches, interviews, commercials, and news feeds as well as compiled bibliographies on such topics as women in broadcasting and minorities in broadcasting. Another important role of the library is to serve as a clearinghouse and reference center for materials of all sorts connected with radio broadcasting. The Web site for the library is located at www.lib.umd.edu and can be used to search these resources and gain information on how to reproduce them for educational use. In person, the library features a very sophisticated data retrieval system and has a staff devoted to researching in the area of broadcast history.

The University of Maryland is also home to the National Public Broadcasting Archives, which combine the annals of such noncommercial broadcast institutions as America's Public Television Stations (APTS), Children's Television Workshop (CTW), Corporation for Public Broadcasting (CPB), National Public Radio (NPR), and Public Broadcasting Service (PBS). The result is an impressive resource of text information including pamphlets, journals, clippings, and personal papers as well as audio and video offerings of noncommercial programming. Again, a search of the archives is possible at www.lib.umd.edu.

The Smithsonian is obviously a primary research center, especially the Clark Collection of Radioana in the Museum of History and Technology Branch Library. The Clark Collection is especially strong on very early radio developments. The Manuscript Division of the Library of Congress also has substantial radio materials, including the Eric Sevareid papers. The special Motion Picture, Broadcasting and Recorded Sound Division of the Library of Congress has one of the major research holdings in the country. In addition, the National Association of Broadcasters (NAB) has its own library collection located in the NAB building.

Just outside Washington in Fairfax, Virginia, George Mason University houses the Federal Theatre Project Research Center, which has a huge collection of scripts and research materials prepared by the radio branch of Roosevelt's Works Project Administration (WPA)-sponsored Federal Theatre Project.

Founded in 1975 by William S. Paley, the Museum of Television and Radio in Manhattan is the centerpiece of research collections in New York. To fulfill the goal of preserving radio and television programs and making them available to the public, the collection includes more than 95,000 programs of "artistic, cultural, and historical significance" from virtually every genre, including news, drama, public affairs, documentaries, performing arts, children's shows, sports, comedy, and advertising. The museum offers exhibitions, screenings, comfortable listening rooms, and an extensive educational program including the satellite distribution of its seminars to universities and other learning centers. The museum has a Radio Collection of 10,000 cassette tape programs available for listening by the public. The holdings in the museum are virtually all tape holdings; it is not a manuscript or book library. A second location of the museum opened in Beverly Hills in 1996 to present the same services to West Coast patrons. The Web site associated with the museum, located at www.mtr.org, is well organized and helpful (it even provides directions!).

ABC, CBS, and NBC have their official libraries and archives located in New York. These are not public libraries in the conventional sense, but staff members do respond to inquiries, and the networks have a history of working cooperatively with scholars. The David Sarnoff Library in Princeton, New Jersey, is a major source of information on the business aspect of radio, and in Philadelphia, Temple University Library houses a substantial collection of scripts and other radioana. Other notables in the Northeast are the Belfer Audio Laboratory and Archive at Syracuse University, which features the largest collection—some 300,000—of sound recordings in North America, including, but far from limited to, early radio broadcasts, and the Fred Allen Collection at the Boston Public Library.

At the forefront of broadcast collections in the Midwest is the Museum of Broadcast Communications in Chicago, located in the landmark Chicago Cultural Center. The site offers some 49,000 archived radio programs and numerous interactive exhibits. Its Radio Hall of Fame branch lives up to its mission to "recognize and preserve radio's rich history" through its continuing practice of archiving radio programming from *Amos n' Andy* to *All Things Considered*. Its working radio studio, the Lynne "Angel" Harvey Radio Center, is available for free live remotes. For on-line information about the museum, its exhibits, and events, the Web site at www.mbcnet.org is of modest utility.

Another well-known and widely used research center in the region is the State Historical Society of Wisconsin in Madison. Its Mass Communication History Center contains a collection of several thousand recordings (discs) of network radio shows, and the library also has the National Association of Broadcasters papers as well as other substantial holdings in the form of private and corporate papers of various radio personalities and organizations. It also contains substantial film and tape holdings for television and advertising.

Another regional standout is the Radio Archive of the University of Memphis, governed by Dr. Marvin R. Bensman, which allows the researcher to access a sampling of old-time radio programs through a sizable archive of transcriptions and collections. To search the database, the interested researcher can visit www. people.memphis.edu/~mbensman/.

In California, the most important collections are housed in the new outpost of the Museum of Television and Radio and at University of California, Los Angeles'

(UCLA) libraries. UCLA houses the National Academy of Television Arts and Sciences Television Library, which includes, among many other things, a Jack Benny Collection. Also, UCLA's Theater Arts Library has a collection of over 1,500 radio scripts and a major collection of books and periodicals. The North American Radio Archives Library, located in San Francisco, has archives that include tapes of 15,000 radio programs and substantial slide, script, and book holdings. Other substantial collections in the West include the Archives of Recorded Sound at Brigham Young University, the University of Southern California (USC) Special Collections at the Doheny Library in Los Angeles, and the American Library of Radio and Television at Thousand Oaks Library (California).

HISTORY AND CRITICISM

Histories of broadcasting are so many and so varied that a good-sized bibliography could be devoted exclusively to this one type of literature. They come in a variety of types ranging from the ponderously academic and scholarly to the breezily informal and anecdotal, and when biography, autobiography, and memoir are included, as they should be, the number of works legitimately identifiable as radio history swells to the hundreds. Obviously, this chapter does not attempt comprehensive treatment, but a representative selection should indicate the nature of the field.

General History

The premier work on radio history remains Erik Barnouw's three-volume *History of Broadcasting in the United States*. Volume 1, entitled *Tower in Babel*, appeared in 1966 and covers the period from Marconi's first experiments to 1933. Volume 2, *The Golden Web*, covers the "golden age" and the rise of television up to 1953. Volume 3 focuses primarily on television but covers the decline of network radio as well; entitled *The Image Empire*, it also covers the experiments and efforts made by local stations and small groups through the mid-1960s. Barnouw writes well, and his volumes are enlivened by many of the more remarkable anecdotes and stories about radio personalities and programs, but his real concern is with the development of the total broadcast system. His scholarly thoroughness makes him indispensable, and his inclusion of bibliographies, indexes, chronological tables, and summaries of regulations and laws makes his volumes absolutely central to any inquiry into radio's history.

Lewis Coe's *Wireless Radio: A Brief History* employs a broad definition of "radio," cataloging all of the uses of the radio spectrum, including radio at sea, amateur radio, radio-controlled toys, military radio, police radio, and cellular and satellite phones. The book provides a useful and rarely addressed reminder of all the less obvious ways that radio technology is used to improve quality of life and provides a nontechnical description of the development of each.

Hugh G. J. Aitken provides a descriptive timeline of the major technological advances in the development of radio in his work *The Continuous Wave: Technology and American Radio, 1900–1932*. Aitken traces with detail the origins of the steps involved in progressing from creating radio waves by sparks through and beyond the breakthrough innovation of the continuous wave. The report is a highly technical and somewhat arcane account of the equipment and science behind radio.

Another resource for a broad overview of the early days of radio is George H. Douglas' *The Early Days of Radio Broadcasting*. Douglas provides an "informal history" of the period after the birth of radio and before its golden age, with an emphasis on the human elements that supplement the factual accounts. This approach makes for an engaging, though somewhat less substantive, perspective. Chapters include information on early stations (how they formed, what they offered), the development of the audience, growth of sets sold, development of advertising practices, early radio news and sports broadcasting, and brief discussions of select music and dramatic programs.

Philip T. Rosen's *The Modern Stentors: Radio Broadcasters and the Federal Government, 1920–1934* tells of the dilemma encountered regarding how to regulate and standardize the newly born broadcast industry. The author provides careful analysis of the relationship between each federal administration and the industry and chronicles the laws, rulings, conflicts, and reactions that characterized the struggle.

J. Fred MacDonald's *Don't Touch That Dial: Radio Programming in American Life from 1920 to 1960* is a superb, scholarly history and criticism of radio programming (drama, mystery, soap opera, adventure, etc.) and is probably the best single treatment of radio programming of the "golden age" currently available.

Among the most important of the previous era of works on radio history are Gleason L. Archer's *A History of Radio to 1926* and *Big Business and Radio*. Archer's concern, like Barnouw's, is essentially an academic interest in the development of the total broadcasting spectrum, especially the roles of RCA and NBC. A more enjoyable, "popular" approach is that of Francis Chase Jr., an excellent raconteur. His *Sound and Fury: An Informal History of Broadcasting* concentrates heavily on the development of programming and the effects of personalities on radio shows. E.P.J. Shurick's *The First Quarter Century of American Broadcasting* is another important early history of radio whose strength lies in its demonstration of how programming capability in news and information grew with the earliest technological advances in radio broadcasting. Able Green and Joe Laurel Jr. also produced an excellent light history of radio based on *Variety*'s coverage of the medium in *Show Biz' From Vaude to Video*.

Another popular book, really a folio-sized coffee-table book, is Lowell Thomas' *Magic Dials: The Story of Radio and Television*, a collection of impressive, but meaningless, color photographs with a brief, no-nonsense history of the medium, written in Thomas' characteristic style. One of the best popular histories is Sam J. Slate and Joe Cook's collaboration *It Sounds Impossible*, which includes very detailed chapters on soap opera, comedy, and so on, each one emphasizing the pioneer developers in the form. Both Slate and Cook were active in early radio, and they frequently include firsthand reminiscences and anecdotes about programs and personalities. Jim Harmon's nostalgic *The Great Radio Heroes* and *The Great Radio Comedians* do a good job of pulling together interesting information about the actors, writers, sponsors, and distributors of *Gangbusters*, *Inner Sanctum*, *The Shadow*, and so on. Madeleine Edmondson and David Round's book *The Soaps: Daytime Serials of Radio and TV* is a lighthearted, though serious, study of the aesthetic and historical development of soap operas, the first 120 pages of which focus on radio. Similar but more scholarly (though that may be too strong a term) is Raymond William Stedman's *The Serials: Suspense and Drama by Installment*, which highlights the whole pop aesthetic of the cliff-hanger from its first transmutation out of the serialized novel into pulp, film, radio, comic books, and television. Two more works, Lloyd R. Morris' *Not So Long Ago* (a general account of radio) and Robert Campbell's *The Golden Years of Broadcasting: A Celebration of the First 50 Years of Radio and TV on NBC* (a useful, though at times too effusive, account of the accomplishments of NBC) also deserve mention.

Individual Stations

Some serious historical work in the field of radio has focused not on national and network developments but rather on individual stations. Radio stations are often more concrete, stable phenomena with clear histories and a distinctly real existence. Networks, on the other hand, are essentially corporate entities made up of legal contracts and cable linkages. Conceptually and historically, networks are much more difficult to deal with than are actual broadcasting stations. Moreover, since many stations had established themselves as creative, vital programming entities long before RCA created New York City, it is not surprising that many stations are proudly conscious of their histories as separate entities from any network.

Bill Jaker, Frank Sulek, and Peter Kanze, all with professional experience in New York City radio, have authored *The Airwaves of New York: Illustrated Histories of 156 AM Stations in the Metropolitan Area, 1921–1996*. In researching newspaper and magazine articles and interviewing radio veterans, they have uncovered hidden gems in the broadcast history of the city, including such long-forgotten stations as WVFW, begun by the Veterans of Foreign Wars in Brooklyn and running from 1933 to 1941, and the early Madison Square Garden station WMSG on the air in the 1920s. They continue their sketch through the present and include modern niche marketing stations such as the recent WZRC broadcasting in Korean.

Louis M. Bloch Jr.'s *The Gas Pipe Networks: A History of College Radio 1936–1946* is an interesting and unique supplement to the more typical historical accounts of commercial radio. Bloch's account places much emphasis on the people and processes involved in the 1936 founding of the first college radio station, the Brown Network at Brown University in Providence, Rhode Island. It's an account that he can give firsthand, as Bloch himself participated in the early days of "gas pipe" radio, in which engineering students began stringing wire and placing receivers in their dormitory rooms. He also traces the birth and growth of the Intercollegiate Broadcasting System (IBS), which provided program sharing with other early innovators from Harvard, Columbia, and other universities.

One of the most distinctive and interesting accounts of an individual station's history is found in Louis Cantor's *Wheelin' on Beale: How WDIA-Memphis Became the Nation's First All-Black Radio Station and Created the Sound That Changed America*. The station boasts many reasons to be famous; it featured both the first black DJ in the South (Nat D. Williams) and a young B. B. King playing for free to promote club appearances. But the most compelling tale told by Cantor is of how what began as merely an attempt to reverse money losses at the white-owned

Old-time battery radio, ca. 1920. Photo by Harry M. Rhoads. Courtesy of the Denver Public Library

station by appealing to previously ignored black audiences resulted in a social and cultural phenomenon in which WDIA became a voice for the growing black community as well as an important player in the roots of blues and rhythm and blues (R&B) music.

Nathan Godfried's *WCFL, Chicago's Voice of Labor, 1926–78* chronicles an attempt to secure a voice for the working class in the emerging broadcast media. The book examines how a part of the organized labor movement gained a foothold in the media business in 1926 with the establishment of WCFL, which broadcast, along with popular entertainment, labor and public affairs programming. Godfried describes the compromise made between broadcasting labor programming and remaining commercially viable by appealing to advertisers, a precarious balance that was carefully achieved until the station's demise is 1978.

For a glimpse of the past of Texas radio, former local broadcast personality Lynn Woolley has written *The Last Great Days of Radio*. The personal account runs the gamut in content from regional news and sports coverage to comedy and musical programming and is written in an accessible and amiable style.

A number of other station histories have been written from a more partisan viewpoint, frequently by principals in a station's development. Elliott M. Sanger, for instance, wrote *Rebel in Radio: The Story of WQXR*. Sanger was general manager of the "radio station of the *New York Times*" for nearly thirty years, and his tracing of the station's development from a garage-based hobby to the best-known classical music station in the century is told with some understandable bias. Similarly, Steve Post's *Playing in the FM Band: A Personal Account of Free Radio* tells the story of listener-sponsored Pacifica radio's New York station from the viewpoint of an advocate and primary participant in the "underground" or "counterculture" programming for which the station became widely known.

More commercial but no less biased is Dick Perry's *Not Just a Sound: The Story of WLW*. This strange book offers a laudatory history of "the nation's station," the huge 500,000-watt WLW (which broadcast during the 1920s and 1930s from its Cincinnati tower with ten times the power of any station in the country), of some interest to radio fans. Also falling within this category is the critical examination of "the Man" responsible for commercial, corporate-supported radio by Los Angeles disc jockey Jim Ladd in *Radio Waves: Life and Revolution on the FM Dial*. The book chronicles the birth of "free-form" radio through Ladd's own experiences at KMET, a California station that temporarily bucked both authority and strict playlists. As long as the reader does not expect a purely factual, unbiased historical account, the book can be humorous and provocative.

Among the best-known earlier works on an individual station is William Peck Banning's *Commercial Broadcasting Pioneer: The WEAF Experiment 1922–1926*. WEAF was AT&T's broadcast outlet in the early 1920s and was deeply involved in the development of both the "toll" broadcasting concept and early multistation hookups using cables. Banning's study is a scholarly and thorough analysis of early attempts to commercialize radio.

Radio News

For the development of radio news there is one primary source from which, despite its age, almost any inquiry can be launched. David Holbrook Culbert's *News for Everyman: Radio and Foreign Affairs in Thirties America* is a book of limited scope, focusing on the careers of six news commentators who came to prominence during the last years of the 1930s. The twenty-page bibliographic essay that he includes with the volume, however, is so thorough that it amounts to a guidebook for research into the historical development of newscasting.

The Culbert source is well supplemented by several more recent additions. Taking its place as an instant classic, for example, is *Now the News: The Story of Broadcast Journalism* by Edward Bliss Jr., providing a detailed and complete picture of the history of broadcast journalism. Beginning with a persuasive argument for when to place the birth of news heard over the air (Bliss votes for 1898, when Marconi's wireless company gave minute-to-minute coverage of the Kingstown Regatta), this impressive tome uncovers subtle details and remembers to include less obvious, though important, players. Special attention is given to coverage of major historical events: the Scopes trial, Lindbergh's flight, FDR's Fireside Chats. Few works match the eye for detail and thoroughness seen here. Bliss describes not only the contributions of Walter Winchell and Ed Murrow but also those of Fulton Lewis Jr. and Elmer Davis. He describes foreign coverage not only of Munich and Paris during World War II but also of Ethiopia and Spain in the 1930s.

The Murrow Boys: Pioneers on the Front Lines of Broadcast Journalism by Stanley Cloud and Lynne Olson tells the stories of the ten men and one woman who reported for CBS during World War II under the direction of Murrow. The account is, above all else, a study of the character of those people—the idealism through which they hoped to make a difference, the intellectualism through which they honed the craft of broadcast journalism, the bravery through which they defied orders in hopes of capturing the story, and the innovation through which they carved the way and set historic standards for journalism and reportage. Cloud and Olson also provide critical commentary on the loosened ideals of journalism that the correspondents found upon their return to the United States.

Three other books about the inestimable Edward R. Murrow deserve special mention. *Edward R. Murrow: An American Original* by Joseph E. Persico is a comprehensive and dramatic telling of the traits and accomplishments that made a legend, including anecdotes and insight into the professional and personal life of Murrow. A. M. Sperber's massive *Murrow: His Life and Times* is almost unwieldy in its thoroughness, but it is without question a definitive work on the man who all but created modern broadcast news. Also, Murrow's own *This Is London*, a collection of many of the London-based reports prior to World War II, is notable as a rich, though not complete, collection of Murrow's historic 1939–1940 coverage of the bombing of London.

As Good as Any: Foreign Correspondence on American Radio, 1930–1940 by David H. Hosley details the foreign news coverage heard on American network radio over this tumultuous time period, with special attention on reporting of Nazi movements in Europe. Hosley makes a persuasive case that by 1940, CBS, NBC, and to a lesser extent Mutual had secured foreign correspondence as "a key element in the Golden Age of radio." He also brings to life the accounts and actions of the groundbreaking individuals who would serve to inform Americans of events abroad, such as Cesar Saerchinger, William L. Shirer, Mary Marvin Breckinridge, and, of course, Edward R. Murrow.

Outside of a celebrity tell-all, it is a rare occasion when a book on broadcasting finds its way to the *New York Times* best-sellers list. But such is the case with Joe Garner's book/CD package *We Interrupt This Broadcast: Relive the Events That Stopped Our Lives . . . from the Hindenburg to the Death of Princess Diana*. This volume recounts news coverage of major breaking stories from television and radio (including the crash of the Hindenburg, D-Day, the resignation of Richard Nixon, and the death of Franklin Roosevelt) with brief text, dazzling pictures, and two accompanying CD recordings of original news broadcasts. Garner is not a scholar, but rather a pioneer in commercial audio book development. As such, he neither offers new information nor synthesizes the information that he has. But the sight and sound combination suits the subject matter perfectly, and the stylish presentation makes for an engaging, if pricey, educational tool.

Media at War: Radio's Challenge to the Newspapers, 1924–1939 by Gwenyth L. Jackaway is a historical examination of the attempts of the established newspaper industry to block the efforts of growth of radio journalism. The book covers the period from the first broadcast reports of election returns, to the eventual decision by the Associated Press to distribute its services to radio stations. It frames the press-radio war as more than just a battle for profits but also a struggle for power over communicating to the public and thereby perhaps exerting an influence on opinion or agenda. In doing so, it provides a useful and unique niche of radio history scholarship.

Serving to extend knowledge and criticism of radio journalism to global proportions is Timothy Crook's *International Radio Journalism: History, Theory and Practice*. Crook's work employs a comparative analysis of radio in the United States, United Kingdom, and Australia with particular attention to influences of government, multinational conglomerate owners, and new technologies as well as to coverage of international events like the Holocaust.

Linda Wertheimer's *Listening to America: Twenty-five Years in the Life of a Nation, as Heard on National Public Radio* was published in celebration of NPR's 1970 founding. Wertheimer—a founder and news veteran herself—is exceedingly credible and qualified to take this retrospective, which features selections of originally run interviews coupled with the author's insightful commentary to place them in proper historical context. The resulting collection of scripts is a vast and handy resource and covers such diverse topics as Watergate, the fall of Saigon, the Iranian hostage crisis, the AIDS epidemic, and the murder of John Lennon. Organized chronologically, the reader can choose a year and have the events of the day come to life through these accounts.

Other important, though aging, books in the history of radio news include Charles Siepmann's *Radio's Second Chance* and Mitchell V. Charnley's *News by Radio*, both providing solid analysis of early efforts of radio news.

Music Programming

The very broad field of music programming has produced several valuable books. Among the premier books is Tom DeLong's *The Mighty Music Box: The Golden Age of Musical Radio*, a highly successful effort to cover the history of music programming from classical, to country, to all forms of popular music. Disappointing only in his sketchy handling of jazz, DeLong is probably the best single source for the general history of radio music programming.

More narrow in scope, but more thorough in analysis, is Philip Eberly's *Music in the Air: America's Changing Tastes in Popular Music*, which treats not only contemporary music but also the FM-Top 40 formats, jazz, swing, and black popular music of the 1920s and 1930s. Eberly offers some useful social insights as he deftly negotiates the tricky issue of middle-class taste and the evolution of American popular music. Perhaps the most beneficial aspect of the Eberly book for the radio history buff is the appendixes that list the newspapers, periodicals, encyclopedias, newsletters, air checks, and discographies that he drew upon as well as tables and charts of record sales, early ads, format schedules, music charts, ratings, and a useful flowchart of rock and roll history.

The Hits Just Keep on Coming: The History of Top 40 Radio by Ben Fong-Torres is a pithy description of the energetic burst in popularity of Top 40 radio that began in the 1950s. The work features interviews with such legendary figures as Dick Clark, Casey Kasem, and "Cousin Brucie" Morrow. Though at times it borders on the inconsequential in merely focusing on celebrity profiles of the DJs, it contains occasional substantive remarks as well as a brief sketch of historical context and is written in a solid and engaging manner.

Other useful histories and criticism in the overtrodden field of radio and rock music include Michael C. Keith's *Voices in the Purple Haze: Underground Radio and the Sixties*, which tells the tale of the 1960s revolution by disc jockeys who railed against the fast-talking rock and roll disc jockeys of the 1950s to adopt a more mellow, languid attitude and play music that radically departed from the prior Top 40 formats.

No discussion of radio music would be complete without a source on the payola scandals. A key source on the history of payola and its evolution through the natural tensions between radio programmers and music producers is Russell Sanjet's splendid book *From Print to Plastic: Publishing and Promoting America's Popular Music*. Sanjet traces the scandals of 1959 to their earliest roots in the ASCAP/BMI feuds. A well-written update on the topic was provided a decade later by Kerry Segrave in the 1993 *Payola in the Music Industry: A History, 1880–1991*, a well-researched and finely detailed work that makes for engaging and informative reading.

The far less fertile field of radio and classical music does offer useful resources, including Irving Sablosky's *American Music*, which discusses lucidly the role of radio in forming the transition between nineteenth- and twentieth-century serious music. John Briggs' *Requiem for a Yellow Brick Brewery: A History of the Metropolitan Opera* treats at length how the Met's desire for an audience and radio's early desire for respectability helped forge a sixty-year relationship. Of course, the major biographies of Arturo Toscanini, such as Howard Taubman's *Maestro: The Life of Arturo Toscanini*, devote large sections to Sarnoff's bold decision to bring class and the flammable Toscanini to NBC—a relationship that lasted for seventeen intense and fascinating years.

Several new encyclopedias chronicle the events and performers who contributed to the rise of country music from its humble beginnings to its recent swell in popularity. *The Encyclopedia of Country Music: The Ultimate Guide to the Music*, edited by Paul Kingsbury, Laura Garrard, and Daniel Cooper, in 1998, contains over 1,200 alphabetical listings, hundreds of photographs, and entries by over 130 contributors as it spans country music's eight-decade history. The emphasis in Barry McCloud's *Definitive Country: The Ultimate Encyclopedia of Country Music and Its Performers* is decidedly more biographical in nature, containing details on the personal and professional lives of major and minor players in country music's history. Irwin Stambler's *Country Music: The Encyclopedia* (with Grelun Landon) also contains largely biographical entries of performances as well as recordings of note by a wide variety of country music artists along with helpful subject, artist, album title, and song title indexes.

Other recent collections have a stronger emphasis on the role of the radio industry in country music. For a source that combines biographical sketches of performers with entries on radio shows and disc jockeys as well as on instrument-producing companies and geographic locations, the editors of *Country Music Magazine* have produced *The Comprehensive Country Music Encyclopedia*. Similarly, Horace Logan and Bill Sloan's *Elvis, Hank, and Me: Making Musical History on the Louisiana Hayride* details the entertainers and guests appearing on this live country music program broadcast by the CBS radio network beginning in 1948. Told from a true insider's perspective by Logan, who produced the show for most if its ten-year life span, and Sloan, a former editor of *Country Rambler* magazine, the account is at once informative, funny, and touching.

Arguably the best earlier book on radio and country music is Nick Tosches' *Country: The Biggest Music in America*. The lowbrow title notwithstanding, this is a serious study of country music, highlighting the early influence of key radio stations and disc jockeys and their role in the maturity of both the music and the country music industry. Tosche has also provided 1996's *Country: The Twisted Roots of Rock 'n' Roll*, in which he describes the seedy underbelly of the country music industry throughout its history and the relationship between the wild, dark side of the music and American culture. The result is a provocative and truly unique perspective that makes for a fascinating and enlightening read of such topics as sex and drugs in the industry and the often self-destructive paths of its artists.

Biography and Autobiography

Biography and autobiography are major forms of historical information about radio, and scores of works have been produced about the stars of network shows. Frequently, as with Charles J. Correl and Freeman Gosden's *All about Amos 'n Andy*, biography is not only romanticized but also confounded with fictional biography of radio characters associated with performers. Also, many of the biographical works produced during radio's heyday are manifestly unreliable, being designed more to tell the fans what they wanted to hear than to convey significant information. Robert Eichberg's *Radio Stars of Today: Behind the Scenes in Broadcasting* is an example of such a work.

On the other hand, first-rate biographical materials have become more readily available. Two books on David Sarnoff, for instance, open real channels of understanding about this incredibly influential man. Eugene Lyons' *David Sarnoff: A Biography* is a thorough and sympathetic study of the outlines of Sarnoff's career, and the anthology of Sarnoff's own writings, speeches, memoranda, reports, collected in 1968, *Looking Ahead: The Papers of David Sarnoff*, constitutes a major addition to biographical studies.

R. L. Bannerman's *Norman Corwin and Radio: The Golden Years* provides both biographical information on the life and contributions of writer-director-producer Corwin and a social history of the centrality of radio in American life. Bannerman highlights the works for which Corwin stands out as a "radio poet," especially those shows in which he tackled political and social issues as well as the comedies and fantasies that he penned. Bannerman also provides information on Corwin's fascinating nonprofessional life, including the accusations that he withstood during the Red Scare. The book features a foreword from broadcast historian Erik Barnouw.

Tom Lewis provides in-depth profiles of three radio innovators in *Empire of the Air: The Men Who Made Radio*. Those featured are Lee De Forest (discoverer of the audion tube), Edwin Armstrong (whose inventions allowed the superior FM radio), and David Sarnoff (president of Radio Corporation of America, RCA). Lewis describes them not as mutually exclusive entities but rather as interrelated and occasionally warring forces and makes a powerful case that they constituted the end of an era in which a single, independent innovator worked alone to outdistance competitors and to become the sole "father" of a form of technology.

National Public Radio: The Cast of Characters by Mary Collins with photographs by Jerome Liebling and Murray Bognovitz is a collection of prose and photographs detailing the growth of NPR through financial crisis in the 1970s and development in the 1980s to its present position of comparative fame and accolades. The work contains many anecdotes and behind-the-scenes details that—when combined with the photos—make this much-respected and beloved institution come to life. But above all, Collins' work is a very personal, low-key look at the people who make up NPR, both on and off the air, including such luminaries as Bob Edwards, Susan Stamberg, Cokie Roberts, and Linda Werthheimer.

Autobiography and memoirs are also excellent sources of history, provided they are taken with the appropriate dosage of salt. Fred Allen's *Treadmill to Oblivion*, for instance, includes not only inside information but also some genuinely penetrating criticism of the medium and its personalities. Similarly, James Critchlow's *Radio Hole-in-the-Head. Radio Liberty: An Insider's Story of Cold War Broadcasting* bears mention. Critchlow was one of the founders in 1953 of Radio Liberty, a station committed to presenting news of events in the former Soviet Union that was neither censored nor distorted to counter news broadcast by official government stations. The author speaks firsthand of Radio Liberty's struggles and eventual acceptance after the Cold War ended. Former CBS news president Sig Mickelson's *America's Other Voice: The Story of Radio Free Europe and Radio Liberty* also gives a fascinating insider's perspective on the efforts to keep residents of communist bloc nations accurately informed through stations staffed largely by American intellectuals and Russian émigrés.

Frequently, the reminiscences of behind-the-scenes people are more illuminating than the memoirs of better-known personalities. Carroll Carroll's *None of Your Business; or, My Life with J. Walter Thompson (Confessions of a Renegade Radio Writer)* gives some real insight into what it was like to work in program production during the years when advertising agencies were the primary producers of commercially successful shows. Ben Gross' *I Looked and I Listened: Information Recollections of Radio and Television* offers a lucid and rancorless account of radio from an actor's point of view, and he is particularly enlightening about how the networks responded to Joseph McCarthy's efforts to "clean up" the media in the early 1950s. A truly singular book about the creation of one of radio's most spectacular programs is Kenneth Koch's *The Panic Broadcast: Portrait of an Event*, which tells about the *Mercury Theater of the Air* legendary production of H. G. Wells' *War of the Worlds*, narrated by Orson Welles. Koch wrote the script (which is included in the book), and his account of the preparation and aftermath of the production makes fascinating reading for anyone concerned with this famous broadcast's genesis.

The memoirs of announcers give a very special perspective on the medium that is often insightful and spans program categories. Red Barber, for instance, concentrates on sports announcers in his *The Broadcasters*, but his memoirs touch upon a wide range of prominent figures in radio history. Ted Husing's *Ten Years before the Mike* has a similarly wide-ranging set of interests, especially if read in conjunction with the maudlin autobiography *My Eyes Are in My Heart*, which was based on the *This Is Your Life* television show done after Husing lost his sight due to a brain tumor. Graham McNamee's autobiography *You're on the Air*, although burdened by spates of self-congratulation, provides some substantial insights into early radio history and on the nature of early radio "celebrity." Lindsay Nelson, the erstwhile voice of the New York Mets, is the author of *Hello, Everybody, I'm*

Lindsay Nelson, which offers several engaging chapters on his life among the vagabond radio broadcasters in the 1930s and 1940s.

Howard Stern's *Private Parts* merits mention as a bona fide autobiography of a significant radio career and one of the few radio books ever to achieve major stature in the commercial book and film world. Stern also revolutionized various aspects of the radio business, such as introducing aggressive syndication practices and expanding the limits of mainstream talk content and approach.

Criticism

While radio is long on historical account, it is rather short on criticism. Surprisingly few book-length works have been published with the intention of explaining the artistic dimensions of the medium, evaluating psychological responses, or assessing its role in society.

Journalists have been among the best nonacademics to write good, intelligent books about radio. *Washington Post* reporter and award-winning author Howard Kurtz, for instance, takes a critical look at radio and television talk shows in his 1996 *Hot Air. All Talk, All the Time: An Inside Look at the Performers and the Pundits*. Kurtz lends his extensive knowledge of the political arena in explaining how these programs became so powerful, identifying their major players, and arguing for their negative repercussions on politics and the media. The book includes extensive analysis of such figures as Rush Limbaugh, Phil Donahue, Michael Kinsley, Don Imus, Larry King, and others who constitute the talk show circuit that Kurtz convincingly argues is "insidious" and "corrupted by self-promotion." Kurtz amasses colorful and provocative evidence—insults, controversial phrases, and one-liners broadcast by hosts—that talk shows jeopardize the ideals of journalism and reduce the quality of national discourse regarding politics.

John Crosby was the *New York Herald*'s radio critic after World War II, and his *Out of the Blue: A Book about Radio and Television* collects some of his most provocative and enjoyable comments. Similarly, Albert N. Williams' *Listening: A Collection of Critical Articles on Radio* collects columns and articles originally written for the *Saturday Review of Literature*. Unlike Crosby, Williams is at his best when he looks at the principles and policies governing network program patterns rather than individual shows or persons, and his commentary sheds real light on the character and style of various network programming policies.

Gilbert Seldes wrote two excellent books, *The Great Audience* and *The Public Arts*, that deal with radio, and he brings to his trenchant criticisms both the bite of the satirist and the affection of a practitioner. In the former, Seldes is heavily concerned with radio. He scourges the medium for such things as its penchant to write scripts "in order to be forgotten" (so that the audience will tune in for the next show) while also giving credit where due in his praise of soap opera as an original and serious literary form.

Representative of most early radio criticism by media academics is Erik Barnouw's *Mass Communications: Television, Radio, Film, Press; The Media and Their Practice in the United States of America*. Insightful and intelligent, Barnouw offers some extremely useful points for understanding how radio functions and its proper nature as both an aesthetic form and a communications medium. He points to its unique ability to serve an active audience, for instance, and its inherent leaning toward narrative rather than dramatic presentations. For an understanding of the craftsmanship of radio and the process by which programs are brought into being, he is unsurpassed as a critic.

No treatment of criticism would be complete without some mention of Marshall McLuhan. In *Understanding Media: The Extensions of Man*, for instance, McLuhan lays out his vision of people's extension and definition of themselves through their communications media, shedding light on the essential natures of all the electronic media. His chapter on radio looks harder at the whole medium than anything since 1930s art critic Rudolf Arnheim. McLuhan's vision of radio as "tribal drums" carrying the electrical impulses of the social nervous system was not so totally unprecedented as some have thought it; but it was new and radical enough to influence the thinking of many later critics.

A series of other critical works argues for societal and cultural influences on the development of the radio industry. Ralph Engelman's *Public Radio and Television in America: A Political History* adopts a critical studies approach to give an interpretive view of public broadcasting in the context of political, economic, ideological, and social factors of the day. He also provides a useful explanation of each of the major historical, legal maneuvers that have affected public broadcasting.

Michele Hilmes takes a unique bent in the 1990 *Hollywood and Broadcasting: From Radio to Cable*, in which she critically examines the interrelationship between broadcasting (both radio and television) and film. For the period from network radio to the present, Hilmes demonstrates the considerable influence that the Hollywood studios had and continue to have over the economic structure, program forms, and means of distribution of broadcasting. Hilmes provides careful detail regarding the often overlooked attempts by the studios to gain control over the nascent radio industry, detailing both successes and failures.

Susan Smulyan provides protracted argument for how things could have been if noncommercial forces had prevailed at the onset of American broadcasting. In *Selling Radio: The Commercialization of American Broadcasting 1920–1934* she details the power struggles among such disparate elements as AT&T, RCA, educational entities, interest groups, and the U.S. government that ultimately resulted in an advertising-based system that, she argues, was far from inevitable. Susan J. Douglas presents another view of the forces that shaped broadcasting upon its birth in *Inventing American Broadcasting 1899–1922*. Her approach is fourfold, assessing the contributions and attempts at influence of the existing press industry, the inventors, the technology itself, and the military.

Other critical contributions—even fewer in number—attack broad social and psychological questions of paramount importance to historians and critics. Two names of unparalleled historical significance in this area are Hadley Cantril and Paul F. Lazarsfeld. Cantril and Gordon A. Allport, for instance, wrote *The Psychology of Radio*, which was the first major attempt to analyze the psychological process by which listeners respond to radio. Cantril also published (with Hazel Gaudet and Herta Herzog) *The Invasion from Mars: A Study in the Psychology of Panic*, which was the first of a long list of scholarly and critical publications about Orson Welles' phenomenal Halloween prank. Cantril is best known as a public opinion researcher, of course, and he was among the earliest people to develop scientific methodologies for dealing with radio audiences.

Even more prolific than Cantril, Paul F. Lazarsfeld was probably the most assiduous sociological researcher of the "golden age." In *Radio and the Printed Page*, subtitled *An Introduction to the Study of Radio and Its Role in the Communication of Ideas*, he discussed the nature of the complex interplay between the aural medium and the visual media of books and newspapers. Although vitiated by lack of a sophisticated concept of information as a measurable substance, Lazarsfeld's study remains an interesting attempt to see radio as a medium of exchange and change in opinion. Lazarsfeld also worked with Frank N. Stanton to edit two volumes of *Radio Research*, which attempted to digest developments in the field, and he later worked on two studies of public opinion about radio. With Harry Field he produced an extensive survey of public opinion on radio entitled *The People Look at Radio*. Two years later he worked with Patricia Kendall to produce a follow-up study entitled *Radio Listening in America: The People Look at Radio—Again*. In both studies, he was primarily interested in both the content of programming and the nature of public response to programs and advertisement. Characteristically, he was also interested in the effect of criticism on public response.

Vincent M. Ditingo's *The Remaking of Radio* is a well-written and thoughtful analysis of the factors responsible for radio's survival in the face of so much change in the communications industry. Ditingo, a former editor of *Broadcasting & Cable*, describes in full and accurate detail the adaptations that radio experienced, including the use of satellites and other technological innovations to share programming and the growth of FM radio and recent recovery of AM radio in popularity. He also assesses the role of the climate of deregulation as responsible for much of radio's continuing financial survival.

Edward C. Pease and Everette E. Dennis' edited compilation of essays entitled *Radio: The Forgotten Medium* shows why—though it is "no longer as glamorous or important as its shinier successors" (xi)—radio remains a vital and resilient medium. The compilation was originally issued as a special edition (Summer 1993) of *Media Studies Journal*, published by the Freedom Forum Media Studies Center, which was altered and expanded and now features detailed essays by media scholars, public opinion specialists, and industry professionals. Sample essays in the book include Former Radio Television News Directors' Association president David Bartlett on news radio, Times Mirror Center for the People and the Press' Andrew Kohut and Carol Bowman on "The Vocal Minority in U.S. Politics," record company executive Sean Ross on music radio and audience fragmentation, former FCC commissioner Andrew C. Barrett on radio regulation, and longtime American Public Radio (APR) president Steven L. Salyer on public radio. The compilation ends with a discussion of seven books useful as resources on radio (many included here).

Since the late 1940s, social scientists have tended to focus their attention on television as the primary grounds for research, and in this trend they are typical of all criticism. With the exception of occasional anomalies, more criticism today subsumes radio within a larger concern with television, and thus the field of radio criticism is a relatively dead issue with most periodicals and publishers. Research inquiries into the effects of radio on American popular culture will always be complicated. The interplay of business, government, technology, and art, for instance, causes part of the creative tension within which radio has always existed, and this is an extremely difficult interplay to understand. Yet, understanding of the evolution of this chameleon-like medium and its present position in American popular culture remains vitally important.

BIBLIOGRAPHY

Books and Articles

Aitken, Hugh G. J. *The Continuous Wave: Technology and American Radio, 1900–1932*. Princeton, N.J.: Princeton University Press, 1985.

Allen, Fred. *Treadmill to Oblivion*. Boston: Little, Brown, 1954.

Archer, Gleason L. *Big Business and Radio*. New York: American Historical Society, 1939.

———. *A History of Radio to 1926*. New York: American Historical Society, 1938.

Arnheim, Rudolf. *Radio*. Trans. Margaret Ludwig and Herbert Read. London: Faber and Faber, 1936.

Ash, Lee. *Subject Collections: A Guide to Special Book Collections and Subject Emphases as Reported by University, College, Public, and Special Libraries and Museums in the United States of America and Canada*. 5th ed. New York: R. R. Bowker, 1985.

Bannerman, R. L. *Norman Corwin and Radio: The Golden Years*. University: Alabama University Press, 1986.

Banning, William Peck. *Commercial Broadcasting Pioneer: The WEAF Experiment 1922–1926*. Cambridge: Harvard University Press, 1946.

Barber, Walter L. ("Red"). *The Broadcasters*. New York: Dial Press, 1970.

Barfield, Ray E., and M. Thomas Inge. *Listening to Radio, 1920–1950*. New York: Praeger, 1996.

Barnouw, Erik. *History of Broadcasting in the United States*. 3 vols. New York: Oxford University Press, 1966–1970.

———. *Mass Communications: Television, Radio, Film, Press; The Media and Their Practice in the United States of America*. New York: Rinehart, 1956.

Barnouw, Erik, George Gerbner, Wilbur Schramm, Tobia L. Worth, and Larry Gross, eds. *International Encyclopedia of Communications*. Vols. 1–4. New York: Oxford University Press, 1989.

Berg, Gertrude. *The Rise of the Goldbergs*. New York: Barse, 1931.

Bliss, Edward, Jr. *Now the News: The Story of Broadcast Journalism*. New York: Columbia University Press, 1991.

Bloch, Louis M., Jr. *The Gas Pipe Networks: A History of College Radio 1936–1946*. Cleveland, Ohio: Bloch, 1980.

Blum, Eleanor. *Basic Books in the Mass Media: An Annotated, Selected Booklist Covering General Communications, Book Publishing, Broadcasting, Editorial Journalism, Film, Magazines, and Advertising, Indexes, and Scholarly and Professional Periodicals*. Urbana: University of Illinois Press, 1980.

Brennecke, Paul, ed. *America before TV: A Day in Radio, September 21, 1939*. Middlebury, Vt.: Great Tapes, 1998.

Briggs, John. *Requiem for a Yellow Brick Brewery: A History of the Metropolitan Opera*. Boston: Little, Brown, 1969.

Buxton, Frank, Bill Owen, and Henry Morgan. *The Big Broadcast 1920–1950*. 2nd ed. Lanham, Md.: Scarecrow Press, 1996.

———. *Radio's Golden Age: The Programs and the Personalities.* New York: Easton Valley Press, 1966.

Campbell, Robert. *The Golden Years of Broadcasting: A Celebration of the First 50 Years of Radio and TV on NBC.* New York: Scribner's, 1972.

Cantor, Louis. *Wheelin' on Beale: How WDIA-Memphis Became the Nation's First All-Black Radio Station and Created the Sound That Changed America.* New York: Pharos Books, 1992.

Cantril, Hadley, and Gordon W. Allport. *The Psychology of Radio.* New York: Harper and Brothers, 1935.

Cantril, Hadley, Hazel Gaudet, and Hertz Herzog. *The Invasion from Mars: A Study in the Psychology of Panic.* Princeton, N.J.: Princeton University Press, 1940.

Carroll, Carroll. *None of Your Business; or, My Life with J. Walter Thompson (Confessions of a Renegade Radio Writer).* New York: Cowles, 1970.

Catsis, John R. *Sports Broadcasting.* Chicago: Nelson-Hall, 1996.

Charnley, Mitchell V. *News by Radio.* New York: Macmillan, 1948.

Chase, Francis, Jr. *Sound and Fury: An Informal History of Broadcasting.* New York: Harper and Brothers, 1942.

Chicorel, Marietta, ed. *Chicorel Index to the Spoken Arts on Discs, Tapes, and Cassettes.* 3 vols. Chirocel Index Series, vols. 7, 7a, 7b. New York: Chicorel Library, 1973–1974.

Cloud, Stanley, and Lynne Olson. *The Murrow Boys: Pioneers on the Front Lines of Broadcast Journalism.* Boston: Houghton Mifflin, 1996.

Coe, Lewis. *Wireless Radio: A Brief History.* Jefferson, N.C.: McFarland, 1996.

Collins, Mary, with photographs by Jerome Liebling and Murray Bognovitz. *National Public Radio: The Cast of Characters.* Washington, D.C.: Seven Locks Press.

The Comprehensive Country Music Encyclopedia. Spokane, Wash.: Timeless Books, 1994.

Correl, Charles J., and Freeman Gosden. *All about Amos n' Andy.* New York: Rand McNally, 1929.

Critchlow, James. *Radio Hole-in-the-Head. Radio Liberty: An Insider's Story of Cold War Broadcasting.* Washington, D.C.: American University Press, 1995.

Crook, Timothy. *International Radio Journalism: History, Theory and Practice.* New York: Routledge, 1998.

Crosby, John. *Out of the Blue: A Book about Radio and Television.* New York: Simon and Schuster, 1952.

Culbert, David H. *News for Everyman: Radio and Foreign Affairs in Thirties America.* Westport, Conn.: Greenwood Press, 1976.

DeLong, Tom. *The Mighty Music Box: The Golden Age of Musical Radio.* Los Angeles: Amber Crest Book, 1980.

Ditingo, Vincent M. *The Remaking of Radio.* Boston: Focal Press, 1995.

Douglas, George H. *The Early Days of Radio Broadcasting.* Jefferson, N.C.: McFarland, 1987.

Douglas, Susan J. *Inventing American Broadcasting 1899–1922.* Baltimore: Johns Hopkins University Press, 1997.

Duncan, James, H., Jr. *American Radio: Sixteenth Anniversary Issue, 1976–1992: A Statistical History.* Indianapolis: Duncan's American Radio, 1992.

Dunning, John. *On the Air: The Encyclopedia of Old-Time Radio*. New York: Oxford University Press, 1998.

———. *Tune in Yesterday: The Ultimate Encyclopedia of Old Time Radio 1925–1976*. Englewood Cliffs, N.J.: Prentice-Hall, 1976.

Eberly, Philip. *Music in the Air: America's Changing Tastes in Popular Music*. New York: Hastings House, 1982.

Edmondson, Madeleine, and David Round. *The Soaps: Daytime Serials of Radio and TV*. New York: Stein and Day, 1973.

Eichberg, Robert. *Radio Stars of Today; Behind the Scenes in Broadcasting*. Boston: L. C. Page, 1937.

Ely, Melvin Patrick. *The Adventures of Amos n' Andy: A Social History of an American Phenomenon*. New York: Free Press, 1992.

Emery, Walter B. *National and International Systems of Broadcasting: Their History, Operation, and Control*. East Lansing: Michigan State University Press, 1969.

Engelman, Ralph. *Public Radio and Television in America: A Political History*. Thousand Oaks, Calif.: Sage, 1996.

Fong-Torres, Ben. *The Hits Just Keep on Coming: The History of Top 40 Radio*. San Francisco: Miller Freeman Books, 1998.

Fornatale, Peter and Joshua E. Mills. *Radio in the Television Age*. Woodstock, N.Y.: Overlook Press, 1980.

Frost, S. E., Jr. *Education's Own Stations: The History of Broadcast Licenses Issued to Educational Institutions*. Chicago: University of Chicago Press, 1937.

Garner, Joe. *We Interrupt This Broadcast: Relive the Events That Stopped Our Lives . . . from the Hindenburg to the Death of Princess Diana*. Naper, Ill.: Sourcebooks Trade, 1998.

Godfried, Nathan. *WCFL, Chicago's Voice of Labor, 1926–78*. Urbana: University of Illinois Press, 1997.

Green, Able, and Joe Laurel Jr. *Show Biz: From Vaude to Video*. New York: Henry Holt, 1951.

Greenfield, Thomas A. *Radio: A Reference Guide*. Westport, Conn.: Greenwood Press, 1989.

Gross, Ben. *I Looked and I Listened: Informal Recollections of Radio and Television*. New York: Random House, 1954.

Harmon, Jim. *The Great Radio Comedians*. Garden City, N.Y.: Doubleday, 1970.

———. *The Great Radio Heroes*. Garden City, N.Y.: Doubleday, 1967.

Harwood, Kenneth. "World Bibliography of Selected Periodicals on Broadcasting (Revised)." *Journal of Broadcasting* 16 (1972), 131–46.

Head, Sydney, and Christopher H. Sterling. *Broadcasting in America: A Survey of Electronic Media*. 7th ed. Boston: Houghton Mifflin, 1994.

Head, Sydney, Christopher H. Sterling, and Lemuel B. Schofield. *Broadcasting in America: A Survey of Electronic Media. Brief Version*. 2nd ed. Boston: Houghton Mifflin, 1996.

Hilliard, Robert L., with Michael C. Keith. *The Broadcast Century: A Biography of American Broadcasting*. Boston: Focal Press, 1997.

Hilmes, Michele. *Hollywood and Broadcasting: From Radio to Cable*. Urbana: University of Illinois Press, 1990.

Hosley, David H. *As Good as Any: Foreign Correspondence on American Radio, 1930–1940.* Westport, Conn.: Greenwood Press, 1984.

Howeth, S. L. *History of Communications-Electronics in the United States Navy.* Washington, D.C.: Government Printing Office, 1963.

Husing, Ted. *My Eyes Are in My Heart.* New York: Simon and Schuster, 1941.

———. *Ten Years before the Mike.* New York: Farrar and Rinehart, 1935.

Jackaway, Gwenyth L. *Media at War: Radio's Challenge to the Newspapers, 1924–1939.* New York: Praeger, 1995.

Jaker, Bill, Frank Sulek, and Peter Kanze. *The Airwaves of New York: Illustrated Histories of 156 AM Stations in the Metropolitan Area, 1921–1996.* Jefferson, N.C.: McFarland, 1998.

Keith, Michael C. *Voices in the Purple Haze: Underground Radio and the Sixties.* New York: Praeger, 1997.

Keith, Michael C., and Joseph M. Krause. *The Radio Station.* Boston: Focal Press, 1989.

Kingsbury, Paul, Laura Garrard, and Daniel Cooper, eds. *The Encyclopedia of Country Music: The Ultimate Guide to the Music.* New York: Oxford University Press, 1998.

Koch, Kenneth. *The Panic Broadcast: Portrait of an Event.* Boston: Little, Brown, 1970.

Kurtz, Howard. *Hot Air. All Talk, All the Time: An Inside Look at the Performers and the Pundits.* New York: Times Books, 1996.

Lackmann, Ronald. *Remember Radio.* New York: G. P. Putnam's Sons, 1970.

———. *Same Time . . . Same Station: An A-Z Guide to Radio from Jack Benny to Howard Stern.* New York: Facts on File.

Ladd, Jim. *Radio Waves: Life and Revolution on the FM Dial.* New York: St. Martin's Press.

Lazarsfeld, Paul F. *Radio and the Printed Page: An Introduction to the Study of Radio and Its Role in the Communication of Ideas.* New York: Duell and Sloan, 1940.

Lazarsfeld, Paul F., and Harry Field. *The People Look at Radio.* Chapel Hill: University of North Carolina Press, 1946.

Lazarsfeld, Paul F., and Patricia L. Kendall. *Radio Listening in America: The People Look at Radio—Again.* Englewood Cliffs, N.J.: Prentice-Hall, 1946.

Lazarsfeld, Paul F., and Frank N. Stanton, eds. *Radio Research 1941.* New York: Duell, Sloan, and Pearce, 1942.

———. *Radio Research 1942–43.* New York: Duell, Sloan, and Pearce, 1944.

Lewis, Tom. *Empire of the Air: The Men Who Made Radio.* New York: Edward Burlingame Books, 1991.

Logan, Horace, and Bill Sloan. *Elvis, Hank, and Me: Making Musical History on the Louisiana Hayride.* New York: St. Martin's Press, 1998.

Lord, Phillips H. *Seth Parker's Sunday Evening Meeting: An Entertainment in One Act.* New York: Samuel French, 1930.

Lyons, Eugene. *David Sarnoff: A Biography.* New York: Harper and Row, 1966.

MacDonald, J. Fred. *Don't Touch That Dial: Radio Programming in American Life from 1920 to 1960.* Chicago: Hall, 1979.

MacDonald, J. Fred, ed., *Richard Durham's Destination Freedom: Scripts from Radio's Black Legacy, 1948–1950.* New York: Praeger, 1989.

Maltin, Leonard. *The Great American Broadcast: A Celebration of Radio's Golden Age*. New York: Dutton, 1997.

Marx, Herbert Lewis, Jr., ed. *Television and Radio in American Life*. Reference Shelf, Vol. 25, No. 2. New York: H. W. Wilson, 1953.

McCloud, Barry. *Definitive Country: The Ultimate Encyclopedia of Country Music and Its Performers*. Berkeley, Calif.: Perigee, 1995.

McLuhan, Marshall. *Understanding Media: The Extensions of Man*. New York: McGraw-Hill, 1964.

McNamee, Graham, with Robert Gordon Anderson. *You're on the Air*. New York: Harper Brothers, 1926.

Mickelson, Sig. *America's Other Voice: The Story of Radio Free Europe and Radio Liberty*. New York: Praeger, 1983.

Morris, Lloyd R. *Not So Long Ago*. New York: Random House, 1949.

Mott, Robert L. *Radio Sound Effects: Who Did It, and How, in the Era of Live Broadcasting*. Jefferson, N.C.: McFarland, 1993.

Murrow, Edward R. *This Is London*. New York: Simon and Schuster, 1941.

Nachman, Gerald. *Raised on Radio*. New York: Pantheon Books, 1998.

Nelson, Lindsay. *Hello, Everybody, I'm Lindsay Nelson*. New York: William Morrow, 1985.

Pease, Edward C., and Everette E. Dennis, eds. *Radio: The Forgotten Medium*. New Brunswick, N.J.: Transaction, 1995.

Perry, Dick. *Not Just a Sound: The Story of WLW*. Englewood Cliffs, N.J.: Prentice-Hall, 1971.

Persico, Joseph E. *Edward R. Murrow: An American Original*. New York: Da Capo Press, 1997.

Pitts, Michael R. *Radio Soundtracks: A Reference Guide*. Metuchen, N.J.: Scarecrow Press, 1976.

Post, Steve. *Playing in the FM Band: A Personal Account of Free Radio*. New York: Viking, 1974.

Poteet, G. Howard. *Published Radio, Television, and Film Scripts*. Troy, N.Y.: Whitston, 1975.

Rosen, Philip T. *The Modern Stentors: Radio Broadcasters and the Federal Government, 1920–1934*. Westport, Conn.: Greenwood Press, 1980.

Sablosky, Irving. *American Music*. Chicago: University of Chicago Press, 1969.

Sanger, Elliott M. *Rebel in Radio: The Story of WQXR*. New York: Hastings House, 1973.

Sanjet, Russell. *From Print to Plastic: Publishing and Promoting America's Popular Music 1900–1980*. Brooklyn, N.Y.: Institute for Studies in American Music, 1983.

Sarnoff, David. *Looking Ahead: The Papers of David Sarnoff*. New York: McGraw-Hill, 1968.

Schiffer, Michael B. *The Portable Radio in American Life*. Tucson: University of Arizona Press, 1991.

Segrave, Kerry. *Payola in the Music Industry: A History, 1880–1991*. Jefferson, N.C.: McFarland, 1993.

Seldes, Gilbert. *The Great Audience*. Reprint. Westport, Conn.: Greenwood Press, 1970.

———. *The Public Arts*. New York: Simon and Schuster, 1956.

Sennett, Andrew G., ed. *The World Radio TV Handbook*. New York: Billboard Directories, 1995.

Shurick, E.P.J. *The First Quarter Century of American Broadcasting*. Kansas City, Mo.: Midland, 1946.

Siepmann, Charles. *Radio's Second Chance*. Boston: Little, Brown, 1946.

Slate, Sam J., and Joe Cook. *It Sounds Impossible*. New York: Macmillan, 1963.

———. *Of Mikes and Men: From Ray Scott to Curt Gowdy: Broadcast Tales from the Pro Football Booth*. South Bend, Ind.: Diamond Communications, 1998.

Smith, Curt. *The Storytellers: From Mel Allen to Bob Costas: Sixty Years of Baseball Tales from the Broadcast Booth*. New York: Macmillan USA, 1995.

———. *Voices of the Game: The First Full-Scale Overview of Baseball Broadcasting, 1921 to the Present*. South Bend, Ind.: Diamond Communications, 1987.

Smulyan, Susan. *Selling Radio: The Commercialization of American Broadcasting 1920–1934*. Washington, D.C.: Smithsonian Institution Press, 1994.

Sperber, A. M. *Murrow: His Life and Times*. New York: Freundlich Books, 1986.

Stambler, Irwin, with Grelun Landon. *Country Music: The Encyclopedia*. New York: St. Martin's Press, 1997.

Stedman, Raymond William. *The Serials: Suspense and Drama by Installment*. Norman: University of Oklahoma Press, 1971.

Sterling, Christopher H., James K. Bracken, and Susan M. Hill, eds. *Mass Communications Research Resources: An Annotated Guide*. Mahwah, N.J.: Erlbaum, 1998.

Stern, Howard. *Private Parts*. New York: Pocket Star Books, 1994.

Summers, Harrison B. *A Thirty Year History of Programs Carried on National Radio Networks in the United States 1926–1956*. Columbus: Ohio State University Press, 1958.

Swartz, Jon D. and Robert C. Reinehr. *Handbook of Old-Time Radio: A Comprehensive Guide to Golden Age Radio Listening and Collecting*. Lanham, Md.: Scarecrow Press, 1993.

Taubman, Howard. *Maestro: The Life of Arturo Toscanini*. New York: Simon and Schuster, 1961.

Thomas, Lowell. *Magic Dials: The Story of Radio and Television*. New York: Lee Furman, 1939.

———. *Country: The Twisted Roots of Rock 'n' Roll*. New York: Da Capo Press, 1996.

Tosches, Nick. *Country: The Biggest Music in America*. New York: Stein and Day, 1977.

Tyler, Poyntz, ed. *Television and Radio*. The Reference Shelf, Vol. 36, No. 2. New York: H. W. Wilson, 1961.

Wertheimer, Linda, ed. *Listening to America: Twenty-five Years in the Life of a Nation, As Heard on National Public Radio*. New York: Houghton Mifflin, 1995.

Williams, Albert N. *Listening: A Collection of Critical Articles on Radio*. Reprint. Freeport, N.Y.: Books for Libraries Press, 1968.

Woolley, Lynn. *The Last Great Days of Radio*. Plano, Tex.: Wordware, 1994.

Periodicals

Broadcast Bibliophile's Booknotes. Philadelphia, 1969–1974.
Broadcasting and Cable (originally *Broadcasting*). Washington, D.C., 1931– .
Broadcasting and Cable Yearbook (originally *Broadcasting Yearbook*). Washington, D.C., 1935– .
Communication Abstracts. Beverly Hills, Calif., 1978– .
Communication Booknotes Quarterly. Washington, D.C., 1982– .
Dimensions of Radio. Washington, D.C., 1960– .
Journal of Broadcasting and Electronic Media (originally *Journal of Broadcasting*). Washington, D.C., 1956– .
Journal of Communication. Philadelphia, 1951– .
Journal of Popular Culture. Bowling Green, Ohio, 1966– .
Journal of Radio Studies. Washington, D.C., 1998– .
Journalism Quarterly. Columbia, S.C., 1924– .
Mass Media Booknotes (originally *Broadcast Bibliophiles Booknotes*). Washington, D.C., 1974–1982.
Radio Annual. New York, 1938–1964.
Radio Broadcast. New York, 1922–1930.
Radio Daily. New York, 1937–1964.
Radio Directory. New York, 1938–1941.
Radio Programming Profile. BF/Communication Services, Glen Head, N.Y., 1968.
Radio Programming Profile. Alan Torbet Associates, N.Y., 1975.

Audio Recordings

50 Old Time Radio Commercials. Metacom, 1985.
Four Decades with Studs Terkel. Highbridge Company, 1994.
Golden Age of Radio: Radio's All-Time Greatest Shows. Dove Books Audio, 1996.
Laughter from the Golden Age of Radio. West Audio, 1990.
Nostalgia Radio. Metacom, 1994.
Old Time Radio Comedy. Soundelux Audio, 1994.
Radio's Golden Years. Metacom, 1988.
Smithsonian Collection of Old Time Radio. Radio Spirits, 1997.

RECORDING INDUSTRY

James A. Von Schilling

"I was never taken so aback in life," was Thomas Alva Edison's reaction to the initial sounds coming from the machine that he had hastily designed to repeat the spoken word, its first words being Edison's own rendition of "Mary Had a Little Lamb." Amazing as that premier performance of recording must have been in 1876, even to its inventor, perhaps much more amazing has been the industry's performance in the century and a quarter since. Recordings have survived patent struggles and labor disputes, two world wars and a Great Depression, the breakup of monopolies and the breakdown of distribution systems, and the advent of motion pictures, radio, television, and cyberspace, along with the rise and fall of musical tastes, styles, and superstars. At times sales may have dipped, and there were even moments when the industry seemed on its last leg and tipping over, but the general trend for over a century has been continuous growth in product, audience, and profits.

Even in recent times, some argued that the emergence of home video technology posed a serious threat to the recording industry. But this argument ignored two of the basic principles that have governed the complex history of recordings. First, the industry has survived and prospered partly by taking advantage of any new medium that appeared to be its rival or even conqueror. When radio boomed in the 1920s, for example, it seemed to mark the demise of the record industry. Aided by the onset of the depression, radio was making the notion of paying to hear music at home obsolete or at least foolish. Within a few years, though, radio had introduced America to "swing" music, a style so popular that it triggered as a side effect a whole new boom in record buying. Similarly, the later notion that television might doom the recording industry was disproved in the aftermath of the 1964 appearances of the Beatles on the *Ed Sullivan Show*, if not the appearances of Elvis Presley on the same show a decade earlier. Not surprisingly, the video revolution of the 1980s actually helped rescue the recording industry from an economic slump, with album and cassette sales spurred by "music videos" of performers shown on television.

The second principle behind the remarkable growth and survival of the record industry reaches all the way back to Edison's reaction to his "child's" first words. At the very heart of recording's relationship to American culture has been its power to take each of us aback, as Edison was, throughout our personal lives. Historians of the industry have noted that each new development in recording technology was heralded as introducing the ultimate in lifelike sound, only to be rendered hopelessly "tiny" by newer technologies, sometimes just a few years later. This suggests that we take such claims with a certain skepticism, but it also illustrates an important point. Despite how inferior the recording techniques and results of the past may seem to us now, they created powerful emotional experiences for the audiences of their time. The essential bond has always been between the listener and the recorded sound, and everything else—the technology, the marketing, the profits—has resulted from that bond and its basic power.

In other words, recorded sound does something of great significance to people, and so it has for over 100 years of American culture. The variety of styles and performers that has been recorded and the variety of audiences affected by these recordings makes it difficult to determine exactly what this significance is and where its real power resides. "It's got a good beat and you can dance to it," goes the classic explanation for what makes a rock-and-roll record a memorable experience to its audience, but that hardly works with recordings of other genres: jazz, country, Broadway, opera, and so forth. Regardless of genre, however, most recordings do one thing in common: they capture in time a unique combination of music, performance, and artistry and then enable us to make this "timepiece" part of our personal experience.

When we purchase a recording, we generally have little knowledge of the history, technology, or economics behind it. But all that may be incidental; the essence of recorded sound may simply be the personal actions of bringing that recording home, slitting the cellophane wrapping, placing the product into the machine, initiating the electricity and machinery, and then experiencing internally the timepiece of music, performance, and artistry awaiting us in the grooves. A nursery rhyme in his own voice took Edison aback; today it may require a multitracked, million-dollar electronic production, but the results are the same. We are taken hold of, and a truly memorable recording transcends all the history, technology, and business and does not let us back into that other world—at least until the music ends.

HISTORICAL OUTLINE

Thomas Edison invented the phonograph the way Columbus discovered America—accidentally, while looking for something else entirely. Edison was actually seeking to improve the newly emerging telephone system by making it more accessible to the middle and lower classes in America. Home telephone equipment was expensive back in 1876; Edison hoped to design a machine for recording messages, with the results capable of being replayed and transmitted at a centrally located telephone. Precisely why anybody would need to record the message beforehand rather than simply speak into the centrally located phone (as we do today

Native American being recorded, ca. 1900. © Smithsonian Institution

at public telephones) has never been completely established, not that it really mattered. Edison's idea, which was tendered into a working mechanism by an assistant, John Kruesi, in November 1876, quickly took on new applications when introduced to the public the following year. Edison himself soon envisioned a list of ten general uses for his invention, of which only the tenth dealt with telephones. The others included "letter writing and all kinds of dictation," the "reproduction of music" (fourth on his list), and "clocks that announce in accurate speech the time for going home, going to meals, etc."

At first the phonograph generated great publicity as Edison's assistants conducted public demonstrations around the country. But by 1880 Edison had re-channeled his energies and redirected his laboratory toward a new idea, the electric lightbulb, and the phonograph slipped into a state of suspended animation for most of the decade. In October 1887, however, Edison switched gears again, "confessing" to America that, despite his apparent fixation on what he called "the electric business. . . . Nevertheless, the phonograph has been more or less constantly in my mind." Edison's apparent fickleness was, in reality, a shrewd businessman's response to a rapidly changing commercial climate, as his short-lived monopoly over the machine, the industry, and its future was about to end.

Edison's invention was facing a stiff, serious competitor in 1887, the Alexander Graham Bell-sponsored Graphophone; the following year yet a third rival emerged, Emile Berliner's gramophone. The stage was set for the next thirty years of the fledgling industry's history and a series of complex, exhaustive struggles among the pioneering individuals and companies that emerged from these first three rivals. From a technological perspective, the machine that eventually dominated the market after this "thirty years' war" was a far cry from Edison's mechanism. Instead, it more closely resembled Emile Berliner's gramophone, recording on discs rather than Edison's cylinder products.

From a business viewpoint, two major companies survived out of the dozen or so that played key roles during these early years; although the ranks of "majors" have changed throughout the decades, these two have always made the list. The first company, Victor Talking Machine, came to life in 1901, when Eldridge R. Johnson, who had been Berliner's equipment supplier, staked his own claim in the industry. Twenty-five years later Johnson sold his controlling interest in Victor for $28 million to a firm that soon merged with the Radio Corporation of America (RCA). Columbia Phonograph, the other permanent leg of the record industry, had its origins back in 1878, as a subsidiary distributor for Bell's Graphophone. Columbia suffered through periods of hard times and one clear case of bankruptcy. Propped up in 1923 by new owners, it survived the depression and eventually found a safe haven in the early 1930s under the corporate umbrella of RCA's archrival, the Columbia Broadcasting System (CBS).

From a musical standpoint, no single style dominated these early years of the record industry as rock music has since the 1950s. Rather, the catalogs of the pioneer companies featured everything from the arias of Enrico Caruso, to the popular ditties whistled by George W. Johnson. Popular music in general, however, clearly dominated the market, no doubt partly because many early phonographs were coin-operated and served as amusements in public locations. But classical performers, particularly opera stars (orchestras fared poorly under the early recording techniques), became crucial weapons in the fierce publicity battles fought between the pioneer companies. Signing a top European tenor or soprano could help establish a company as an industry leader, even though most of that company's sales were likely to fall in the popular market.

Linked so closely to America's popular culture, however, the record industry was subject to the fluctuations of public taste. The medium experienced its first real boom during the dance mania of the mid-1910s. Victor scored a coup by signing the period's ballroom royalty, Vernon and Irene Castle, to "supervise" the recording of dance music, while Columbia trumpeted its own expert, G. Hepburn Wilson, who "dances while the band makes the record." Sales of newly designed phonograph consoles, with prices ranging up to $2,000, soared in the United States and Europe and continued strong through the early 1920s, aided by a popular, shocking, and liberating style of music and dance: hot jazz.

But the focus of popular culture shifted unexpectedly in the mid-1920s to a new medium for speech and music—the radio, with one clear technical advantage over the phonograph. The radio was electric: the amplification processes involved in radio transmission produced sounds far superior in quality to the mechanical diaphragm and stylus system that the early phonograph employed. That technological edge gave radio a jump start and forced the record industry to adapt by adding radio sets to its consoles and developing electrical recording and playback processes itself. But these changes weren't enough to carry the record industry through a second upheaval later that decade, as the Great Depression placed phonograph records on its list of obviously expendable purchases.

Record sales by 1932 had dropped incredibly—to just 6 percent of the 1927 rate—and sales of phonographs sank to similar depths. The industry did climb back, of course, but doing so took the rest of the decade and involved a number of factors, not the least of which was the New Deal's gradual restoration of consumer confidence in general. Within the industry itself, however, several key developments aided the recovery, most notably, the sudden leap to sales prominence of Decca Records, founded by an American, Jack Kapp, and financed by a London stockbroker. With the current industry "majors"—Victor, Columbia, and Brunswick—all selling their discs for seventy-five cents apiece, Decca managed to corral some top performers and sell their records for only thirty-five cents. "Decca Scoops Music World" headlined their ads, and they did indeed scoop up such pop stars as Bing Crosby, the Mills Brothers, and the Dorseys for their roster. RCA-Victor also contributed significantly to the recovery by marketing a popular, budget-priced phonograph called the Duo, Jr., designed to use the home radio for amplification.

Perhaps the biggest boost to the record industry, however, came from America's popular culture, as the "hot jazz" craze of the 1920s settled into a more mainstream, socially acceptable style of entertainment. America thus entered the "swing" or "Big Band" era, when purchasing the latest tunes by Benny Goodman, Glenn Miller, Harry James, and others became a basic part of life for a whole generation of young Americans. Radio may have popularized the music in the first place, and jukeboxes whetted the public's appetite, but actually owning an "In the Mood" 78 rpm to play in the parlor was the next best thing to jitterbugging in front of the bandstand. Sales of records picked up slowly at first and then dramatically, reaching a peak of 127 million in 1941—and then the bubble burst again.

The problem this time, at first, was World War II and the restrictions imposed on the record industry. All manufacturers of electrical equipment were redirected to the war effort, and 70 percent of the nation's shellac resources (from which records were being produced) were devoted to strictly military purposes. But a heavier bomb fell on the home front in the summer of 1942, when the American Federation of Musicians (AFM) voted to strike the record industry on the grounds that recorded music was putting the professional musician out of business, or at least severely curtailing the need for live performances. With its sales concentrated solely in the popular market, Decca suffered the most by not being able to record the latest styles and hits (which could still be heard in live performances on the radio) and was forced to capitulate the following year. The terms of the Decca agreement involved the payment of royalties to the AFM, for the support of unemployed musicians, for every record sold. Columbia and RCA held out for a second year but eventually surrendered on the same day that Germany signed its peace pact with the Allies.

With conflicts both national and international finally settling down, the record industry may have anticipated a relatively calm postwar period. Instead, the following decade featured an upheaval in technology, a disruption of the industry's economic structure, and a shift in American popular culture of earthquake proportions. The revolution in technology surfaced to the public as the "battle of the speeds," with the new 33⅓ rpm album from CBS in one corner and the new 45 rpm "single" from RCA in the other. Actually, a great deal more than different turntable speeds was involved since Peter Goldmark, the CBS engineer who developed the long-playing 33⅓ album, had virtually reinvented the entire recording and production process along the way. Nothing would ever be the same after Goldmark's album caught on with the public: not the recording studio, with its dramatically improved microphone system; not the records themselves, with their contents expanded up to ten times the two- or three-minute span of the old 78; not even the industry's long-established hierarchy, with Columbia now the leader and RCA playing "catch up." Countering with its own 45 rpm recording format, RCA weakly described the little disc's virtues as the ideal form for the popular single. They were in luck, though, as a figure emerged in America's popular culture (conveniently signed to an RCA contract) who would link the 45, with its oversized hole and its undersized playing time, to millions of young people: the "Hillbilly Cat" from Tupelo, Mississippi—Elvis Presley.

RCA may have reaped the most benefits from the rise of Elvis Presley from Tupelo to stardom, but the fact is that neither Elvis, Chuck Berry, or Little Richard nor any of the pioneers of rock and roll would have affected our popular culture had it not been for a new force that developed in the postwar record industry: the independent record company, or "indie." These businesses ranked far below the "majors" in total sales, production, and promotional budgets, as well as access to distribution (the majors at that time being RCA, Columbia, Decca, Capitol, Mercury, and MGM). Yet, for several key reasons, such relatively small-scale operations as Chess, Savoy, and Atlantic Records came to assume positions of great importance and, in fact, permanently changed the direction of popular music and the entire record industry. First and perhaps foremost, these independent companies recorded black music performed by black artists in a style that was known as rhythm and blues (R&B), out of which developed rock and roll. With but a few exceptions (e.g., Louis Jordan on Decca), the majors either disavowed black music entirely, shunted it onto less-supported subsidiary labels, or recorded black artists like Nat King Cole who were closer to the white mainstream.

In neglecting to record rhythm-and-blues performers, the majors were simply following a pattern that had been established and reestablished throughout the century, in which black artists influenced—and often determined—the course of America's popular music, but white artists profited commercially once the new music reached the public. From the industry's viewpoint, the history of recorded music up to that point had clearly shown that any new music emerging from the black subculture could be directed into the mainstream by the majors, with the ensuing profits diverted from the original sources. Such had been the case with hot jazz and swing music; thus, there was every reason to believe that the system would prevail with rhythm and blues, despite the presence of the independent companies. After all, the majors in the early 1950s were holding a tight grip over all possible distribution routes: jukeboxes, radio airplay, record stores, sheet music—or so they thought.

As it turned out, the majors failed to assess two additional factors, one sociological, and the other commercial, that nearly toppled the whole system. In sociological terms, the majors failed to adjust to the new realities of America's racial structure, for World War II had brought blacks and whites into much greater proximity. This was clearly the case in America's northern cities, where thousands of southern blacks had relocated during the war to seek jobs and had remained afterward. Segregation and discrimination were still in force, but the music of a people can sometimes penetrate where the people themselves cannot, especially if an ideal commercial means for that penetration exists.

In this case, the music—rhythm and blues—found the perfect means in a handful of young and daring radio disc jockeys, such as Alan Freed, Hal Jackson, and Bill Randle, who felt its power and promoted it to anyone who would listen, black or white. Thus, radio undermined the ability of the majors to orchestrate this new popular music, for the one thing that RCA, Columbia, and the others couldn't control was the tuning of the American teenager's bedroom or car radio.

Considering all that the majors could control, however, it is a testimony to the power of rhythm and blues that performers such as Chuck Berry, Fats Domino, Ray Charles, the Coasters, Little Richard, Frankie Lymon, and Bo Diddley—all recording for indies—ever managed to gain a white audience. The majors had direct influence and often outright control over the entire production, promotion, and distribution stages in the life of most popular tunes up through the 1950s, and they used all their power to fight for the continued success of their performers, many of whom were holdovers from the Big Band era. Their most infamous tactic was the "cover" record: a white version of a black hit, quickly recorded, released, and promoted in the mainstream white markets and on leading white radio stations (e.g., Perry Como's cover of "Kokomo," originally recorded by Gene and Eunice). One especially heavy-handed tactic involved public denunciation of the new music by established mainstream figures. Frank Sinatra, for example, used the words "brutal, ugly, desperate, vicious" to describe rock and roll at a 1958 congressional hearing. With less publicity but perhaps more effectiveness, the industry developed a third key tactic: revamping its commercial operations and strengthening its promotion departments, especially involving radio airplay. The majors now recognized the importance of releasing pop singles quickly, to capitalize on popular trends, and of marketing their releases thoroughly from coast to coast.

In the short run, the majors lost the struggle with the indies. The number of hit singles produced by independent companies at the close of the 1950s was twice that of the majors, a remarkable shift from the immediate postwar years, when only 5 out of 162 million-sellers belonged to indies. In the long run, however, the majors won the fight, as few of the independent companies survived the 1960s and the industry retrenchment of that decade. Once again, the forces behind the new shift were numerous and complex. A well-publicized factor was the 1960 congressional investigation into record industry "payola," or the bribing of radio disc jockeys by record personnel to spur airplay for new releases. The big losers in the scandal weren't the major record companies but the freewheeling rock-and-roll disc jockeys who had played such key roles in the rise of the new music, especially Alan Freed, whose career and personal life crumbled after the hearings. The indies themselves suffered, too, losing whatever respectability they might have gained during the 1950s. Also, any curtailment of payola activities would hurt the indies more than the majors, which could still rely on their own extensive distribution systems and, in the case of RCA and Columbia, their own nationwide home record clubs.

In addition, the style of popular music had by then progressed from the early years of rock and roll and in a direction that benefited the mainstream industry. With a surprising number of rock pioneers removed from the scene for various reasons (e.g., Elvis Presley drafted, Chuck Berry jailed), the sound was decidedly less black R&B and more white "pop." Top hits, for example, were recorded by numerous television situation-comedy stars, ranging from Shelley Fabares to Walter Brennan. Another portion of the market belonged to the young performers who recorded for the Philadelphia-centered labels associated with Dick Clark's *American Bandstand* television show. Few members of either group remained successful through the mid-1960s; however, their brief tenure at the top clearly presaged two trends that have characterized the record industry ever since. First, the record industry had developed economically to the point where cross-ownership and conglomeration were influencing the musical results; that is, television's nonsingers owed their recording careers to the tangled webs being woven during the 1960s among the various entertainment industries. Second, the record industry was now profiting heavily from the "cult of personality" approach to producing and marketing performers. Whether it was the pompadoured teenage idol or the cashmere-sweatered girl-next-door, the *image* of the performing artist was selling records, perhaps more than the music or performance itself.

Neither trend was new to the record industry. After all, RCA and CBS had been media conglomerates for decades, and numerous recording stars had developed careers in other entertainment fields or had public images that boosted their sales. But it was during the 1960s that the record industry's corporate structure and its promotional apparatus became as important, if not more so, than the recording technology or the music itself. Under such conditions, the companies that did the best weren't necessarily the most inventive or even the most talented but rather the ones with the strongest economic bases and skills of promotion.

A company whose rise to major status typified the changes in the industry was Warner Records, an independent label purchased in the 1960s by Kinney Services, a New York-based conglomerate. With a stock of reasonably talented young performers (based largely in Southern California) but with lots of promotional campaigning and enough capital to support its own operations and also acquire Atlantic and Elektra Records, Warner spent the 1960s climbing toward the top of the industry in sales. Warner is often cited as the company best illustrating how the "baby boom" generation and its fixation on popular music brought enormous growth and success to the record industry during the 1960s. Although this sociological approach has obvious validity, it misses the point that neither Warner nor the other 1960s majors could have capitalized on the boom and the fixation without their corporate structures and promotional efforts.

Even the Beatles, when viewed in retrospect, were not as spontaneously welcomed by American youth as our popular myths would have us believe. In 1963, the year before "Beatlemania" struck our shores, several Beatles singles were released in the United States on independent labels and caused little reaction. It wasn't until a major company, Capitol, bought the distribution rights and launched one of the most extensive promotional campaigns in the history of recorded music that the Beatles attracted their massive following. In other words, Beatlemania—along with the other waves of popular music intensity during the last four decades—developed from a combination of factors all present in contemporary Amer-

RCA logo. Courtesy of the Library of Congress

ica: a large population of young people with spending money; the close links that have existed between popular music and the social and emotional lives of young Americans, at least since the mid-1950s and the advent of rock music, although probably extending back through the "swing" and "hot jazz" years; and the existence of well-financed, promotion-oriented record companies to feed huge amounts of product to the vast young audience.

With a collection of recordings and a playback system having become basic commodities among American youth, with recordings sold everywhere from local supermarkets to coast-to-coast chain stores, and with top performers rating "cover story" prominence in our national newsmagazines, it's no surprise that the recording industry climbed past both the radio and the motion picture industry in total annual income. Whether the products on which that climb was based—the recorded music from the 1960s on—truly deserve so much promotion, sales, and recognition is subject to debate. Some would draw an imaginary line in the 1970s to separate the "good" from the "bad"—1960s rock, for example, from 1970s disco. Some would draw the line a few years earlier or later, and others would make a distinction throughout recent decades between "genuine" popular music expression and "hyped" industry product.

Still others would argue that all such lines and distinctions are more a reflection of social-and peer-group attitudes than of the relative quality of any of the music. According to this line of thinking, most recorded music since 1960, when the majors began operating on a grander economic scale, has been fashioned with the same basic principles in mind. The ever-present goal is to maximize profits, as the media conglomerates that now own recording companies used all the money generated by all the music to support their acquisitions. Thus, every trend—even the hint of a trend—is picked up by the industry, worked into salable products, heavily promoted, and eventually dropped by the wayside when a new trend emerges. In the 1970s, 1980s, and 1990s, trends that followed this pattern included country rock, punk rock, New Wave, heavy metal, disco, and "grunge" music.

In the early 1980s, the recording industry lost much of the momentum that came with the surge of Beatlemania among baby boomers in the 1960s and "discomania" in the 1970s. Record sales flattened out, and the rush to sign new artists and press new recordings slowed. But two unexpected developments in the mid-1980s brought new life to the industry. The first was a technological innovation: the compact disc (CD), combining computer and laser technology to create wear-proof, smaller-sized albums with clear and dynamically strong sounds. Sold at double the average price of record albums, the new CDs boosted industry profits—especially when the cost of pressing individual CDs dropped to the level of vinyl recordings. The switchover to CD technology led many Americans to buy new CDs that were reissues of their favorite vinyl records or "greatest hits" collections of their favorite performers (thus paying a second—or third—time for a recording, and at a higher price).

The other boost to the industry in the mid-1980s came from television, with the rapid rise in popularity of MTV, a cable channel devoted to "music videos." These short productions evolved from the promotional films shown on television in the 1960s and 1970s to stimulate sales of new records. The Beatles, for example, had produced video versions of their hit singles from 1966 on. But the popularity of MTV in the mid-1980s—especially among the "Generation Xers," who grew up in the shadows of the baby boomers—transformed music videos into a trendy new art form. Soon, the video versions of new recordings became as popular as the CDs themselves—and more expensive to produce. Despite the costs, the recording industry reaped benefits from MTV, its "spin-off" channel VH1, and music videos in general, as popular music reasserted its leading role in the cultural lives of young Americans.

Moreover, African American performers now had a direct means of showcasing their music, ideas, style, and fashions to the rest of the country. At first, MTV mainly featured white performers, but the megahit album of the mid-1980s, Michael Jackson's *Thriller*, changed all that. The multitalented Jackson was the ideal MTV performer—stylish, dramatic, physical, and sensual—and his videos were stunningly visual. His popularity opened doors into American homes for Prince, Hammer, his sister Janet Jackson, and similar black artists, while another branch of African American culture—"hip-hop"—slipped in with them. Hip-hop culture had blossomed in the black quarters of American cities during the 1980s, and with it had arisen "rap" music, in which performers recited their lyrics in syncopated rhythms. The music that accompanied these rap artists ranged from vocal effects to vinyl records that were "scratched" and "sampled" to actual musicians. The end results were as fresh and lively and as entertaining and controversial as new developments in popular music have typically been.

One of the controversial aspects of rap music was at least as old as ragtime and jazz: its focus on the seamier side of life. The "rapped" lyrics were often harsh, violent, jarring, and obscene, and they led in part to a backlash against the recording industry. Congressional hearings in the mid-1980s had precipitated a movement to monitor the contents of song lyrics that were popular among young people. The recording industry responded with its own self-imposed code system, in which new releases with violent and/or obscene lyrics carried "parental warning" stickers. In 1992, many stores and radio stations banned a rap song, "Cop Killer," that spoke of violence against corrupt police.

The rap music industry itself became controversial after a series of violent incidents in the 1990s involving rap producers and performers. Of course, the recording industry already had a checkered history of criminal actions, from payola scandals to jailed performers. The rap incidents, however, involved lethal weapons and even killings; unfortunately, they helped cast the music in a bad light. As of this writing, rap music remains an unrecognized giant among popular music forms. For over twenty years, rap artists have given our culture a gritty, forceful, and rhythmic style of musical performance. They have captured a big audience that crosses racial, economic, and generational lines, influencing our language and fashions. In other words, they've done everything that America's other major forms of popular music have done—except earn much recognition.

Also in the 1980s and 1990s, after decades of selling American popular music in foreign countries, the recording industry sold itself to foreign corporations. First, RCA Records, with its origins as the first record company (Victor Talking Machine), was purchased by Bertlesmann, a German media conglomerate. Then Japan's Sony bought CBS Records, including the storied Columbia label. PolyGram of the Netherlands acquired A&M in 1989 and Motown in 1993, then was purchased itself in the late 1990s by Seagram's, headquartered in Canada, which had already bought MCA Records. The one remaining major label still owned by Americans was Warner, which merged with Time and then Turner Broadcasting. The selling of America's recording industry to foreign interests suggests how valuable a commodity our popular music and performers have become in the world market. It raises the question, however, of just who'll be "in charge" of American popular music as we progress into the twenty-first century. At the very least, a new international dimension will be added to a partnership between artists and executives in the recording industry that's long been uneasy and at times oppressive.

On the other hand, foreign control of America's recording companies may become a moot point in the twenty-first century, as a monumental piece of 1990s technology threatens to restructure the business: the Internet. The same "digitalization" of music that led to the rise of CDs also allows songs to be transmitted in cyberspace to computers all over the world. Software to play these musical "files," to save them on discs and hard drives, and to sort and arrange them as the listener pleases—all can be downloaded off the Internet at little or no cost. As of this writing, the recording industry is scrambling to develop a means of encoding its popular music to prevent widespread distribution for free over the Internet.

At stake, of course, are the billions of dollars that recordings generate annually in sales around the world. On the other hand, the recording industry has already survived free distribution of popular music on the radio and on television. If the industry's future, in fact, is to serve as a division within a vast international entertainment conglomeration, then its profits from selling CDs and cassettes may no longer be needed. If a popular song entices the public to attend a movie or a concert, buy a product, watch a television program, or visit a Web site, that may be enough to satisfy the corporate profit-makers.

The medium of recorded music today is in many ways vastly different from what it was even just one generation past. Yesterday's hi-fi in the parlor may now be today's compact disc player in the dashboard, complete with laser beam and computer chips. The music itself may have passed through synthesizers, equalizers, digital analyzers, and even satellite transponders before reaching the compact disc as an embossed spiral of electronic dots, written in binary computer code. Before reaching the radio stations and retail outlets, the disc's commercial potential may have been debated by market researchers, video producers, and top executives of foreign conglomerates.

Today's top recordings earn "gold" and "platinum" status not after weeks of high sales but often right at the point of release; some CDs cost over $1 million to produce, sell over 10 million units, and bring in over $100 million in gross profits. Today's top recording stars influence fashions, hairstyles, sexual mores, drug usage, even social and political decision making. Today's industry scandals are less likely to involve small sums of money paid to freewheeling disc jockeys than millions of dollars raked in by well-organized "pirates" of illegally copied recordings—and even killings of some recording stars and executives.

In other ways, however, the more things have changed, the more they've remained the same. It took Thomas Edison only months to begin speculating how his new invention, originally a telephone accessory, might expand into new fields and directions: the expansion continues. The industry's early years featured intensely fought struggles between competing companies: the struggles continue with all their intensity. Those first recordings were a mixed lot, mostly based on popular tastes and often disdained by cultural critics: the mixture continues, along with the popular emphasis and critical disdain. From "Mary Had a Little Lamb" up through Madonna, the sounds of recorded music and voice have continued to hold a power all their own, transcending changes in technology and styles of performance. For the future, we can expect both technology and styles to continue changing, with the power remaining strong. It has been a century and a quarter now since America played its first recording; right now, despite all that has happened to the culture and the industry during those 125 years, there is no sign that the music is about to end.

REFERENCE WORKS

The most common reference work on recorded music is the discography, which comes in a variety of sizes, styles, and time periods. Two discographies might more accurately be labeled "cylinderographies," for they deal solely with the early years of the record industry and the wax cylinders produced for Edison's machines: Brian Rust's *Discography of Historical Records on Cylinders and 78s* and Allen Koenigsberg's *Edison Cylinder Records: 1889–1912*. Other discographies concentrate on smaller movements within the realm of popular music, such as Tom Lord's multivolume *Jazz Discography*, Frank Scott's *Down Home Guide to the Blues*, and *Blues and Gospel Records: 1890–1943*, by John Godrich and Robert M. W. Dixon. Similar one-genre discographies include *The Trouser Press Guide to '90s Rock*, focusing on punk and New Wave and edited by Ira A. Robbins, *Ethnic Music on Records: 1893–1942*, by Richard K. Spottswood, and Richard C. Lynch's *Broadway, Movie, TV and Studio Cast Musicals on Record: A Discography of Recordings, 1985–1995*. Also, *Incredibly Strange Music*, by V. Vale, compiles lounge music, sound-effect records, and similar oddities, as does the colorful *Forever Lounge*, by John Wooley et al.

The prolific Michael Ruppli has compiled a series of discographies for Greenwood Press; currently in print are volumes that focus on the following record labels: Aladdin/Imperial, Atlantic, Blue Note, Clef-Verve, Decca, King, Mercury, and MGM. Another subgenre of the discography is the chronological listing of record releases, usually hit singles and albums. The work of one researcher in this field is particularly noteworthy: Joel Whitburn, who has compiled a series of books listing top pop and rhythm-and-blues records of the last few decades, based on Billboard charts. Another variation on the discography is the guide to record prices, such as Jerry Osbourne's *Official Price Guide to Records*, which details the value of over 100,000 recordings, and Tim Neely's *Goldmine Price Guide to 45 Rpm Records*.

A useful type of discography is the expert guide to recordings, in which the authors select and comment on the best recordings, usually from one genre. Robert Pruter has compiled *The Blackwell Guide to Soul Recordings*, with similar volumes for jazz and blues compiled by Barry Kernfeld and John Cowley, respectively. The *All Music Guide to Rock* is also part of a set of expert guides, with over 10,000 entries per volume. Its editor, Michael Erlewine, has produced other guides to jazz and country recordings. Robert Santelli's *The Best of the Blues* and *Musichound Blues: The Essential Album Guide*, by Leland Rucker, are other good choices for blues recordings; Musichound also offers expert guides to folk music, edited by Neal Walters, and lounge and swing recordings, edited by Steve Knopper. One book that attempts to select the best recordings in a variety of genres is the *Rolling Stone Album Guide: The Definitive Guide to the Best of Rock, Rap, Jazz, Blues, Country, Soul, Folk and Gospel*, by Anthony DeCurtis and James Henke.

Music critic Robert Christgau offers his authoritative choices for the best pop recordings in several volumes of his *Christgau's Record Guide*. Two excellent books focus on just the "single" recording: *Heart of Rock and Soul: The 1001 Greatest Singles Ever Made*, by Dave Marsh, and *Rock and Roll: The 100 Best Singles*, by Paul Williams. For punk, New Wave, grunge, and hip-hop recordings, a comprehensive guide is the *Spin Alternative Press Record Guide*, by Eric Westband and Craig Marks; for heavy metal music, two choices are Chuck Eddy's *Stairway to Hell: The 500 Best Heavy Metal Albums in the Universe* and Martin Strong's *The Great Metal Discography*. Readers of these and any other expert guides should keep in mind that taste in recordings and performers is subjective and that the favorites of one critic can be summarily dismissed by another.

The second leading category of reference works is the so-called encyclopedia, which attempts to catalog information about performers, styles, and other recorded music topics. Colin Larkin's multivolume *Virgin Encyclopedias of Popular Music* is a good example of this reference work, but with a British slant; the books are based on Larkin's *The Guinness Encyclopedia of Popular Music*. Patricia Romanowski and Holly George Warren focus on rock music in *The New-Rolling Stone Encyclopedia of Rock & Roll*, as does Jim Miller in the earlier *The Rolling Stone Illustrated History of Rock n' Roll, 1950–80*. Offering a generous selection of visuals along with its text is *The Billboard Illustrated Encyclopedia of Rock*. A good supplement to these works would be Scott Schinder's *Rolling Stone's Alternative Rock-a-Rama*. Other general reference works in genres include *Encyclopedia of the Blues*, by Gerard Herzhaft, and one of the first books of this kind, Leonard Feather's reissued *Encyclopedia of Jazz*.

Country music has produced several worthwhile encyclopedias, including another "classic" that's still in print: L. Brown and G. Fredrich's *Encyclopedia of Country & Western Music*. Two good reference books with similar contents and titles are Barry McCloud's *Definitive Country: The Ultimate Encyclopedia of Country Music and Its Performers* and Paul Kingsbury's *The Encyclopedia of Country Music: The Ultimate Guide to the Music*, published by the Country Music Foundation with Oxford University Press. Another good selection as a general reference work is *Country: The Music and the Musicians: From the Beginnings to the '90s*, and for a recent trend that's been called "alt-country," the choice is Grant Alden and Peter Blackstock's *No Depression*.

An interesting variation on the encyclopedia is the almanac, which uses calendars, lists, and other formats to present a wealth of material. Mark Bego's *Rock and Roll Almanac* is a good example of this approach, as is *The Chronicle of Jazz*, by Mervyn Cooke, Roy Carr's *A Century of Jazz*, and Hugh Gregory's *A Century of Pop: A Hundred Years of Music That Changed the World*. A truly valuable reference book is *The Rock and Roll Reader's Guide*, by Gary Krebs, which provides annotated bibliographies on hundreds of rock performers and other general categories, such as chronologies, concert events, and magazines. B. Lee Cooper's *Rock Music in American Popular Culture: Rock 'n' Roll Resources* draws connections between recordings and various themes and topics in American culture, such as sports and medicine.

Several reference works consist of photographs, generally of the performers themselves, in concert, in the studio, or in public or personal settings. *Rolling Stone Images of Rock & Roll*, by Fred Woodward and Anthony DeCurtis, is a compilation of photos from the pages and files of the rock and social magazine, *Rolling Stone*. Michael Ochs has compiled a cocktail-table collection of photographs entitled *Rock Archives: A Photographer's Journey through the First Two Decades of Rock & Roll*. Ochs has also published a collection of album-cover art, *1000 Rock Covers*.

Books that focus solely on record album covers are a category in themselves, reflecting the artwork, photography, and graphic design that helped sell records in the first place. In particular, a set of beautiful books by Graham Marsh spotlights the record jackets from the respected Blue Note jazz label; another Marsh book is *The Blues: Album Cover Art*. Other appealing books of recording jackets are *The Album Cover Art of Soundtracks*, by Stefan Kassel and Frank Jastfelder, *Album Covers from the Vinyl Junkyard*, with an emphasis on lounge and easy-

Elvis Presley. Courtesy of the National Archives

listening albums, and Burkhardt Seiler's *Album Cover Art of Punk*. For a "cocktail table" book on older album artwork, Eric Kohler has produced *In the Groove: Vintage Record Graphics: 1940–1960*. For a diverse compilation of artwork related to rock recordings in general, a good choice is Spencer Drate's *Rock Art, CDs, Albums and Posters*.

RESEARCH COLLECTIONS

For those to whom popular music is something of a religion, the third floor of the Jerome Library at Bowling Green State University is nothing short of Mecca, for housed there in the flatlands of Ohio is the best collection of purely popular music in the country. The Sound Recording Archives (http://www.bgsu.edu/colleges/library/music/music.html), closely linked to the Center for the Study of Popular Culture, was developed on a shoestring budget by William L. Schurk in 1967 with the object of collecting an actual copy of every popular record ever made. So far Schurk has gathered over 650,000 LP albums, single 45s, old 78s, CDs, and Edison cylinders. Other libraries may house more jazz or folk or country records, but no single collection has Bowling Green's range and variety, with the exception of the Library of Congress, which is not a strictly popular archive. Schurk's secret in building such a collection on a limited budget has been to take full advantage of donations, trading opportunities, auctions, and sales. His holdings in rock and roll and obscure, limited issues are particularly noteworthy, as are his rare "soundies," musical motion picture shorts used in a form of early 1940s jukebox.

Another strong asset of the Bowling Green collection is its accessibility to the public. Although the stacks themselves are closed, with all recordings handled only by the staff, listening facilities make it possible for the user to hear virtually any request in a matter of minutes. The Sound Recording Archives provides taping services for the university community and research opportunities, under certain conditions, for outside groups and individuals. The archives also maintains a diverse collection of reference materials, including discographies, industry promotional material, record sleeves, sheet music, and back issues of many popular music magazines.

The Library of Congress in Washington, D.C., began collecting popular and classical records in 1924, largely through the donations of Victor and the other early major companies. The industry donations continued for decades, while the library's Music Division began developing special collections in folk music and in such government recordings as the World War II "V-discs." In 1972, legislation brought recorded music within the provisions of the copyright law, with one result being that most record companies began automatically submitting their new releases to the library's Recorded Sound Division (http://lcweb.loc.gov/rr/record).

Today, the Recorded Sound Division has accumulated the world's largest collection, with over 1 million recordings and additional tens of thousands acquired each year. An important boost to the library's collection came when a private citizen donated some 40,000 discs and 500 cylinders of mostly pre-1926 material. According to the library, these new holdings are particularly strong in popular music, especially jazz, humor, minstrel, and vaudeville recordings.

The services provided by the Library of Congress for the recorded music researcher are numerous and include the production of listening tapes, under certain strict conditions, by the division's own recording laboratory. The division is also involved in recording production on a small-scale commercial basis, with special anthologies of some of its holdings available to the general public. Limited listening facilities are provided on the premises for researchers and advanced students, who are advised to schedule time well in advance. Also, catalogs of recordings and of printed works on music are distributed twice a year through the library's Descriptive Cataloguing Division, as well as lists of all recordings received for copyright purposes from 1972 on, the latter service provided by the library's Copyright Office and the U.S. Government Printing Office. An exciting new feature of the Recorded Sound Division is its on-line American Variety Stage collection, which brings recordings from the early 1900s onto the Internet.

Another major collection of classical and popular recorded music, the Rodgers and Hammerstein Archives of Recorded Sound (http://www.nypl.org/research/lpa/rha/rha.html), is housed at the New York Public Library's Performing Arts Research Center at Lincoln Center. The library itself had been building a collection since the 1930s, but it took a large grant from the Rodgers and Hammerstein Foundation in 1965 to create the efficient, extensive, multiservice facilities that presently exist. The archives holds over 10,000 printed items and 500,000 recordings "from Mozart . . . to Motown," including Edison cylinders and the record library of WNEW-AM, formerly a top New York popular radio station. The archives also has rock videos, public television broadcasts, and tapes of NBC's *Bell Telephone Hour* radio shows from 1941 to 1968.

The Rodgers and Hammerstein Archives offers easy public access to their recording collections through the use of headphones and listening carrels, with taping services provided at a fee for study and research purposes. Also, the Lincoln Center facility contains assorted reference material on the recording business, including industry catalogs, clipping files, and scores of related periodicals. In addition, examples of early phonographs and gramophones are on permanent display, and the archives often presents special exhibits from its collection.

Over 100,000 recordings of popular music are kept in the Center for Popular Music at Middle Tennessee State University (http://www.mtsu.edu/~ctrpopmu/research.html). The center's collection is particularly strong in the areas of gospel, rock, rhythm and blues, music from Tennessee and the Southeast, minstrelsy, sheet music and songbooks, and music industry catalogs. The center's staff conducts and assists in research for a fee, with a lower rate charged for nonprofit and academic clients.

Other noteworthy collections specialize in certain types of popular music. A major collection of jazz records, with some 50,000 LPs and 78s, is housed at the Institute for Jazz Studies (http://libraries.rutgers.edu/rulib/abtlib/danlib/jazz.htm) at Rutgers University's John Cotton Dana Library in Newark, New Jersey. The institute, which offers an academic program and publishes the *Journal of Jazz Studies*, also maintains a book collection, clipping files, and back issues of various jazz and jazz-related magazines. Listening facilities are available; in addition, taping services are offered for the researcher (who must supply the blank tape). For the specialist interested in New Orleans jazz, a strong collection is maintained at the William Ransom Hogan Archive of New Orleans Jazz at Tulane University (http://www.tulane.edu/~lmiller/JazzHome.html), with "oral histories, recorded music, photographs and film, and sheet music and orchestrations."

Another music collection is housed at the New York Public Library's Schomburg Center, which specializes in African American and related cultures. The collection ranges from "the earliest recordings of the classic blues singers and jazz bands, through gospel and rhythm and blues offerings, to contemporary popular forms, such as rap music." Along with listening carrels, the center offers videotaped performances and interviews featuring both past and present African American recording artists. The University of Michigan also houses a collection of African American recordings, with a great number of 78s from the 1920s through the 1950s.

For music from the American South, an excellent resource is the Southern Folklife Collection in the Wilson Library at the University of North Carolina at Chapel Hill (http://cadmus.lib.unc.edu/mss/sfc1). Its holdings include "string band and old timey music, bluegrass, blues, early country music, religious music, fiddle tunes [and] interviews with performers." Also, the D. K. Wilgus Archive of Folksong and Music at UCLA (http://www.humnet.ucla.edu/humnet/folklore/archives) houses 8,000 recordings of "traditional music, song, and narrative as well as 1,000 field-recorded tapes," including some of Southern California's folk festivals in the 1960s and 1970s.

Among major universities that house important collections of popular music are Yale, Stanford, and Syracuse. Yale's Historical Sound Recordings collection (http://www.library.yale.edu:80/histsoun.html) is housed in the Sterling Memorial Library and specializes in early spoken-word recordings and the American musical theater. The Stanford Archive of Recorded Sound (http://www-sul.stanford.edu/depts/ars), established in 1958, has 200,000 recordings, including "wax cylinders, . . . vinyl discs, acetate and aluminum transcription discs [and] magnetic wire recordings," and over 4,000 print and manuscript items. Of particular interest are tape archives of the Monterey Jazz Festival. The Belfer Audio Laboratory and Archive at Syracuse University (http://libwww.syr.edu/information/belfer/index.-

htm) has over 300,000 recordings, including cylinders, phonodiscs, and early radio broadcasts.

HISTORY AND CRITICISM

The definitive story of the recording industry and recorded music has yet to be written. There have been, however, more books published recently on this vital aspect of our popular culture than ever before. Until the 1990s, perhaps the best analysis of the recording industry was *Tarnished Gold: The Record Industry Revisited*, by R. Serge Denisoff, an updated version of Denisoff's *Solid Gold* and written with William Schurk. *Tarnished Gold* has excellent chapters on the industry of the late 1970s and early 1980s, including the early years of MTV. Another noteworthy pre-1990 analysis of the recording industry is *Rock 'n' Roll Is Here to Pay*, by Steve Chapple and Reebee Garofalo, which explores racism, media conglomeration, and other controversial topics.

As the recording industry expanded in the 1990s, so did the selection of books that examine the business of popular music in America. Russell and David Sanjek's *Pennies from Heaven: American Popular Music in the 20th Century* provides an extensive and detailed history of America's music industry. The Sanjeks are closely associated with Broadcast Music, Inc. (BMI), a major trade group in music publishing, and their analysis is slanted toward the organizational side of this field. A classic reference book on the record industry as a business is Sidney Shemel and M. William Krasilovsky's *This Business of Music*, now in its seventh edition. Two other good texts are *Music, Money, and Success: The Insider's Guide to the Music Industry*, by Jeffrey and Todd Brabec, and Geoffrey P. Hull's *The Recording Industry*, from the Allyn & Bacon Series in Mass Communication. Another basic text on commercial aspects of the recording industry is Tad Lathrup and Jim Pettigrew Jr.'s *The Business of Music Marketing and Promotion*.

A colorful book that investigates the wheelings and dealings of the modern recording industry is *Hit Men: Power Brokers & Fast Money inside the Music Business*, by Fredric Dannen and Erroll McDonald. A popular variation of the investigative analysis is the "insider" book, such as Bruce Haring's *Off the Charts: Ruthless Days and Reckless Nights inside the Music Industry*, focusing on the 1980s and 1990s. Fred Goodman's *The Mansion on the Hill: Dylan, Young, Geffen, Springsteen, and the Head-On Collision of Rock and Commerce* manages to weave a cohesive tale out of some twenty years of recording history, media and concert promoting, intricate business dealings, and social and personal sagas.

Other business-related books are intended for readers who hope to enter the recording field themselves and need practical advice on contracts, managers, royalties, and so on. For these readers, Donald Passman has written *All You Need to Know about the Music Business*—not to be confused with *Everything You'd Better Know about the Record Industry*, by Kashif and Gary Greenberg. Also for the aspiring recording artist, another good book is *Sound Advice: The Musician's Guide to the Record Industry*, by Wayne Wadhams. *Confessions of a Record Producer*, written under the pseudonym of Moses Avalon, offers a more cynical approach to careers in the recording industry. Also, a pair of worthwhile books focuses on the business of country music: *Nashville's Unwritten Rules: Inside the Business of Country Music*, by Dan Daley, and *The View from Nashville*, by Ralph Emery, a country impresario.

Good Vibrations: A History of Record Production, by Mark Cunningham, focuses more on technology and the recording industry, with profiles of Les Paul, Phil Spector, and other innovators in musical sound. Michael Chanan's *Repeated Takes: A Short History of Recording and Its Effects on Music* also focuses on technology, but in the broad context of popular music and society. Two books focus on the famous music industry awards: *The Grammys*, by Thomas O'Neil and Peter Bart, and Henry Schipper's investigative *Broken Record: The Inside Story of the Grammy Awards*. Stan Soocher's *They Fought the Law: Rock Music Goes to Court* gives detailed accounts of lawsuits and other cases involving the Beatles, Elvis Presley, Michael Jackson, 2 Live Crew, and others. For a closer look at two of the industry's un-lawful practices, readers can select Kerry Segrave's *Payola in the Music Industry: A History, 1880–1991* and Clinton Heylin's *Bootleg: The Secret History of the Other Recording Industry*.

Another category of general introductory works deserves consideration: the collection of essays. The most outstanding examples now available have one thing in common: they all focus on rock music and the rock recording industry. *Psychotic Reactions & Carburetor Dung* is a lively set of writings by rock critic Lester Bangs, who championed exciting music and very creative prose. Other worthy collections are *Rocking My Life Away: Writing about Music & Other Matters*, by Anthony DeCurtis, and *Not Fade Away: A Backstage Pass to 20 Years of Rock & Roll*, by Ben Fong-Torres. In his *Music to My Ears: The Billboard Essays: Portraits of Popular Music in the '90s*, journalist Timothy White mixes interviews and personality profiles. A set of essays entitled *The Country Reader: Twenty Five Years of the Journal of Country Music*, edited by Paul Kingsbury, offers readable and scholarly writing within this genre.

A number of worthwhile books focus on individual companies of significance in the history of recorded music. Rick Kennedy's *Jelly Roll, Bix, and Hoagy: Gennett Studios and the Birth of the Recorded Jazz* is the detailed story of an early record company from Indiana that helped make jazz the popular music of the 1920s and 1930s. Colin Escott and Martin Hawkins' *Good Rockin' Tonight: Sun Records & the Birth of Rock 'n' Roll* studies the small Memphis operation that brought the world Elvis Presley, Carl Perkins, Jerry Lee Lewis, Roy Orbison, and Johnny Cash. *Little Labels, Big Sound*, by Rick Kennedy and Randy McNutt, examines the independent companies, such as King, Riverside, and Ace, that played crucial roles in the production and spread of both jazz and early rock and roll.

In Rob Bowman's extensive and detailed history of the Stax label, *Soulsville, U.S.A: The Story of Stax Records*, readers can follow the rise and fall of a company that produced soulful and "funky" music in the 1960s and 1970s from the likes of Otis Redding, Wilson Pickett, and Booker T. and the MGs. Another influential label from that era was Elektra, which housed a diverse collection of performers and cultural icons, for example, the Doors, Phil Ochs, Judy Collins, Iggy Pop, and Harry Chapin. In *Follow the Music: The Life and High Times of Elektra Records*, the company's founder and CEO, Jac Holzman, relates Elektra's story in conversations with many of the participants. Two other books focus on labels that share in common a commitment to recording "people's music," but with drastically different outcomes. Peter Goldsmith's *Making People's Music: Moe Asch and Folkways Records* studies a man and a label that brought the recordings of Woody Guthrie, Leadbelly, and Pete Seeger into American culture. *Have Gun Will Travel:*

The Spectacular Rise & Violent Fall of Death Row Records, by Ronin Ro, explores the wild and sometimes criminal behavior of this "rap" label's executives and artists.

A number of highly skilled and intelligent writers have focused their energies on presenting the story of African American music in American culture—and for good reason. It's complex, emotional, and fascinating and perhaps one of the best stories thus far in the history of our country. Peter Guralnick's *Sweet Soul Music: Rhythm and Blues and the Southern Dream of Freedom* and Gerri Hershey's *Nowhere to Run: The Story of Soul Music* are two thoughtful works from the 1980s that detail the music, lives, and recording careers of famous and not-so-famous black performers, with Guralnick narrowing in on southern soul and Memphis' Stax Records. Also during that period, one of the field's most prolific and accessible writers, Arnold Shaw, produced two books on African American music, *Black Popular Music in America* and *Honkers and Shouters: The Golden Years of Rhythm and Blues*. More recently, excellent books on this subject have been written by Hugh Gregory (*The Real Rhythm and Blues*) and Craig Werner (*A Change Is Gonna Come: Music, Race & the Soul of America*), with the latter also incorporating the story of the African American social movement. A much more visual work on African American music is *Heart & Soul: A Celebration of Black Music Style in America 1930–1975*, by Bob Merlis and Davin Seay, with an appealing assortment of record covers, publicity photos, and other promotional material.

Although disco music accounted for a large percentage of the record industry's business during the late 1970s, there is currently no study in print of the disco industry and its recordings. *Boogie Night: The Disco Age*, produced by the Friedman-Fairfax and Sony Music staff, a combination of text and CD recording, will have to suffice for now. On the other hand, it took Latin music almost a century of influencing American popular recordings before it inspired a critical study: John Storm Roberts' *The Latin Tinge: The Impact of Latin American Music on the United States*, first published in 1979 but with an extensive updated section in the 1999 edition. Another study of Latin music (which gave us the rumba, samba, tango, mambo, cha-cha, bugaloo, bamba, and the hustle) is *Hot Sauces: Latin and Caribbean Pop* by Billy Bergman.

As might be expected, the field of jazz has inspired a number of critical studies. A leading jazz writer is Gary Giddens, and his knowledge and understanding of this music are in strong evidence in his book *Visions of Jazz: The First Century*. Another extensive critical study of jazz is Ted Gioia's *The History of Jazz*. Critical studies of Big Band music are rare in recent years (George Simon's *The Big Bands*, in its fourth edition, remains a good choice), but a renewed interest in "swing" dancing in the late 1990s resulted in the publishing of V. Vale's *Swing! The New Retro Renaissance*. A similar renewed cultural interest—in this case, in the "groovy" music of the late 1960s—is evidenced in *I Want to Take You Higher: The Psychedelic Era, 1965–1969*, by James Henke.

Several authors have taken a geographical approach to writing about recordings and performers by focusing on key areas of the country. The most popular choice is Memphis, the city that helped launch the blues, jazz, rhythm and blues, soul, and rock and roll, and whose Beale Street and Graceland are now music-related tourist attractions. Along with the previously mentioned books on Stax and Sun Records, two other books that describe the music and sociology of this Mississippi River city are *Memphis Beat*, by Larry Nagler, and *It Came from Memphis*, by

Robert Gordon. Another key geographic area for the recording industry for decades has been Southern California. In *Waiting for the Sun: Strange Days, Weird Scenes, and the Sound of Los Angeles*, Barney Hoskyns portrays the artistry, dealings, and lifestyles of a vast array of characters, including West Coast jazzmen, Beach Boys, Mamas and Papas, hippy singer-songwriters, and hard-core punk performers.

Countless books that deal with the recording industry focus on the musical groups or individuals themselves. Whether it's a book-length biography or a collection of critical studies, the subject is most often a rock performer. Timothy White's *Rock Lives: Profiles & Interviews*, for example, covers most of the major names in the rock recording industry with well-written and interesting essays. *All Roads Lead to Rock: Legends of Early Rock 'n' Roll*, edited by Colin Escott, focuses on the pioneers of rock music, including Screamin' Jay Hawkins and Big Mama Thornton. Brock Helander's *The Rockin' '50s: The People Who Made the Music* profiles many of the pioneers, too, along with other popular performers from that era, such as Rick Nelson, Jackie Wilson, and the Everly Brothers.

Several works are devoted exclusively to females in the recording industry. James L. Dickerson's *Women on Top: The Quiet Revolution That's Rocking the American Music Industry* mixes executives and producers with performers. *Trouble Girls: The Rolling Stone Book of Women in Rock*, edited by Barbara O' Dair, spotlights a diverse selection of female rock performers, while David Nathan's *The Soulful Divas* offers chapters on African American female performers, from Nina Simone to Whitney Houston. Two books feature portraits and essays of some of the industry's less-celebrated women, such as Joan Jett and Chrissie Hynde in Andrea Juno's *Angry Women in Rock* and Holly Near and the group Sweet Honey in the Rock in Laura Post's *Backstage Pass*.

Other collections focus entirely on lesser-known performers and groups, male or female, whose recordings have been influential, critically acclaimed, or just unique. Nick Tosches' *Unsung Heroes*, for example, has chapters on Louis Prima, Johnnie Ace, Louis Jordan, and the Treniers. Roni Sarig's *The Secret History of Rock: The Most Influential Bands You've Never Heard* features such cult and alternative performers as Van Dyke Parks, Big Star, Captain Beefheart, and Television, as does *Unknown Legends of Rock 'n' Roll: Psychedelic Unknowns, Mad Geniuses, Punk Pioneers, Lo-Fi Mavericks & More*, by Richie Unterberger. Jim Payne's noteworthy book focuses on performers of a key instrument in popular recordings, the percussionists, in *Give the Drummers Some! The Great Drummers of R&B, Funk & Soul*.

Hundreds of biographies and critical studies have been written about individual performers and groups; again, the majority of subjects are rock musicians. A notable exception is Frank Sinatra, one of the great figures of American popular culture, who left the world an enormous legacy of wonderful recordings. An excellent study of these recordings is Ed O'Brien's *Sinatra 101: The 101 Best Recordings and the Stories Behind Them*. Another legendary nonrock performer is Les Paul, the subject of Mary Alice Shaughnessy's *Les Paul: An American Original*; his recordings in the 1940s and 1950s transformed the sound of popular music. *Let the Good Times Roll: The Story of Louis Jordan and His Music*, by John Chilton, relates the life and career of another major figure in the prerock era; in fact, Jordan may well be the link between the big bands and rock and roll.

Just as Elvis Presley dominated the early years of rock, so, too, does he dominate the books written about performers from that era. His definitive biography has been written in two volumes by Peter Guralnick, *Last Train to Memphis: The Rise of Elvis Presley* and *Careless Love: The Unmaking of Elvis Presley*. Guralnick's works on Presley are exceptional in their detail, writing, and clear intelligence. For a study of the remarkable recordings of Elvis Presley, Johnny Mikkelson's *Reconsider Baby: The Definitive Elvis Sessionography* is an excellent source, as is *Elvis Presley: A Life in Music*, by Ernst Jorgensen. *Elvis Album: 1954–1977* relates the Presley life and work in mostly visual images, with photographs, movie stills, record jackets, and so on, while *Elvis Culture: Fans, Faith & Image*, by Erika Doss, documents and analyzes his amazing popularity in the years since his death.

Elvis Presley was one of several recording "legends" to have emerged in the 1950s. Another was the multitalented Chuck Berry, whose life story and colorful writing style can be found in his own *Chuck Berry: The Autobiography*. A good companion piece to Berry's autobiography is Howard DeWitt's *Chuck Berry's Rock 'N' Roll Music*. The legendary Buddy Holly, who died young in 1959, is the subject of *Remembering Buddy*, by John Goldrosen and John Beecher. Carl Perkins, a rival of Presley in the 1950s, accomplished something that Elvis unfortunately never did: he wrote his autobiography, with the help of David McGee entitled *Go, Cat, Go! The Life and Times of Carl Perkins, the King of Rockabilly*. Also, a fascinating alternative story of a 1950s pioneer is *Miss Rhythm: The Autobiography of Ruth Brown*, written by another influential recording star from that era.

The radio disc jockey and promoter most responsible for bringing the records of Ruth Brown and others to the public's attention in the 1950s was Alan Freed. His life and career tumbled after the payola scandal, but they've been re-created in John Jackson's *Big Beat Heat: Alan Freed and the Early Years of Rock & Roll*. The same scandal also put the career of Dick Clark in jeopardy, but he escaped with a slap on the wrist and went on to become an entertainment mogul. Clark's story is told evenhandedly in *American Bandstand*, by John Jackson, and much more subjectively in Clark's own collection of visuals and texts, *Dick Clark's American Bandstand*.

Recordings of the 1960s were strongly influenced by producer Phil Spector, known for the "wall of sound" that he created for the East Coast vocal groups of that era. Spector is the subject of Mark Ribowsky's *He's a Rebel: The Truth about Phil Spector*, as well as the major supporting character (and villain, at times) in *Be My Baby*, the autobiography of the lead singer of the Ronettes—his wife, Ronnie Spector. Second only to Spector in his influential recording studio work from the 1960s is Brian Wilson of the Beach Boys. Timothy White's *The Nearest Faraway Place: Brian Wilson, the Beach Boys, and the Southern California Experience* is a perceptive critical study of Wilson and the Beach Boys, framed in the context of postwar American culture.

Also emerging from the recording industry of the 1960s was soul music, the artistic reflection of African American social and cultural movements of the era. Sam Cooke was one of the 1960s first soul singers; his life and his controversial death in 1964 are covered in detail in *You Send Me: The Life and Times of Sam Cooke*, by Daniel Wolff. Cooke was one of the first African Americans to develop his own recording company, SAR Records, but it was Berry Gordy who created the most famous black-owned label, Motown Records. Gordy has told his own story in *To Be Loved: The Music, the Magic, the Memories of Motown*; so, too, has one of Motown's best singers, Martha Reeves (of Martha and the Vandellas) with Mark Bego, in *Dancing in the Street: Confessions of a Motown Diva*.

Motown's most tragic story is the life of Marvin Gaye, a troubled artist who made soulful and memorable recordings, as detailed in *Divided Soul: The Life of Marvin Gaye*, by David Ritz. The same author is also the cowriter of *Brother Ray*, the autobiography of Ray Charles, who may be considered the "king" of soul music—or at least its genius. His most recent biography, *Ray Charles: Man and Music*, is the product of one of the best writers in this field, Michael Lydon. The female counterpart to Ray Charles is Aretha Franklin, and her story is told by Mark Bego in *Aretha Franklin: The Queen of Soul*. Country music, too, has its own "royalty," and their recommended biographies are Colin Escott's *Hank Williams: The Biography* and Ellis Nassour's *Honky Tonk Angel: The Intimate Story of Patsy Cline*.

America's dominance of rock music ended in early 1964, with the "invasion" of the Beatles and other British performers, whose recordings, ironically, were heavily influenced by the music that they had heard from the States. The Beatles themselves are the subject of scores of biographies and critical studies. Their studio work, for example, is detailed meticulously in a fascinating book by Mark Lewisohn, *The Beatles Recording Sessions*. Lewisohn also coauthored *The Complete Beatles Chronicles*, which covers more topics and includes more visuals. The rise and fall of the Beatles' own label, Apple Records, are described in Richard Di-Lello's graphic *The Longest Cocktail Party*; another failed Beatles project is the subject of *Get Back: The Unauthorized Chronicle of the Beatles' Let It Be Disaster*, by Doug Sulpy and Ray Schweighardt.

The Beatles were enormously successful in America, of course—not only as recording artists but also as agents of cultural change. Their remarkable career and influence are described and analyzed by Philip Norman in *Shout! The Beatles in Their Generation* and in Mark Hertsgaard's *A Day in the Life: The Music and Artistry of the Beatles*, which emphasizes their recordings. *The Ultimate Beatles Encyclopedia*, by Bill Harry, is a one-volume reference book on the group, while William McKeen's *The Beatles* is a bibliography to a multitude of additional sources. Back in the 1970s and 1980s, Harry Castleman and Walter Podrazik produced an extensive set of reference books on the Beatles for Pierian Press; still in print is *The Beatles Again*, from 1977.

Also in the 1970s, the famed producer of the Beatles, George Martin, wrote his autobiography, *All You Need Is Ears*, which was updated and reissued in 1995. *A Cellarful of Noise: The Autobiography of the Man Who Made the Beatles*, by Brian Epstein, the Beatles' manager, was reissued in 1984 with no updating possible, since Epstein died in 1998, just three years after the book was written. In recent years, Barry Miles wrote a detailed biography of Paul McCartney, entitled *Paul McCartney: Many Years from Now*, based on hours of interviews with the ex-Beatle, and his great collaborator, John Lennon, was the subject of Ray Coleman's *Lennon: The Definitive Biography*.

Among the other "British invasion" recording artists, the Rolling Stones have gathered the most books in print, including a comprehensive biography written by their bass player, Bill Wyman, entitled *Stone Alone: The Story of a Rock 'n' Roll Band*. The group's spectacular tours of America in the 1970s, after the Beatles had broken up, are detailed in Robert Greenfield's firsthand account, *A Journey through*

America with the Rolling Stones. Even more color can be found in *The Early Stones: Legendary Photographs of a Band in the Making*, by Michael Cooper and Terry Southern. In *X-Ray: The Unauthorized Autobiography*, the story of another British-invasion group, the Kinks, is told in a striking narrative by their leader and acclaimed songwriter, Ray Davies.

Several American groups and performers arising from the 1960s have also generated a substantial number of biographies and studies. Bob Dylan, in particular, is the subject of dozens of books, including Clinton Heylin's *Bob Dylan: The Recording Sessions 1960–1994* and Michael Krogsgaard's *Positively Bob Dylan: A Thirty-Year Discography, Concert and Recording Session Guide, 1960–1991*. Offering a good selection of articles, reviews, and other critical studies of Dylan is *The Bob Dylan Companion: Four Decades of Commentary*, edited by Carl Benson. Generating nearly as many books in print are the Grateful Dead and their leading performer, Jerry Garcia. For a basic overview of the Dead, David Gans' *Conversations with the Dead: The Grateful Dead Interview Book* provides a wealth of information from the group, their entourage, and dedicated fans. Carol Brightman's *Sweet Chaos: The Grateful Dead's American Adventure* is a scholarly work that explores the Dead and the unusual "Deadhead" subculture that they generated from the early 1970s through the 1990s. Focusing on the Dead's charismatic leader is *Dark Star: An Oral Biography of Jerry Garcia*, written by Robert Greenfield.

Three American rock performers from the 1960s era are forever linked by the triumph of the brilliant recordings they made and the tragedy of their shortened lives. The musical genius of guitarist Jimi Hendrix can be traced in John McDermott's *Jimi Hendrix Sessions: The Complete Studio Recordings Sessions, 1963–1970*. In *Scars of Sweet Paradise*, Alice Echols tells the story of the short, meteoric life and career of Janis Joplin, who symbolized the freedom and excesses of her era. The life of Jim Morrison of the Doors has been chronicled in several books and on film; in *Moonlight Drive: The Stories behind Every Doors Song*, Chuck Crisafulli focuses on the group's inventive recordings. Another performer from that era, David Crosby, fell into some of the vices that shortened the careers of his compatriots. He survived, however, and has written of his own ups and downs with Carl Gottlieb in *Long Time Gone: The Autobiography of David Crosby*.

Other American recording artists and groups from the late 1960s and 1970s have noteworthy or unusual careers that have been detailed in print. *Midnight Riders: The Story of the Allman Brothers Band* edited by Scott Freeman and Michael Pietsch focuses on a popular southern rock band that ceased abruptly upon the tragic death of their lead guitarist, Greg Allman. The tale of another popular American group that collapsed from the weight of its business, personnel, and recording problems is told in *Bad Moon Rising: The Unauthorized History of Creedence Clearwater Revival*, by Hank Bordowitz. Two well-traveled rock sidemen from that era relate the trials and tribulations of their own careers in *Backstage Passes & Backstabbing Bastards*, by keyboardist Al Kooper, and *Road Stories & Recipes*, by Memphis musician and songwriter Don Nix.

One of the musical genuises who recorded from the late 1960s into the 1980s is Frank Zappa, who left a legacy of rock and avant-garde compositions and a wealth of socially conscious writing. His biography can be found in David Walley's *No Commercial Potential: The Saga of Frank Zappa*, as well as in Zappa's own book, aptly titled *The Real Frank Zappa Book*. For a broader selection of writings both by Zappa, including his testimony before Congress against censorship of record-ings, and by reviewers, journalists, and scholars, a good choice is *The Frank Zappa Companion: Four Decades of Commentary* edited by Richard Kostelanetz and John Rocco. An interesting collection of material on performers who were the opposite of Frank Zappa—the teen and preteen idols of the 1960s–1980s—is *Who's Your Fave Rave?* by Randi Reisfeld and Danny Fields, with scores of short features and photographs from teen music magazines.

In the 1980s, several "superstars" emerged from the recording industry to cap-ture cult status in American culture and around the world. The career of Michael Jackson, formerly the child-prodigy lead singer for the Jackson Five, reached a high point in the mid-1980s with the phenomenal success of his solo album *Thriller* and his mesmerizing videos and stage shows. As great as his success was, so, too, was the drop that he experienced in the 1990s; all these twists and turns and more are detailed in Randy J. Taraborrelli's *Michael Jackson: The Magic and the Madness*. Jackson's female counterpart in onstage charisma and offstage controversy thus far is Madonna; her story is told by Matthew Rettenmund in *Encyclopedia Madon-nica*, a combination of visuals and text. For a more extensive and scholarly look at this former dance student who's become an international cultural icon, a good choice is *Desperately Seeking Madonna: In Search of the Meaning of the World's Most Famous Woman*, edited by Adam Sexton. Also charismatic but far less controversial is singer/songwriter Bruce Springsteen; David Marsh's reissued biography *Born to Run: The Bruce Springsteen Story* remains a recommended biography. Springsteen himself has published a lavish book of song lyrics, recording notes, photographs, text, and other material, with the simple title *Songs*.

Among the groups that recorded in the 1990s, Nirvana garnered much critical attention, especially after the suicide of their young singer/songwriter, Kurt Co-bain. The group and the rock movement that they represented are the subject of *Guitar World Presents Nirvana and the Grunge Revolution*; another recommended work is Michael Azerrad's *Come As You Are: The Story of Nirvana*. Coexisting with grunge and other alternative rock movements of the 1990s are the rap and hip-hop artists, such as Chuck D., who expresses his social and cultural views in *Fight the Power: Rap, Race, and Reality* written with Yusuf Jahr. The recordings of all of these performers are part of the "growing tip" of American culture at the turn of the millennium. Their creative works and their stories bring us into the future, when there will undoubtedly be hundreds more books written about the record-ings and performers that give American culture its catchy, long-playing sound track.

BIBLIOGRAPHY

Books

Album Covers from the Vinyl Junkyard. Hamburg: Gingko, 1997.
Alden, Grant, and Peter Blackstock. *No Depression*. Nashville: Dowling, 1998.
Arnold, Gina. *Kiss This: Punk in the Present Tense*. New York: St. Martin's, 1997.
———. *Route 666: On the Road to Nirvana*. New York: St. Martin's, 1993.
Avalon, Moses. *Confessions of a Record Producer*. San Francisco: Miller Freeman, 1998.

Azerrad, Michael. *Come As You Are: The Story of Nirvana*. New York: Doubleday, 1994.

Bangs, Lester. *Psychotic Reactions & Carburetor Dung*. New York: Vintage, 1988.

Becker, Scott, ed. *We Rock So You Don't Have To*. San Diego: Incommunicado, 1998.

Bego, Mark. *Aretha Franklin: The Queen of Soul*. New York: St. Martin's, 1989.

———. *Rock and Roll Almanac*. New York: Macmillan, 1996.

Benson, Carl, ed. *The Bob Dylan Companion: Four Decades of Commentary*. New York: Schirmer, 1998.

Bergman, Billy. *Hot Sauces: Latin and Caribbean Pop*. New York: Quill, 1985.

Berry, Chuck. *Chuck Berry: The Autobiography*. New York: Harmony Books, 1987.

Bordowitz, Hank. *Bad Moon Rising: The Unauthorized History of Creedence Clearwater Revival*. New York: Schirmer, 1998.

Bowman, Rob. *Soulsville, U.S.A.: The Story of Stax Records*. New York: Macmillan, 1997.

The Billboard Illustrated Encyclopedia of Rock. New York: Billboard, 1998.

Brabec, Jeffrey, and Todd Brabec. *Music, Money, and Success: The Insider's Guide to the Music Industry*. New York: Schirmer, 1994.

Brightman, Carol. *Sweet Chaos: The Grateful Dead's American Adventure*. New York: Clarkson Potter, 1998.

Brown, L., and G. Fredrich. *Encyclopedia of Country & Western Music*. New York: Tower Books, 1971.

Brown, Ruth. *Miss Rhythm: The Autobiography of Ruth Brown*. New York: Da Capo, 1999.

Carr, Roy. *A Century of Jazz*. New York: Da Capo, 1997.

Castleman, Harry, and Walter Podrazik. *The Beatles Again*. Ann Arbor, Mich.: Pierian, 1977.

Chanan, Michael. *Repeated Takes: A Short History of Recording and Its Effects on Music*. New York: Verso, 1997.

Chapple, Steve, and Reebee Garofalo. *Rock 'n' Roll Is Here to Pay*. Chicago: Nelson-Hall, 1978.

Charles, Ray, with David Ritz. *Brother Ray*. New York: Da Capo, 1992.

Chilton, John. *Let the Good Times Roll: The Story of Louis Jordan and His Music*. Ann Arbor: University of Michigan Press, 1997.

Christgau, Robert. *Christgau's Record Guide*. New York: Da Capo, 1994.

———. *Christgau's Record Guide: Rock Albums of the 70's*. New York: Houghton Mifflin, 1985.

Chuck D., and Yusuf Jah. *Fight the Power: Rap, Race, and Reality*. New York: Delta, 1998.

Clark, Dick. *Dick Clark's American Bandstand*. New York: Collins, 1997.

Coleman, Ray. *Lennon: The Definitive Biography*. New York: HarperPerennial, 1992.

Collins, Ace. *Disco Duck and Other Adventures in Novelty Music*. New York: Berkley Boulevard, 1998.

Cooke, Mervyn. *The Chronicle of Jazz*. New York: Abbeville, 1998.

Cooper, B. Lee. *Rock Music in American Popular Culture: Rock 'n' Roll Resources*. Binghamton, N.Y.: Haworth, 1994.

Cooper, Michael, and Terry Southern. *The Early Stones: Legendary Photographs of a Band in the Making*. New York: Hyperion, 1973.

Country: The Music and the Musicians: From the Beginnings to the '90s. New York: Abbeville, 1994.

Cowley, John. *The New Blackwell Guide to Recorded Blues*. Oxford: Blackwell, 1996.

Crisafulli, Chuck. *Moonlight Drive: The Stories behind Every Doors Song*. Miami Springs, Fla.: MBS, 1995.

Crosby, David, and Carl Gottlieb. *Long Time Gone: The Autobiography of David Crosby*. New York: Doubleday, 1988.

Cunningham, Mark. *Good Vibrations: A History of Record Production*. London: Sanctuary, 1999.

Daley, Dan. *Nashville's Unwritten Rules: Inside the Business of Country Music*. Woodstock, N.Y.: Overlook, 1999.

Dannen, Fredric, and Erroll McDonald. *Hit Men: Power Brokers & Fast Money inside the Music Business*. New York: Vintage, 1991.

Davies, Hunter. *The Beatles*. New York: Norton, 1996.

Davies, Ray. *X-Ray: The Unauthorized Autobiography*. Woodstock N.Y.: Overlook, 1995.

Dawidoff, Nicholas. *In the Country of Country*. New York: Vintage, 1998.

Dawson, Jim. *The Twist: The Story of the Song and Dance That Changed the World*. Boston: Faber and Faber, 1995.

DeCurtis, Anthony. *Rocking My Life Away: Writing about Music & Other Matters*. Durham, N.C.: Duke University Press, 1998.

DeCurtis, Anthony, and James Henke. *Rolling Stone Album Guide: The Definitive Guide to the Best of Rock, Rap, Jazz, Blues, Country, Soul, Folk and Gospel*. New York: Random House, 1992.

DeCurtis, Anthony, and Jim Miller. *The Rolling Stone Illustrated History of Rock 'n' Roll*. New York: Random House, 1992.

Denisoff, R. Serge, and William L. Schurk. *Tarnished Gold: The Record Industry Revisited*. New Brunswick, N.J.: Transaction Books, 1987.

DeWitt, Howard A. *Chuck Berry's Rock 'n' Roll Music*. Ann Arbor, Mich.: Pierian Press, 1985.

Dickerson, James L. *Women on Top: The Quiet Revolution That's Rocking the American Music Industry*. New York: Watson-Guptill, 1998.

DiLello, Richard. *The Longest Cocktail Party*. Ann Arbor, Mich.: Popular Culture Ink, 1997.

Doss, Erika. *Elvis Culture: Fans, Faith & Image*. Lawrence: University of Kansas Press, 1999.

Drate, Spencer. *Rock Art, CDs, Albums and Posters*. Glen Cove, N.Y.: Pbc International, 1994.

Echols, Alice. *Scars of Sweet Paradise: The Life and Times of Janis Joplin*. New York: Metropolitan, 1999.

Eddy, Chuck. *Stairway to Hell: The 500 Best Heavy Metal Albums in the Universe*. New York: Da Capo, 1998.

Eliot, Mark. *Rockonomics: The Money behind the Music*. New York: Citadel, 1993.

Elvis Album; 1954–1977. Lincolnwood, Ill.: Publication International, 1997.

Emery, Ralph. *The View from Nashville*. New York: William Morrow, 1998.

Epstein, Brian. *A Cellarful of Noise: The Autobiography of the Man Who Made the Beatles*. New York: Byron, 1998.

Erlewine, Michael, et al., eds. *All Music Guide to Country*. San Francisco: Miller Freeman, 1997.

———. *All Music Guide to Jazz*. San Francisco: Miller Freeman, 1998.

———. *All Music Guide to Rock*. San Francisco: Miller Freeman, 1997.

Escott, Colin. *Hank Williams: The Biography*. Boston: Little, Brown, 1995.

———. *Tattooed on Their Tongues: A Journey through the Backrooms of American Music*. New York: Schirmer, 1998.

Escott, Colin, ed. *All Roads Lead to Rock: Legends of Early Rock 'n' Roll*. New York: Schirmer, 1999.

Escott, Colin, and Martin Hawkins. *Good Rockin' Tonight: Sun Records & the Birth of Rock 'N' Roll*. New York: St. Martin's, 1992.

Faragher, Scott. *Music City Babylon: Inside the World of Country Music*. New York: Carol, 1992.

Feather, Leonard. *Encyclopedia of Jazz*. New York: Da Capo, 1988.

Fernando, S. H. *New Beats: Exploring the Music, Culture, & Attitudes of Hip-Hop*. New York: Anchor, 1994.

Fong-Torres, Ben. *Not Fade Away: A Backstage Pass to 20 Years of Rock & Roll*. San Francisco: Miller Freeman, 1999.

Freeman, Scott, and Michael Pietsch, eds. *Midnight Riders: The Story of the Allman Brothers Band*. New York: Little, Brown, 1996.

Friedman-Fairfax, and Sony Music Staff. *Boogie Night: The Disco Age*. New York: Michael Friedman/Fairfax, 1995.

Gans, David. *Conversations with the Dead: The Grateful Dead Interview Book*. New York: Citadel, 1991.

Giddens, Gary. *Visions of Jazz: The First Century*. New York: Oxford, 1998.

Gioia, Ted. *The History of Jazz*. New York: Oxford, 1998.

Godrich, John, and Robert M. W. Dixon. *Blues and Gospel Records: 1890–1943*. Oxford: Clarendon, 1997.

Goldrosen, John, and John Beecher. *Remembering Buddy*. New York: Da Capo, 1996.

Goldsmith, Peter D. *Making People's Music: Moe Asch and Folkways Records*. Washington, D.C.: Smithsonian, 1998.

Goodman, Fred. *The Mansion on the Hill: Dylan, Young, Geffen, Springsteen, and the Head-On Collision of Rock and Commerce*. New York: Vintage, 1998.

Gordon, Robert. *It Came from Memphis*. Boston: Faber and Faber, 1996.

Gordy, Berry. *To Be Loved: The Music, the Magic, the Memories of Motown*. New York: Warner, 1994.

Graff, Gary, ed. *Musichound R&B: The Essential Album Guide*. Farmington Hills, Mich.: Visible Ink, 1997.

Greenfield, Robert. *Dark Star: An Oral Biography of Jerry Garcia*. New York: Broadway, 1997.

———. *A Journey through America with the Rolling Stones*. London: Helter Skelter, 1998.

Gregory, Hugh. *A Century of Pop: A Hundred Years of Music That Changed the World*. Albuquerque: Acapella, 1998.

———. *The Real Rhythm and Blues*. London: Blandford, 1998.

Gribin, Anthony J. and Matthew M. Schiff. *Doo Wop: The Forgotten Third of Rock 'n' Roll*. Iola, Wis.: Kraus, 1992.

Guitar World Presents Nirvana and the Grunge Revolution. Milwaukee: Hal Leonard, 1998.

Guralnick, Peter. *Careless Love: The Unmaking of Elvis Presley*. Boston: Little, Brown, 1999.

———. *Last Train to Memphis: The Rise of Elvis Presley*. Boston: Little, Brown, 1994.

———. *Sweet Soul Music: Rhythm and Blues and the Southern Dream of Freedom*. New York: Harper and Row, 1986.

Hammond, John. *John Hammond on Record*. New York: Ridge Press, 1977.

Haring, Bruce. *Off the Charts: Ruthless Days and Reckless Nights inside the Music Industry*. New York: Birch Lane, 1996.

Harry, Bill. *The Ultimate Beatles Encyclopedia*. New York: Hyperion, 1992.

Helander, Brock. *The Rockin' '50s: The People Who Made the Music*. New York: Schirmer, 1998.

Henke, James, ed. *I Want to Take You Higher: The Psychedelic Era, 1965–1969*. San Francisco: Chronicle, 1997.

Hershey, Gerri. *Nowhere to Run: The Story of Soul Music*. New York: Times Books, 1984.

Hertsgaard, Mark. *A Day in the Life: The Music and Artistry of the Beatles*. New York: Delta, 1996.

Herzhaft, Gerard. *Encyclopedia of the Blues*. Fayetteville: University of Arkansas Press, 1997.

Heylin, Clinton. *Bob Dylan: The Recording Sessions 1960–1994*. New York: St. Martin's, 1997.

———. *Bootleg: The Secret History of the Other Recording Industry*. New York: St. Martin's, 1996.

Holzman, Jac, and Gavan Daws. *Follow the Music: The Life and High Times of Elektra Records*. Santa Monica, Calif.: First Media, 1998.

Hoskyns, Barney. *Waiting for the Sun: Strange Days, Weird Scenes, and the Sound of Los Angeles*. New York: Griffin, 1996.

Hull, Geoffrey P. *The Recording Industry*. Needham Heights, Mass.: Allyn and Bacon, 1998.

Jackson, John A. *American Bandstand*. New York: Oxford University Press, 1997.

———. *Big Beat Heat: Alan Freed and the Early Years of Rock & Roll*. New York: Schirmer, 1991.

Jorgensen, Ernst. *Elvis Presley: A Life in Music*. New York: St. Martin's, 1998.

Juno, Andrea. *Angry Women in Rock*. San Francisco: Juno, 1996.

Kashif, and Gary Greenberg. *Everything You'd Better Know about the Record Industry*. Venice, Calif.: Brooklyn Boy, 1996.

Kassel, Stefan, and Frank Jastfelder. *The Album Cover Art of Soundtracks*. Boston: Little, Brown, 1997.

Kennedy, Rick. *Jelly Roll, Bix, and Hoagy: Gennett Studios and the Birth of the Recorded Jazz*. Bloomington: Indiana University Press, 1999.

Kennedy, Rick, and Randy McNutt. *Little Labels, Big Sound*. Bloomington: Indiana University Press, 1999.

Kernfeld, Barry, ed. *The Blackwell Guide to Recorded Jazz*. Oxford: Blackwell, 1995.

Kingsbury, Paul, ed. *The Country Reader: Twenty Five Years of the Journal of Country Music*. Nashville: Country Music Foundation and Vanderbilt University, 1996.

———. *The Encyclopedia of Country Music: The Ultimate Guide to the Music*. New York: Oxford, 1998.

Knopper, Steve, ed. *Musichound Lounge: The Essential Album Guide to Martini Music and Easy Listening*. Farmington Hills, Mich.: Visible Ink, 1998.

———. *Musichound Swing*. Farmington Hills, Mich.: Visible Ink, 1999.

Koenigsberg, Allen. *Edison Cylinder Records: 1889–1912*. New York: Allen Koenigsberg, 1988.

Kohler, Eric. *In the Groove: Vintage Record Graphics: 1940–1960*. San Francisco: Chronicle, 1999.

Kooper, Al. *Backstage Passes & Backstabbing Bastards*. New York: Billboard, 1998.

Kostelanetz, Richard, and John Rocco, eds. *The Frank Zappa Companion: Four Decades of Commentary*. New York: Schirmer, 1997.

Krebs, Gary M. *The Rock and Roll Reader's Guide*. New York: Billboard, 1997.

Krogsgaard, Michael. *Positively Bob Dylan: A Thirty-Year Discography, Concert and Recording Session Guide, 1960–1991*. Ann Arbor: Popular Culture Ink, 1991.

Larkin, Colin. *The Guinness Encyclopedia of Popular Music*. London: Guinness, 1995.

———. *Virgin Encyclopedias of Popular Music*. London: Virgin, 1998.

Lathrup, Tad, and Jim Pettigrew Jr. *The Business of Music Marketing and Promotion*. New York: Billboard, 1999.

Lewisohn, Mark. *The Beatles Recording Sessions*. New York: Harmony, 1990.

Lewisohn, Mark, and Peter Guzzardi, eds. *The Complete Beatles Chronicles*. New York: Harmony, 1992.

Lord, Tom. *The Jazz Discography*. Skandia, Mich.: North Country, 1997.

Lydon, Michael. *Ray Charles: Man and Music*. New York: Riverhead, 1999.

Lynch, Richard C. *Broadway, Movie, TV and Studio Cast Musicals on Record: A Discography of Recordings, 1985–1995*. Westport, Conn.: Greenwood, 1996.

MacNeil, Legs, and Gillian McCain. *Please Kill Me: The Uncensored History of Punk*. New York: Penguin, 1996.

Marcus, Greil. *Ranters & Crowd Pleasers: Punk in Pop Music, 1977–1992*. New York: Anchor, 1993.

Marsh, Dave. *Born to Run: The Bruce Springsteen Story*. New York: Thunder's Mouth, 1996.

———. *Heart of Rock and Soul: The 1001 Greatest Singles Ever Made*. New York: Da Capo, 1999.

Marsh, Graham, ed. *Blue Note: The Album Cover Art*. San Francisco: Chronicle, 1991.

———. *Blue Note 2: The Album Cover Art: The Finest in Jazz since 1939*. San Francisco: Chronicle, 1997.

———. *The Blues: Album Cover Art*. San Francisco: Chronicle, 1996.

Martin, George. *All You Need Is Ears*. New York: St. Martin's, 1995.

McCloud, Barry. *Definitive Country: The Ultimate Encyclopedia of Country Music and Its Performers*. New York: Perigee, 1995.

McDermott, John. *Jimi Hendrix Sessions: The Complete Studio Recordings Sessions, 1963–1970*. Boston: Little, Brown, 1996.

McKeen, William. *The Beatles*. Westport, Conn.: Greenwood, 1990.

Merlis, Bob, and Davin Seay. *Heart & Soul: A Celebration of Black Music Style in America 1930–1975*. New York: Stewart Tabori and Chang, 1997.

Mikkelson, Johnny. *Reconsider Baby: The Definitive Elvis Sessionography 1954–1977*. Ann Arbor, Mich.: Popular Culture Ink, 1986.

Miles, Barry. *Paul McCartney: Many Years from Now*. New York: Owl, 1998.

Miller, Jim, ed. *The Rolling Stone Illustrated History of Rock n' Roll*. New York: Random House, 1980.

Morrison, Gary. *Go Cat Go! Rockabilly Music and Its Makers*. Urbana: University of Illinois Press, 1998.

Nagler, Larry. *Memphis Beat*. New York: St. Martin's, 1998.

Nassour, Ellis. *Honky Tonk Angel: The Intimate Story of Patsy Cline*. New York: St. Martin's, 1993.

Nathan, David. *The Soulful Divas*. New York: Watson-Guptill, 1999.

Neely, Tim. *Goldmine Price Guide to 45 Rpm Records*. Iola, Wis.: Kraus, 1999.

Nix, Don. *Road Stories & Recipes*. New York: Macmillan, 1997.

Norman, Philip. *Shout! The Beatles in Their Generation*. New York: Fireside, 1996.

O'Brien, Ed. *Sinatra 101: The 101 Best Recordings and the Stories Behind Them*. New York: Boulevard Books, 1996.

Ochs, Michael. *1000 Rock Covers*. London: Taschen, 1997.

———. *Rock Archives: A Photographer's Journey through the First Two Decades of Rock and Roll*. New York: Doubleday, 1984.

O'Dair, Barbara, ed. *Trouble Girls: The Rolling Stone Book of Women in Rock*. New York: Random, 1997.

O'Neil, Thomas, and Peter Bart. *The Grammys: The Ultimate Unofficial Guide to Music's Highest Honor*. New York: Perigee, 1999.

Osboune, Jerry. *Official Price Guide to Records*. New York: House of Collectibles, 1999.

Passman, Donald S. *All You Need to Know about the Music Business*. New York: Simon & Schuster, 1997.

Payne, Jim. *Give the Drummers Some! The Great Drummers of R&B, Funk & Soul*. New York: Warner Brothers, 1996.

Perkins, Carl, and David McGee. *Go, Cat, Go! The Life and Times of Carl Perkins, the King of Rockabilly*. New York: Hyperion, 1997.

Post, Laura. *Backstage Pass: Interviews with Women in Music*. Norwich, Vt.: New Victoria, 1997.

Pruter, Robert. *The Blackwell Guide to Soul Recordings*. Oxford: Blackwell, 1993.

Reeves, Martha, and Mark Bego. *Dancing in the Street: Confessions of a Motown Diva*. New York: Hyperion, 1994.

Reisfeld, Randi, and Danny Fields. *Who's Your Fave Rave?* New York: Boulevard, 1997.

Rettenmund, Matthew. *Encyclopedia Madonnica: Madonna—the Woman and the Icon—from A to Z*. New York: St. Martin's 1995.

Ribowsky, Mark. *He's a Rebel: The Truth about Phil Spector*. New York: Dutton, 1989.

Ritz, David. *Divided Soul: The Life of Marvin Gaye*. New York: Da Capo, 1991.

Ro, Ronin. *Have Gun Will Travel: The Spectacular Rise & Violent Fall of Death Row Records*. New York: Doubleday, 1998.

Robbins, Ira A. *The Trouser Press Guide to '90s Rock*. New York: Fireside, 1997.

Roberts, John Storm. *The Latin Tinge: The Impact of Latin American Music on the United States.* New York: Oxford, 1999.

Rolling Stone: The Complete Covers. New York: Harry Abrams, 1998.

The Rolling Stone Interviews: 1967–1980: Talking with the Legends of Rock and Roll. New York: St. Martin's, 1989.

Romanowski, Patricia, and Holly George Warren. *The New Rolling Stone Encyclopedia of Rock & Roll.* New York: Fireside, 1995.

Rose, Tricia. *Black Noise: Rap Music and Black Culture in Contemporary America.* Hanover, N.H.: Wesleyan University Press, 1994.

Rucker, Leland, ed. *Musichound Blues: The Essential Album Guide.* Farmington Hills, Mich.: Visible Ink, 1997.

Rule, Greg. *Electro Shock: Groundbreakers of Synth Music.* San Francisco: Miller Freeman, 1999.

Ruppli, Michel. *The Aladdin/Imperial Labels.* Westport, Conn.: Greenwood, 1991.

———. *Atlantic Records: A Discography.* Westport, Conn.: Greenwood, 1979.

———. *The Blue Note Label.* Westport Conn.: Greenwood, 1988.

———. *The Clef-Verve Labels.* Westport Conn.: Greenwood, 1986.

———. *The Decca Labels.* Westport Conn.: Greenwood, 1996.

———. *The King Labels.* Westport Conn.: Greenwood, 1986.

———. *The Mercury Labels.* Wesport Conn.: Greenwood, 1993.

———. *The MGM Labels.* Westport Conn.: Greenwood, 1998.

Rust, Brian. *Discography of Historical Records on Cylinders and 78s.* Westport, Conn.: Greenwood, 1979.

Sanjek, Russell, and David Sanjek. *Pennies from Heaven: American Popular Music in the 20th Century.* New York: Da Capo, 1996.

Santelli, Robert. *The Best of the Blues: The 101 Essential Albums.* New York: Penguin, 1997.

Sarig, Roni. *The Secret History of Rock: The Most Influential Bands You've Never Heard.* New York: Watson-Guptill, 1998.

Schinder, Scott. *Rolling Stone's Alternative Rock-A-Rama: An Outrageous Compendium of Facts, Fiction, Trivia, and Critiques on Alternative Rock.* New York: Delta, 1996.

Schipper, Henry. *Broken Record: The Inside Story of the Grammy Awards.* Ontario: Birch Lane, 1992.

Scott, Frank. *Down Home Guide to the Blues.* Albuquerque: Acapella, 1991.

Segrave, Kerry. *Payola in the Music Industry: A History, 1880–1991.* Jefferson, N.C.: McFarland, 1993.

Seiler, Burkhardt, ed. *Album Cover Art of Punk.* Corte Madera, Calif.: Gingko, 1998.

Sexton, Adam, ed. *Desperately Seeking Madonna: In Search of the Meaning of the World's Most Famous Woman.* New York: Dell, 1993.

Shaughnessy, Mary Alice. *Les Paul: An American Original.* New York: William Morrow, 1993.

Shaw, Arnold. *Black Popular Music in America.* New York: Schirmer, 1986.

———. *Honkers and Shouters: The Golden Years of Rhythm and Blues.* New York: Macmillan, 1978.

Shemel, Sidney, and M. William Krasilovsky. *This Business of Music.* New York: Billboard, 1985.

Simon, George T. *The Big Bands*. New York: Schirmer, 1981.

Soocher, Stan. *They Fought the Law: Rock Music Goes to Court*. New York: Schirmer, 1998.

Spector, Ronnie. *Be My Baby*. New York: Hamony, 1990.

Spottswood, Richard K. *Ethnic Music on Records: 1893–1942*. Champaign: University of Illinois, Press, 1990.

Springsteen, Bruce. *Songs*. New York: Avon, 1998.

Stancell, Steven. *Rap Whoz Who: The World of Rap Music*. New York: Schirmer, 1996.

Strong, Martin C. *The Great Metal Discography*. Edinburgh: Canongate, 1998.

Sulpy, Doug, and Ray Schweighardt. *Get Back: The Unauthorized Chronicle of the Beatles' Let It Be Disaster*. New York: St. Martin's, 1999.

Taraborrelli, J. Randy. *Michael Jackson: The Magic and the Madness*. New York: Ballantine, 1991.

Tosches, Nick. *Unsung Heroes*. New York: Da Capo, 1999.

Unterberger, Richie. *Unknown Legends of Rock 'n' Roll: Psychedelic Unknowns, Mad Geniuses, Punk Pioneers, Lo-Fi Mavericks & More*. San Francisco: Miller-Freeman, 1998.

Vale, V. *Incredibly Strange Music*. San Francisco: V/Search, 1994.

———. *Swing! The New Retro Renaissance*. San Francisco: V/Search, 1998.

Wadhams, Wayne. *Sound Advice: The Musician's Guide to the Record Industry*. New York: Schirmer, 1990.

Walley, David. *No Commercial Potential: The Saga of Frank Zappa*. New York: Da Capo, 1996.

Walters, Neal, ed. *Musichound Folk: The Essential Album Guide*. Farmington Hills, Mich.: Visible Ink, 1998.

Werner, Craig. *A Change Is Gonna Come: Music, Race & the Soul of America*. New York: Plume, 1998.

Westband, Eric, and Craig Marks. *Spin Alternative Press Record Guide*. New York: Vintage, 1995.

Whitburn, Joel. *The Billboard Book of Top 40 Hits*. Menomonee Falls, Wisc.: Record Research, 1996.

———. *Joel Whitburn's Top Pop Singles 1955–1996*. Menomonee Falls, Wisc.: Record Research, 1997.

———. *Joel Whitburn's Top R&B Singles: 1942–1995*. Menomonee Falls, Wisc.: Record Research, 1996.

White, Timothy. *Music to My Ears: The Billboard Essays: Portraits of Popular Music in the '90s*. New York: Henry Holt, 1997.

———. *The Nearest Faraway Place: Brian Wilson, the Beach Boys, and the Southern California Experience*. New York: Henry Holt, 1996.

———. *Rock Lives: Profiles & Interviews*. New York: Henry Holt, 1991.

Williams, Paul. *Rock and Roll: The 100 Best Singles*. New York: Carroll and Graf, 1993.

Wilson, Robert, and Ed O'Brien. *Sinatra 101: The 101 Best Recordings & the Stories behind Them*. New York: Boulevard, 1996.

Wolff, Daniel. *You Send Me: The Life and Times of Sam Cooke*. New York: Morrow, 1995.

Woodward, Fred, and Anthony DeCurtis. *Rolling Stone Images of Rock & Roll*. New York: Little, Brown, 1997.

Wooley, John, et al. *Forever Lounge*. Dubuque, Iowa: Antique Trader, 1999.

Wyman, Bill. *Stone Alone: The Story of a Rock 'n' Roll Band*. New York: Viking Penguin, 1990.

Zappa, Frank. *The Real Frank Zappa Book*. New York: Poseidon, 1990.

Periodicals

General

Billboard
Grammy Magazine
Hit Parader
Pop Star!
Shout Out!
Stereo Review
Teen Beat
Uncut
Vibe

Rock

Circus
Metal Maniac
Mojo
Rolling Stone

Alternative

CMJ New Music Monthly
Punk Planet
Spin
Urb

Rap/Hip-Hop

Black Beat
Blaze
Rap Pages
Right On!
The Source

Jazz

Coda Magazine
Down Beat
Jazziz
Jazz Times

Blues

Blues Access
Blues Review
Living Blues

Country/Bluegrass/Folk

Bluegrass Unlimited
Country Music
The Old-Time Herald

Academic

Journal of Country Music
Journal of Jazz Studies
Popular Music and Society

Recording Technology

Audio
EQ
Future Mix
Mix
Recording

Miscellaneous

American Record Guide (Classical/Collecting)
Backstreets (Bruce Springsteen)
Blue Suede News (Oldies)
Dirty Linen (Folk/World)
Goldmine (Oldies/Collecting)
Insider (Club/Urban)
Modern Lounge (Lounge/Easy-Listening)
Relix (Psychedelic)
XLR8R (Electronic)

REGIONALISM

Anne Rowe

Although regionalism in literature and the arts has long been the subject of numerous studies by scholars and critics, only in the past three decades has any significant attention been given to regionalism as it relates to popular culture. A survey of the handbooks and anthologies of popular culture reveals increasing concern with regionalism. Recently, a number of articles on popular culture and regionalism have appeared, and formal theories concerning regionalism in popular culture are steadily being developed.

The chief thrust of this chapter is to survey the studies that have been made of regionalism and to define where these studies have intersected with those of popular culture. A seminal work that treats regionalism as it relates to popular culture is Jack Temple Kirby's *Media-Made Dixie: The South in the American Imagination*, an exploration of the image of the South as it has been created and presented in the popular media. *Geography, the Media and Popular Culture*, edited by Jacquelin Burgess and John R. Gold, also explores the importance of the relationship between a place and its culture. The *Encyclopedia of Southern Culture*, edited by Charles Reagan Wilson and William Ferris, provides a comprehensive look at many aspects of popular culture in a particular region. In the past decade works such as *Dominant Symbols in Popular Culture*, edited by Ray B. Browne, Marshall W. Fishwick, and Kevin O. Browne, have also taken a new look at the relationship between regionalism and popular culture.

Much of the important work on regionalism and popular culture has appeared in such journals as *Studies in Popular Culture*, *Journal of American Popular Culture*, and the *Journal of Popular Culture*. The latter has devoted several in-depth sections to the topic. For example, volume 11 (Spring 1978) contains a number of essays on cultural geography and popular culture. Volume 16 (Winter 1982) is devoted to the topic "The South and Popular Culture." The western novel has also been the subject of several numbers of the *Journal of Popular Culture*, including volume 4 (Fall 1970). Volume 23 (Summer 1989) of the *Journal of Popular Culture* is, in large part, devoted to a study of Cajun life and culture. A 1996 issue of *Studies in Popular Culture* (19:2) also has a regional emphasis, containing twenty-three essays treating the culture of the American South.

With the advent of the *Journal of Regional Culture* in 1981, the subject of regionalism and popular culture finally began to receive the treatment that it deserves. Volume 1 (Fall/Winter 1981) treats the South. Other issues include volume 4 (Spring/Summer 1984), which contains essays on Florida, including Jerome Stern's perceptive essay "Florida as Popular Culture." Volumes 4–5 (Fall/Winter 1984; Spring/Summer 1985) contain essays on the topic "New Jersey Culture: The View from the Disciplines." Volume 3 of the *Journal of American Culture* (Summer 1980) contains essays on the "Cultural History of the American West," and volume 14 (Summer 1991) has essays on "The American West as Image in Literature, Language, Painting and Films." Volume 11 (Fall 1988) is an in-depth issue on Georgia. With the increasing attention given to regionalism and popular culture in these journals, it seems likely that book-length studies of the subject will also grow in number.

HISTORICAL OUTLINE

Although an awareness of regions or sections has existed in America from the colonial period to the present, regionalism in literature and the arts generally refers to two periods: the local color period of the late nineteenth century and regionalism of the 1930s and after. More recently, the argument has been set forth that since the 1970s a newer form of regionalism has emerged.

The beginning of the local color movement is usually cited as 1868, when Bret Harte began publishing stories of California mining camps in the *Overland Monthly*. Many provincial sketches and stories appeared in large-circulation magazines during the 1870s, and the local color vogue reached its height during the 1880s and 1890s, tapering off near the end of the century.

Only after the end of the Civil War, when it became clear that the battle for nationalism had been won, was there a dramatic growth of interest in the many sectional differences of the United States. Local color writing, which emphasized the unique setting of a particular region and reproduced the dialect, customs, provincial types, and other qualities of that region, seemed to satisfy the desire of the American people to take a nostalgic look at the good old days of the preindustrialized, prewar period. Thus, much local color writing was rural-based but intended for city consumption. Local color writing grew out of every region, and representative local colorists included Mary E. Wilkins Freeman and Sarah Orne Jewett of New England, Bret Harte of the West, and George Washington Cable and Thomas Nelson Page of the South. After the fall of the Confederacy there were much national interest in, and curiosity about, the South, and southern local colorists were heavily represented in nationally circulated magazines. Local color writing usually appeared as short stories. Plots were highly contrived, and characterization was generally superficial, characters often not transcending the stereotype.

In contrast to the term *local color*, *regionalism* is generally used to refer to an intellectual movement of the 1930s that posited that each of the regions of the United States is a geographical, cultural, and economic entity. This new concept of regionalism, which was as much sociological as literary, was apparent particularly in the South. The publication of *I'll Take My Stand: The South and the Agrarian Tradition* by Twelve Southerners in 1930 expressed the desire of its authors to resist standardization and to preserve, as far as possible, an agrarian-based culture. Although the agrarians, as they were called, including John Crowe Ransom, Robert Penn Warren, Donald Davidson, Allen Tate, and others, did not believe that the South could remain an entirely agricultural society, they argued for a set of values that supported a human rather than a machine-dominated society.

During the 1930s a number of works appeared that explored the relationship of the regions to the literary and social culture of America. Carey McWilliams' *The New Regionalism in American Literature* was an early attempt at defining regionalism. *The Attack on Leviathan: Regionalism and Nationalism in the United States* by Donald Davidson posited an agrarian point of view. *American Regionalism: A Cultural-Historical Approach to National Integration* by Howard W. Odum and Harry Estill Moore argued for an integration of cultural, geographical, and historical factors. In a recent article Robert H. Brinkmeyer Jr. notes of this period, "Most regionalists eventually came to see that regionalism's power derived less from concrete political platforms than from its ideological posture against modernity" (648).

One of the most important literary movements related to regionalism in the 1930s was the Southern Renaissance, out of which came the work of William Faulkner, Thomas Wolfe, Robert Penn Warren, Eudora Welty, and others. In novels, short stories, poetry, and essays, the literary productivity of the South loomed great. Other major writers of the 1930s, Willa Cather and John Steinbeck, for example, also employed a regional base for their works.

Regionalism as a cultural force has continued to receive attention since the 1930s. For some artists and critics regionalism has a pejorative connotation, implying limitation. Regionalism, it is argued, must necessarily limit the universal message of the work of art. Proponents of regionalism argue, perhaps more convincingly, that all art must come out of a particular region or culture.

A number of recent works have also made significant contributions to the study of the relationship between regionalism and women's writing. Donna M. Campbell in *Resisting Regionalism: Gender and Naturalism in American Fiction, 1885–1915* explores the "decline of women's local color fiction and the rise of American naturalism at the turn of the century" and argues that these "should not . . . be seen as discrete events"; rather than a single "transition" from one to the other there was "a genteelly pitched battle between the two, a conflict ended by the successful subversion and banishment of local fiction" (12). In *Breaking Boundaries: New Perspectives on Women's Regional Writing* Sherrie A. Inness and Diana Royer bring together essays that show "the many ways that women writers have used a regional writing to critique dominant societal norms" (3). They make a strong case for viewing women's regional writing as a vehicle for representing a marginalized point of view. Judith Fetterley in " 'Not in the Least American': Nineteenth-Century Literary Realism" also argues that regionalism should not be subsumed under realism and emphasizes the importance of regionalism in the work of women writers.

An argument is set forth in the Introduction to *The New Regionalism*, edited by Charles Reagan Wilson, that the new regionalism as described in Carey Mc-

Eudora Welty. Courtesy of the Library of Congress

Williams' book has been supplanted since the 1970s with a "new" new regionalism that "shows special interest in the environmental context of regions, cultural diversity, socially constructed identities, and the ways social relationships shape the exercise of and resistance to power" (xxiii). In a recent essay in *American Literary History* Michael Kowalewski also refers to a "revitalized interest in American literary regionalism and the literature of place (171).

An essay by John G. Cawelti in *Dominant Symbols in Popular Culture*, "Regionalism and Popular Culture: From Social Force to Symbolism," argues for "the importance of regionalism as a symbol, if not an actual social and political force, in twentieth century American popular culture." Arguing that "technology has made it possible for Americans to recreate essentially the same life styles anywhere in the country," Cawelti concludes, "Once actual geographical places and subculture, the great American regions have become part of a landscape of the imagination." He explores this idea in four areas: the commercial and political uses of regional symbols, regionalism as related to mass entertainment, and, finally, "the use of artifacts, styles, dress, foods, and other patterns symbolically connected with the traditional regions to establish some sense of identity and continuity in a culture which seems increasingly to lack these qualities."[1] Cawelti's catalog of elements of regionalism includes excellent examples of the areas of focus for contemporary explorations of regionalism and popular culture.

REFERENCE WORKS

Although many works provide bibliographical information on regional writings, and a number of general guides to popular culture are available, only in recent years have studies devoted to regionalism *and* popular culture appeared. Standard sources for critical material dealing with earlier regional studies are three volumes compiled by Lewis Leary, *Articles on American Literature, 1900–1950, Articles on American Literature, 1950–1967*, and *Articles on American Literature, 1968–1975*. These volumes have special sections on regionalism, which provide an invaluable listing of the articles pertaining to the topic. Another standard research tool, edited by Robert E. Spiller et al., is the *Literary History of the United States*, which contains chapters on the various sections of the United States as well as extensive bibliographical material on regionalism, including general studies, New England, New York to Delaware, the South and the Deep South, the Midwest, the Southwest, the Pacific Northwest, and California and the Far West. Other useful bibliographical works on regionalism, although limited to the South, are Louis D. Rubin Jr., *A Bibliographical Guide to the Study of Southern Literature*, and the volume that updates it, *Southern Literature, 1968–1975: A Checklist of Scholarship*, edited by Jerry T. Williams. The *Columbia Literary History of the United States* treats regionalism, although an essay by James M. Cox, "Regionalism: A Diminished Thing," is dismissive of the role of regionalism in the national literature. More recently, works such as *The Encyclopedia of Southern Culture*, edited by Charles Reagan Wilson and William Ferris, *A Literary History of the American West* edited by J. Golden Taylor, and *The New Regionalism*, edited by Charles Regan Wilson, have appeared as important reference tools.

RESEARCH COLLECTIONS

The description of research collections that follows must of necessity be eclectic because no comprehensive index to library holdings in popular culture is available. Much of the material cited here includes manuscript holdings of regional materials, only a portion of which pertain to popular culture as such.

Volume 6 of the Popular Culture Association *Newsletter*, edited by Michael T. Marsden, contains a compilation of popular culture holdings of various sizes related to regionalism. A representative listing follows. The Oral History Collection at Brookens Library in Springfield, Illinois, emphasizes regional history of Springfield and Central Illinois. Lees Junior College Library, Jackson, Kentucky, has an Appalachian Oral History Project, which includes 600 taped interviews with mountain residents. Louisiana State University Library, Baton Rouge, has a collection of Acadian folk material and folk music. Northern Arizona University Library, Flagstaff, has a collection of western pulp novels and western pulp magazines. Northern Arizona University English Department has original tape recordings of southwestern folk songs and ballads.

One of the most extensive collections of western Americana is found in the Bancroft Library of the University of California at Berkeley. The collection includes manuscripts assembled by Hubert Howe Bancroft that center on the history of California and Mexico. Also contained in the Bancroft Library are regional oral histories of North Californians. Norlin Library of the University of Colorado at

Boulder has published Ellen Arguimbau's *A Guide to Manuscript Collections: Western Historical Collections*, which describes the 480 individual collections of material relating to western culture. The Autry Museum of Western Heritage in Los Angeles has a collection of more than 40,000 objects. The Northern Arizona University Cline Special Collections and Archives Department contains more than 700 interviews, many with Arizona pioneers.

The *Subject Directory of Special Libraries and Information Centers*, edited by Margaret Labash Young, Harold Chester Young, and Anthony T. Kruzas, provides listings of many collections that relate, in part at least, to regionalism in popular culture. For example, Beik Library, Appalachian State University, Boone, North Carolina, has an Appalachian Regional Collection (music library). The Sam Houston State University Library, Huntsville, Texas, has a collection of 10,000 volumes of Texana and Confederate materials. The Indiana University Lilly Library, Bloomington, contains the Ellison Far West Collection. The Walter Havighurst Special Collections Library at Miami University, Oxford, Ohio, has more than 4,000 volumes pertaining to Ohio Valley history. Johnson Camden Library at Morehead State University, Morehead, Kentucky, holds a Kentucky Collection of 2,560 volumes. The library of the Pacific-Union Club, San Francisco, has a special collection of 2,000 items of Californiana. The Special Collections Department of Rutgers University, New Brunswick, New Jersey, has a special collection of New Jerseyana. The Special Collections Department of the University of Arizona Library, Tucson, contains extensive collections of southwest material. The Department of Special Collections in the University of California at Los Angeles Research Library contains a Southern California Regional Oral History Interviews Collection. The Special Collections Library of the University of Idaho, Moscow, has a collection of Pacific Northwest materials. The Kerlan Collection of the University of Minnesota Library, Minneapolis, includes a collection of Minnesota authors and settings. The Special Collections Department/University Archives of the University of Nevada's Reno Library has a collection of material on Nevada and the West. The library of the University of Texas at El Paso contains several collections, the most prominent being the Sonnichsen Collection of Southwestern Literature and Fiction, the McNeely Collection of southwestern and Mexican works, and the Southern Pacific Collection. The Virginia Commonwealth University James Branch Cabell Library, Richmond, has a collection of contemporary Virginia authors. The Pacific Northwest Collection of the University of Washington, Seattle, has materials relating to the anthropology, history, economics, and social conditions of the Pacific Northwest, including Washington, Oregon, Idaho, western Montana, Yukon, British Columbia, and Alaska.

During the 1930s and 1940s, when regional writing was at its peak, southern writers dominated the market. Following are some special collections of southern regional materials listed in Thomas H. English, *Roads to Research: Distinguished Library Collections of the Southeast*. The Aldermann Library of the University of Virginia, Charlottesville, has a large collection of writings of southern authors. The George W. Cable Collection of Tulane University includes more than 20,000 items, among them letters, manuscripts, and typescripts. The Joel Chandler Harris Collection at Emory University is very large and includes an extensive manuscript collection. The joint University Libraries at Vanderbilt University in Nashville,

Tennessee, have a collection of the Fugitive Group. The University of Florida Library has the Marjorie Kinnan Rawlings Collection and a collection of Floridiana. The Southern Historical Collection at the University of North Carolina at Chapel Hill has over 3.6 million items that are private records pertaining to southern culture and history. The George Washington Flowers Collection of Southern Americana at Duke University has over 2.5 million items covering the entire South for every period of its history. The Georgiana Collection in the University of Georgia Library at Athens provides a record of all phases of history and culture from the colonial period to the present. In the Department of Archives and Manuscripts at the Louisiana State University Library are nearly 3 million items related to contemporary life in the Lower Mississippi Valley for the past 200 years. The North Carolina Collection at the University of North Carolina at Chapel Hill has more than 200,000 items relating to every aspect of life in North Carolina. Also, the Main Library System of the University of North Carolina at Chapel Hill has "Documenting the American South," a full-text database of primary materials, including southern culture, spanning the colonial period to the twentieth century. A collection of Tennesseeiana is held at the Manuscript Division of the Tennessee State Library and Archives.

Special Collections in Libraries of the Southeast, edited by J. B. Howell, cites a collection of 500 cheap editions of fiction, "displayed for sale in railway bookstalls from the mid-19th century" (82) in the Robert W. Woodruff Library at Emory University. Hutchins Library of Berea College at Berea, Kentucky, has a collection of "8,000 volumes and 250 linear feet of archival and manuscript materials relating to the history and culture of the Southern highlands" (112–13). The collection includes books, pamphlets, manuscripts, photographs, tapes, and films. Another extensive collection is the Folk-lore, Folk-life and Oral History Archives at the Helm-Cravens Library of Western Kentucky University, Bowling Green. The Mississippi Department of Archives and History, Jackson, has a collection of Mississippiana including the Works Progress Administration (WPA) Collection of material assembled by WPA workers on the history and culture of Mississippi. At the University of Mississippi Library is the Mississippi Collection, consisting of 20,000 cataloged volumes as well as thousands of uncataloged items pertaining to the culture and history of the state. The Carol Grotnes Belk Library at Appalachian State University, Boone, North Carolina, contains the William Leonard Eury Appalachian Collection comprising over 10,000 volumes, clippings, slides, oral history tapes, original manuscripts, and four extensive collections of ballads. The Library and Media Center of the Country Music Foundation, Nashville, Tennessee, has an extensive collection of items related to country music, including more than 70,000 recordings, as well as songbooks, oral tapes, photographs, and newspaper clippings.

Beginning in the 1970s, a number of centers devoted to regional studies have been established, including the Center for Great Plains Studies (1976, University of Nebraska), the Center for the Study of Southern Culture (1977, University of Mississippi), and the Appalachian Center (1978, University of Kentucky). A growing number of Web sites are also devoted to regional culture.

HISTORY AND CRITICISM

The works treated here are arranged chronologically, and the majority of those focusing strictly on popular culture appear among the more recent critical works. The earlier works cited are important to the understanding of the concept of regionalism as it has influenced American life and art.

Provincial Types in American Fiction, by Horace Spencer Fiske, published in 1907, is an early work describing various types of American provincial life as treated since the Civil War by writers in New England, the South, the Midwest, and the Far West. Fiske describes provincial types in fiction according to region, and there are separate introductory sections for each of the regions as well as explication and discussion of the stories by these authors.

Another early work, *The New Regionalism in American Literature* (1930), by Carey McWilliams, reflects the growing interest in regionalism. McWilliams provides useful discussions of early journals and collections of writings of the various regions. He concludes that regional writers are trying to create a sense of community through their work.

A foundational study of regionalism in many aspects—geographical and political as well as cultural—is Howard W. Odum and Harry Estill Moore, *American Regionalism: A Cultural-Historical Approach to National Integration* (1938). Odum and Moore find that "the older authentic literary regionalism stands in direct opposition to our premise of regionalism as a constituent part of the whole and as a tool for national integration of all parts of the nation" (vi). Part One traces the general rise and incidence in American regionalism; Part Two .provides a theoretical-historical account from the perspective of the social sciences; and Part Three enumerates and describes each region. Odum and Moore make a distinction between local color and regionalism. Local color they find to be a pejorative term, whereas regionalism has positive connotations. They also note, "Next to metropolitan regionalism and sectionalism the rise and characterization of American regionalism have perhaps been more often identified with literary regionalism than with anything else" (168).

An important early statement about regionalism from a perspective very different from that of Odum and Moore is made by Donald Davidson in his collection of essays, *The Attack on Leviathan: Regionalism and Nationalism in the United States* (1938). Davidson's premise is that in attacking Leviathan (the monolithic nationalism in writing), artists and others are "seeking . . . a definition of the terms on which America may have both the diversity and the unity that gives soundness to a tradition" (12). In a chapter entitled "Regionalism in the Arts," Davidson argues that artistic regionalism "is like the regionalism of the social scientists in so far as it is a new attempt to meet an old problem. . . . To one wing of American criticism regionalists seem to subscribe to some narrow and confining principle of art." Some regionalists, on the other hand, "are too ready to elevate the word regional . . . into a slogan and a panacea" (65). In an essay entitled "Regionalism and Nationalism in American Literature," Davidson concludes, "The national literature is the compound of the regional impulses, not antithetical to them, but embracing them and living in them as the roots, branch, and flower of its being" (232–33).

The Tennessee Valley Authority: A National Experiment in Regionalism (1938) by Clarence Lewis Hodge is a study of the significance of the Tennessee Valley

Authority as a new regional unit in the field of government. Hodge's central premise is that "regionalism is a trend the importance of which has been inadequately recognized by students in the field of government" (vii). Although this work does not address regionalism in popular culture as such, it is important for stressing the concept of regionalism as a major influence in people's lives.

Regionalism in America (1951), edited by Merrill Jensen, provides important historical information. Part One treats the development and use of the concept of regionalism from its beginnings in the eighteenth century until the present. Part Two offers an account of three historic regions of the United States: the South, Spanish Southwest, and Pacific Northwest. Part Three surveys regionalism in American culture and includes a survey of literature, architecture, painting, and linguistics; this section of Jensen's book is of special interest because it treats a variety of genres and disciplines in terms of their regional qualities. Part Four surveys contributions on those who have dealt with regionalism as a practical concept. Part Five, "The Limitations and the Promise of Regionalism" contains essays arguing for the continuation of discrete regions and for regionalism as leading to the integration of region.

Leo Lowenthal's *Literature, Popular Culture, and Society* (1961) provides in its introduction a historical account of popular culture, which Lowenthal says is "probably as old as human civilization" (xvii). Four chapters deal with literature as commodity, and the final chapter treats literature as art. Although not focused on regionalism, the historical account of popular culture is useful.

Regionalism and Beyond: Essays of Randall Stewart (1968), edited by George Core, excludes a consideration of popular literature but does treat American regions extensively, including New England and the Tidewater and Frontier South. Another work appearing in 1968, *Frontiers of American Culture*, edited by Ray B. Browne, Richard H. Crowder, Virgil L. Lokke, and William T. Stafford, contains an essay by Leslie Fiedler entitled "The New Western: Or, the Return of the Vanishing American," in which Fiedler posits that "geography in the United States is mythological. From the earliest times, at any rate, American writers have tended to define their own country—and, much of our literature has, consequently, tended to define itself—topologically, as it were, in terms of the four cardinal directions: mythicized North, South, East and West."[2] Another essay in the collection, Richard M. Dorson's "Folklore in Relation to American Studies," comments on the humor of the Old Southwest and finds that it is "clearly an expression of the popular culture. . . . One reason . . . this humorous literature disappeared from sight when its vogue had passed was its lack of recognition or even awareness by highbrow literary critics."[3] Dorson argues that the folklorist can correct the overly exclusive definition of southwest humor made by literary historians.

Challenges in American Culture (1970), edited by Ray B. Browne, Larry N. Landrum, and William K. Bottorff, is a potpourri of popular culture interests. Related to the study of regionalism in popular culture is an essay by Esther K. Birdsall, "The FWP and the Popular Press." Birdsall gives a brief history of the Federal Writers Project (FWP), which "spent 27,189,370 dollars to fill seven twelve foot shelves in the library of the Department of the Interior with publications ranging from the state guides to pamphlets of regional interest," and discusses contemporary reaction to the FWP.[4]

Raymond D. Gastil in *Cultural Regions of the United States* (1975) cites the great interest in regionalism in the 1930s. Gastil draws on studies of dialect, house styles and architecture, settlement patterns, and regional history and concludes that we have exaggerated the disappearance of regionalism.

Western Popular Theatre (1977), edited by David Mayer and Kenneth Richards, is the proceedings of a symposium sponsored by the Manchester University Department of Drama and contains a paper of interest to students of regionalism in popular culture. "The Wild West Exhibition and the Drama of Civilization" by William Brasmer traces the history of the development of the Wild West exhibit.

Jeffrey Schrank's *Snap, Crackle, and Popular Taste: The Illusion of Free Choice in America* (1977) contains a chapter entitled "The Packaged Environment: Illusions of Quality and Culture," which discusses kitsch as "a package of phony culture. Kitsch is something ordinary, cheap or simply mass produced but packaged to appear as culture or art with a capital A" (117). *Snap, Crackle, and Popular Taste* deals not so much with regionalism as with its replacement—a packaged sameness that may be found in every part of the United States.

Marshall W. Fishwick's *Springlore in Virginia* (1978) treats a very specific aspect of regionalism in popular culture: the culture that grows up around springs. Fishwick defines springlore as "what we know, think, and say about flowing waters, springs and spas, and the people who gather around them. Springs can and do serve as healing places, stage sets, touchstones, cyphers, icons—even tombstones of a class or culture" (2). Fishwick's book focuses on a close cluster of Virginia springs and discusses the culture of the South as it relates to these springs.

Another project that treats regionalism in popular culture is the special issue of the *Journal of Popular Culture* (1978), "In-Depth: Cultural Geography and Popular Culture," edited by Alvar Carlson. In an essay titled "The Contributions of Cultural Geographers to the Study of Popular Culture," Carlson points out that "cultural geographers, knowingly or unknowingly, have long had an interest in some aspects of popular culture, although the discipline of popular culture was formally established only within the last decade."[5] Following Carlson's essay are twelve articles treating topics ranging from a geographical examination of alcoholic drink in the United States, to massage parlors in the nation's capital.

Media-Made Dixie: The South in the American Imagination (1978) by Jack Temple Kirby is one of the few extended works specifically to evaluate regionalism in popular culture. Kirby states that the main object of his inquiry is the "*popular* historical images of the South since the advent of feature movies and annual best-seller lists" (xiv). Kirby surveys the images of the South in the mass communication media, including films, best-sellers, popular histories, school texts, television, music, radio, drama, sports, and advertising.

Several studies offer perceptive analyses of regionalism and art of the 1930s. Joseph S. Czestochowski's *John Steuart Curry and Grant Wood: A Portrait of Rural America* (1981) contains prints of representative art of the period and analyzes the role of these two artists. Mary Scholz Guedon's *Regionalist Art: Thomas Hart Benton, John Steuart Curry, and Grant Wood: A Guide to the Literature* (1982) is an annotated bibliography of regionalism in art during the 1920s and 1930s. M. Sue Kendall's *Rethinking Regionalism: John Steuart Curry and the Kansas Mural Controversy* (1986) uses a case study, the confrontation between the artist and the region that he depicted, to explore the relationship between art and culture and to "suggest several ways in which we need a rethinking of the phenomenon of regionalism in American art" (14).

Regionalism and the Female Imagination (1985), edited by Emily Toth, contains essays treating women writers and a variety of regions: New England, the Midwest, the Appalachian Mountain region, and the South. Of special interest are essays in a section of the book entitled "Psychology, Religion, and Regionalism." Works such as Toth's point the way to increasingly specialized treatments of culture and region.

Recasting America: Culture and Politics in the Age of Cold War (1989), edited by Lary May, contains essays that treat aspects of popular culture during the Cold War period. A notable essay by Erika Doss, "The Art of Cultural Politics: From Regionalism to Abstract Expressionism," traces the "remarkable shift . . . in American art from the anecdotal art of regionalism to the nonobjective art of abstract expressionism" (195).

Faulkner and Popular Culture (1990), edited by Doreen Fowler and Ann J. Abadie, includes papers from the 1988 conference on "Faulkner and Popular Culture." In the introduction Doreen Fowler notes, "If Faulkner's responses to mass culture were ambivalent, he nonetheless contributed to its cluttered content by promoting his own popular image." She continues, "On the one hand, Faulkner distrusted and even despised the vulgar meretriciousness of some formulations of popular culture; on the other, his art was rooted in the culture of the folk" (ix, xiii).

Sense of Place: American Regional Cultures (1990), edited by Barbara Allen and Thomas J. Schlereth, notes the recent emphasis on regionalism as an interdisciplinary field and brings together essays that the editors say are representative of the "mature stage of regional folklore scholarship. At the heart of each is a concern with how people construct a sense of place, of region, for themselves through cultural expression" (12).

Mapping American Culture (1992), edited by Wayne Franklin and Michael Steiner, contains papers presented at the 1990 meeting, "Place in American Culture," of the California American Studies Association. A central premise of this work is that American studies is, among other things, grounded in place.

Regionalism Reconsidered: New Approaches to the Field (1994), edited by David Jordan, contains essays contributing to the argument of the importance of regionalism today. Jordan asserts, "After languishing on the periphery of critical discourse for several decades, regionalism has recently begun to contribute a significant voice to some of the most urgent debates of our day. . . . regionalism is more than just nostalgic 'local color,' . . . it comprises a dynamic interplay of political, cultural, and psychological forces" (ix).

A Certain Slant of Light: Regionalism and the Form of Southern and Midwestern Fiction (1995) by David Marion Holman offers the argument that regionalism is not a limiting term. Holman writes, "I would define regional writers, as opposed to writers who are simply from a geographical region of the country, by the extent to which they participate in the communal psychology of the region—the extent to which their works manifest the values of the region and the extent to which those values inform the world of literature" (13).

Wanted Dead or Alive: The American West in Popular Culture (1996), edited by Richard Aquila, contains chapters focusing on different aspect of popular culture. Aquila asserts that "the pop culture West—like the American West itself—has played an important role in American life and thought. The pop culture West enables us to explore the development and meaning of the mythic West, which has been one of America's most enduring national myths" (11).

In *Reading the West: New Essays on the Literature of the American West* (1996), the editor, Michael Kowalewski, takes note of "the extraordinary resilience of popular visions of the West" and argues that "despite this seeming embarrassment of riches, a fully informed criticism of western writing as a whole has remained fitful and infrequent" (3, 5).

In *Dixie Rising: How the South Is Shaping American Values, Politics, and Culture* (1996), Peter Applebome argues that the South exerts enormous influence on American culture: "[T]he most striking aspect of American life at century's end—in a way that would have been utterly unimaginable three decades ago at the height of the civil rights era—is how much the country looks like the South" (6).

Breaking Boundaries: New Perspectives on Women's Regional Writing (1997), edited by Sherrie A. Inness and Diana Royer, is an essay collection dedicated, as the editors state, to reenvisioning and expending the traditional genre of realism. They note that the essays treat "the multiplicity of connections between women and regional writing" (1).

A Sense of Place: Re-Evaluating Regionalism in Canadian and American Writing (1998), edited by Christian Riegel, Herb Wyile, Karen Overbye, and Don Perkins, is a collection of essays containing an introduction in which the editors assert, "The image of regionalism . . . has been a divided one, especially because regionalism has been largely defined in relation to nationalism, sometimes as a centrifugal, even corrosive force undermining the cohesion of the nation-state, sometimes as a more organic alternative to the nation-state with its arbitrary borders" (x).

The sampling of books noted here demonstrates that, although regionalism and popular culture will continue to elude simple definitions, the topic remains of vital interest.

ANTHOLOGIES AND REPRINTS

Because regionalism in popular culture is such an all-inclusive topic, only a sampling of representative anthologies is treated. The following discussion is based on a sampling of works that contain local color and regional stories. A full listing, of course, would number in the hundreds. A selective list is included in the bibliography at the end of this chapter.

Some early regional anthologies include *American Local-Color Stories*, edited by Harry R. Warfel and G. Harrison Orians, which has selections from the works of thirty-eight writers. Kendall B. Taft's *Minor Knickerbockers: Representative Selections, with Introduction, Bibliography, and Notes* contains selections of the work of early New York writers. Robert Penn Warren's *A Southern Harvest: Short Stories by Southern Writers* is a good anthology of southern writing. Midwestern and western anthologies are represented by Benjamin S. Parker's *Poets and Poetry of Indiana*; Mary H. Marable and Elaine Boylan's *A Handbook of Oklahoma Writers*; Thomas M. Pearce and A. P. Thomason's *Southwesterners Write*; Stewart Hall Holbrook's *Promised Land: A Collection of Northwest Writing*; and Levette J. Davidson and Prudence Bostwick's *The Literature of the Rocky Mountain West, 1803–1903*.

John Steinbeck. Courtesy of the Library of Congress

Tall Tales of the Southwest: An Anthology of Southern and Southwestern Humor, 1830–1860, edited by Franklin J. Meine and published in 1930, collects stories written between 1830 and 1860 and provides brief biographical sketches and bibliographical information for each writer. Meine's introduction gives a historical account of the development of frontier humor. Of special interest is a summary of the range of subjects treated in southwest humor. A distinction must be made, of course, between humor of the old Southwest, as treated here, including the old southwest frontier—Alabama, Mississippi, western Georgia—and the modern Southwest.

Claude M. Simpson's *The Local Colorists: American Short Stories, 1857–1900* is a seminal study of the local color period. Representative writers of the Northeast, Midwest, South, and West are included, and Simpson's introduction to the collection provides what has become a standard definition of local color. A historical account of the rise of the local color movement is included as well.

Walter Blair's *Native American Humor*, first published in 1937 and published in a revised edition in 1960, is also a standard work. The first half of the book contains essays dealing with nineteenth-century developments in American humor, which Blair groups as follows: changing attitudes of humorists toward comic native characters, changes in humorous techniques, and changing reader attitudes toward this humor. Representative selections of Down East humor (1830–1867), humor of the old Southwest (1830–1867), literary comedians (1855–1900), local colorists (1869–1900), and writings of Mark Twain are included.

E. N. Brandt has edited *The Saturday Evening Post Reader of Western Stories*. The collection, published in 1960, contains eighteen short stories and two novelettes.

Brandt's preface catalogs the "many Wests—the West of the explorers, the West of the Mountain Men and the Indian Wars, the West of the wagon trains, the gold seekers, the homesteaders, the ranchers, and the cowboys. Each one has had its faithful chroniclers" [vii].

Another work published in 1960, *Southern Stories*, edited by Arlin Turner, chronologically presents stories by southern writers. In his introduction Turner provides a brief historical outline of the development of the short story in southern writing and says that, for southerners, "the regional affiliation is conspicuous" (xiii).

Representative of contemporary editions of the works of a single regional writer is M. Thomas Inge's edition of *Sut Lovingood's Yarns* by George Washington Harris (1966). Inge provides an extensive introduction to Harris' life and gives the publication history of his work. Inge considers Harris probably the foremost writer of the southwest humor school and includes in his edition the best of the Sut Lovingood sketches written between 1854 and 1869.

A book that is representative of the works that collect popular culture materials is Ray B. Browne's *The Alabama Folk Lyric: A Study in Origins and Media of Dissemination* (1979). Browne provides a working definition for the folk song and notes that the songs collected in this work are part of a collection of 2,500 ballads and songs made in the summers of 1951, 1952, and 1953, a collection that Browne describes as one of the largest ever assembled for any state. The 192 pieces included in this work (328, counting variants) represent all classes and geographical sections of the state.

American Women Regionalists, 1850–1910 is edited by Judith Fetterley and Marjorie Pryse (1992), who note in their introduction that "in creating this anthology, we are asserting the existence of a tradition among nineteenth-century American women writers that we term regionalism" (xi).

American Local Color Writing, 1880–1920, edited by Elizabeth Ammons and Valerie Rohy (1998), is divided by regions and contains an introduction that treats the development of a critical study of local color.

NOTES

1. John G. Cawelti, "Regionalism and Popular Culture: From Social Force to Symbolism," in *Dominant Symbols in Popular Culture*, edited by Ray B. Browne, Marshall W. Fishwick, and Kevin O. Browne (Bowling Green Ohio: Bowling Green State University Popular Press, 1990), 97–98, 105.

2. Leslie A. Fiedler, "The New Western: Or, The Return of the Vanishing American," in *Frontiers of American Culture*, ed. Ray B. Browne, Richard H. Crowder, Virgil L. Lokke, and William T. Stafford (Lafayette, Ind.: Purdue Research Foundation, 1968), 114.

3. Richard M. Dorson, "Folklore in Relation to American Studies," in *Frontiers of American Culture*, 183.

4. Esther K. Birdsall, "The FWP and the Popular Press," in *Challenges in American Culture*, ed. Ray B. Browne, Larry N. Landrum, and William W. Bottorff (Bowling Green, Ohio: Bowling Green University Popular Press, 1970), 101.

5. Alvar Carlson, "The Contribution of Cultural Geographers to the Study of Popular Culture," in "In Depth: Cultural Geography and Popular Culture," ed. Alvar Carlson, special issue, *Journal of Popular Culture* 11 (Spring 1978), 830.

BIBLIOGRAPHY

Books and Articles

Allen, Barbara, and Thomas J. Schlereth, eds. *Sense of Place: American Regional Cultures.* Lexington: University Press of Kentucky, 1990.

Applebome, Peter. *Dixie Rising: How the South Is Shaping American Values, Politics, and Culture.* New York: Times Books, 1996.

Aquila, Richard, ed. *Wanted Dead or Alive: The American West in Popular Culture.* Urbana: University of Illinois Press, 1996.

Arguimbau, Ellen, comp., and John A. Brennan, ed. *A Guide to Manuscript Collections: Western Historical Collections.* Boulder: Western Historical Collections, University of Colorado, 1977.

Bargainnier, Earl F. "The Falconhurst Series: A New Popular Image of the Old South." *Journal of Popular Culture* 10 (Fall 1976), 298–314.

Batteau, Allen W. *The Invention of Appalachia.* Tucson: University of Arizona Press, 1990.

Bigsby, C.W.E., ed. *Approaches to Popular Culture.* Bowling Green, Ohio: Bowling Green State University Popular Press, 1976.

Boney, Nash. "The American South." *Journal of Popular Culture* 10 (Fall 1976), 290–97.

Brinkmeyer, Robert H., Jr. "Modern American Regionalism." *Mississippi Quarterly* 47 (1994), 645–650.

Browne, Ray B. *The Alabama Folk Lyric: A Study in Origins and Media of Dissemination.* Bowling Green, Ohio: Bowling Green State University Popular Press, 1979.

Browne, Ray B., Richard H. Crowder, Virgil L. Lokke, and William T. Stafford, eds. *Frontiers of American Culture.* Lafayette, Ind.: Purdue Research Foundation, 1968.

Browne, Ray B., Marshall W. Fishwick, and Kevin O. Browne, eds. *Dominant Symbols in Popular Culture.* Bowling Green, Ohio: Bowling Green State University Popular Press, 1990.

Browne, Ray B., Larry N. Landrum, and William K. Bottorff, eds. *Challenges in American Culture.* Bowling Green, Ohio: Bowling Green State University Popular Press, 1970.

Burgess, Jacquelin, and John R. Gold, eds. *Geography, the Media and Popular Culture.* London: Croom Helm, 1985.

Campbell, Donna M. *Resisting Regionalism: Gender and Naturalism in American Fiction, 1885–1915.* Athens: Ohio University Press, 1997.

Carlson, Alvar W. "Cultural Geography and Popular Culture." *Journal of Popular Culture* 9 (Fall 1975), 482–83.

Carlson, Alvar W. ed. "In-Depth: Cultural Geography and Popular Culture." *Journal of Popular Culture* 11 (Spring 1978), 829–997 (12 articles).

Core, George, ed. *Regionalism and Beyond: Essays of Randall Stewart.* Nashville, Tenn.: Vanderbilt University Press, 1968.

Cox, James M. "Regionalism: A Diminished Thing." In *Columbia Literary History of the United States,* ed. Emory Elliot. New York: Columbia University Press, 1988, 761–784.

Czestochowski, Joseph S. *John Steuart Curry and Grant Wood: A Portrait of Rural America*. Columbia: University of Missouri Press, 1981.

Davidson, Donald. *The Attack on Leviathan: Regionalism and Nationalism in the United States*. Chapel Hill: University of North Carolina Press, 1938.

Elliot, Emory, ed. *Columbia Literary History of the United States*. New York: Columbia University Press, 1988.

Engler, Richard E., Jr. *The Challenge of Diversity*. New York: Harper and Row, 1964.

English, Thomas H. *Roads to Research: Distinguished Library Collections of the Southeast*. Athens: University of Georgia Press, 1968.

Fetterley, Judith. " 'Not in the Least American': Nineteenth-Century Literary Realism." *College English* 56 (December 1994), 877–895.

Fishwick, Marshall W. *Springlore in Virginia*. Bowling Green, Ohio: Bowling Green State University Popular Press, 1978.

Fiske, Horace Spencer. *Provincial Types in American Fiction*. Chautauqua, N.Y.: Chautauqua Press, 1907.

Fowler, Doreen, and Ann J. Abadie, eds. *Faulkner and Popular Culture*. Jackson: University Press of Mississippi, 1990.

Franklin, Wayne, and Michael Steiner, eds. *Mapping American Culture*. Iowa City: University of Iowa Press, 1992.

Gastil, Raymond D. *Cultural Regions of the United States*. Seattle: University of Washington Press, 1975.

Griffin, Larry J. and Don H. Doyle. *The South as an American Problem*. Athens: University of Georgia Press, 1995.

Guedon, Mary Scholz. *Regionalist Art: Thomas Hart Benton, John Steuart Curry, and Grant Wood: A Guide to the Literature*. Metuchen, N.J.: Scarecrow Press, 1982.

Hodge, Clarence Lewis. *The Tennessee Valley Authority: A National Experiment in Regionalism*. New York: American University Press, 1938. Reprint. New York: Russell and Russell, 1968.

Holman, David Marion. *A Certain Slant of Light: Regionalism and the Form of Southern and Midwestern Fiction*. Baton Rouge: Louisiana State University Press, 1995.

Howard, June. "Unravellling Regions, Unsettling Periods: Sarah Orne Jewett and American Literary History." *American Literature* 68 (June 1996), 365–384.

Howell, J. B., ed. *Special Collections in Libraries of the Southeast*. Jackson, Miss.: Howick House, 1978.

Inness, Sherrie A., and Diana Royer, eds. *Breaking Boundaries: New Perspectives on Women's Regional Writing*. Iowa City: University of Iowa Press, 1997.

Jensen, Merrill, ed. *Regionalism in America*. Madison: University of Wisconsin Press, 1951.

Jordan, David. *Regionalism Reconsidered: New Approaches to the Field*. New York: Garland, 1994.

Kendall, M. Sue. *Rethinking Regionalism: John Steuart Curry and the Kansas Mural Controversy*. Washington, D.C.: Smithsonian Institution Press, 1986.

Kirby, Jack Temple. *Media-Made Dixie: The South in the American Imagination*. Baton Rouge: Louisiana State University Press, 1978. Rev. ed. Athens: University of Georgia Press, 1987.

Kowalewski, Michael, ed. *Reading the West: New Essays on the Literature of the American West*. Cambridge: Cambridge University Press, 1996.

———. "Writing in Place: The New American Realism." *American Literary History* 6 (1994), 171–183.

Leary, Lewis. *Articles on American Literature, 1900–1950*. Durham, N.C.: Duke University Press, 1954.

———. *Articles on American Literature, 1950–1967*. Durham, N.C.: Duke University Press, 1970.

———. *Articles on American Literature, 1968–1975*. Durham, N.C.: Duke University Press, 1979.

Lowenthal, Leo. *Literature, Popular Culture, and Society*. Englewood Cliffs, N.J.: Prentice-Hall, 1961.

Marsden, Michael T., ed. "National Finding List of Popular Culture Holdings Special Collections." *Popular Culture Association Newsletter* 6 (March 1977), 2–6.

May, Lary, ed. *Recasting America: Culture and Politics in the Age of Cold War*. Chicago: University of Chicago Press, 1989.

Mayer, David, and Kenneth Richard, eds. *Western Popular Theatre*. London: Methuen, 1977.

McWilliams, Carey. *The New Regionalism in American Literature*. Seattle: University of Washington Book Store, 1930. Reprint. Folcroft, Pa.: Folcroft Library Editions, 1974.

Odum, Howard W., and Harry Estill Moore. *American Regionalism: A Cultural-Historical Approach to National Integration*. New York: Holt, 1938.

Riegel, Christian, Herb Wyile, Karen Overbye, and Don Perkins, eds. *A Sense of Place: Re-Evaluating Regionalism in Canadian and American Writing*. Edmonton: University of Alberta Press, 1998.

Rubin, Louis D., Jr. *A Bibliographical Guide to the Study of Southern Literature*. Baton Rouge: Louisiana State University Press, 1969.

Schrank, Jeffrey. *Snap, Crackle, and Popular Taste: The Illusion of Free Choice in America*. New York: Dell, 1977.

Simpson, Claude M., ed. *The Local Colorists: American Short Stories, 1857–1900*. New York: Harper and Row, 1960.

Spiller, Robert E., Willard Thorp, Thomas H. Johnson, Henry Seidel Canby, and Richard Ludwig, eds. *Literary History of the United States*. 2 vols. 3rd rev. ed. New York: Macmillan, 1963.

Stern, Jerome. "Florida as Popular Culture." *Journal of Regional Cultures* 4 (Spring/Summer 1984), 1–14.

Taylor, J. Golden, ed. *A Literary History of the American West*. Fort Worth: Texas Christian University Press, 1987.

Toth, Emily, ed. *Regionalism and the Female Imagination: A Collection of Essays*. New York: Human Sciences Press, 1985.

Twelve Southerners. *I'll Take My Stand: The South and the Agrarian Tradition*. New York: Harper and Brothers, 1930.

Vance, Mary A., ed. *Regionalism: Monographs*. Monticello, Ill.: Vance Bibliographies, 1987.

Watkins, Floyd C. *In Time and Place: Some Origins of American Fiction*. Athens: University of Georgia Press, 1977.

Williams, Jerry T., ed. *Southern Literature, 1968–1975: A Checklist of Scholarship*. Boston: G. K. Hall, 1978.

Wilson, Charles Reagan, ed. *The New Regionalism*. Jackson: University Press of Mississippi, 1998.

Wilson, Charles Reagan, and William Ferris, co-eds., and Ann J. Abadie and Mary L. Hart, assoc. eds., *Encyclopedia of Southern Culture*. Chapel Hill: University of North Carolina Press, 1989.

Wolfe, Margaret Ripley. "The Southern Lady: Long Suffering Counterpart of the Good Ole' Boy." *Journal of Popular Culture* 1 (Summer 1977), 18–27.

Young, Margaret Labash, Harold Chester Young, and Anthony T. Kruzas, eds. *Subject Directory of Special Libraries and Information Centers*. Detroit: Gale Research, 1975.

Anthologies

Ammons, Elizabeth, and Valerie Rohy, eds. *American Local Color Writing, 1880–1920*. New York: Penguin Books, 1998.

Blair, Walter. *Native American Humor*. New York: American Book, 1937. Rev. ed. San Francisco: Chandler, 1960.

Brandt, E. N., ed. *The Saturday Evening Post Reader of Western Stories*. Garden City, N.Y.: Doubleday, 1960.

Browne, Ray B., ed. *The Alabama Folk Lyric: A Study in Origins and Media of Dissemination*. Bowling Green, Ohio: Bowling Green State University Popular Press, 1979.

Davidson, Levette J., and Forester Blake, comps. *Rocky Mountain Tales*. Norman: University of Oklahoma Press, 1947.

Davidson, Levette J., and Prudence Bostwick, comps. *The Literature of the Rocky Mountain West, 1803–1903*. Caldwell, Idaho: Caxton Printers, 1939.

Fetterley, Judith, and Marjorie Pryse, eds. *American Women Regionalists, 1850–1910*. New York: W. W. Norton, 1992.

Harris, George Washington. *Sut Lovingood's Yarns*. Ed. M. Thomas Inge. New Haven, Conn.: College and University Press, 1966.

Holbrook, Stewart Hall, ed. *Promised Land: A Collection of Northwest Writing*. New York: McGraw-Hill, 1945.

Marabale, Mary H., and Elaine Boylan, eds. *A Handbook of Oklahoma Writers*. Norman: University of Oklahoma Press, 1939.

Meine, Franklin J., ed. *Tall Tales of the Southwest: An Anthology of Southern and Southwestern Humor, 1830–1860*. 3rd ed. New York: Alfred A. Knopf, 1946.

Parker, Benjamin S., ed. *Poets and Poetry of Indiana*. New York: Silver, Burdett, 1900.

Pearce, Thomas M., and A. P. Thomason, comps. *Southwesterners Write*. Albuquerque: University of New Mexico Press, 1947.

Simpson, Claude M., ed. *The Local Colorists: American Short Stories, 1857–1900*. New York: Harper and Row, 1960.

Taft, Kendall B., ed. *Minor Knickerbockers: Representative Selections, with Introduction, Bibliography, and Notes*. New York: American Book, 1947.

Turner, Arlin, ed. *Southern Stories*. 2nd ed. New York: Holt, Rinehart, and Winston, 1965.

Warfel, Harry R., and G. Harrison Orians, eds. *American Local-Color Stories*. New York: American Book, 1941. Reprint, New York: Cooper Square, 1970.
Warren, Robert Penn, ed. *A Southern Harvest: Short Stories by Southern Writers*. Boston: Houghton Mifflin, 1937.

Periodicals

Journal of American Culture. Bowling Green, Ohio, 1979– .
Journal of Popular Culture. Bowling Green, Ohio, 1967– .
Journal of Regional Cultures. Bowling Green, Ohio, 1981– .
Studies in Popular Culture. Tallahassee, Fla., 1978– .

ROMANCE FICTION

Kay Mussell

Romance fiction comprises a group of related literary genres defined by a focus on courtship or marriage, in which the course of a love story provides both the structure and the value system for the plot. Because the issues inherent in love stories are traditionally women's concerns, romance fiction is almost entirely a female form of escape reading. The heroine's quest for fulfillment through a lasting marriage has been dramatized in fiction extensively from Samuel Richardson's *Pamela* (1741), to the most recent Silhouette romance; yet, despite superficial changes, the shape and conventions of the popular romance have remained similar over time, even in an era where women's experience is significantly shaped by middle-class feminism.

Romances frequently have close affinities to other kinds of popular novels: the gothic, historical fiction, mysteries, romantic suspense, science fiction, fantasy, and thrillers or novels of adventure, many explicitly incorporating elements from other genres in their plots. Historical romances relate the events of history from the vantage point of a female protagonist with a focus on her relationships with men. In gothic romances, the love story is intertwined with a story of a woman's peril and finally reaffirms the romantic belief in love as cure for, and defense against, evil. Particularly popular subgenres of the romance in the 1990s were the "futuristic" and "paranormal" romances, which derive from science fiction and fantasy fiction. Also popular are "time travel" romances, which feature relationships between heroes and heroines from different periods of time. A few romance novels, more accurately called "anti-romances," invert the love plot while reinforcing the assumptions of the form. In anti-romances, the value structure is unchanged, but the heroine behaves in such a way that she cannot be rewarded with a good marriage. These, too, are romances, although they serve as cautionary tales rather than as models to be emulated. Examples include such well-known books as *Gone with the Wind* and *Forever Amber*.

A major difficulty in understanding the romance is that it is such an ephemeral form. It is particularly hard to find romances published before 1900 because so many left very little trace, and some cannot be identified as romances from a mere title or author's name. Many early romances have certainly been lost forever as the last cracked and crumbling copy, published by a local printer as a favor to a neighboring author, has disappeared in the trash after an attic was cleaned. But even contemporary romances may be difficult to find once the initial print run is exhausted, since most romances are issued in a single printing and rarely go back to press. Until recently, romances were not routinely reviewed and almost never appeared on best-seller lists. Although public libraries frequently buy hardback romances, they do not always acquire paperback originals; and when they do, these books are not always cataloged as part of the collection. Scholars searching for out-of-print romances must rely on used-book stores or on-line book services (such as New and Previously Owned Books, http://www.newandusedbooks.com/). An especially convenient source for older romances is the on-line auction Web site eBay, which frequently features hardback romances published since the late nineteenth century as well as lightly read paperbacks published more recently.

Scholars studying the romance always face the problem of how to define the scope of their work. How many books must be read to define a portion of the field? How can those books be obtained? Which books or authors are most important? What selection criteria should be used, and how do the criteria then shape analysis and conclusions? Many studies are limited by the writer's assumption that since romances are "all alike," only a few need to be read in order to draw conclusions about all romances. The more useful studies are those that concentrate on one or more subgenres in order to define and evaluate the varieties of romance.

HISTORICAL OUTLINE

Romance novels from England were imported to America in the eighteenth century, and some were reprinted by American printers, including Benjamin Franklin, who issued an edition of Samuel Richardson's *Pamela* (1741) as early as 1744. The first romance to become widely popular in America, however, was Susanna Haswell Rowson's *Charlotte Temple*, one of the great best-sellers of literary history. First published in England in 1791, the novel's American edition was printed in Philadelphia in 1794. It went through numerous editions throughout the nineteenth century and, as recently as the early twentieth century, was still in print for general readers. In the past decade, it has returned to print in at least two paperback editions designed for classroom use. A classic seduction story, *Charlotte Temple* tells the tale of a young English girl seduced and abandoned by an officer. He lures her to America, where she dies giving birth to their child. Although the seduction novel was primarily a British form, American authors also wrote them. Hannah W. Foster's *The Coquette* (1797), like *Charlotte Temple*, has attracted the attention of scholars and has been reprinted for classroom use. Other examples are Eliza Vicery's *Emily Hamilton* (1803) and several anonymous novels, such as *Fidelity Rewarded* (1796) and *Amelia, or the Faithless Briton* (1798). After the early nineteenth century, a full-blown seduction story was hard to find. The tensions of the precarious position of "fallen women" were still important in later romance novels, but the conventions of the seduction story—the explicit warnings about male predation, the overt if somewhat euphemistic story about sexuality—were less significant as ingredients of romance fiction.

Another popular form of the romance in the late eighteenth and early nineteenth centuries derived from the gothic novel. Although the eighteenth-century gothic novels were roughly synonymous with the novel of horror, a subgenre focused on women beset by terrors in a sensationalized romantic context. In the worldview of the female gothic novel, heroines are cast as victims in a world of danger and deception; but through the demonstration of conventional female virtues, the victim proves herself worthy of the love of the hero, who becomes her deliverer from peril. The gothic villain, who manipulates terrifying props and produces fear and danger, is defeated by the power of true love. Among the notable American titles are Isaac Mitchell's *The Asylum, or Alonzo and Melissa* (1804) and Sally Woods' *Julia, or the Illuminated Baron* (1800). Other early American gothic romance writers included Ann Eliza Bleecker and the women who used the pseudonyms "A Lady of Massachusetts" and "A Lady of Philadelphia."

From the 1820s until after the Civil War, romance fiction was dominated by a group of women novelists usually called the "domestic sentimentalists." They included such writers as Catharine Maria Sedgwick, Lydia Maria Child, Fanny Fern (Ruth Payton Willis), Mary Jane Holmes, Ann Sophia Stephens, and Maria Susanna Cummins. The work of these women has been more thoroughly documented than that of most other romance writers, particularly by feminist scholars. Some works by these writers have been returned to print in paperback editions, including Sedgwick's *Hope Leslie* (1827), Child's *Hobomok* (1824), and Cummins' *The Lamplighter* (1854), notably in the American Women Writers series of Rutgers University Press. A good sample of work by many of these authors appears in *Hidden Hands*, an anthology edited by Lucy M. Freibert and Barbara A. White. Although critics disagree about the meaning of "domestic sentimentalism," the novels are often structured as love stories, and almost all the heroines are married, happily, at the end of the books. Between the beginning and end, males may be less in evidence than are females, as the heroines spend their time solving domestic difficulties and improving their characters, saving souls, learning to be "true women," and sometimes having adventures. But despite the trials and adventures of these novels, most end in reconciliation with the heroine's place in a good marriage.

After the Civil War, romances were found among dime novel series and story papers, as well as in full-length novels, which were frequently serialized in newspapers and magazines before book publication. Augusta Jane Evans Wilson's *St. Elmo* (1867) and novels by Mrs. E.D.E.N. Southworth were especially popular. Works by both authors are now in print. The prolific Southworth, whose work incorporated many gothic elements, wrote such well-known romances as *The Hidden Hand* (1859) and *The Curse of Clifton* (1852). Bertha M. Clay was the pseudonym for a group of writers, beginning with Charlotte M. Breame, who wrote romances for Street and Smith's dime novel series. Other writers of dime novel romances included Charlotte May Stanley, Laura Jean Libbey, Ida Reade Allen, and Emma Garrison Jones. Around the turn of the century, historical romances were common, including work by Mary Johnston. Her *To Have and to Hold* (1900), one of the most popular historical novels in American publishing history, was set in Jamestown; *The Fortunes of Garin* is a medieval romance. Several authors of

Scene from the film *Gone with the Wind*, 1939. Kobal Collection/Selznick/MGM

anti-Mormon novels portraying the evils of polygamy also adopted romance conventions in telling their stories.

Lists of best-sellers are available from 1895 onward, so it becomes an easier task to identify romance novels that did well in the marketplace. Those books that did not sell widely enough to appear in these compilations are still hard to retrieve, but enough information is available to indicate that the love story remained in style. In the first half of the century, Kathleen Norris' novels of family and domestic drama were especially popular, as were Mary Roberts Rinehart's romantic mysteries and Grace Livingston Hill's novels of romance and traditional religious faith. Other popular writers included Temple Bailey, Maisie Greig, and Berta Ruck. The racier books of Fannie Hurst and Faith Baldwin also sold well, as did the romantic suspense novels of Emilie Loring. Many of these authors' works were reprinted by Triangle Books, which specialized in inexpensive hardback editions. Another well-known writer was E. M. Hull, whose books about Arab sheiks and Anglo women were more openly erotic than most other romances. Her best-known book, *The Sheik* (1919), was made into a popular film with Rudolph Valentino. In addition, romances by Ethel M. Dell, Elinor Glyn, and Gene Stratton Porter attracted many readers.

Only a very few romances, however, were great best-sellers. An exception was *Gone with the Wind* (1936), which appealed to a much wider audience than most—to men as well as to women. After *Gone with the Wind*, the next romance sensation was Daphne du Maurier's *Rebecca* (1938), followed in 1944 by Kathleen Windsor's *Forever Amber*. Another romance of the period was Marcia Davenport's family saga *The Valley of Decision* (1942). In each of these, the traditional happy ending of the romance is either missing or flawed. It appears probable that anti-romances hold more appeal for male readers than do more straightforward love stories, and wider readership no doubt accounts for higher sales.

The post–World War II period has been very fruitful for the popular romance novel in America. Particularly popular between the 1950s and the 1970s were British or Commonwealth authors Mary Stewart, Victoria Holt, Evelyn Anthony, Dorothy Eden, Georgette Heyer, and Barbara Cartland, as well as Americans Anya Seton and Phyllis Whitney. Stewart wrote novels of romantic suspense with contemporary settings; important titles include *My Brother Michael* (1959) and *Nine Coaches Waiting* (1958). Holt (who also wrote historical romances as Jean Plaidy and Philippa Carr) set off a boom in modern gothic romances with the publication of *Mistress of Mellyn* (1960), a Victorian romance that paid homage to both *Jane Eyre* and *Rebecca*. Evelyn Anthony's early work was largely in historical romance, but she also wrote romances about espionage and terrorism. Dorothy Eden began as a gothic romance writer and later wrote historical romances. Georgette Heyer was the creator of one of the most popular contemporary subgenres—the Regency romance, set in the early nineteenth century in Britain. Regencies are short, comic romances that frequently draw on the world of Jane Austen. Barbara Cartland, a prolific writer, also made her mark in the Regency romance but without Heyer's originality or flair. Seton specialized in heavily researched historical novels that interpreted British or American history from a female perspective; especially noteworthy were *Katherine* (1954), *The Winthrop Woman* (1958), and *Devil Water* (1962). Whitney wrote romantic mysteries with strong gothic overtones, often with American settings. Other popular historical romance writers of the 1950s and 1960s were Margaret Campbell Barnes and Jan Westcott.

Romance genres changed again in the mid-1970s with the emergence of a new generation of American writers who dramatically expanded the range of subjects and the conventions appropriate to the romance—most notably in a more permissive view of female sexuality. The first major change emerged with a new subgenre, called variously the "bodice-ripper," "sweet-savage romance," or "erotic romance." Represented by two wildly popular authors, Rosemary Rogers and Kathleen Woodwiss, these new romances quickly earned a following of readers. While sensation and eroticism had shaped earlier romances, Rogers and Woodwiss altered the conventions in three important ways. First, the heroines were allowed premarital sex without incurring the punishment that was usually meted out to earlier heroines who transgressed the sexual code for women. Within a few years, even the most conservative publisher of romances, Mills and Boon/Harlequin, had allowed authors to feature some heroines whose sexual experience was not a bar to a satisfying conclusion in marriage. Second, the sexual acts were described much more fully than in the past, although the euphemistic treatment still fell far short of the specificity of pornography. Third and most controversial, there was often an element of violence in the sexual relationships, with the occasional outright rape and frequent physical overpowering of the heroine during the act. Romance writers today still struggle with this issue, although most writers deny that violence has a role in the portrayals of sexuality in their books.

The second major change was the result of business decisions and competition among publishers in the late 1970s and early 1980s. Harlequin Romances were inexpensive paperback original novels published in Canada by arrangement with

Mills and Boon, based in London, which acquired and edited the books for publication. With the exception of American Janet Dailey, all the authors were from Britain or the Commonwealth countries, as were the settings of the books themselves. The American firm of Simon & Schuster held the contract for distributing Harlequin novels in the United States. In 1980, Simon & Schuster broke with Harlequin and inaugurated a competing series called Silhouette Books. In addition to attracting some of Mills and Boon/Harlequin's longtime authors, Silhouette cultivated a new generation of American writers. Other American firms, such as Dell, Jove, and Bantam, jumped into the competition, and for a few years the romance market became glutted with series romances. As publishers vied for the audience, competition led to the emergence of a new generation of romance authors and a rapid change in the level of sophistication and complexity of the plots, especially in portrayals of sexuality but also in character types, settings, and topics. Category romances that confronted difficult personal crises proliferated, including books about infertility, rape recovery, widowhood, and illegitimacy. The most intense competition ended in 1984, when Harlequin and Silhouette merged, leaving a field that was less competitive but far more open to new and controversial subject matter.

Since the early 1980s, the romance genres have continued to change, and today they represent a significant portion of the market for paperback novels and a growing portion of hardbacks. Although romances were almost never found on major best-seller lists in the past, now the most popular authors—such as Nora Roberts, Danielle Steel, Jayne Ann Krentz, Judith McNaught, and others—achieve recognition on those lists with regularity. The field is divided into a variety of subgenres. Category romances, primarily published by Harlequin and Silhouette, account for a large part of the monthly output. Single-title romances are divided into contemporary, historical (with its subgenre of Regency romances), and futuristic or paranormal. Any of these varieties can incorporate gothic, mystery, or adventure conventions as well. Among the more innovative romance writers of the past decade are Jo Beverley, Mary Jo Putney, and Mary Balogh in Regency romance; Sue Civil-Brown (Rachel Lee), Eileen Dreyer (Kathleen Korbel), and Barbara Samuel (Ruth Wind) in category romance; Susan Krinard in paranormal romance; Sandra Kitt in multiethnic romance; Diana Gabaldon in time-travel; and Jennifer Crusie in humorous romance.

The drama of courtship and marriage has had a strong hold on the imaginations of many women readers for two centuries. The specifics of the plot have changed over the years, but the shape of the narrative and the value structure have altered relatively little. Although heroines of contemporary series romances may now be allowed a wider range of sexual experience and professional ambition, at heart they remain as committed to marriage and family as were their predecessors.

REFERENCE WORKS

Only a few reference works are dedicated to romance novels, but some general reference sources are useful, especially for the periods before the 1950s. Since a major task for any researcher studying the romance is the identification of relevant novels, both traditional reference sources and general studies of American fiction can be helpful. An important tool for identifying early romance novels is a twenty-five-volume guide entitled *Chronological Bibliography of English Language Fiction in the Library of Congress through 1950*, subdivided into three separate and complete bibliographies compiled by R. Glenn Wright and composed of reproduced cards from the Library of Congress shelf list. The sets are organized, respectively, by author, title, and chronology; and because the cards themselves are reproduced, they contain much information that might not be available in a standard bibliographical format. The guides are organized in each set by nationality and include indexes to translators and translations. For the early period, when few novels were being published in America, the chronological bibliography is especially valuable. Several general studies of eighteenth- or early nineteenth-century American fiction provide information about popular novels and include romances. Henri Petter's *The Early American Novel* contains valuable bibliographical sections for works before 1820, including synopses of plots. Cathy N. Davidson's *Revolution and the Word* also includes information on titles and authors of the period. Nina Baym's *Woman's Fiction: A Guide to Novels by and about Women in America 1820–1870* contains useful bibliographical materials for the era of the domestic sentimentalists.

A good reference guide to contemporary romance authors and titles, James Vinson's *Twentieth-Century Romance and Gothic Writers* was published in 1982. The third and larger edition, *Twentieth-Century Romance and Historical Writers*, edited by Aruna Vasudevan and published in 1994, is much larger and more comprehensive. *Twentieth-Century Crime and Mystery Writers*, edited by John M. Reilly, includes modern gothic writers such as Joan Aiken, Dorothy Eden, Elizabeth Peters, Phyllis Whitney, and Mary Stewart. Eileen Fallon's *Words of Love: A Complete Guide to Romance Fiction* (1984) contains chapters on romance history, the "romance boom," subgenres, resources for writers, information on writers and pseudonyms, and a bibliography.

A major resource for the history of writing by American women is *The Oxford Companion to Women's Writing in the United States*, edited by Cathy N. Davidson and Linda Wagner-Martin. The volume contains many useful essays and bibliographical references despite its lack of emphasis on popular writers and popular fiction. The entry on "romance novels" was written by Linda K. Christian-Smith. Entries on writers who used romance conventions include Lydia Maria Child, Maria Susanna Cummins, Augusta Jane Evans, Hannah Webster Foster, Fannie Hurst, Laura Jean Libbey, Margaret Mitchell, Mary Roberts Rinehart, Susanna Rowson, Catharine Maria Sedgwick, E.D.E.N. Southworth, and Susan Warner. The book contains considerable information on multicultural women's writing, including Amy Ling's entry on Winnifred Eaton, who wrote romance novels in the early twentieth century under the "Japanese" pseudonym of Onoto Watanna. Other entries that pertain to romance novels include "gothic fiction," "domestic fiction," "epistolary novel," "sentimental novel," and "southern women's writing." Entries on "readership" and "beginnings of the novel" document the importance of women writers and readers in the history of American fiction.

A particularly rich resource is Mary Ellen Zuckerman's *Sources on the History of Women's Magazines, 1792–1960: An Annotated Bibliography*. Since many magazines intended for women published romantic stories, popular authors frequently wrote for them. Women's magazines have not been studied thoroughly, and Zuckerman's excellent compilation is a good place to start. *Fiction in American Magazines before 1800: An Annotated Catalogue* by Edward W. R. Pitcher is a comprehensive bibliography of fiction in seventy-six American magazines published before 1800. The annotations refer to the sources of the items but only rarely to content or plot. Some gothic or romantic stories are evident from the context, so the volume is a useful finding guide.

Information for romance fans can also be of use to scholars. *Romantic Times* and *Affaire de Coeur* are monthly magazines for romance readers, which include information on favorite authors and upcoming titles. *Romance Reader's Handbook*, compiled by Melinda Helfer, Kathryn Falk, and Kathe Robin, includes information on romance writers' pseudonyms, recommends favorite books to read and bookstores that are romance-friendly, and provides miscellaneous information on romance writers. Peggy J. Jaegly's *Romantic Hearts: A Personal Reference for Romance Readers*, now in its third edition, is a large reference compendium of pseudonyms, authors, and titles. It also includes some short author profiles.

Genreflecting: A Guide to Reading Interests in Genre Fiction, originally published in 1982, has appeared in three additional revised editions. The romance section is fairly similar in each edition, with timely updates consisting of brief commentary on types of romances and listing selected annotated titles under such categories as "womanly romances," "soap opera," "doctor and nurse," "romantic-suspense," "historical romances," "historical novels," "sagas," "period fiction," "glitz and glamour," "gothic," "sweet and savage," "spicy," "supernatural," "time travel," and "inspirational." It also contains a bibliographic section on romance critiques and a list of publications for romance readers. Diana Tixier Herald updates the fiction listings regularly with new on-line reviews posted at the Genreflecting site on the World Wide Web (http://www.genrefluent.com/).

The Twilight Publishing Group Ltd. (c/o Central Boursource, 14817 Central Woods Avenue, Baton Rouge La. 70818) publishes finding guides for fans looking for complete lists of books by romance authors. *Essence of Romance* features more than 5,000 writers and a total of more than 25,000 romance titles, including lists of pseudonyms and bibliographical information on multiauthored romance anthologies. *Essence of Romance Update V* supplements the original volume with romance releases through December 1996. Other Twilight publications include *Romance by the Number* (10,000 titles issued in romance series), *The Story Continues II* ("series, spinoffs, sequels, sagas, related characters"), and *Romance by the Title* (more than 30,000 titles arranged alphabetically). The authors of all these volumes are Pattie Blouin, Claire Gipson, and Helen Gipson.

The two volumes of *Enchanted Journeys beyond the Imagination: An Annotated Bibliography of Fantasy, Futuristic, Supernatural, and Time-Travel Romances*, by Susan W. Bontly and Carol J. Sheridan, identify more than 700 books in the emerging subgenres of "futuristic" and "paranormal" romance. These subgenres have captured increasing market segments in recent years and have influenced category romance lines as well. Categories include fantasy ("myths, legends, and make-believe such as fairies, leprechauns, unicorns"), futuristic ("earth-related," "other worlds," and "UFO"), supernatural ("angel or guardian angel," "ghost," "powers," "vampire or werewolf," "witchcraft or magic"), and time travel (by historical period). A paperback combining the two volumes was issued in July 1996.

Reference books compiled by librarian Kristin Ramsdell are particularly useful to researchers. *Happily Ever After: A Guide to Reading Interests in Romance Fiction* offers a brief history of the genre, annotated lists of novels by subgenre, and a bibliography of criticism. A similar, but more recent, work is *Romance Fiction: A Guide to the Genre*. Ramsdell's two volumes of *What Romance Do I Read Next? A Reader's Guide to Recent Romance Fiction* are guides for romance readers. *Collecting Romance Novels* by Dawn Reno and Jacque Tiegs is a useful little volume aimed at readers who want to become collectors. The book includes guides to finding old romances, values for some books by especially popular writers, a discussion of romance series and categories, a long list of authors and their pseudonyms, advice on how to evaluate used romances, and suggestions for keeping track of a collection.

RESEARCH COLLECTIONS

The most comprehensive research collection on contemporary romance fiction is in the Popular Culture Library at Bowling Green State University. The collection includes thousands of romance novels in all genres as well as reference guides, critical works, manuscripts, correspondence, and ephemera. Since 1996, the Popular Culture Library has been the repository for the Romance Writers of America archives; contributions from contemporary romance writers make this collection particularly valuable to researchers.

The Library of Congress has many examples of romance novels throughout the collection. The Rare Book Room hosts a large collection of dime novels with many romance writers represented, including E.D.E.N. Southworth and Bertha M. Clay. Other dime novel collections are located at the University of California at Los Angeles, Yale University, the New York Public Library, and New York University. Northern Illinois University, DeKalb, has the Albert Johannsen Collection of 1,100 cataloged volumes and some related material; the University of Alberta, Canada, collection is especially strong in penny dreadfuls and gothics. The Hess Collection at the University of Minnesota holds 70,000 dime novels. Several special collections in the New York Public Library include popular fiction. The Berg Collection of English and American literature is excellent; the Rare Book Division offers both the Frank P. O'Brien Collection of Beadle Dime Novels and a chapbook file. The Arents Collection of books in parts also includes romances.

Manuscripts and personal papers of romance writers are frequently difficult to find, although some library collections reflect scholarly interest in popular culture materials. The Special Collections of the University of Virginia Alderman Library hold materials relating to such nineteenth-century writers as E.D.E.N. Southworth, Susanna Rowson, Catharine Maria Sedgwick, Lydia Maria Child, Susan Warner, Amelia E. Barr, Mary Johnston, Frances Parkinson Keyes, Mary Jane Holmes, Maria Susanna Cummins, and Augusta Jane Evans Wilson. Boston University's Mugar Memorial Library collects literary and personal papers, correspondence, and published articles by and about modern published authors, including materials on such romance writers as Barbara Cartland, Emilie Loring, Anya Seton, and Phyllis Whitney. Ellen B. Brandt, a biographer of Susanna Haswell Rowson, notes that the best collection of Rowson material is at the American Antiquarian Society, although she also found items at the University of Pennsylvania Rare Book Room, the Pennsylvania Historical Society, the Philadelphia Free

Scene from *The Sheik*, 1921. Kobal Collection/
Famous Players/Paramount

Library, and the New York Historical Society. Catharine Maria Sedgwick, who
wrote *Hope Leslie* (1827) and *A New England Tale* (1822), lived in Stockbridge,
Massachusetts, where her papers, manuscripts, and other memorabilia are depos-
ited in the Stockbridge Library Association's Sedgwick Family Collection. Caro-
line Lee Hentz has diaries and letters in the Southern Historical Collection at the
University of North Carolina at Chapel Hill, as well as letters in the Chamberlain
Collection of the Boston Public Library. Papers of Lydia Maria Child, whose
romances include *Hobomok* (1824) and *A Romance of the Republic* (1867), are in the
Hofstra University Library, the Ellis Gray Loring Collection of the New York
Public Library, the P. G. and S. B. Shaw Papers of the Houghton Library at
Harvard University, and the Schlesinger Library at Radcliffe College. Ann Sophia
Stephens' papers are located at the New York Public Library. E.D.E.N. South-
worth, one of the most prolific late-nineteenth-century romance writers, can be
studied at the Duke University Library and the Library of Congress Manuscript
Division. Susan Warner and her sister Ann, authors of a number of books written
separately or together, lived on Constitution Island in the Hudson River near
West Point. The Constitution Island Association maintains their home and some
memorabilia and papers. Susan (under the name Elizabeth Wetherell) wrote one
of the period's most popular novels, *The Wide, Wide World* (1850). The memorabilia of Mary Jane Holmes, author of more than forty books between 1854 and
1905, is in the Seymour Library in Brockport, New York.

Helen Hunt Jackson, author of *Ramona* (1884), is represented in the collections
of the Huntington Library and the Jones Library in Amherst, Massachusetts. Amelia E. Barr emigrated to the United States from England and wrote more than

sixty novels. Her papers are in the Archives Division of the Texas State Library; the collection is restricted. The New York Public Library and Rutgers University hold the papers of Laura Jean Libbey. Correspondence of Temple Bailey, Anya Seton, Mary Johnston, and Mary Roberts Rinehart can be found in the Houghton Mifflin Company collection in the Houghton Library Manuscript Department at Harvard University. Kathleen Norris' papers are at Stanford University. Frances Parkinson Keyes' papers are located at Tulane University. Materials on Fannie Hurst can be found at the Olin Library, Washington University, St. Louis, at the Special Collection of the Goldfarb Library at Brandeis University, and at the University of Texas Library. Faith Baldwin papers are in the Knox College Seymour Library in Galesburg, Illinois. Materials relating to Margaret Mitchell can be found at the University of Georgia, the Atlanta Public Library, the Atlanta History Center, Agnes Scott College in Georgia, and Boston University. The papers of Marcia Davenport are in the Manuscript Division of the Library of Congress, including approximately 3,500 items—literary manuscripts, galley proofs, press clippings, working drafts, notes, and 100 items of correspondence with Maxwell Perkins, her editor on her major work of romance fiction, *The Valley of Decision* (1942). Legal briefs and records of the attempt by the Commonwealth of Massachusetts to ban Kathleen Winsor's *Forever Amber* on grounds of obscenity can be found in the Library of Congress Law Library. Additional materials on Margaret Mitchell and Kathleen Winsor are in the Macmillan Collection at the New York Public Library. Some Georgette Heyer papers are at the University of Tulsa.

INTERPRETATION AND CRITICISM OF ROMANCES

General Studies

Since the earliest version of this bibliographical survey was completed in the late 1970s, the field of romance fiction studies has changed dramatically. Twenty years ago, much of the commentary on romances appeared in more general studies of fiction or popular culture. (See Kay Mussell, *Women's Gothic and Romantic Fiction: A Reference Guide*, 1981.) In the ensuing years, many scholars—particularly feminist scholars—have turned their attention to this form of entertainment, which appeals primarily to women. Romance criticism now appears in scholarly monographs, articles in scholarly journals, and a growing number of anthologies of criticism focused on a particular aspect of the genre or a significant critical question.

Some of the older or more general studies still contribute important information or criticism. Henry Petter's *The Early American Novel* includes a long section on "the love story" with extensive description of romance conventions. Michael Davitt Bell's *Hawthorne and the Historical Romance of New England* traces the connections between Hawthorne and contemporary women writers in their use of the Puritan past. A major theoretical work for the study of popular fiction, including romance, is John Cawelti's *Adventure, Mystery, and Romance: Formula Stories as Art and Popular Culture*. Cawelti is exceptionally insightful on the definition of the popular romance and particularly suggestive on the relationship between the romance and what he calls the "social melodrama."

Some general scholarly studies also include criticism of popular romances. For example, Linda Bayer-Berenbaum, in her study of gothic fiction and art, *The Gothic Imagination*, includes a chapter on Mary Shelley's *Frankenstein* and Victoria Holt's *On the Night of the Seventh Moon* as complementary gothic tales. Kate Ferguson Ellis' *The Contested Castle: Gothic Novels and the Subversion of Domestic Ideology* examines the language of domestic violence and the sense of precariousness for women displayed in gothic fiction. The book provides background for discussion of popular gothic romances from the eighteenth and nineteenth centuries but concentrates on male writers and more canonical female writers such as Ann Radcliffe, Mary Wollstonecraft, Mary Shelley, and Emily Brontë rather than on popular romance writers of the period. Ellis' 1987 article, "Gimme Shelter: Feminism, Fantasy, and Women's Popular Fiction," however, examines the popular gothic revival of the 1960s and the emergence of "bodice-rippers" or, as she calls them, "spectaculars" that characterized the romances of the 1970s.

Two other studies by British scholars refer briefly to romances. *Female Desires: How They Are Sought, Bought and Packaged* by Rosalind Coward looks at how female desires are represented in a variety of forms (including ads, images of homemaking and food, film, and novels). In an essay on Mills and Boon romances, linking them to *Pride and Prejudice*, she argues that the romance fantasy is regressive, resembling Freudian notions about the search for the ideal father. In *Into the Mainstream: How Feminism Has Changed Women's Writing*, Nicci Gerrard examines the influence of feminism on women's writing and publishing. In a chapter on genre fiction, she discusses women writers of detective novels, romance and blockbusters, and science fiction.

Patricia Raub's *Yesterday's Stories: Popular Women's Novels of the Twenties and Thirties* analyzes patterns and conventions in a wide variety of novels by women between the wars. Focusing on such issues as attitudes about marriage, divorce, and work, Raub includes fiction by Temple Bailey, Faith Baldwin, Daphne Du Maurier, E. M. Hull, Fannie Hurst, Margaret Mitchell, and Kathleen Norris. Raub's essay "Issues of Passion and Power in E. M. Hull's *The Sheik*" in *Women's Studies* argues that the novel is far more important than it has frequently been judged. The novel, while reflecting its milieu in the 1920s, serves as a precursor to the contemporary Harlequin Romance.

Mary Cadogan, inspired by Rachel Anderson's *The Purple Heart Throbs* (1974) wrote *And Then Their Hearts Stood Still: An Exuberant Look at Romantic Fiction Past and Present*. Aimed at a popular audience, the volume is a wide-ranging defense of the romance genre, broadly defined, with many plot summaries. It has no notes or bibliography. Chapters cover such topics as "governesses and gothics," "piety and passion," "taming the beast," "still smiling through," and "the great husband hunt." Cadogan's relatively uncritical analysis includes some interesting commentary on Edith M. Hull's "sheik romances." Other authors range from Ann Radcliffe and Charlotte M. Yonge, to Elinor Glyn, Barbara Cartland, Baroness Orczy, Judith McNaught, Janet Dailey, Judith Krantz, Rosalind Pilcher, and Danielle Steel. The book is particularly useful as a survey of a wide range of romance categories and writers over time.

Feminist Critiques and Defenses

As women's studies gained ground in the academy, many new studies of women's popular culture emerged. Since the late 1970s, scholars of both literature and history have addressed issues relating to romance fiction, usually in an attempt to explain the popularity of the form. Ellen Moers' *Literary Women* defined the conventions, concerns, and experiences that take shape in literature by women, including romances. Eugenia C. DeLamotte's *Perils of the Night: A Feminist Study of Nineteenth-Century Gothic* is a fine study of both canonical and popular works in the gothic tradition.

A growing list of works by women scholars, primarily historians of New England, has added to our knowledge of romance fiction between 1820 and 1870, although they sometimes discuss novels of the period as if their romance conventions were insignificant or absent. Ann Douglas' *The Feminization of American Culture* suggests that both nineteenth-century clergymen and women experienced a progressive loss of power leading to a debased religious sensibility. Women writers turned to fiction to work out the implications of daily problems, expressed in a pervasive and evasive sentimentality and convention. Nina Baym's *Women's Fiction: A Guide to Novels by and about Women in America, 1820–1870* analyzes a number of important forgotten romances. Mary Kelley's studies of nineteenth-century women writers have added to our knowledge of female authorship. Kelley argues in "The Sentimentalists: Promise and Betrayal in the Home" that women authors felt serious conflict between their intentions and the form of their fiction. Her book *Private Women, Public Stage: Literary Domesticity in Nineteenth-Century America* is a study of twelve important writers: Maria Susanna Cummins, Charlotte Perkins Gilman, Caroline Lee Hentz, Mary Jane Holmes, Maria McIntosh, Sara Parton, Catharine Maria Sedgwick, Mrs. E.D.E.N. Southworth, Harriet Beecher Stowe, Mary Virginia Terhune, Susan Warner, and Augusta Evans Wilson.

The introduction to Susan K. Harris' *19th-Century American Women's Novels: Interpretative Strategies* offers an excellent brief history of scholarly approaches to these books, many of which included romance conventions even when they were not fully courtship stories. Harris sees these novels as frequently subversive of contemporary expectations for women. Describing them as "exploratory" novels because of their "function as a means of testing women's possibilities for alternative modes of being" (19), she traces their development from the didactic novels of such early writers as Susannah Rowson and Catherine Maria Sedgwick, to the more ambiguous work of Augusta Evans Wilson, Susan Warner, Fanny Fern, and E.D.E.N. Southworth. Unlike some other critics who have examined these novels, Harris seeks out contemporary commentary on them, from reviews to readers' diaries, thus drawing a clear distinction between the texts' interpretation by nineteenth- and twentieth-century readers. For nineteenth-century writing by women, including romances, the major scholarly source since 1984 has been the journal *Legacy: A Journal of Nineteenth-Century American Women's Writing*, originally published as a newsletter. Although its focus remains the nineteenth century, in 1991 the journal changed its subtitle to *A Journal of American Women's Writing* and began publishing work on earlier and later periods. Each issue includes articles, reviews, profiles of writers, and a bibliography of recent books and articles.

The profiles, which frequently focus on relatively unknown writers, are especially useful.

An important and controversial argument about romances has been waged by some feminist scholars who label romances "porn for women." The issue was first raised by Ann Douglas and Ann Barr Snitow in two influential articles. Although Snitow, writing about Mills and Boon romances in "Mass Market Romance: Pornography for Women Is Different," argues that romances are pornographic because they are acutely sexualized, Douglas, in "Soft-Porn Culture" in the *New Republic*, appears to use the term as if it had no necessary connection to sex at all. Using as her examples Harlequin Romance and Presents novels of the late 1970s, Douglas labels as "porn" male-centered representations of male–female relations or male domination of women, with or without sexual content. She argues that the gains of women's liberation are under siege from popular culture and that readers and viewers will see representations of men and women that she believes will undermine female autonomy and that are therefore injurious to women. Similar arguments are charted in "The Critic as Pornographer: Male Fantasies of Female Reading in Eighteenth-Century Germany" by Stephan K. Schindler, who documents the German literary and cultural establishment's efforts to control female reading by arguing that women who read novels might engage in autoerotic pleasure that would threaten the male role.

Beatrix Faust, in her 1980 book *Women, Sex, and Pornography*, writes about rape scenes in bodice-rippers by Rosemary Rogers, Kathleen Woodiwiss, and Valerie Sherwood, which have both sexual and violent content. Among these early critics of romance as pornography, Faust has the most complex notion of how romances work and what pornography might be; and she distinguishes between differing sexual representations that appeal to men and to women. Like Faust, Alison Assiter in her book *Pornography, Feminism, and the Individual* adopts a concrete definition that links sexuality with domination. In effect, however, she agrees with Douglas and Snitow that romances glorify male domination of women. Because these critics read romances as promoting female submissiveness to male dominance and because conventional pornography is characterized by objectification of the female by the male, romances and pornography are conflated. In *The Princess at the Window*, Donna LaFramboise analyzes the sexual content in a novel by Johanna Lindsey and suggests that the increase in explicit sex scenes and the acknowledgment that women, too, are capable of desire are due in part to the very feminism that often continues to denigrate them as harmful to women. Turning the feminist critique of romances as pornography on its head, Helen Hazen's *Endless Rapture: Rape, Romance, and the Female Imagination* defends sexual violence in romance novels. Hazen argues that the aspects of romance that most offend feminists—the implied violence against women, rape fantasies—are precisely the needs and desires of women that feminists conventionally ignore.

Less politically charged than other examinations of sexuality in romances, Carol Thurston's *The Romance Revolution: Erotic Novels for Women and the Quest for a New Sexual Identity* charts the rapid changes in romance formulas that began with the original "bodice-rippers" in the 1970s. Thurston used a variety of methods to study these changes, including content analysis, reader questionnaires, mail surveys of romance readers, and interviews with authors and editors (12). Thurston believes that the erotic romance that emerged in the early 1980s represented a new synthesis of women's concerns and behavior that empowered women to seek alternatives to traditional roles, especially expressions of sexuality. Carol Thurston and Barbara Doscher's "Supermarket Erotica: 'Bodice Busters' Put Romantic Myths to Bed" argues that the erotic romances of Woodiwiss and Rogers express covert female protest against patriarchy in a form acceptable to readers who might be uncomfortable with overt feminism.

The most influential scholarly study of the romance to date is Janice A. Radway's *Reading the Romance: Women, Patriarchy, and Popular Literature* (1984). Based in ethnography and reader-response criticism, the study examines romance reading as an act within a social context. After a chapter on the history of publishing practices (or "institutional matrix") of romances, Radway turns to an ethnographic study of forty-two romance readers in a midwestern city that she calls "Smithton." Guided in their reading by a bookstore employee whose expertise had led her to begin writing a review newsletter with a national distribution, these readers represented to Radway a resource for understanding how readers apprehend the reading experience, choose their books, and explain their preferences. Radway explicitly rejects close reading of romance texts as a strategy for understanding their meaning and appeal, although she does engage in analysis of some specific texts identified as either "ideal" or "failed" romances by the readers whom she studied. She found considerable differences between the two groups of novels and uses those differences to understand how the romance fantasy appeals to readers. Additionally, she examines the narrative and linguistic strategies of romances in the context of interpretations of the readers' responses on questionnaires and in interviews.

Radway concludes that romance reading for the Smithton women is an act that is at once "combative" and "compensatory." The readers whom she studied saw their reading as something that they did for themselves, as a refusal for a period of time to enact their expected nurturing roles in the family. Using Nancy Chodorow's psychoanalytical theories of female development, she also examines the dynamics of gender relations in a patriarchal culture and concludes that readers identify with the heroine and seek in the hero a figure who will satisfy the readers' own needs for nurturing. Romances, she argues, in focusing on male behavior in regard to female heroines, serve to explain male aloofness and strength as benign and to ameliorate readers' fears of being hurt or dominated by men, thus reconciling women to their traditional role in patriarchy. An earlier article by Radway, published in 1982, examines the language of the popular gothic romance in a semiotic analysis of its effect on the reader. "The Aesthetic in Mass Culture: Reading the 'Popular' Literary Text" argues that, unlike serious readers who revel in ambiguity and the aesthetics of language, readers of popular literature look for transparency, predictability, and reassurance. The clichéd and familiar language of mass market novels responds to that desire.

While Radway's conclusions were quite similar to those of other feminist critics, her methodology was decidedly different. By drawing on and interpreting the responses of romance readers, she grounded her findings in the experience of reading. In the years since its publication, most romance criticism has referred to *Reading the Romance*; and although it has been criticized, it remains an important influence in the field. In *Feminism and Youth Culture*, Angela McRobbie, for example, applauds Radway's attention to the act of reading instead of focusing on the text itself, specifically, her recognition that readers partially produce their own meaning in the process. She criticizes Radway, however, for her methodology, which places too much emphasis on self-reporting and does not place readers in an economic or class structure. McRobbie, like many other British scholars, is far more committed to class analysis than are most American critics. In *Feminist Media Studies*, Liesbet van Zoonen includes an extensive section on *Reading the Romance* in a chapter on reception studies. Situating studies of romance in the larger context of how women experience and create meaning from popular entertainment, van Zoonen finds merit in reception studies but believes that they will be incomplete until similar studies of male reception of male genres are added.

Another influential study, Tania Modleski's *Loving with a Vengeance: Mass-Produced Fantasies for Women*, argues that such female entertainment forms as Harlequin romances, gothic novels, and soap operas are fantasies that contain strategies for release of covert anger against men and a patriarchal culture. Like Radway, Modleski attributes readers' attraction to romances and gothics to the subservient position of women in patriarchy. Drawing on Chodorow and other critics, Modleski suggests that women who read romances seek both a better understanding of what appears threatening in male behavior and a new vision of themselves through the hero's eyes. Gothic novels, while sharing some characteristics with Harlequins, deal more directly with women's fears and the need to identify and destroy the source of the danger to the self. Modleski's study also pays particular attention to the literary history of romances and gothics since the eighteenth century and locates modern novels in the context of enduring literary patterns. Both Radway and Modleski assume that romance reading is a response to real conditions experienced by women in culture and that it is an effective mechanism for defusing anger and fear. As feminists, both argue that women would be better served if they faced the consequences of their discontent directly rather than ameliorating it through repetitive fantasy. Because of her focus on a wider range of texts over time, Modleski's study takes into account some of the more subtle distinctions among types of romances. Because most of the books that her readers recommended were sensual historical romances, Radway's analysis is based on a narrower sample of romances published within a short time span.

In *Romance and the Erotics of Property: Mass Market Fiction for Women*, Jan Cohn examines category romances of the early 1980s. Arguing that romance is more about power than about love, Cohn sees the elements of romance as addressing women's search for economic viability against changing social conditions. Her understanding of the role of sexuality in romance is particularly acute; she rejects, for example, the notion that sex in popular romance is "soft porn." Instead, she sees it as the means through which a heroine understands herself and negotiates the journey to economic security through love and marriage. Arguing that contemporary women in fiction do not have the option of individual economic power without threatening their femininity, she asserts that the fantasy of the romance accepts society's limits on women and makes them seem inevitable and right. Although her sample of contemporary romances is narrow, she uses them effectively to demonstrate how authors and readers negotiate cultural dilemmas in a time of change in women's expectations.

Catherine Belsey's postmodern study, *Desire: Love Stories in Western Culture*, examines Mills and Boon romances in the context of Western notions about desire, sexuality, and love as a utopian ideal. Belsey notes that the metaphors of sexuality are more reminiscent of disaster (floods, volcanoes, storms) than of gentler emotions, as romances appear to attribute the passions of desire to external forces that buffet the lovers into relinquishing control of the mind over the body. Despite the power of the union, however, Belsey attributes the repetitive reading habits of romance readers to the inherent dissatisfaction of the romance ending, which can never quite achieve the wholeness of its promise. Kay Mussell's *Fantasy and Reconciliation: Contemporary Formulas of Women's Romance Fiction* argues that romances respond to female interests and concerns that are only rarely met or satisfied in the society at large. The book covers several romance subgenres from the mid-1950s through the early 1980s. *Good-bye Heathcliff: Changing Heroes, Heroines, Roles, and Values in Women's Category Romances* by Mariam Darce Frenier charts the changes in Harlequin and Silhouette Romances from 1970 to the mid-1980s. In *The Alienated Reader: Women and Romantic Literature in the Twentieth Century*, Bridget Fowler discusses romance genres between the 1930s and the 1980s as literature for a lower-class female audience. Fowler examines the ideology of romances, the role of publishing, and the consumption of mass culture, using as representative texts magazine fiction of the 1930s, the novels of British writer Catherine Cookson, and the variety of romance formulas in the 1970s and 1980s.

Suzanne Juhasz, in her essay "Texts to Grow On: Reading Women's Romance Fiction," sees romances as exemplifying specifically female ways of experiencing the world, rooted in relationships and centered on notions about mother–daughter dynamics. Novels that aspire to verisimilitude, she says, must show female failure in realizing the self, while romances show successful development with marriage as its reward. Positing the love story against the quest motif, which she identifies as a male pattern, Juhasz defends the romance as a maternal form suited to female concerns. In *Reading from the Heart: Women, Literature, and the Search for True Love*, Juhasz extends her argument and shifts to first person. Although the book grows out of the psychological theory delineated in the earlier article, Juhasz's monograph makes explicit that she is writing about the literature that she loves to read and that her own perception of her reading experience is the subject of the book. An appendix discusses the theoretical underpinnings of her argument, but the text itself is written from the point of view of an engaged reader rather than that of a critic. Almost alone among critics of romance fiction, Juhasz integrates her reading of lesbian romances into her overall analysis of the appeal of the romance to women readers. Although she addresses popular romance only tangentially, this is an important book for understanding the genre.

Because it changes the terms of discussion, one of the most interesting recent scholarly books on the romance is George Paizis' *Love and the Novel: The Poetics and Politics of Romance Fiction* (1998). Noting correctly that most previous romance criticism was concerned with attacking or defending the romance, Paizis sets out to situate the romance in its commercial context and, especially, its formalistic tradition. Based on a carefully selected sample of about thirty novels, primarily published by the Mills and Boon/Harlequin/Silhouette complex, Paizis closely analyzes the semiotic and structural elements of the romance narrative, concentrating on the "first meeting," the "obstacles" that must be overcome by the heroine, and the "happy ending." Building on previous studies, Paizis contributes an unusual, valuable, and long-overdue male perspective to romance criticism.

Scholarly articles on romances usually focus more narrowly on particular sub-genres or significant problems in romance criticism. Examining category romances of the mid-1980s, Harriet Margolis argues in "Feminist Irony or Poisonous FAN-TASY?: Category Romance and the Conscious Reader" that emerging romances exhibited far more feminist notions than many critics assumed. She suggests that these changes were largely a product of reader preferences and that readers were developing a more self-conscious and sometimes ironic view of romance conventions that made them more perceptive critics and more selective consumers of the fiction. In another brief, but provocative, essay "The Lover's Value(s)," Margolis confronts the uneasiness that she feels as an academic feminist who also reads romances, particularly in regard to the critical distance that many critics assume when writing about romance writers and readers.

In 1990, *Continuum: The Australian Journal of Media and Culture* published a special issue on "The Media of Publishing." In "Popular Romance in the Post-modern Age. And an Unknown Australian Author," Ann Curthoys and John Docker recount their surprise at discovering the variety and the intertextuality of romance novels, particularly those by Australian writers. Drawing on the post-modernist criticism of Andreas Huyssen and work on romance by Radway and Thurston, the article rejects modernist notions of high and low culture in favor of a more holistic, cultural understanding of popular genres. The authors situate popular romance in literary history and offer a close reading of an Australian Mills and Boon novel that derives from Jane Austen's *Persuasion*. " 'No More Virgins': Writing Romance—An Interview with Emma Darcy" profiles the Australian romance writing team that uses the pseudonym Emma Darcy. The interview by Albert Moran focuses on their writing practice and on their sense of how closely linked popular fiction must be to its audience.

In "The Wonderful-Terrible Bitch Figure in Harlequin Novels," Susan Ostrov Weisser examines the contrast between the heroine and her rival for the hero's love in category romances. Weisser argues that the Bitch figure not only is a foil for the heroine but embodies traits that are more conventionally ascribed to men, such as materialism, aggression, authoritarianism, and aloofness. Although Weisser covers ground that has previously been explored by others and uses only two novels for examples, the essay offers insight into the motif in the context of feminist thought. Kate McCafferty's "Palimpsest of Desire: The Re-Emergence of the American Captivity Narrative as Pulp Romance" examines romances featuring Native American heroes and white American heroines as a transformation of the American captivity narrative. Focusing on books that she calls the "Savage Series," published by Zebra, McCafferty argues that these books refigure the captivity narrative with the Native American lover as the hero. White males, for example, are seen as repressive and evil, while the Native American lover is linked to family and domestic values.

Lillian S. Robinson's essay, "On Reading Trash," describes the work of Georgette Heyer as a modern fantasy that appeals to some readers who also enjoy Jane Austen. An article by Angela Miles, "Confessions of a Harlequin Reader: Learning Romance and the Myth of the Male Mother," begins with the author's description of her own guilty pleasure in reading romances, particularly when under stress. Miles set out to understand why she, as a feminist scholar, responded so strongly to a fantasy with characteristics that she had expected to scorn. She concludes that the "enormous emotional power of the Harlequin reading, and the romance fantasy in general, can be explained by the fact that the hero is in fact a mother figure for the reader/woman" (2). Although the motif of hero-as-nurturer has been noted by other commentators, Miles' analysis is more thoroughly rooted in feminist theory and the emerging literature on mother–daughter relationships, which derives largely from Nancy Chodorow's influential *The Reproduction of Mothering: Psychoanalysis and the Sociology of Gender* (1978). While drawing on Radway's primary research with romance readers, Miles disagrees with Radway's contention that academic critics do not read romances in the same way as do nonacademic readers. Instead, Miles explicitly grounds her analysis in her own perceptions of her pleasure in reading, as well as in the reception that her ideas have received from other readers. Unlike many other academic critics, Miles has read widely and understands Harlequins' variety as well as their conventions.

Writing in *The Cream City Review*, Katherine Wikoff argues that feminist critiques of the romance genre as pathological nostalgia miss the point. Instead, in "Readings in Romance Fiction: Nostalgia as Pathology?" she suggests that the yearning for the romantic happy ending is a yearning for wholeness as women grow older and realize that certain choices are closed to them. Stephanie Wardrop, in "The Heroine Is Being Beaten: Freud, Sado-Masochism, and Reading the Romance," offers a close reading of Linda Howard's *MacKenzie's Mission* to support her contention that the appeal of romance might well be understood through its ritualization of sado-masochistic sexuality, which is then broken down through commitment to marriage. Drawing on psychoanalytic theorists, Wardrop's essay takes into account the way that readers interpret even relatively violent sex scenes as opportunities for dominant males to relinquish control to females through the force of their passion. In this nuanced interpretation, she surveys the major critical stances on romances and explains how feminist critics have frequently misunderstood what readers experience as they read.

Amal Treacher, in "What Is Life without My Love?: Desire and Romantic Fiction," describes two typical feminist approaches to female fantasies about sexuality. The first suggests that once women understand the extent to which their desires are shaped by patriarchy, they can control and change their fantasies. The second, to which Treacher herself subscribes, believes that fantasy and desire are both shaped by socialization and deeply buried in the psyche and therefore are less subject to individual control. Although she offers a close reading of only one Mills and Boon novel, Treacher's essay identifies and analyzes many of the more controversial aspects of the genre.

In *Rewriting English: Cultural Politics of Gender and Class*, Janet Batsleer, Tony Davies, Rebecca O'Rouke, and Chris Weedon include a chapter on romance, called "Gender and Genre: Women's Stories." Focusing primarily on work by Barbara Cartland and Catherine Cookson, two of Britain's most popular romance writers, they suggest that romances appeal to readers because they place women and their sphere, the home, at the center of the action. Moreover, romance conventions allow women to fantasize about sexual desire under the guise of true love and reinforce social proscriptions of premarital sex for women. Romances are fundamentally about the passage from girlhood to female adulthood through resolving conflicts related to monogamy and the double standard, which still control much social discourse about femininity. Finally, the authors contend that popular romances in England disseminate values of lineage and class as determiners of value, despite the preponderance of lower-class readers.

Anthologies of romance criticism usually focus on a particular subgenre of romance or a significant issue about the romance. Ellen Moers' concept of "female gothic" inspired Juliann E. Fleenor's groundbreaking anthology, *The Female Gothic*. Fleenor's introduction to the anthology provides an excellent analytical survey of scholarly theories about women and the gothic tradition and argues that the gothic has been appropriate to female literary purposes in both serious and popular works. Many of the articles in the volume are relevant to popular romance formulas. Among the most pertinent is Joanna Russ' classic critique, "Somebody's Trying to Kill Me and I Think It's My Husband," originally published in the *Journal of Popular Culture* in 1973. Kay Mussell's " 'But Why Do They Read Those Things?': The Female Audience and the Gothic Novel" argues that the modern gothic enacts and gives meaning to the traditional activities of the female sphere in a context of great excitement and danger. Barbara Bowman's "Victoria Holt's Gothic Romances: A Structuralist Inquiry" identifies the character types and plot structure of Holt's novels and concludes that they "dramatize a crucial choice in a woman's life between being cared for by her parents and caring for others" (81). Kathleen L. Maio's "Had-I-But-Known: The Marriage of Gothic Terror and Detection" discusses the strong female protagonists of romantic detective novels by Mary Roberts Rinehart and Mabel Seeley in contrast to the weaker women of modern romantic suspense novels.

The Progress of Romance, edited by Jean Radford, is a collection of essays on the romance as a genre, seen historically. Anna Clark in "The Politics of Seduction in English Popular Culture, 1748–1848" argues that the image of the seduction of a poor, innocent maid by an aristocratic rake became a powerful instrument of the class struggle in England. Helen Taylor, in "*Gone with the Wind*: The Mammy of Them All," offers an uneasy feminist reading of the novel and film's popularity that points out the guilty pleasure of experiencing a racist and sexist text. In "Mills & Boon Meets Feminism," Ann Rosalind Jones writes about the conventional conflict between mass-market romances and feminism and says that while the novels refer to feminist notions, their approach is frequently incoherent in narrative, setting, and dialogue.

Lynne Pearce and Jackie Stacey's collection of essays *Romance Revisited* grew from a 1993 conference at the Center for Women's Studies at Lancaster University. Although the essays address issues of romance as a concept in the context of feminism, many of the essays address romance fiction. The editors' introduction, "Heart of the Matter: Feminists Revisit Romance," sets the stage for a feminist reconsideration of romance by looking at ways that feminist critics have theorized the romance. Stevi Jackson's "Women and Heterosexual Love: Complicity, Resistance and Change" cautions that many previous feminist critiques have fallen into the essentialist trap or failed to take into account the durability of the romance in an age of feminist change. Rosalynn Voaden in "The Language of Love: Medieval Erotic Vision and Modern Romance Fiction" links the drama of courtship in the contemporary romance novel with the female visionary experience in medieval narrative. In both of these disparate forms, women are the center of attention, there is a focus on the body, and the process of waiting for consummation is intensely eroticized. In "Literature beyond Modernism: Middlebrow and Popular Romance," Bridget Fowler examines novels by Danielle Steel and Virginia Andrews as examples of romances of the 1990s. Joan Forbes argues in "Anti-Romance Discourse as Resistance: Women's Fiction 1775–1820" that some of the courtship novels of the period also contain a contrary discourse that undermines and challenges the conventional story and its ending.

In 1997, the journal *Para*doxa: Studies in World Literary Genres* published a special issue devoted to the romance, entitled, "Where's Love Gone? Transformations in the Romance Genre." In the introductory essay, Kay Mussell provides an overview of romance criticism since the 1970s as well as the changes in romance fiction during the same period. Tania Modleski writes in "My Life as a Romance Reader" about her own experiences as both reader and critic. In "Accidental Authors, Random Readers, and the Art of Popular Romance," Beth Rapp Young delineates the often gender-based dualities of romance criticism. Lynn Coddington, in "Wavering between Worlds: Feminist Influences in the Romance Genre," surveys feminist criticism of romances and writes about herself as a writer of both romances and a dissertation on the composition practices of romance writers. Another practicing romance writer who is also a doctoral candidate, Jennifer Crusie Smith, contributed "Romancing Reality: The Power of Romance to Reinforce and Re-Vision the Real," which evaluates the appeal of the romance for women. Sandra Booth's "Paradox in Popular Romances of the 1990s: The Paranormal versus Feminist Humor" contrasts two especially popular subgenres of this decade. Several scholars wrote single-author studies for the collection, including Deborah K. Chappel on LaVyrle Spencer ("LaVyrle Spencer and the Anti-Essentialist Argument"), Harriet Margolis on Emma Darcy ("A Child in Love, or Is It Just Fantasy? The Values of Women's Genres"), Pamela Regis on Nora Roberts ("Complicating Romances and Their Readers: Barrier and Point of Ritual Death in Nora Roberts's Category Fiction"), Sylvia Kelso on Barbara Michaels ("Stitching Time: Feminism(s) and Thirty Years of Gothic Romances"), and Julia Bettinotti and Marie-Françoise Truel on E. M. Hull ("Lust and Dust: Desert Fabula in Romances and Media"). Gabriele Linke compares Mills & Boon with Harlequin romances in "Contemporary Mass Market Romances as National and International Culture." Patricia Koski, Lori Holyfield, and Marcella Thompson offer a sociological analysis of "Romance Fiction as Women's Myth." Sarah Webster Goodwin chronicles her experiences teaching a course on romances in "Romance and Change: Teaching the Romance to Undergraduates." Kay Mussell conducted interviews with Jayne Ann Krentz, Barbara G. Mertz (Barbara Michaels/Elizabeth Peters), Nora Roberts, and Janet Dailey. Norbert Spehner contributed an annotated bibliography on the romance.

Romantic Conventions, edited by Anne K. Kaler and Rosemary E. Johnson-Kurek, "centers on the analysis of a limited number of aspects of the romance genre and attempts to pinpoint the specific conventions, patterns, themes, and images that make it work" (3). Sections include essays on "Archetypes and Stereotypes," "Time and Place," and "Language and Love." Pamela Marks in "The Good Provider in Romance Novels" examines the hero's role in romances as necessary for preservation of the traditional domestic unit. Abby Zidle's "From Bodice-Ripper to Baby-Sitter: The New Hero in Mass-Market Romance" examines changing male roles in contemporary romances. Rosemary E. Johnson-Kurek, in " 'I Am Not a Bimbo: Persona, Promotion, and the Fabulous Fabio," looks at the image of the

Scene from *Jane Eyre*, 1996. Kobal Collection/Coote, Clive/Rochester/Miramax

male model who has posed for countless romance novel covers and whose public persona incites much ridicule of the genre. "This Is Not Your Mother's Cinderella: The Romance Novel as Feminist Fairy Tale," by award-winning romance writer Jennifer Crusie Smith, argues that romances take the familiar elements of fairy tales and rework them for a contemporary and more feminist audience. In "Cavewoman Impulses: The Jungian Shadow Archetype in Popular Romantic Fiction," Amber Botts posits romances as the female equivalent of the male quest plot and suggests that they provide a means for women of experiencing darker impulses in a "safe" fantasy environment. "Medieval Magic and Witchcraft in the Popular Romance Novel" by Carol Ann Breslin examines female power in romance fiction. Anne K. Kaler's "Conventions of Captivity in Romance Novels" is a wide-ranging look at the common motif of heroines threatened by male power and the threat of rape. Her reading of E. M. Hull's classic *The Sheik* is especially insightful. In "Time-Travel and Related Phenomena in Contemporary Popular Romance Fiction," Diane M. Calhoun-French finds the conventions of this popular subgenre of the 1990s to be problematic because it allows romance writers and readers to enjoy antifeminist behavior and values by displacing them onto past time periods. Rosemary E. Johnson-Kurek's "Leading Us into Temptation: The Language of Sex and the Power of Love" examines the increasingly explicit language common to some contemporary romances, specifically the Harlequin Temptation series. In "Changing Ideologies in Romance Fiction," Dawn Heinecken looks at the influence of feminism on recent romances. In "Postmodern Identity (Crisis): Confessions of a Linguistic Historiographer and Romance Writer," Julie Tetel Andresen discusses her experience as a successful academic at a prestigious university and a successful romance writer. Anne K. Kaler, in "Hero,

Heroine, or HERA: A New Name for an Old Problem," proposes a new term for a female hero.

Social Science Approaches

While most romance criticism has emerged from literature and history, other fields have also contributed. Rita C. Hubbard's "Relationship Styles in Popular Romance Novels, 1950 to 1983" uses fantasy theme analysis methodology to compare changes in category romances over four decades. Selecting ten novels from each decade since the 1950s, Hubbard concludes that considerable change in relationships has occurred. J. K. Alberts published an article in *Communication Quarterly* that analyzed the conversational patterns in Harlequin Romances. "The Role of Couples' Conversations in Relational Development: A Content Analysis of Courtship Talk in Harlequin Romance Novels" identifies common verbal exchanges between heroes and heroines. Alberts identifies and explains the significance of four stages of conversation that culminate in the act of saying, "I love you." Mary M. Talbot's *Fictions at Work: Language and Social Practice in Fiction* is a linguistic analysis of such popular genres as romance, horror, and feminist science fiction. Talbot's linguistic method analyzes typical linguistic markers of romance fiction, the interactions that occur within the texts, and the intertextual references to such classic romances as *Pride and Prejudice* and *Pamela*.

In *Popular Reading and Publishing in Britain, 1914–1950*, Joseph McAleer traces the history of three British mass market publishing firms, including Mills and Boon. Although the firm published romances along with other genres from its founding in 1980, he argues that only in the 1930s did it begin to specialize in romantic fiction aimed at a female audience. The success of this new direction was based on several factors: the company's preference for nonerotic romances appealing to the middle class, emphasis on the product as a "brand name" rather than books by individuals, development of a stable group of authors rather than reliance on "stars," distribution through catalogs, and heavy marketing of hardback romances to libraries. A more extensive study of Mills and Boon was published by jay Dixon in 1999. *The Romance Fiction of Mills and Boon: 1909–1990s* surveys the history of the major British publisher of romances. Dixon, an enthusiastic reader of romances as well as a former employee of Mills and Boon, has an encyclopedic knowledge of the firm and its products. She is also a feminist who challenges many of the popular notions about romance conventions. This is an important survey of almost a century of romance novels, particularly valuable for its detailed coverage of the earlier decades of the period. Margaret Ann Jensen's *Love's Sweet Return: The Harlequin Story* is a scholarly study of the Canadian firm of Harlequin Books. In 1979, to commemorate its thirtieth anniversary of publishing paperback fiction, Harlequin issued *Harlequin 30th Anniversary: 1949–1979*, a volume that lists all the novels published to date along with a history of the company. The lists chart the company's gradual transition from publishing general popular fiction to publishing, exclusively, romance reprints from Mills and Boon. Profiles of particularly popular Harlequin authors are included. Paul Grescoe's *The Merchants of Venus: Inside Harlequin and the Empire of Romance* is a longer and more recent study of the firm.

John Markert's "Romance Publishing and the Production of Culture" is a detailed examination of the rise of romance publishing in the United States, from the mid-1950s through about 1984. Based largely on interviews with publishing executives, the study concludes that changes in romance content and the romance market were the product of factors within the book publishing industry as well as changes in the society at large. Markert appears to place more emphasis on internal factors. Markert's article includes two useful charts that show the relative sales of different kinds of romances from the early 1970s through the mid-1980s. These charts show the virtual disappearance of gothics and the rapid rise to dominance of contemporary sensual romances after 1980. Moreover, his interviews with romance publishing executives make his study particularly valuable in understanding how the romance market changed so rapidly during the early 1980s.

Controversies over romances also appear in publications for librarians. In "Trash or Treasure? Pop Fiction in Academic and Research Libraries," Robert G. Sewell reports that even libraries that collect popular fiction frequently do not circulate romances. Mary K. Chelton's "Unrestricted Body Parts and Predictable Bliss: The Audience Appeal of Formula Romances," published in *Library Journal*, offers a guide for librarians interested in serving patrons' interest in romances. A longer, but similar, article in *Public Libraries*, entitled "Exploring the World of Romance Novels," explains recent trends in the genre, including more hardcover publication, fewer "clinch" covers, and ethnic characters. The authors, Cathie Linz (a romance writer), Ann Bouricius, and Carole Byrnes, discuss in some detail how romances should be acquired, cataloged, and circulated. The May 1995 issue of *Wilson Library Bulletin* contains three articles on romances and libraries. The main article, "A Fine Romance: How to Select Romances for Your Collection," by Johanna Tuñón, suggests a variety of ways to identify popular writers whose romances should be included in library collections. She also provides a useful resource list and bibliography. An opinion piece in the same issue, "The Librarian as Effete Snob: Why Romance?" by Shelley Mosley, John Charles, and Julie Havir, refutes common stereotypes and makes a positive case for why librarians should provide romances for readers.

Writing in the *Journal of Advanced Composition*, Joseph Harris takes to task those critics who assume that "normal" readers of any popular genre are seduced by manipulative art while serious critics understand the "true meaning" of such work. "The Other Reader" looks at academic critics of advertisements, soap operas, and romances who interpret the responses of the general public to popular materials as somehow less perceptive than those of trained critics. He argues that such criticism stems from critics' social and political commitments and are rarely based on listening carefully to the reactions of others, which might fruitfully test the unfounded assumptions of such analysis.

Psychologist Cynthia Whissell, of Laurentian University, has contributed several studies of romance fiction from a more statistical, empirical model. Using a computer program that tests samples of text for emotional markers, Whissell compared adventure and romance novels in "Objective Analysis of Text." She found some of the predicted gender markers—but not so many as she expected, given the difference in audiences for these two forms of popular fiction. In "Mate Selection in Popular Women's Fiction," she uses evolutionary theory on mate selection to determine that romance novels fit the predicted model. Drawing on both classic romances, such as *Pride and Prejudice* and *Jane Eyre*, and contemporary romances, Whissell finds that males and females fit predicted gender-based personality models and that they choose mates according to predicted factors. Men choose women for reproductive capacity and sexual exclusivity, while women choose mates who exhibit strong economic potential and inclination toward parenting. In "The Formula behind Women's Romantic Formula Fiction," Whissell uses a computer program that she wrote that generates romance plots. By identifying elements of the formula and showing the variations possible within the rules, Whissell provides the basis for a firmer analysis of the romance genre.

During the 1980s and early 1990s, educators engaged in a lively debate over the value of romance reading for adolescent girls. Reminiscent of earlier disputes over whether parents and teachers should encourage or discourage children from reading "fluff," this new debate was also infused with literacy theory and feminist scholarship. Typical is a volume of essays edited by Linda K. Christian-Smith, entitled *Texts of Desire: Essays on Fiction, Femininity and Schooling*. Two main themes tie together the volume's essays: the assumption that literacy is not neutral but exists in a social context that shapes readers' interpretation and self-identity and the assertion that the reading of romance novels acts as a means of both socialization into, and resistance to, patriarchy. Essays focus on book clubs for adolescents and teen romance novels. *Texts of Desire* builds on previous work by Christian-Smith. In a 1987 article, "Gender, Popular Culture, and Curriculum: Adolescent Romance Novels as Gender Texts," Christian-Smith reported on a semiotic analysis of thirty-four romance novels written for adolescents by American authors between 1942 and 1982. Christian-Smith's "Power, Knowledge and Curriculum: Constructing Femininity in Adolescent Romance Novels" is an ethnographic report similar to her essay in *Texts of Desire*. Her most elaborated analysis, which includes some of the work already described, is her 1990 monograph *Becoming a Woman through Romance*. In analyzing forty-two adolescent romance novels published between 1942 and 1982, Christian-Smith identifies the common codes of romance, sexuality, and beautification conveyed by the novels, discusses how young readers experience them, and suggests ways in which teachers can use students' interest in these novels to encourage reading development.

Two of the contributors to *Texts of Desire*, Australian scholars Pam Gilbert and Sandra Taylor, published a study on the construction of gender identity, *Fashioning the Feminine: Girls, Popular Culture, and Schooling*. Gilbert and Taylor review many of the major feminist critiques of romance reading, discuss adolescent readers' responses to romances, and conclude that the discourse of romance is harmful and limiting to girls as they develop their adult identities. The most important chapter for analysis of romance is Chapter 4, "Romancing the Girl: Fiction, Fantasy, and Femininity." In an anthology entitled *Pleasure and Danger*, Sharon Thompson's "Search for Tomorrow: On Feminism and the Reconstruction of Teen Romance" is a study of the stories that teenage girls told her when asked about their experiences with sex and romance. Thompson conducted her interviews between 1978 and 1983 and identified her subjects as young women raised in the context of the second wave of feminism, expecting independence but frequently in conflict or confused over expectations for romance and family.

Early readership studies established information about romance readers in the 1960s and 1970s. The most important were by Jan Hajda, Peter H. Mann, and the research firm of Yankelovich, Skelly, and White. The 1978 Yankelovich studies were expanded in 1983 into the three volumes of the *Consumer Research Study on Reading and Book Purchasing*, commissioned by the book industry and focusing on the demographics of reading and book buying, influences on reading, and the reasons for reading. Subtitled *Focus on Juveniles*, *Focus on the Elderly*, and *Focus on Adults*, the 1983 studies show, as expected, that romance reading is an overwhelmingly female pastime. Among juveniles, romance reading increases as children enter the teenage years. Mann's work was updated in an article, "Romantic Fiction and Its Readership," reporting on a survey of British book reading that contains data on the popularity of romance fiction. Mann also writes about the prejudice against romance fiction that has kept scholars and critics from understanding the phenomenon or the readers. Also dated, but interesting for its counterintuitive findings is a 1980 study of adult reading habits in Canada, Kenneth F. Watson's *Leisure Reading Habits: A Survey of the Leisure Reading Habits of Canadian Adults with Some International Comparisons*. As predicted, most romance readers were female, but relatively high proportions of male readers were also represented at all age levels. Moreover, romance reading in Canada differed according to geography, with higher levels of readership in Quebec than in Atlantic Canada or the areas west of Quebec.

Writing in *Women's Studies*, Lynda L. Crane reported on a survey of romance readers in Baltimore in an essay entitled, "Romance Novel Readers: In Search of Feminist Change?" The readers in the study responded to an invitation in the newspaper. The first stage was a questionnaire, and the second, a smaller number of interviews. Respondents indicated that a major impetus for reading romance novels was to experience an intimacy that was seldom true of their own relationships with men. Many, however, identified with strong and independent heroines. Most agreed that feminism had been good for women. There was considerable disagreement about the role of explicit or aggressive sex scenes, with some readers finding them pleasurable and others expressing disgust. Crane concludes that the pleasure of reading romances is more complex than many critics have suggested.

Although there are very few studies of romance in cross-cultural perspective, some individual studies are useful. Two works by feminist scholars have been published only in French. Both focus on French translations of Harlequin publications. Marie-Andrée Dubrule's *Le Cas Harlequin* includes evaluation of work by such classic Mills and Boon/Harlequin authors as Janet Dailey, Anne Hampson, Flora Kidd, Anne Mather, Carole Mortimer, Lilian Peake, Anne Weale, Mary Wibberley, and Violet Winspear, among others. *La Corrida de l'Amour: Le Roman Harlequin* by Hélène Bédard-Cazabon, Julia Bettinotti, Jocelyn Gagnon, Pascale Noizet, and Christian Provost includes information on the business side of Harlequin Enterprises as well as analysis of character types, point of view, setting, plot dynamics, and the heroine's perspective on, and experience of, romance in Harlequin novels. Both studies include bibliographies of work on romances, mostly in French and rarely cited in the scholarship in English.

Unlike these French-Canadian studies, which deal with translations of British and American romances into French, "Japanese Harlequin Romances as Transcultural Woman's Fiction" by Chieko Irie Mulhern charts the development of original romances in Japan. (The author is using the name "Harlequin" here as a generic term. Harlequin Romances have been translated for a Japanese audience, but this article is about romances written in Japanese by Japanese authors.) Deliberately modeled on the Harlequin and Silhouette models, the Sanrio New Romances debuted in 1984 and featured work by Japanese women writers who consciously set out to write category romances for a contemporary Japanese audience. Many conventions are shared by Japanese and Western romances, but Chieko points out some significant distinctions as well. For example, of the first twenty-six titles, published between 1984 and 1988, about half have heroes who are either Caucasian or Eurasian, although most heroines are Japanese. The proportion of mixed-race romances in Japan is far higher than those in comparable American or British novels, although in the 1990s more mixed couples have appeared in the United States. Mulhern also points out a pattern of mutilation of both male and female characters as a convention of Japanese romances. Heroines in Japanese romances frequently have female friends or confidantes and overtly desire positive relationships with their in-laws. Despite differences, however, Mulhern's analysis is most notable for the many linkages and similarities that she finds between Japanese romances and those of Western cultures.

SOURCES ON ROMANCE WRITERS

A few novelists who wrote romance have been the subject of major studies, but comprehensive critical studies of individual romance writers are still relatively rare. Ellen B. Brandt's *Susanna Haswell Rowson: America's First Best-Selling Novelist* is a biography with a critical analysis of Rowson's books and a good bibliography. Another study is Patricia L. Parker's *Susanna Rowson*, a biographical treatment of Rowson's work in the Twayne United States Authors Series. Twayne's English Authors Series includes a useful volume on Mary Stewart by Lenemaja Friedman; although much of the book concerns Stewart's later historical series about Merlin and King Arthur, a chapter on Stewart's life and analyses of her romantic suspense work offer solid information about her career. Jan Cohn's *Improbable Fiction: The Life of Mary Roberts Rinehart* is a fine critical biography of Rinehart's life and work. *Grace Livingston Hill* is a biography of the author, told by her grandson, Robert Muncie. *The Lives of Danielle Steel* by Vickie L. Bane and Lorenzo Benet (of *People* magazine) is a gossipy introduction to the best-selling writer.

Barbara Cartland has been the subject of full-length biographies for a general audience. Henry Cloud's *Barbara Cartland: Crusader in Pink* was published in paperback. Gwen Robyns' *Barbara Cartland*, published in hardback, is an official biography written with Cartland's assistance. More interesting and valuable, however, is an essay about Cartland by Rosalind Brunt. "A Career in Love: The Romantic World of Barbara Cartland" includes a biographical sketch that succinctly locates Cartland in her social context, explains how she consciously constructed celebrity persona expresses a coherent philosophy, and offers a close reading of one of her novels. Brunt contends that, rather than supporting a belief in the primacy of love for women, Cartland's novels instead represent a materialistic notion of the world in which a woman's virginity is her only commodity of value.

The Janet Dailey Companion: A Comprehensive Guide to Her Life and Her Novels consists primarily of Sonja Massie and Martin N. Greenberg's extended interview with the author, who was one of the first North Americans to succeed in the category romance market. Dailey began writing for Mills and Boon/Harlequin in the mid-1970s. In a series of Harlequin Presents novels, Dailey used each of the fifty United States as a setting, in the process demonstrating the possibilities of North American settings for category romance. With her first single title novels for Pocket Books in the late 1970s, she also demonstrated that successful category romance authors could break into mass market paperback publishing. The interview covers Dailey's life, her writing, and her ideas about romance fiction. It also contains interviews with her husband (and research assistant), her mother, and her agent. Many of her books are summarized in the final section.

Autobiographical writing by romance writers is occasionally available. Among these are Fannie Hurst's *Anatomy of Me*, Frances Parkinson Keyes' *Roses in December* and *All Flags Flying*, and Kathleen Norris' *Noon* and *Family Gathering*. Mary Kelley has edited a biography and journal by Catharine Maria Sedgwick in *The Power of Her Sympathy*. Marcia Davenport's *Too Strong for Fantasy* includes background information about her novel *The Valley of Decision*.

An unusual study of a book that is usually discussed as a romance is Sally Beauman's "Rereading *Rebecca*," published in the *New Yorker* in 1993. Beauman argues that generations of readers and critics have misread Daphne du Maurier's *Rebecca* (1938). In her reading, Beauman suggests that the nameless narrator (usually read as the heroine) is actually the double of Rebecca (read as the villain) and that both women are victims of patriarchy in the person of Maxim de Winter. Rebecca threatens the patriarchal order (primogeniture) by becoming pregnant by another man, and she dies for her transgression. The narrator, in assisting her husband to cover up his crime, condemns herself to a living death of exile and boredom. In this long essay, Beauman also reviews an authorized biography of du Maurier as well as a sequel to *Rebecca* written by another author.

Beginning in the late 1970s, when competition among paperback romance publishers increased, romance authors began to seek professional affiliations and publicity. In Romance Writers of America, authors had a new organization with a newsletter, *Romance Writers' Report*, to keep in touch with fellow writers and publishing opportunities. The association's annual convention brings together published and aspiring romance writers along with editors, publishers, and agents. The organization's Web site, which includes current news about the field along with lists of award-winning novels, is http://www.rwanational.com. The organization gives awards to both published novels and unpublished manuscripts in many romance subgenres, along with Hall of Fame and Lifetime Achievement awards, as well as naming a Librarian of the Year and honoring a journalist who reported on the romance.

Also since the late 1970s, "how-to-write-a-romance" books have proliferated, and valuable information on contemporary romance conventions can be found in books like Marilyn M. Lowery's *How to Write Romance Novels That Sell*, Yvonne McManus' *You Can Write a Romance! and Get It Published!*, Kathryn Falk's *How to Write a Romance and Get It Published*, Jean Kent and Candace Shelton's *The Romance Writers' Phrase Book*, and Helene Schellenberg Barnhart's *Writing Romance Fiction for Love and Money*. More recent guidance for aspiring romance writers appears in Eve Paludin's *Romance Writer's Pink Pages*, Vanessa Grant's *Writing Romance*, and David H. Borcherding's *Romance Writer's Sourcebook*. The Falk and Borcherding books also include brief "how-to" essays by successful romance authors. More recently, the Romance Writers of America issued a handbook for aspiring writers entitled *Writing Romances*, edited by Rita Gallagher and Rita Clay

Estrada. The book includes essays by many of the most popular and innovative contemporary writers, including Roberta Gellis, Karen Robards, Jude Deveraux, Jo Beverley, Diana Gabaldon, Eileen Dreyer, Susan Wiggs, Kathleen Eagle, and Janet Dailey.

Mills and Boon author Mary Wibberley published a manual for aspiring romance writers entitled *To Writers with Love: On Writing Romantic Novels*. Part advice and part defense of the genre, Wibberley offers suggestions on such issues as character types, setting, plotting, dialogue, and sexual tension. Wibberley repeats a list of familiar defenses, including the prevalence of romantic themes in literature from Homer to Shakespeare to the Brontës, the respect awarded to male escape fantasy fiction and television, and the success of romance fiction in the marketplace. A much earlier example of the advice-for-writers genre is Anne Britton and Marion Collin's *Romantic Fiction*, published in 1960 in the New Writers' Guide series. Phyllis A. Whitney includes many examples from romance novels in her *Guide to Fiction Writing*.

The Writer and *Writer's Digest*, two popular magazines for writers, occasionally publish articles on romance writing and markets, far too many to summarize. A typical example is Silhouette editor Wendy Corsi Staub's "When Not to Try, Try Again," which explains how writers should interpret rejection letters. Some aspiring romance writers do not recognize the finality of a rejection, while others fail to understand when an editor would like to see a different manuscript. Staub also contributed "Writing the Category Romance Novel," which takes on the controversial issue of whether there is a "formula" for romance or not. Academic critics of popular culture, following John Cawelti, tend to use the term "formula" in a descriptive sense, but the term is frequently read by romance writers as pejorative. Staub argues that there is no rigid formula but that readers expect certain elements to appear in work labeled "romance." Rosalyn Alsobrook offers advice in "When You Write a Historical Romance." Laura Baker outlines what editors are seeking in new romance manuscripts. "The Changing Face of Romance Novels" surveys recent trends in the industry, focusing on the emerging paranormal romance categories of time travel, futuristic, fantasy, and supernatural romances.

The most important resource for understanding the point of view of romance writers on their craft and their audience is the anthology *Dangerous Men, Adventurous Women: Romance Writers on the Appeal of the Romance*, edited by best-selling writer Jayne Ann Krentz, published by the University of Pennsylvania Press in 1992 and reprinted in paperback by HarperCollins in 1996. The volume includes essays by nineteen romance writers exploring a variety of issues in the genre. These writers are keenly aware of the critical controversies surrounding their genre. Many of the essays refer, not always negatively, to published scholarly works on romances.

Linda Barlow and Jayne Ann Krentz's essay, "Beneath the Surface: The Hidden Codes of Romance" outlines the mythic nature of the romance fantasy and analyzes the language of romance fiction, focusing on dialogue and description. Echoing, for example, recent studies of male and female discourse, Barlow and Krentz believe that the barbed, sometimes antagonistic dialogue between romance hero and heroine contrasts with the common female perception that men don't really communicate with women. Romantic description, which may seem trite and repetitive, actually calls upon mythic and archetypal images familiar to readers.

The figurative language in romances is "highly connotative" and frequently paradoxical, which hints at the reconciliation of the ending. In perhaps the most controversial essay in the *Dangerous Men* volume, "The Androgynous Reader: Point of View in the Romance," Laura Kinsale argues that the common notion that the female reader identifies with the heroine is in error. Instead, the heroine is merely a "place-holder," allowing the reader to step into the story and identify with the more interesting and powerful hero. Disagreeing partly with Kinsale, Linda Barlow in "The Androgynous Writer: Another View of Point of View" believes that readers identify primarily with the heroine but are also engaged by the romantic hero. This dual identification allows a reader to explore both the female journey to adulthood and the masculine portion of herself.

Susan Elizabeth Phillips, in "The Romance and the Empowerment of Women," discusses the widespread notion that romances and feminism are antithetical and concludes that, contrary to stereotypes, romances are about female power, not male domination. She argues that to accuse romance of being unrealistic misses the point, since readers are looking for entertainment, not reality. Mary Jo Putney, in "Welcome to the Dark Side," explores the appeal of the "wounded hero" rescued by a woman and discusses her own use of realistic "issues" such as alcoholism, rape, and epilepsy in her historical novels. Jayne Ann Krentz's "Trying to Tame the Romance: Critics and Correctness" is a fascinating look at the attempt by some romance editors to make the romance genre more "respectable," against the will of the more successful writers in the field. Krentz says that some of the young editors in the 1980s wanted writers to stop using the "alpha male" figure (the strong, domineering, macho male) that Krentz believes essential to the conflict in romances. Other targets were the "aggressive seduction" of heroine by hero, sometimes mislabeled as a rape fantasy, and the heroine's conventional virginity, a source of female power. Finally, romance writers were advised to give up conventional and familiar plot structures, which Krentz says derive from deeply felt ancient myths of female bonding. All these elements, she argues, are essential to the romance as a genre; and although some romances came to use the more politically correct or "respectable" forms, they have never sold as well as the more conventional novels.

In "Women Do," Judith Arnold suggests that women enjoy reading romances because they are the one form of fiction in which women get to act, to "do." Kathleen Gilles Seidel, in "Judge Me by the Joy I Bring," takes on feminist critics who, while claiming sisterhood, continue to see romance readers and writers as "the Other." Such critics, she believes, assume that romance reading is damaging and that women who read romances would better spend their time actually confronting their problems. She also discusses the elements of successful romances and defines qualities that make a good romance, including an understanding of the reader's fantasies and literary ability. Finally, she believes that successful romance writers see their audience as "sisters" and can therefore empathize with their needs and fantasies as women.

Another collection of essays by romance writers is *North American Romance Writers*, edited by Kay Mussell and Johanna Tuñón. Thirty romance writers are represented, with a bibliography of their works, listings of their major awards, a biographical sketch, and an essay on the subject of their own work. Kay Mussell contributed an introduction, and Johanna Tuñón added an extensive bibliography of both scholarly and popular commentary on romances. The authors were selected for variety and for their innovative contributions to the genre over the past two decades. Included are Judith Arnold (Ariel Berk, Thea Frederick), Mary Balogh, Jo Beverley, Loretta Chekani (Loretta Chase), Sue Civil-Brown (Rachel Lee), Judy Cuevas (Judith Ivory), Sharon and Tom Curtis (Laura London, Robin James), Justine Dare Davis, Eileen Dreyer (Kathleen Korbel), Kathleen Eagle, Patricia Gaffney, Alison Hart (Jennifer Greene, Jeanne Grant, Jessica Massey), Lorraine Heath, Tami Hoag, Susan Johnson (Jill Barkin), Dara Joy, Lynn Kerstan, Sandra Kitt, Susan Krinard, Jill Marie Landis, Pamela Morsi, Maggie Osborne (Margaret St. George), Mary Jo Putney, Alicia Rasley, Emilie Richards, Paul Detmer Riggs, Nora Roberts (J. D. Robb), Barbara Samuel (Ruth Wind), Kathleen Gilles Seidel, and Jennifer Crusie Smith. Key essays include Kerstan's "In Praise of Love and Folly," Rasley's "Paradox in Balance," Riggs' "Taboo or Not Taboo: That Is the Question," and Kathleen Gilles Seidel's " 'I Can Pay the Rent': Money in the Romance Novel."

BIBLIOGRAPHY

Books and Articles

Alberts, J. K. "The Role of Couples' Conversations in Relational Development: A Content Analysis of Courtship Talk in Harlequin Romance Novels." *Communication Quarterly* 34 (Spring 1986), 127–42.

Alsobrook, Rosalyn. "When You Write a Historical Romance." *Writer* (March 1990), 20–21.

Anderson, Rachel. *The Purple Heart Throbs: The Sub-Literature of Love*. London: Hodder and Stoughton, 1974.

Andresen, Julie Tetel. "Postmodern Identity (Crisis): Confessions of a Linguistic Historiographer and Romance Writer." In *Romantic Conventions*, ed. Anne K. Kaler and Rosemary E. Johnson-Kurek. Bowling Green, Ohio: Bowling Green State University Popular Press, 1999, 173–86.

Arnold, Judith. "Women Do." In *Dangerous Men, Adventurous Women: Romance Writers on the Appeal of the Romance*, ed. Jayne Ann Krentz. Philadelphia: University of Pennsylvania Press, 1982, 133–39.

Assiter, Alison. *Pornography, Feminism, and the Individual*. London: Pluto Press, 1989.

Baker, Laura. "The Changing Face of Romance Novels." *Writer's Digest* (March 1995), 35–37.

Bane, Vickie L., and Lorenzo Benet. *The Lives of Danielle Steel*. New York: St. Martin's, 1994.

Barlow, Linda. "The Androgynous Writer: Another View of Point of View." In *Dangerous Men, Adventurous Women: Romance Writers on the Appeal of the Romance*, ed. Jayne Ann Krentz. Philadelphia: University of Pennsylvania Press, 1982, 45–52.

Barlow, Linda, and Jayne Ann Krentz. "Beneath the Surface: The Hidden Codes of Romance." In *Dangerous Men, Adventurous Women: Romance Writers on the Appeal of the Romance*, ed. Jayne Ann Krentz. Philadelphia: University of Pennsylvania Press, 1982, 15–29.

Barnhart, Helene Schellenberg. *Writing Romance Fiction for Love and Money*. Cincinnati, Ohio: Writer's Digest Books, 1983.

Batsleer, Janet, Tony Davies, Rebecca O'Rourke, and Chris Weedon. *Rewriting English: Cultural Politics of Gender and Class*. London: Methuen, 1985.

Bayer-Berenbaum, Linda. *The Gothic Imagination: Expansion in Gothic Literature and Art*. Rutherford, N.J.: Fairleigh Dickinson University Press, 1982.

Baym, Nina. *Woman's Fiction: A Guide to Novels by and about Women in America 1820–1870*. Ithaca, N.Y.: Cornell University Press, 1978.

Beauman, Sally. "Rereading *Rebecca*." *New Yorker* (November 8, 1993), 127–38.

Bédard-Cazabon, Hélène, Julia Bettinotti, Jocelyn Gagnon, Pascale Noizet, Christian Provost. *La Corrida de l'Amour: Le Roman Harlequin*. Montreal: Université de Quebec à Montréal, 1986.

Bell, Michael Davitt. *Hawthorne and the Historical Romance of New England*. Princeton, N.J.: Princeton University Press, 1971.

Belsey, Catherine. *Desire: Love Stories in Western Culture*. Oxford: Blackwell, 1994.

Bettinotti, Julia, and Marie-Françoise Truel. "Lust and Dust: Desert Fabula in Romances and Media." *Para*doxa: Studies in World Literary Genres* 3: 1–2 (1997), 184–194.

Blouin, Pattie, Claire Gipson, and Helen Gipson, eds. *Essence of Romance*. Baton Rouge: Twilight, 1993.

———. *Essence of Romance Update V*. Baton Rouge: Twilight, 1996.

———. *Romance by the Number*. Baton Rouge: Twilight, 1993.

———. *Romance by the Title*. Baton Rouge: Twilight, 1997.

———. *The Story Continues II*. 2nd ed. Baton Rouge: Twilight, 1993.

Bontly, Susan W., and Carol J. Sheridan, eds. *Enchanted Journeys beyond the Imagination: An Annotated Bibliography of Fantasy, Futuristic, Supernatural, and Time-Travel Romances*. Vol. 1. San Antonio: Blue Diamond, May 1995.

———. *Enchanted Journeys beyond the Imagination: An Annotated Bibliography of Fantasy, Futuristics, Supernatural, and Time-Travel Romance*. Vol. 2. San Antonio: Blue Diamond, May 1996.

Booth, Sandra Marie. "Paradox in Popular Romances of the 1990s: The Paranormal versus Feminist Humor." *Para*doxa: Studies in World Literary Genres* 3: 1–2 (1997), 94–106.

Borcherding, David H., ed. *Romance Writer's Sourcebook*. Cincinnati, Ohio: Writer's Digest Books, 1996.

Botts, Amber. "Cavewoman Impulses: The Jungian Shadow Archetype in Popular Romantic Fiction." In *Romantic Conventions*, ed. Anne K. Kaler and Rosemary E. Johnson-Kurek. Bowling Green, Ohio: Bowling Green State University Popular Press, 1999, 62–74.

Bowman, Barbara. "Victoria Holt's Gothic Romances: A Structuralist Inquiry." In *The Female Gothic*, ed. Juliann E. Fleenor. Montreal: Eden Press, 1983, 69–81.

Brandt, Ellen B. *Susanna Haswell Rowson: America's First Best-Selling Novelist*. Chicago: Serbra Press, 1975.

Breslin, Carol Ann. "Medieval Magic and Witchcraft in the Popular Romance Novel." In *Romantic Conventions*, ed. Anne K. Kaler and Rosemary E. Johnson-Kurek. Bowling Green, Ohio: Bowling Green State University Popular Press, 1999, 75–85.

Britton, Anne, and Marion Collin. *Romantic Fiction*. London: T. V. Boardman, 1960.

Brunt, Rosalind. "A Career in Love: The Romantic World of Barbara Cartland." In *Popular Fiction and Social Change*, ed. Christopher Pawling. London: Macmillan, 1984.

Cadogan, Mary. *And Then Their Hearts Stood Still: An Exuberant Look at Romantic Fiction Past and Present*. London: Macmillan, 1994.

Calhoun-French, Diane M. "Time-Travel and Related Phenomena in Contemporary Popular Romance Fiction." In *Romantic Conventions*, ed. Anne K. Kaler and Rosemary E. Johnson-Kurek. Bowling Green, Ohio: Bowling Green State University Popular Press, 1999, 100–112.

Cawelti, John. *Adventure, Mystery, and Romance: Formula Stories as Art and Popular Culture*. Chicago: University of Chicago Press, 1976.

Chappel, Deborah K. "LaVyrle Spencer and the Anti-Essentialist Argument." *Para*doxa: Studies in World Literature Genres* 3: 1–2 (1997), 107–20.

Chelton, Mary K. "Unrestricted Body Parts and Predictable Bliss: The Audience Appeal of Formula Romances." *Library Journal* 116 (July 1991), 44–49.

Child, Lydia Maria. *Hobomok and Other Writings on Indians*. 1824. Ed. Carolyn L. Karcher. New Brunswick, N.J.: Rutgers University Press, 1986.

Christian-Smith, Linda K. *Becoming a Woman through Romance*. New York: Routledge, 1990.

———. "Gender, Popular Culture, and Curriculum: Adolescent Romance Novels as Gender Texts." *Curriculum Inquiry* 17 (Winter 1987), 365–406.

———. "Power, Knowledge and Curriculum: Constructing Femininity in Adolescent Romance Novels." In *Language, Authority and Criticism: Readings on the School Textbook*, ed. Suzanne de Castell, Allan Luke, and Carmen Luke. London: Falmer, 1989, 17–31.

Christian-Smith, Linda K., ed. *Texts of Desire: Essays on Fiction, Femininity and Schooling*. London: Falmer, 1993.

Chodorow, Nancy. *The Reproduction of Mothering: Psychoanalysis and the Sociology of Gender*. Berkeley: University of California Press, 1978.

Clark, Anna. "The Politics of Seduction in English Popular Culture, 1748–1848." In *The Progress of Romance: The Politics of Popular Fiction*, ed. Jean Radford. New York: Routledge and Kegan Paul, 1986, 47–70.

Cloud, Henry. *Barbara Cartland: Crusader in Pink*. New York: Bantam, 1979.

Coddington, Lynn. "Wavering between Worlds: Feminist Influences in the Romance Genre." *Para*doxa: Studies in World Literary Genres* 3:1–2 (1997), 58–77.

Cohn, Jan. *Improbable Fiction: The Life of Mary Roberts Rinehart*. Pittsburgh: University of Pittsburgh Press, 1980.

———. *Romance and the Erotics of Property: Mass-Market Fiction for Women*. Durham, N.C.: Duke University Press, 1988.

Coward, Rosalind. *Female Desires: How They Are Sought, Bought and Packaged*. New York: Grove Weidenfeld, 1985.

Crane, Lynda L. "Romance Novel Readers: In Search of Feminist Change?" *Women's Studies* 23 (1994), 257–69.

Cummins, Maria Susanna. *The Lamplighter*. 1854. Ed. Nina Baym. New Brunswick, N.J.: Rutgers University Press, 1988.

Curthoys, Ann and John Docker. "Popular Romance in the Postmodern Age. And an Unknown Australian Author." *Continuum: The Australian Journal of Media and Culture* 4: 1 (1990).

Davenport, Marcia. *Too Strong for Fantasy*. New York: Scribner's, 1967.

Davidson, Cathy N. *Revolution and the Word: The Rise of the Novel in America*. New York: Oxford University Press, 1986.

Davidson, Cathy N., and Linda Wagner-Martin, eds. *The Oxford Companion to Women's Writing in the United States*. New York: Oxford University Press, 1995.

DeLamotte, Eugenia C. *Perils of the Night: A Feminist Study of Nineteenth-Century Gothic*. New York: Oxford University Press, 1990.

Dixon, jay. *The Romance Fiction of Mills and Boon: 1909–1990s*. London: UCL Press, 1999.

Douglas, Ann. *The Feminization of American Culture*. New York: Alfred A. Knopf, 1978.

———. "Soft-Porn Culture." *New Republic* 183 (August 30, 1980), 25–29.

Dubrule, Marie-Andrée. *Le Cas Harlequin*. Quebec: Les Cahiers de recherche du GREMF. Groupe de recherche multidisciplinaire féministe. Université Laval, 1986.

Ellis, Kate Ferguson. *The Contested Castle: Gothic Novels and the Subversion of Domestic Ideology*. Urbana: University of Illinois Press, 1989.

———. "Gimme Shelter: Feminism, Fantasy, and Women's Popular Fiction." In *American Media and Mass Culture: Left Perspectives*, ed. Donald Lazere. Berkeley: University of California Press, 1987, 216–30.

Evans, Augusta Jane. *St. Elmo*. 1866. Ed. Diane Roberts. Tuscaloosa: University of Alabama Press, 1992.

Falk, Kathryn, ed. *How to Write a Romance and Get It Published*. New York: Crown, 1983. (Updated New York: Signet, 1989.)

Fallon, Eileen, ed. *Words of Love: A Complete Guide to Romance Fiction*. New York: Garland, 1984.

Faust, Beatrix. *Women, Sex, and Pornography: A Controversial and Unique Study*. New York: Macmillan, 1980.

Fleenor, Juliann E., ed. *The Female Gothic*. Montreal: Eden, 1983.

Forbes, Joan. "Anti-Romantic Discourse as Resistance: Women's Fiction 1775–1820." In *Romance Revisited*, ed. Lynne Pearce and Jackie Stacey. New York: New York University Press, 1995, 293–305.

Foster, Hannah W. *The Coquette*. Ed. and intro. Cathy N. Davidson. New York: Oxford University Press, 1986.

Fowler, Bridget. *The Alienated Reader: Women and Romantic Literature in the Twentieth Century*. New York: Harvester Wheatsheaf, 1991.

———. "Literature beyond Modernism: Middlebrow and Popular Romance." In *Romance Revisited*, ed. Lynne Pearce and Jackie Stacey. New York: New York University Press, 1995, 89–99.

Freibert, Lucy M., and Barbara A. White, eds. *Hidden Hands: An Anthology of American Women Writers, 1790–1870*. New Brunswick, N.J.: Rutgers University Press, 1985.

Frenier, Mariam Darce. *Good-bye Heathcliff: Changing Heroes, Heroines, Roles, and Values in Women's Category Romances*. New York: Greenwood, 1988.

Friedman, Lenemaja. *Mary Stewart*. Boston: Twayne, 1990.

Gallagher, Rita, and Rita Clay Estrada, eds. *Writing Romances: A Handbook by the Romance Writers of America*. Cincinnati: Writer's Digest Books, 1997.

Gerrard, Nicci. *Into the Mainstream: How Feminism Has Changed Women's Writing*. London: Pandora, 1989.

Gilbert, Pam, and Sandra Taylor. *Fashioning the Feminine: Girls, Popular Culture, and Schooling*. North Sydney, NSW: Allen and Unwin, 1991.

Goodwin, Sarah Webster. "Romance and Change: Teaching the Romance to Undergraduates." *Para*doxa: Studies in World Literary Genres* 3: 1–2 (1997), 233–41.

Grant, Vanessa. *Writing Romance*. North Vancouver, B.C.: International Self-Counsel Press, 1997.

Grescoe, Paul. *The Merchants of Venus: Inside Harlequin and the Empire of Romance*. Vancouver: Raincoast Books, 1996.

Hackett, Alice Payne, and James Henry Burke. *80 Years of Best-Sellers*. New York: R. R. Bowker, 1977.

Hajda, Jan. "A Time for Reading." *Trans-Action* 4 (June 1967), 45–50.

Harlequin Books. *Harlequin 30th Anniversary: 1949–1979*. Toronto: Harlequin Books, 1979.

Harris, Joseph. "The Other Reader." *Journal of Advanced Composition* 12 (Winter 1992), 27–37.

Harris, Susan K. *19th-Century American Women's Novels: Interpretative Strategies*. Cambridge: Cambridge University Press, 1990.

Hazen, Helen. *Endless Rapture: Rape, Romance, and the Female Imagination*. New York: Scribner's, 1983.

Heinecken, Dawn. "Changing Ideologies in Romance Fiction." In *Romantic Conventions*, ed. Anne K. Kaler and Rosemary E. Johnson-Kurek. Bowling Green, Ohio: Bowling Green State University Popular Press, 1999, 149–72.

Helfer, Melinda, Kathryn Falk, and Kathe Robin, eds. *Romance Reader's Handbook*. Brooklyn Heights, N.Y.: Romantic Times, 1989.

Herald, Diana Tixier. *Genreflecting: A Guide to Reading Interests in Genre Fiction*. 4th ed. Littleton, Colo.: Libraries Unlimited, 1995.

Hubbard, Rita C. "Relationship Styles in Popular Romance Novels, 1950 to 1983." *Communication Quarterly* 33 (Spring 1985), 113–25.

Hurst, Fannie. *Anatomy of Me*. Garden City, N.Y.: Doubleday, 1958.

Jackson, Stevi. "Women and Heterosexual Love: Complicity, Resistance and Change." In *Romance Revisited*, ed. Lynne Pearce and Jackie Stacey. London: Lawrence and Wishart, 1995, 49–62.

Jaegly, Peggy J. *Romantic Hearts: A Personal Reference for Romance Readers*. 3rd ed. Lanham, Md.: Scarecrow Press, 1997.

Jensen, Margaret Ann. *Love's Sweet Return: The Harlequin Story*. Toronto: Women's Educational Press, 1984.

Johnson-Kurek, Rosemary E. " 'I Am Not a Bimbo': Persona, Promotion, and the Fabulous Fabio." In *Romantic Conventions*, ed. Anne K. Kaler and Rosemary E. Johnson-Kurek. Bowling Green, Ohio: Bowling Green State University Popular Press, 1999, 35–50.

———. "Leading Us into Temptation: The Language of Sex and the Power of

Love." In *Romantic Conventions*, ed. Anne K. Kaler and Rosemary E. Johnson-Kurek. Bowling Green, Ohio: Bowling Green State University Popular Press, 1999, 113–148.

Jones, Ann Rosalind. "Mills & Boon Meets Feminism." In *The Progress of Romance: The Politics of Popular Fiction*, ed. Jean Radford. New York: Routledge and Kegan Paul, 1986, 195–218.

Juhasz, Suzanne. *Reading from the Heart: Women, Literature, and the Search for True Love*. New York: Viking, 1994.

———. "Texts to Grow On: Reading Women's Romance Fiction." *Tulsa Studies in Women's Literature* 7 (Fall 1988), 239–59.

Kaler, Anne K. "Conventions of Captivity in Romance Novels." In *Romantic Conventions*, ed. Anne K. Kaler and Rosemary E. Johnson-Kurek. Bowling Green, Ohio: Bowling Green State University Popular Press, 1999, 86–99.

———. "Hero, Heroine or HERA: A New Name for an Old Problem." In *Romantic Conventions*, ed. Anne K. Kaler and Rosemary E. Johnson-Kurek. Bowling Green, Ohio: Bowling Green State University Popular Press, 1999, 187–92.

Kaler, Anne K., and Rosemary E. Johnson-Kurek, eds. *Romantic Conventions*. Bowling Green, Ohio: Bowling Green State University Popular Press, 1999.

Kelley, Mary. *The Power of Her Sympathy: The Autobiography and Journal of Catharine Maria Sedgwick*. Boston: Massachusetts Historical Society (Northeastern University Press), 1993.

———. *Private Women, Public Stage: Literary Domesticity in Nineteenth-Century America*. New York: Oxford University Press, 1984.

———. "The Sentimentalists: Promise and Betrayal in the Home." *Signs* 4 (Spring 1979), 434–46.

Kelso, Sylvia. "Stitching Time: Feminism(s) and Thirty Years of Gothic Romances." *Para*doxa: Studies in World Literary Genres* 3:1–2 (1997), 164–79.

Kent, Jean and Candace, Shelton. *The Romance Writers' Phrase Book*. New York: Perigee Books (Berkley), 1984.

Kerstan, Lynn. "In Praise of Love and Folly." In *North American Romance Writers*, ed. Kay Mussell and Johanna Tuñón. Lanham, Md.: Scarecrow Press, 1999, 124–29.

Keyes, Frances Parkinson. *All Flags Flying: Reminiscences of Frances Parkinson Keyes*. New York: McGraw-Hill, 1972.

———. *Roses in December*. Garden City, N.Y.: Doubleday, 1960.

Kinsale, Laura. "The Androgynous Reader: Point of View in the Romance." In *Dangerous Men, Adventurous Women: Romance Writers on the Appeal of the Romance*, ed. Jayne Ann Krentz. Philadelphia: University of Pennsylvania Press, 1982, 31–44.

Koski, Patricia, Lori Holyfield, and Marcella Thompson. "Romance Fiction as Women's Myth." *Para*doxa: Studies in World Literary Genres* 3: 1–2 (1997), 219–32.

Krentz, Jayne Ann, ed. *Dangerous Men, Adventurous Women: Romance Writers on the Appeal of the Romance*. Philadelphia: University of Pennsylvania Press, 1992. Reprint. HarperCollins, 1996.

———. "Trying to Tame the Romance: Critics and Correctness." In *Dangerous Men, Adventurous Women: Romance Writers on the Appeal of the Romance*, ed.

Jayne Ann Krentz. Philadelphia: University of Pennsylvania Press, 1982, 107–14.

LaFramboise, Donna. *The Princess at the Window: A New Gender Morality*. Toronto: Penguin, 1996.

Linke, Gabriele. "Contemporary Mass Market Romances as National and International Culture: A Comparative Study of Mills & Boon and Harlequin Romances." *Para*doxa: Studies in World Literary Genres* 3: 1–2 (1997), 195–213.

Linz, Cathie, Ann Bouricius, and Carole Byrnes. "Exploring the World of Romance Novels." *Public Libraries* 34 (May–June 1995), 144–51.

Lowery, Marilyn M. *How to Write Romance Novels That Sell*. New York: Rawson Associates, 1983.

MacManus, Yvonne. *You Can Write a Romance! And Get It Published!* New York: Pocket Books, 1983.

Maio, Kathleen L. "Had-I-But-Known: The Marriage of Gothic Terror and Detection." In *The Female Gothic*, ed. Julian E. Fleenor. Montreal: Eden, 1983, 82–90.

Mann, Peter H. *A New Survey: The Facts about Romantic Fiction*. London: Mills and Boon, 1974.

———. "Romantic Fiction and Its Readership." *Poetics* 14 (1985), 95–105.

———. *The Romantic Novel: A Survey of Reading Habits*. London: Mills and Boon, 1969.

Margolis, Harriet. "A Child in Love, or Is It Just Fantasy? The Values of Women's Genres." *Para*doxa: Studies in World Literary Genres* 3: 1–2 (1997), 121–44.

———. "Feminist Irony or Poisonous FANTASY?: Category Romances and the Conscious Reader." *Yearbook of Interdisciplinary Study in the Fine Arts* 3 (1992): 165–78.

———. "The Lover's Value(s): Women's Romance Novels in an Exchange-Based Society." *Women's Studies Association (NZ) Conference Papers* (Wellington, August 1994), 78–82.

Markert, John. "Romance Publishing and the Production of Culture." *Poetics* 14 (1985), 69–93.

Marks, Pamela. "The Good Provider in Romance Novels." In *Romantic Conventions*, ed. Anne K. Kaler and Rosemary E. Johnson-Kurek. Bowling Green, Ohio: Bowling Green State University Popular Press, 1999, 10–22.

Massie, Sonja, and Martin N. Greenberg. *The Janet Dailey Companion: A Comprehensive Guide to Her Life and Her Novels*. New York: HarperCollins, 1996.

McAleer, Joseph. *Popular Reading and Publishing in Britain, 1914–1950*. Oxford: Clarendon Press, 1992.

McCafferty, Kate. "Palimpsest of Desire: The Re-Emergency of the American Captivity Narrative as Pulp Romance." *Journal of Popular Culture* 27 (Spring 1994), 43–56.

McRobbie, Angela. *Feminism and Youth Culture*. Boston: Unwin Hyman, 1991.

Miles, Angela. "Confessions of a Harlequin Reader: Learning Romance and the Myth of the Male Mother." *Canadian Journal of Political and Social Theory* 12: 1–2 (1988), 1–37.

Modleski, Tania. *Loving with a Vengeance: Mass-Produced Fantasies for Women*. Hamden, Conn.: Archon, 1982.

———. "My Life as a Romance Reader." *Para*doxa: Studies in World Literary Genres* 3: 1–2 (1997), 15–28.

Moers, Ellen. *Literary Women*. Garden City, N.Y.: Doubleday, 1977.

Moran, Albert. " 'No More Virgins': Writing Romance—An Interview with Emma Darcy." *Continuum: The Australian Journal of Media and Culture* 4: 1 (1990).

Mosley, Shelley, John Charles, and Julie Havir. "The Librarian as Effete Snob: Why Romance?" *Wilson Library Bulletin* 69 (May 1995), 24–25, 114–15.

Mulhern, Chieko Irie. "Japanese Harlequin Romances as Transcultural Woman's Fiction." *The Journal of Asian Studies* 48 (February 1989), 50–70.

Muncie, Robert. *Grace Livingston Hill*. Wheaton, Ill.: Tyndale House, 1986.

Mussell, Kay. " 'But Why Do They Read Those Things?': The Female Audience and the Gothic Novel." *The Female Gothic*, ed. Juliann E. Fleenor. Montréal: Eden Press, 1983, 57–68.

———. *Fantasy and Reconciliation: Contemporary Formulas of Women's Romance Fiction*. Westport, Conn.: Greenwood Press, 1984.

———. Interviews. "Jayne Ann Krentz" (46–57), "Nora Roberts" (155–63), "Barbara G. Mertz" (180–83), "Janet Dailey" (214–18). *Para*doxa: Studies in World Literary Genres* 3: 1–2, (1997).

———. "Where's Love Gone? Transformations in Romance Fiction and Scholarship." *Para*doxa: Studies in World Literary Genres* 3, no. 1–2 (1997), 3–14.

———. *Women's Gothic and Romantic Fiction: A Reference Guide*. Westport, Conn.: Greenwood Press, 1981.

Mussell, Kay, and Johanna Tuñón, eds. *North American Romance Writers*. Lanham, Md.: Scarecrow Press, 1999.

1983 Consumer Research Survey on Reading and Book Purchasing: Focus on Adults. Conducted by Market Facts. Interpreted by Research and Forecasts. Prepared for Book Industry Study Group. New York: Study Group, 1984.

1983 Consumer Research Survey on Reading and Book Purchasing: Focus on the Elderly. Conducted by Market Facts. Interpreted by Research and Forecasts. Prepared for Book Industry Study Group. New York: Study Group, 1984.

1983 Consumer Research Survey on Reading and Book Purchasing: Focus on Juveniles. Conducted by Market Facts. Interpreted by Research and Forecasts. Prepared for Book Industry Study Group. New York: Study Group, 1984.

Norris, Kathleen. *Family Gathering*. Garden City, N.Y.: Doubleday, 1959.

———. *Noon: An Autobiographical Sketch*. Garden City, N.Y.: Doubleday, Page, 1925.

Paizis, George. *Love and the Novel: The Poetics and Politics of Romance Fiction*. New York: St. Martin's, 1998.

Paludin, Eve. *Romance Writer's Pink Pages*. Rocklin, Calif.: Prima, 1994, 1996.

Parker, Patricia L. *Susanna Rowson*. Boston: Twayne, 1986.

Pearce, Lynne, and Jackie Stacey, eds. *Romance Revisited*. New York: New York University Press, 1995.

Petter, Henri. *The Early American Novel*. Columbus: Ohio State University Press, 1971.

Phillips, Susan Elizabeth. "The Romance and the Empowerment of Women." In *Dangerous Men, Adventurous Women: Romance Writers on the Appeal of the Romance*, ed. Jayne Ann Krentz. Philadelphia: University of Pennsylvania Press, 1982, 53–59.

Pitcher, Edward W. R. *Fiction in American Magazines before 1800: An Annotated Catalogue*. Schenectady: Union College Press in conjunction with Lexington, Ky.: Antoca Press, 1993.

Putney, Mary Jo. "Welcome to the Dark Side." In *Dangerous Men, Adventurous Women: Romance Writers on the Appeal of the Romance*, ed. Jayne Ann Krentz. Philadelphia: University of Pennsylvania Press, 1982, 99–105.

Radford, Jean, ed. *The Progress of Romance: The Politics of Popular Fiction*. London: Routledge and Kegan Paul, 1986.

Radway, Janice A. "The Aesthetic in Mass Culture: Reading the 'Popular' Literary Text." In *The Structure of the Literary Process: Studies Dedicated to the Memory of Felix Vodička*. Amsterdam: John Benjamins, 1982, 397–429.

———. *Reading the Romance: Women, Patriarchy, and Popular Literature*. Chapel Hill: University of North Carolina Press, 1984.

Ramsdell, Kristin. *Happily Ever After: A Guide to Reading Interests in Romance Fiction*. Littleton, Colo.: Libraries Unlimited, 1987.

———. *Romance Fiction: A Guide to the Genre*. Littleton, Colo.: Libraries Unlimited, 1999.

———. *What Romance Do I Read Next? A Reader's Guide to Recent Romance Fiction*. Detroit: Gale Research, 1997, 1999.

Rasley, Alicia. "Paradox in Balance." In *North American Romance Writers*, ed. Kay Mussell and Johanna Tuñón. London: Scarecrow, 1999, 168–71.

Raub, Patricia. "Issues of Passion and Power in E. M. Hull's *The Sheik*." *Women's Studies* 21 (1992), 119–28.

———. *Yesterday's Stories: Popular Women's Novels of the Twenties and Thirties*. Westport, Conn.: Greenwood, 1994.

Regis, Pamela. "Complicating Romances and Their Readers: Barrier and Point of Ritual Death in Nora Roberts's Category Fiction." *Para*doxa: Studies in World Literary Genres* 3: 1–2 (1997), 145–54.

Reilly, John M., ed. *Twentieth-Century Crime and Mystery Writers*. New York: St. Martin's Press, 1980.

Reno, Dawn and Jacque Tiegs. *Collecting Romance Novels*. Brooklyn, N.Y.: Alliance, 1995.

Riggs, Paula Detmer. "Taboo or Not Taboo: That Is the Question." In *North American Romance Writers*, ed. Kay Mussell and Johanna Tuñón. London: Scarecrow, 1999, 183–89.

Robinson, Lillian S. "On Reading Trash." In *Sex, Class, and Culture*. Bloomington: Indiana University Press, 1978.

Robyns, Gwen. *Barbara Cartland*. Garden City, N.Y.: Doubleday, 1985.

Rowson, Susanna Haswell. *Charlotte Temple*. Ed. and intro. Cathy N. Davidson. New York: Oxford University Press, 1986.

———. *Charlotte Temple and Lucy Temple*. Ed. and intro. Ann Douglas. New York: Penguin Books, 1991.

Russ, Joanna. "Somebody's Trying to Kill Me and I Think It's My Husband: The Modern Gothic." *Journal of Popular Culture* 6 (Spring 1973), 666–91. Reprint. *The Female Gothic*, ed. Juliann E. Fleenor. Montréal: Eden Press, 1983, 31–56.

Schindler, Stephan K. "The Critic as Pornographer: Male Fantasies of Female Reading in Eighteenth-Century Germany." *Eighteenth-Century Life* 20: 3 (1996), 66–80. On-line: Project Muse.

Sedgwick, Catharine Maria. *Hope Leslie*. 1827. Ed. Mary Kelley. New Brunswick, N.J.: Rutgers University Press, 1987.

Seidel, Kathleen Gilles. " 'I Can Pay the Rent': Money in the Romance Novel." In *North American Romance Writers*, ed. Kay Mussell and Johanna Tuñón. Lanham, Md.: Scarecrow, 1999, 211–19.

———. "Judge Me by the Joy I Bring." In *Dangerous Men, Adventurous Women: Romance Writers on the Appeal of the Romance*, ed. Jayne Ann Krentz. Philadelphia: University of Pennsylvania Press, 1996, 159–79.

Sewell, Robert G. "Trash or Treasure? Pop Fiction in Academic and Research Libraries." *College and Research Libraries* 46 (November 1984), 450–61.

Smith, Jennifer Crusie. "Romancing Reality: The Power of Romance to Reinforce and Re-vision the Real." *Para*doxa: Studies in World Literary Genres* 3: 1–2 (1997), 81–93.

———. "This Is Not Your Mother's Cinderella: The Romance Novel as Feminist Fairy Tale." *Romantic Conventions*, ed. Anne K. Kaler and Rosemary E. Johnson-Kurek. Bowling Green, Ohio: Bowling Green State University Popular Press, 1999, 51–61.

Snitow, Ann Barr. "Mass-Market Romance: Pornography for Women Is Different." 1979. In *Powers of Desire: The Politics of Sexuality*, ed. Ann Snitow, Christine Stansell, and Sharon Thompson. New York: Monthly Review Press, 1983.

Southworth, Mrs. E.D.E.N. *The Hidden Hand*. 1859. Ed. Joanne Dobson. New Brunswick, N.J.: Rutgers University Press, 1988.

Spehner, Norbert. "L'Amour, toujours l'amour . . . The Popular Love Story and Romance: A Basic Checklist of Secondary Sources." *Para*doxa: Studies in World Literary Genres* 3: 1–2 (1997), 253–68.

Staub, Wendy Corsi. "When Not to Try, Try Again." *Writer* (January 1993), 19+. On-line. Available Electric Library. March 14, 1996.

———. "Writing the Category Romance Novel." *Writer* (June 1995, 29+. On-line. Available Electric Library. March 14, 1996.

Talbot, Mary M. *Fictions at Work: Language and Social Practice in Fiction*. London: Longman, 1995.

Taylor, Helen. "*Gone with the Wind*: The Mammy of Them All." In *The Progress of Romance: The Politics of Popular Fiction*, ed. Jean Radford. New York: Routledge and Kegan Paul, 1986, 113–36.

Thompson, Sharon. "Search for Tomorrow: On Feminism and the Reconstruction of Teen Romance." In *Pleasure and Danger: Exploring Female Sexuality*, ed. Carole S. Vance. Boston: Routledge and Kegan Paul, 1984, 350–84.

Thurston, Carol. *The Romance Revolution: Erotic Novels for Women and the Quest for a New Sexual Identity*. Urbana: University of Illinois Press, 1987.

Thurston, Carol, and Barbara Doscher. "Supermarket Erotica: 'Bodice-Busters' Put Romantic Myths to Bed." *Progressive* (April 1982), 49–51.

Treacher, Amal. "What Is Life Without My Love?: Desire and Romantic Fiction."

In *Sweet Dreams: Sexuality, Gender and Popular Fiction*, ed. Susannah Radstone. London: Lawrence and Wishart, 1988, 73–90.

Tuñón, Johanna. "Bibliography." *North American Romance Writers*. Ed. Kay Mussell and Johanna Tuñón. London: Scarecrow, 1999, 227–70.

———. "A Fine Romance: How to Select Romances for Your Collection." *Wilson Library Bulletin* 69 (May 1995), 31–34.

Van Zoonen, Liesbet. *Feminist Media Studies*. London: Sage, 1994.

Vasudevan, Aruna, ed. *Twentieth-Century Romance and Historical Writers*. London: St. James Press, 1994.

Vinson, James, ed. *Twentieth-Century Romance and Gothic Writers*. London: Macmillan, 1982.

Voaden, Rosalynn. "The Language of Love: Medieval Erotic Vision and Modern Romance Fiction." In *Romance Revisited*, ed. Lynne Pearce and Jackie Stacey. London: Lawrence and Wishart, 1995, 78–88.

Wardrop, Stephanie. "The Heroine is Being Beaten: Freud, Sado-Masochism, and Reading the Romance." *Style* (Fall 1995), 459–73. On-line. Available First Search. July 3, 1996.

Watson, Kenneth F. *Leisure Reading Habits: A Survey of the Leisure Reading Habits of Canadian Adults with Some International Comparisons*. Commissioned by the Department of the Secretary of State of Canada. Researched by Statistics Canada. Analyzed by Abt Associates Research. Ottawa: Infoscan, 1980.

Weisser, Susan Ostrov. "The Wonderful-Terrible Bitch Figure in Harlequin Novels." In *Feminist Nightmares: Women at Odds: Feminism and the Problem of Sisterhood*, ed. Susan Ostrov Weisser and Jennifer Fleischner. New York: New York University Press, 1994, 269–82.

Whissell, Cynthia. "The Formula behind Women's Romance Formula Fiction." *Arachne* (1997).

———. "Mate Selection in Popular Women's Fiction." *Human Nature* 7 (1996), 427–47.

———. "Objective Analysis of Text: I. A Comparison of Adventure and Romance Novels." *Perceptual and Motor Skills* 79 (1994), 1567–70.

Whitney, Phyllis A. *Guide to Fiction Writing*. Boston: Writer, 1982.

Wibberley, Mary. *To Writers with Love: On Writing Romantic Novels*. London: Buchan and Enright, 1985.

Wikoff, Katherine, "Readings in Romance Fiction: Nostalgia as Pathology?" *The Cream City Review* 18: 2. On-line. Available http://www.uwm.edu/People/noj/tccr/smp18–2c.htm#wikoff. March 14, 1996.

Wright, R. Glenn, comp. *Author Bibliography of English Language Fiction in the Library of Congress through 1950*. Boston: G. K. Hall, 1973.

———. *Chronological Bibliography of English Language Fiction in the Library of Congress through 1950*. Boston: G. K. Hall, 1974.

———. *Title Bibliography of English Language Fiction in the Library of Congress through 1950*. Boston: G. K. Hall, 1976.

Yankelovich, Skelly, and White. *Consumer Research Study on Reading and Book Purchasing*. Darien, Conn.: The Group, 1978, 1983 (3 vols.).

Young, Beth Rapp. "Accidental Authors, Random Readers, and the Art of Popular

Romance." *Para*doxa: Studies in World Literary Genres* 3: 1–2 (1997), 29–45.

Zidle, Abby. "From Bodice-Ripper to Baby-Sitter: The New Hero in Mass Market Romance." In *Romantic Conventions*, ed. Anne K. Kaler and Rosemary E. Johnson-Kurek. Bowling Green, Ohio: Bowling Green State University Popular Press, 1999, 23–34.

Zuckerman, Mary Ellen, comp. *Sources on the History of Women's Magazines, 1792–1960: An Annotated Bibliography.* New York: Greenwood, 1991.

Periodicals

Affaire de Coeur. Oakland, Calif. 1979– .
Legacy. Amherst, Mass. 1984– .
Publishers Weekly. New York, 1872– .
Romance Writers' Report. Houston, Tex., 1981– .
Romantic Times. Brooklyn Heights, N.Y., 1982– .

SCIENCE

George F. Spagna Jr. and
Elizabeth Barnaby Keeney

The nature and power of science as a cultural force in modern America are profound. Coexistence with the payoffs and fallouts from modern science—the space race, nuclear weaponry and power, the miracles and dilemmas of genetics, global communications technology, and the explosive growth of the Internet—has bred a culture in which science is pervasive in content, style, and imagery. Yet, it is a culture in which the underlying science can seemingly be ignored by most, much as one need not understand the principles of the internal combustion engine in order to drive a modern car. This chapter explores some of the routes by which science came to play an important role in modern culture and assesses the current place of science.

Several themes are of sufficient importance to be laid out from the start. The most obvious revolves around the transmission of science into popular culture. How does the nonexpert gain access to scientific knowledge? Who generates it? Who receives it? Why? What happens to it and to them in the process? What is the perceived importance or meaning of science as popular culture? A second broad theme focuses on the popular image of science and the scientist. What is the perceived importance of science as an intellectual pursuit? How is it seen as relating to other areas of knowledge, especially religion? What is the image of science and the scientist? What is the perceived impact of science and scientists on society? The themes of transmission and image are traced over the course of American history with the aim of steering the reader to the relevant questions, figures, and literature. This exposition is by no means complete. Rather, it is intended to guide the reader to further exploration.

HISTORICAL OUTLINE

As Europeans first began to settle in the New World, they turned to the exploration and exploitation of the natural resources of their new home. Their interest was driven in large part by the need to survive, which was obviously linked to the environment. Curiosity also played a major part. The New World was populated and covered with unfamiliar plants, animals, and geological productions that mystified and delighted not only the settlers but also those Europeans lucky enough to be the recipients of shipments of specimens and accounts. Religious interest—spawned by the widespread belief that by studying nature one could find evidence of the existence and character of its designer and creator—also proved to be an important motivation. The intellectual elite of the day—ministers, physicians, lawyers, and other scholars—maintained a strong interest in science. As cities emerged in the clearings and on the hillsides, so, too, did the trappings of learned culture that science needs to thrive—learned societies, libraries, schools, and the like. European naturalists encouraged those colonists whom they knew to be interested in natural history by arranging for shipments of specimens, providing books, supplies, equipment, and ensuring the publication of findings. This encouragement evolved into an informal network, the "natural history circle," which consisted of naturalists up and down the East Coast and in Europe. Many colonists corresponded less formally about natural history. Still others sent astronomical observations and descriptions of native American life. Twenty-five colonists were rewarded for their contributions by election to the Royal Society of London. Accounts of the New World written by colonists—for example, Thomas Jefferson's *Notes on the State of Virginia*—which included careful descriptions of natural history, were popular reading in America and in Europe.

More accessible writings, among them almanacs and newspapers, were far more important to the spread of scientific culture in the colonies than were these longer narratives. Almanacs sprinkled comments on astronomy, medicine, and natural history among the agricultural and meteorological advice that formed their cores. The new heliocentric astronomy, for example, found its way into American culture via this medium. Newspaper reporting of scientific matters was even more diverse, as were popular lectures, which provided both education and entertainment. Toward the end of the colonial period, attempts began at the publication of magazines with varying degrees of interest in science, but financial problems meant that few lasted long.

For those seriously interested in science, the late colonial period saw the emergence of American, rather than colonial, learned and scientific institutions. Learned colonists banded together to share their interests and encourage each other first and most successfully in Philadelphia in Benjamin Franklin's Junto (1727) and slowly in other cities as well. In 1769 the Junto merged with Franklin's American Philosophical Society (1744) to become the American Philosophical Society Held at Philadelphia for Promoting Useful Knowledge, which remains one of the nation's leading learned societies today. Colonial libraries, among them those of the American Philosophical Society, the young colleges, and the library companies like the Redwood Library at Newport, Rhode Island, began to develop collections that included scientific tracts. At the colleges, where young men were primarily trained for the ministry and other learned callings, science played a small, but significant, role in the curriculum as a piece of learned culture that was important to a full understanding of God's natural creations. As it became a reality that, in the words of Benjamin Franklin in 1743, "the first drudgery of settling new colonies which confines the attention of people to mere necessaries is now

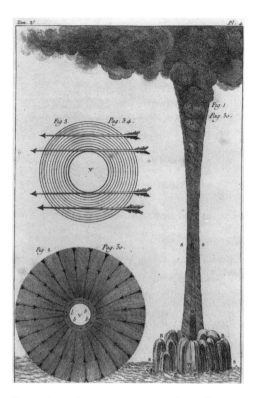

Engraving of a waterspout used to illustrate
Benjamin Franklin's discussion of terrors at
sea, ca. 1753. Courtesy of the Library of Congress

pretty well over; and there are men in every province in circumstances that set
them at ease, and afford them the leisure to cultivate the finer arts and improve
the common stock of knowledge," the institutions of science and the interest and
support needed to sustain them emerged (qtd, in Hindle, 1974: 1).

Science still remained primarily an activity or interest of the elite of society on
the eve of the Revolution. Newspaper science and popular lectures aside, few
Americans had the luxury of interest in science for its own sake. In the colonial
upper class, men, and occasionally women, as Joan Hoff Wilson has observed,
could pursue science. But most colonists, male or female, were occupied with more
immediate and practical concerns (225).

In the wake of the Revolution, science became secondary in the public mind to
the creation of a new nation. Indeed, not all Americans saw science as a positive
aspect of American life. Young William Cullen Bryant was expressing a sentiment
popular among his elders in his 1809 poem "The Embargo" when he chastised
President Thomas Jefferson for his scientific interests:

> Go, wretch, resign the presidential chair,
> Disclose thy secret measures, fowl or fair.
> Go, search with curious eye, for horned frogs,

> Mid the wild wastes of Louisianian bogs;
> Or, where Ohio rolls his turbid stream,
> Dig for huge bones, thy glory and thy theme. (40)

British support, once so important, was no more, and no American structure was yet in place. The challenge, in the words of Franklin in 1785, was to make a reality of "the favorable influence that Freedom has upon the growth of useful Sciences and Arts." Science was shaped by nationalism and at the same time became a tool of nationalism. On the one hand, the promise of the utility of science and the potential national gain associated with scientific advance served to promote science. On the other, these same motivations dictated specific sorts of science and scientific culture over others. Geographic and observational sciences, most especially botany, zoology, and geology, which held dual promises of utility and illustration of the Creator's hand, thrived. Theoretical science, for example, chemistry and physics, did less well.

The early nineteenth century saw the emergence of a new American science in terms of both its intellectual structure and its social structure. Emphasis on Scottish commonsense realism and adherence to an approach to science promoted long before by Francis Bacon, stressing fact gathering and observation, produced a peculiarly American science, perceived as the handmaiden of religion. Nascent professionals and amateurs alike took interest in geology or botany not only because it would potentially yield practical knowledge that would better the nation but also because it would lend an understanding of God. Discussions about the relationship of science and religion centered not over conflicts but rather over reconciliation. Scientists and theologians were more likely to argue that because one Creator was behind both revealed theology (based on the Bible) and natural theology (based on God's creations and works in the natural world) any conflicts between science and religion must be with errors of interpretation, than they were to assert that their field was correct to the exclusion of the other or that the two spheres were unrelated.

Among the institutions of the new nation were many that supported education and entertainment in a variety of fields, including science. The antebellum period saw the growth of formal education of all sorts from primary schools through colleges. Science came out a winner at all levels. Children's readers were filled with essays on science and on natural theology, the academy curricula for both male and female students included heavy doses of science, and the antebellum colleges increasingly added courses in natural history and natural philosophy (physical sciences), while keeping classes in natural theology, all during a period when enrollment at each level was growing. In the 1820s public lecturing became organized into the *lyceum* movement, which sponsored lecture series in towns across the country on a range of topics, many of them scientific. By the 1840s Boston's Lowell Institute could attract audiences of 2,000 when a popular lecturer like Yale professor Benjamin Silliman held forth on science. Antebellum America was abuzz with reform movements and self-improvement schemes, and the promoters of science, not surprisingly, cast their pastime in this light. Scientific culture was woven into a larger mesh of piety, industriousness, and socially acceptable behavior. A regional perspective is provided in Thomas Johnson's *Scientific Interests in the Old South*. While institutions certainly encouraged this, they were not alone.

Scientific textbooks, especially those that could be used equally well at home for self-instruction, became best-sellers, and other publications followed suit. With a popular text such as Mrs. Almira Hart Lincoln Phelp's *Familiar Lectures on Botany* or *Botany for Beginners*, both best-sellers, and a local field guide in hand, many antebellum Americans pursued science on their own as a valued pastime. This interest in self-improvement, whether institutional or individual, led to a boom in publishing and shaped the nature of what was published.

The antebellum period saw the first long-lived American periodicals, including the first dedicated to science, the *Medical Repository* (1797), which covered both medicine and science, and Benjamin Silliman's *American Journal of Science* (1818). The *American Journal of Science* (known as *Silliman's Journal*, for its editor) never had particularly wide circulation even by standards of the day, but its impact on amateurs and professionals alike was nonetheless great. Throughout the nineteenth century, it served to keep those interested in science abreast of the latest news and developments, though by late century it had begun to specialize in geology and was joined by a host of other periodicals. Some, like the *American Naturalist* (1867) and the *Scientific American* (1845), which began as a technical journal, focused on one area of science. Others, like the *Popular Science Monthly* (1872) (now *Popular Science*) and *Popular Astronomy* (1893), targeted laypeople, while still others, like the *Botanical Gazette* (1875), targeted professionals.

Many of the new periodicals were organs of the new scientific societies, which flourished and grew as the century progressed. In towns and cities across the new nation the scientifically literate and merely curious banded together. Joining the ranks of general learned and scientific societies were specialized clubs—the Torrey Botanical Club and the Nuttall Ornithological Club, to name but two—as well as, increasingly, societies that catered only to professionals, such as the Botanical Society of America. Often one of the activities of a society was to publish a magazine—for example, the Torrey Botanical Club's *Bulletin* (1870). *Science* (1883) emerged as the organ of the American Association for the Advancement of Science and today remains among the nation's most important scientific periodicals.

Popular periodicals of a more general nature also included science and indeed found it to be a topic that appealed to readers. Relatively intellectual periodicals like the *North American Review* (1815), *Southern Literary Messenger* (1834), *Harper's Magazine* (1850), or the *Atlantic Monthly* (1857) found scientific coverage to be well worth the space in terms of reader interest. Women's magazines, for example, *Godey's Lady's Book* (1830), and even children's, for example, the *Youth's Companion* (1827) and *Merry's Museum and Parley's Magazine* (1842), or farmers', for example, *The Country Gentleman* (1853), all filled their pages with science. At the turn of the century, nature magazines sponsored by institutions gained importance. *National Geographic* (1888) emerged as a way for enthusiasts to support exploration, both scientific and general, from their armchairs. *Audubon Magazine* (1899) gave them a way to support preservation. Museum publications like *Natural History* (1900) gave them a way to support research and education. More recently, *Smithsonian* (1970/1971) continues the trend.

Museums, botanical gardens, zoological parks, and observatories all walked the line between education and entertainment as well. Originally seen as a chance to display the wonders of God's handiwork as found in the objects of creation, they soon became not merely places for research and self-improvement but places for

WALDEN;

OR,

LIFE IN THE WOODS.

By HENRY D. THOREAU,

AUTHOR OF "A WEEK ON THE CONCORD AND MERRIMACK RIVERS."

I do not propose to write an ode to dejection, but to brag as lustily as chanticleer in the morning, standing on his roost, if only to wake my neighbors up. — Page 92.

BOSTON:

TICKNOR AND FIELDS.

M DCCC LIV.

Henry David Thoreau's *Walden*, 1854. Courtesy of the Library of Congress

entertainment as well. In part, this reflected the nation's collecting mania on a grand scale. Children were exhorted to begin their own "museums" in books like Jacob Abbott's *Rollo's Museum*, and adults to support more formal institutions financially. Colleges, cities, private groups, and eventually the federal government as guardian of the bequest of James Smithson, a British enthusiast, all became the keepers of an array of scientific institutions that combined education and entertainment. From these sprang yet more periodicals, books, lecture series, expeditions, and, in more recent times, television shows, motion pictures, and Internet sites.

The interest in nature spawned here gave rise to a literary genre of popular nature writing, which followed from the early accounts of colonists like Jefferson through the transcendentalists, most notably, Henry David Thoreau and Ralph Waldo Emerson. Later in the century, more realistic and less romantic writers, including John Muir and John Burroughs, became popular. This viewpoint also finds its way into the fiction of the nineteenth and twentieth centuries, as discussed in Norman Foerster's *Nature in American Literature: Studies in the Modern View of Nature* and in Charles Walcutt's *American Literary Naturalism: A Divided Stream*. The social sciences also found outlet, as described in Jean Pfaelzer's *The Utopian Novel in America, 1886–1896* and in Robert Shurter's broader *The Utopian Novel in America, 1865–1900.* In the twentieth century, Aldo Leopold, Rachel Carson, and a host of modern writers on nature, including Lewis Thomas, Carl Sagan, and Annie Dillard, carried on the popular expository tradition. This tradition has been explored in *Expository Science: Forms and Functions of Popularization*, edited by Terry Shinn and Richard Whitley. Timothy Ferris, Stephen Hawking, Roger Penrose, Stephen Jay Gould, and P.C.W. Davies continue writing today.

Over time science became increasingly professionalized, and the directions in which professionals chose to push science were not always ones that sat well with the public. With the coming of Darwinian evolution and the nineteenth- and twentieth-century revolutions in physics, increasingly science became both the threat and the promise that it is in modern America. Thermodynamics, which many American intellectuals felt implied decay, not progress, in the natural world and human society, and organic evolution, which heated already brewing controversies that remain with us yet today about the relationship of science and religion, cast an increasing shadow over science and the scientist.

The relationship between science and religion in American thought is immensely complex. On the one hand, religion can provide a motivation for studying science, as the two can be, and often have been, seen to be talking about one and the same material, and hence each can enhance the other. Well into the nineteenth century, scientific leaders and laypeople alike saw natural theology as one of the strongest reasons to pursue science. In this paradigm, any conflicts between science and religion must be due to errors in interpretation, as one great Author lay behind both the book of Nature and the written Scripture. The American religious response to scientific theories in the nineteenth century thus was in large part determined by the role that they left, implicitly or explicitly, for God in creating and governing the world. In the case of organic evolution, the responses ranged from complete acceptance of Darwinian evolution, to acceptance of evolution but not of natural selection, to rejection on the grounds of biblical literalism. By late century, what had once been a comfortable relation between science and religion was strained in some quarters, though certainly not all. Cornell University's founder, Andrew D. White, wrote *A History of the Warfare of Science with Theology in Christendom* in 1896, and it is still available in reprint. A recent contribution is found in Brook and Cantor's *Reconstructing Nature: The Engagement of Science and Religion.* Contemporary studies of the relation between scientific and religious worldviews include Alister McGrath's *Foundations of Dialogue in Science and Religion* and *Science and Religion: An Introduction.*

In the early twentieth century, conservative Christians began to worry about a variety of challenges to biblical literalism, including public school teaching of evolutionary theory, especially the notion that humans have evolved. Legislative attempts to ban the teaching of evolution ensued, and the Scopes "monkey trial" in Dayton, Tennessee, in 1925 became a major media event and brought the movement to the public eye. Paul Conkin looks beyond the political arena in *When All the Gods Trembled: Darwinism, Scopes, and American Intellectuals.* In the wake of the creationists' legal victory in Dayton, textbook publishers softened or removed discussions of evolution from high school biology texts, and the issue quieted down until the early 1960s, when a National Science Foundation-funded textbook project (the Biological Sciences Curriculum Study) forcefully reintroduced evolution. Succeeding decades have seen repeated attempts by creationists either to ban the teaching of evolution or to present it alongside the biblical account of creation. End-run tactics, such as the introduction of so-called creation science, continue to this day. Ronald L. Numbers has contributed to recent studies of this phenomenon. Ivan Zabilka's *Scientific Malpractice: The Creaton/Evolution Debate* and Delos McKown's *The Mythmaker's Magic: Behind the Myth of "Creation Science"* offer selective viewpoints on the debate.

A fairly recent phenomenon is the reappearance of a viewpoint that does not place science and religion at odds. Anglican priest and particle physicist John Polkinghorne argues for a *Belief in God in an Age of Science*. Other contributions may be found in *Cosmos, Bios, Theos*, edited by Henry Margenau and Roy Abraham Varghese. Ian Barbour provides an overview in *Religion in an Age of Science*, and Chet Raymo offers another viewpoint in *Skeptics and True Believers: The Exhilarating Connection between Science and Religion*.

Through the works of one of Darwin's chief popularizers, Herbert Spencer, Americans became familiar with a dark side of evolution, competition and struggle. Spencer's essays were widely read in both collected volumes and in the *Popular Science Monthly*, wherein he adapted and modified Darwin's ideas to discuss human society. His followers, so-called social Darwinists, believed that competition and survival of the fittest were phenomena not merely of nature but of human society as well. Literary naturalists, most especially Jack London, reflected the horror of this realization in their fiction, while social theorists used it to justify reform schemes that equated poverty and illness with "unfitness" and hence unworthiness to survive. This reached its nadir in America in the eugenics movement, a British import that sought to influence the human gene pool and hence society by immigration quotas and forced sterilization of groups perceived as "unfit" because of ethnicity, social class, or alleged "feeble-mindedness" or "criminal character" and through attempts to encourage the reproduction of the "fit." Changes in scientific understanding of heredity and the horrors of World War II brought these sorts of attempts largely to an end, though eugenics laws remained on the books in some states well into the latter half of the century.

Despite this underlying negative image, the early twentieth century also saw the zenith of the public perception of science and scientists in which scientists were portrayed as heroes and science as the key to all social reform. Throughout the Progressive Era this positive image of science became reified in everything from food and drug legislation and workplace reforms to programs to help mothers and infants. Sinclair Lewis' *Arrowsmith* (1925) and Upton Sinclair's *The Jungle* (1906) stand as literary pillars of this imagery.

As the war era loomed, science was seen as the nation's best tool not only to win war but perhaps to prevent it. In the wake of World War II, however, such optimism was challenged by the growing realization that science could at once create and destroy. Concerns about nuclear weaponry and power, about genetic engineering, and about the environment all led to major debates about the nature and value of science. Even the space program, which stood as a symbol of what science could accomplish, has seen dramatic shifts in public approbation. The *Challenger* disaster in 1986 can be balanced by the spectacular successes of the thrice-refitted Hubble space telescope, but a fickle public remembers the more recent failure of Mars *Polar Lander* and Mars *Climate Observer* in 1999 in more detail than successful Mars *Pathfinder* and the plucky rover *Sojourner* in 1997.

The means by which Americans learn about science have changed dramatically. Books and periodicals are still chief agents. Stephen Jay Gould has joined the ranks of Loren Eisley, Isaac Asimov, Carl Sagan, and the host of other post–World War II writers whose scientific works have captured a popular audience. Science magazines have multiplied, and the older standard-bearers, like *Scientific American* and *National Geographic*, have been joined by a series of new journals. *Sky and Telescope* (1941), *Environment* (1959), and many other specialized popular periodicals emerged in midcentury. *Smithsonian* (which is a general magazine with a high science content) began in the 1970s, a decade that saw a number of new science periodicals, most notably *Omni* (1978). The trend appeared to be continuing in the 1980s, when *Discover* (1980) began publication, but the mid-1980s saw a number of science magazines die, perhaps because of waning interest but more probably because of competition not only among the many periodicals but from other media as well.

Print media are no longer the only show, or perhaps even the dominant show, in town. From its earliest days television attempted to combine education and entertainment with Don Herbert, aka *Mr. Wizard*, and other science shows. *National Geographic* specials began running in 1965, and the 1970s and 1980s saw a dramatic increase in both the quantity and quality of science shows. *NOVA* and other series and specials too numerous to list cater to all ages. *Newton's Apple* and *3–2–1 Contact* have brought children's science television a long way from the early days of *Mr. Wizard*. The explosive growth of cable and direct satellite connections brings access to commercial (e.g., the Discovery Channel) and noncommercial (e.g., NASA Direct) science presentations. Entering the keywords "Popular Science" into almost any Internet search engine generates tens of thousands of hits to World Wide Web sites. The challenge for the Net searcher, as for the television watcher, is to discriminate between real science and junk science. Martin Gardner's *Fads and Fallacies in the Name of Science* and *Science: Good, Bad, and Bogus* show that this phenomenon is not new or unique to the era of global Internet communication. Indeed, Taylor Stoehr demonstrates the deep literary tradition of pseudoscience in *Hawthorne's Mad Scientists: Pseudoscience and Social Science in Nineteenth-Century Life and Letters*.

Increasingly in the post World War II era, mass media have played a major role in determining the public's reaction to science. Breaking news on science and its effects are often presented as either miraculous or disastrous. Medical breakthroughs are often cast in the former light, though stories of failed gene therapies or drug trials gone awry can tarnish the halo. Accidents like those at Three Mile Island or Chernobyl are typically remembered long after their effects have been ameliorated. Often, though, the situation is more complicated, with the potential of both great benefit and significant threat, as in the case of pesticides that can both improve crop production and cause environmental harm. Science and its byproducts have become neither savior nor demon but both, a Dr. Jekyll and Mr. Hyde in public imagination.

That the scientific enterprise has risen to the level of cultural icon is undeniable. That popular understanding of science is often off-target is also likely. Greg De Young describes the popularity of science themes in "Postage Stamps and the Popular Iconography of Science." Dorothy Nelkin and M. Susan Lindee examine the promise and hype in *The DNA Mystique: The Gene as a Cultural Icon*. Or, with obvious reference to Mary Shelley's *Frankenstein*, science and scientists remain what Robert de Ropp describes in *The New Prometheans: Creative and Destructive Forces in Modern Science*.

REFERENCE WORKS

The general neglect of popular science is nowhere felt so clearly as in the dearth of reference works specifically aimed at the phenomenon. The most practical approach is to begin with the many works that aim at science generally and to winnow out popular works and studies of science and popular culture from among the mass of literature.

Finding one's way around the many bibliographies, encyclopedias, and other reference works on science is facilitated by Ching-Chih Chen's *Scientific and Technical Information Sources*, which is an annotated guide. Older primary and secondary sources on natural history can be located through Max Meisel's *Bibliography of American Natural History: The Pioneer Century, 1769–1865*. The McGraw-Hill *Encyclopedia of Science and Technology* and *The Harper Encyclopedia of Science*, edited by James R. Newman, provide good introductions to many subjects, as does the *Encyclopaedia Britannica*. Works like S. Parker's *McGraw-Hill Dictionary of Scientific and Technical Terms* and M. J. Clugston's *The New Penguin Dictionary of Science* are useful tools for deciphering specialized terminology. Recent advances and accomplishments may be followed in *Science Year: The World Book Science Annual*.

Several guides to the historical sources are useful. The journal *Isis* publishes an annual critical bibliography of the history of science that includes works on science in American culture. Four cumulations of these bibliographies—Magda Whitrow's *ISIS Cumulative Bibliography*, which covers 1913–1965, and John Neu's three volumes (*Isis Cumulative Bibliography, 1966–1975, 1976–1985*, and *1986–1995*)—include detailed subject breakdowns by area of science, culture, and historical period. Hamilton Cravens' "Science, Technology, and Medicine" and Marc Rothenberg's two volumes on *The History of Science and Technology in the United States: A Critical and Selective Bibliography* offer excellent guides to the literature on American science. The essays in Sally Gregory Kohlstedt and Margaret W. Rossiter's *Historical Writing on American Science: Perspectives and Prospects* offer critical appraisal of a number of fields and topics of interest, although none of the essays deals directly with science and popular culture. Kohlstedt et al. have also written for the American Association for the Advancement of Science (AAAS) a history of that organization and its relation to American society, *The Establishment of Science in America: 150 Years of the American Association for the Advancement of Science*. Clark A. Elliot's *History of Science in the United States* is another useful source. Theodore Besterman has compiled two bibliographic references, *Biological Sciences: A Bibliography of Bibliographies* and *Physical Sciences: A Bibliography of Bibliographies*. Denis Grogan's *Science and Technology: An Introduction to the Literature* and Malinowsky's *Science and Engineering Literature: A Guide to Reference Sources* are also useful starting points. To begin studying the relation between science and the broader citizenry, one can start with Marcel La Follette's *The Citizen and Science: Almanac and Annotated Bibliography*.

Biographical studies of scientists abound. Living scientists are described briefly in *American Men and Women of Science*. Clark Elliot's *Biographical Dictionary of*

American Science: The Seventeenth through the Nineteenth Centuries provides a short sketch and bibliography for all but the most obscure. The most prominent deceased scientists are included in the *Dictionary of Scientific Biography*. The *Isis Cumulative Bibliographies* by Whitrow include biographical volumes. The University of Alabama Press sponsors a growing series on "The History of American Science and Technology," containing both monographs and collections.

RESEARCH COLLECTIONS

Many libraries in the United States have fine collections of popular science holdings. The Library of Congress and major public libraries are particularly apt to have popular—as opposed to academic—works. University and college libraries vary considerably in their approach to collecting popular works, though those with education schools often have very good collections. Those interested in the pre–Civil War period will find that since the lines between popular and scholarly science had not yet been firmly drawn, any major science collection with historic holdings is apt to be of interest. The best academic libraries in this regard are generally found at institutions with programs in the history of science. Those specifically interested in areas that touch on medicine should not overlook the National Library of Medicine in Bethesda, Maryland. Those interested in natural history will find valuable libraries at many museums, most notably, the Academy of Natural Sciences in Philadelphia. Lee Ash has compiled an updated listing of library and museum resources in *Subject Collections: A Guide to Special Book Collections and Subject Emphasis as Reported by University, College Public and Special Libraries and Museums in the United States and Canada*. Similarly, Huelmantel's *Directory of Special Libraries and Information Centers* is a current compilation.

Those interested in specific scientists may find their papers and correspondence of interest. The location of collections can be found in the biographical sketches in Clark Elliot's *Biographical Dictionary of American Science* and the *Dictionary of Scientific Biography*. Pre-twentieth-century collections can be especially revealing about popular science, as many amateurs corresponded with national luminaries. The Library of Congress and the American Philosophical Society in Philadelphia each holds extensive collections, but state historical societies, colleges, and universities also have important collections. Those specifically interested in women in science will find the holdings of the Schlesinger Library on the History of Women at Harvard University immensely valuable.

HISTORY AND CRITICISM

The closing decades of the twentieth century saw a revolution in the historical study of science that included a growing realization that science is both culturally bound and part of popular culture. The result is growing literatures on American science and science in American culture, both of which deserve our attention here. American historians have generally devoted little interest to science, even in their social and intellectual histories, but there are exceptions, and recent works suggest that the situation is improving. Merle Curti's *The Growth of American Thought* speaks eloquently about science as both intellectual and popular culture. Perry Miller's *The Life of the Mind in America: From the Revolution to the Civil War*, an unfinished posthumous work, provides an intriguing outline. Similarly, historians of American science have been more concerned with the scientific community and its work than with popular culture. George Daniels' *Science in American Society: A Social History*, though problematic, provides an introduction. The essays in Nathan Reingold's *The Sciences in the American Context: New Perspectives* explore a number of areas of science from different perspectives. Reingold's two volumes of documentary history, the second coedited with Ida Reingold, provide insights to both professional and amateur scientists, but mostly the former.

More focused, chronological studies from both disciplines offer more on science in popular culture. Louis B. Wright's chapter on "Scientific Interest and Observation," in his *The Cultural Life of the American Colonies*, remains a classic. Brooke Hindle's *The Pursuit of Science in Revolutionary America* and the volume of essays from *Isis* that he edited, *Early American Science*, cover both popular and professional science in the colonial era. Older, but still valuable and lively, is Dirk Struik's *Yankee Science in the Making*. Antebellum America has received major attention from historians of American science. John C. Greene's *American Science in the Age of Jefferson* joins George Daniels' *American Science in the Age of Jackson* to survey scientific developments. Greene's essay "Popular Science in the Age of Jefferson" (reprinted in Hindle, *Early American Science*) remains, with Donald Zochert's essays "Science and the Common Man in Ante-bellum America" (reprinted in Reingold, *Science in America from 1820–1940*) and "The Natural History of an American Pioneer: A Case Study," as well as Walter Hendrickson's "Science and Culture in the American Middle West" (also reprinted in Reingold), the most explicit treatment of popular science. Howard Miller's *Dollars for Research* and A. Hunter Dupree's *Science in the Federal Government* offer insight into why Americans chose to fund science in the nineteenth century.

Robert Bruce's *The Launching of Modern American Science, 1846–1876* carries us through the Civil War in Pulitzer Prize-winning style. Paul Carter's *The Spiritual Crisis of the Gilded Age* provides a sense of American thought in the era. Cynthia Russett's *Darwin in America* and Paul Boller Jr.'s *American Thought in Transition*, while topical, offer many insights into the relationship of science and social thought in this period, as does the more diverse collection of essays by Charles Rosenberg, *No Other Gods: On Science and American Social Thought*. Douglas Sloan's "Science in New York City" explores the place of science in one American city, while Oleson and Brown present essays on a variety of places and disciplines in *The Pursuit of Knowledge in the Early American Republic: American Scientific and Learned Societies from Colonial Times to the Civil War*.

Samuel Hays' *Conservation and the Social Gospel of Efficiency* illuminates the Progressives' concern with science. Ronald Tobey's *The American Ideology of National Science, 1919–1930* and his *Saving the Prairies: The Life Cycle of the Founding School of American Plant Ecology, 1895–1955* explore the interfaces of science and society. In his *Technology as Freedom: The New Deal and the Electrical Modernization of the American Home*, Tobey examines an entirely twentieth-century aspect of the same question. As even the rather narrow focus of these works suggests, for other aspects of the twentieth century one is best off exploring the topical histories. Everett Mendelsohn's "Science in America: The Twentieth Century," though somewhat dated, provides an introduction to the era.

Daniel J. Kevles' *The Physicists*, which focuses on the emergence of a profession

Rachel Carson. Courtesy of the Library of Congress

in America, provides a fine introduction and bibliography. Kevles also provides a look at the interactions between science and society in his 1985 monograph *In the Name of Eugenics.* One area of physical science where amateurs have participated, and continue to participate is astronomy. Marc Rothenberg's "Organization and Control: Professionals and Amateurs in American Astronomy, 1899–1918" explores one aspect of this participation; Russell McCormmach's "Ormsby Mac-Knight Mitchell's *Sidereal Messenger,* 1846–48" explores another. Hyman Kuritz's "The Popularization of Science in Nineteenth-Century America" emphasizes physics, as does Linda Kerber's "Science in the Early Republic."

Natural history has had many chroniclers. Max Meisel's *Bibliography of American Natural History* offers a useful introduction and guide to sources. Joseph Kastner's general *A Species of Eternity* and his history of bird-watching, *A World of Watchers,* nicely blend the professional and amateur interests. Smallwood and Smallwood, *Natural History and the American Mind,* and Huth, *Nature and the American,* remain classics and are now complemented by Charlotte Porter's *The Eagles Nest: Natural History and American Ideas, 1812–1842.* Clive Bush's *The Dream of Reason* is a more recent exploration of the cultural meaning of nature in America. Donald Worster's *Nature's Economy: A History of Ecological Ideas* explores the transformation of interest in nature into interest in the environment, as does his *The Wealth of Nature: Environmental History and the Ecological Imagination.* Lynn Barber's *The Heyday of*

Natural History, 1820–1870 focuses heavily on Great Britain but does provide insight into America as well, while Wayne Hanley's *Natural History in America* provides biographical sketches of a handful of prominent figures. Peter Schmitt's *Back to Nature* provides an insightful look into why turn-of-the-century Americans grew so interested in the natural world.

Emanuel Rudolph's essays on amateur botany and botany education provide glimpses into one popular field. Marianne Ainley's "The Contribution of the Amateur to North American Ornithology" explores another field in which amateurs are still heavily involved. John Warner's " 'Exploring the Inner Labyrinths of Creation' " details popular microscopy in turn-of-the-century America.

It is at least arguable that no area of science has had more impact on popular culture than organic evolution, and historians have approached the topic from a number of angles. R. J. Wilson's *Darwinism and the American Intellectual* and Ronald L. Numbers' *Darwinism Comes to America* both collect primary documents, including reviews, responses, and reflections. Numbers' essay "Science and Religion" in the Kohlstedt and Rossiter volume is a good introduction to both the broad intellectual response and the religious dimensions. Bert Loewenberg has also used the title *Darwinism Comes to America*, exploring the issue from the side of the religious community. Thomas Glick's *The Comparative Reception of Darwinism* includes valuable essays by Edward Pfeifer and Michele Aldrich on the United States. Stow Persons' *Evolutionary Thought in America* and Paul Boller's *American Thought in Transition* join Cynthia Russett's volume mentioned earlier to cover many aspects of evolutionary thought in America. William Coleman's essay on evolutionary themes in Frederick Jackson Turner's "frontier thesis" and Richard Hofstadter's classic *Social Darwinism in American Thought* explore some of the ways in which American intellectuals used evolutionary thought in nonbiological arenas. The reflection of biological thought in social theory predates Darwinism, as William Stanton's *The Leopard's Spots: Scientific Attitudes towards Race in America, 1815–1859* amply demonstrates. Daniel Kevles' *In the Name of Eugenics* talks about the use and misuse of understandings of human heredity in America and Great Britain, while Stephen J. Gould's *The Mismeasure of Man* specifically outlines problems with early and contemporary attempts to quantify fitness, especially intelligence. Dorothy Nelkin's *The Creation Controversy: Science or Scripture in the Schools*, Edward Larson's *Trial and Error*, and Ronald Numbers' "The Creationists" all discuss the debates between evolutionists and creationists in the twentieth century.

The interest in gardens, zoos, and museums spawned by natural history is now being documented. Charles Sellers' *Mr. Peale's Museum* presents a lively account of one of America's first natural history museums. Neil Harris' *Humbug: The Art of P. T. Barnum* and John Richards Betts' "P. T. Barnum and the Popularization of Natural History" recount one man's very successful attempt to blend entertainment and education. George Brown Goode's *The Smithsonian Institution, 1846–1896* and Paul Oehser's *Sons of Science: The Story of the Smithsonian Institution and Its Leaders* are old but invaluable. Geoffrey Hellman provides a more modern account in *The Smithsonian: Octopus on the Mall*. William Deiss' "Spencer F. Baird and His Collectors," Phillip Kopper's *National Museum of Natural History*, and Curtis Hinsley's *Savages and Scientists: The Smithsonian Institution and the Development of American Anthropology, 1846–1910* provide more focused accounts. Philip J. Pauly's "The World and All That Is in It: The National Geographic Society,

1888–1918" and Nancy Lurie's *A Special Style: The Milwaukee Public Museum, 1882–1982* describe two other institutions. Ronald Rainger bridges biography and museum history in *An Agenda for Antiquity: Henry Fairfield Osborn and Vertebrate Paleontology at the American Museum of Natural History, 1890–1935*. Ann Leighton's volumes on gardens and Jeffery Stott's "The Historical Origins of the Zoological Park in American Thought" are among the only historical treatments of these forms of entertainment and education.

Well into the nineteenth century, learned and scientific societies served as an interface between popular culture and academic science. The standard source on American scientific societies is Ralph Bates' *Scientific Societies in the United States*, which, while somewhat dated, remains the only survey. Max Meisel's *Bibliography* lists many of the smaller societies, as well as the more major ones, and provides bibliographical material. Douglas Sloan's "Science in New York City, 1867–1907" provides a good account of the cultural meaning and import of scientific societies in one time and place. A similar, but broader, work is Simon Baatz's history of the New York Academy of Science, *Knowledge, Culture, and Science in the Metropolis*. Many individual societies have been the subject of study. Raymond Stearns' *Science in the British Colonies of North America* focuses on the role of the Royal Society of London. The American Association for the Advancement of Science, modern America's most important scientific society, is the subject of Sally Gregory Kohlstedt's *The Formation of the American Scientific Community*. Alexandra Oleson and Sanborn Brown's *The Pursuit of Knowledge in the Early American Republic* and Alexandra Oleson and John Voss' *The Organization of Knowledge in Modern America, 1860–1920* both contain many useful articles on societies. Walter Hendrickson's *The Arkites, and Other Pioneer Natural History Organizations of Cleveland* details both the learned and the social activities of a Cleveland society. Sally Gregory Kohlstedt's "The Nineteenth-Century Amateur Tradition: The Case of the Boston Society of Natural History" discusses the changing role of amateurs as science became increasingly professionalized.

Schools are an immensely important vehicle for the dissemination of popular science. Ruth Elson's *Guardians of Tradition* explores the content of nineteenth-century textbooks. Emanuel Rudolph's "The Introduction of the Natural System of Classification of Plants to Nineteenth Century American Students" examines the importance of one idea. Stanley Guralnick's *Science and the AnteBellum American Colleges* explores how and why science made its way into higher education.

In the days before mass communication, public lecturing on science was a popular form of entertainment and edification. Carl Bode's *The American Lyceum: Town Meeting of the Mind* chronicles the popular lecture movement of the nineteenth century. Margaret Rossiter's "Benjamin Silliman and the Lowell Institute" discusses the most important of the sponsors of public lectures.

The popular magazine still awaits a history. Frank Luther Mott's *A History of American Magazines* is an invaluable tool (despite being dated and sometimes inaccurate) because it has not been surpassed. Donald Beaver's "Altruism, Patriotism and Science: Scientific Journals in the Early Republic" and Matthew D. Whalen and Mary F. Tobin's "Periodicals and the Popularization of Science in America, 1860–1910" are two of the few studies of scientific periodicals specifically. Two popular periodicals have been the subject of individual studies. The *Popular Science Monthly* and its editor are the subject of William E. Leverette Jr.'s "E. C. Youmans' Crusade for Scientific Autonomy and Respectability." Russell Mc-Cormmach's "Ormsby MacKnight Mitchell's *Sidereal Messenger, 1846–48*" examines a short-lived, but important, popular astronomy magazine. Dorothy Nelkin examines contemporary science journalism in *Selling Science: How the Press Covers Science and Technology*. Thomas Maugh's "The Media: The Image of the Scientist Is Bad" examines the content of reporting, rather than the format.

A number of specific issues have caught the media's attention over the years. The relationship of science and religion has in recent years galvanized around controversies surrounding the teaching of evolution, as described earlier, but the background and setting for that debate are too often overlooked. Wendell Glick's "Bishop Paley in America" recounts the teaching of natural theology in early America. Theodore Bozeman's *Protestants in an Age of Science* and Herbert Hovenkamp's *Science and Religion in America, 1800–1860* both explore the interaction of Protestant theology and Baconian science. Ronald Numbers' *Creation by Natural Law* explores the religious influence on, and reaction to, one scientific theory, Laplace's "nebular hypothesis." Herbert Leventhal's *In the Shadow of the Enlightenment: Occultism and Renaissance Science in Eighteenth-Century America* and Laurence Moore's *In Search of White Crows: Spiritualism, Parapsychology, and American Culture* examine two aspects of the relationship of pseudoscience and religion. Dorothy Nelkin also explores the controversy over the teaching of evolution versus teaching "creation science" in two works, *The Creation Controversy: Science or Scripture in the Schools* and *Science Textbook Controversies and the Politics of Equal Time*. In *The Baltimore Case*, Kevles explores the political and mass media impact of possible scientific dishonesty.

Other aspects of science have also attracted much public attention. In modern America, concern about the real or potential perils of science has led to a situation where potential benefits must be weighed against possible risk. Nuclear power and weaponry, developments in genetics, and environmental concerns are but three of the best documented. Paul Boyer's *By the Bomb's Early Light: American Thought and Culture at the Dawn of the Atomic Age* surveys the popular response to the promise and the threat of nuclear weaponry. Clifford Grobstein's *A Double Image of the Double Helix: The Recombinant-DNA Debate* and John Richards' *Recombinant DNA: Science, Ethics, and Politics* chronicle public and professional response to advances in genetics. Society's periodic attention span may be well illustrated by the recurrence of concern with specific technologies. Jackson and Stitch also provide a pre-1980 chronicle in their *Recombinant DNA Debate*, and Sheldon Krimsky examines the same issues in *Genetic Alchemy: The Social History of the Recombinant DNA Controversy*. More recently, Horace Judson returns to similar issues in *The Eighth Day of Creation: Makers of the Revolution in Biology*. Rachel Carson's *Silent Spring* touched off public concern about the environment that had been smoldering beneath the surface. James Whorton's *Before Silent Spring* and Thomas Dunlap's *DDT: Scientists, Citizens, and Public Policy* recount the background to Carson's concerns. Frank Graham's *Since Silent Spring* describes the aftermath.

Many of the best entryways to popular science are biographies of both prominent and lesser-known scientists. Works on prominent scientists are so numerous that only a few of the best can be listed here. The Berkeleys' biographies of naturalist John Bartram and geologist George William Featherstonhaugh provide a glimpse of early American scientific culture. A. Hunter Dupree's life of botanist

Stephen Jay Gould. Courtesy of Harvard University

Asa Gray and Edward Lurie's of zoologist Louis Agassiz illustrate a fascinating contrast in scientific style and reaction to Darwinism. Tamara Haygood's biography of botanist Henry William Ravenel locates science in its southern context, while David Livingstone's biography of Nathaniel Southgate Shaler illustrates how those on the border of science and culture translated science to the broader world in the late nineteenth century. Peggy Champlin contributes *Raphael Pumpelly: Gentleman Geologist of the Gilded Age* to this genre, as does Patsy Gerstner's *Henry Darwin Rogers, 1808–1866: American Geologist.* Joseph Ewan has provided a look at *Rocky Mountain Naturalists* and *John Banister and His Natural History of Virginia, 1678–1692,* the latter coauthored by Nesta Ewan. Kenneth Manning has eloquently described the life of a black biologist, Ernest Just, in *Black Apollo of Science.* The impact of science on women's lives in nineteenth-century America is explored in Deborah Jean Warner's biography of Graceanna Lewis and also in Maxine Benson's *Martha Maxwell, Rocky Mountain Naturalist.*

Other aspects of women's interaction with science have recently begun to receive attention from historians. Margaret Rossiter's *Women Scientists in America: Struggles and Strategies to 1940* discusses the pursuit of science by women and includes an extensive bibliography. Patricia Siegel and Kay Finley's *Women in the Scientific Search* provides further bibliographic help. Joan Hoff Wilson's "Dancing Dogs" makes a case that colonial women were surprisingly involved in science.

Deborah Jean Warner describes the entry of science into the female academy curriculum in "Science Education for Young Women in Ante-bellum America." Emanuel Rudolph has explored the special relationship of women and botany, especially the role of Almira Hart Lincoln Phelps, in a series of articles. Laura Shapiro examines the impact of modern nutrition on female nonscientists in *Perfection Salad: Women and Cooking at the Turn of the Century*.

In late 1987, the role of science in American popular culture, long treated in the fragmentary fashion previously suggested, was the subject of a book: John C. Burnham's *How Superstition Won and Science Lost: Popularizing Science and Health in the United States*. In it, Burnham explores how popular science diverged from professional science to the detriment of public understanding. Superstition, Burnham argues, is alive and well in the public mind, having beaten out scientific enlightenment, in large part because of the nature of popularization. The volume offers a very rich plate of ideas and is well documented. Those interested in science as popular culture in America would do well to begin here.

The manner in which scientists interact with the broader culture or more narrowly with other intellectuals in nonscientific disciplines is also a subject of some interest to the broader public. In what is now a classic tale from 1996, physicist Alan Sokal published an essay in *Social Text*, a journal of cultural studies, purportedly exploring the similarities between quantum gravitational theory and postmodernism. He subsequently revealed that the entire article was a parody and a hoax, perpetrated solely to challenge the intellectual credibility of the editors. While such interdisciplinary squabbles are not new—indeed, the rift between the scientific and humanitarian disciplines has been well explored (and deplored) since C. P. Snow's *Two Cultures*—this tiff received much attention in the popular press, including front-page coverage by the venerable *New York Times*.

ANTHOLOGIES AND REPRINTS

Few collections of either primary or secondary works have appeared, but those that have are valuable. Ronald Numbers' *Darwinism Comes to America* and Robert Wilson's *Darwinism and the American Intellectual: An Anthology* both contain reviews and reflections. They present startlingly different focuses that remind the reader how much more we have to learn about the reception of Darwinism. Two collections of articles previously printed in *Isis* are also of special interest: Nathan Reingold's *Science in America from 1820–1940* and Brooke Hindle's *Early American Science*.

BIBLIOGRAPHY

Books and Articles

Abbott, Jacob. *Rollo's Museum*. Boston: Weeks, Jordon, 1839.

Ainley, Marianne Gostonyi. "The Contribution of the Amateur to North American Ornithology: A Historical Perspective." *The Living Bird* 18 (1979), 161–77.

Aldrich, Michele L. "United States Bibliographic Essay." In *The Comparative Re-*

ception of Darwinism, ed. Thomas F. Glick. Austin: University of Texas Press, 1972.

Asimov, Isaac. *Asimov's New Guide to Science*. New York: Basic Books, 1984.

Baatz, Simon. *Knowledge, Culture, and Science in the Metropolis: The New York Academy of Sciences, 1817–1970*. New York: New York Academy of Sciences, 1990.

Barber, Lynn. *The Heyday of Natural History, 1820–1870*. Garden City, N.Y.: Doubleday, 1980.

Barbour, Ian G. *Religion in an Age of Science*. San Francisco: HarperCollins, 1990.

Basalla, George. "Pop Science: The Depiction of Science in Popular Culture." In *Science and Its Public: The Changing Relationship*, ed. Gerald Holton and William A. Blanpied. Dordrecht, Holland: Reidel, 1976.

Beaver, Donald deB. "Altruism, Patriotism and Science: Scientific Journals in the Early Republic." *American Studies* 12 (1971), 5–19.

———. *The American Scientific Community, 1800–1860: A Statistical-Historical Study*. New York: Arno Press, 1980.

Bell, Whitfield J., Jr., and L. H. Butterfield. *Early American Science*. New York: Russell and Russell, 1971.

Bender, Thomas. "Science and the Culture of American Communities: The Nineteenth Century." *History of Education Quarterly* 16 (1976), 63–77.

Benson, Maxine. *Martha Maxwell, Rocky Mountain Naturalist*. Lincoln: University of Nebraska Press, 1970.

Berkeley, Edmund, and Dorothy Smith Berkeley. *George William Featherstonhaugh: The First U.S. Government Geologist*. Tuscaloosa: University of Alabama Press, 1988.

———. *The Life and Travels of John Bartram: From Lake Ontario to the River St. John*. Tallahassee: University Presses of Florida, 1990.

Betts, John Richards. "P. T. Barnum and the Popularization of Natural History." *Journal of the History of Ideas* 20 (1959), 353–68.

Black, George W., Jr. *American Science and Technology: A Bicentennial Bibliography*. Carbondale and Edwardsville: Southern Illinois University Press, 1979.

Bode, Carl. *The American Lyceum: Town Meeting of the Mind*. New York: Oxford University Press, 1956.

Boller, Paul, Jr. *American Thought in Transition: The Impact of Evolutionary Naturalism, 1865–1900*. Reprint. Lanham, Md.: University Press of America, 1981.

Boyer, Paul S. *By the Bomb's Early Light: American Thought and Culture at the Dawn of the Atomic Age*. Reprint. Chapel Hill: University of North Carolina Press, 1994.

Bozeman, Theodore Dwight. *Protestants in an Age of Science: The Baconian Ideal and Antebellum American Religious Thought*. Chapel Hill: University of North Carolina Press, 1977.

Bronowski, Jacob. *The Ascent of Man*. Boston: Little, Brown, 1984.

Brook, John, and Geoffrey Cantor. *Reconstructing Nature: The Engagement of Science and Religion*. Edinburgh: T and T Clark, 1998.

Bruce, Robert. *The Launching of Modern American Science, 1846–1876*. Ithaca, N.Y.: Cornell University Press, 1988.

Bryant, William Cullen. *The Embargo*. Facsimile of 1808 and 1809 editions, with introduction and notes by Thomas O. Mabbott. Gainesville, Fla.: Scholar's Facsimiles and Reprints, 1955.

Burnham, John C. *How Superstition Won and Science Lost: Popularizing Science and Health in the United States*. New Brunswick, N.J.: Rutgers University Press, 1987.

Burroughs, John. *The Gospel of Nature*. Bedford, Mass.: Applewood Books, 1990.
———. *In the Catskills*. Temecula, Calif.: Reprint Services, 1993.
———. *Writings of John Burroughs*. Temecula, Calif.: Reprint Services, 1993.

Burroughs, John, and Farida A. Wiley. *John Burroughs' America: Selections from the Writings of the Naturalist*. New York: Dover, 1997.

Bush, Clive. *The Dream of Reason: American Consciousness and Cultural Achievement from Independence to the Civil War*. New York: St. Martin's Press, 1978.

Carson, Rachel. *Silent Spring*. Boston: Houghton Mifflin, 1962.

Carter, Paul A. "Science and the Common Man." *American Scholar* 45 (1975–1976), 778–94.
———. *The Spiritual Crisis of the Gilded Age*. DeKalb: Northern Illinois University Press, 1971.

Champlin, Peggy. *Raphael Pumpelly: Gentleman Geologist of the Gilded Age*. Tuscaloosa: University of Alabama Press, 1994.

Coleman, William. "Science and Symbol in the Turner Frontier Hypothesis." *American Historical Review* 72 (1966), 22–49.

Conkin, Paul K. *When All the Gods Trembled: Darwinism, Scopes, and American Intellectuals*. Lanham, Md.: Rowman and Littlefield, 1998.

Cravens, Hamilton. "Science, Technology, and Medicine." In *American Studies: An Annotated Bibliography*, ed. J. Salzman. Cambridge: Cambridge University Press, 1988.

Cravens, Hamilton, Alan I. Marcus, and David M. Katzman, eds. *Technical Knowledge in American Culture: Science, Technology, and Medicine since the Early 1800s*. Tuscaloosa: University of Alabama Press, 1996.

Curti, Merle. *The Growth of American Thought*. 3rd ed. Reprint. Piscataway, N.J.: Transaction, 1991.

Daniels, George H. *American Science in the Age of Jackson*. Tuscaloosa: University of Alabama Press, 1994.
———. *Nineteenth-Century American Science: A Reappraisal*. Evanston, Ill.: Northwestern University Press, 1972.
———. *Science in American Society: A Social History*. New York: Alfred A. Knopf, 1971.

Davies, P.C.W. *God and the New Physics*. New York: Simon and Schuster, 1983.
———. *The Mind of God: The Scientific Basis for a Rational World*. New York: Simon and Schuster, 1992.

Deiss, William A. "Spencer F. Baird and His Collectors." *Journal of the Society for the Bibliography of Natural History* 9 (1980), 635–45.

de Ropp, Robert S. *The New Prometheans: Creative and Destructive Forces in Modern Science*. New York: Dell, 1973.

de Tocqueville, Alexis. *Democracy in America*. Ed. Henry Reeve, Francis Bowen, and Philips Bradley. New York: Alfred A. Knopf, 1966.

De Young, Greg. "Postage Stamps and the Popular Iconography of Science." *Journal of American Culture* 9 (Summer 1986), 1–13.

Dillard, Annie. *Pilgrim at Tinker's Creek*. Anniversary ed. New York: Harper-Collins, 1998.

Drees, Willem B. *Religion, Science, and Naturalism*. New York: Cambridge University Press, 1998.

Dunlap, Thomas R. *DDT: Scientists, Citizens, and Public Policy*. Princeton, N.J.: Princeton University Press, 1981.

Dupree, A. Hunter. *Asa Gray, American Botanist, Friend of Darwin*. Baltimore: Johns Hopkins University Press, 1988.

———. *Science in the Federal Government: A History of Policies and Activities*. Baltimore: Johns Hopkins University Press, 1988.

Eiseley, Loren. *Darwin's Century: Evolution and the Men Who Discovered It*. Garden City, N.Y.: Doubleday, 1961.

———. *The Firmament of Time*. Lincoln: University of Nebraska Press, 1999.

———. *The Immense Journey*. New York: Random House, 1959.

———. *The Invisible Pyramid*. Lincoln: University of Nebraska Press, 1998.

———. *The Unexpected Universe*. New York: Harcourt, Brace, 1972.

Elliot, Clark A. *History of Science in the United States*. New York: Garland Press, 1996.

Elson, Ruth Miller. *Guardians of Tradition: American Textbooks of the Nineteenth Century*. Lincoln: University of Nebraska Press, 1964.

Etzioni, Amitai, and Clyde Nunn. "The Public Appreciation of Science in Contemporary America." In *Science and Its Public: The Changing Relationship*, ed. Gerald Holton and William A. Blanpied. Dordrecht, Holland: Reidel, 1975.

Ewan, Joseph. *Rocky Mountain Naturalists*. Denver: University of Denver Press, 1950.

Ewan, Joseph, and Nesta Ewan. *John Banister and His Natural History of Virginia, 1678–1692*. Urbana: University of Illinois Press, 1970.

Ferris, Timothy. *Coming of Age in the Milky Way*. New York: Doubleday, 1989.

———. *Galaxies*. San Francisco: Sierra Club Books, 1982.

———. *The Red Limit: The Search for the Edge of the Universe*. New York: Harper Trade, 1983.

———. *The Whole Shebang: A State of the Universe(s) Report*. New York: Simon and Schuster, 1998.

Feynman, Richard P. *The Meaning of It All: Thoughts of Citizen Scientist*. Reading, Mass.: Perseus Books, 1998.

Foerster, Norman. *Nature in American Literature: Studies in the Modern View of Nature*. New York: Russell and Russell, 1958.

Gardner, Martin. *Fads and Fallacies in the Name of Science*. New York: Dover, 1957.

———. *The New Ambidextrous Universe*. New York: W. H. Freeman, 1991.

———. *Science: Good, Bad, and Bogus*. Amherst, Mass.: Prometheus, 1990.

Geiser, Samuel Wood. *Naturalists of the Frontier*. 2nd ed, enlarged, rev. Ann Arbor: Books on Demand, 1937.

Gerstner, Patsy. *Henry Darwin Rogers, 1808–1866: American Geologist*. Tuscaloosa: University of Alabama Press, 1995.

Glass, Bentley. "The Scientist in Contemporary Fiction." *Scientific Monthly* 85 (1957), 288–93.

Glick, Thomas F., ed. *The Comparative Reception of Darwinism.* Chicago: University of Chicago Press, 1988.

Glick, Wendell. "Bishop Paley in America." *New England Quarterly* 27 (1954), 347–54.

Goetzman, William H. *Exploration and Empire: The Explorer and the Scientist in the Winning of the American West.* Austin: Texas Historical Association, 1994.

Goode, George B. *The Smithsonian Institution, 1846–1896: The History of Its First Half Century.* Washington, D.C.: Smithsonian Institution, 1897. Reprint. Manchester, N.H.: Ayer, 1980.

Gould, Stephen Jay. *Ever since Darwin: Reflections in Natural History.* New York: W. W. Norton, 1992.

———. *The Flamingo's Smile: Reflections in Natural History.* New York: W. W. Norton, 1987.

———. *Hen's Teeth and Horse's Toes.* New York: W. W. Norton, 1994.

———. *The Mismeasure of Man.* New York: W. W. Norton, 1996.

———. *The Panda's Thumb: More Reflections in Natural History.* New York: W. W. Norton, 1992.

———. *Rocks of Ages: Science and Religion in the Fullness of Life.* New York: Ballantine, 1999.

Graham, Frank. *Since Silent Spring.* New York: Fawcett, 1976.

Green, Harvey. "Popular Science and Political Thought Converge: Colonial Survival Becomes Colonial Revival, 1830–1910." *Journal of American Culture* 6 (Fall 1983), 3–24.

Greene, John C. *American Science in the Age of Jefferson.* Ames: Iowa State University Press, 1984.

Greene, Mott T. *Geology in the Nineteenth Century: Changing Views of a Changing World.* Ithaca, N.Y.: Cornell University Press, 1982.

Grobstein, Clifford. *A Double Image of the Double Helix: The Recombinant-DNA Debate.* San Francisco: Freeman, 1979.

Grogan, Denis J. *Science and Technology: An Introduction to the Literature.* London: C. Bingley, 1982.

Guralnick, Stanley M. *Science and the AnteBellum American Colleges.* Memoirs, Vol. 109. Philadelphia: American Philosophical Society, 1975.

Handlin, Oscar. "Science and Technology in Popular Culture: A Study of Cohesive and Disjunctive Forces." *Daedalus* 94 (Winter 1965), 156–70. Reprinted in *Science and Culture,* ed. Gerald Holton. Boston: Houghton Mifflin, 1965.

Hanley, Wayne. *Natural History in America: From Mark Catsby to Rachel Carson.* New York: Quadrangle/New York Times Books, 1977.

Harris, Neil. *Humbug: The Art of P. T. Barnum.* New York: Little, Brown, 1973.

Hawking, Stephen. *A Brief History of Time.* New York: Bantam Books, 1998.

Haygood, Tamara Miner. *Henry William Ravenel, 1814–1887: South Carolina Scientist in the Civil War Era.* Tuscaloosa: University of Alabama Press, 1987.

Hays, Samuel P. *Conservation and the Gospel of Efficiency: The Progressive Conservation Movement, 1890–1920.* Pittsburgh: University of Pittsburgh Press, 1999.

Hellman, Geoffrey. *The Smithsonian: Octopus on the Mall.* Westport, Conn.: Greenwood, 1978.

Hendrickson, Walter. *The Arkites, and Other Pioneer Natural History Organizations of Cleveland*. Makers of Cleveland series, No. 1. Cleveland: Press of Western Reserve University, 1962.

Herbert, Don. *Mr. Wizard's Experiments for Young Scientists*. New York: Doubleday, 1990.

———. *Mr. Wizard's Science Secrets*. 2nd ed. New York: Hawthorne Books, 1973.

———. *Mr. Wizard's Supermarket Science*. New York: Random House, 1980.

Herbert, Don, and Hy Ruchlis. *Mr. Wizard's Science Activities*. New York: Book-Lab, 1973.

Hindle, Brooke. *The Pursuit of Science in Revolutionary America*. 1956. Reprint. New York: W. W. Norton, 1974.

Hindle, Brooke, ed. *Early American Science*. New York: Science History, 1976.

Hinsley, Curtis J. *Savages and Scientists: The Smithsonian Institution and the Development of American Anthropology, 1846–1910*. Washington, D.C.: Smithsonian Institution Press, 1981.

Hofstadter, Richard. *Social Darwinism in American Thought*. Rev. ed. Boston: Beacon Press, 1992.

Holton, Gerald. *The Advancement of Science, and Its Burdens*. Cambridge: Harvard University Press, 1998.

———. "Modern Science and the Intellectual Tradition." *Science* 131 (1960), 1187–93.

———. *Science and AntiScience*. Cambridge: Harvard University Press, 1994.

Holton, Gerald, and William A. Blanpied. *Science and Its Public: The Changing Relationship*. Dordrecht, Holland: Reidel, 1975.

Hovenkamp, Herbert. *Science and Religion in America, 1800–1860*. Philadelphia: University of Pennsylvania Press, 1978.

Huth, Hans. *Nature and the American: Three Centuries of Changing Attitudes*. Berkeley: University of California Press, 1957.

Jackson, David A., and Stephen P. Stitch. *Recombinant DNA Debate*. New York: Prentice-Hall, 1979.

Jaffe, Bernard. *Men of Science in America*. New York: Simon and Schuster, 1944.

Jefferson, Thomas. *Notes on the State of Virginia*. New York: Viking Penguin, 1998.

Jenkins, Frances B. *Science Reference Sources*. 5th ed. Cambridge: MIT Press, 1969.

Johnson, Thomas C., Jr. *Scientific Interests in the Old South*. New York: Appleton-Century, 1936.

Judson, Horace F. *The Eighth Day of Creation: Makers of the Revolution in Biology*. Plainview, N.Y.: Cold Spring Harbor Laboratory Press, 1996.

———. *Science in Crisis at the Millennium*. New York: New York Academy of Sciences, 1998.

Kastner, Joseph. *A Species of Eternity*. New York: Alfred A. Knopf, 1986.

———. *A World of Watchers*. New York: Alfred A. Knopf, 1986.

Kerber, Linda K. "Science in the Early Republic: The Society for the Study of Natural Philosophy." *William and Mary Quarterly* 29 (1972), 263–80.

Kevles, Daniel J. *The Baltimore Case: A Trial of Politics, Science, and Character*. New York: W. W. Norton, 1988.

———. *In the Name of Eugenics: Genetics and the Uses of Human Heredity*. Cambridge: Harvard University Press, 1985.

———. *The Physicists: The History of a Scientific Community in Modern America.* Cambridge: Harvard University Press, 1995.

Kohlstedt, Sally Gregory. *The Formation of the American Scientific Community: The American Association for the Advancement of Science, 1848–60.* Urbana: University of Illinois Press, 1976.

———. "The Nineteenth-Century Amateur Tradition: The Case of the Boston Society of Natural History." In *Science and Its Public: The Changing Relationship*, ed. Gerald Holton and William A. Blanpied. Dordrecht, Holland: Reidel, 1976.

Kohlstedt, Sally Gregory, and Margaret W. Rossiter. *Historical Writing on American Science: Perspectives and Prospects.* Baltimore: Johns Hopkins University Press, 1986.

Kohlstedt, Sally Gregory, Michael M. Sokal, Bruce V. Lewinster, and AAAS Staff. *The Establishment of Science in America: 150 Years of the American Association for the Advancement of Science.* Piscataway, N.J.: Rutgers University Press, 1999.

Krimsky, Sheldon. *Genetic Alchemy: The Social History of the Recombinant DNA Controversy.* Cambridge: MIT Press, 1984.

Kuritz, Hyman. "The Popularization of Science in Nineteenth-Century America." *History of Education Quarterly* 21 (1981), 259–74.

La Follette, Marcel Chotkoski. *The Citizen and Science: Almanac and Annotated Bibliography.* Bloomington, Ind.: Poynter Center on American Institutions, 1977.

———. *Creationism, Science, and the Law.* Cambridge: MIT Press, 1983.

Larson, Edward J. *Trial and Error: The American Controversy over Creation and Evolution.* New York: Oxford University Press, 1985.

Leighton, Ann. *American Gardens in the Eighteenth Century: "For Use or for Delight."* Amherst: University of Massachusetts Press, 1986.

———. *American Garden of the Nineteenth Century: "For Comfort and Affluence."* Amherst: University of Massachusetts Press, 1987.

———. *Early American Gardens: "For Meat or Medicine."* Amherst: University of Massachusetts Press, 1986.

Leventhal, Herbert. *In the Shadow of the Enlightenment: Occultism and Renaissance Science in Eighteenth-Century America.* New York: New York University Press, 1976.

Leverette, William E., Jr. "E. C. Youmans' Crusade for Scientific Autonomy and Respectability." *American Quarterly* 17 (1965), 12–32.

Lewis, Sinclair. *Arrowsmith.* New York: Harcourt, Brace, 1990.

Livingstone, David N. *Nathaniel Southgate Shaler and the Culture of American Science.* Tuscaloosa: University of Alabama Press, 1987.

Leopold, Aldo. *For the Health of the Land: Previously Unpublished Essays and Other Writings.* Washington, D.C.: Island Press, 1999.

———. *The River of the Mother of God and Other Essays.* Madison: University of Wisconsin Press, 1993.

———. *A Sand County Almanac: With Essays on Conservation from Round River.* New York: Ballantine, 1991.

Loewenberg, Bert J. *Darwinism Comes to America.* Minneapolis: Augsburg Fortress, 1969.

London, Jack. *Martin Eden*. Murrieta, Calif.: Classic Books, 1998.

Lurie, Edward. *Louis Agassiz: A Life in Science*. Baltimore: Johns Hopkins University Press, 1988.

Lurie, Nancy Oestereich. *A Special Style: The Milwaukee Public Museum, 1882–1982*. Milwaukee: Milwaukee Public Museum, 1984.

———. *Women and the Invention of American Anthropology*. Prospect Heights, Ill.: Waveland Press, 1999.

Manning, Kenneth. *Black Apollo of Science: The Life of Ernest Everett Just*. New York: Oxford University Press, 1985.

Margenau, Henry, and Roy Abraham Varghese, eds. *Cosmos, Bios, Theos: Scientists Reflect on Science, God, and the Origins of the Universe, Life, and Homo Sapiens*. LaSalle, Ill.: Open Court, 1993.

Maugh, Thomas H., II. "The Media: The Image of the Scientist Is Bad." *Science* 200 (April 7, 1978), 37.

McCormmach, Russell. "Ormsby MacKnight Mitchell's *Sidereal Messenger*, 1846–48." *Proceedings of the American Philosophical Society* 110 (1960), 35–47.

McGrath, Alister E. *The Foundations of Dialogue in Science and Religion*. Malden, Mass.: Blackwell, 1998.

———. *Science and Religion: An Introduction*. Malden, Mass.: Blackwell, 1999.

McKown, Delos Banning. *The Mythmaker's Magic: Behind the Myth of "Creation Science."* Buffalo, N.Y.: Prometheus Books, 1993.

Meisel, Max. *Bibliography of American Natural History: The Pioneer Century, 1769–1865*. 3 vols. 1924. Reprint. Mansfield Center: Martino, 1994.

Mendelsohn, Everett. "Science in America: The Twentieth Century." In *Paths of American Thought*, ed. A. M. Schlesinger Jr. and M. White. Boston: Houghton Mifflin, 1963.

Miller, Howard S. *Dollars for Research: Science and Its Patrons in Nineteenth-Century America*. Seattle: University of Washington Press, 1970.

Miller, Perry. *The Life of the Mind in America: From the Revolution to the Civil War*. New York: Harcourt, Brace, and World, 1970.

Moore, R. Laurence. *In Search of White Crows: Spiritualism, Parapsychology, and American Culture*. New York: Oxford University Press, 1977.

Mott, Frank Luther. *A History of American Magazines*. 5 vols. Cambridge: Harvard University Press, 1938–1968.

Muir, John. *Nature Writings*. New York: Library of America, 1997.

———. *Northwest Passages*. Truckee, Calif.: Coldstream Press, 1998.

———. *To Yosemite and Beyond*. Salt Lake City: University of Utah Press, 1999.

———. *The Wilderness Journeys*. London: Canongate Books, 1996.

Nelkin, Dorothy. *The Creation Controversy: Science or Scripture in the Schools*. Boston: Beacon Press, 1984

———. *Science Textbook Controversies and the Politics of Equal Time*. Cambridge: MIT Press, 1977.

———. *Selling Science: How the Press Covers Science and Technology*. New York: Freeman, 1995.

Nelkin, Dorothy, and M. Susan Lindee. *The DNA Mystique: The Gene as a Cultural Icon*. New York: W. H. Freeman, 1996.

Numbers, Ronald L. *Creation by Natural Law: Laplace's Nebular Hypothesis in America*. Seattle: University of Washington Press, 1977.

———. "The Creationists." In *God and Nature: Historical Essays on the Encounter between Christianity and Science*, ed. David C. Lindberg and Ronald L. Numbers. Berkeley: University of California Press, 1986.

———. *The Creationists*. Berkeley: University of California Press, 1993.

———. *Darwinism Comes to America*. Cambridge: Harvard University Press, 1998.

———. *Disseminating Darwinism: The Role of Place, Race, Religion, and Gender*. New York: Cambridge University Press, 1999.

———, ed. *Creationism-Evolution Debates*. New York: Garland, 1995.

———, ed. *Early Creationist Journals*. New York: Garland, 1995.

Numbers, Ronald L., and Charles E. Rosenberg. *The Scientific Enterprise in America: Readings from Isis*. Chicago: University of Chicago Press, 1996.

Oehser, Paul H. *Sons of Science: The Story of the Smithsonian Institution and Its Leaders*. Reprint. Westport, Conn.: Greenwood, 1969.

Oleson, Alexandra, and Sanborn C. Brown, eds. *The Pursuit of Knowledge in the Early American Republic: American Scientific and Learned Societies from Colonial Times to the Civil War*. Baltimore: Johns Hopkins University Press, 1976.

Oleson, Alexandra, and John Voss, eds. *The Organization of Knowledge in Modern America, 1860–1920*. Baltimore: Johns Hopkins University Press, 1979.

Pauly, Philip J. "The World and All That Is in It: The National Geographic Society, 1888–1918." *American Quarterly* 31 (1979), 517–32.

Pennock, Robert T. *Tower of Babel: The Evidence against the New Creationism*. Cambridge: MIT Press, 1999.

Penrose, Roger. *The Emperor's New Mind*. New York: Oxford University Press, 1989.

———. *The Emperor's Tour of the Physical Universe*. New York: Vintage Books, 1998.

———. *The Large, the Small, and the Human Mind*. Cambridge: Cambridge University Press, 1999.

Persons, Stow, ed. *Evolutionary Thought in America*. New Haven, Conn.: Yale University Press, 1950. Reprint. New York: Archon Books, 1968.

Pfaelzer, Jean. *The Utopian Novel in America, 1886–1896*. Pittsburgh: University of Pittsburgh Press, 1984.

Pfeifer, Edward J. "United States." In *The Comparative Reception of Darwinism*, ed. Thomas F. Glick. Austin: University of Texas Press, 1972.

[Phelps,] Almira Hart Lincoln. *Botany for Beginners*. Hartford, Conn.: F. J. Huntington, 1833.

———. *Familiar Lectures on Botany*. Hartford, Conn.: H. and F. J. Huntington, 1829.

Polkinghorne, J. C. *Belief in God in an Age of Science*. New Haven, Conn.: Yale University Press, 1998.

Porter, Charlotte. *The Eagles Nest: Natural History and American Ideas, 1812–1842*. University: University of Alabama Press, 1986.

Rainger, Ronald. *An Agenda for Antiquity: Henry Fairfield Osborn and Vertebrate Paleontology at the American Museum of Natural History, 1890–1935*. Tuscaloosa: University of Alabama Press, 1991.

Raymo, Chet. *Skeptics and True Believers: The Exhilarating Connection between Science and Religion*. New York: Walker, 1998.

Reingold, Nathan. *Science, American Style*. Piscataway, N.J.: Rutgers University Press, 1991.

Reingold, Nathan, ed. *Science in America from 1820–1940*. New York: Watson Publishing International, 1976.

———. *Science in Nineteenth-Century America: A Documentary History*. Chicago: University of Chicago Press, 1985.

———. *The Sciences in the American Context: New Perspectives*. Washington, D.C.: Smithsonian Institution Press, 1979.

Reingold, Nathan, and Ida H. Reingold, eds. *Science in America: A Documentary History, 1900–1939*. Chicago: University of Chicago Press, 1981.

Reingold, Nathan, and Marc Rothenberg, ed. *Scientific Colonialism: A Cross-Cultural Comparison*. Washington, D.C.: Smithsonian Institution Press, 1986.

Richards, John, ed. *Recombinant DNA: Science, Ethics, and Politics*. New York: Academic Press, 1978.

Rosenberg, Charles E. *No Other Gods: On Science and American Social Thought*. Baltimore: Johns Hopkins University Press, 1976.

Rossiter, Margaret W. "Benjamin Silliman and the Lowell Institute: The Popularization of Science in Nineteenth-Century America." *New England Quarterly* 44 (December 1971), 602–26.

———. *Women Scientists in America: Struggles and Strategies to 1940*. Baltimore: Johns Hopkins University Press, 1982.

Rothenberg, Marc. *The History of Science and Technology in the United States: A Critical and Selective Bibliography*. New York: Garland, 1983.

———. *The History of Science and Technology in the United States*. Vol. 2: *A Critical and Selective Bibliography*. New York: Garland, 1993.

———. "Organization and Control: Professionals and Amateurs in American Astronomy, 1899–1918." *Social Studies of Science* 11 (1918), 305–25.

Rudolph, Emanuel D. "Almira Hart Lincoln Phelps (1793–1884) and the Spread of Botany in Nineteenth Century America." *American Journal of Botany* (1984), 1161–67.

———. "Botany in American and British Chapbooks before 1860." *Plant Science Bulletin* 19 (1973), 34–36.

———. "How It Developed That Botany Was the Science Thought Most Suitable for Victorian Young Ladies." *Children's Literature* 2 (1973), 92–97.

———. "The Introduction of the Natural System of Classification of Plants to Nineteenth Century American Students." *Archives of Natural History* 10 (1982), 461–68.

———. "Women in Nineteenth Century American Botany: A Generally Unrecognized Constituency." *American Journal of Botany* 69 (1982), 1346–55.

Russett, Cynthia E. *Darwin in America: The Intellectual Response, 1865–1912*. San Francisco: Freeman, 1976.

Sagan, Carl. *Billions and Billions: Thoughts on Life and Death at the Brink of the Millennium*. New York: Macmillan, 1998.

———. *Broca's Brain: Reflections on the Romance of Science*. New York: Ballantine Books, 1993.

———. *Cosmos*. New York: Ballantine Books, 1993.

———. *The Dragons of Eden: Speculations on the Evolution of Human Intelligence*. New York: Ballantine Books, 1993.

———. *Pale Blue Dot*. New York: Random House, 1995.

Schmitt, Peter J. *Back to Nature: The Arcadian Myth in Urban America*. Baltimore: Johns Hopkins University Press, 1990.

Scott, Janny. "Postmodern Gravity Deconstructed, Slyly." *New York Times*, May 18, 1996: 1, 22.

Sellers, Charles Coleman. *Mr. Peale's Museum: Charles Wilson Peale and the First Popular Museum of Natural History and Art*. New York: W. W. Norton, 1980.

Shapiro, Laura. *Perfection Salad: Women and Cooking at the Turn of the Century*. New York: North Point Press, 1995.

Shelley, Mary Wollstonecraft. *Frankenstein, or the Modern Prometheus*. New York: Doubleday, 1999.

Shinn, Terry, and Richard Whitley, eds. *Expository Science: Forms and Functions of Popularization*. Dordrecht, Holland: Reidel, 1985.

Shurter, Robert L. *The Utopian Novel in America, 1865–1900*. New York: AMS Press, 1973.

Siegel, P. J., and Kay T. Finley. *Women in the Scientific Search: An American Bibliography, 1724–1979*. Metuchen, N.J.: Scarecrow Press, 1984.

Sinclair, Upton. *The Jungle*. New York: Doubleday, Page, 1906.

Sloan, Douglas. "Science in New York City, 1867–1907." *Isis* 71 (1980), 35–76.

Smallwood, William Martin, and Mabel Sarah Coon Smallwood. *Natural History and the American Mind*. Reprint. New York: AMS Press.

Snow, C. P. *The Physicists*. Boston: Little, Brown, 1981.

———. *The Two Cultures and the Scientific Revolution*. New York: Cambridge University Press, 1959.

———. *The Two Cultures: and a Second Look*. 2nd ed. New York: Cambridge University Press, 1964.

———. *The Sokal Hoax: The Sham That Shook the Academy*. Lincoln: University of Nebraska Press, 2000.

Sokal, Alan. "Transgressing the Boundaries: Toward a Transformative Hermeneutics of Quantum Gravity." *Social Text* 46/47 (1996), 217–52.

Sokal, Alan, and Jean Bricmont. *Fashionable Nonsense: Postmodern Intellectuals' Abuse of Science*. New York: Picador USA, 1998.

Stanton, William. *The Great United States Exploring Expedition of 1838–1842*. Berkeley: University of California Press, 1975.

———. *The Leopard's Spots: Scientific Attitudes towards Race in America, 1815–1859*. Chicago: University of Chicago Press, 1982.

Stearns, Raymond P. *Science in the British Colonies of North America*. Urbana: University of Illinois Press, 1970.

Stern, Madeleine. *Heads and Headlines: The Phrenological Fowlers*. Norman: University of Oklahoma Press, 1971.

Stoehr, Taylor. *Hawthorne's Mad Scientists: Pseudoscience and Social Science in Nineteenth-Century Life and Letters*. Hamden, Conn.: Archon Books, 1978.

Stott, Jeffery R. "The Historical Origins of the Zoological Park in American Thought." *Environmental Review* 5 (1981), 52–65.

Struik, Dirk J. *Yankee Science in the Making*. New York: Viking, 1974.

Thomas, Lewis. *The Lives of a Cell: Notes of a Biology Watcher*. New York: Viking Press, 1984.

———. *The Medusa and the Snail: More Notes of a Biology Watcher*. New York: Bantam, 1979.

———. *TV, Science, and Kids: Teaching Our Children to Question*. New York: Addison-Wesley, 1984.

Thoreau, Henry D. *The Journal of Henry D. Thoreau*. Timecula, Calif.: Reprint Services, 1991.

Tobey, Ronald C. *The American Ideology of National Science, 1919–1930*. Pittsburgh: University of Pittsburgh Press, 1971.

———. *Saving the Prairies: The Life Cycle of the Founding School of American Plant Ecology, 1895–1955*. Berkeley: University of California Press, 1981.

———. *Technology as Freedom: The New Deal and the Electrical Modernization of the American Home*. Berkeley: University of California Press, 1996.

Tucher, Andrea J., ed. *Natural History in America, 1609–1860*. New York: Garland, 1985.

Turner, James. *Without God, without Creed: The Origins of Unbelief in America*. Baltimore: Johns Hopkins University Press, 1986.

Van Tassel, David, and Michael G. Hall, eds. *Science and Society in the United States*. Homewood, Ill.: Dorsey, 1966.

Walcutt, Charles C. *American Literary Naturalism: A Divided Stream*. Westport, Conn.: Greenwood Publishing Group, 1974.

Warner, Deborah Jean. *Graceanna Lewis: Scientist and Humanitarian*. Washington, D.C.: Smithsonian Institution Press, 1979.

———. "Science Education for Women in Ante-bellum America." *Isis* 69 (1978), 58–67.

Warner, John Harley. " 'Exploring the Inner Labyrinths of Creation': Popular Microscopy in Nineteenth-Century America." *Journal of the History of Medicine and Allied Sciences* 37 (1982), 7–33.

Watson, James D. *The Double Helix: A Personal Account of the Discovery of the Structure of DNA*. New York: N.A.L. Dutton, 1999.

Wenk, E. *Technology, Democracy, and Civic Discourse in the American Future*. New York: Ablex, 1999.

Whalen, Matthew D. "Science, the Public and American Culture: A Preface to the Study of Popular Science." *Journal of American Culture* 4 (Winter 1981), 14–26.

Whalen, Matthew D., and Mary F. Tobin. "Periodicals and the Popularization of Science in America, 1860–1910." *Journal of American Culture* 3 (1980), 195–203.

White, Andrew D. *A History of the Warfare of Science with Theology in Christendom*. Reprint. Herndon, Va.: Thoemmes Press, 1997.

Whorton, James C. *Before Silent Spring: Pesticides and Public Health in Pre-DDT America*. Princeton, N.J.: Princeton University Press, 1974.

Wilson, Joan Hoff. "Dancing Dogs of the Colonial Period: Women Scientists." *Early American Literature* 7 (1973), 225–35.

Wilson, Robert J., ed. *Darwinism and the American Intellectual: An Anthology*. Belmont, Calif.: Wadsworth, 1988.

Worster, Donald. *Nature's Economy: A History of Ecological Ideas*. Cambridge: Cambridge University Press, 1994.

———. *The Wealth of Nature: Environmental History and the Ecological Imagination*. New York: Oxford University Press, 1994.

Wright, Louis B. *The Cultural Life of the American Colonies*. New York: HarperCollins, 1983.

Zabilka, Ivan L. *Scientific Malpractice: The Creation/Evolution Debate*. Lexington, Ky.: Bristol Books, 1992.

Zochert, Donald. "The Natural History of an American Pioneer: A Case Study." *Transactions of the Wisconsin Academy of Sciences, Arts, and Letters* 60 (1972), 7–15.

Reference Works

AAAS Science Book List: A Selected and Annotated List of Science and Mathematics Books for Secondary School Students, College Undergraduates and Nonspecialists. Ed. Katheryn Wolff, Susan M. O'Connell, and Valerie J. Montenegro. Washington, D.C.: AAAS, 1986.

AAAS Science Book List Supplement. Ed. Katheryn Wolff and Jill Story. Washington, D.C.: AAAS, 1978.

AAAS Science Book List for Children: A Selected and Annotated List of Science and Mathematics Books for Children in Elementary Schools, and for Children's Collections in Public Libraries. Comp. Hillary J. Deaason, Washington, D.C.: AAAS, 1972.

AAAS Science Film Catalog. Comp. Ann Seltz-Petrash and Katheryn Wolff. New York: R. R. Bowker and AAAS, 1975.

American Men and Women of Science. Ed. R. R. Bowker Staff. 20th ed. 15 vols. New York: R. R. Bowker, 1998.

Ash, Lee. *Subject Collections: A Guide to Special Book Collections and Subject Emphasis as Reported by University, College, Public and Special Libraries and Museums in the United States and Canada*. 7th rev. ed. New York: R. R. Bowker, 1993.

Asimov, Isaac. *Asimov's Biographical Encyclopedia of Science and Technology*. 2nd rev. ed. Garden City, N.Y.: Doubleday, 1982.

Bates, Ralph S. *Scientific Societies in the United States*. 3rd ed. Cambridge: MIT Press, 1965.

Besterman, Theodore. *Biological Sciences: A Bibliography of Bibliographies*. Totowa, N.J.: Rowman and Littlefield, 1971.

———. *Physical Sciences: A Bibliography of Bibliographies*. Totowa, N.J.: Rowman and Littlefield, 1971.

*Catalog of Motion Pictures and Filmstrips for Rent and Sale by the National Audiovisual Center, 1969. Supplements, 1971– . Washington, D.C.: National Audiovisual Center, 1971.

Chen, Ching-Chih. *Scientific and Technical Information Sources*. Cambridge: MIT Press, 1987.

Clapp, Jane, ed. *Museum Publications*. 2 vols. Metuchen, N.J.: Scarecrow Press, 1962.

Clugston, M. J. *The New Penguin Dictionary of Science*. New York: Viking Penguin, 1999.

Considine, Douglas M. *Van Nostrand's Scientific Encyclopedia.* 8th ed. New York: John Wiley and Sons, 1995.

Dictionary of Scientific Biography. Set. New York: Macmillan Library Reference, 1990.

Documentary Film Classics Produced by the United States Government. Washington, D.C.: National Audio Visual Center, 1980.

Elliot, Clark A. *Biographical Dictionary of American Science: The Seventeenth through the Nineteenth Centuries.* Westport, Conn.: Greenwood Press, 1979.

Encyclopaedia Britannica. 1st ed., rev. Chicago: Encyclopaedia Britannica, 1997.

Encyclopaedia Britannica Online. http://www.search.eb.com.

Huelmantel. *Directory of Special Libraries and Information Centers.* 2nd ed. Detroit: Gale Research, 1998.

McGraw-Hill Encyclopedia of Science and Technology. 8th ed. 20 vols. New York: McGraw-Hill, 1997.

McGraw-Hill. *Modern Scientists and Engineers.* 3 vols. New York: McGraw-Hill, 1980.

Malinowsky, H. Robert. *Science and Engineering Literature: A Guide to Reference Sources.* 3rd ed. Littleton, Colo.: Libraries Unlimited, 1980.

National Geographic Index, 1888–1946; 1947–1983. 2 vols. Washington, D.C.: National Geographic Society, 1984.

Neu, John, ed. *Isis Cumulative Bibliography, 1966–1975.* London: Cassell Academic, 1985.

———. *Isis Cumulative Bibliography, 1976–1985.* New York: Macmillan, 1989.

———. *Isis Cumulative Bibliography, 1986–1995.* Canton, Mass.: Watson, 1997.

Newman, James R., ed. *The Harper Encyclopedia of Science.* Rev. ed. New York: Harper and Row, 1967.

NOVA: Science Adventures on Television. Boston: Boston Public Library, 1974.

NOVA: Science Adventures on Television II. Boston: Boston Public Library, 1975.

Parker, S. *McGraw-Hill Dictionary of Scientific and Technical Terms.* 5th ed. New York: McGraw-Hill, 1993.

Pure and Applied Science Books, 1876–1982. New York: R. R. Bowker, 1982.

Science Year: The World Book Science Annual. Chicago: Field Enterprises Educational, 1965– .

Sill, William B., ed. *The New Popular Science Encyclopedia of the Sciences.* Rev. ed. New York: Grosset and Dunlap, 1968.

Smithsonian Year: Programs and Activities. Washington, D.C.: Smithsonian Institution Press, 1971– . Annual.

Subramanan, K. *Scientific and Technical Information Resources.* New York: Marcel Decker, 1981.

Thornton, John L., and R. I. Tully Jr. *Thornton and Tully's Scientific Books, Libraries and Collectors: A Study of Bibliography and the Book Trade in Relation to Science.* 4th ed. Brookfield, Vt.: Ashgate, 1999.

Wasserman, Paul, ed. *Catalog of Museum Publications and Media.* 2nd ed. Detroit: Gale Research, 1979.

Whitrow, Magda, ed. *ISIS Cumulative Bibliography: A Bibliography of the History of Science Formed from ISIS Critical Bibliographies 1–90, 1913–1965.* 6 vols. London: Mansell, 1971–1984.

Yule, John-David. *Concise Encyclopedia of the Sciences*. New York: Facts on File, 1981.

Periodicals

American Journal of Science. New Haven, Conn., 1818– .

American Naturalist. New York and Chicago, 1867– .

American Scientist. New Haven, Conn. 1943– . Continues *Sigma Xi Quarterly*. New Haven, Conn. 1913–1942.

Astronomy. Milwaukee, 1973– .

Atlantic Monthly. New York, 1857– .

Audubon Magazine. New York, 1899– .

Botanical Gazette. Crawfordsville, Ind., and Chicago, 1875–1919.

The Country Gentleman. Philadelphia, 1853–1955.

Discover. New York, 1980– .

Environment. St. Louis and Washington, D.C., 1959– .

Godey's Lady's Book. Philadelphia, 1830–1898.

Harper's Magazine. New York, 1850– .

Isis. Philadelphia and Belstville, Md., 1913– .

Journal of the Franklin Institute. Philadelphia, 1826– .

Medical Repository. New York, 1797–1824.

Merry's Museum and Parley's Magazine. Boston, 1842–1872.

National Geographic. Washington, D.C., 1888– .

Natural History. New York, 1900– .

North American Review. Boston, 1815–1940.

Omni. New York, 1978– .

Popular Astronomy. Northfield, Minn., 1893–1941.

Popular Science Monthly. New York, 1872– .

Science. Lancaster, Pa., etc., 1883– .

Science Books and Films. Washington, D.C., 1965– .

Science News. Washington, D.C., 1921– .

Scientific American. New York, 1845– .

Sky and Telescope. Cambridge, Mass., 1941– .

Smithsonian. Washington, D.C., 1970/1971– .

Southern Literary Messenger. Richmond, Va., 1834–1864.

Southern Quarterly Review. New Orleans and Columbia, S.C., 1842–1857.

Torrey Botanical Club, *Bulletin*. New York, 1870– .

Youth's Companion. Boston, 1827–1929.

SCIENCE FICTION

Donald E. Palumbo

With roots in the gothic novel and seventeenth- and eighteenth-century European tales of imaginary moon voyages, which have their own antecedents in ancient Greek satire, science fiction flourished in the twentieth and twenty-first centuries—and nowhere more so than in America. SF (the abbreviation favored by scholars and most serious adherents) has seen an astonishing growth in status in the last half century in particular, in which time it has become one of the most popular specialized literary genres, colonized all aspects of the entertainment industry from films to computer games, and achieved solid academic respectability. In 1950, there was no such thing as a college class in science fiction; now, it is the rare university that does not offer regularly at least one SF course. It is no longer possible, as Dena Brown once joked, to "take science fiction out of the classroom and put it back in the gutter where it belongs." The number of original SF novels published annually hovered at about 300 throughout the past decade; and well over 2,500 reviews of science-fiction books, including books of criticism, appear each year. But what is science fiction?

Science fiction exists on the continuum of fantastic narrative that also includes myth and fantasy, horror, gothic, and utopian literature; but no precise definition that completely separates SF from these related genres has gained broad acceptance. Science fiction is fantastic (or nonmimetic) in that it always describes a reality that is clearly not our own. Although many specific works, such as Daniel Keyes' *Flowers for Algernon*, are character-driven and stylistically innovative, SF tends to prioritize setting and plot over character and style, and setting is the decisive indicator. Whether a world exactly like ours except that it is possible in it to increase a man's intelligence temporarily, as in Keyes' novel, or a galaxy of millions of inhabited worlds that have long forgotten earth tens of thousands of years from now, as in Isaac Asimov's *Foundation* series or Frank Herbert's *Dune* series, the SF setting includes crucial features that would not exist in realistic fiction. But these differences must hinge, at least implicitly, on some scientific principle or technological innovation. Thus, if a tale involves dragons of unexplained origin, it may be fantasy; but if the dragons are the result of genetic engineering, it may be science fiction. If a machine enables its inventor to travel in time, it's SF; if a bump on the head sends the protagonist back 1,000 years, it isn't. But the focus of the story is more likely to be the impact of technological developments on individuals and societies, rather than the nuts and bolts of technology or science itself.

HISTORICAL OUTLINE[1]

Science fiction had its beginnings at least as early as the second century, when Lucian satirized Greek society through the device of an imaginary moon voyage. American science fiction has more immediate antecedents in the popular British and some French imaginary voyage fictions of the seventeenth and eighteenth centuries. Andrae's *Christianopolis* (1619), Tommaso Campanella's *The City of the Sun* (1623), and Sir Francis Bacon's *The New Atlantis* (1627)—all involving earthbound voyages—were among the precursors to Jonathan Swift's *Gulliver's Travels* (1726–1727), which was more skeptical of science than these earlier works. The first English translation of Lucian's *True History* (1634), the second-century Greek account of moon voyages, was followed by Bishop Francis Godwin's *The Man in the Moon* (1638), the first of many English-language lunar-voyage narratives; Bishop John Wilkins' *A Discourse Concerning a New World and Another Planet* (1638), which predicts trips to the moon and lunar colonies; Cyrano de Bergerac's parody of imaginary voyages, *Histoire comique . . . contenant les etats et empires de la lune* (1657), in which the moon is reached via rocket ship; and David Russen's *Iter Lunare: Or, A Voyage to the Moon* (1703), an extended critique of Cyrano's book. The first American lunar-voyage narrative was Joseph Atterley's (George Tucker's) *A Voyage to the Moon* (1827). In the late nineteenth century, with the discovery of the Martian moons and "canals," Mars replaced the moon as the preferred destination for imaginary voyages; but by then the interior of the earth was also a popular location for such fiction. Like their Greek prototype, these early scientific fantasies were often social satire or criticism.

Two optimistic eighteenth-century British works, *The Reign of George VI, 1900–1925* (1763) and Samuel Madden's *Memoirs of the Twentieth Century* (1733), were the first fictional narratives to attempt to predict the future. It was not until the beginning of the Industrial Revolution in the eighteenth century, with its vision of a future altered for the better by technology, that science fiction could exist as a distinct literary form, but the growing belief in the potential for technological miracles was tempered in literature by the more pessimistic tone of the gothic.

Brian W. Aldiss contends in *Trillion Year Spree* that science fiction had its beginnings in the English Romantic movement with the publication of Mary Shelley's *Frankenstein* (1817), which replaced the supernatural elements of the gothic horror tale with "science." *Frankenstein* enunciated the theme of the scientist's creating life and reaping the inevitable retribution that follows trespass into areas of knowledge that humanity was not meant to explore. This "mad scientist" trope is a contrast to the utopian themes of many of the earlier, imaginary-voyage narratives. Although preceded by Jean-Baptiste Cousin de Granville's *Le Dernier Homme* (*The Last Man*, 1805), perhaps the earliest secular example of apocalyptic fiction, Mary Shelley sounded yet another pessimistic, but enduring, science-fiction theme in *The Last Man* (1826), in which a plague wipes out humanity. Each of these early motifs—the scientific discovery that brings disaster, the natural catastrophe, and the utopia (with its inversion, the dystopia)—thrived in American science fiction throughout its history. Mature versions of both the human-made and natural catastrophe motifs, for example, include George R. Stewart's *Earth Abides* (1949), Pat Frank's *Alas, Babylon* (1959), Walter M. Miller's *A Canticle for Leibowitz* (1960), and Vonda N. McIntyre's *Dreamsnake* (1978) and tend to focus not so much on the catastrophe itself as on the type of society that will develop after the cataclysm.

The nineteenth century exhibited a fascination with the idea of scientific progress, and its mood was generally optimistic. Popular magazines such as *Century*, *Cosmopolitan*, *Harper's*, *Atlantic Monthly*, and *Saturday Evening Post* published numerous stories featuring new mechanical devices and scientific marvels. Nearly every major writer in America and many in Europe—Nathaniel Hawthorne, Edgar Allan Poe, Fritz-James O'Brien, Edward Bellamy, Ambrose Bierce, and Mark Twain among them—experimented with writing stories about the new sciences and the possibilities of the future, but Jules Verne epitomized the nineteenth century's romantic interest in science and technology. With his numerous variations on the still-popular imaginary-voyage narrative—his *Les Voyages extraordinaires*, such works as *Cinq semaines en ballon* (*Five Weeks in a Balloon*, 1863), *Voyage au centre de la terre* (*A Journey to the Center of the Earth*, 1864), *De la terre a la lune* (*From the Earth to the Moon*, 1865), *Autour de la lune* (*Round the Moon*, 1870), and *Vingt mille lieues sous les mers* (*Twenty Thousand Leagues under the Sea*, 1870)—Verne was the earliest highly successful pioneer, if not the originator, of science fiction.

By the turn of the century, the imaginary-voyage narrative had incorporated the lost-race motif. An early American example is Albert Bigelow Paine's *The Great White Way* (1901), in which an expedition discovers a lost race of telepathic neo-primitives inhabiting an Antarctic utopia. Popular on both sides of the Atlantic, the lost-race tale developed out of a contemporary interest in geology, archaeology, paleontology, and exploration. Sir H. Rider Haggard—author of *King Solomon's Mines* (1885), *She: A History of Adventure* (1887), and *Allan Quartermain* (1887)—was the pioneer who established the most imitated formula for this type of story, but Edgar Rice Burroughs, an American, was its most popular practitioner. Burroughs was a master storyteller, and his Tarzan series made him the most widely read English-language author of his time.[2] Many of the Tarzan novels involved lost cities and lost races, but—like other Haggard imitators—Burroughs also found lost races in outer space. "Under the Moons of Mars" (1912), his first published story, appeared later in book form as *A Princess of Mars* (1917), the first of a series of novels in which what remains of a once-mighty Martian civilization is depicted with color, vigor, and exotic splendor. Other series took the reader to Venus (*Pirates of Venus*, 1934), to the moon (*The Moon Maid*, 1926), and to the much-visited Antarctica (*The Land That Time Forgot*, 1924) and the center of the earth (the Pellucidar of *At the Earth's Core*, 1922), which in this and several nineteenth-century imaginary voyages can be reached via Antarctica. His adventures were light, his characterizations superficial, his science almost nonexistent, and his plots endlessly repetitious; but Burroughs' striking settings and spellbind-

Scene from the film *The Time Machine*, 1960.
© The Del Valle Archive

ing adventures freed the lost-race and imaginary-journey narratives from their antiquated themes.

Two other motifs emerged in the late nineteenth century: the portrayal of future warfare (the most popular type of story about the future published in England prior to World War I) and the investigation of psychological abnormalities. In Britain, George Chesney's *The Battle of Dorking* (1871) predicted that technological innovation would decide the outcome of future wars, thus establishing imaginary warfare as a viable theme for science-fiction writers. This piece and similar future-war stories published in Germany and France may have influenced public opinion prior to World War I. Early American treatments of this motif include Pierton W. Dooner's *Last Days of the Republic* (1880), in which China conquers the United States; Stanley Waterloo's *Armageddon* (1898), in which Yankee scientists develop a superweapon, defeat Europe, and take over the world in an alliance with Great Britain; and Cleveland Moffett's *The Conquest of America* (1916), in which Germany invades the United States but is defeated through the efforts of Thomas Edison. Many future-war novels exhibit a strikingly racist tone evident in those by Dooner and Waterloo. Eventually, their enemy nations would be replaced by alien invaders. In *Anatomy of Wonder 4*, Thomas Clareson points out that nineteenth-century tales about abnormal mental states, such as Robert Louis Stevenson's *Strange Case of Dr. Jekyll and Mr. Hyde* (1886) and other stories exploring multiple personality disorder, "were replaced by the motif dealing over the years with mutants, androids, 'supermen,' and clones." This type of character suffuses American SF—from Jerry Siegel and Joe Shuster's Superman (1938), the first among hundreds in the pantheon of American comic-book superheroes, to

Jommy Cross in A. E. van Vogt's *Slan* (1940), the Mule in Asimov's "Foundation Trilogy" (1951–1953), and Paul Atreides in Herbert's *Dune* (1965).

Surely the most profound influence on science fiction at the turn of the century, Herbert George Wells wrote stories featuring both human-made supermen, as in *The Food of the Gods* (1904), and future warfare, as in *The War in the Air* (1908) and *The World Set Free* (1914). While not set in the future, his *The War of the Worlds* (1898) does take this latter theme interplanetary. In 1895 Wells published his first and perhaps best "scientific romance," *The Time Machine*, which introduced a new species of imaginary voyage. While ostensibly about time travel, this short novel actually yokes two less-outlandish scientific theories—evolution and entropy—to conjure up a terminal vision of humanity's and the universe's destiny. In doing so, it projects into the far future turn-of-the-century concerns about the strict stratification of the British class system and the exploitation of the working class. Wells challenged nineteenth-century notions of progress and repeatedly undermined the comforting assumptions of his time in dramatizing the idea that humanity's tenure on earth was ever threatened by unknown dangers and very likely temporary.

In the aftermath of World War I, the tones of American and European science fiction diverged. Physically, economically, and psychologically gutted by the war, Europe abandoned the utopian optimism that had characterized much of its nineteenth-century speculative fiction. Highly influential non-English SF of this period includes Czech writer Karel Capek's play *R. U. R* (*Rossum's Universal Robots*, 1920), which coined the word "robot," and Russian author Yevgeny Zamiatin's brilliant antiutopia *We* (1924). Post–World War I British future-war stories were strikingly pessimistic. Prominent British SF novels of the 1930s and 1940s include such famous dystopias as Aldous Huxley's *Brave New World* (1932) and George Orwell's *Nineteen Eighty-four* (1949), as well as such seminal and highly philosophical works as Olaf Stapledon's *Last and First Men* (1930), which spans 2 billion years, and *Star Maker* (1937), which spans 100 billion years. American SF did display an atypical sober side between the wars, mostly in novels by nongenre writers, as in Sinclair Lewis' antifascist *It Can't Happen Here* (1935) and Ayn Rand's antisocialist dystopia *Anthem* (1938). But, physically untouched by the war and its economic beneficiary during the boom years of the 1920s, America reflected a tone of confident optimism in its various genres of adventure fiction. Moreover, an increased demand for popular fiction after the war enabled American SF to find its audience, reached through new specialty magazines, and to develop its distinctive character.

The term "science fiction" first appeared in Hugo Gernsback's editorial for the premier issue of *Science Wonder Stories*, dated June 1929. Gernsback, a Luxembourg immigrant, had previously published a series of electrical magazines[3] that had regularly featured science-fiction stories; but the genre entered the era of pulp science fiction in 1926, when he produced the first issue of *Amazing Stories*, the earliest magazine devoted exclusively to "scientifiction," as Gernsback had at first called it. *Amazing Stories* adhered to an editorial policy of teaching and promoting science and of presenting an optimistic vision of a technological future through its stories. The magazine's very success led to the quick isolation of SF from mainstream literature and other genre fiction, as its many successors and imitators soon marketed science fiction to a growing number of readers almost exclusively through the vehicle of a long list of specialist pulp titles.[4] Since 1953, each year's most popular works of science fiction have been awarded "Hugos" in honor of the man who invented the term "science fiction" and encouraged the development of the field's early writers.

Gernsback steadfastly promoted SF, at first filling his magazines with reprints of classic tales by Verne, Wells, and Poe. Later, he featured the stories of Edward E. Smith, Ray Cummings, A. Merritt, Jack Williamson, Edmond Hamilton, and Murray Leinster, among others. Most of the SF appearing in *Amazing Stories* emphasized the wonders of science. Other pulp adventure magazines of the 1930s and 1940s likewise featured tales of robots, space exploration, catastrophes, and alien encounters. While they still relied on fantastic adventures reminiscent of the exotic romances of Edgar Rice Burroughs, their stories were filled with futuristic hardware and also developed new SF settings. Cummings took readers to sub-atomic worlds in a series of stories beginning with "The Girl in the Golden Atom" (1919). Merritt, although primarily a fantasy writer, popularized the parallel-world setting in such works as *The Ship of Ishtar* (1924). The best known of these authors, E. E. "Doc" Smith, popularized the "space opera" with exuberant, dreamlike, galaxy-spanning sagas of heroic adventure such as *The Skylark of Space* (1928; as a novel, 1946) and its three sequels, his "Skylark" series, and *Triplanetary* (1934; as a novel, 1948) and its five sequels, his "Lensman" series.

Science fiction began to change shape and direction when John W. Campbell Jr. assumed the editorship of *Astounding Stories* in 1937.[5] A regular contributor to the magazine himself, Campbell recruited authors who could write more realistically about science and scientists, and he demanded from them a more rigorous treatment of a broader range of ideas as well as greater sophistication in style and technique. He urged writers to refine their plots and characters, to place more emphasis on human relationships, and to tap psychology, philosophy, politics, and other soft sciences for new SF story ideas. *Astounding* gradually became the foremost science-fiction magazine and one of the few to survive the economic hardships and wartime shortages of the 1930s and 1940s. Among the new writers to appear in the pages of *Astounding* during the early years of Campbell's editorship were Isaac Asimov, Robert A. Heinlein, A. E. van Vogt, Theodore Sturgeon, Lester del Rey, and Clifford D. Simak, many of whom would remain prominent for the next half century. Guided by Campbell's demands for quality and serious scientific conjecture—several *Astounding* stories from the early 1940s predicted the atomic bomb—science fiction matured and entered its "golden age," roughly the period from 1938 to 1950.

Like "Doc" Smith's Skylark and Lensman books, many other classic SF novels that would later reappear in "fixup" paperbacks (and eventually in hard covers) were initially published serially in SF magazines during the "golden age"—as were many individual stories and interrelated stories that would later be republished in unified collections. Prominent examples by Asimov alone include "Strange Playfellow" (1940), the first of the stories that, as "Robbie," would later be incorporated into *I, Robot* (1950); "Nightfall" (1941), probably the single best-known American SF story; and the five stories and four novellas (1942–1950) later to be republished as *Foundation* (1951), *Foundation and Empire* (1952), and *Second Foundation* (1953). Other notable work that first appeared during the "golden age" includes Asimov's first published novel, *Pebble in the Sky* (1950); Heinlein's "Future

History" stories, such as "Requiem" and "The Roads Must Roll" (both 1940), other stories that would later be republished in *Beyond This Horizon* (1948; serially, 1942) and *Methuselah's Children* (1958; serially, 1941), his earliest SF novels for children, and *Sixth Column* (1949); van Vogt's *Slan* (1946; serially, 1940), *The Weapon Shops of Isher* (1951; serially, 1941–1942), *The Weapon Makers* (1946; serially, 1943), *The World of Null-A* (1948; serially, 1945), and *The Pawns of Null-A* (1956; serially, 1948–1949); Sturgeon's "It" (1940) and *The Dreaming Jewels* (1950): del Rey's "Helen O'Loy" (1938) and "Nerves" (1942); Simak's "City" and its sequel "Huddling Place" (both 1944), the first tales in his *City* (1952) sequence; L. Sprague de Camp's *Lest Darkness Fall* (1941); Arthur C. Clarke's *Against the Fall of Night* (1953; serially, 1948); Ray Bradbury's short-story collections *Dark Carnival* (1947) and *The Martian Chronicles* (1950); Hal Clement's *Needle* (1950); Cordwainer Smith's "Scanners Live in Vain" (1950); and Jack Vance's *The Dying Earth* (1950).

At about midcentury American SF broadened and improved yet again, with the appearance of such influential pulps as the *Magazine of Fantasy & Science Fiction* (1949), edited by Anthony Boucher and J. Francis McComas, and the more satiric *Galaxy* (1950), edited by Horace L. Gold and later by Frederik Pohl. Doubleday launched its Science Fiction Book Club, and SF began to appear in Ace and Dell paperbacks. While pre–World War II American science fiction had reveled in technical wonders and scientific advances, after the war writers began to examine the human consequences of these advances and the possibility that humanity might become their victims. As the social sciences became important subjects for American SF writers in the 1950s and 1960s, the social criticism that had reappeared during the "golden age" enjoyed a full revival, and the dystopian future became a staple, as it long had been in Europe. In 1953, Pohl and Cyril Kornbluth satirized advertising and capitalism in *The Space Merchants*, while Bradbury envisioned a totalitarian, book-burning America in *Fahrenheit 451*. Other dystopias appeared in such American novels as Kornbluth's *Not This August* (1955), William Burroughs' *Naked Lunch* (1959), Harry Harrison's *Make Room! Make Room!* (1966), and Philip K. Dick's *Do Androids Dream of Electric Sheep?* (1968)—and continued to appear in such British works as Anthony Burgess' *A Clockwork Orange* (1962) and John Brunner's *Stand on Zanzibar* (1968).

"Golden age" writers continued to produce more, and often more literary, work for the booming post–World War II market. Examples include Asimov's first robot novels, *The Caves of Steel* (1954) and *The Naked Sun* (1957); Heinlein's *Double Star* (1956), *Starship Troopers* (1959), *The Moon Is a Harsh Mistress* (1966), and *Stranger in a Strange Land* (1961), which attracted a large cult following in the 1960s; Sturgeon's *More than Human* (1953) and *Venus Plus X* (1960); Clarke's *Childhood's End* (1953) and *Rendezvous with Rama* (1973); and Clement's *Mission of Gravity* (1954). Simultaneously, new American authors became more prominent. Memorable SF from this period also includes Alfred Bester's *The Demolished Man* (1953) and *The Stars My Destination* (originally *Tiger! Tiger!*, 1956); Poul Anderson's *Brain Wave* (1954); Frank Herbert's *The Dragon in the Sea* (1956) and *Dune* (1965), the most popular science-fiction novel ever written and the first of six Dune books; Philip Jose Farmer's *The Green Odyssey* (1957) and *To Your Scattered Bodies Go* (1971), the first of six Riverworld books; Walter M. Miller Jr.'s *A Canticle for Liebowitz* (1959); Kurt Vonnegut's *The Sirens of Titan* (1959) and *Slaughterhouse-*

Five (1969); Gordon R. Dickson's *Dorsai* (1960); Fritz Leiber's *The Big Time* (1961) and *The Wanderer* (1964); Dick's *The Man in the High Castle* (1962) and *Ubik* (1969); and Keyes' *Flowers for Algernon* (1966), which first appeared as a short story (1959) and is very likely this characteristically cerebral genre's most emotionally engaging work.

Attention to social issues intensified in the 1960s, when the highly influential "New Wave" writers—led by Michael Moorcock, J. G. Ballard, and Aldiss, in England, and including Norman Spinrad, Harlan Ellison, Samuel R. Delany, Joanna Russ, Thomas M. Disch, Roger Zelazny, and Robert Silverberg, in America—reacted against the existing SF "establishment" with more technophobic, leftist, and stylistically innovative works that tended to depict technological disasters, moral corruption, and social decay. Key works by these authors include Aldiss' *Non-Stop* (1958) and his Helliconia trilogy (1982–1985); Ballard's *The Burning World* (1964) and *Crash* (1973); Ellison's " 'Repent, Harlequin!' Said the Tick-Tock Man" (1965), "I Have No Mouth, and I Must Scream" (1967), and his multiple-author collection *Dangerous Visions* (1967); Delany's *Babel-17* (1966) and *The Einstein Intersection* (1967); Zelazny's *This Immortal* (1966) and *Lord of Light* (1967); Disch's *334* (1972); the prolific Silverberg's *Dying Inside* (1972); and Russ' *The Female Man* (1975), which John Clute's *Science Fiction: The Illustrated Encyclopedia* lauds as "the single greatest feminist SF novel."

In the late 1960s through the early 1980s, with an ever-growing number of women entering the field, feminism and gender issues became prominent new themes. James Tiptree Jr. (Alice Sheldon) published such short stories and novellas as "And I Awoke and Found Me Here on the Cold Hill's Side" (1971), "The Women Men Don't See" (1973), *The Girl Who Was Plugged In* (1973), and *Houston, Houston, Do You Read?* (1977); Ursula K. Le Guin, *The Left Hand of Darkness* (1969) and *The Dispossessed* (1974); Suzy McKee Charnas, *Walk to the End of the World* (1974) and *Motherlines* (1978); and Marge Piercy, *Woman on the Edge of Time* (1976). Other women who wrote cutting-edge science fiction at this time include Kate Wilhelm, Pamela Sargent, Marion Zimmer Bradley, Octavia Butler, C. J. Cherryh, Vonda McIntyre, and Joan Vinge.

Simultaneously, Pohl reestablished himself as a major SF writer with *Man Plus* (1976) and *Gateway* (1977), the first of five Gateway books. Still other truly noteworthy works to appear during this period include Alexei Pashin's *Rite of Passage* (1968), Larry Niven's *Ringworld* (1970), Joe Haldeman's Vietnam-inspired *The Forever War* (1975), and Gene Wolfe's extraordinarily literate and imaginative five-volume "Book of the New Sun" (1980–1987). Having written little science fiction in over a quarter century, Asimov returned to SF in the 1980s with two new robot and four additional Foundation novels (the last published posthumously in 1993) to unify with astonishing success all his robot, Empire, and Foundation stories and novels into a monumental fifteen-volume series. By this time novels by Asimov, Herbert, Heinlein, and Clarke were appearing regularly on best-seller lists.

But the tone of science fiction in the 1980s was set by the "cyberpunk" movement, which obtained its name from the title of a 1983 Bruce Bethke story. Derived to some extent from works by Bester, Burgess, William Burroughs, and several "New Wave" writers and from the hard-boiled detective novel and film noir, cyberpunk deals with the human/computer interface in a dystopic future setting of sprawling urban ghettos festering in a world dominated by multinational conglomerates; its other, distinctive setting is "cyberspace" itself, a virtual-reality representation of the networked electronic "space" in which all computerized data exist. The prototype cyberpunk novel is William Gibson's much-imitated *Necromancer* (1984), which was followed by two sequels; the definitive cyberpunk anthology is Bruce Sterling's multiple-authored collection *Mirrorshades* (1986). Other authors strongly associated with cyberpunk include Pat Cadigan, Greg Bear, Michael Swanwick, George Alec Effinger, and Rudy Rucker.

By 1990 the tropes and conventions of cyberpunk had already been reabsorbed into the SF mainstream, which was itself broadening out even further and becoming even harder to distinguish from related genres and even from mainstream fiction. Cyberpunk-related concepts such as nanotechnology and cyborgs, a continuing interest in gender issues and ecology, a resurgence of interests in cloning and genetic manipulation, and a general updating of all the themes from science fiction's long and complex history (including several reinterpretations of Mars) characterize the state of SF at the end of the twentieth century. The best representative works from newer American authors of the past twenty years include Gregory Benford's *Timescape* (1980), Orson Scott Card's *Ender's Game* (1985), Bear's *Blood Music* (1985) and *Moving Mars* (1993), David Brin's *The Uplift War* (1987), Sheri Tepper's *The Gate to Women's Country* (1988), Dan Simmon's *Hyperion* (1989), Lois McMaster Bujold's *The Vor Game* (1990), Connie Willis' *Doomsday Book* (1992), Vernor Vinge's *Fire upon the Deep* (1992), and Kim Stanley Robinson's Mars trilogy—*Red Mars* (1992), *Green Mars* (1993), and *Blue Mars* (1994).

But American SF is hardly confined to the printed page. In addition to its long association with comic books, film, radio, and television, science fiction has more recently colonized such sites as amusement parks, board games, role-playing games, computer games, and collectible card games. SF cartooning has European roots going back 200 years, and Winsor McCay's drowsing hero dreams of adventures on other planets in the early American comic strip *Little Nemo in Slumberland* (1905–1914). Decidedly SF comics date back to the depression-era *Buck Rodgers* (1929) and *Flash Gordon* (1934) newspaper strips, and the modern comic book discovers its most famous icon in an extraterrestrial, Superman (*Action Comics* #1, 1938). These characters were inspired by the early SF pulps; and the first successful comic book to publish original science fiction was *Planet Comics* (1940–1953), a spin-off of the SF pulp *Planet Stories*. Comic books omnivorously adapt science fiction from other media—from *Classics Illustrated* versions of the works of Verne and Wells in the 1940s and 1950s, to the *Star Trek* and *Star Wars* comics and the "graphic novel" versions of SF classics by Bester and Delany in the 1970s, original graphic novels like *The Watchmen* series in the 1980s, and Dark Horse Comics' adaptations of contemporary SF films in the 1990s. Still, the superhero is the mainstay of the American comic book, such as those published by industry giants DC and Marvel; and superhero comics are full of aliens, mutants, and characters who acquire their powers through exposure to radiation. But, while the superhero has science-fiction roots, and while much legitimate SF has appeared in American comics, the superhero comic book is essentially a fantasy medium that has successfully appropriated and absorbed into itself every conceivable science-fiction theme, concept, trope, or icon.[6]

Although over 100 SF films were produced before 1930, the most significant were European movies such as Georges Melie's *La voyage dans la lune* (French, 1902) and Fritz Lang's *Metropolis* (German, 1926). Memorable American science-fiction films from the 1930s include James Whale's *Frankenstein* (1931), *The Invisible Man* (1932), and *The Bride of Frankenstein* (1935), as well as the Universal serials featuring Flash Gordon (1936, 1938, 1940) and Buck Rogers (1939). The American SF film enjoyed its first boom in the 1950s, which yielded such classics as *The Day the Earth Stood Still* (1951), *The War of the Worlds* (1953), *This Island Earth* (1955), *Forbidden Planet* (1956), *Invasion of the Body Snatchers* (1956), and *The Incredible Shrinking Man* (1957). The only great American science-fiction film of the 1960s is Stanley Kubrick's *2001: A Space Odyssey* (1968), a cerebral, big-budget masterpiece whose realistic effects irrevocably changed the look and scope of the SF movie. (Kubrick's *Dr. Strangelove*, 1964, is British.) The best science-fiction films of the early 1970s include Kubrick's *A Clockwork Orange* (1971) and John Carpenter's low-budget black comedy *Dark Star* (1974). But SF cinema was then revolutionized again by George Lucas' *Star Wars* (1977), which featured a brilliant, relentlessly allusive plot and state-of-the-art special effects—and remains one of the most popular movies ever made, as demonstrated by its highly successful rerelease in 1997. *Star Wars* not only had a profound impact on American popular culture (of which it is profoundly derivative) but also inaugurated the second science-fiction film boom of the late 1970s and early 1980s.

This second boom featured less paranoia, friendlier aliens, much better effects, and bigger budgets than the 1950s boom but still displayed a gritty underside, not only in its numerous, often darker remakes of 1950s classics (the best of which is Cronenberg's *The Fly*, 1986) but also in such films as Ridley Scott's *Alien* (1979), Carpenter's *Escape from New York* (1981), Scott's cyberpunk-styled *Blade Runner* (1982), and James Cameron's seamlessly plotted *The Terminator* (1984). Other landmark films from this second boom include *Close Encounters of the Third Kind* (1977), *Superman* (1978), *Star Wars* sequels *The Empire Strikes Back* (1980) and *Return of the Jedi* (1983), *E. T. the Extraterrestrial* (1982), the first four (of nine) Star Trek movies (of which *The Wrath of Kahn*, 1982, and *The Voyage Home*, 1986, are the best), and the first of Robert Zemeckis' three intricate *Back to the Future* time-travel comedies (1985, 1989, 1990). Australia's *Mad Max 2 (The Road Warrior*, 1981) and two British films, Terry Gilliam's *Time Bandits* (1981) and *Brazil* (1985), are also noteworthy. While the pace of SF film production has hardly slackened, the 1990s featured an unfortunate revival of the evil-alien and cosmic-catastrophe film as big-budget blockbusters; the relatively few memorable films of the decade include the subtly P. K. Dickian's *Total Recall* (1990), Coppola's controversial *Mary Shelley's Frankenstein* (1994), Gilliam's innovative *12 Monkeys* (1995), and Zemeckis' genre-transcending *Contact* (1997). Anticipating the 1999 release of the first of three planned *Star Wars* prequels, *Episode 1: The Phantom Menace*, Lucas predicted that "digital technology is the thing that's going to allow science-fiction and fantasy in film to flourish as it never has before" in the twenty-first century.[7]

The most famous radio broadcast in history is Orson Welles' 1938 transmission of *War of the Worlds*, which many listeners believed was actual news coverage of an alien invasion. The heyday of SF radio coincided with the "golden age," but such radio series as *Dimension X* (1950–1951) were supplanted in the early 1950s by numerous low-budget, cardboard-set television series like *Captain Video* (1949–1956). Trailing the 1950s and 1980s booms in science-fiction films, the two boom periods for SF on television are the 1960s and the 1990s. The best televised SF from the 1960s appeared on Rod Serling's *The Twilight Zone* (1959–1964); *The Outer Limits* (1963–1966); Gene Roddenberry's *Star Trek* (1966–1969), which spawned a huge cult following that still persists thirty years later; and the British series *The Avengers* (1961–1969), which was widely rebroadcast in the United States. Although SF never disappeared from the small screen, the appropriation of special-effects technology pioneered in films, culminating in the skillful use of computer animation, led to a resurgence of science-fiction television in the past decade—most notably on *Star Trek: The Next Generation* (1987–1994), *Quantum Leap* (1989–1994), *The X-Files* (1993–   ), Roddenberry's posthumous *Earth: Final Conflict* (1997–   ), and *Babylon 5* (1993–1998), which is arguably the best SF series yet to appear on television. Numerous science-fiction/comedy series, such as *My Favorite Martian* (1963–1966) or *Mork and Mindy* (1978–1982), also ran on television from the 1960s onward; the wittiest and most entertaining of these are *The Adventures of Brisco County, Jr.* (1993–1994), an SF/comedy/western, and Great Britain's *Red Dwarf* (1988–   ), which (like *Dr. Who*, 1963–1992) is available on some U.S. public television stations.

With the worldwide production of nearly 2,000 science-fiction movies in the past century, scores of SF television shows airing thousands of original episodes over the past fifty years, and the advent in the past decade of a "Sci-Fi Channel" devoted exclusively to SF, fantasy, and horror programming, film and television have brought science fiction to a far larger (if less discriminating) audience than was ever reached via print media. This has greatly accelerated science fiction's colonization of those leisure-time popular-culture sites that have seen tremendous growth in the past two decades: amusement parks, board games, role-playing games, collectible card games, and computer games. Films and TV have inspired such amusement-park attractions as MGM Studio's *Star Tours* and Universal's *Back to the Future* and *Terminator 3-D* rides, and even the Las Vegas Hilton's *Star Trek Experience*. Board games based on SF novels, such as Avalon Hill's *Starship Troopers*, and original SF board games, such as *Imperium* and Steve Jackson's *Ogre*, have been around since the 1970s; but more recent SF board games are often based on comics, films or film versions, and television series, such as TSR's *Buck Rogers*, Parker Brothers' *Dune*, numerous *Star Trek* games, and CGS's *Babylon 5*.

Role-playing games, introduced in the 1980s, and collectible card games, invented in the 1990s, are primarily fantasy media. Yet there are also many original SF role-playing games, such as *RIFTS*, Steve Jackson's *GURPS* (Generic Universal RolePlaying System), *Robotech*, and *Cyberpunk: 2020*; collectible card games based on SF novels, like *Dune*, and television series, like *Babylon 5* and *The X-Files*; as well as both RPGs and CCGs based on *Star Trek* and *Star Wars*. Finally and appropriately, computer games have recently become yet another locus for science fiction, with original strategy games like the Logic Factory's *Ascendancy* and Microprose's *Master of Orion II*—both of which feature futuristic technological development, galactic exploration, and encounters with alien species—sharing the market with a wide variety of SF computer games, including Westwood's *Dune 2000* and many based on the ubiquitously merchandised *Star Trek* and *Star Wars* franchises.

REFERENCE WORKS

In the past forty years, alongside its growth as popular literature, science fiction has gradually emerged as a recognized academic discipline. In 1958, Scott Osborne organized the first scholarly conference on science fiction at the Modern Language Association meeting in New York; Thomas D. Clareson founded the genre's first academic journal, *Extrapolation*, in 1959; and in that same year English poet and author Kingsley Amis presented a series of lectures at Princeton University— published in 1960 as *New Maps of Hell*—in which he proclaimed his longtime admiration for science fiction. Clareson's establishment of the Science Fiction Research Association in 1970 provided interested academicians with an annual forum for professional study of the genre. Simultaneously, college courses in SF began to proliferate, and the publication of science-fiction criticism and reference works increased noticeably to meet the needs of scholars and teachers. Sessions on science fiction now appear perennially in the national, state, and regional programs of such broad-based academic organizations as the Modern Language Association and the National Council of Teachers of English. Somewhat more specialized academic gatherings, such as the Popular Culture Association's meetings and the International Conference on the Fantastic in the Arts, feature thriving SF areas that schedule scores of paper presentations every year, and specialized scholarly journals such as *Extrapolation*, *Science-Fiction Studies*, and *Foundation* each publish dozens of academic articles on science fiction annually.

In the decades before the acceptance of science fiction as a legitimate academic discipline, dedicated enthusiasts with little training in bibliographic methodology indexed and classified SF materials and published their research in ephemeral fan magazines and pamphlets. These pioneering efforts constitute an important body of core documents and helped to establish the bibliography as a mainstay in science-fiction research. Robert E. Briney and Edward Wood's *SF Bibliographies* (1972), the first attempt to document and preserve early bibliographic work in the field, lists and annotates approximately 100 books and pamphlets published between 1923 and 1971. Marshall B. Tymn, Roger Schlobin, and L. W. Currey's *A Research Guide to Science Fiction Studies* (1977) provides a comprehensive, annotated listing of the important scholarly tools published in English through 1976. The most recent encyclopedic overview of SF research materials is Michael Burgess' authoritative *Reference Guide to Science Fiction, Fantasy, and Horror* (1992), which lists, annotates in detail, evaluates, and cross-references 551 encyclopedias, dictionaries, bibliographies, indexes, and other research tools.

The pioneer bibliography of primary works in science fiction and fantasy is Everett F. Bleiler's *The Checklist of Fantastic Literature* (1948), which contains approximately 5,200 prose titles published from 1764 through 1947 and remains an indispensable reference tool for this period; thirty years later Bleiler issued a revised edition, titled *The Checklist of Science-Fiction and Supernatural Fiction*, that drops 600 titles and adds 1,150 others to extend coverage through 1978. In 1990 Bleiler and his son, Richard J. Bleiler, published the definitive annotated list of pre-pulp-era SF, *Science-Fiction, the Early Years*, which provides detailed descriptions—with historical contexts, bibliographical details, and author, title, motif, and chronological cross-references—of over 3,000 titles published prior to 1930. A complementary resource and another important seminal bibliography, Donald H.

Darth Vader from the film *Star Wars*, 1977. © The Del Valle Archive

Tuck's three-volume *The Encyclopedia of Science Fiction and Fantasy through 1968* (1974, 1978, 1983) contains alphabetical listings of authors, anthologists, editors, artists, and others, with compilations of their works and brief biographical sketches, as well as series descriptions and full listings of the contents of story collections and anthologies. Superseding Tuck's bibliography, R. Reginald's (Michael Burgess) two-volume *Science Fiction and Fantasy Literature* (1979) and its supplement, *Science Fiction and Fantasy Literature 1975–1991*, together constitute the "essential" checklist for fantastic literature, including science fiction, to date. Volume 1 lists 15,884 English-language first editions of books published between 1700 and 1974; volume 2 presents 1,443 biographical sketches of modern SF and fantasy authors, editors, and critics; and the supplement lists an additional 22,000 English-language works. An even more comprehensive bibliography for the eight-year period that it encompasses is Charles N. Brown and William G. Contento's *Science Fiction, Fantasy, & Horror*, an annual covering 1984 through 1991—a continuation of Contento's *Index to Science Fiction Anthologies and Collections*—that is a revised and supplemented index of books, shorter fiction, and the contents of anthologies, collections, and magazines treated in the previous year's issues of *Locus*.

SF magazines have been well indexed since the 1952 publication of Donald B. Day's *Index to the Science-Fiction Magazines: 1926–1950*, which catalogs the contents of fifty-eight SF magazines from their first issues through December 1950. The next fifteen years are treated in Erwin S. Strauss' *The MIT Science Fiction Society's Index to the S-F Magazines, 1951–1965*, which covers 100 English-language magazines. The New England Science Fiction Association (NESFA) subsequently issued Anthony Lewis' *Index to the Science Fiction Magazines 1966–1970*, which treats all American and British magazines of the late 1960s. Coverage was extended to include original anthologies in the 1971–1972 supplement, and NESFA has since issued annual volumes at irregular intervals. The most comprehensive reference work for SF magazines up to 1984 is Tymn and Mike Ashley's *Science Fiction, Fantasy, and Weird Fiction Magazines*, which provides the publishing histories of 279 twentieth-century English-language magazines and includes sections on anthology series, academic periodicals, fanzines, and non-English-language magazines. However, this massive volume and all earlier efforts are superseded by Stephen T. Miller and Contento's meticulously thorough three-volume *Science Fiction, Fantasy & Weird Magazine Index: 1890–1990*, which encompasses more than 11,000 issues of 767 magazines, including many rare or obscure titles. Complementing the magazine indexes is Contento's *Index to Science Fiction Anthologies and Collections*, which contains contents listings of 1,900 books containing 12,000 different English-language stories by 2,500 authors published through June 1977; a 1984 supplement covers an additional 8,550 short stories, poems, and plays through 1983.

Three reference works constitute an essential set of resources for locating biographical, critical, and bibliographical information on SF writers. *Twentieth-Century American Science Fiction Writers* (1981), edited by David Cowart and Thomas L. Wymer, contains biographical information, bibliographical data, and critical evaluations of ninety authors who began writing after 1900 and (mostly) before 1970. Everett F. Bleiler's *Science Fiction Writers: Critical Studies of the Major Authors from the Early Nineteenth Century to the Present Day* (1982) contains essays on the life and works of seventy-six important SF writers and provides the most astute critical commentary of any such reference book. Noelle Watson and Paul Schellinger's third edition of *Twentieth-Century Science-Fiction Writers* (1991)—an expanded version of Curtis C. Smith's 1981 and 1986 reference handbooks—provides similar, but less-detailed, information on more than 640 English and foreign-language authors. Complementing these reference works on SF writers is Robert Weinberg's *A Biographical Dictionary of Science Fiction and Fantasy Artists* (1988), which includes 279 entries that span the twentieth century while emphasizing the pulp era.

By far the most useful and popular general reference work on science fiction as a whole is Neil Barron's *Anatomy of Wonder*, now in its fourth edition as *Anatomy of Wonder 4: A Critical Guide to Science Fiction* (1995). *Anatomy of Wonder* is the major source for content descriptions of science-fiction novels, story collections, anthologies, reference works, and critical studies and was heavily consulted in revising this chapter. The fourth edition annotates over 1,000 fiction and 500 nonfiction works, both English-language and foreign, and contains extensive essays by knowledgeable authorities that provide historical contexts for the annotations. Coverage of film and television, science-fiction art, comic books, magazines, and teaching aids is also included, as are numerous lists. An even more ambitious, but less up-to-date, survey of the genre is Frank N. Magill and Keith

Neilson's five-volume *Survey of Science Fiction Literature* (1979), which contains 513, 2,000-word essays covering 280 authors (including about ninety foreign-language titles by seventy-two authors) and is published with a separately bound *Bibliographical Supplement* (1982) by Tymn.

An unparalleled one-volume work covering all aspects of science fiction is John Clute, Peter Nicholls, and Brian Stableford's *The Encyclopedia of Science Fiction* (1993, 1995 update), a revised and expanded edition of Nicholls' *The Science Fiction Encyclopedia* (1979) that supersedes James Gunn's *The New Encyclopedia of Science Fiction* (1988). The lengthiest single volume yet published on SF and unmatched in scope by any other book in the field, it contains about 1.4 million words in its over 4,000 alphabetical entries on authors, editors, critics, publishers, magazines, themes, terminology, film, television, art, and more. An on-line corrigenda is continuously updated (at http://www.dcs.gla.ac.uk/SF-Archives/Misc/sfec.html), and a CD-ROM version (1995) is also available from Grolier Electronic Publishing. A colorful companion volume is Clute's *Science Fiction: The Illustrated Encyclopedia* (1995), which contains far less information arranged in a more interesting and apprehensible format; featuring hundreds of color photos and art reproductions, as well as comprehensive timelines, this coffee-table book views SF in terms of themes, historical contexts, magazines, major authors, classic titles, artwork, film, and television. The first true dictionary of science-fiction terminology is Gary K. Wolfe's wide-ranging *Critical Terms for Science Fiction and Fantasy* (1986), a glossary of about 700 cross-referenced concepts and terms preceded by a lengthy history of SF and fantasy scholarship.

Of all the SF film reference books, the most encyclopedic and sophisticated is Phil Hardy's *Science Fiction* (1984, 1991), volume 2 of the Aurum Film Encyclopedia series. The 1991 edition contains 1,500 chronologically arranged, annotated entries on silent, English-language, and foreign films from 1895 to 1990; box-office data; lists of "best" and award-winning films; and a selective bibliography. Entries include credits, a synopsis of the plot, and informed critical commentary. With the comprehensive statistical overview provided in the appendixes and over 500 black-and-white stills and dozens of color plates, this spectacular volume is the standard reference on science-fiction films. Bryan Senn and John Johnson's less-comprehensive *Fantastic Cinema Subject Guide* (1992) alphabetically categorizes 2,500 science-fiction, fantasy, and horror films under eighty-one subject areas.

The comprehensive record of reviews of SF books and of secondary literature on science fiction and fantasy generally is contained in Hal W. Hall's series of "Book Review Indexes" and "Reference Indexes." Hall's *Science Fiction Book Review Index* (*SFBRI*), published annually from 1970 to 1989, cites book reviews in SF magazines, in selected fanzines, and in general reviewing media such as *Library Journal*, *Publishers Weekly*, and *Choice*. In 1975 Hall published a compilation of the first four *SFBRI* annuals, which also extends back nearly fifty years to the beginnings of the pulp era, his *Science Fiction Book Review Index, 1923–1973*, which cites close to 14,000 reviews (of nearly 7,000 books) appearing in SF magazines since 1923 and in this broader range of magazines since 1970. This was followed by *Science Fiction Book Review Index, 1974–79*, a compilation of six *SFBRI* annuals that cites 16,700 reviews of over 5,000 books, and by *Science Fiction and Fantasy Book Review Index, 1980–1984*, a compilation of five *SFBRI* annuals that cites over 13,800 reviews appearing in over seventy periodicals and also contains a 16,000-

item "Science Fiction and Fantasy Research Index" to secondary literature. Hall subsequently published the two-volume *Science Fiction and Fantasy Research Index, 1878–1985* (1987), a comprehensive index to 19,000 books, articles, and interviews about fantastic literature organized by author and subject, and *Science Fiction and Fantasy Research Index, 1985–1991* (1993), which contains an additional 16,000 citations.

CRITICAL STUDIES[8]

The volume of science-fiction criticism published since 1970 is overwhelming and, as Gary Wolfe points out in *Anatomy of Wonder 4*, "has evolved out of three distinct traditions": fan feedback in pulp magazine letters columns and fanzines from the 1920s and 1930s; SF writers' published commentaries on the field and on each other's work, which emerged in the 1940s; and the ever-increasing attention that numerous academic scholars and the odd mainstream commentator have afforded SF since the 1950s. The first comprehensive background study is J. O. Bailey's *Pilgrims through Space and Time* (1947), a thematically arranged survey of the scientific and utopian romance that focuses almost exclusively on pre–World War I fiction. Reginald Bretnor's *Modern Science Fiction* (1953) is an important document on the "golden age" and the first collection of critical essays on SF from a mainstream publisher. Kingsley Amis' *New Maps of Hell* (1960), which gave direction to current criticism by emphasizing SF's role as an instrument of social diagnosis and warning, is the first book-length study by a prominent writer not already associated with science fiction as well as the first to reach a broad audience. Robert M. Philmus' *Into the Unknown* (1970), a survey of eighteenth- and nineteenth-century English science fiction that relates the genre to utopian satire and mythology, is the first historical study of SF published by a scholarly press.

Aldiss and David Wingrove's *Trillion Year Spree* (1986), a thoroughly revised and updated version of Aldiss' *Billion Year Spree* (1973), is the definitive single-volume critical history of science fiction, from *Frankenstein* through the mid-1980s; as a comprehensive survey of SF's development as a genre, *Trillion Year Spree* supplants James Gunn's *Alternate Worlds* (1975), an informed historical study of the scientific, social, and philosophical forces that shaped science fiction from its early beginnings to the mid-1960s. Robert Scholes and Eric S. Rabkin's *Science Fiction: History, Science, Vision* (1977) is an excellent textbook overview of SF for the general reader that examines the genre's history, relationship to scientific premises, and themes. Another important genre survey, author Barry Malzberg's *The Engines of the Night* (1982) offers a thoughtful consideration of the pulps and science fiction's early publishing history, the 1950s, fandom and conventions, and the plight of the professional SF writer. A publisher's reader-friendly perspective on the genre is provided in editor David Hartwell's *Age of Wonders* (1984), which eschews history to examine such issues as discovering and becoming addicted to science fiction, SF fandom, publishing, academic criticism, and science fiction as a reflection of contemporary culture.

Supplementing these more-general histories and surveys of the genre, there has been a proliferation of SF period studies in the past twenty years. Two quite recent books in Twayne's Studies in Literary Themes and Genres series, which neatly divide the history of SF between them, are Paul Alkon's *Science Fiction before 1900*

(1994) and Brooks Landon's *Science Fiction after 1900* (1997). Both follow the same format: a Chronology, four or five chapters of analysis, and a concluding Bibliographic Essay and Recommended Titles. Alkon's history focuses on the seventeenth- and eighteenth-century *voyages extraordinaires* and key nineteenth-century works. Landon's treatment of twentieth-century SF is a history of the genre developed in the context of contemporary critical theory and provides a useful generic overview when read in conjunction with Edward James' more straightforward *Science Fiction in the Twentieth Century* (1994).

Clareson's *Some Kind of Paradise* (1985), which views American SF from 1870 to 1930 as a popular response to world events, is the most comprehensive history of early American science fiction. Two of the many volumes that focus on the pulp era are Paul A. Carter's *The Creation of Tomorrow: Fifty Years of Magazine Science Fiction* (1977), a historical survey of thematic trends apparent in pulp SF from 1919 through the 1950s, and Alexei and Cory Panshin's *The World beyond the Hill* (1989), most of which is an incomparable history of the "golden age" that provides a detailed analysis of the evolution of the SF magazine in general and of Campbell's editorship of *Astounding* in particular. Clareson's *Understanding Contemporary American Science Fiction* (1990) is primarily a history of American SF of the 1950s and 1960s. David Pringle's *Science Fiction: The 100 Best Novels* (1985) is a judicious and sometimes surprising work-centered survey of the genre that consists of 100 two-page essays on influential English-language SF novels from Orwell's *Nineteen Eighty-Four* to Gibson's *Neuromancer*. George E. Slusser and Tom Shippey's *Fiction 2000* (1992) is an edited collection that zeroes in on the cyberpunk movement. Disch's *The Dreams Our Stuff Is Made Of* (1998) sees American science fiction from 1950 to the present as being inextricably bound to the wretched excesses of the late twentieth century. Excellent period studies of the history of British SF include Darko Suvin's *Victorian Science Fiction in the UK* (1983), an especially detailed and rigorous overview and analysis of science fiction in England from 1848 to 1900; Stableford's *Scientific Romance in Britain 1890–1950* (1985), which argues that this British literary tradition is quite separate from American SF; Nicholas Ruddick's *Ultimate Island: On the Nature of British Science Fiction* (1993), which provides an intertextual study that is a contrast to Stableford's and traces influences in British SF from those that shape H. G. Wells' work to those informing the 1960s "New Wave"; and Colin Greenland's *The Entropy Exhibition* (1983), a history of the "New Wave" itself.

Even more than period studies, theoretical criticism of science fiction has also boomed in the past quarter century. The following are among the most rewarding of these analyses. David Ketterer's *New Worlds for Old* (1974), the first such study to provide sustained explications of contemporary texts, places SF within the broader category of "apocalyptic" literature concerned with the "destruction of an old world and the coming of a new order" to argue that "science fiction and mainstream American literature share many significant features." A major contribution to the intellectual history of SF, Suvin's *Metamorphoses of Science Fiction* (1979) is a dense and insightful examination of the concepts of "cognition" (science) and "estrangement" (fiction)—undertaken to separate science fiction from naturalistic fiction, fiction dealing with the supernatural, and utopian fiction—followed by a history of European and American SF from More's *Utopia* to Slavic science fiction of the 1950s. Gary Wolfe's *The Known and the Unknown* (1979) examines the evolution and meaning of key science-fiction images—spaceships, the city, wastelands, robots, and monsters—and relates them to the fundamental beliefs and values of the genre to reveal its complex and sophisticated ideology concerning the meaning of technology and humanity's role in the universe. While Wolfe argues that the juxtaposition of the known and the unknown, mediated by a barrier, is SF's crucial paradigm, Mark Rose asserts in *Alien Encounters* (1981) that the essential science-fiction archetype is the human encounter with the non-human, and Carl Malmgren views SF in terms of alien-encounter, alternate-society, gadget, and alternate-world stories to contend in *Worlds Apart* (1991) that science fiction is best defined by the worlds that it creates. Colin Manlove's *Science Fiction: Ten Explorations* (1986) sees the themes of identity and self as common threads in SF from Asimov's *Foundation* series to Gene Wolfe's *Book of the New Sun* but eschews any universal theorizing to marvel instead at science fiction's thesis-thwarting inventiveness. Casey Fredericks' interdisciplinary *The Future of Eternity* (1982) examines the impact of mythology on modern SF and fantasy to argue that the crucial confrontations informing science fiction are those between human and superman, human and machine, and human and alien.

The study of specific science-fiction themes has likewise experienced explosive growth in the past few decades, particularly studies of utopias and dystopias (including examinations of feminist utopias and dystopias), studies of such related themes as nuclear war and the end of the world, and broader investigations of feminism and gender issues in SF. Mark R. Hillegas' *The Future as Nightmare: H. G. Wells and the Anti-Utopians* (1967) is the first systematic study of twentieth-century dystopian fiction. The most comprehensive study of modern utopian fiction is Krishan Kumar's lengthy *Utopia and Anti-Utopia in Modern Times* (1987). Sarah Lefanu's *In the Chinks of the World Machine: Feminism and Science Fiction* (1988), which Gary Wolfe notes "is perhaps the most coherent exposition of feminist themes in SF," is only one of over a dozen recent works that focus on gender issues in science fiction, including feminist utopias and dystopias. Preeminent among a half-dozen recent studies of future-war and nuclear-war fiction are I. F. Clarke's *Voices Prophesying War* (1992), which Wolfe identifies as "the standard history of future war literature"; Paul Brians' *Nuclear Holocausts* (1987), a historical treatment that traces all themes related to nuclear war from 1885 to 1984; and Martha Bartter's *The Way to Ground Zero* (1988), a more extensive and focused treatment of such themes in American SF. Wolfe points out that "a useful complementary text" is H. Bruce Franklin's *War Stars: The Superweapon and the American Imagination* (1988), which raises "SF themes to the level of political and social commentary, and . . . is crucial to understanding the historical impact of SF-type visions." The most comprehensive treatment of the related end-of-the-world theme is W. Warren Wagar's *Terminal Visions: The Literature of Last Things* (1982), which examines this prominent SF motif in 300 works from Mary Shelley's *The Last Man* to Ballard's disaster novels.

Walter E. Meyers' *Aliens and Linguistics: Language Study and Science Fiction* (1980) is a well-documented analysis of SF's treatment of linguistics. Meyers' approach is speculative but firmly grounded in current techniques of language analysis and informed by a wide acquaintance with SF literature. The first in-depth treatment of artificial intelligence (robots and computers) in science fiction, Patricia Warrick's *The Cybernetic Imagination in Science Fiction* (1980) is both a history of cybernetic SF and an analysis of its recurring images, patterns, and meanings based on a study of 225 short stories and novels written between 1930 and 1977. Analysis of this theme is continued in two essay collections edited by Richard D. Erlich and Thomas P. Dunn, *The Mechanical God: Machines in Science Fiction* (1982) and *Clockwork Worlds: Mechanized Environments in SF* (1983).

Finally, the past two decades have also yielded a sprinkling of essay collections by, and a torrent of full-length critical studies about, individual SF authors. Books of insightful essays by science-fiction writers include Delany's *The Jewel-Hinged Jaw* (1977), Stanislaw Lem's *Microworlds* (1985), Spinrad's *Science Fiction in the Real World* (1990), Le Guin's *The Language of the Night* (1992), and Russ' *To Write like a Woman* (1995). The best-edited collections of essays by a variety of SF authors are Nicholls' *Science Fiction at Large* (1977) and Maxim Jakubowski and Edward James' *The Profession of Science Fiction* (1993).

Three ongoing series that have among them published nearly 100 critical volumes on individual SF and fantasy authors are Borgo Press' *The Milford Series: Popular Writers of Today*, edited by Reginald since 1977; Starmont House's *The Starmont Reader's Guides to Contemporary Science-Fiction and Fantasy Authors*, edited by Schlobin from 1979 to 1992 and currently being published by Borgo; and Greenwood Press' *Contributions to the Study of Science Fiction and Fantasy* series, initiated by Tymn in 1982 and edited by Donald Palumbo and C. W. Sullivan III since 1992. Among the best volumes on individual SF authors in the Borgo series are Margaret Aldiss' treatment of Brian Aldiss, Albert Berger's of Campbell, and Slusser's studies of Clarke and Ellison. The best of the more than sixty volumes in the Starmont series include Rabkin's *Arthur C. Clarke*, Lance Olsen's *William Gibson*, John Kinnaird's *Olaf Stapledon*, and Robert Crossley's *H. G. Wells*. Michael Collings' volume on Card, Patrick McCarthy et al.'s edited collection of essays on Stapledon, and Elkins and Greenberg's edited collection of essays on Silverberg are among the most insightful single-author studies in the Greenwood series. Among the best of another 100 or so critical studies of individual SF authors not contained in these three series are Pringle's treatment of Ballard; David Mogen's of Bradbury; Douglas Barbour's of Delany; two studies of Dick, by Lawrence Sutin and Douglas Mackey, and a collection of essays on Dick edited by R. D. Mullen, Istvan Csicserny Jr., and Arthur B. Evans; Franklin's *Robert A. Heinlein*; Manlove's *C. S. Lewis*; Elizabeth Cummins' *Understanding Ursula K. Le Guin*; two treatments of Orwell, by Patrick Reilly and Michael Sheldon, and a collection of essays on Orwell edited by Irving Howe; four studies of Mary Shelley, by Chris Baldick, Ann K. Mellor, Emily W. Sunstein, and Martin Tropp; Jerome Kinkowitz's *Kurt Vonnegut* and Robert Merrill's edited collection, *Critical Essays on Kurt Vonnegut*; two treatments of Wells, by John Huntington and David Smith, and a collection of essays on Wells edited by Suvin and Philmus; and Arthur B. Evans' *Jules Verne Rediscovered*.

In addition to author studies, Greenwood's *Contributions to the Study of Science Fiction and Fantasy* series focuses on historical and thematic studies (many of which are also noted earlier) and also includes volumes of selected papers from each year's International Conference on the Fantastic in the Arts. Now numbering nearly 100 items, 20 of them proceedings volumes, it is the largest critical series on science fiction and fantasy in the English language. To date, thirteen proceedings volumes from the Eaton Conference on Science Fiction and Fantasy Liter-

Poster for the film *It Came from Outer Space*, 1953.
© The Del Valle Archive

ature—the Alternatives series, edited primarily by Slusser, Rabkin, Scholes, and Gary Westfahl—have also been published by Southern Illinois University Press between 1980 and 1989 and by the University of Georgia Press since 1992. Among the best of the Eaton Conference volumes is Slusser and Rabkin's *Shadows of the Magic Lamp* (1985), a collection of fourteen pieces from the 1982 conference that exhibit a full range of critical methodologies applied to fantastic films, particularly the science-fiction film.

There has been no shortage of books on SF films since the first serious study by John Baxter—*Science Fiction in the Cinema*, which outlines the history of the genre from 1895 to 1968—appeared in 1970. John Brosnan's *The Primal Screen: A History of Science Fiction Film* (1991)—a vastly expanded version of his *Future Tense: The Cinema of Science Fiction* (1979)—is a better and more recent historical treatment. Bill Warren's two-volume *Keep Watching the Skies! American Science Fiction Movies of the Fifties* (1982, 1986) is a survey of all 287 films produced in the United States between 1950 and 1962 that contain some SF element crucial to the plot. Vivian Sobchack's *Screening Space* (1987), a revision of her *The Limits of Infinity* (1980) that adds a lengthy chapter on "Postfuturism," is a highly sophisticated aesthetic analysis of the American SF film from the early 1950s through its renaissance in the late 1970s and early 1980s; it considers the relationship between science-fiction and horror films, imagery, sound, electronic technology, and contemporary perceptions of time and space. Much influenced by Sobchack, Landon's *The Aesthetics of Ambivalence* (1992) zeroes in on the relationship between SF film and SF literature, focusing specifically on adaptations and special effects as well as on electronic technology. For an overview of SF television, see John Javna's *The Best of Science Fiction TV*, which actually considers the ten "worst" series as well as better ones. Among the best books on SF art are Anthony Frewin's *One Hundred Years of Science Fiction Illustration, 1840–1940* (1975), which focuses on SF pulp art from the 1920s and 1930s; Aldiss' *Science Fiction Art* (1975), which emphasizes magazine illustrations from 1920 to 1975; and Ian Summers' *Tomorrow and Beyond: Masterpieces of Science Fiction Art* (1978), which features American paperback covers from the 1970s and contains over 300 color reproductions.

ANTHOLOGIES AND REPRINTS

The Science Fiction Book Club has been publishing inexpensive hardcover reprints of original SF paperbacks, as well as various omnibus editions, since the 1950s. In the past decade, Eaton Press' Masterpieces of Science Fiction series has begun providing expensive, leather-bound, and gilt-edged reprints of SF classics to subscribers. Numerous paperback editions of *Frankenstein* and the best-known works by such authors as Verne, Wells, Asimov, Heinlein, Clarke, Herbert, and Dick—and a host of other, more recent SF writers—remain constantly in print and are readily available. Indiana University Press publishes notable critical editions of early science fiction, such as *Twenty Thousand Leagues under the Sea* (1992), translated by Emanuel J. Mickel; *A Critical Edition of The War of the Worlds* (1993), edited by David Y. Hughes and Harry M. Geduld; and Geduld's *The Definitive Time Machine* (1987). *Who Goes There?* (1948), seven stories by Campbell, and *A Martian Odyssey and Other Science Fiction Tales* (1974), an omnibus edition of Stanley G. Weinbaum's stories, are excellent collections of "golden age" pulp fiction by two prominent SF figures.

Anthologies have been the ubiquitous mainstay of science-fiction reprints, particularly of the short story, since the 1940s, and, due to the genre's emphasis on short fiction, anthologies have also been an important vehicle for the publication of original SF since the 1960s. The 1940s boom in paperback publication led immediately to the anthologized republication of SF stories that had originally appeared in the pulp-era magazines, and these magazine reprints continued to be the most common form of SF book publication throughout the 1950s. Well over fifty SF reprint anthologies appeared in the late 1940s and early 1950s, but the popularity of SF anthologies peaked in 1973, when 105 new titles were published in a single year. This number declined to seventy-eight in 1974, but by then most new anthologies contained original stories rather than reprints, for dozens of original SF anthologies and anthology series had appeared in the 1960s and early 1970s as the result of a continuing decline in magazine publication coupled with the mid-1960s SF boom. Science-fiction reprint anthologies and anthology series have appeared primarily as (1) collections of stories published originally in a specific magazine in a given year, on a given theme, or as a retrospective, (2) "best" stories published in a given year from a variety of original sources, (3) collections of award-winning stories, and (4) collections focusing on a particular theme, period, or some unique editorial criteria. Such collections organized around a specific theme often contain both reprinted and original stories, and numerous individual anthologies and anthology series publish only original SF.

Some of the most important single-magazine reprint anthologies are those derived from *Astounding Stories* and *Analog* (the name was changed in 1960), *The Magazine of Fantasy and Science Fiction*, and *Galaxy Science Fiction*, each of which began publishing collections in 1952. Campbell edited *The Astounding Science Fiction Anthology* (1952), *Prologue to Analog* (1962), and *Analog 1* through *Analog 8* (1963–1971); several successors—including Ben Bova, Harrison, and Aldiss—have edited numerous annual and retrospective *Analog* volumes since. Boucher and McComas edited the first three volumes of *The Best from Fantasy and Science Fiction* (1952–54), and Boucher alone edited the next five. This series was published annually until 1982 under a variety of other editors; and, beginning with a *Twenty-fifth Anniversary Anthology* (1974), a retrospective volume has continued to appear every five years. Gold edited ten volumes in the *Galaxy Reader of Science Fiction* series from 1952 to 1962, including three volumes of novelettes; Pohl and others subsequently edited an additional dozen *Galaxy* volumes, concluding with a thirty-year retrospective, *Galaxy Magazine*, that appeared in 1980.

There have been four prominent "year's best" anthology series—edited by Judith Merril, Terry Carr, Gardner Dozois, and David Hartwell—two of which continue to publish annual volumes. Merril's *SF: The Year's Greatest*, which became *The (5th) Annual of the Year's Best SF* in 1960, published American and British SF by genre and nongenre writers from 1956 to 1968, except in 1967. Carr's *The Best Science Fiction of the Year*, which featured both established and emerging writers, appeared from 1965 to 1987. Dozois' Hugo-award-winning and roomy *The Year's Best Science Fiction* has been the dominant year's-best collection since its debut in 1984. The latest such annual series is Hartwell's *Years Best SF*, which began publication in 1996. Each of these series reprints stories that had first been published the previous year. A different approach is taken by *Isaac Asimov Presents the Great Science Fiction Stories*, edited by Asimov and Greenberg: Volume 1, *1939* was published in 1979 and thus contained only stories that had first appeared forty years earlier. Succeeding volumes persisted in utilizing about four decades of hindsight; the last, chronicling 1963, appeared in 1990. Asimov also edited *The Hugo Winners* and, with Greenberg, *The New Hugo Winners*. The five *Hugo Winners* volumes (1962, 1971, 1977, 1985, 1986) contain all the short stories, novellas, and novelettes to win a Hugo from its inception in 1955 through 1982, excluding 1957; the two *New Hugo Winners* volumes (1989, 1991) cover 1983 to 1988. A comparable series is *Nebula Awards*, which has reprinted each year's Nebula-winning short stories since its 1966 debut, edited by Damon Knight; subsequent editors have included Aldiss, Harrison, Zelazny, Anderson, Simak, Asimov, Wilhelm, Gunn, Le Guin, Dickson, Delany, Pohl, Herbert, Haldeman, Silverberg, and Bova, who edited a *Best of the Nebulas* retrospective volume in 1989.

Five notable SF anthology series have printed original stories only. Pohl captured the tenor of 1950s SF in his six *Star Science Fiction Stories* collections, published from 1953 to 1960. Knight's twenty-one *Orbit* anthologies, 1966 to 1980, favored a polished literary style and featured emerging writers. Silverberg and Marta Randall's *New Dimensions* series, 1971–1981, and Carr's *Universe* series, 1971–1987, also promoted new writers; Silverberg and Karen Haber revived the

Universe series in 1990. Lou Aronica and Shawna McCarthy began editing the *Full Spectrum* series in 1988.

Finally, there have been a large number of excellent period-based and general SF anthologies. Franklin's *Future Perfect: American Science Fiction of the Nineteenth Century* (rev. ed., 1978), which contains extensive critical commentary, remains the most perceptive survey of nineteenth-century American SF. Stableford identifies Asimov's *Before the Golden Age* (1974), which contains stories from the 1930s, as being "easily the best introduction to . . . early pulp SF." Other great collections of pulp-era SF include Raymond J. Healy and McComas' *Adventures in Time and Space* (1946) and Groff Conklin's frequently reprinted *A Treasury of Science Fiction* (1948). Boucher's two-volume *A Treasury of Great Science Fiction* (1959), a magnificent collection of four novels and twenty-one stories from 1938 to 1958, introduced many readers to the genre. Silverberg and Bova's two-volume *Science Fiction Hall of Fame* (1971, 1974) contains twenty-six short stories and twenty-two novellas selected by the Science Fiction Writers of America as the best published before 1965. Ellison's *Dangerous Visions* (1967), which was followed by *Again, Dangerous Visions* (1972), is the major hardcover anthology of original SF stories that launched the American New Wave; self-consciously "taboo-breaking," it contained several explicitly sexual stories that could not have been published at the time in SF magazines. The best recent SF anthologies include Hartwell's *The World Treasury of Science Fiction* (1989), which contains numerous non-English-language stories in translation as well as classic American stories; Le Guin and Brian Attebery's *The Norton Book of Science Fiction* (1993), which contains North American SF from 1960 to 1990 and features stories by women and minorities; Hartwell and Kathryn Cramer's *The Ascent of Wonder* (1994), a hard-SF anthology; Hartwell's *The Science Fiction Century* (1997), the self-styled "mother of all definitive anthologies" that contains forty-five stories by as many authors, from Wells and E. M. Forster to Nancy Kress and Stanislaw Wisniewski; and Dozois' *The Good Old Stuff: Adventure SF in the Grand Tradition* (1998), a chronological collection of sixteen stories published between 1948 and 1971.

NOTES

1. For a quite recent and far more detailed discussion of the history of science fiction, see the first four chapters in *Anatomy of Wonder 4: A Critical Guide to Science Fiction*, edited by Neil Barron: Chapter 1—"The Emergence of Science Fiction: The Beginnings through 1915," by Thomas D. Clareson, 3–61; Chapter 2—"Science Fiction between the Wars: 1916–1939," by Brian Stableford, 62–114; Chapter 3—"From the Golden Age to the Atomic Age: 1940–1963," by Paul A. Carter, 115–221; and Chapter 4 "The New Wave, Cyberpunk, and Beyond: 1963–1994," by Michael M. Levy and Brian Stableford, 222–377. The discussion in Clareson's chapter is especially thorough and was consulted heavily, with John Clute, Peter Nicholls and Brian Stableford's *The Encyclopedia of Science Fiction* and other reference works, in the revision of this section.

2. *Tarzan of the Apes*, Burroughs' second published novel, first appeared in the October 1912 issue of *All-Story*. His first novel, *Under the Moons of Mars*, appeared in the February 1912 issue of the same magazine and ran as a six-part series; for its book publication in 1917 the title was changed to *A Princess of Mars*.

3. Gernsback published science fiction as early as 1911, when his own story, "Ralph 124C41+," appeared in *Modern Electrics*. He also published science fiction in *Electrical Ex-*

perimenter (1915–1920), *Science and Invention* (1920–1928), *Radio News* (1919–1928), and *The Experimenter* (1924–1926).

4. Gernsback launched *Amazing Stories Annual* in 1927, *Amazing Stories Quarterly* in 1928, and *Science Wonder Stories* in 1929. These were followed by *Air Wonder Stories*, *Scientific Detective Monthly*, and *Science Wonder Quarterly*; in 1953 he published his last title, *Science Fiction Plus*, a large-format magazine.

5. *Astounding Stories of Super Science* began publication in January 1930 under the editorship of Harry Bates; the next editor was F. Orlin Tremaine (1933–1937), who was replaced by John W. Campbell. The magazine changed its name to *Astounding Science Fiction* in 1938, to *Analog Science-Fact Fiction* in 1960, and to *Analog Science Fiction-Science Fact* in 1965.

6. For a more extensive recent discussion of the history of science fiction in the comics, see Peter M. Coogan's "Science Fiction Comics" in Neil Barron's *Anatomy of Wonder 4*. For a closer look at the use of SF material in Marvel comics, see Donald Palumbo's "Science Fiction and Comic Books" in C. W. Sullivan III's *Young Adult Science Fiction*.

7. Interview following *Return of the Jedi*, contained in the 1997 twentieth-anniversary boxed-set video rerelease of "The Star Wars Trilogy."

8. For a thorough, judicious, and recent annotated list of books on science-fiction criticism and history, see Gary K. Wolfe's chapter on "History and Criticism," 483–546, in Neil Barron's *Anatomy of Wonder 4*, which was consulted heavily in the revision of this section. For the most up-to-date, comprehensive evaluation of SF criticism, see the four-article feature on "The History of Science Fiction Criticism" in the July 1999 issue of *Science-Fiction Studies*; Veronica Hollinger provided extensive prepublication notes from her essay for this issue, on SF criticism since 1980, that were also helpful in the revision of this section.

BIBLIOGRAPHY

Reference, History, and Criticism

Aldiss, Brian W. *Billion Year Spree: The True History of Science Fiction*. Garden City, N.Y.: Doubleday, 1973.
———. *Science Fiction Art*. New York: Crown, 1975.
Aldiss, Brian W., with David Wingrove. *Trillion Year Spree: The History of Science Fiction*. New York: Atheneum, 1986.
Aldiss, Margaret. *The Work of Brian W. Aldiss: An Annotated Bibliography and Guide*. San Bernardino, Calif.: Borgo Press, 1992.
Alkon, Paul K. *Science Fiction before 1900: Imagination Discovers Technology*. Studies in Literary Themes and Genres, No. 3. New York: Twayne, 1994.
Amis, Kingsley. *New Maps of Hell: A Survey of Science Fiction*. New York: Harcourt, Brace, 1960; North Stratford, N.H.: Arno Press, 1975.
Bailey, J. O. *Pilgrims through Space and Time: Trends and Patterns in Scientific and Utopian Fiction*. New York: Argus Books, 1947; Westport, Conn.: Greenwood Press, 1972.
Baldick, Chris. *In Frankenstein's Shadow: Myth, Monstrosity, and Nineteenth-Century Writing*. New York: Oxford University Press, 1987.
Barbour, Douglas. *Worlds Out of Words: The SF Novels of Samuel R. Delany*. Frome, Canada: Bran's Head Books, 1979.
Barron, Neil, ed. *Anatomy of Wonder: Science Fiction*. New Providence, N.J.: R. R. Bowker, 1976; rev. ed., 1981, as *Anatomy of Wonder: A Critical Guide to*

Science Fiction; 3rd ed., 1987; 4th ed., 1995, as *Anatomy of Wonder 4: A Critical Guide to Science Fiction*.

Bartter, Martha A. *The Way to Ground Zero: The Atomic Bomb in American Science Fiction*. Westport, Conn.: Greenwood, 1988.

Baxter, John. *Science Fiction in the Cinema*. London: Zwemmer, 1970.

Berger, Albert I. *The Magic That Works: John W. Campbell and the American Response to Technology*. San Bernardino, Calif.: Borgo Press, 1993.

Bleiler, Everett F. *The Checklist of Fantastic Literature: A Bibliography of Fantasy, Weird and Science Fiction Books Published in the English Language*. Chicago: Shasta, 1948; West Linn, Oreg.: Fax Collector's Editions, 1972.

———. *The Checklist of Science-Fiction and Supernatural Fiction*. Glen Rock, N.J.: Firebell Books, 1978.

Bleiler, Everett F., ed. *Science Fiction Writers: Critical Studies of the Major Authors from the Early Nineteenth Century to the Present Day*. New York: Scribner's, 1982.

Bleiler, Everett F., and Richard J. Bleiler. *Science-Fiction, the Early Years: A Full Description of More than 3,000 Science-Fiction Stories from Earliest Times to the Appearance of the Genre Magazines in 1930, with Author, Title, and Motif Indexes*. Kent, Ohio: Kent State University Press, 1990.

Bretnor, Reginald, ed. *Modern Science Fiction: Its Meaning and Its Future*. New York: Coward-McCann, 1953; 2nd ed., Chicago: Advent, 1979.

Brians, Paul. *Nuclear Holocausts: Atomic War in Fiction, 1895–1984*. Kent, Ohio: Kent State University Press, 1987.

Briney, Robert E., and Edward Wood. *SF Bibliographies: An Annotated Bibliography of Bibliographical Works on Science Fiction and Fantasy Fiction*. Chicago: Advent, 1972.

Brosnan, John. *Future Tense: The Cinema of Science Fiction*. New York: St. Martin's Press, 1979.

———. *The Primal Screen: A History of Science Fiction Film*. Poughkeepsie, N.Y.: Orbit, 1991.

Brown, Charles N., and William G. Contento. *Science Fiction, Fantasy, & Horror: A Comprehensive Bibliography of Books and Short Fiction Published in the English Language*. Oakland, Calif.: Locus Press, 1984–1991.

Burgess, Michael. *Reference Guide to Science Fiction, Fantasy, and Horror*. Englewood, Colo.: Libraries Unlimited, 1992.

Carter, Paul A. *The Creation of Tomorrow: Fifty Years of Magazine Science Fiction*. New York: Columbia University Press, 1977.

Ciofi, Frank. *Formula Fiction? An Anatomy of American Science Fiction, 1930–1940*. Contributions to the Study of Science Fiction and Fantasy, No. 3. Westport, Conn.: Greenwood Press, 1982.

Clareson, Thomas D. *Science Fiction Criticism: An Annotated Checklist*. Kent, Ohio: Kent State University Press, 1972.

———. *Some Kind of Paradise: The Emergence of American Science Fiction*. Westport, Conn.: Greenwood Press, 1985.

———. *A Spectrum of Worlds*. New York: Doubleday, 1972.

———. *Understanding Contemporary American Science Fiction: The Formative Period (1926–1970)*. Columbia: University of South Carolina Press, 1990.

Clarke, I. F. *Voices Prophesying War: Future Wars, 1763–3746*. New York: Oxford University Press, 1992.

Clute, John. *Science Fiction: The Illustrated Encyclopedia*. London: Dorling Kindersley, 1995.

Clute, John, Peter Nicholls, and Brian Stableford, eds. *The Encyclopedia of Science Fiction*. New York: St. Martin's Griffin, 1993; update, 1995.

Collings, Michael R. *In the Image of God: Theme, Characterization, and Landscape in the Fiction of Orson Scott Card*. Westport, Conn.: Greenwood Press, 1990.

Contento, William G. *Index to Science Fiction Anthologies and Collections*. Boston: G. K. Hall, 1978.

———. *Index to Science Fiction Anthologies and Collections 1977–1983*. Boston: G. K. Hall, 1984.

Cowart, David, and Thomas L. Wymer, eds. *Twentieth-Century American Science Fiction Writers*. 2 vols. Detroit: Gale Research, 1981.

Crossley, Robert. *H. G. Wells*. Mercer Island, Wash.: Starmont House, 1986.

Cummins, Elizabeth. *Understanding Ursula K. Le Guin*. Columbia: University of South Carolina Press, 1990.

Day, Donald B. *Index to the Science-Fiction Magazines: 1926–1950*. Portland, Oreg.: Perri Press, 1952; rev. ed., Boston: G. K. Hall, 1982.

Delany, Samuel R. *The Jewel-Hinged Jaw: Notes on the Language of Science Fiction*. Marina Del Rey, Calif.: Dragon Press, 1977.

Disch, Thomas M. *The Dreams Our Stuff Is Made Of: How Science Fiction Conquered the World*. New York: The Free Press, 1998.

Dunn, Thomas P., and Richard D. Erlich, eds. *The Mechanical God: Machines in Science Fiction*. Westport, Conn.: Greenwood Press, 1982.

Elkins, Charles L., and Martin H. Greenberg, eds. *Robert Silverberg's Many Trapdoors: Critical Essays on His Science Fiction*. Westport, Conn.: Greenwood Press, 1992.

Erlich, Richard D., and Thomas P. Dunn, eds. *Clockwork Worlds: Mechanized Environments in SF*. Westport, Conn.: Greenwood Press, 1983.

Evans, Arthur B. *Jules Verne Rediscovered: Didacticism and the Scientific Novel*. Westport, Conn.: Greenwood Press, 1988.

Franklin, H. Bruce. *Robert A. Heinlein: America as Science Fiction*. New York: Oxford University Press, 1980.

———. *War Stars: The Superweapon and the American Imagination*. New York: Oxford University Press, 1988.

Franklin, H. Bruce, ed. *Future Perfect: American Science Fiction of the Nineteenth Century*. New York: Oxford University Press, 1966; rev. ed., 1978.

Fredericks, Casey. *The Future of Eternity: Mythologies of Science Fiction and Fantasy*. Bloomington: Indiana University Press, 1982.

Frewin, Anthony. *One Hundred Years of Science Fiction Illustration, 1840–1940*. Burbank, Calif.: Pyramid, 1975.

Geduld, Harry M., ed. *The Definitive Time Machine*. Bloomington: Indiana University Press, 1987.

Greenland, Colin. *The Entropy Exhibition: Michael Moorcock and the British "New Wave" in Science Fiction*. New York: Routledge, 1983.

Gunn, James. *Alternate Worlds: The Illustrated History of Science Fiction*. Englewood Cliffs, N.J.: Prentice-Hall, 1975.

Gunn, James, ed. *The New Encyclopedia of Science Fiction*. New York: Viking, 1988.

Hall, Hal W. *Science Fiction and Fantasy Book Review Index, 1980–1984: An Index to More than 13,800 Book Reviews Appearing in Over 70 Science Fiction, Fantasy, and General Periodicals from 1980 to 1984 and Containing "Science Fiction and Fantasy Research Index," an Index to Secondary Literature, Providing Nearly 16,000 Subject and Author Access Points to Articles, Essays, and Books Featuring the History of, or Criticism on, Science Fiction and Fantasy Literature, Television Programs, Motion Pictures, and Graphic Arts*. Detroit: Gale Research, 1985.

———. *Science Fiction and Fantasy Research Index, 1878–1985: An International Author and Subject Index to History and Criticism*. 2 vols. Detroit: Gale Research, 1987.

———. *Science Fiction Book Review Index 1923–1973*. Detroit: Gale Research, 1975.

———. *Science Fiction Book Review Index, 1974–1979*. Detroit: Gale Research, 1979.

———, ed. *Science Fiction and Fantasy Research Index, 1985–1991: An International Author and Subject Index to History and Criticism*. Englewood, Colo.: Libraries Unlimited, 1993.

———. *Science/Fiction Collections: Fantasy, Supernatural & Weird Tales*. New York: Haworth, 1983.

Hardy, Phil, ed. *Science Fiction*. London: Aurum Press, 1984; 2nd ed., 1991. (The Aurum Film Encyclopedia, Volume 2). U.S. ed.: *The Overlook Film Encyclopedia: Science Fiction*. New York: Overlook, 1994.

Hartwell, David. *Age of Wonders: Exploring the World of Science Fiction*. New York: Walker, 1984; McGraw-Hill, 1985.

Hillegas, Mark R. *The Future as Nightmare: H. G. Wells and the Anti-Utopians*. Carbondale: Southern Illinois University Press, 1967, 1974.

Howe, Irving, ed. *Orwell's Nineteen Eighty-Four: Text, Sources, Criticism*. 2nd ed. New York: Harcourt Brace Jovanovich, 1963.

Hughes, David Y., and Harry M. Geduld, eds. *A Critical Edition of The War of the Worlds*. Bloomington: Indiana University Press, 1993.

Huntington, John. *The Logic of Fantasy: H. G. Wells and Science Fiction*. New York: Columbia University Press, 1982.

Jakubowski, Maxim, and Edward James, eds. *The Profession of Science Fiction: SF Writers on Their Craft and Ideas*. New York: St. Martin's Press, 1993.

James, Edward. *Science Fiction in the Twentieth Century*. New York: Oxford University Press, 1994.

Javna, John. *The Best of Science Fiction TV*. New York: Harmony, 1987.

Ketterer, David. *New Worlds for Old: The Apocalyptic Imagination, Science Fiction, and American Literature*. Bloomington: Indiana University Press, 1974.

Kinnaird, John. *Olaf Stapledon*. Mercer Island, Wash.: Starmont House, 1986.

Klinkowitz, Jerome. *Kurt Vonnegut*. New York: Routledge, 1982.

Kumar, Krishan. *Utopia and Anti-Utopia in Modern Times*. Malden, Mass.: Basil Blackwell, 1987.

Landon, Brooks. *The Aesthetics of Ambivalence: Rethinking Science Fiction Film in the Age of Electronic (Re)Production*. Westport, Conn.: Greenwood Press, 1992.

———. *Science Fiction after 1900: From the Steam Man to the Stars*. Studies in Literary Themes and Genres, No. 12. New York: Twayne, 1997.

Lefanu, Sarah. *In the Chinks of the World Machine: Feminism and Science Fiction.* London: Woman's Press, 1988.

Le Guin, Ursula K. *The Language of the Night: Essays on Fantasy and Science Fiction.* Rev. ed. London: Harper, 1992.

Lem, Stanislaw. *Microworlds: Writings on Science Fiction and Fantasy.* Ed. Franz Rottensteiner. New York: Harcourt Brace Jovanovich, 1985.

Lewis, Anthony. *Index to the Science Fiction Magazines 1966–1970.* Cambridge, Mass.: New England Science Fiction Association, 1971.

Mackey, Douglas A. *Philip K. Dick.* New York: Twayne, 1988.

Magill, Frank N., ed., and Keith Neilson, assoc. ed. *Survey of Science Fiction Literature: Five Hundred 2,000-Word Essay Reviews of World-Famous Science Fiction Novels with 2,500 Bibliographical References.* 5 vols. Englewood Cliffs, N.J.: Salem Press, 1979.

Malmgren, Carl. *Worlds Apart: Narratology of Science Fiction.* Bloomington: Indiana University Press, 1991.

Malzberg, Barry. *The Engines of the Night: Science Fiction in the Eighties.* Garden City, N.Y.: Doubleday, 1982; Bluejay Books, 1984.

Manlove, Colin N. *C. S. Lewis: His Literary Achievement.* New York: Macmillan, 1987.

———. *Science Fiction: Ten Explorations.* Kent, Ohio: Kent State University Press, 1986.

McCarthy, Patrick A., Martin H. Greenberg, and Charles Elkins, eds. *The Legacy of Olaf Stapledon: Critical Essays and an Unpublished Manuscript.* Westport, Conn.: Greenwood Press, 1989.

Mellor, Ann K. *Mary Shelley: Her Life, Her Fiction, Her Monsters.* New York: Routledge, 1987.

Merrill, Robert, ed. *Critical Essays on Kurt Vonnegut.* Boston: G. K. Hall, 1990.

Meyers, Walter E. *Aliens and Linguistics: Language Study and Science Fiction.* Athens: University of Georgia Press, 1980.

Mickel, Emanuel J., trans. *The Complete Twenty Thousand Leagues under the Sea.* Bloomington: Indiana University Press, 1991.

Miller, Stephen T., and William G. Contento. *Science Fiction, Fantasy & Weird Magazine Index: 1890–1990.* 3 vols. New York: Garland, 1995.

Mogen, David. *Ray Bradbury.* New York: Twayne, 1986.

Mullen, R. D., Istvan Csicserny, Jr., and Arthur B. Evans, eds. *On Philip K. Dick: 40 Articles from Science-Fiction Studies.* Greencastle, Ind.: SF-TH, 1992.

Nicholls, Peter, ed. *Science Fiction at Large.* London: Gollancz, 1976; New York: Harper, 1977.

———. *The Science Fiction Encyclopedia.* Garden City, N.Y.: Doubleday, 1979.

Olsen, Lance. *William Gibson.* Mercer Island, Wash.: Starmont House, 1992.

Panshin, Alexei, and Cory Panshin. *The World beyond the Hill: Science Fiction and the Quest for Transcendence.* New York: Jeremy P. Tarcher, 1989.

Philmus, Robert M. *Into the Unknown: The Evolution of Science Fiction from Francis Godwin to H. G. Wells.* Berkeley: University of California Press, 1970, 1983.

Pringle, David. *J. G. Ballard: A Primary and Secondary Bibliography.* Boston: G. K. Hall, 1984.

———. *Science Fiction: The 100 Best Novels—An English-Language Selection, 1949–1984.* New York: Carroll and Graf, 1985.

Rabkin, Eric S. *Arthur C. Clarke*. 2nd rev. ed. Mercer Island, Wash.: Starmont House, 1980.

Reilly, Patrick. *Nineteen Eighty-Four: Past, Present, and Future*. New York: Twayne, 1989.

Reginald, R., pseud. [Michael Burgess], ed. *The Milford Series: Popular Writers of Today*. Series. San Bernardino, Calif.: Borgo Press, 1977-present.

———. *Science Fiction and Fantasy Literature: A Checklist, 1700–1974, with Contemporary Science Fiction Authors II*. 2 vols. Detroit: Gale Research, 1979.

———. *Science Fiction and Fantasy Literature 1975–1991: A Bibliography of Science Fiction, Fantasy, and Horror Fiction Books and Nonfiction Monographs*. Detroit: Gale Research, 1992.

Rose, Mark. *Alien Encounters: Anatomy of Science Fiction*. Cambridge: Harvard University Press, 1981.

Ruddick, Nicholas. *Ultimate Island: On the Nature of British Science Fiction*. Westport, Conn.: Greenwood, 1993.

Russ, Joanna. *To Write like a Woman: Essays in Feminism and Science Fiction*. Bloomington and Indianapolis: Indiana University Press, 1995.

Schlobin, Roger C., ed. *The Starmont Reader's Guides to Contemporary Science-Fiction and Fantasy Authors*. Series. Mercer Island, Wash.: Starmont House, 1979-present.

Scholes, Robert, and Eric S. Rabkin. *Science Fiction: History, Science, Vision*. New York: Oxford University Press, 1977.

Senn, Bryan, and John Johnson. *Fantastic Cinema Subject Guide: A Topical Index to 2,500 Horror, Science Fiction, and Fantasy Films*. Jefferson, N.C.: McFarland, 1992.

Sheldon, Michael. *Orwell: The Authorized Biography*. London: Harper, 1991.

Slusser, George Edgar. *Harlan Ellison: Unrepentant Harlequin*. San Bernardino, Calif.: Borgo Press, 1977.

———. *The Space Odysseys of Arthur C. Clarke*. San Bernardino, Calif.: Borgo Press, 1978.

Slusser, George E., and Eric S. Rabkin, eds. *Shadows of the Magic Lamp: Fantasy and Science Fiction in Film*. Carbondale: Southern Illinois University Press, 1985.

Slusser, George E., Eric S. Rabkin, Robert Scholes, Gary Westfahl, and Colin Greenland, eds. *Alternatives*. Series. Carbondale: Southern Illinois University Press, 1980–1989; Athens: University of Georgia Press, 1992–present.

Slusser, George E., and Tom Shippey, eds. *Fiction 2000: Cyberpunk and the Future of Narrative*. Athens: University of Georgia Press, 1992.

Smith, Curtis C., ed. *Twentieth-Century Science-Fiction Writers*. New York: St. Martin's Press, 1981; 2nd ed., Chicago: St. James Press, 1986.

Smith, David. *H. G. Wells: Desperately Mortal*. New Haven, Conn.: Yale University Press, 1986.

Sobchack, Vivian. *Screening Space: The American Science Fiction Film*. 2nd, enlarged ed. New York: Ungar, 1987

Spinrad, Norman. *Science Fiction in the Real World*. Carbondale and Edwardsville: Southern Illinois University Press, 1990.

Stableford, Brian. *Scientific Romance in Britain 1850–1950*. New York: St. Martin's Press, 1985.

Strauss, Erwin S. *The MIT Science Fiction Society's Index to the S-F Magazines, 1951–1965*. Cambridge: MIT Science Fiction Society, 1965.

Sullivan, C. W., III, ed. *Young Adult Science Fiction*. Westport, Conn.: Greenwood Press, 1999.

Summers, Ian. *Tomorrow and Beyond: Masterpieces of Science Fiction Art*. New York: Workman, 1978.

Sunstein, Emily W. *Mary Shelley: Romance and Reality*. New York: Little, Brown, 1989.

Sutin, Lawrence. *Divine Invasions: A Life of Philip K. Dick*. New York: Harmony, 1989.

Suvin, Darko. *Metamorphoses of Science Fiction: On the Poetics of a Literary Genre*. New Haven, Conn.: Yale University Press, 1979.

———. *Victorian Science Fiction in the UK: The Discourse of Knowledge and Power*. Boston: G. K. Hall, 1983.

Suvin, Darko, and Robert M. Philmus, eds. *H. G. Wells and Modern Science Fiction*. Cranbury, N.J.: Bucknell University Press, 1977.

Tropp, Martin. *Mary Shelley's Monster: The Story of Frankenstein*. Boston: Houghton Mifflin, 1976.

Tuck, Donald H. *The Encyclopedia of Science Fiction and Fantasy through 1968*. 3 vols. Chicago: Advent, 1974, 1978, 1982.

Tymn, Marshall B., and Mike Ashley, eds. *Science Fiction, Fantasy and Weird Fiction Magazines*. Westport, Conn.: Greenwood Press, 1985.

Tymn, Marshall B., Donald Palumbo, and C. W. Sullivan III, eds. *Contributions to the Study of Science Fiction and Fantasy*. Series. Westport, Conn.: Greenwood Press, 1982–present.

Tymn, Marshall B., and Roger C. Schlobin. *The Year's Scholarship in Science Fiction and Fantasy: 1972–1975*. Kent, Ohio: Kent State University Press, 1979.

———. *The Year's Scholarship in Science Fiction and Fantasy: 1976–1979*. Kent, Ohio: Kent State University Press, 1983.

Tymn, Marshall, Roger C. Schlobin, and L. W. Currey. *A Research Guide to Science Fiction Studies: An Annotated Checklist of Primary and Secondary Sources for Fantasy and Science Fiction*. New York: Garland, 1977.

Wagar, W. Warren. *Terminal Visions: The Literature of Last Things*. Bloomington: Indiana University Press, 1982.

Warren, Bill. *Keep Watching the Skies! American Science Fiction Movies of the Fifties*. Vol. 1: 1950–1957, Jefferson, N.C.: McFarland, 1982; Vol. 2: 1958–1962, Jefferson, N.C.: McFarland, 1986.

Warrick, Patricia. *The Cybernetic Imagination in Science Fiction*. Cambridge: MIT Press, 1980.

Watson, Noelle, and Paul E. Schellinger, eds. *Twentieth-Century Science-Fiction Writers*. 3rd ed. Chicago: St. James Press, 1991.

Weinberg, Robert. *A Biographical Dictionary of Science Fiction and Fantasy Artists*. Westport, Conn.: Greenwood Press, 1988.

———. *Horror and Science Fiction Films II*. Metuchen, N.J.: Scarecrow Press, 1982.

———. *Horror and Science Fiction Films III*. Metuchen, N.J.: Scarecrow Press, 1984.

Wolfe, Gary K. *Critical Terms for Science Fiction and Fantasy: A Glossary and Guide to Scholarship*. Westport, Conn.: Greenwood Press, 1986.

————. *The Known and the Unknown: The Iconography of Science Fiction*. Kent, Ohio: Kent State University Press, 1979.

Anthologies and Reprints

Aronica, Lou, and Shawna McCarthy, eds. *Full Spectrum*. Original anthology series. New York: Bantam, 1988– .

Asimov, Isaac, ed. *Before the Golden Age*. Garden City, N.Y.: Doubleday, 1974.

————. *The Hugo Winners*. 5 vols. Garden City, N.Y.: Doubleday, 1962, 1971, 1977, 1985, 1986.

Asimov, Isaac, and Martin H. Greenberg, eds. *Isaac Asimov Presents the Great Science Fiction Stories*. Vol. 1: *1939*. New York: DAW, 1979.

————. *The New Hugo Winners*. 2 vols. Winwood, 1989; Bronx, N.Y.: Baen, 1991.

Boucher, Anthony, ed. *A Treasury of Great Science Fiction*. 2 vols. Garden City, N.Y.: Doubleday, 1959.

Boucher, Anthony, and J. Francis McComas, eds. *The Best from Fantasy and Science Fiction*. New York: Little, Brown, 1952–1955.

Campbell, John W., Jr., ed. *The Astounding Science Fiction Anthology*. New York: Simon and Schuster, 1952.

————. *Who Goes There?* Chicago: Shasta, 1948.

Carr, Terry, ed. *The Best Science Fiction of the Year*. Anthology series. Ballantine, Holt, Pocket Books, Timescape, Baen, Tor, 1965–1987.

————. *Universe*. Original anthology series. Garden City, N.Y.: Doubleday, 1971–1987.

Conklin, Groff, ed. *A Treasury of Science Fiction*. New York: Crown, 1948.

Dozois, Gardner, ed. *The Good Old Stuff: Adventure SF in the Grand Tradition*. New York: St. Martin's Griffin, 1998.

————. *The Year's Best Science Fiction*. Anthology series. New York: St. Martin's Press, 1984– .

Ellison, Harlan, ed. *Again, Dangerous Visions*. Garden City, N.Y.: Doubleday, 1972.

————. *Dangerous Visions*. Garden City, N.Y.: Doubleday, 1967.

Franklin, H. Bruce. *Future Perfect: American Science Fiction of the Nineteenth Century*. New York: Oxford, 1966; rev. ed., 1978.

Gold, H. L., ed. *Galaxy Reader of Science Fiction*. New York: Crown, 1952.

Hartwell, David, ed. *The Science Fiction Century*. New York: Tor, 1997.

————. *The World Treasury of Science Fiction*. New York: Little, Brown, 1989.

————. *Years Best SF*. Anthology series. New York: Harper Prism, 1996– .

Hartwell, David, and Kathryn Cramer, eds. *The Ascent of Wonder*. New York: Tor, 1994.

Healy, Raymond J., and J. Francis McComas, eds. *Adventures in Time and Space*. New York: Random House, 1946. As *Famous Science-Fiction Stories*, 1957.

Knight, Damon, ed. *Orbit*. Original anthology series. Putnam, Berkley, Harper, 1966–1980.

Le Guin, Ursula, and Brian Attebery, eds. *The Norton Book of Science Fiction*. New York: W. W. Norton, 1993.

Merril, Judith, ed. *SF: The Year's Greatest*. Anthology series. New York: Dell, 1956–1966, 1968.

Pohl, Frederik, ed. *Star Science Fiction Stories*. Original anthology series. New York: Ballantine, 1953–1960.

Silverberg, Robert, and Ben Bova, eds. *Science Fiction Hall of Fame*. 2 vols. Garden City, N.Y.: Doubleday, 1971, 1974.

Silverberg, Robert, and Marta Randall, eds. *New Dimensions*. Original anthology series. Doubleday, Signet, Harper, Pocket Books, 1971–1981.

Verne, Jules. *Twenty Thousand Leagues under the Sea*. Trans. Emanuel J. Mickel. Bloomington: Indiana University Press, 1992.

Weinbaum, Stanley G. *A Martian Odyssey and Other Science Fiction Tales*. New York: Hyperion, 1974.

Wells, H. G. *A Critical Edition of the War of the Worlds*. Ed. David Y. Hughes and Harry M. Geduld. Bloomington: Indiana University Press, 1993.

———. *The Definitive Time Machine*. Ed. Harry M. Geduld. Bloomington: Indiana University Press, 1987.

Selected Periodicals

Cinefantastique. Oak Park, Ill., 1970–   .
Extrapolation. Kent, Ohio, 1959–   .
Foundation: The Review of Science Fiction. London, 1972–   .
The Journal of the Fantastic in the Arts. Stow, Ohio, 1989–   .
Locus: The Newspaper of the Science Fiction Field. Oakland, Calif., 1968–   .
Monad. Eugene, Oreg., 1991–   .
The New York Review of Science Fiction. Pleasantville, N.Y., 1988–   .
Para*doxa: Studies in World Literary Genres. Vashon Island, Wash., 1995–   .
Science Fiction Chronicle. Brooklyn, N.Y., 1979–   .
Science Fiction Eye. Asheville, N.C., 1987–   .
Science-Fiction Studies. Greencastle, Ind., 1973–   .

SELF-HELP AND POPULAR RELIGION

David Fillingim

The American religious/spiritual landscape at the turn of the millennium is vast and densely populated. Simply to list and describe the active groups and movements, from AA (Alcoholics Anonymous) to Zoroastrianism, would require most of the space assigned to this topic. Compiling such a list would also beg questions of definition: exactly what counts as "religious" or "spiritual"? A growing body of literature, for instance, is devoted to analyzing the religious dimensions of secular culture,[1] suggesting that all of popular culture can be interpreted religiously. Moreover, given that devout practitioners within most religious traditions would insist that proper religious devotion is purely for the sake of the deity—not for one's own benefit—just what is the relationship between "religion" and "self-help"?

Charles Lippy develops the notion of "popular religiosity"—broader, more inclusive, and more dynamic than mere "religion"—to describe what transpires where the religious and the popular converge. In any given society, popular religiosity draws from a "central zone" of shared symbols and values to create and maintain "worlds of meaning" for individuals and groups within that society.[2] The central zone of symbols and values may derive from the society's dominant formal religious traditions, as well as from less formally religious sources, such as the cluster of political ideals that function as America's "civil religion."[3] Popular religiosity also draws from various "subsidiary zones" of symbols and values associated with subcultures or countercultures active in the society and even from individual idiosyncrasies, so that popular religiosity is syncretistic and far from uniform, but because a central zone of symbols always exerts its influence, broad descriptions of a society's popular religiosity are possible.

In America, according to Lippy, the predominant force driving popular religiosity has been the widely held perception that "supernatural powers"—forces beyond ordinary human control—influence and even determine the course of events in one's life. Consequently, American popular religiosity has been "largely an attempt to gain access to that realm of power and to use that power to benefit the individual."[4] In other words, American popular religiosity has most often been an effort at self-help. Lippy traces this effort to gain power over one's destiny through a variety of popular phenomena. For example, during the colonial period, almanacs were constantly among the most popular printed materials as individuals (including Puritans and other Christians, to the dismay of their religious leaders) consulted astrological charts in search of greater access to the unseen forces that shaped their destiny. Similarly, in the nineteenth century, as the rise of science called into question traditional Christian beliefs about the supernatural, new occult and esoteric movements promised superior access than science or Christianity to the powers that shape individual destiny. Apparently, Americans judge religious practices, like other activities in which Americans indulge, predominantly in terms of their instrumental value.

The self-help movement can be construed as a mid-twentieth-century phenomenon, exemplified in Norman Vincent Peale's gospel of success. Peale's 1952 best-selling book, *The Power of Positive Thinking*, with its anecdotal and sloganeering style, has become a model for the thousands of self-help books that have ensued. Peale amalgamates elements of evangelical Christianity, occult science, capitalist industriousness, Freudian psychology, and commonsense pragmatism into a system of personal self-improvement. Self-help tradition, then, draws on various streams of American popular religiosity. Its antecedents include secular programs of self-improvement such as Benjamin Franklin's method of thrift and Horatio Alger's rags-to-riches formula, formal religious teaching such as the Puritanism of Cotton Mather and the revivalistic traditions embodied in Billy Graham and other early media preachers, and nineteenth-century spiritual/occult movements such as New Thought and Christian Science.

Perhaps most significantly, we find in Peale's system the same quest for access to unseen powers that Lippy identifies as the hallmark of American popular religiosity. In the twentieth century, the supernatural spiritual powers courted and feared by sixteenth- and seventeenth-century American colonists were replaced in most people's minds by less metaphysical, but equally remote, realities. One of the places where the unseen powers believed to control the lives of modern individuals reside is in the deep recesses of the unconscious. We must remember that among Peale's accomplishments is the cofounding with Smiley Blanton (who had undergone analysis with Freud himself) of a psychiatric clinic that later evolved into the Institutes of Religion and Health.[5] Another location of inexorable power in the modern world is in the institutions of advanced capitalism.[6] As liberation theologians have noted, social institutions and the ideologies that drive them function in the modern world much the same way that angels, demons, and elemental spirits functioned in the world of the New Testament era—as unseen forces that control people's lives.[7] To the individual overwhelmed by seemingly hostile economic forces or debilitating unconscious psychological deficiencies (such as Peale's own inferiority complex), "positive thinking" offers a formula for gaining control of one's own destiny.

Of course, the reality of American popular religiosity is more complex than a simple utilitarian effort at self-mastery and success. Observers from Tocqueville to the present have expressed amazement at the high level of religiosity among Americans. Despite expectations that religious activity would decline with mod-

ernization, the percentage of Americans who are church members has risen steadily throughout American history, from around 16 percent at the time of the
Revolution to around 60 percent today (some estimates place the highest rate of
church membership at around 80 percent in the 1950s).[8] Thus, Gary Wills could
argue convincingly in 1990 that religion is all-pervasive in American politics. Yet,
just three years later, Stephen Carter received rave reviews for his argument that
religious values had been excluded from serious consideration in American public
discourse. How can they both be right? A Brookings Institution report notes the
paradox: "Collectively, we seem suspicious of politicians who are too religious,
and suspicious of politicians who are not religious at all."[9]

HISTORICAL OUTLINE

Marshall Fishwick schematizes American popular religion as unfolding cyclically
through a series of five "awakenings." These awakenings, Fishwick suggests, happen about every fifty years. The first three correspond with the three streams of
revival discussed by church historians—the New England awakening in the mid-
eighteenth century, the frontier revivals at the dawn of the nineteenth, and the
urban revivals of Finney and Moody in the second half of the nineteenth century.
The fourth awakening that Fishwick identifies is the rise of fundamentalism in the
first quarter of the twentieth century, while the fifth, beginning to wane at press
time, is the electronic awakening witnessed in televangelism. The five movements
that Fishwick identifies have to do primarily with evangelical Christianity (though
he does discuss Catholic use of the media). Other forms of American popular
religiosity seem to undergo similar cycles. For example, esoteric traditions have
experienced surges in popularity with the explosion in astrological almanac sales
in the mid-eighteenth century, the popularity of phrenology, mesmerism, and
spiritualism in the first half of the nineteenth, the development of Christian Science and theosophy toward the end of the nineteenth century, the American appropriation of the teachings of Swami Vivekenanda and of Rudolph Steiner's
anthroposophy in the first quarter of the twentieth century, and the emergence
of New Age spirituality as the turn of the millennium approached.

Popular religiosity, then, is at least repetitive, if not cyclical, and popular relig-
ious/spiritual trends often move in diametrically opposite directions simultaneously. For example, the resurgent Fundamentalism embodied in the rise of the
religious right in the 1980s corresponds with the rise of New Age spirituality and
with continued conservative complaints about secularization, to which both Fundamentalism and New Age belief stand as counterexamples. Wuthnow argues that
what has occurred in American spirituality since the 1950s is a transition from a
dominant "spirituality of dwelling" to a "spirituality of seeking." The older approach emphasized belonging or being "at home" in church and in one's community; spirituality was understood primarily as being a member in good standing
of one's local congregation. With the rise of consumerism in an increasingly mo-
bile and fragmented society, Americans no longer experience their lives as a seam-
less fabric in which home, work, church, and community are intertwined.
Americans now are spiritual seekers, seeking spiritual practices that are meaningful
and helpful as they negotiate their way among the plethora of roles and locations
in which they live and work.[10] Looking backward through Wuthnow's lens, one

sees that there have always been those who were not at home in the dominant American spiritual traditions; that is, statistically small numbers of dissenters have always participated in diverse spiritual movements. But in the postdenominational era, pluralism itself has become dominant.

The story of American popular religiosity can be encapsulated as the story of four overlapping dialogues or dialectics: between religion and superstition, between religion and science, between religion and therapy, and between religion and market forces. Along the way, some account must be given for the fact that, through it all, an apocalyptic or millenarian strain has persisted. Keeping in mind Lippy's contention that American popular religiosity is largely about gaining access to a realm of supernatural power and using that power for personal benefit, some attention to how this dynamic fits the religiosity of marginalized groups is in order.

Religion and Superstition

An opposition between religion and superstition may seem an odd place to begin. After all, to the modern mind shaped by Freud's and Marx's dismissals, religion *is* superstition. Besides, superstition is a relative term. Evangelical Protestants in the Reformed tradition would tend to look down upon Pentecostal experience of the Spirit and popular Catholic devotion to the saints as superstition, while adherents to these latter two practices might label as superstitious Mormon belief in God's revelation to Joseph Smith. As R. Lawrence Moore notes, "superstition is a label for the other man's religion."[11] In response to the supposition that the proper opposition is between science and superstition (understanding "superstition" to include religion), Samuel Southard notes that "the original meaning of the word experimental in the American vocabulary" was set not by scientists but by Puritan divine Jonathan Edwards to describe his method of discerning the authenticity of "religious affections" observed among participants in the revivals of the first Great Awakening.[12]

Recognizing that superstition is a relative term, let me posit as a starting point and case study an opposition between formal religion in the form of seventeenth-century Puritanism and some practices that Puritan leaders viewed as superstition. The Puritan approach to life was (officially, at least) rational, systematic, and highly ordered, very "scientific" in contrast to the haphazard reliance on talismans, omens, and astrological signs that characterized religiosity among the larger portion of the colonial populace.[13] But Puritan leaders proved unable to thwart the intense popularity of almanacs and other devices and practices through which colonists sought access to the realm of supernatural power. Puritans, of course, also believed in the supernatural but preferred a more ordered access to it. Ironically, by preaching against occult practices, often equating them with the domain of Satan, Puritan preachers confirmed not only the reality of supernatural power but also the effectiveness of the condemned practices.

What has been called the Puritan "double vision" evolved. Occult practice came to be popularly viewed as compatible with Christian doctrine because the whole created order is of God, the supernatural realm must be under God's control, and occult practices are merely another means through which God communicates to created beings.[14] This validation of occult practice was aided, in fact, by the emer-

Cotton Mather. Courtesy of the Library of Congress

gence of science. John Winthrop, after all, was a contemporary of Galileo and Francis Bacon. Scientific observation of the orderly motions of the heavenly bodies lent popular credence to the conviction that astrology was both scientifically valid and theologically acceptable. If an intelligent Creator had built an observable pattern into the motions of the stars and planets, it seemed reasonable to imbue that pattern with communicative significance.

The Puritan double vision was a popular phenomenon; official Puritanism remained opposed to astrology and other occult practices. Official Puritanism also had its own low points on the superstition scale, the hysteria embodied in the Salem witch trials being a case in point. But Puritan notables leaned in the direction of science more than superstition. Increase Mather preached against witch hysteria, while Cotton Mather advocated inoculation against smallpox. Cotton Mather's *Essays to Do Good* can be read as a partly secularized Puritan ethic emphasizing the earthly benefits of godly living. In response to the waning influence of religious doctrine in the growing urban centers, Mather makes a case that virtuous living brings not only heavenly rewards but also earthly success.[15] Benjamin Franklin read Mather's *Essays* as a young man and was deeply influenced by them. Franklin's "experimental" program of self-improvement carries the secularization of Puritan ethics to its logical conclusion: virtue is purely a means of material success.[16]

Eighteenth-century science, then, favored religion ever so slightly over superstition as a means of gaining control over one's destiny. Some theoretical credence was lent to the popular practice of astrology. But "experimental" investigation showed Puritan discipline and virtue to be more effective in producing wealth. On the other hand, the same experimental investigation, when carried a bit further at the dawn of the nineteenth century, showed the supernatural underpinnings of Puritan ethics to be unnecessary. However, despite the fact that Franklin was a successful publisher who reached a broad popular audience, his program of ethics proved too austere for the tastes of many. Wayne Oates notes that near the turn of the nineteenth century, a popular belief was that "fortuitous events"—dumb luck—could outweigh all other factors in determining the course of one's life.[17] So astrology and other superstitions perdured alongside the simple vices of sloth and profligacy that so worried Franklin, as did the Calvinist doctrines that Franklin and other Deists found unnecessary.

The Puritan struggle against superstition demonstrates the inadequacy of approaches to religious history that focus only on the official beliefs of organized religious groups or the intellectual debates among theologians and other religious elites. The study of popular religiosity focuses instead on how "official" doctrine is appropriated by the populace and synthesized with other beliefs and practices. Indeed, astrology and Calvinist doctrine have perdured in America even to the present, alongside a host of other beliefs and practices. As science continued to gain influence over the course of the nineteenth century, religion made adjustments to keep pace.

Religion and Science

With the dissemination of the theories of Darwin, Marx, and Freud, scientific materialism became the accepted cosmology in American intellectual circles and wherever conditions were right for the new ideas to trickle down to the masses. Materialist science was not the only nineteenth-century trend that loosened the de facto Protestant establishment's stranglehold on American culture. Denominational schisms over slavery and the Civil War shook the foundations of the institutions of formal religion in America, while Catholic and Jewish immigrants brought increased religious diversity to the American continent. But the new science, especially Darwin's theory of evolution, caused the most obvious stir in the American religious melting pot.

The problem with Darwinism was not merely that it contradicted the Genesis Creation story, though that alone might have been enough to galvanize Fundamentalism into an identifiable movement. Due to the influence of the historical criticism of the Bible that Fundamentalists also opposed, most churches had already gained some degree of comfort with less than literal readings of Scripture. The problem with evolution was that it seemed to threaten the very basis of religion by denying that humans are fundamentally different from other animals. If humans evolved from lower forms of animals, then we are only so much tissue, and we don't have immaterial souls in need of saving. So, while Fundamentalists could simply deny the truth of the new theory, mainline Protestants accustomed to accommodating mainstream culture faced a difficult task in trying to negotiate some sense in which religion could have any significant meaning.

A number of new movements appeared as offshoots of the negotiation between science and religion. Movements such as Christian Science, phrenology, mesmerism, theosophy, and spiritualism emerged from the intellectual confusion brought about by scientific questioning of religious assumptions to offer techniques through which people could gain access to that otherwise inaccessible realm of power that was now seen as the domain not only of religion but also of science. Phrenology, for example, was consistent with a scientific materialist cosmology and thus promised to unlock the technical mysteries of the new science to the uninitiated, while mesmerism claimed to offer a more scientific view of the relation between the material and immaterial realms than religion offered.[18] Theosophy and Christian Science, on the other hand, sought to replace the new materialism with a philosophical idealism and claimed to be both the true science and the true religion. All of these movements made their claims to truth on a landscape increasingly influenced by the rise of science.

In other words, "scientific" discourse proved to be hegemonic. Christian Science practitioners claimed a better cure ratio than physicians and posited this as evidence that their cosmology was correct. Phrenologists similarly claimed empirical evidence for the accuracy of their diagnoses and prescriptions. Conversely, the Shakers saw their lucrative commerce in mail-order remedies diminish when they refused to speak in the language of scientific discourse.[19] Even Fundamentalists, who have ostensibly opposed modernist science, have adopted scientific discourse. Books, pamphlets, videos, seminars, and radio programs offering scientific evidence for the Genesis account of creation and other biblical teachings have become a cottage industry among Fundamentalists and Evangelicals. Contemporary Fundamentalists remain true to their Calvinist roots by promoting a rational, ordered access to supernatural power. Behind conservative political activism on abortion, homosexuality, and other issues lies a conviction that righteousness is the only path to peace and prosperity. Bringing the nation into conformity with "God's laws," it is believed, will bring God's blessings on the nation, while allowing America to slide further into moral and spiritual decay will bring the nation closer to God's wrathful judgment. The assumption that following God's law is the path to prosperity is individualized in myriad ways.

So, then, though scientific discourse was hegemonic, scientific materialist cosmology was not. Belief in a supernatural or spiritual realm remained strong throughout the nineteenth century and even to the present. All of the movements associated with the occult tradition in nineteenth-century America promised some type of access to this spiritual realm. Spiritualism offered direct communication with those who had passed on to the other realm. Madame Blavatsky's theosophy and Mary Baker Eddy's Christian Science both functioned as modern gnosticisms, offering secret knowledge of true spiritual reality that lay beyond the reach of the uninitiated, and, while church historians may speak of the "Fundamentalist-modernist controversy," it seems more accurate to speak of a Fundamentalist-modernist compromise, as Fundamentalists continue to deploy scientific methods to assert modernist truth claims on behalf of a premodern cosmology.

The same factors that facilitated the proliferation of occult movements in the first half of the nineteenth century also facilitated the emergence of Mormonism.

Into an arena in which competing views of ultimate reality vied for the attention of confused spiritual seekers, Joseph Smith offered a new revelation from God tailor-made for the American continent. Smith, who had dabbled in the occult, claimed that in 1827 he had been shown golden plates inscribed with the text of *The Book of Mormon* and that he had also been supernaturally enabled to translate the ancient text into English. As Lippy notes, acceptance of Smith's claims by others depended first on a widespread belief in the reality of the supernatural and, second, on Smith's ability to convince others that he had been granted unique access to the realm of supernatural power, accomplished in part through Smith's reputation as a healer and exorcist.[20]

The advancement of science also played a role in the emergence of millennial movements during the nineteenth century. Millennialism had arrived on the American continent at least as early as John Winthrop's vision of a city on a hill; in fact, it might be argued that all American religious history is millennial in some broad sense of the term. But the nineteenth-century technological advances that facilitated industrialization and westward expansion planted the seeds of a secular faith in progress that would parallel an increase in millennial fervor among the faithful. The doctrine of Manifest Destiny stands as an embodiment of this secular millennialism. The secular faith in progress found a religious parallel in the Social Gospel movement, which dominated liberal theology toward the end of the nineteenth century. Social Gospelers such as Washington Gladden and Walter Rauschenbusch taught that Christian social action could accomplish gradual improvement through which the Kingdom of God would be realized in American society.

The Social Gospel text that reached—and continues to reach—the widest popular audience was Charles Sheldon's *In His Steps*. Sheldon was a pastor in Topeka who in 1897 began preaching a serialized story of a group of parishioners who resolve to do nothing without first asking themselves the question, "What would Jesus do?" The novel was first published in installments in a weekly Christian newspaper. The characters are led to respond to their self-questioning by conducting a series of revival services in the local saloon district and, of course, campaigning for Prohibition. The continuing influence of Sheldon's novel is seen in the marketing of "WWJD?" [What would Jesus do?] bracelets, books, and trinkets in the 1990s. The appeal of the Sheldonian question is in its hypothetical and subjunctive mode: neither the characters in Sheldon's novel nor the more recent WWJD youth ministry materials indulge in any serious investigation of what Jesus actually did or did not do. Sheldon and the Social Gospelers assume that people generally possess all the power that they need. With a little redirection and incremental change, the world can be brought under the banner of Christ. Among the ironies in popular evangelicalism is the fact that those who are buying the WWJD merchandise hold a doctrine of human depravity that should render any WWJD ethic meaningless.

More apocalyptic versions of millennialism appeared in the first half of the nineteenth century among the Millerites and the Shakers. Near the end of the nineteenth century, the cluster of ideas began to emerge that would become known as dispensational premillennialism upon the publication of the Scofield Reference Bible in 1907. Just as Fundamentalism represents a reaction against certain modernist trends, so premillennialism represents a reaction against liberal

Mormons arrive at Salt Lake. Courtesy of the Library of Congress

and humanistic strains within the Social Gospel movement. The pattern unfolding in human history, the premillennialists argue, is not gradual progress toward the realization of the Kingdom of God on earth, but rather increasing wickedness leading to a coming judgment. All of this will transpire according to God's preordained plan for the ages.

Premillennialism reestablishes the realm of ultimate power as supernatural. The human choice is simply to choose sides—to join the faithful who will share in God's ultimate victory or remain aligned with the present evil age, which will soon pass away. The emotional appeal of premillennialism is the same as that of the less doctrinaire but equally eschatological gospel song tradition that emerged from the revivals of D. L. Moody. Gospel songs about heaven reflect the awareness that this world is a jungle operating according to principles antithetical to Christianity. Those who seek to live by Christian principles will never have power in this world; therefore, they must postpone gratification to the next world, trusting Jesus to calm their inner anxieties in the here and now. Premillennialist ideas were popularized in Hal Lindsey's 1970 best-seller *The Late Great Planet Earth* and are consistent with the teachings of television preachers Pat Robertson and Jerry Falwell.

The advancement of science had the effect of broadening the spiritual marketplace. As older religious ideas were brought into question, new ideas emerged, often claiming scientific justification. But the old ideas refused to die and reasserted themselves sometimes by questioning science on scientific grounds. At any rate, scientific discourse came to shape the playing field on which religious and spiritual debates would be played out. The true test of spiritual or religious teachings, however, remained the pragmatic one, as it had been in the "experimental" systems of Franklin and the Puritans. Americans want a religiosity that works, that gives individuals access to a realm of power and enables them to use that power for some beneficial purpose, whether that purpose be physical health, material wealth, or simply greater peace and confidence in the face of the chaos and anxiety of life in modern industrial society.

Religion and Therapy

Science, of course, seeks to explain not only the outward universe in which humans and other animals reside but also the inner world of human functioning. Science offers its own versions of ultimate power. Oates suggests that with the growing influence of scientific determinism, DNA and behavioral conditioning have come to play in the modern mind the role that the three Fates played in classical Greece and Rome. Human behavior is seen to be determined by genetic makeup or social conditioning or some combination of the two.[21] Therapy has become the "scientific" means of gaining access to a realm of unseen power and reversing the negative effects of these determining factors as much as possible. So great has been the influence of the therapeutic ethos in an American culture that social critic Philip Rieff in 1968 declared *The Triumph of the Therapeutic*.

Therapy also greatly influenced the practices of both organized religion and popular religiosity in the twentieth century. The second half of the twentieth century witnessed the growth of myriad practices and movements that blur the distinction between religion and therapy. Peale's "Positive Thinking," for example, though ostensibly the preaching of a Christian minister, is in practice a simple formula for thought conditioning leading to increased self-esteem and material success accessible to anyone, regardless of religious conviction or lack thereof. Alcoholics Anonymous and other twelve-step programs posit a spiritual journey as the only effective treatment for addiction. Jungian therapy, transcendental meditation, scientology, and a host of other practices combine the religious with the therapeutic in pursuit of more complete human well-being. The pastoral counseling movement has brought therapy into the churches; many large urban and suburban congregations house counseling centers staffed with trained therapists whose practice is indistinguishable from that of "secular" therapists. Preaching often reflects the therapeutic mood as what has been called "the counseling sermon"[22] becomes ever more prevalent in American pulpits.

Critics have complained that the uncritical acceptance by religious leaders of certain therapeutic practices paved inroads into religion for the individualistic and even narcissistic ethos that lies behind popular psychology. But such criticisms overlook two important factors. First, the therapeutic or self-help ethos was not new to religiosity in the twentieth century. Nineteenth-century movements such as New Thought and Christian Science betray a similar concern that religious practice facilitate mental as well as physical healing. Some, in fact, have traced the introspective conscience that made American religiosity open to therapeutic concerns to Puritan "practical divinity"—particularly the Puritan practice of self-examination in search of signs of one's own election.[23] Individualism has never been foreign to American religion.

Second, the American theological appropriation of behavioral science was actually quite intentional and deliberative, not at all haphazard or unintentional. Allison Stokes describes this intentional engagement of religion and psychology as the "Religion and Health Movement," which is discernible throughout the first half of the twentieth century. Early efforts to link religion and mental health, such as the Emmanuel movement in Boston in the early 1900s, reflected the Social Gospel movement's concern that Christianity be practically helpful in alleviating human suffering. The same concern to alleviate human suffering motivated psychiatric chaplain and sometime psychiatric patient Anton Boisen to posit that theological students who are training for ministry should study not only the dry texts of theological tomes but also the "living human documents" of suffering individuals. Boisen is recognized as the founder in 1925 of the Clinical Pastoral Education movement, a program of chaplaincy internships for ministry students that continues to influence (critics say it dominates) American theological education.

In the years following World War II years, the Religion and Health movement continued to expand. Norman Vincent Peale's collaboration with Smiley Blanton (and the degree to which awareness of depth psychology appears in Peale's books) represents the popular side of the movement. On the theoretical level, a series of monthly meetings of the loosely organized New York Psychology Group brought leading figures in American theology such as Paul Tillich and Seward Hiltner and leading figures in psychology, psychiatry, and behavioral science such as Rollo May, Erich Fromm, Carl Rogers, and Ruth Benedict together in regular discussions on the integration of religion and psychology. Other leading figures in American theology, such as Reinhold Niebuhr, also engaged the thought of Freud in their own work. Though trends in theological ivory towers are not always directly related to popular religiosity, it cannot be denied that the Religion and Health movement as outlined by Stokes has been a major force in shaping American theological education. So, when American congregants sought religious practices that were more oriented toward therapeutic effectiveness, they often found a clergy trained and ready to oblige.

Outside the institutions of formal religion, the link between spirituality and therapy is even more strongly evident. The "Twelve-Step" or "Recovery" movement was perhaps the most significant new spiritual movement in terms of participation in twentieth-century America. The Recovery movement originated with Alcoholics Anonymous, founded in 1935 by Bill Wilson. AA posits as the method for overcoming addiction a twelve-step spiritual journey, in which the basic elements of American popular religiosity as analyzed by Lippy are evident. First, a power beyond the individual is seen as being in control of one's life and destiny, as seen in step 1: "We admitted that we were powerless over alcohol and that our lives had become unmanageable." Second, a realm of supernatural power that might be marshaled toward the individual's benefit is identified, as seen in step 2: "Came to believe that a power greater than ourselves could restore us to sanity."[24] Finally, a method of gaining access to that power is prescribed; by participating in the group and following the remaining steps, the individual is empowered to remain sober.

The twelve-step approach was soon generalized to treat other forms of addiction. By replacing the word "alcohol" in step 1 with the names of other addictive substances or practices, groups such as Narcotics Anonymous, Gamblers Anony-

Alcoholics Anonymous meeting, ca. 1950. © Bett-mann/CORBIS

mous, Love and Sex Addicts Anonymous, and Emotions Anonymous found the twelve-step program equally effective for their needs. During the 1980s, Melodie Beattie began applying the Recovery philosophy to healing the emotional wounds suffered by family members of addicted persons, and the Codependency move-ment was born. The Recovery movement spread like wildfire. By 1991, 4 percent of the United States population belonged to an organized recovery group, and many others read the hundreds of recovery books published each year. Many of the groups met in churches, specifically, Christian recovery groups, the vague higher power of AA now being specifically identified with the God of the Bible. Some even began to substitute the word "sin" for a specific addiction in step 1, making the twelve steps a generic treatment program for the human condition.[25]

As a self-help movement, twelve-step spirituality exhibits two factors that ac-count for its appeal that are also characteristic of Norman Vincent Peale's "Pos-itive Thinking." First, both approaches are developed in practical, commonsense terms accessible to their target audience. Peale speaks in anecdotes and slogans, and his anecdotes more often than not have to do with individuals who gain success in business. Twelve-step spirituality also relies heavily upon slogans and anecdotes. Some two-thirds of nearly 600 pages of the AA "Big Book" are devoted to stories of individuals who found hope and healing thorough AA, and most of the time in AA meetings is given to testimonials. Second, both approaches em-phasize individual responsibility. In Peale's system, the individual is capable of, and responsible for, performing the daily thought conditioning that changes neg-ative thinking into positive thinking. Similarly, in AA, it is the individual who must recognize his or her condition, resolve to do something about it, perform the self-examination required in AA's "searching and fearless moral inventory" (step 4), and stick with the program "one day at a time" (to borrow a favorite AA slogan).

Religion as therapy continues to be a powerful metaphor shaping organized religion as well as the practices of the growing number of postmodern Americans who describe themselves as "spiritual but not religious." Scott Peck, whose *The Road Less Traveled* spent several years atop the *New York Times* best-seller list, can be seen as a Norman Vincent Peale for the post-Vietnam era. Peck refuses to gloss over the fact that life is complex and often difficult and offers a program of spiritual growth through self-examination and self-acceptance in the face of the trials and conflicts of (post)modern life.[26] New Age spirituality is similarly characterized by introspection—a search for one's true self using a variety of spiritual tools. The irony of such approaches is that they respond to the isolation and alienation of modern life by intensifying the focus on the individual.[27]

Religion as therapy is also evident among evangelicals, where "small-group" ministries are displacing Sunday school as the focus of church programming. Small groups combine the bonding that smaller congregations (or families) once provided with the therapeutic benefits of recovery groups. During the 1990s, four out of ten Americans participated in small groups, the majority of these being sponsored by churches. Among the needs met by small groups is the need to be empowered to negotiate the complexities of (post)modern life. The groups, Wuthnow notes, give participants a sense of divine power: the group itself "can become a manifestation of the sacred" as the support that members receive from one another increases their confidence and decreases their anxiety, leaving them emotionally equipped to manage the stress and strain of their complicated lives.[28] In other words, the small group movement reflects the central dynamic of American popular religiosity—the desire to be empowered to have greater control over one's life.

In addition to small group ministries, Evangelicalism displays its therapeutic proclivities through its own self-help tradition. Psychologist James Dobson rose to fame offering self-help advice to parents and, though his Focus on the Family organization has received more public attention for its conservative political activism, self-help continues to occupy much of its radio time. Larry Burkett offers Christian financial counseling through a radio program and several books. The Minirth-Meier clinics seek to combine biblical counsel with psychiatry in their treatment centers. David Seamands, perhaps the most psychologically astute of the Evangelical self-help writers, offers techniques for healing damaged emotions through self-acceptance based on the individual's awareness of having been accepted by Christ. The small groups, radio advice, Christian treatment centers, and self-help books that meet Evangelical believers' felt personal needs reflect the larger trend among Evangelicals of attempting to construct an alternative Christian economy that offers believers everything that they can get in the larger economy with the dirt and stains of worldliness removed. Christian bookstores with coffee shops, Christian concerts, Christian T-shirts, Christian music and videos, and a variety of other products offer the opportunity to enjoy all the goods of advanced capitalism without the usual attendant sins and temptations. As popular religiosity, this trend, too, reflects the desire for empowerment. Rather than negotiate the difficult and hostile chaos of the secular economy, Evangelical Christians can increasingly shop in a safer, sanitized, more controllable version. There are, of course, those voices in the wilderness that suggest that consumerism is not exactly consistent with the teachings of Jesus of Nazareth. But consumerism is yet another area in which American Christians have tended to be more American than Christian.

Religion and the Market

The Weberian thesis that American capitalism has its roots in the Puritan character is well known, and observers of popular Evangelicalism cannot but be aware of the "church marketing" trend that began in the 1980s. But few are aware of the degree to which American Christianity has participated in shaping American consumer markets, particularly in entertainment and leisure. As R. Lawrence Moore argues compellingly in *Selling God: American Religion in the Marketplace of Culture*, the relationship between religious and market values in American history has been mutual. Throughout American history, Moore demonstrates, "[c]hurches interacted with, influenced, and were influenced by popular trends in commercial culture" (55). According to Moore, the constitutional disestablishment of religion created an atmosphere in which religious ideas would have to compete with each other and with nonreligious ideas for the attention of a populace free to choose how and whether to practice religious devotion. In other words, the First Amendment creates a marketplace in religion.

Into this marketplace, American religious leaders entered boldly. Moore characterizes the Second Great Awakening as one of the great marketing successes of the colonial era. George Whitefield, after all, is credited by one biographer with presenting religion as "a product that could be marketed" and described by another as a "peddlar in divinity."[29] Other early American marketing successes came in the area of publishing. Benjamin Franklin marketed Whitefield's sermons. Lesser-known clerics published tracts presenting their religious views. More significantly, religious leaders shaped the rules by which nonreligious materials would be marketed. Publishers of sensational pamphlets describing in graphic detail the dangers of licentious living sought and received the blessing of Protestant ministers by emphasizing the hortatory benefits of such reading material in warning impressionable young men and women away from dangers into which otherwise they might fall. The assurance that a pamphlet (or later, a novel) had such positive moral effects enabled consumers to purchase materials for their titillating appeal with religious sanction.

Religious leaders continued to take an active role in shaping the market in entertainment. When theater promoters desired to market their product to the middle class, Moore notes, they had first to make a convincing case that theater could be morally uplifting. Henry Ward Beecher began affirming the potential value of the theater experience, other liberal or progressive ministers followed suit, and the path was opened for "respectable" theater to displace the more prominent earlier version, which catered to working-class audiences through bawdy productions and liquor sales. The Chautaqua movement promoted the idea that leisure was a good in itself, perhaps even a Christian duty, a notion that facilitated the acceptance of city parks as valuable public investments. Similarly, the development of the Young Men's Christian Association (YMCA) popularized the idea that it was the atmosphere in which an activity took place, not the activity itself, that determined its moral value.

The first church marketing manuals appeared during the first decade of the twentieth century. Dwight L. Moody had cemented the relationship between Christianity and business by recruiting business leaders to organize his local crusades, but it was the more liberal churches attuned to the Social Gospel doctrine of human progress that brought the church into the advertising age. Among the slogans recommended in a 1921 church advertising manual was "Christianity Makes People Healthy, Happy, and Prosperous."[30] The way was paved for Peale and others to market material success and emotional well-being as the chief benefits of religious devotion. What evolved in the second half of the twentieth century is a variety of niche markets in religious devotion. One such niche market is New Age spirituality, which, Moore notes, is statistically insignificant but aesthetically appealing and thus gets more scholarly and media attention than other movements with larger numbers of participants. Other spiritual niche markets offering different paths of access to the supernatural or different explanations of how the supernatural invades modern life include the angel craze of the 1990s and its converse, the new demonology in the novels of Frank Peretti.

A large part of the story of the marketing of religion in the twentieth century involved the rise of religious broadcasting.[31] During radio's early days, airtime was donated to religious groups as part of radio stations' public service obligation. The beneficiaries of this largesse were groups that reflected the dominant values of the urban/suburban middle class, the mainline Protestant denominations. Fundamentalist and Pentecostal preachers, whose natural audience was drawn from the rural and working-class population, found that purchasing airtime was their only way to gain access to the airwaves. Mainline Protestants resisted this move toward purchased airtime as being somehow distasteful, which, Moore notes, is quite ironic given their previous forays into the marketing of religion. So conservatives, following the lead of Charles Fuller's pioneering *Old Fashioned Revival Hour*, soon dominated the religious airwaves. Conservative Evangelical dominance continued into the age of television, with some notable exceptions, such as Catholic Bishop Fulton Sheen in the 1950s and "Possibility Thinker" Robert Schuller from the 1970s onward.

The rise of televangelism has centered on dynamic personalities who, enacting some latter-day "Horatio Alger finds Jesus" rags-to-riches scenario, have built (and sometimes lost) their own media empires. Billy Graham's *Hour of Decision*, begun in 1950, was the first successful Evangelical television program. Graham, however, did not cross over completely into the new medium but retained the crusade as his primary focus, and his television broadcasts to this day consist primarily of videotaped segments of his crusades. Graham's focus on his evangelistic mission, combined with his organizational prowess, makes him the only televangelist to remain untouched by scandal. Oral Roberts similarly began his television career in the 1950s by filming his crusades, but his crusades offered the spectacle and attendant controversy of faith healing. After a two-year hiatus, Roberts retooled his approach to broadcasting and in 1969, from studios at the university that he founded, launched the first Christian talk/variety program. Producing a state-of-the-art variety show was much more expensive than filming a crusade, so it is not surprising that Roberts developed the first theology of television fund-raising. Roberts promised a "Blessing Pact" whereby God was virtually guaranteed to return every contributor's gift from an unexpected source as a result of Roberts' prayers on behalf of his benefactors. This idea was soon expanded into the idea of "Seed Faith," whereby a gift to the evangelist was likened to planting a seed, which would eventually grow and produce blessings in the form of material gain or physical healing in the life of the donor.

Pat Robertson began what would evolve into the Christian Broadcasting Network (CBN) in 1961. His *700 Club* program has followed a format resembling a morning news/talk show, complete with fund-raising appeals and intercessory prayer on the air. Robertson's prayers have the power not only to provide blessings to his listeners and donors but even to move hurricanes. Jim Bakker left Robertson's CBN in 1974 to launch his own ill-fated *PTL Club* in a gaudier version of Roberts' variety show format. Bakker took fund-raising to new heights (or depths), and it is plausibly argued that his own greed and narcissism were his undoing. Jerry Falwell evokes the heritage of his Fundamentalist forebears by entitling his television broadcast *The Old Time Gospel Hour*. Despite his staunch social and fiscal conservatism, Falwell was drawn briefly into the *PTL* cesspool but quickly discovered that Bakker's Disneyfication of Christianity did not suit him.

Neil Postman argues that television trivializes, and in religious broadcasting is seen a trivialization of popular religiosity: one gains access to supernatural power simply by sending a check to a well-coifed emissary who will beseech the deity on behalf of financial supporters. Christian television offers "Jesus Lite," a version of Christianity that promises blessings but makes no demands (other than offering financial support to the television preacher of your choice). The dark night of the soul through which Christian tradition teaches Christians to pass, the "fear and trembling" with which the Apostle Paul advises believers to "work out your own salvation (Philippians 2: 12)," are absent from the religious airwaves. The implication is similar to that of New Age spirituality: the spiritual life is a smorgasbord from which one can take what one likes and leave the rest.[32]

Moore's account of the active participation of religion in the commercialization culture should be seen as enriching, rather than contradicting, any account that emphasizes the hegemony of market values. As political philosopher Michael Walzer argues, market values have tended to become dominant in all spheres of American culture. Moreover, as Erica Rand has demonstrated, capitalist hegemony is itself a dialogical process: consumers appropriate market values on their own terms, while the market appropriates acts of resistance and transforms resistance itself into a market commodity. Religious leaders, Moore concludes, "deserve more credit than they usually get as major architects of American experience."[33] Yet, Moore notes with resignation, the ascendancy of accommodation limits religion's potential for social transformation. Fishwick concludes his account of the relationship between popular religion and the popular with similar resignation: the options appear to be reduced to the polar opposites by which Benjamin Barter characterizes extremist religion and extreme commercialization: "jihad vs. McWorld."[34]

Popular religiosity, however, as the processes by which individuals and groups create meaning and negotiate channels of power in their surrounding environment can never be reduced to polar opposites. As Moore notes at the beginning of his chronicle, religious intellectuals and elites may draw hard distinctions between sacred and secular, but "ordinary people" simply live their lives. Negotiating the "marketplace of culture" is one of the avenues through which Americans seek access to a realm of power by which they can control their own destiny. For most of American history, religious (read Protestant Christian) values have been indistinguishable from middle-class values—hence, the easy religious endorsement of "respectable" forms of leisure and entertainment. The link between religion and middle-class values also makes plausible the assumption that religion should lead to material success; "respectable" people are respectable precisely because of their social status. Thus, a program like Peale's positive thinking functions as popular religiosity precisely because of its easy marketability: Peale's audience "suffered not from sin, . . . but from unawareness of the practical power of their faith. They believed in Christ, but they did not know how to use him to construct prosperous lives for themselves and their families."[35] Positive thinking, in other words, offers access to that realm of power by which persons can become or remain middle-class. In a market economy, supernatural power is in the service of social power.

Supernatural Power and the Less Powerful

A number of American groups and individuals, of course, have lacked the same access to social power that the dominant Protestant middle class has held. Yet the experience of these individuals and groups is also part of the story of American popular religiosity. African Americans, Native Americans, and the working class (which included most American Catholics and Jews during the nineteenth century and the early decades of the twentieth) have lived and practiced their religions outside the cultural mainstream. To what extent do those at the margins of American society exemplify Lippy's depiction of popular religiosity as the seeking of access to supernatural power to be used for individual benefit?

African American slaves found themselves in a position of utter social powerlessness on the American continent. African slaves were brought to the American colonies beginning in 1619. During the first century of chattel slavery in America, African slaves developed practices such as conjuring, which offered access to the powerful realm of spirits, and slave "trickster" narratives, which constructed a type of subversive power that could be exerted by slaves amid the dehumanizing conditions of the institution of slavery. Both of these practices had antecedents in African traditions and would later be amalgamated into African American Christianity. Concerted efforts to convert slaves to Christianity began with the first Great Awakening in the mid-eighteenth century. White owners overcame their reluctance to evangelizing slaves in hope that slaves would exhibit such "Christian" virtues as meekness and submission to authority. But the slaves themselves found other aspects of the Christian message, such as God's liberation of slaves in the book of Exodus, more relevant to their situation.

Thus, the evolution of African American Christianity followed a double path. Slaves gave the outward appearance of conforming to the ethos of white Christianity while developing their own practice of Christianity as an "invisible institution."[36] Through secret "hush harbor" meetings, double messages embedded in the spirituals, and other methods, slaves exerted the subversive power to control their own religious practice. By the time slaves were allowed to officiate at public religious meetings and build their own churches, the African American church was well established as a locus of power. Donald Swift suggests that the church functioned for early African Americans as "the only institution over which they could exert some control while slaves in a racist society" (30). After the Civil War, the African American church continued to function as one of few social institutions under African American control and thus as a source of social power for African American believers. The type of empowerment emphasized in African American religiosity differs from the individual self-help emphasized in the popular religiosity dominant in the larger society. The African American church has focused much of its energy on social reform and "moral uplift." As Anthony Pinn notes, "Black churches never restricted their activities to the realm of spiritual health."[37] African American religiosity, then, is more communal than individualistic and eschews much of the dualism (such as sacred vs. secular or this-worldly vs. otherworldly) associated with mainstream American religion.

For much of its history, American Catholicism demonstrated a stronger thrust toward communal empowerment than Protestantism, as Catholic parishes also functioned as enclaves in which immigrants could experience a stronger sense of belonging and control than they had in the larger society. During the last quarter of the nineteenth century, the number of American Catholics quadrupled. The vast majority of Catholic immigrants at the turn of the century held low-paying, working-class jobs, and the sudden influx coupled with the explosive growth of urban populations inspired fear and often loathing among middle-class Protestants. The Catholic Church resisted Protestant hegemony by establishing parochial schools and publishing devotional materials. Catholic parishes and lay organizations also served as ready-made networks for labor organizers. The success of the labor movement ameliorated many of the socioeconomic disparities between the American middle and working classes, and second- and third-generation immigrants naturally moved into the middle class through education and hard work, so that by the 1950s, Catholics were incorporated into the banal generic Americanism criticized by Herberg.

American Jews have followed a path from a marginal immigrant community to assimilation into the cultural mainstream similar to that of Catholics, to the extent that some observers fear that American Judaism is in danger of disappearing through intermarriage. American women constitute yet another group for whom religion has functioned as a source of social empowerment, as the "first wave" of the women's movement arose out of Christian women's groups organized to support benevolence, missions, and temperance. The belief that women's influence needed to be felt more strongly in society led to the suffrage movement. Native Americans have combined native traditions with the Christianity visited upon them by missionaries in myriad ways. While Native Americans certainly exhibited greater respect for their surroundings than, say, the nineteenth-century industrialists who embarked on a conquest of nature, the mythical perfect harmony idealized in New Age and ecofeminist appropriations of Native American traditions is a distortion. Among the Native American movements that exhibit an effort at social empowerment in response to being pushed to the margins of an alien culture is the apocalyptic Ghost Dance movement at the end of the nineteenth century, which, not unlike the slave spirituals, promoted a mode of living successfully amid white dominance with a promise that Native peoples would ultimately be vindicated.[38] It seems reasonable to conclude that persons at the margins of American culture have tended to develop religiosities that are as syncretistic as American popular religiosity but not as individualistic.

REFERENCE WORKS

The study of popular religiosity is the purview of a number of academic disciplines, including religious studies and theology, history, sociology, communication studies, psychology, and others. The major journals in each of these fields run the occasional article on popular religion, as do the interdisciplinary popular culture and American culture journals. But no academic journal devoted to the study of popular religion exists. The boundaries between academic disciplines play a variety of roles in the study of American religion. Scholars in theology and religious studies often find common ground with scholars in the disciplines from which theology and religious studies borrow methodologies. For example, a panel of scholars presenting sociological analyses of some aspect of American religion might include a member of a university sociology department, a member of a university religious studies department, and a member of a theological seminary faculty, and all three scholars might submit their work to the same journal, in either sociology or religious studies. Similar convergence between historians and church historians might occur. Sometimes disagreement about a work's merit breaks down along disciplinary lines. For example, *The Churching of America, 1776–1990: Winners and Losers in Our Religious Economy* by sociologists Roger Finke and Rodney Stark has been lauded by scholars of quantitative ilk but scorned by historians for relying on outdated historical arguments.[39]

Though no scholarly journal devoted to popular religion exists, a number of religious periodicals aimed at religious professionals and educated laypersons merit attention by scholars. The *Christian Century* is a biweekly newsmagazine that serves as the mouthpiece of mainline Protestantism. *Christianity Today*, founded in 1956 by Billy Graham, serves the same function among Evangelicals. *America* and *Commonweal* are similar Catholic periodicals. All four of these magazines are characterized by thoughtful analysis of cultural and religious trends (often by recognized scholars), careful news reporting, and insightful book reviews. *Christianity Today* is essential reading for persons interested in monitoring the pulse of popular Evangelicalism. The monthly magazines *Sojourners* and *The Other Side* offer cultural criticism from the perspective of radical Christianity—Christians from various denominational backgrounds devoted to working for social justice. *Sojourners'* regular "Culture Watch" column will be of particular interest to students of popular culture. The Episcopal publication *The Witness* and the Jewish magazine *Tikkun* similarly offer radical social criticism. The Jewish publication *Commentary* features social criticism from a more politically conservative perspective, as does *First Things*, edited by neoconservative Richard John Neuhaus.

A number of relevant general reference works have appeared in recent years. The 1988 *Encyclopedia of the American Religious Experience*, edited by Charles Lippy and Peter Williams, is extremely helpful, as is *Twentieth-Century Shapers of American Popular Religion*, a biographical dictionary edited by Lippy. J. Gordon Melton's *Encyclopedia of American Religions* includes thematic overviews on various "families" of religious groups followed by an alphabetical listing of the individual groups. Frank S. Mead's *Handbook of Denominations in the United States*, revised by Samuel S. Hill, is a standard updated every five years. The *Encyclopedia of Religion & Society*, edited by William Swatos, contains thorough entries on the categories through which sociologists analyze religion but is not limited to the American experience.

Scholars interested in quantitative analysis will also want to visit the American Religion Data Archive (www.arda.tm).

Elise Chase's 1985 work, *Healing Faith: An Annotated Bibliography of Christian Self-Help Books*, remains useful as a guide to primary source self-help materials up to its date of publication, as do earlier surveys of self-help tradition such as Donald B. Meyer's *The Positive Thinkers: A Study of the American Quest for Health, Wealth, and Personal Power from Mary Baker Eddy to Norman Vincent Peale* and Richard Weiss' *The American Myth of Success: From Horatio Alger to Norman Vincent Peale*. A more recent survey of self-help ideology is Wendy Kaminer's *I'm Dysfunctional, You're Dysfunctional: The Recovery Movement and Other Self-Help Fashions*, which, like Meyer's work, is characterized by invective against the turn toward pop psychology in American religion. Carol George's *God's Salesman: Norman Vincent Peale and the Power of Positive Thinking* is a thorough account of Peale's life and thought. Peale's own writings, like those of other self-help luminaries, remain readily available. Linda A. Mercandite's *Victims and Sinners: Spiritual Roots of Addiction and Recovery* analyzes theological themes that account for the popularity of twelve-step programs in America.

HISTORY AND CRITICISM

As a survey of American popular religiosity, Charles Lippy's *Being Religious, American Style: A History of Popular Religiosity in the United States* is unparalleled. Lippy's account, remarkable for its breadth of coverage and depth of research as well as for its lucid and cogent style, is as valuable for the bibliographic guidance found in its notes and references as for the compelling argument that it makes. Lippy includes analysis of trends in African American religion, Native American religion, and American Judaism for each time period that he discusses. R. Lawrence Moore places the story of popular religion within the larger narrative of the rise of advanced capitalism in *Selling God: American Religion in the Marketplace of Culture*. Marshall Fishwick offers a cyclical interpretation in *Great Awakenings: Popular Religion and Popular Culture*. An excellent earlier survey of American popular religion is *Popular Religion in America: Symbolic Change and the Modernization Process in Historical Perspective* by Peter Williams, published in 1980.

Sidney Ahlstrom's 1972 *A Religious History of the American People* remains the standard history of religion in America, though excellent surveys abound. In *Religion and the American Experience: A Social and Cultural History, 1765–1997*, historian Donald C. Swift treats American religious pluralism as fully as possible in a brief survey. Mark Knoll gives a comprehensive account of North American Christianity in *A History of Christianity in the United States and Canada*, while R. Lawrence Moore highlights the large cultural influence of nonmainstream religious movements in *Religious Outsiders and the Making of Americans*. In *The Democratization of American Christianity*, Nathan Hatch demonstrates how the populist ideals that have dominated American politics have also shaped American religious life. The essays compiled by Harry S. Stout and D. G. Hart in *New Directions in American Religious History* offer a convenient overview of recent trends in the field. For a treatment of women's religious history, see Susan Hill Lindley's *"You Have Stept Out of Your Place": A History of Women and Religion in America*.

The subtitle of *Under God: Religion and American Politics*, by Garry Wills, is deceptively narrow (as is the fact that Wills takes the 1988 presidential election as his starting point). Wills effectively demonstrates the pervasiveness of religion in American culture, and his exposition of millennial/apocalyptic dimensions of the American religious psyche are particularly helpful. As the turn of the millennium approached, the surge in popular interest in apocalypticism was accompanied by a spate of scholarly attention. Especially helpful is *Apocalypticism in the Modern Period and the Contemporary Age*, edited by Stephen J. Stein (volume 3 of the three-volume *Encyclopedia of Apocalypticism*). An excellent anthology analyzing newer apocalyptic movements is *Millennium, Messiahs, and Mayhem: Contemporary Apocalyptic Movements*, edited by Thomas Robbins and Susan J. Palmer. Lippy's earlier essay, "Waiting for the End: The Social Context of American Apocalyptic Religion," provides an excellent overview and is accompanied by fine treatments of various aspects of American apocalyptic in *The Apocalyptic Vision in America: Interdisciplinary Essays on Myth and Culture*, edited by Lois Parkinson Zamora. See also the essays compiled by Malcolm Bull in *Apocalypse Theory and the Ends of the World* and those assembled by Douglas Robinson in *American Apocalypses: The Image of the End of the World in American Literature*.

On popular religiosity in the colonial era, see *Worlds of Wonder, Days of Judgment: Popular Religious Belief in Early New England* by David Hall. Notable studies of Puritanism include *The Puritan Origins of the American Self* by Sacvan Bercovitch; *God's Caress: The Psychology of Puritan Religious Experience* by Charles Lloyd Cohen; and *The Spiritual Self in Everyday Life: The Transformations of Personal Religious Experience in Nineteenth Century New England* by Richard Rabinowitz. Three titles in the Library of Religious Biography series that shed light on seventeenth- and eighteenth-century American religion are Edwin S. Gaustad's *Liberty of Conscience: Roger Williams in America* and *Sworn on the Altar of God: A Religious Biography of Thomas Jefferson*, and Harry S. Stout's *The Divine Dramatist: George Whitefield and the Rise of Modern Evangelicalism*. Another biography of Whitefield, Frank Lambert's *Peddlar in Divinity: George Whitefield and the Transatlantic Revivals, 1737–1770*, ties the story of early revivalism to the rise of market forces, while John H. Wigger's *Taking Heaven by Storm: Methodism and the Rise of Popular Christianity in America* highlights the influence of Whitefield and his successors on the development of American Christianity. For a general survey of American revivalism, see *Revivals, Awakenings, and Reform: An Essay on Religion and Social Change in America, 1607–1977* by William G. McGloughlin.

The antebellum period was characterized by a diversity of religious and spiritual movements. Alexis de Tocqueville's classic account of religion's place in antebellum America in *Democracy in America* should not be overlooked; see also *The Voluntary Church: American Religious Life, 1740–1860, Seen through the Eyes of European Visitors*, edited by Milton B. Powell. For accounts of the frontier revivals that dominated antebellum Protestant Christianity, see *And They All Sang Hallelujah: Plain-Folk Camp-Meeting Religion, 1840–1845* by Dickson Bruce, and *Charles G. Finney and the Spirit of American Evangelicalism* by Charles E. Hambrick-Stowe. Protestant Christianity was also dominated by battles leading to schism over slavery. John Lee Eighmy's *Churches in Cultural Captivity* presents a compelling case study of southern Baptists' capitulation to the dominant forces in southern culture on the issue of slavery.

The standard history of Mormonism, which emerged in the early nineteenth century, is *The Mormon Experience: A History of the Latter-Day Saints* by Leonard J. Arrington and Davis Bitton. Important analyses of the place of Mormonism in American culture include *Mormons and the Bible: The Place of the Latter-Day Saints in American Religion* by Philip Barlow and *The Angel and the Beehive: The Mormon Struggle with Assimilation* by Armand L. Mauss. Richard Ouellette's 1999 *Religious Studies Review* essay, "Mormon Studies," provides an excellent overview of recent Mormon historiography, while Claudia and Richard Bushman's essay, "Latter-Day Saints: Home Can Be a Heaven on Earth," links Mormonism's move into the cultural mainstream with the resurgence of conservative "family values" in the 1980s. Craig Blomberg and Stephen Robinson discuss the similarities and differences between Mormons and Evangelicals in *How Wide the Divide? A Mormon and Evangelical in Conversation*.

The second half of the nineteenth century witnessed the third Great Awakening in the urban revivals led by Dwight L. Moody. James F. Findlay Jr. chronicles Moody's career in *Dwight L. Moody: American Evangelist, 1837–1899*. Sandra Sizer analyzes the cultural impact of Moody's message in *Gospel Hymns and Saving Religion: The Rhetoric of Nineteenth Century Revivalism*, arguing that the domestication/privatization/feminization of religious devotion in America can be traced to the revivals. Ted Ownby's *Subduing Satan: Religion, Recreation, and Manhood in the Rural South, 1865–1920* traces the process of the domestication of religion in the South during the post–Civil War era to deeper currents dividing male and female cultures. Roger Lundin's *Emily Dickinson: The Fate of Theology in American Culture* elucidates the place of religion in mainstream culture during the late nineteenth century, while Paul S. Boyer's essay, "*In His Steps*: A Reappraisal," analyzes the values and conflicts of middle-class Protestants during the same period.

The second half of the nineteenth century also witnessed a revival of occult or esoteric spirituality in America, spearheaded by the emergence of Helena P. Blavatsky's theosophy and Mary Baker Eddy's Christian Science. The essays collected by Howard Kerr and Charles L. Crow in *The Occult in America: New Historical Perspectives* provide insight into American occultism from seventeenth-century witch trials to twentieth-century unidentified flying object (UFO) phenomena. See also R. Lawrence Moore's *In Search of White Crows: Spiritualism, Parapsychology, and American Culture*. Steven Gottschalk's sympathetic *The Emergence of Christian Science in American Religious Life* remains the most thorough analysis of the thought of Mary Baker Eddy and of the movement that she founded, while Moore's scattered discussions (see especially the chapter on Christian Science in *Religious Outsiders*) are more critical. On theosophy, Mark Bevir's recent *Journal of the American Academy of Religion* article places Blavatsky's own thought in its cultural context, while Steven Prothero's *Religious Studies Review* essay provides invaluable guidance through recent secondary sources. See also Michael Gomes, *Theosophy in the Nineteenth Century: An Annotated Bibliography*.

On American religion in the first half of the twentieth century, see Martin Marty's three-volume *Modern American Religion*, which covers the period from 1893 to 1961. Herberg's *Protestant, Catholic, Jew* is a classic account of how the three religious traditions of mainstream American culture had melted into generic civil religion by the 1950s. The best account of the rise of Fundamentalism is George M. Marsden's *Fundamentalism and American Culture: The Shaping of Twentieth Century Evangelicalism, 1870–1925*. Edward J. Larson analyzes Fundamentalism's most publicized moment and its enduring cultural significance in *Summer for the Gods: The Scopes Trial and America's Continuing Debate over Science and Religion*. The massive five-volume Fundamentalism Project, edited by Martin Marty and Scott Appleby, aims at comparative perspectives on a global scale, and many of the essays included elucidate aspects of American Protestant Fundamentalism during its formative years as well as during its more recent resurgence. On twentieth-century revivalism, see Edith Blumhofer's *Aimee Semple McPherson: Everybody's Sister*, Lyle W. Dorsett's *Billy Sunday and the Redemption of Urban America*, and Richard M. Riss' *A Survey of 20th-Century Revival Movements in North America*.

On American religiosity since World War II, the work of sociologist Robert Wuthnow is recommended. His *After Heaven: Spirituality in America since the 1950s* is the best general survey. The distinction between a spirituality of seeking and a spirituality of dwelling that Wuthnow develops in *After Heaven* corresponds on some points with the distinction that he develops in *Poor Richard's Principle* between "ascetic moralism" associated with Calvinist tradition in American and the more Romantic "expressive moralism" focused on self-fulfillment and embodied in the small group movement and other recent spiritual trends. Wuthnow further analyzes the cultural significance of the small group movement in *Sharing the Journey: Small Groups and America's New Quest for Community*. Sociologist and practical theologian Tex Sample provides an excellent overview of Wuthnow's work, as well as an indictment of his theological writing that fails to take sociological reality adequately into account. Sample discusses the tensions between the cultural left, right, and middle as they relate to American Protestantism in *U.S. Lifestyles and Mainline Churches*.

Sociologist Robert Bellah and colleagues analyze "expressive individualism" as the typical belief system in late twentieth-century America in *Habits of the Heart: Individualism and Commitment in American Life*. The disintegration of common values inherent in American individualism prompts James Davidson Hunter to posit a war between right and left in *Culture Wars: The Struggle to Define America*. Wuthnow broadens the field of contenders in the culture wars in *The Struggle for America's Soul: Evangelicals, Liberals, and Secularism*, while Erling Jorstad softens the culture wars idea by proposing a dialectical tension between the impulse to preserve tradition and the impulse toward progress in *Holding Fast/Pressing On: Religion in America in the 1980s*. William Martin surveys the 1980s resurgence of Fundamentalism in *With God on Our Side: The Rise of the Religious Right in America*. Randall Balmer combines scholarly analysis with journalistic description in *Mine Eyes Have Seen the Glory: A Journey into the Evangelical Subculture in America*. On televangelism, see *Prime Time Religion: An Encyclopedia of Religious Broadcasting*, edited by J. Gordon Melton and Gary Ward. See also *Oral Roberts: An American Life* by David Edwin Harrell Jr. and *A Prophet With Honor: The Billy Graham Story* by William Martin. On American religiosity in the 1960s, see Robert S. Ellwood's *The Sixties Spiritual Awakening: American Religion Moving from Modern to Postmodern*.

The standard history of African American Christianity is *The Black Church in the African American Experience* by C. Eric Lincoln and Lawrence H. Mamiya. Lincoln's 1961 work, *The Black Muslims in America*, though dated, remains a useful survey. A more recent treatment of Islam among African Americans is Richard

Brent Turner's *Islam in the African American Experience*, which focuses on political thought. Claude Andrew Clegg's *An Original Man: The Life and Times of Elijah Muhammad* serves not only as a biography of Muhammad, who led the Nation of Islam from 1934 to 1975, but also as a history of the organization. Leading African American theologian James Cone discusses the cultural significance of Malcolm X and Martin Luther King in *Martin and Malcolm and America: A Dream or a Nightmare*. The standard account of slave religion is *Slave Religion: The Invisible Institution in the Antebellum South* by Albert Raboteau. Also available is the *Encyclopedia of African-American Religions*, edited by Larry G. Murphy, J. Gordon Melton, and Gary L. Ward.

On African American popular religiosity, the work of Anthony Pinn is a good place to start. In *Why Lord? Suffering and Evil in Black Theology*, Pinn discusses various ways in which the African American community has sought to construct some meaning out of the experience of extreme and unjust suffering. While Pinn discusses academic theology at some length, his discussion of popular movements in the African American church and his analysis of the theological message of blues and rap are extremely relevant to understanding African American popular religiosity. In *Varieties of African American Religious Experience*, Pinn interprets non-Christian religious movements such as voodoo, Islam, and the Black Humanism that Pinn himself endorses. On the religious significance of African American musical traditions, the work of Jon Michael Spencer is unparalleled; see his *Blues and Evil* and *Re-Searching Black Music*. Cone's 1972 work, *The Spirituals and the Blues*, analyzing the theological significance of the two musical forms mentioned in its title, has become a classic. Other treatments of the spirituals that merit attention include Cheryl Kirk-Duggan's *Exorcizing Evil: A Womanist Perspective on the Spirituals* and David Goatley's *Were You There? Godforsakenness in Slave Religion*.

On American Catholicism, see *Catholics and American Culture: Fulton Sheen, Dorothy Day, and the Notre Dame Football Team* by Mark Massa; *The Encyclopedia of American Catholic History*, edited by Michael Glazier and Thomas P. Shelley; *A Short History of American Catholicism* by Martin Marty; *Parish School: A History of American Catholic Parochial Education from Colonial Times to the Present* by Timothy Walch; and *The History of Black Catholics in the United States* by Cyprian Davis. On Judaism, see *A History of the Jews in America* by Howard Sachar and "American Jewry: Families of Tradition in American Culture" by Sylvia Barak Fishman. On Native American religion, see *The Spiritual Legacy of the American Indian* Joseph Epes Brown; *God Is Red: A Native View of Religion* and *Red Earth: Native Americans and the Myth of Scientific Fact* by Vine Deloria; and *Native and Christian: Indigenous Voices on Religious Identity in the United States and Canada*, edited by James Treat.

To place the movement in historical context, Catherine Albanese links New Age spirituality to a long tradition of seeking wholeness through harmony with nature in *Nature Religion in America: From the Algonkian Indians to the New Age*, while Robert S. Ellwood links the late twentieth-century interest in Eastern spirituality to nineteenth-century occultism in *Alternative Altars: Unconventional and Eastern Spirituality in America*. Richard Kyle's *The Religious Fringe: A History of Alternative Religions in America* is a fair and thorough survey from an Evangelical Christian perspective. Jacob Needleman's 1970 *The New Religions* remains a useful survey, while *America* editor David Toolan's *Facing West from California's Shores: A Jesuit Journey into New Age Consciousness* is a thoughtful and sympathetic assessment. More recently, Michael Brown links New Age spirituality to nineteenth-century spiritualism in *The Channeling Zone: American Spirituality in an Anxious Age*. See also *The Encyclopedia of Cults, Sects, and New Religions*, edited by James R. Lewis, and the essays compiled by Lewis and Melton, *Perspectives on the New Age*.

RESEARCH COLLECTIONS

The situation regarding research collections in this realm remains as Roy Anker reported in the second edition of this *Handbook*: research collections of either secular or religious self-help literature are almost nonexistent. Because of its great popularity in its day, much of the literature discussed in this chapter can be found in major public or university libraries as well as in bookstores that specialize in old and used books.

Bridwell Library of Southern Methodist University has established a New Thought collection, collecting books, pamphlets, periodicals, personalia, archives, and miscellaneous documents of people and organizations associated with the New Thought Alliance.

Materials on Christian Science—periodicals and unpublished primary source materials—are located at the Mother Church in Boston. While it is generally believed that the collection of unpublished documents is extensive, there is a sizable and important portion of the holdings to which the public is not permitted access, as many scholars have complained. In the past, access has been granted in proportion to the scholar's likely fealty to Christian Science.

Since many of the recent declaimers of self-help have been prominent churchmen, full collections of their writings and electronically recorded messages are retained in the archives and libraries of the congregations served. Hence, Norman Vincent Peale's numerous books and a full run of his magazine, *Guideposts*, can be found at Marble Collegiate Church in New York City. Similarly, the Robert H. Schuller Televangelism Association, which produces Schuller's weekly *Hour of Power*, retains tapes of all broadcasts and regularly prints in pamphlet form Schuller's sermons. Free access is permitted at the association's offices on the campus of Garden Grove Community Church, Garden Grove, California.

The Billy Graham Center at Wheaton College in Wheaton, Illinois, houses the Center for the Study of American Evangelicals, which houses research collections of primary materials for the study of all phases of American Fundamentalism and Evangelicalism. Oral Roberts University in Tulsa, Oklahoma, holds a significant collection of Pentecostal material. The problems of research in the area are acute because revivalist traditions usually thrived on the spoken word, and evangelists often did not bother to retain notes or printed texts of their work. Often the best resources for information about revivalist events and traditions are participants or observers of the events and personalities.

NOTES

1. See, for example, Chidester; Spencer, "Overview of American Popular Music in a Theological Perspective," and *Blues and Evil*.
2. Charles Lippy, *Being Religious, American Style*, pp. 9–10.
3. Will Herberg noted a confluence of beliefs and values among Americans regardless

of religious tradition in *Protestant, Catholic, Jew*. Robert Bellah popularized the term "civil religion" in "Civil Religion in America." On the shared beliefs of Americans in the 1990s, see Bellah, "Is There a Common American Culture?"

4. Lippy, *Being Religious*, 10–11.

5. On Peale's role in the appropriation of Freudian theory into American religion and theology, see Stokes, Chapter 5. George presents an excellent critical account of Peale's life and thought in *God's Salesman*.

6. On Peale and capitalism, see Orwig, 131–149.

7. See Franz Hinkelammert, *The Ideological Weapons of Death* (Maryknoll, N.Y.: Orbis Books, 1986), 140–43; Wink, *The Powers That Be*.

8. Ostling, 11; Wuthnow, *After Heaven*, 30.

9. Dionne and J. DiIulio, 9.

10. Wuthnow, *After Heaven*.

11. Moore, "The Occult Connection?" 136.

12. Southard, 10.

13. Weintraub, 230.

14. Lippy, *Being Religious*, 26–27. Lippy borrows the term "double vision" from Stowell, 42.

15. Bernhard; Griswold.

16. Griswold; Weintraub; Jehlen; Fiering.

17. Oates, *Luck*, xii.

18. See McCandless; Morse.

19. See Ash.

20. Lippy, *Being Religious*, 80.

21. Oates, *Luck*, 28.

22. Oates, "The Cult of Reassurance," 335.

23. See Schneider.

24. The steps are quoted from *Alcoholics Anonymous*, 59.

25. See, for example, Miller; Alsdurf and Alsdurf.

26. For a theological analysis and critique of Peck's work, see Wink, "Walking M. Scott Peck's Less-Traveled Road"; a less sympathetic critique is in Kaminer, "Saving Therapy."

27. Peck, though, turned his attention to community building in his subsequent work.

28. Wuthnow, "How Small Groups Are Transforming Our Lives."

29. Stout, quoted in Moore, *Selling God*, 42; Lambert.

30. Moore, *Selling God*, 215.

31. For a brief, but thoughtful survey and analysis, see Leonard.

32. For a critique of New Age spirituality along these lines, see Zaleski.

33. Moore, *Selling God*, 275.

34. Fiswick, *Great Awakenings*, 217–19.

35. Moore, *Selling God*, 242.

36. See Raboteau.

37. Pinn, *Why Lord?*, 39.

38. See Thatcher.

39. See Ostling; Goff.

BIBLIOGRAPHY

Books and Articles

Ahlstrom, Sydney E. *A Religious History of the American People*. New Haven, Conn.: Yale University Press, 1972.

Albanese, Catherine. *Nature Religion in America: From the Algonkian Indians to the New Age*. Chicago: University of Chicago Press, 1990.

———. "Religion and Popular American Culture: An Introductory Essay." *Journal of the American Academy of Religion* 69 (1996), 733–42.

Alcoholics Anonymous: The Story of How Many Thousands of Men and Women Have Recovered from Alcoholism. 3rd ed. New York: Alcoholics Anonymous World Services, 1976.

Alsdurf, Jim, and Phyllis Alsdurf. "The Generic Disease." *Christianity Today* 32 (December 9, 1988), 30–38.

Arrington, Leonard J., and Davis Bitton. *The Mormon Experience: A History of the Latter-Day Saints*. Urbana: University of Illinois Press, 1992.

Ash, Scott. "The Shakers and the AMA: Two Models of Republican Textuality." *Paradigms: Theological Trends of the Future* 10 (1995), 1–5.

Balmer, Randall. *Mine Eyes Have Seen the Glory: A Journey into the Evangelical Subculture in America*. New York: Oxford University Press, 1989.

Barlow, Philip. *Mormons and the Bible: The Place of the Latter-Day Saints in American Religion*. New York: Oxford University Press, 1991.

Bellah, Robert N. "Civil Religion in America." *Daedalus* 96 (1967), 1–21.

———. "Is There a Common American Culture?" *Journal of the American Academy of Religion* 66 (1998), 613–25.

Bellah, Robert N., et al. *Habits of the Heart: Individualism and Commitment in American Life*. Berkeley: University of California Press, 1985.

Bercovitch, Sacvan. *The Puritan Origins of the American Self*. New Haven, Conn.: Yale University Press, 1975.

Bernhard, Virginia. "Cotton Mather and the Doing of Good: A Puritan Gospel of Wealth." *New England Quarterly* 49 (1976), 225–41.

Bevir, Mark. "The West Turns Eastward: Madame Blavatsky and the Transformation of the Occult Tradition." *Journal of the American Academy of Religion* 62 (1994), 747–67.

Blomberg, Craig L., and Stephen E. Robinson. *How Wide the Divide? A Mormon and Evangelical in Conversation*. Downers Grove, Ill.: InterVarsity Press, 1997.

Blumhofer, Edith. *Aimee Semple McPherson: Everybody's Sister*. Library of Religious Biography. Grand Rapids, Mich.: William B. Eerdmans, 1996.

Boyer, Paul S. "*In His Steps*: A Reappraisal." *American Quarterly* 23 (1971), 60–71.

Brown, Joseph Epes. *The Spiritual Legacy of the American Indian*. New York: Crossroad, 1982.

Brown, Michael. *The Channeling Zone: American Spirituality in an Anxious Age*. New York: Oxford University Press, 1997.

Bruce, Dickson D., Jr. *And They All Sang Hallelujah: Plain-Folk Camp-Meeting Religion, 1840–1845*. Knoxville: University of Tennessee Press, 1974.

Bull, Malcolm, ed. *Apocalypse Theory and the Ends of the World*. Cambridge, Mass.: Blackwell, 1995.

Bush, Trudy. "On the Tide of Angels." *Christian Century* 112 (March 1, 1995), 236–38.

Bushman, Claudia L., and Richard L. Bushman. "Latter-Day Saints: Home Can Be a Heaven on Earth." In *Faith Traditions and the Family*, ed. Phyllis D.

Airhart and Margaret Lamberts Bendroth. The Family, Religion, and Culture Series. Louisville: Westminster John Knox Press, 1996.

Butler, Jon. *Awash in a Sea of Faith: Christianizing the American People*. Cambridge: Harvard University Press, 1990.

Carter, Stephen. *The Culture of Disbelief: How American Law and Politics Trivialize Religious Devotion*. New York: Anchor Doubleday, 1993.

Chase, Elise. *Healing Faith: An Annotated Bibliography of Christian Self-Help Books*. Westport, Conn.: Greenwood, 1985.

Chidester, David. "The Church of Baseball, the Fetish of Coca-Cola, and the Potlatch of Rock 'n' Roll: Theoretical Models for the Study of Religion in American Popular Culture." *Journal of the American Academy of Religion* 69 (1996), 743–65.

Clegg, Claude Andrew. *An Original Man: The Life and Times of Elijah Muhammad*. New York: St. Martin's Press, 1997.

Cohen, Charles Lloyd. *God's Caress: The Psychology of Puritan Religious Experience*. New York: Oxford University Press, 1986.

Cone, James H. *Martin and Malcolm and America: A Dream or a Nightmare*. Maryknoll, N.Y.: Orbis, 1991.

———. *The Spirituals and the Blues*. Maryknoll, N.Y.: Orbis, 1991.

Davis, Cyprian. *The History of Black Catholics in the United States*. New York: Crossroad, 1990.

Deloria, Vine, Jr. *God Is Red: A Native View of Religion*. Golden, Colo.: Fulcrum, 1994.

———. *Red Earth: Native Americans and the Myth of Scientific Fact*. New York: Scribner, 1995.

Dionne, E.J., Jr. and John J. DiIulio Jr. "What's God Got to Do with the American Experiment?" *The Brookings Review* 17:2 (Spring 1999), 4–9.

Dorsett, Lyle W. *Billy Sunday and the Redemption of Urban America*. Library of Religious Biography. Grand Rapids, Mich.: William B. Eerdmans, 1991.

Eighmy, John Lee. *Churches in Cultural Captivity: A History of the Social Attitudes of Southern Baptists*. Knoxville: University of Tennessee Press, 1972.

Ellwood, Robert S. *Alternative Altars: Unconventional and Eastern Spirituality in America*. Chicago: University of Chicago Press, 1979.

———. *The Sixties Spiritual Awakening: American Religion Moving from Modern to Postmodern*. New Brunswick, N.J.: Rutgers University Press, 1994.

Fiering, Norman S. "Benjamin Franklin and the Way to Virtue." *American Quarterly* 30 (1978), 199–223.

Findlay, James F. *Dwight L. Moody: American Evangelist, 1837–1899*. Chicago: University of Chicago Press, 1969.

Finke, Roger, and Rodney Stark. *The Churching of America, 1776–1990: Winners and Losers in Our Religious Economy*. New Brunswick, N.J.: Rutgers University Press, 1992.

Fishman, Sylvia Barak. "American Jewry: Families of Tradition in American Culture." In *Faith Traditions and the Family*, ed. Phyllis D. Airhart and Margaret Lamberts Bendroth. The Family, Religion, and Culture Series. Louisville: Westminster John Knox Press, 1996.

Fishwick, Marshall W. *Great Awakenings: Popular Religion and Popular Culture*. New York: Haworth Press, 1995.

Gaustad, Edwin S. *Liberty of Conscience: Roger Williams in America*. Library of Religious Biography. Grand Rapids, Mich.: William B. Eerdmans, 1991.

———. *Sworn on the Altar of God: A Religious Biography of Thomas Jefferson*. Library of Religious Biography. Grand Rapids, Mich.: William B. Eerdmans, 1996.

George, Carol V. R. *God's Salesman: Norman Vincent Peale and the Power of Positive Thinking*. New York: Oxford University Press, 1993.

Glazier, Michael, and Thomas P. Shelley, eds. *The Encyclopedia of American Catholic History*. Collegeville, Minn.: Liturgical Press, 1997.

Goatley, David. *Were You There? Godforsakenness in Slave Religion*. Maryknoll, N.Y.: Orbis, 1996.

Goff, Philip K. "Spiritual Enrichment and the Bull Market: Balancing the Books of American Religious History." *Religious Studies Review* 22 (1996), 106–12.

Gomes, Michael. *Theosophy in the Nineteenth Century: An Annotated Bibliography*. New York: Garland, 1994.

Gottschalk, Steven. *The Emergence of Christian Science in American Religious Life*. Berkeley: University of California Press, 1973.

Griswold, A. Whitney. "Three Puritans on Prosperity." *New England Quarterly* 7 (1934), 475–93.

Hall, David D. *Worlds of Wonder, Days of Judgment: Popular Religious Belief in Early New England*. New York: Knopf, 1989.

———, ed. *Lived Religion in America: Toward a History of Practice*. Princeton, N.J.: Princeton University Press, 1997.

Hambrick-Stowe, Charles E. *Charles G. Finney and the Spirit of American Evangelicalism*. Library of Religious Biography. Grand Rapids, Mich.: William B. Eerdmans, 1996.

Harrell, David Edwin, Jr. *Oral Roberts: An American Life*. Bloomington: Indiana University Press, 1985.

Hatch, Nathan O. *The Democratization of American Christianity*. New Haven: Yale University Press, 1989.

Herberg, Will. *Protestant, Catholic, Jew: An Essay in American Religious Sociology*. Garden City, N.Y.: Doubleday, 1950.

Hunter, James Davidson. *Culture Wars: The Struggle to Define America*. New York: HarperCollins, 1990.

Jehlen, Myra. " 'Imitate Jesus and Socrates': The Making of a Good American." *South Atlantic Quarterly* 89 (1990), 501–24.

Jorstad, Erling. *Holding Fast/Pressing On: Religion in America in the 1980s*. Westport, Conn.: Greenwood Press, 1990.

Kaminer, Wendy. *I'm Dysfunctional, You're Dysfunctional: The Recovery Movement and Other Self-Help Fashions*. Reading, Mass.: Addison-Wesley, 1992.

———. "Saving Therapy: Exploring the Religious Self-Help Literature." *Theology Today* 48 (1991), 301–25.

Kerr, Howard, and Charles L. Crow, eds. *The Occult in America: New Historical Perspectives*. Urbana: University of Illinois Press, 1983.

Kirk-Duggan, Cheryl. *Exorcizing Evil: A Womanist Perspective on the Spirituals*. Maryknoll, N.Y.: Orbis, 1997.

Knoll, Mark A. *A History of Christianity in the United States and Canada*. Grand Rapids, Mich.: W. B. Eerdmans, 1992.

Kyle, Richard. *The Religious Fringe: A History of Alternative Religions in America.* Downers Grove, Ill.: InterVarsity Press, 1993.

Lambert, Frank. *Peddlar in Divinity: George Whitefield and the Transatlantic Revivals, 1737–1770.* Princeton, N.J.: Princeton University Press, 1994.

Larson, Edward J. *Summer for the Gods : The Scopes Trial and America's Continuing Debate over Science and Religion.* New York: Basic Books, 1997.

Leonard, Bill. "The Electric Church: An Interpretive Essay." *Review and Expositor* 81 (1984), 43–57.

Lewis, James R., ed. *The Encyclopedia of Cults, Sects, and New Religions.* Amherst, N.Y.: Prometheus, 1998.

Lewis, James R., and J. Gordon Melton, eds. *Perspectives on the New Age.* Albany: State University of New York Press, 1992.

Lincoln, C. Eric. *The Black Muslims in America.* Boston: Beacon Press, 1961.

Lincoln, C. Eric, and Lawrence H. Mamiya. *The Black Church in the African American Experience.* Durham, N.C.: Duke University Press, 1990.

Lindley, Susan Hill. *"You Have Stept Out of Your Place": A History of Women and Religion in America.* Louisville: Westminster John Knox Press, 1996.

Lippy, Charles H. *Being Religious, American Style: A History of Popular Religiosity in the United States.* Westport, Conn.: Praeger, 1994.

———. "Waiting for the End: The Social Context of American Apocalyptic Religion." In *The Apocalyptic Vision in America: Interdisciplinary Essays on Myth and Culture,* ed. Lois Parkinson Zamora. Bowling Green, Ohio: Bowling Green State University Popular Press, 1982.

Lippy, Charles H., ed. *Twentieth-Century Shapers of American Popular Religion.* Westport, Conn.: Greenwood, 1989.

Lippy, Charles H., and Peter Williams, eds. *Encyclopedia of the American Religious Experience.* New York: Charles Scribner's Sons, 1988.

Lundin, Roger. *Emily Dickinson: The Fate of Theology in American Culture.* Library of Religious Biography. Grand Rapids, Mich.: William B. Eerdmans, 1996.

Marsden, George M. *Fundamentalism and American Culture: The Shaping of Twentieth Century Evangelicalism, 1870–1925.* New York: Oxford University Press, 1980.

Martin, William. *A Prophet with Honor: The Billy Graham Story.* New York: Morrow, 1991.

———. *With God on Our Side: The Rise of the Religious Right in America.* New York: Broadway Books, 1996.

Marty, Martin. *The Irony of It All, 1893–1919.* Vol. 1 of *Modern American Religion.* Chicago: University of Chicago Press, 1986.

———. *The Noise of Conflict, 1919–1941.* Vol. 2 of *Modern American Religion.* Chicago: University of Chicago Press, 1991.

———. *A Short History of American Catholicism.* Allen, Tex.: Thomas More, 1995.

———. *Under God Indivisible, 1941–1960.* Vol. 3 of *Modern American Religion.* Chicago: University of Chicago Press, 1996.

Marty, Martin, and R. Scott Appleby, eds. *Fundamentalisms Observed.* Vol. 1 of the Fundamentalism Project. Chicago: University of Chicago Press, 1991.

———. *Fundamentalisms and Society: Reclaiming the Sciences, the Family, and Education.* Vol. 2 of the Fundamentalism Project. Chicago: University of Chicago Press, 1993.

————. *Fundamentalisms and the State: Remaking Polities, Economies, and Militance.* Vol. 3 of the Fundamentalism Project. Chicago: University of Chicago Press, 1993.

————. *Accounting for Fundamentalisms: The Dynamic Character of Movements.* Vol. 4 of the Fundamentalism Project. Chicago: University of Chicago Press, 1993.

————. *Fundamentalisms Comprehended.* Vol. 5 of the Fundamentalism Project. Chicago: University of Chicago Press, 1995.

Massa, Mark. *Catholics and American Culture: Fulton Sheen, Dorothy Day, and the Notre Dame Football Team.* New York: Crossroad, 1999.

Mauss, Armand L. *The Angel and the Beehive: The Mormon Struggle with Assimilation.* Urbana: University of Illinois Press, 1992.

McCandless, Peter. "Mesmerism and Phrenology in Antebellum Charleston: 'Enough of the Marvellous.'" *Journal of Southern History,* 58 (1992), 199–230.

McGloughlin, William G. *Revivals, Awakenings, and Reform: An Essay on Religion and Social Change in America, 1607–1977.* Chicago: University of Chicago Press, 1978.

Mead, Frank Spencer. *Handbook of Denominations in the United States.* New York: Abingdon Press, 1961–1980. Revised by Samuel S. Hill, 1985– .

Melton, J. Gordon, ed. *Encyclopedia of American Religions.* 6th ed. Farmington Hills, Mich.: Gale Research, 1999.

Melton, J. Gordon, and Gary Ward, eds. *Prime Time Religion: An Encyclopedia of Religious Broadcasting.* Phoenix: Oryx Press, 1997.

Mercandite, Linda A. *Victims and Sinners: Spiritual Roots of Addiction and Recovery.* Louisville: Westminster John Knox Press, 1996.

Meyer, Donald B. *The Positive Thinkers: A Study of the American Quest for Health, Wealth, and Personal Power from Mary Baker Eddy to Norman Vincent Peale.* Garden City, N.Y.: Doubleday, 1965.

————. *The Positive Thinkers: A Study of the American Quest for Health, Wealth, and Personal Power from Mary Baker Eddy to Norman Vincent Peale and Ronald Reagan.* Middletown, Conn.: Wesleyan University Press, 1988.

Miles, Margaret. *Seeing and Believing: Religion and Values in the Movies.* Boston: Beacon Press, 1998.

Miller, Keith. *A Hunger for Healing: The Twelve Steps as a Classic Model for Christian Spiritual Growth.* San Francisco: Harper, 1991.

Moore, R. Lawrence. *In Search of White Crows: Spiritualism, Parapsychology, and American Culture.* New York: Oxford University Press, 1977.

————. "The Occult Connection? Mormonism, Christian Science, and Spiritualism." In *The Occult in America,* ed. Howard Kerr and Charles L. Crow. Urbana: University of Illinois Press, 1983.

————. *Religious Outsiders and the Making of Americans.* New York: Oxford University Press, 1986.

————. *Selling God: American Religion in the Marketplace of Culture.* New York: Oxford University Press, 1994.

Morse, Minna. "Facing a Bumpy History: The Much Maligned Theory of Phrenology Gets a Tip of the Hat from Modern Neuroscience." *Smithsonian,* 28:7 (October 1997), 24–29.

Murphy, Larry G., J. Gordon Melton, and Gary L. Ward, eds. *Encyclopedia of African-American Religions*. New York: Garland, 1993.

Needleman, Jacob. *The New Religions*. New York: E. P. Dutton, 1970.

Oates, Wayne E. "The Cult of Reassurance." *Review and Expositor* 51 (1954), 335–47.

———. *Luck: A Secular Faith*. Louisville: Westminster John Knox Press, 1995.

Orwig, Sarah Forbes. "Paradigm for Religion in Business: The Ministry of Norman Vincent Peale." *Book of Proceedings*, Fifth Annual Conference Promoting Business Ethics. Chicago: Vincentian Universities in the United States, 1998.

Ostling, Richard N. "America's Ever-Changing Religious Landscape." *Brookings Review* 17:2 (Spring 1999), 10–13.

Ouellette, Richard. "Mormon Studies." *Religious Studies Review* 25 (1999), 161–169.

Ownby, Ted. *Subduing Satan: Religion, Recreation, and Manhood in the Rural South, 1865–1920*. Chapel Hill: University of North Carolina Press, 1990.

Peck, M. Scott. *The Road Less Traveled*. New York: Simon and Schuster, 1978.

Pinn, Anthony B. *Varieties of African American Religious Experience*. Minneapolis: Fortress Press, 1998.

———. *Why Lord? Suffering and Evil in Black Theology*. New York: Continuum, 1995.

Powell, Milton B., ed. *The Voluntary Church: American Religious Life, 1740–1860, Seen through the Eyes of European Visitors*. New York: Macmillan, 1967.

Prothero, Stephen. "Theosophy's Sinner/Saint: Recent Books on Madame Blavatsky." *Religious Studies Review* 23 (1997), 257–62.

Rabinowitz, Richard. *The Spiritual Self in Everyday Life: The Transformations of Personal Religious Experience in Nineteenth Century New England*. Boston: Northeastern University Press, 1989.

Raboteau, Albert J. *Slave Religion: The Invisible Institution in the Antebellum South*. New York: Oxford University Press, 1978.

Rand, Erica. *Barbie's Queer Accessories*. Durham, N.C.: Duke University Press, 1995.

Rieff, Philip. *The Triumph of the Therapeutic*. New York: Harper and Row, 1968.

Riss, Richard M. *A Survey of 20th-Century Revival Movements in North America*. Peabody, Mass.: Hendrickson, 1988.

Robbins, Thomas, and Susan J. Palmer, eds. *Millennium, Messiahs, and Mayhem: Contemporary Apocalyptic Movements*. New York: Routledge, 1997.

Robinson, Douglas. *American Apocalypses: The Image of the End of the World in American Literature*. Baltimore: Johns Hopkins University Press, 1985.

Sachar, Howard. *A History of the Jews in America*. New York: Knopf, 1993.

Sample, Tex. *U.S. Lifestyles and Mainline Churches*. Louisville, Ky.: Westminster John Knox Press, 1990.

Schneider, A. Gregory. "In Search of the Evangelical Self: History, Psychology, and Religious Subcultures in America." *Religious Studies Review*, 23 (1997), 135–40.

Sizer, Sandra. *Gospel Hymns and Saving Religion: The Rhetoric of Nineteenth Century Revivalism*. Philadelphia: Temple University Press, 1978.

Southard, Samuel. *Religious Inquiry: An Introduction to the Why and How*. Nashville: Abingdon Press, 1976.

Spencer, John Michael. *Blues and Evil*. Knoxville: University of Tennessee Press, 1993.

———. "Overview of American Popular Music in a Theological Perspective." *Black Sacred Music* 8 (Spring 1994), 205–17.

———. *Re-Searching Black Music*. Knoxville: University of Tennessee Press, 1994.

Stein, Stephen J., ed. *Apocalypticism in the Modern Period and the Contemporary Age*. Volume 3 of *Encyclopedia of Apocalypticism*. New York: Continuum, 1999.

Stokes, Allison. *Ministry after Freud*. Cleveland: Pilgrim Press, 1985.

Stout, Harry S. *The Divine Dramatist: George Whitefield and the Rise of Modern Evangelicalism*. Library of Religious Biography. Grand Rapids, Mich.: William B. Eerdmans, 1991.

Stout, Harry S., and D. G. Hart, eds. *New Directions in American Religious History*. New York: Oxford University Press, 1997.

Stowell, Marion. *Early America Almanacs: The Colonial Weekday Bible*. New York: Burt Franklin, 1977.

Swatos, William, ed. *Encyclopedia of Religion & Society*. Walnut Creek, Calif.: Alta Mira Press, 1998.

Swift, Donald C. *Religion and the American Experience: A Social and Cultural History, 1765–1997*. Armonk, N.Y.: M. E. Sharpe, 1998.

Thatcher, Tom. "Empty Metaphors and Apocalyptic Rhetoric." *Journal of the American Academy of Religion*, 66 (1998), 549–570.

Tocqueville, Alexis de. *Democracy in America*. Trans. George Lawrence. Ed. J. P. Mayer and Max Lerner. New York: Doubleday, 1969.

Toolan, David. *Facing West from California's Shores: A Jesuit Journey into New Age Consciousness*. New York: Crossroad, 1987.

Treat, James, ed. *Native and Christian: Indigenous Voices on Religious Identity in the United States and Canada*. New York: Routledge, 1996.

Turner, Richard Brent. *Islam in the African American Experience*. Bloomington: Indiana University Press, 1997.

Walch, Timothy. *Parish School: A History of American Catholic Parochial Education from Colonial Times to the Present*. New York: Crossroad, 1996.

Walzer, Michael. *Spheres of Justice*. New York: Basic Books, 1983.

Weintraub, Karl J. "The Puritan Ethic and Benjamin Franklin." *Journal of Religion* 56 (1976), 223–37.

Weiss, Richard. *The American Myth of Success: From Horatio Alger to Norman Vincent Peale*. New York: Basic Books, 1969.

Wigger, John H. *Taking Heaven by Storm: Methodism and the Rise of Popular Christianity in America*, Urbana: University of Illinois Press, 1998.

Williams, Peter. *Popular Religion in America: Symbolic Change and the Modernization Process in Historical Perspective*. Englewood Cliffs, N.J.: Prentice-Hall, 1980.

Wills, Gary. *Under God: Religion and American Politics*. New York: Simon and Schuster, 1990.

Wink, Walter. *The Powers That Be: Theology for a New Millennium*. New York: Doubleday, 1998.

———. "Walking M. Scott Peck's Less-Traveled Road." *Theology Today* 48 (1991), 279–89.

Wuthnow, Robert. *After Heaven: Spirituality in America since the 1950s*. Berkeley: University of California Press, 1998.

———. "How Small Groups Are Transforming Our Lives." *Christianity Today*, 38 (February 7, 1994), 20–24.

———. *Poor Richard's Principle: Restoring the American Dream by Recovering the Moral Dimension of Work, Business, and Money*. Princeton, N.J.: Princeton University Press, 1996.

———. *Sharing the Journey: Small Groups and America's New Quest for Community*. New York: Free Press, 1994.

———. *The Struggle for America's Soul: Evangelicals, Liberals, and Secularism*. Grand Rapids, Mich.: William B. Eerdmans, 1989.

Zaleski, Philip. "No Easy Answers." *Parabola* 13 (Fall 1988), 84–91.

Zamora, Lois Parkinson, ed. *The Apocalyptic Vision in America: Interdisciplinary Essays on Myth and Culture*. Bowling Green, Ohio: Bowling Green State University Popular Press, 1982.

Periodicals

America. New York, 1917– .

American Quarterly. Baltimore, 1948– .

Christian Century. Chicago, 1901– .

Christianity Today. Stream, Ill., 1956– .

Church History. Wallingford, Pa., 1931– .

Commentary. New York, 1945– .

Commonweal. New York, 1924– .

First Things. New York, 1990– .

Guideposts. New York, 1945– .

The Other Side. Philadelphia, 1965– .

Religious Studies Review. Macon, Ga., 1974– .

Sojourners. Washington, D.C., 1971– .

Tikkun Magazine. San Francisco, 1986– .

The Witness. Boston, 1908– .

SPORTS

Robert J. Higgs and Ralph Lamar
Turner

What is sport? The truth is that no one knows, and the challenge to define it, or at least to describe its characteristics, has engaged the attention of some of the best scholars of our time, always with beneficial results but never with answers that satisfy completely. Johan Huizinga in *Homo Ludens*, a sine qua non on sport, says, "In our heart of hearts we know that none of our pronouncements is absolutely conclusive" (212). Like Tennyson's flower in the crannied wall, we know that sport is, but we do know with certainty what it is. Nevertheless, we are compelled to seek understanding of anything that so engages the interest of humankind as sport or play. In fact, play has become so important that it can no longer be left exclusively to the players. The influence of games on societies, from the bloody Roman spectacles to the staged demonstrations of the modern Olympiad and the Super Bowl, is simply staggering. Sport, as one observer has claimed, is the new opiate of the masses, as it has probably always been, though never so freely administered as in the modern world.

A distinction must be made between sport, play, and game. Play conjures up an image of childlike abandon, an expression of the sublime detached from encumbering rules and standards of conduct, without preconceived ideas of form or function. Play, for a brief expanse of time, the period of its engagement, seemingly reunites us with the divine in ourselves, unfettering our earthly bonds, our cares and woes, made manifest by the reality of life. During the moment of play, children—and even adults when they allow themselves to truly participate—enter into another world, a world of bliss interrupted only by time. According to Hugo Rahner, earthly play and dance can provide glimpses of heavenly joy yet even in their purest form remain distinct from worship and meditation, which require focus of the spirit as well as abandonment of worldly concerns.

" 'Sport,' 'athletics,' 'games,' and 'play,' " says Paul Weiss, "have in common the idea of being cut off from the workaday world" (134). Here he is in agreement with Huizinga, as he is with Roger Caillois, who claims that play is free, separate, uncertain, unproductive, and governed by both rules and make-believe (9–10). "Sport," as Weiss reminds us, "means to disport . . . that is, to divert and amuse." Hence, sport is that aspect of culture by which people divert themselves from labor as opposed to work. This important distinction is well made by Hannah Arendt in *The Human Condition* in her discussion of the difference between *animal laborans*, laboring animal, and *homo faber*, man the maker or artist, which is succinctly implied in the phrase "the work of our hands and the labor of our body" (85). The "game" lies somewhere between play and sport. It is play with the constraints of sport, that is, a ruled endeavor where structure has been placed upon it for the sake of conformity with preconceived ideas of form and function. Today, however, it is essential to realize, in professional sports especially, that the athlete is quite often player, laborer, and artist, one who laboriously sculpts a life of meaning out of his or her physical nature. Though lines between different activities frequently become blurred, we consider sports as "unnecessary" action in the sense that they are not *required* for survival as are forms of labor such as farming. We also regard sports as activities that require expenditures of substantial amounts of physical energy, more than that needed to play a game of bridge or checkers, which are also forms of play and diversions from labor. "Sports" are generally synonymous with athletics, while "sport" refers to broader pursuits such as fishing and hunting.

HISTORICAL OUTLINE

"What is play? What is serious?" Huizinga asks. The Puritans would have had less difficulty in answering these questions than we would today. For them, any effort not devoted to the good of the colony was to be eschewed, and games did not seem to lend themselves to the general welfare. In 1621 Governor William Bradford rebuked the young men whom he found "in ye streete at play, openly; some pitching ye barr and some at stooleball, and such like sports." There should not be, in the governor's view, any "gameing or revelling in ye streets," nor if we are to judge from the incident of the Maypole of Merry Mount, any reveling in the country either.

Though there is a debate as to the degree of hostility that the Puritans held toward games, it seems safe to say that they were not exactly sports fans.[1] In 1647, for instance, a court order was issued against shuffleboard in Massachusetts Bay, and in 1650 the same injunction was extended against "bowling or any other play or games in or about houses of common entertainment."[2] In 1693 in eastern Connecticut a man "was fined twelve shillings and sentenced to six hours in the stocks for playing ball on the Sabbath. . . . Apparently, either he was playing alone or his teammates were let go with a warning, since he was the only man convicted."[3] The Puritan attitude toward fun and games in the view of many is perhaps best illustrated in Macaulay's remark that bear-baiting was stopped not because it gave pain to the bear but because it provided pleasure to the spectators.

The "Detestation of Idleness" was not confined to New England. In Virginia in 1619 "the assembly decreed that any person found idle should be bound over to compulsory work; it prohibited gaming at dice or cards, strictly regulated drinking, provided penalties for excess in apparel and rigidly enforced Sabbath observance."[4] Interdictions against racing within the city limits of New Amsterdam were

Native Americans playing stickball in Colorado, ca. 1910. © Smithsonian Institution

issued in 1657, and two years later Governor Peter Stuyvesant proclaimed a day of fast on which would be forbidden "all exercise and games of tennis, ball-playing, hunting, fishing, plowing, and sewing, and moreover all unlawful practices such as dice and drunkenness."[5] Restrictions of activities in some form on Sunday could be found wherever the new American civilization was extended on the frontier.

As John A. Krout, Foster Rhea Dulles, and others have pointed out, the theocracy did not represent all of New England, and the narrow sanctions of the ruling class had in the long run little chance of being obeyed. The human propensity to play could not be stilled. Sport grew not only in New England but all along the frontier. Hunting and fishing flourished, frequently as a means for gaining food but also as a form of diversion. Forests and rivers seemed to contain an endless supply of game and fish, and many availed themselves of the abundance: "Even Cotton Mather fished. Samuel Sewall tells of the time when the stern old Puritan went out with line and tackle and fell into the water at Spy Pond, 'the boat being ticklish.' "[6] For those who have read Mather's prose, this is a pleasing image indeed.

The growth of recreation, even during the latter part of the seventeenth century, can be inferred from the journal of Sarah Kembell Knight, who wrote of her travels through Connecticut in 1704:

Their diversions in this part of the country are on lecture days and training days mostly: on the former there is riding from town to town . . . and on training days the youth divert themselves by shooting at the targets, as they call it (but it very much resembles a pillory). When he that hits nearest the white has some yards of red ribbon presented to him, which being tied to his hattband, he is led away in triumph, with great applause, as the winners of the Olympiak Games.[7]

At the beginning of the nineteenth century there was a wide diversity of amusements in the North, as reported by President Timothy Dwight of Yale:

The principal amusements of the inhabitants are visiting, dancing, music, conversation, walking, riding, sailing, shooting at a mark, draughts, chess, and unhappily, in some of the larger towns, cards and dramatic exhibitions. . . . Our countrymen also fish and hunt. Journeys taken for pleasure are very numerous, and are a very favorite object. Boys and young men play at football, cricket, quoits, and at many other sports of an athletic cast, and in the winter are peculiarly fond of skating. Riding in a sleigh, or sledge, is also a favorite diversion in New England.[8]

Ninepins, skittles, and bowls were common at inns in the North for the convenience of the guests,[9] while in the South shooting matches were preferred, with "beef shooting" being one of the favorite forms.[10] The sports that seemed to attract the most attention in the South, however, were cockfighting and horse racing. According to Hugh Jones in 1724, "The common planters don't much admire labour or any other manly exercise except Horse racing, nor diversion, except Cock-Fighting, in which some greatly delight." In tones suggestive of William Byrd, he adds, "This Way of Living and the Heat of the Summer make some very lazy, who are then said to be Climate-struck."[11]

While the foreign traveler, especially the English, as Henry Adams notes,

charged the Virginians with fondness for horse-racing and cockfighting, betting and drinking, . . . the popular habit which most shocked them, and with which books of travel filled pages of description was the so-called rough and tumble fight. The practice was not one on which authors seemed likely to dwell; yet foreigners like Weld, and Americans like Judge Longstreet in "Georgia Scenes" united to give it a sort of grotesque dignity like that of the bull-fight, and under their treatment it became interesting as a popular habit.[12]

The rough-and-tumble, Adams argues, did not originate in Virginia but came to America from England, as did, according to Jennie Holliman, most American sports, excepting those practices learned from the Indians, such as methods of hunting and trapping deer and bear, the use of bows and arrows, fishing at night with lights on canoes, lacrosse, and even rolling the hoop. Still, the predominant influence was from abroad. The gun itself is a good example. "Up to 1830," says Holliman, "a few fine guns had been made in America, but they did not sell to an advantage simply because they were not imported." The same was true for fishing equipment, twine, tackles, hooks, flies, and rods, which came from Holland as well as England. Sleighs also came from Holland, while bridles, harnesses, and saddles came from England (6–7).

The history of horse racing has, to a large extent, been the history of selective breeding, of which Diomed and Messenger provide excellent examples. Diomed was brought to Virginia in 1789 and came to be held in such esteem that his death in 1808 caused almost as much mourning as that for Washington in 1799.[13] Messenger, bred by the earl of Grosvenor on his Yorkshire farm, was brought to America a few years after the Revolution by Thomas Berger of Pennsylvania. Prized as a stud, Messenger was the sire of a long line of racing immortals, including American Eclipse, who defeated Sir Henry of Virginia at the Union course on Long Island in 1823, the first intersectional race that illustrated once and for all the popular appeal of the sport. Another offspring of Messenger was Hambletonian, the horse that turned harness racing into a national mania: "In the 1850s, the nation worshipped Hambletonian. It bought commemorative plates on which his likeness was inscribed. Children talked about him as if he were human."[14] Spurred on by the creation of jockey clubs, the establishment of racecourses, and the support of the aristocracy, horse racing became America's first organized sport and has remained unquestionably one of its most popular.

The wide interest in the turf helped to bring about the rise of sporting literature in the three decades before the Civil War. The first sporting magazine in America was the *American Turf Register*, published in Baltimore in 1829 by John Stuart Skinner. Ten years later Skinner sold the *Register* to William Trotter Porter, who had already begun his own weekly sporting publication called *Spirit of the Times*, one of the most famous of all American publications and a reservoir of the history of American popular culture from 1831 to 1861. Prominent among contributors to this magazine were Thomas B. Thorpe, who inaugurated the "Big Bear school of humor," and the Englishman Henry William Herbert, who wrote under the pen name "Frank Forester" and who introduced "something of the English point of view of sport for sport's sake."[15]

Baseball, like horse racing, has its roots in the nineteenth century and, also like horse racing, owes more perhaps to the English than we are inclined to admit. The myth that Abner Doubleday invented baseball is totally without foundation. According to Wells Twombly, "The rules of baseball attributed to Doubleday in 1839 were identical to those in a rule book for the English game of rounders published in London in 1827" (43). In America rounders became known as "town ball" and was played at Harvard as early as 1829. In *The Book of Sport* (1827) Robert Carver related that many Britons, like the Americans, were calling the game by a new name, "base ball," and that it was "becoming a distinct threat to cricket."[16] Both the game and the new name caught on quickly in America, and by the 1850s the *Spirit of the Times* was calling it "The National Game."[17] By the 1880s daily attendance at the games was some 60,000. It had become "far and away the leading spectator sport."[18]

As Foster Rhea Dulles has observed, the role of colleges in the rise of sports in the decades after the Civil War was not one of leadership. The only sport that undergraduates developed was football, and again the English influence is incontrovertible. Basketball, in fact, is the only popular American ball game whose origins are not English, being invented by James A. Naismith in Springfield, Massachusetts, in 1891. American football evolved from soccer, to rugby, to "American" rugby, and finally to the game we know today. While the basic forms derived from England, the Americans had long demonstrated a fondness for games of mayhem. Harvard, for example, "had a festival in the early 1800s which qualified vaguely as football. It was called Bloody Monday, but the upperclassmen mostly kicked the freshman and only occasionally the ball."[19] Though it was essentially soccer instead of rugby, what is called the first intercollegiate football game took place in 1869 between Princeton and Rutgers at New Brunswick. Rutgers won, no thanks to the player who, becoming confused and endearing himself to all future generations, kicked the ball through the opposing Princeton's goal. The first contest was played before a small crowd, but approximately twenty years later Princeton played Yale before a crowd of almost 40,000.[20] Thus, long before the turn of the century football was well established as a mass spectator sport.

The one overriding fact concerning sport in America is its phenomenal growth. From William Bradford's injunction against games on Christmas Day in 1621 to Super Sunday of any year there has been a complete reversal of attitudes. We have gone from Sabbath bans to Super Sunday. Why did such changes occur? No one seems to be able to offer any conclusive answers except the human love of sport and the need for heroes. One thing is undeniable, however, and that is the argument that the widespread growth of sport was brought about in part by the revolution in technology in the decades after the Civil War. Says John R. Betts, "Antebellum sport had capitalized on the development of the steamboat, the railroad, the telegraph, and the penny press, and in succeeding decades the role of technology in the rise of sport proved even more significant" (69).

Of major importance in the promotion of sports has been the press, a major product of technology. Following the lead of the *Spirit of the Times*, new periodicals drawing attention to sport began to appear after the war. Among these were *Baseball Magazine*, *Golfer's Magazine*, *Yachting*, and the *Saturday Evening Post*. Newspapers from coast to coast began to devote more and more space to sports, until finally they had a section of their own. According to Betts, "Frank Luther Mott designated the years 1892–1914 as a period in newspaper history when sporting news underwent remarkable development, being segregated on special pages, with special makeup pictures, and news writing style" (68). Books, too, continued to arouse interest, especially among the younger generation. Among the many writers bringing dreams of fair play and heroism to millions of American youth were Gilbert Patten (Burt L. Standish), Henry Barbour, Zane Grey, and Edward Stratemeyer (237). Perhaps the champion producer of all in this group of juvenile writers was Gilbert Patten, who wrote a Frank Merriwell story once a week for nearly twenty years and had only one nervous breakdown. Estimates of the sales of Merriwell novels run as high as 500 million copies.[21]

The press helped bring together heroes and hero worshipers, but other developments also played crucial roles in the expansion of sports. It would be difficult, for example, to overestimate the importance of the railroad and the telegraph in the spread of games. Because of the growing rail network, the Cincinnati Red Stockings could travel from Maine to California, and John L. Sullivan could go on a grand tour of athletic clubs, opera houses, and theaters. Revolution in mass transit meant mass audiences, and for those who could not come to the games, the telegraph provided instant news of results. The Atlantic cable, electrification, radio, and television all influenced sport in profound ways that are still only vaguely understood. Because of technology the city of New Orleans could build in 1974 a bronze-topped stadium with a gigantic screen for instant replays at a total cost of over $285 million. Such technomarvels were only the beginning of a

Charles Atlas. Courtesy of the Library of Congress

new age of sports wherein sports became indistinguishable in many respects from business and entertainment.

REFERENCE WORKS

A basic reference work that librarians will find indispensable and researchers in sport very helpful is *Biography Index*, a multivolume, cumulative index of biographical material in books and magazines dating from 1946 to the present. In the area of sport almost 100 categories and associated fields are listed, and further distinction is made between adult and juvenile items. Literally hundreds and perhaps thousands of biographies and autobiographies have been written on American sports figures. Most of the autobiographies are coauthored and seem to follow the same general pattern, describing the hero's or heroine's childhood, early promises and disappointments, and the subsequent rise to fame and success. Joseph Campbell's theory of the monomyth is no doubt confirmed in every account. For facts and bibliographic information on players, managers, officials, coaches, and even executives and administrators, the source to consult is *Biographical Dictionary of American Sports*, with Supplements, edited by David L. Porter, with separate volumes on football, baseball, indoor sports, outdoor sports, and "Sports Talk." Also edited by Porter is *African-American Sports Greats* with entries on such notables as Jesse Owens, Satchel Paige, Jackie Joyner-Kersee, Michael Jordan, and others.

The need for basic information in any research is unending, and in sport the best source is Frank G. Menke's The *Encyclopedia of Sport*, which contains listings of records in both amateur and professional sports as well as attendance figures, all-American teams, money won on horse and dog racing, and other data. *Webster's Sports Dictionary* is well designed to serve another recurring need, that for a quick explanation of the many terms that saturate the world of sports. Other helpful features of the dictionary are diagrams of courts and fields (with measurements) and action illustrations, as well as referee signals and methods of keeping score. *The Oxford Companion to World Sport and Games*, edited by John Arlott, also contains such information in even more detail. For books and articles on the issues of sports, see *Sports: A Reference Guide* by Robert J. Higgs. In the new millennium researchers may avail themselves of a host of research tools via the Internet, aided by increasingly sophisticated search engines, as for example, at Yahoo! (http://www.Yahoo.com), Google (http://www.google.com), LookSmart (http://www.looksmart.com), and the like.

The booming popularity of sport and the quiet dedication of librarians, scholars, and sports enthusiasts have led to a number of fine collections of sporting materials in libraries in various parts of the country. One of the most comprehensive is that of the Citizens Savings Athletic Foundation in Los Angeles. The foundation maintains both a sports museum, which contains perhaps the most complete collection in the world of Olympic Games awards and memorabilia, and a sports library, which is especially strong on Olympic Games publications. It has a large number of sports films, available on a loan basis, and thousands of sports photographs, files of sports magazines, and souvenir programs dating back many years. The foundation has also instituted Halls of Fame, excepting baseball, in various sports. The sites of these institutions, many of which house libraries as well as museums, can be obtained by writing the foundation.

One of the most extensive collections on sporting materials of all kinds is in the Applied Life Studies Library at the University of Illinois at Champaign-Urbana. The library's card catalog of approximately 120,000 entries covers fields in sports medicine, recreation materials, theories of play, health and safety, and dance, to mention only a few. The Chicago Historical Society has a general collection of about 2,000 volumes concerned primarily with team sports in the areas of biography, history, and statistics. For additional information on the collection, see Appendix 2 in *Sports: A Reference Guide* by Robert Higgs.

HISTORY AND CRITICISM

A study of the history of sports tells us what role sports have actually played in our lives; a study of the issues reveals what roles sports should play. Among these many issues are the questions of emphasis, mind–body relationship, professionalism and amateurism, religion, racism, women in sports, language, drugs, and aggression. Before the interested scholar begins study in these or other aspects of sports, however, he or she needs some knowledge of what has already occurred on the American sporting scene, and the few books already referred to are indispensable in this regard.

The basic book to start with is John A. Krout's *Annals of American Sport*, the first full-length study of the subject. The influence of Krout is acknowledged in one way or another by the authors of other important histories, including Jennie Holliman in *American Sports (1785–1835)*, Foster Rhea Dulles in *America Learns to Play*, and John R. Betts in his invaluable *America's Sporting Heritage, 1850–1950*. Betts' book grew out of his 1951 dissertation at Columbia University and is without question the most comprehensive work ever done in the history of American sport. It is a mine of information, and the extensive references are probably the most exhaustive ever published on the popular aspects of sport. An excellent bibliography of sources through the 1850s is Robert W. Henderson's *Early American Sport*, and a good general bibliography can be found in the appendix to Robert Boyle's *Sport: Mirror of American Life*.

Another section of Boyle's book worthy of notice is the chapter on Frank Merriwell entitled "The Unreal Ideal." Merriwell's influence as a hero has been pervasive, and another, more detailed look at this phenomenon can be found in Gilbert Patten's *Frank Merriwell's "Father": An Autobiography*. Another work that sheds a great deal of light on juvenile sports literature is Robert Cantwell's article on Ralph Henry Barbour and William Heyliger, called "A Sneering Laugh with the Bases Loaded," in *Sports Illustrated*. One oversight in almost all bibliographies is the omission of certain sections in Henry Adams' *History of the United States during the Jefferson and Madison Administrations*, especially Chapters 1–6. Not only does Adams offer humorous and penetrating insights of his own, but he summarizes effectively the opinions of a number of foreign travelers commenting upon American culture.

Whether or not sports can build character is debatable, but there is no debating the emerging alliance between sports and religion. In *Sociology of Sport* Harry Edwards has pointed out numerous parallels between sports and religion, and some, such as Charles Prebish, in *Religion and Sport*, have gone as far as to see a "complete identity" between the two. Prebish argues that sports constitute a new American religion, a perspective debated by other contributors in his work. A somewhat broader collection on the same theme is *Sport and Religion*, edited by Shirl Hoffman. In *God in the Stadium*, Robert Higgs traces the history of the relationship between sports and religion through such seemingly diverse venues as education and the military.

The kinship between sports and religion is as old as the beginning of the Olympics and in America was remarked upon most notably at the turn of the century by Thorstein Veblen. In *Theory of the Leisure Class* Veblen sees sports and religion as two of the four occupations of the leisure class and predatory culture, the other two being government and warfare. Veblen's argument is a compelling one and, as far as I know, has never been successfully refuted. Sports and religion were the subject of a three-part series in *Sports Illustrated* in 1976 by Frank Deford, who coined the term "sportianity" and examined the growing phenomenon with the perceptive eye of the reporter. Michael Novak's *The Joy of Sports* is not only a ringing defense of sports but an argument that sports inevitably spring from a religious commitment, regardless of the form that commitment may take.

To what extent sports and religion are allied, or ought to be, is open to question, but that sports generate and reflect social and cultural attitudes and hence values there seems to be little doubt. The commercialism that helped to bring about the proliferation of sports has, ironically, precipitated a widespread criticism of the athletic establishment. At least by the 1920s and probably much earlier, observers were questioning the commercialism of mass sports, and by the 1960s and 1970s the concern had grown to a type of outrage, as seen in such works as Paul Hoch's *Rip Off the Big Game: The Exploitation of Sports by the Power Elite* and Jack Scott's *The Athletic Revolution*. Athletes, too, jumped on the bandwagon. Dave Meggyesy in *Out of Their League* and Gary Shaw in *Meat on the Hoof* voiced trenchant criticism of the way that athletes were being exploited for materialistic ends. While football was the sport generally singled out for attack, baseball has not been completely immune. Even such a devoted fan as Roger Angell in *Five Seasons: A Baseball Companion* registered regret that promotional practices tend to rob the game of its traditional appeal. *Jock Culture, USA* by Neil D. Isaacs and *Sportsworld: An American Dreamland* by Robert Lipsyte not only examine the exploitation of the athlete but also question the pervasiveness of sports in American society and warn against the dangers to values, institutions, and modes of thought.

The purpose of some books is not so much to criticize the current sports establishment as to point to new directions in mind–body relationships. Two engaging examples are works published in the Esalen-Viking series: Michael Murphy's *Golf in the Kingdom* and George Leonard's *The Ultimate Athlete*. Both examine the concept of the "inner body." Leonard's book contains an appendix listing seven new games for the "Sports Adventurers." In *The Psychic Side of Sports* Michael Murphy and Rhea A. White present numerous stories from "the spiritual underground of sports." Well documented, it contains a bibliography of 538 items identified in ten categories of psychic phenomena in sports. As valuable as the book is, the implied parallel between the spirit in religion and the spirit in sport may be askew. The psychic and the sacred are not necessarily synonymous. In his magnum opus, *The Future of the Body*, Michael Murphy presents an informative overview of both Eastern and Western techniques for unlocking the unlimited nature of the human potential.

Both Leonard and Murphy reflect a strong element of Eastern influence, and the classic work on the Oriental approach to sport, indeed the precursor of many others, is Eugene Herrigel's *Zen in the Art of Archery*, which is generally praised but which comes under attack by Arthur Koestler in *The Lotus and the Robot*. In the Zen mastery of archery Koestler finds not the spirit of the Buddha but the basic principles of modern behaviorism. Whether science or religion (or both) is at work in the Zen way, the impact that it has had upon American culture in recent years has been immeasurable, not only upon Americans sitting still and meditating but upon those in action, and not just in aikido. The principles, the theory goes, apply to any undertaking, hence a spate of books and articles in which Eastern methods are applied to Western sports, for example, Fred Rohe's *Zen of Running*. A good discussion of the marriage of East and West is "Sport Is Western Yoga" in *Powers of Mind* by Adam Smith. Another work influenced by Zen, as well as by Shinto and Confucianism, which serves as a guide for businessmen as well as athletes, is *A Book of Five Rings* by Miyamoto Musashi (1584–1645), Japanese "sword-saint." An ancient classic, it has become a modern best-seller, heading every martial arts bibliography. It has been called "Japan's answer to the Harvard MBA." To some, an element of sophistry appears in the ease with which ancient Oriental formulas for strength and wisdom are put to the service of profit. Con-

1984 Olympics in Los Angeles. © Painet

centration is concentration, but a difference in the goals of activities must be considered. Self-defense and self-knowledge, the goals of Oriental martial systems, do not in the long run automatically equate with financial success.

A recurring theme in the plethora of books critical of modern sports has been the status of the black athlete. Notable works on this subject are Harry Edwards' *The Revolt of the Black Athlete*, Jack Olsen's *The Black Athlete: A Shameful Story*, and *Baseball's Great Experiment: Jackie Robinson and His Legacy* by Jules Tygiel. Since much of the controversy over the black athlete has centered not only on forms of exploitation but also on arguments of racial superiority, the researcher should not overlook John Lardner's *White Hopes and Other Tigers*, Martin Kane's *Sports Illustrated* article, "An Assessment of 'Black Is Best,' " Harry Edwards' rebuttal in "The Myth of the Racially Superior Athlete," and the *Time* article, "The Black Dominance." Also instructive in putting the black athlete in perspective is David K. Wiggins' article, "Clio and the Black Athlete in America: Myths, Heroes, and Realities."

The role of women in sports is also a frequently debated issue, supposedly settled by the passage of Title IX of the Education Amendments Act of 1972, which stipulated the withholding of federal funds for those who discriminate on the basis of sex in school programs, including physical education and athletics. Though discriminatory practices may still exist, since 1972 this act has not only revolutionized athletics in the schools but contributed to the rapid growth of, and interest in, women's professional athletics, opening doors once open only for men. Important works in this area are those by Pearl Berlin et al., *The American Woman in Sports*; Eleanor Metheny, *Connotations of Movement in Sport and Dance*; Donna Mae Miller and Katherine R. E. Russell, *Sport: A Contemporary View*; and J. A. Mangan and Roberta J. Park, *From "Fair Sex" to Feminism*. A controversial work touching on sex, sexism, and gender bias in sports is Mariah Nelson's *The Stronger Women Get, the More Men Love Football*. A number of anthologies contain sections on these subjects, often including extensive references and bibliographies. Among these is *Sport in the Socio-cultural Process*, edited by Marie M. Hart. One edition of *Aethlon: The Journal of Sport Literature* (Fall 1997) is devoted to the subject of women in sport and literature, as is the book *Crossing Boundaries*, both edited by Susan Bandy and Anne Darden. Perhaps the most comprehensive reference work, edited by Mary L. Remley, is *Women in Sport: A Guide to Information Sources*.

The student of popular culture will more than likely be interested in the relationship between sports and language, since the abuse of language, especially superlatives, is a daily occurrence. Again, on this subject, as on many others, a good place to start is with John R. Betts in the section entitled "Lingo, Lexicon, and Language" in *America's Sporting Heritage, 1850–1950*. Helpful sources are identified in his notes. A good article on sports and mass communications is "Sportuguese: A Study of Sports Page Communication," which is included in one of the best anthologies on the sociological aspects of sports, *Sports, Culture and Society*, edited by John W. Loy Jr. and Gerald S. Kenyon. Also included in this work is an article on sport in mass society from a foundational book on mass media and popular culture, Reuel Denney's *The Astonished Muse*. There are several how-to books by sports writers; the best of these is *The Red Smith Reader*.

Stirred by the endless use of such terms in sports pages as "scalp," "throttle," and "blast," the controversy over the aggressive nature of sport shows no sign of abating. Again the matter of definitions is crucial. What is aggression? A wide range of answers can be found in the following works: *Aggression: A Social Psychological Analysis* by Leonard Berkowitz; *On Aggression* by Konrad Lorenz; and *Sports Violence*, edited by Jeffrey Goldstein. *Sports in America* by James Michener has a good discussion of violence as it relates to competition.

On the matter of aggression, the central unsolved question seems to be: Do sports enhance aggression or relieve it? This is a difficult question but a compelling one in a world where violence in sports is part of our daily scene. Don Atyeo is convinced, as he shows in *Violence in Sports*, with its sickening accounts of cruelty in competition, that the catharsis or safety valve theory of aggression is wrong. The inherent violence in several sports creates more combative attitudes in spectators. Allen Guttmann in *Sports Spectators* is skeptical of the theory but also points to instances where sports seem to have had a civilizing effect. On the subject of spectators, the student of popular culture will not want to overlook *Fans!* by Michael Roberts, a sobering book but often a funny one, as seen in one chapter title, "Jesus Christ (Pro Football) Superstar." Alfie Kohn's *No Contest* also examines the role of aggression endemic within competition.

Considering the ubiquitous nature of sports in American society and the increasing awareness of their significance by scholars in various disciplines, one is probably safe in predicting that within a few years the study of sport as an aspect of popular culture will be as commonplace in the universities as the study of languages is now.

In practically every discipline in the humanities there are journals devoted to the study of sports, for example, *Aethlon: The Journal of Sports Literature* (formerly *Arete*). Sports also receive their share of attention in the field of popular culture; for example, the Spring 1983 issue of the *Journal of Popular Culture*, "Sports in America," edited by David A. Jones and Leverett T. Smith Jr., is entirely devoted to them. The recently established Center for Research on Sport in Society in the College of Arts and Sciences at the University of Miami reflects in its mission statement the new reality of sports in our culture: "The Center for Research on Sport in Society (CRSS) is founded on the basic principle that sport is an institution that can and does affect our lives and our society in profound and sometimes dramatic ways and, thus, warrants the serious attention of the scholarly community."

ANTHOLOGIES AND REPRINTS

Among several texts in sports history are *American Sports: From the Age of Folk Games to the Age of Spectators* by Benjamin G. Rader; *Saga of American Sport* by John A. Lucas and Ronald A. Smith; *Sport and American Mentality, 1880–1940* by Donald J. Mrozek; *Sports in Modern America* by William J. Baker and John M. Carroll; and *Sports in America: New Historical Perspectives*, edited by Donald Spivey. A number of model studies deal with sport in a specific locale, for example, *The Rise of Sports in New Orleans, 1850–1900* by Dale A. Somers and *A Sporting Time: New York City and the Rise of Modern Athletics, 1820–70* by Melvin L. Adelman.

A student of American sport will frequently find it desirable to know something of attitudes toward sport in other times and places, especially ancient Greece and Rome and nineteenth-century England. E. Norman Gardiner's *Athletics of the Ancient World* is a foundational work on sport in classical times and still of great worth, especially if supplemented by such works as *The Olympic Games: The First Thousand Years* by M. I. Finley and H. W. Plecket, an impressive work that challenges many of the traditional assumptions about ancient sports. David Young, in turn, in *The Olympic Myth of Greek Amateur Athletics* takes Plecket and others to task for imposing, in Young's view, nineteenth-century attitudes toward amateurism on ancient sports, where, he says, the idea did not exist. A valuable bibliography is Rachel Sargent Robinson's *Sources for the History of Greek Athletics*, which should be supplemented by Thomas F. Scanlon's *Greek and Roman Athletics: A Bibliography*, which includes works from 1573 to 1983. For a highly regarded study of the modern Olympic movement and an indispensable sourcebook, turn to *This Great Symbol* by John MacAloon.

Joseph Strutt's *The Sports and Pastimes of the People of England* provides excellent historical background into the role that sport has played in England. A good treatment of sport during the later Victorian period, especially as dealt with in the literature of the period, is Bruce Haley's *The Healthy Body and Victorian Culture*. On the relationship between sports and education, the work to consult is *Athleticism in the Victorian and Edwardian Public Schools* by J. A. Mangan, also the coeditor with James Walvin of *Manliness and Morality*, which deals with the concept of masculinity and class in Britain and America from 1800 to 1940.

An excellent text that traces sports from ancient times to the present is *Sports in the Western World* by William J. Baker. Several observers have noted disturbing parallels between the excesses of ancient and modern sports, most notably, per-

An illustration from Joseph Strutt's *The Sports and Pastimes of the People of England*, 1801. Courtesy of the Library of Congress

haps, Arnold Toynbee in *The Breakdown of Civilizations*, volume 4, *A Study of History*. An excellent treatise on the role that sport played for men and women in the armed services is Wanda Wakefield's *Playing to Win*.

American literature is a vast reservoir of popular culture. William T. Porter's journal *Spirit of the Times: A Chronicle of the Turf, Agriculture, Field Sports, Literature and Stage*, which was published from 1830 to 1861, is itself a mine of sporting stories in the nineteenth century. Sports did not become prominent in fiction until the second decade of this century; the writer who introduced the subject to the American public on a broad scale was Ring Lardner with his stories of bushers. Since Lardner, virtually every major writer and playwright has dealt in some way with the theme of sports. As in history, there are several anthologies, among them *Literature of Sport*, edited by Tom Dodge; *Sport Inside Out*, edited by David L. Vanderwerken and Spencer K. Wertz; and *The Sporting Spirit: Athletes in Literature and Life*, edited by Robert J. Higgs and Neil D. Isaacs. *American Sport Culture: The Humanistic Dimensions*, edited by Wiley Lee Umphlett, is especially suitable for an interdisciplinary approach, as is *Sport Inside Out*. Though some of these may be out of print, they are still helpful for planning and identifying primary materials.

With the rise in popularity of sports literature, there have also appeared a number of critical studies. The first, *The Sporting Myth and the American Experience*, edited by Wiley Lee Umphlett, shows that much American fiction from the early romances to recent neoromanticism makes use of sports figures to give form and meaning to the American experience. *Laurel and Thorn* by Robert J. Higgs examines the types of athletes in American literature as representatives of the balance between body and mind. In *Playful Fiction and Fictional Players*, Neil D. Berman provides an in-depth study of five novels—*Fat City*, *North Dallas Forty*, *End Zone*, *One on One*, and *Universal Baseball Association*—to argue that in order to become a transforming reality in the indoor world, play must be internalized. Christian K. Messenger in *Sport and the Spirit of Play in American Fiction* looks at American literature from Hawthorne to Faulkner in terms of play modes identified by Roger Caillois in *Man, Play, and Games*—"Agon" (competition), "Alea" (chance), "Mimicry" (imitation), and "Ilinx" (irrational whirling)—and concludes that Faulkner's "work with play images is the most complete, for he could create in all the play modes" (313).

Michael Oriard in *Dreaming of Heroes: American Sports Fiction, 1868–1980* treats sports fiction in terms of country and city, youth and age, history and myth, all of which figure prominently in Bernard Malamud's *The Natural*, which Oriard examines at length, relating events in the novel to events in American life as well as to ancient myths. A comprehensive analysis of sport and play as they relate to other manifested aspects of American culture is Oriard's *Sporting with the Gods*. Since a number of colleges now offer courses on literature and the history of sports, there is even a published collection of syllabi entitled *Sport History: Selected Reading Lists and Course Outlines from American Colleges and Universities*, edited by Douglas A. Noverr and Lawrence E. Ziewacz.

Other disciplines have not neglected the study of sports, as seen in such texts as *Philosophic Inquiry in Sport*, edited by William J. Morgan and Klaus V. Meier, and *Studies in the Sociology of Sport*, edited by Aiden O. Dunleavy, Andrew W. Miracle, and C. Roger Rees. A highly acclaimed book on politics is *Sport and Political Ideology* by John M. Hoberman, who seeks to examine why political ideologies such as Marxism and Nazism demonstrate distinctive views of sports. One of the most sobering studies of man's inhumanity to man is depicted in George Eisen's *Children and Play in the Holocaust*. In this work, Eisen examines the inexorable instinct to play, even amid the horrors of the Nazi death camps. Since there have been so many celebrated abuses of sports and even play, it is not surprising that many recent books and articles deal with the ethics of sports in contrast to prevailing rules of sports, which, upon closer inspection, may reflect both social and cultural biases. Among the best of these is *Sports and Social Values* by Robert L. Simon, who believes that competition can be beneficial to all participants if conceived and applied as a mutual quest for excellence as opposed to an egotistical quest for superiority. A contrary view is that of Bruce C. Ogilive and Thomas A. Tutko, as is suggested by the title of their article, "Sports: If You Want to Build Character, Try Something Else." Alfie Kohn essentially expands upon the argument in *No Contest*, in which he indicts competition as the "number one obsession" in the United States and "almost America's new religion," with sports being perhaps its most visible form. Sports not only impact our daily lives but even have international ramifications and transcend cultural boundaries, as noted in Kendall Blanchard's *The Anthropology of Sport*.

Whether or not sports remain an area of intensive investigation in the universities, there is little doubt that they will continue to influence our lives in both obvious and subtle ways, for one thing is certain: humans will play. We may even cease to go to war, but we will never cease to play as long as there is time called leisure after labor is done.

NOTES

1. See, for example, Struna; Wagner.
2. Manchester, 16.

3. Twombly, 18.
4. Dulles, 5.
5. Manchester, 17.
6. Dulles, 25.
7. Sarah Kemball Knight, *Private Journal* (1865), 52–53, quoted in Dulles, 29.
8. Quoted in Henry Adams, "The United States in 1800," in *Henry Adams: The Education of Henry Adams and Other Selected Writings*, ed. Edward N. Saveth (New York: Washington Square Press, 1963), 72–73.
9. Holliman, 81.
10. Ibid., 23.
11. Quoted in Dulles, 35.
12. Adams, 74.
13. Holliman, 108.
14. Twombly, 30.
15. Manchester, 77.
16. Twombly, 46.
17. Manchester, 127.
18. Dulles, 223–24.
19. Kaye, 17.
20. Ibid., 198.
21. Patten, 181.

BIBLIOGRAPHY

Books and Articles

Adams, Henry. *Henry Adams: The Education of Henry Adams and Other Selected Writings*. Ed. by Edward N. Saveth. New York: Washington Square Press, 1963.

Adelman, Melvin L. *A Sporting Time: New York City and the Rise of Modern Athletics, 1820–70*. Urbana: University of Illinois Press, 1986.

Angell, Roger. *Five Seasons: A Baseball Companion*. New York: Simon and Schuster, 1977.

Arendt, Hannah. *The Human Condition*. Chicago: University of Chicago Press, 1958.

Arlott, John, ed. *The Oxford Companion to World Sports and Games*. London: Oxford University Press, 1975.

Atyeo, Don. *Violence in Sports*. New York: Van Nostrand Reinhold, 1979.

Baker, William J. *Sports in the Western World*. Totowa, N.J.: Rowan and Littlefield, 1987.

Baker, William J., and John M. Carroll. *Sports in Modern America*. St. Louis: River City, 1981. Rev. ed. Urbana: University of Illinois Press, 1988.

Bandy, Susan J. and Anne S. Darden. *Crossing Boundaries: An International Anthology of Women's Experiences in Sport*. Champaign, Ill.: Human Kinetics, 1999.

Berkowitz, Leonard. *Aggression: A Social Psychological Analysis*. New York: McGraw-Hill, 1962.

Berlin, Pearl, et al. *The American Woman in Sports*. Reading, Mass.: Addison-Wesley, 1974.

Berman, Neil D. *Playful Fiction and Fictional Players: Games, Sport, & Survival in Contemporary Fiction.* Port Washington, N.Y.: Kennikat Press, 1980.

Betts, John R. *America's Sporting Heritage, 1850–1950.* Reading, Mass.: Addison-Wesley, 1974.

Biography Index. New York: H. W. Wilson, 1946– .

"The Black Dominance." *Time* 109 (May 9, 1977), 57–60.

Blanchard, Kendall. *The Anthropology of Sport: An Introduction.* Westport, Conn.: Greenwood Press, 1995.

Boyle, Robert. *Sport: Mirror of American Life.* Boston: Little, Brown, 1963.

Caillois, Roger. *Man, Play, and Games.* Trans. Meyer Barash. New York: Free Press, 1961.

Cantwell, Robert. "A Sneering Laugh with the Bases Loaded." *Sports Illustrated* 16 (April 23, 1962), 68–76.

Crepeau, Richard. *Baseball: America's Diamond Mind.* Gainesville: University Press of Florida, 1980.

Deford, Frank. "Religion in Sport." *Sports Illustrated* 44 (April 19, 1976), 88–102; see also "Endorsing Jesus," 44 (April 26, 1976), 54–69, and "Reaching for the Stars," 44 (May 3, 1976), 42–60.

Denney, Reuel. *The Astonished Muse.* Chicago: University of Chicago Press, 1975.

Dictionary Catalog of Applied Life Studies Library. Boston: G. K. Hall, 1977.

Dodge, Tom, ed. *Literature of Sport.* Lexington, Mass.: D. C. Heath, 1980.

Dollard, John, et al. *Frustration and Aggression.* New Haven, Conn.: Yale University Press, 1974.

Dulles, Foster Rhea. *America Learns to Play: A History of Popular Recreation, 1607–1940.* New York: Appleton-Century, 1940.

Dunleavy, Aiden O., Andrew W. Miracle, and C. Roger Rees. *Studies in the Sociology of Sport.* Fort Worth: Texas Christian University Press, 1982.

Edwards, Harry. "The Myth of the Racially Superior Athlete." *Black Scholar* 3 (1971), 16–28.

———. *The Revolt of the Black Athlete.* New York: Free Press, 1969.

———. *Sociology of Sport.* Homewood, Ill.: Dorsey Press, 1973.

Eisen, George. *Children and Play in the Holocaust: Games among the Shadows.* Amherst: University of Massachusetts Press, 1988.

Finley, M. I., and H. W. Plecket. *The Olympic Games: The First Thousand Years.* New York: Viking, 1976.

Gardiner, E. Norman. *Athletics of the Ancient World.* London: Oxford University Press, 1930.

Gerber, Ellen W., et al., eds. *The American Woman in Sport.* Reading, Mass.: Addison-Wesley, 1974.

Goldstein, Jeffrey H., ed. *Sports Violence.* New York: Springer-Verlag, 1983.

Guttmann, Allen. *From Ritual to Record: The Nature of Modern Sports.* New York: Columbia University Press, 1978.

———. *Sports Spectators.* New York: Columbia University Press, 1986.

Haley, Bruce. *The Healthy Body and Victorian Culture.* Cambridge: Harvard University Press, 1978.

Hart, Marie M., ed. *Sport in the Socio-cultural Process.* Dubuque, Iowa: William C. Brown, 1972.

Henderson, Robert W. *Early American Sport*. New York: Grolier Club, 1937. Reprint. Cranbury, N.J.: Associated University Presses, 1977.

Herrigel, Eugene. *Zen in the Art of Archery*. Trans. by R.F.C. Hull. 1953. Reprint. New York: Pantheon, 1971.

Higgs, Robert J. *God in the Stadium: Sports & Religion in America*. Lexington: University of Kentucky Press, 1995.

————. *Laurel and Thorn: The Athlete in American Literature*. Lexington: University Press of Kentucky, 1981.

————. *Sports; A Reference Guide*. Westport, Conn.: Greenwood Press, 1982.

Higgs, Robert J., and Neil D. Isaacs, eds. *The Sporting Spirit: Athletes in Literature and Life*. New York: Harcourt Brace Jovanovich, 1977.

Hoberman, John M. *Sport and Political Ideology*. Austin: University of Texas Press, 1986.

Hoch, Paul. *Rip Off the Big Game: The Exploitation of Sports by the Power Elite*. New York: Doubleday, 1972.

Holliman, Jennie. *American Sports (1785–1835)*. 1931. Reprint. Philadelphia: Porcupine Press, 1975.

Hoffman, Shirl J., ed. *Sport and Religion*. Champaign, Ill.: Human Kinetics, 1992.

Huizinga, Johan. *Homo Ludens: A Study of the Play Element in Culture*. Boston: Beacon Press, 1960.

Isaacs, Neil D. *All the Moves: A History of U.S. College Basketball*. Philadelphia: J. B. Lippincott, 1975.

————. *Jock Culture, USA*. New York: W. W. Norton, 1978.

Jones, David A., and Leverett T. Smith Jr., eds. "Sports in America." *Journal of Popular Culture* 16 (Spring 1983), 1–102. Special issue.

Kane, Martin. "An Assessment of 'Black Is Best.'" *Sports Illustrated* 34 (January 18, 1971), 72–76.

Kaye, Ivan N. *Good Clean Violence: A History of College Football*. Philadelphia: J. B. Lippincott, 1973.

Koestler, Arthur. *The Lotus and the Robot*. New York: Macmillan, 1961.

Kohn, Alfie. *No Contest: The Case against Competition*. Boston: Houghton Mifflin, 1986.

Krout, John A. *Annals of American Sport*. Pageant of America series, Vol. 15. New Haven, Conn.: Yale University Press, 1929.

Lardner, John. *White Hopes and Other Tigers*. Philadelphia: J. B. Lippincott, 1956.

Lardner, Ring. *The Portable Ring Lardner*. Ed. Maxwell Geismer. New York: Scribner's, 1963.

Leonard, George. *The Ultimate Athlete*. New York: Viking, 1974.

Lipsyte, Robert. *Sportsworld: An American Dreamland*. New York: Quadrangle, 1975.

Lorenz, Konrad. *On Aggression*. New York: Harcourt, Brace, and World, 1966.

Loy, John W., and Gerald S. Kenyon, eds. *Sports, Culture and Society*. London: Macmillan, 1969.

Lucas, John A., and Ronald A. Smith. *Saga of American Sport*. Philadelphia: Lea and Febiger, 1978.

MacAloon, John J. *This Great Symbol: Pierre de Coubertin and the Origins of the Modern Olympic Games*. Chicago: University of Chicago Press, 1981.

Manchester, Herbert. *Four Centuries of American Sport, 1490–1890*. 1931. Reprint. New York: Benjamin Blom, 1968.

Mangan, J. A. *Athleticism in the Victorian and Edwardian Public Schools: The Emergence and Consolidation of Educational Psychology*. Cambridge: Cambridge University Press, 1981.

Mangan, J. A., and Roberta Park, eds. *From "Fair Sex" to Feminism: Sport and the Socialization of Women in the Industrial and Post-Industrial Eras*. Totowa, N.J.: Frank Cass, 1987.

Mangan, J. A., and James Walvin, eds. *Manliness and Morality: Middle-Class Masculinity in Britain and America, 1800–1940*. Manchester, England: Manchester University Press, 1987.

Meggyesy, Dave. *Out of Their League*. Berkeley, Calif.: Ramparts Press, 1970.

Menke, Frank G. *The Encyclopedia of Sport*. 6th ed. Cranbury, N.J.: A. S. Barnes, 1978.

Messenger, Christian Karl. *Sport and the Spirit of Play in American Fiction*. New York: Columbia University Press, 1981.

Metheny, Eleanor. *Connotations of Movement in Sport and Dance*. Dubuque, Iowa: William C. Brown, 1965.

Michener, James. *Sports in America*. New York: Random House, 1977.

Miller, Donna Mae, and Katherine R. E. Russell. *Sport: A Contemporary View*. Philadelphia: Lea and Febiger, 1971.

Morgan, William J., and Klaus V. Meier, eds. *Philosophic Inquiry in Sport*. Champaign, Ill.: Human Kinetic, 1988.

Mrozek, Donald J. *Sport and American Mentality, 1880–1940*. Knoxville: University of Tennessee Press, 1983.

Murphy, Michael. *The Future of the Body: Explorations into the Further Evolution of Human Nature*. New York: Perigee, 1993.

———. *Golf in the Kingdom*. New York: Viking, 1972.

Murphy, Michael, and Rhea A. White. *The Psychic Side of Sports*. Reading, Mass.: Addison-Wesley, 1978.

Musashi, Miyamoto. *A Book of Five Rings: The Classic Guide to Strategy*. Trans. Victor Harris. New York: Overlook Press, 1974.

Nelson, Mariah B. *The Stronger Women Get, the More Men Love Football: Sexism and the American Culture of Sports*. New York: Harcourt, Brace, 1994.

Novak, Michael. *The Joy of Sports*. New York: Basic Books, 1976.

Noverr, Douglas A., and Lawrence E. Ziewacz, eds. *Sport History: Selected Reading Lists and Course Outlines from American Colleges and Universities*. New York: Markus Wiener, 1987.

Ogilive, Bruce C., and Thomas A. Tutko. "Sports: If You Want to Build Character, Try Something Else." *Psychology Today* 5 (October 1971), 61–63.

Olsen, Jack. *The Black Athlete: A Shameful Story*. New York: Time-Life Books, 1968.

Oriard, Michael. *Dreaming of Heroes: American Sports Fiction 1868–1980*. Chicago: Nelson Hall, 1982.

———. *Sporting with the Gods: The Rhetoric of Play and Game in American Culture*. New York: Cambridge University Press, 1991.

Patten, Gilbert (Burt L. Standish). *Frank Merriwell's "Father": An Autobiography*. Norman: University of Oklahoma Press, 1964.

Porter, David L., ed. *Biographical Dictionary of American Sports*. 8 vols. Westport, Conn.: Greenwood Press, 1987–1992.

———. *African-American Sports Greats*. Westport, Conn.: Greenwood Press, 1995.

Prebish, Charles S. *Religion and Sport: The Meeting of Sacred and Profane*. Westport, Conn.: Greenwood Press, 1993.

Rader, Benjamin G. *American Sports: From the Age of Folk Games to the Age of Spectators*. Englewood Cliffs, N.J.: Prentice-Hall, 1983.

Rahner, Hugo. *Man at Play*. New York: Herder and Herder, 1972.

Remley, Mary L., ed. *Women in Sport: A Guide to Information Sources*. Detroit: Gale Research, 1980.

Roberts, Michael. *Fans! How We Go Crazy over Sports*. Washington, D.C.: New Republic Book, 1976.

Robinson, Rachel S. *Sources for the History of Greek Athletics*. Cincinnati: University of Cincinnati Press, 1955.

Rohe, Fred. *Zen of Running*. New York: Random House, 1975.

Sage, George H., ed. *Sport and American Society: Selected Readings*. Reading, Mass.: Addison-Wesley, 1970.

Scanlon, Thomas F. *Greek and Roman Athletics: A Bibliography*. Chicago: Ares, 1984.

Scott, Jack. *The Athletic Revolution*. New York: Free Press, 1971.

Shaw, Gary. *Meat on the Hoof*. New York: Dell, 1973.

Simon, Robert L. *Sports and Social Values*. Englewood Cliffs, N.J.: Prentice-Hall, 1985.

Slusher, Howard S. *Man, Sport, and Existence: A Critical Analysis*. Philadelphia: Lea and Febiger, 1967.

Smith, Adam. *Power of Mind*. New York: Ballantine, 1975.

Smith, Red. *The Red Smith Reader*. New York: Vintage, 1975.

Somers, Dale A. *The Rise of Sports in New Orleans, 1850–1900*. Baton Rouge: Louisiana State University Press, 1972.

Spivey, Donald, ed. *Sports in America: New Historical Perspectives*. Westport, Conn.: Greenwood Press, 1985.

Struna, Nancy. "Puritans and Sport: The Irretrievable Tide of Change." *Journal of Sport History* 4 (Spring 1977), 1–21.

Strutt, Joseph. *The Sports and Pastimes of the People of England*. 1833. Reprint. New York: A. M. Kelley, 1970.

Toynbee, Arnold. *The Breakdown of Civilizations*. Vol. 4: *A Study of History*. New York: Oxford University Press, 1939.

Twombly, Wells. *200 Years of Sport in America*. New York: McGraw-Hill, 1976.

Tygiel, Jules. *Baseball's Great Experiment: Jackie Robinson and His Legacy*. New York: Vintage, 1984.

Umphlett, Wiley Lee, ed. *American Sport Culture: The Humanistic Dimensions*. Lewisburg, Pa.: Bucknell University Press, 1983.

———. *Mythmakers of the American Dream: The Nostalgic Vision in Popular Culture*. Lewisburg, Pa.: Bucknell University Press, 1983.

———. *The Sporting Myth and the American Experience*. Lewisburg, Pa.: Bucknell University Press, 1975.

Vanderwerken, David L., and Spencer K. Wertz, eds. *Sport Inside Out*. Fort Worth: Texas Christian University Press, 1985.

Veblen, Thorstein. *Theory of the Leisure Class*. 1899. Reprint. New York: Macmillan, 1953.

Voigt, David Q. *American Baseball*. 3 vols. University Park: Pennsylvania State University Press, 1983.

Wagner, Peter. "Puritan Attitudes towards Physical Education in Seventeenth Century New England." *Journal of Sport History* 3 (Summer 1976), 139–51.

Wakefield, Wanda E. *Playing to Win: Sports and the American Military, 1898–1945*. Albany: State University of New York Press, 1997.

Webster's Sports Dictionary. Springfield, Mass.: G. and C. Merriam, 1976.

Weiss, Paul. *Sport: A Philosophic Inquiry*. Carbondale: Southern Illinois University Press, 1969.

Wiggins, David K. "Clio and the Black Athlete in America: Myths, Heroes, and Realities." *Quest* 32 (1980), 217–25.

Young, David C. *The Olympic Myth of Greek Amateur Athletics*. Chicago: Ares, 1984.

Periodicals

Aethlon: The Journal of Sports Literature. Johnson City, Tenn., 1983– .

The International Journal of the History of Sport. London, 1983– .

Journal of Sport History. University Park, Pa., 1973– .

Journal of the Philosophy of Sport. Champaign, Ill., 1973– .

Sports Illustrated. New York, 1954– .

Baseball card collection, 1955. Courtesy of the Library of Congress

Mickey Mantle posing for baseball card. Courtesy of the Library of Congress

"Cap" Anson baseball card, 1887. Courtesy of the Library of Congress

Bob Caruthers baseball card, 1888. Courtesy of the Library of Congress

John Ward baseball card, 1889. Courtesy of the Library of Congress

Honus Wagner baseball card, 1909. © Kit Kittle/CORBIS

STAMP, COIN, AND POSTCARD COLLECTING

John E. Findling and John Bryant

In recent decades Americans have turned to leisure activities with an intensity that nearly belies the function of "rest and relaxation." Like sports, hobbies are for millions an outlet or even a substitute for passion, controlled forms of mania that allow the participant to escape from, or create order in, a restless world. The most popular type of hobby is collecting. Our compulsion to collect, notes W. D. Newgold in the *Encyclopedia Britannica* (1978), probably dates back to those "happy, preliterate days when man foraged for nuts and berries." But today's collector does not forage in order to consume; he catalogs and displays his nuts and berries. The modes of collecting are as numerous as the objects that can be collected, and today anything that is abundant enough to be accessible yet scarce enough to be a challenge can become a "collectible." Some collect natural specimens. (We are told that Howard Hughes collected bits of himself.) Some collect rare books or art. Others collect the detritus of our industrial civilization: tinfoil, beer cans, or barbed wire. More collect antiques or dolls. But most people who collect, collect stamps, coins, or postcards.

The American Philatelic Society reports that its membership now numbers 55,000 individuals. A likelier estimate of serious stamp collectors is more than double that figure, and the number of "nonprofessional" collectors—the child or adult who keeps a cigar box or tidy album of stamps—undoubtedly swells into the millions. The U.S. Postal Service claims that upward of 20 million Americans use its philatelic windows each year. The American Numismatic Association reports 28,000 members, and there are hundreds of local coin clubs with thousands of additional collectors, not to mention the many people who simply throw interesting coins into a box or buy a silver dollar at an estate auction. Postcard collecting is less well organized on a national scale, but many cities and towns have postcard clubs, and many antique shops and flea market dealers do a good business selling postcards to customers.

More impressive than these figures is the remarkable activity that philatelists and numismatists precipitate in both the business and leisure worlds. Many governments maintain philatelic agencies designed to promote collecting and coordinate the year's steady stream of colorful new issues. Coins, too, in recent decades have assumed eye-catching designs. Collectors in both fields belong to local, national, and international associations, nearly all of which hold exhibitions ranging from modest hotel gatherings to major expositions with juried exhibits, lectures, and dealers' tables. Hundreds of stamp, coin, and postcard groups meet regularly to examine special aspects of the hobbies. Each week over 100 syndicated stamp or coin columns address the general reading public. Also, America's presses generate a bewildering array of books, catalog, and at present well over 200 specialized stamp, coin, or postcard periodicals.

To touch the past, to gain mental control over a proliferating world by gathering specimens of it, or simply to research a project—these are human needs that are routinely satisfied by putting a stamp, coin, or postcard in an album. Determining the social and psychological roots of the collecting phenomenon is challenging; equally fascinating are the cultural implications of the stamps and coins themselves. Overtly, stamps, coins, and postcards serve basic economic functions; covertly, stamps and coins at least are modes of governmental propaganda. From an aesthetic perspective, they provide unique popular art forms combining miniature and medallic art, engraving, mass production, and, in some cases, the work of premier American artists and artisans. (At various times, for instance, Americans have been able to purchase an engraved Gilbert Stuart reproduction on a stamp with a coin designed by Augustus St. Gaudens.) Finally, as social icons, stamps, coins, and even postcards reflect shifting American ideologies and may in guarded cases be used as evidence supplementing a scholar's historical or cultural observations.

In the past 150 years, philatelists, numismatists, and deltiologists have published a substantial body of literature. Yet the amount of material published by our universities' cultural historians on these subjects is minute. In the process of reporting the scope and nature of philatelic and numismatic literature, assessing the scant number of publications in the area, and suggesting topics for further study, we hope to confront three problems: the phenomenon of collecting, the aesthetic merits of stamps and coins themselves, and the use of stamps and coins as reliable indicators of cultural development.

HISTORICAL OUTLINE

Since postal history and monetary history are academic fields in their own right, and plump bibliographies exist for them elsewhere, we shall not detail the histories of the mails or money except when such details directly influence the development of the three hobbies. Generally speaking, three factors have shaped the growth of philately, numismatics, and deltiology: democratization, or the spreading of an elite hobby among the masses; commercialization, or the transformation of the hobby into a business; and specialization, or the creation within the hobby of special, even scholarly modes of collecting.

Stamps

Unlike coins, which are as old as sin, postage stamps are an invention of the industrial age and imperial Britain's need for an efficient communication system. Sir Rowland Hill introduced postal reforms and adhesive postage stamps to the public in 1840. Previously, letters bore the price of delivery on them in ink, and that amount was paid by the receiver to the courier on delivery. Numerous private delivery agencies competed in an open market. Hill instituted a government postal monopoly and essentially invented the process of mail delivery. Now senders paid for delivery by purchasing one-cent "Penny Black" stamps, which they then affixed to their letters. The result was more revenues going directly into government coffers and broadened mail circulation. Although an American allegedly introduced the idea of prepaid postage stamps to Hill, Americans were slower to adopt the new system. The first official U.S. stamps were not issued until 1847, and the government did not gain a monopoly until 1863.

Serious stamp collecting began some twenty years after Hill's invention. In the 1840s, stamps were a fad but not a hobby; a socialite in the British colony of Mauritius printed her own "Penny Blacks" to adorn party invitations, and in England something called a "stamp ball" was the rage. The less affluent fancied stamps, too, using them to decorate their walls and lapels. By the 1860s, however, the fad had clearly grown into a hobby. Used stamp transactions were a common sight in the open markets of Europe. London could boast sixty stamp dealers, and French officials, fearing that stamp markets encouraged forgeries and the corruption of youths, closed the Paris markets twice before letting hobbyists be. Philatelic literature (how-to books, catalogs, price lists, and even books on counterfeit detecting) appeared as early as 1862. In 1865, British dealer J. W. Scott set up business in New York, and his new company (still a major U.S. stamp firm) stimulated an already growing market in this country.

From its beginning, philately shared in the democratic spirit of the age. Although more prominent philatelists have generally been wealthy men (John K. Tiffany, Count Ferrari, King Farouk, Franklin Delano Roosevelt), the hobby has been a relatively cheap, accessible, and convenient pastime shared (as handbook authors like to crow) by "kings and kids" alike. Even the earliest guides to the hobby proclaim philately's universal appeal. Stamps were easily packaged and mailed for trade or purchase; they were generally inexpensive and required no costly paraphernalia (such as the traditional coin cabinet). A working-class child with few resources could acquire a modest collection through trade and discovery, if not purchase. Moreover, stamp collecting was seen then as now as a form of play providing moral instruction, knowledge, and good preparation for social advancement. The publisher of Henry Bellars, *The Standard Guide to Postage Stamp Collecting* (1864) for instance, argued that young collectors "have a more perfect knowledge of their studies, and, above all, obtain a quicker experience of actual life, and the value of money." More than a pastime for the idle rich, philately adhered to the Protestant ethic and gave youngsters a boost up the ladder of success.

To be sure, the major advances and research in the nineteenth century were made by the wealthy. The London (now Royal) Philatelic Society, founded in

1869, was followed in 1886 by the American Philatelic Association (now Society), organized by John K. Tiffany, a collector since 1859 and a bibliographer of philatelic literature. J. W. Scott presided over the first years of the Collectors Club of New York, founded in 1896, which listed among its members some of the nation's elite. The backbone of American philately, however, was in the middle and working classes; from 1870 to 1890 interest in the hobby was strong enough to sustain some 300 popular and scholastic periodicals in the United States.

By the turn of the century, major stamp exhibitions in Antwerp (1887) and New York (1889) established philately as an international hobby. In 1890 a third such fair in London celebrated the fiftieth anniversary of Hill's invention and introduced an important decade in the commercialization of the hobby. Until this time governmental postal issues had been predominantly portrait stamps. England had Victoria; America had Washington and Franklin. The first major step in the transformation of the hobby into a big government business occurred when authorities reckoned that prettier stamps might attract the eye and pennies of collectors. In the long run they were right, but the idea did not catch on immediately. As early as 1869 the U.S. government had, in fact, issued a series of seven "pictorial" stamps with vignettes of the signing of the Declaration of Independence, the landing of Columbus, and various "icons" such as a locomotive, steamship, and mounted courier; but these stamps did not sell well. A more notorious "experiment" in stamp marketing occurred in 1893, when N. F. Seebeck of the Hamilton Note Company of New York designed and printed a set of colorful stamps for certain Central and South American nations. Called "Seebecks," these stamps were primarily meant to be sold to collectors. The scheme failed, but in 1894 the republic of San Marino set up its philatelic agency to do precisely what Seebeck had hoped to do—create stamps not as postage but as collector's items.

At first, collectors were scandalized by any government's attempt to capitalize on the hobby, but the trend toward special and commemorative stamps was irreversible, and today most government postal services actively promote stamp collecting. The frequency of special issues has grown slowly but distinctly in the United States since the printing in 1893 of our first commemorative issues celebrating Columbus' landfall in America. By the 1920s the United States was printing only about three special issues a year. However, 1932 was a banner year for U.S. commemoratives; nineteen in all were issued. The average number of issues in the 1950s was eleven; but since the Bicentennial (which produced its own plethora of commemoratives), the figure has steadily grown and by the 1990s exceeded thirty annually. Philatelic sales represent a significant source of income for the U.S. Postal Service, a fact reflected by the opening of philatelic "boutiques" in post offices around the country and the marketing of collateral items for stamp collectors: pins, neckties, and greeting cards all bearing the same image portrayed on a particular stamp. Moreover, the Postal Service has in recent years catered to popular culture interests by immortalizing such figures as Elvis Presley, Marilyn Monroe, James Dean, and Bugs Bunny on commemorative stamps.

The boom in philately during the 1930s and 1940s deeply penetrated various sectors of American culture. Government, entrepreneurs, educators, churches, radio, and universities promoted the hobby. During his administration, Franklin Roosevelt took a great deal of interest in stamp issues, even to the point of suggesting designs for certain stamps, and his flamboyant postmaster general, James

Chief Joseph stamp. © Painet

Farley, was responsible one year for a $1 million profit on the sale of stamps. Also at this time, philately was introduced as a teaching device in public schools. Junior-level history books, for instance, used stamps to "tell the story of America." Church-affiliated stamp clubs sprang up. Bell Telephone encouraged employees to collect, and Ivory Soap sponsored a long-running radio program for collectors. The University of Michigan even offered a course in philately. Since World War II national and local stamp organizations have strengthened their civic-mindedness. The two major associations, the American Philatelic Society (APS) and the American Topical Association (ATA), maintain close ties with civic and educational groups through slide shows, exhibitions, and publications.

For the most part, the 1950s and early 1960s brought a continued expansion of philately's democratization and commercialization. More people were adopting the hobby, and the hobby business, in both private and government sectors, was growing. The notion that stamps make good investments has always been an important part of philately's commercial side, but after World War II, some nationally known investment advisers recommended the purchase of sheets of commemorative stamps from the post office as a sure-fire investment (after all, it was argued, they would never be worth less than face value). Books like Joseph Granville, *Everybody's Guide to Stamp Investment* (1952) and Henry M. Ellis, *Stamps for Fun and Profit* (1953), sent thousands of people out to buy mint stamps. Unfortunately, so many were bought and saved that their investment potential was never realized, and forty years later, in the 1990s, dealers were paying only 80 percent of face value for mint stamps issued in the 1950s.

In the later 1970s, inflationary pressures dating back to the Vietnam War and the Great Society programs of the 1960s created a speculative boom in stamps (as well as in many other collectibles). Pushed along by a number of well-publicized professional speculators, the philatelic market peaked at record high levels in the early 1980s and just as quickly collapsed as the rate of inflation returned to more normal levels by 1984, and the speculators moved on to other conquests. Since the mid-1980s, philatelic values have remained relatively flat, although in the mid-1990s, there was evidence that a slow, but steady, recovery was in progress.

One of the joys of most forms of collecting is that the collector can work out his or her own way to organize his or her collection. This is perhaps more true in stamp collecting than in many other types of collecting because of the vast number of stamps that have been issued by nations around the world. Many beginning collectors start out as generalists, saving any and all stamps that come their way. Soon, if they stick with the hobby, they discover that some stamps are more interesting to them than others, and they move in the direction of specialization, either in the stamps of a particular country (most often their own) or of a particular topic or subject frequently found on stamps, such as horses, trains, sports, or space. This type of collecting is called topical or thematic collecting, and the American Topical Association helps collectors by providing information and checklists on more than 200 different topics.

Most collectors never get beyond this stage, but for those who do, more serious study can be very rewarding. Single-country collectors may gradually add other countries to their collection, or they may decide to specialize in certain issues of their original country, looking for stamps that have color, perforation, or watermark varieties or that have minute differences based on the plates from which they were printed. This type of collecting requires exhaustive research and has led to the publication of highly sophisticated books and articles on individual stamps and their printing history.

Another important branch of philately involves the collecting of stamps on envelopes (called "covers" in the hobby), with an eye toward understanding the postal history of the stamp through the examination of the cancellations and other postal markings on the cover, the destination and the amount of postage used to get the cover there, and the route used to deliver the item (often discernible by additional postmarks on the back of the cover). Other collectors are interested only in particular types of cancellations, particularly those made by late-nineteenth- and early-twentieth-century machine cancelers, or those bearing special slogans, such as "Let's Fight Forest Fires."

Coins

Coin collecting, or numismatics, presents a significantly different pattern of development. Unlike philately, which began in the industrial age as a fad, spread democratically, yet has become as much an academic pursuit as a hobby, numismatics has been from the beginning and until only recently in the provenance of the intellectual and social elite. Old coins have always been attractive to the antiquarian; Petrarch, for instance, was one of the first to have collected antique Roman coins. By the eighteenth century no monarch or even his lesser luminaries could feel properly furnished without a coin cabinet. Men of substance acquired coins as they would art or rare books. Also at this time numismatics entered the university. As early as the Renaissance, gentlemen had written brief treatises on the history of coins, but by the early 1700s in Germany (still the central arena for numismatic research) scholars were beginning to use coins as archaeological and historical evidence. The compulsion that drove Heinrich Schliemann a century later to dig at the layered ruins of Troy was in part the same desire that brought early scholars closer to coins. Since then numismatics has been the all-important handmaiden to the archaeologist and historian as well as the aesthetician. The nineteenth century brought a number of developments that shaped and redefined numismatics from the study of coins to that of money in general and medals. As Elvira E. Clain-Stefanelli remarks in her monograph, *Numismatics—An Ancient Science: A Survey of Its History* (1965), the Napoleonic Wars generated many medals, which were in turn analyzed and cataloged in weighty French volumes. In the New World, British and American governments struck medals to "honor" American Indian peace alliances. The quickly expanding and contracting economies in the world also generated more varieties of currency: paper money, banknotes, scrip, tokens, and even unofficial, yet negotiable, coins. The shortage of coins resulting from President Andrew Jackson's refusal to recharter the Second Bank of the United States in 1834 forced banks and merchants to issue fractional currency and "hard times coins" as late as 1844 in order to make change. With more of such items to collect, numismatists began to focus on material of more recent vintage and of the modern nations. By midcentury, museums as well as universities had become the principal lodgings for major collections. More people were able to see the rarities; more people could also afford modest collections of their own. Yet more scholarly research, publication, and cataloging developed during this period. Thus, numismatics was able to broaden its appeal but also rise in academic respectability.

Although American coinage can be dated back to 1616, we have records of only a few colonial coin collectors. American numismatics dates primarily from the mid-nineteenth century. Philadelphia, home of the U.S. Mint, was logically the first center of numismatic interest. As Clain-Stefanelli records, the mint's chief coiner, Adam Eckfeldt, began a collection at the mint that would become one of the finest in the world. In 1858 several Philadelphians formed the Numismatic and Antiquarian Society. Also founded that year but destined to outlive the Philadelphia organization was the scholarly American Numismatic Society (ANS). This group and the larger, more hobby-oriented American Numismatic Association (ANA), founded in Chicago in 1891, have become the country's principal numismatic organizations. During the latter half of the century, periodicals such as the *American Journal of Numismatics* (no longer published), *The Numismatist*, and other more ephemeral publications provided amateurs and newcomers with an opportunity to prepare themselves for the rigors of numismatic technique. Landmark works in U.S. numismatic scholarship appeared in these decades. Consonant with international scholarship of that age, American numismatists tended to use currency as clues to economic development rather than as archaeological evidence. It has been only recently that scholars have begun to appreciate the artistic merit of America's coinage.

Although by 1900 numismatics was growing, it was still a gentleman-scholar's hobbyhorse. The democratization of the hobby was impeded by certain obvious physical problems. At the time, cumbersome coins required boxes, drawers, and cabinets for storage. Also, modern collecting was inhibited by the fact that governments (which are still conservative when it comes to coinage) rarely minted commemorative, special, or even new issues. At least three developments served to rectify these problems. First, from 1892 to 1934, the U.S. government experimented with commemorative coins, some of which were issued alongside similar commemorative stamps. Also during this period the mint, in an attempt to generate interest in collecting, made available "proof sets" of each year's new or newly dated coins. Unfortunately, the depression and World War II slowed down the collection of such items until the 1950s. A third development was the marketing in the late 1930s of "coin books" made of cardboard pages with holes cut to fit individual coins. The convenient device gave the hobby its biggest boost. At the time, traditional numismatists laughed, but hobbyists today continue to search loose change and coin rolls for that elusive 1931-S cent to place in their album.

Although numismatics preceded philately as an intellectual discipline, coin collectors of the 1930s did well by following commercial techniques that had been in vogue among stamp collectors for decades. Chatty, but reliable, journals such as the *Numismatic Scrapbook Magazine* (1935–) provided trade and sale information. In 1942 Richard S. Yeoman (who first marketed the coin book) began publishing the *Handbook of United States Coins*, "an objective pricing guide" for dealers, and in 1946 he put out the first edition of the *Guidebook of United States Coins*, now an annual mainstay for collectors.

Since World War II the growth of the hobby can be gauged somewhat by the fact that the mint sold nearly 4 million proof sets in 1964, compared with the 50,000 sold in 1950. Part of the reason for that increase in sales was the increasing interest in coins as an investment. Like stamps, coins increased rationally in value until the hobby was crippled in the late 1970s and early 1980s by an unhealthy speculative boom that accompanied a period of high rates of inflation. The efforts of the Hunt brothers, who were wealthy Texans, to corner the silver market at this time and the desire of many others to place their wealth in gold and silver drove the market prices of those two precious metals up by several hundred percent over their mid-1970s levels. This had a direct bearing, of course, on the market prices of gold and silver coins, whose numismatic value rather suddenly was of little significance in comparison with their gold or silver value. Doubtless, some coins were melted down for their metallic value, and many small investors suffered significant losses when the market collapsed in the mid-1980s. Since that time, prices have stabilized (and in some cases, even risen again), but gold and silver values continue to be an important determinant in the valuation of collectible coins. Thus, the twentieth century saw numismatics develop in ways contrary to philately. Beginning as a highly specialized field, coin collecting has enjoyed an age of democratization, which may be cut short by overcommercialization and speculative finance.

Postcards

The first government-issued postcards (called "postal cards" in the hobby) appeared in Vienna in 1869. Since the postage was paid for when one bought the postal card, and a place to write messages was readily available, this was an easy method of correspondence that became popular almost immediately. Within a few years, most nations were issuing postal cards. The U.S. Post Office inaugurated the service in 1873; more than 200,000 postal cards were sold at the post offices in Boston, New York City, and Washington, D.C., in the first two days. By the 1890s, some 500 million government postal cards were sold annually.

In 1893, the first picture postcards (strictly speaking, these were postal cards, since they were prestamped by the U.S. Post Office) were issued in conjunction with the World's Columbian Exposition in Chicago. They too, were very popular, and in 1898, Congress authorized the use of what were called "private mailing cards," printed and sold by private businesses. They were not prestamped; users had to affix the proper postage to the address side of the card prior to mailing. In the language of the hobby, these cards have come to be known as postcards, and from the beginning, they frequently bore pictures of one kind or another, leading to the common term, "picture postcard." The wide variety of colorful and attractive pictures greatly enhanced the desirability of collecting these objects.

Picture postcards owe some of their success to the popularity of trade cards. Trade, or advertising, cards were an early form of marketing in the United States. The free distribution of cards with an attractive or clever illustration on one side and a printed ad on the other side began in the seventeenth century in London and was known in colonial America in the eighteenth century. Improvements in printing techniques, especially involving the use of color lithography, in the late nineteenth century made trade cards much more popular and a collectible in their own right.

In the United States, postal cards had been used for advertising purposes in a limited way since their inception in 1873, but they seldom involved the aesthetic qualities of trade cards. However, the institution of rural free delivery in the 1890s, as well as the authorization of private mailing cards in 1898, led to the rapid demise of the trade card, which became obsolete soon after 1900.

Postcard collecting was popular in the United States by 1905, several years after it had become a craze in Europe, where picture postcards had become widely used in the 1890s. The *Dry Goods Reporter* noted in November 1905, "The demand for illustrated postal [*sic*] cards is daily assuming larger proportions and there are no prospects of the slightest abatement anywhere in sight. Manufacturers have proved themselves fully equal to the enormous demand for an ever increasing supply of new designs, and popular interest has been readily sustained." Others took the postcard collecting mania more lightly. *American Magazine* commented in early 1906:

Postal carditis and allied collecting manias are working havoc among the inhabitants of the United States. The germs of these maladies, brought to this country in the baggage of tourists and immigrants, escaped quarantine regulations, and were propagated with amazing rapidity. . . . By far the worst development of the prevailing pests is postal carditis, which affects the heart, paralyzes the reasoning faculties, and abnormally increases the nerve.

By this time, postcards had become a common fixture in popular culture. In 1913, for example, New York prison officials discovered that heavily embossed cards were convenient vehicles for smuggling drugs to inmates. In 1915, a New Jersey court upheld a will written on a postcard, and art schools assigned postcard designs to their students.

In 1906, the trade publication *Post Card Journal* reported that more than 770 million postcards were mailed in the United States, fewer than in Germany but more than in Great Britain. On a single day during the Christmas season, the St. Louis post office reportedly handled 750,000 postcards, weighing a total of 2.5 tons.

By that time, postcard collecting clubs had been organized. Some, like the Post Card Union of America, published their own cards for members, while others, like the Globe Souvenir Card Exchange, facilitated the trading of cards among its members. Postcard manufacturers recognized the popularity of the hobby and produced elaborate albums designed specifically to hold postcards. Other firms sold frames, wire racks, or wooden cabinets to display or store postcards.

Although domestic production (and sales) of postcards was given a major boost by the protective Payne-Aldrich Tariff of 1909, which placed a sizable customs duty on imported cards, the golden era of the postcard was short-lived. In 1912, the retail giant F. W. Woolworth began selling cards at ten cents a dozen, sharply undercutting the market, and the following year, the folded greeting card and envelope were introduced, offering a more private means of correspondence at very little extra cost. These events forced many independent postcard manufacturers out of business and depressed the hobby as well.

One important aspect of the postcard business during its golden era was the interest in "real photo" postcards. After the government introduced rural free delivery in the 1890s, which provided home mail delivery to millions of rural and small-town residents who previously had been obliged to pick up their mail at a post office, the volume of correspondence from rural areas significantly increased, and the economical postcard became a principal means of keeping in touch with friends and relatives. In 1902, Eastman Kodak, recognizing the appeal of picture postcards, began manufacturing photographic paper in postcard size. This enabled families to exchange pictures of one another through the mail, and professional photographers were quick to add this service to their business. Other technological improvements in printing papers made it possible for amateurs to process their own photographs, and a cottage industry in making picture postcards with photographs soon blossomed. Kodak encouraged this by selling cameras and processing equipment to card makers. Photographers who could make a photographic postcard while the customer waited were often found at tourist sites, in small towns, or on the road as itinerant entrepreneurs.

The photographic (or real photo) postcard business reached its greatest level of popularity after 1907, when postal regulations were changed to allow the writing of messages on the back, or address, side of a postcard. This freed the front of the card for a picture unmarred by a written message. The era of the real photo postcard had passed by the early 1920s, when people could just as easily slip photographs into a greeting card, seal the envelope, and send it away.

Although the golden era of postcards had run its course by World War I, postcards continued to find ample use among Americans who wanted a quick method of writing to friends and relatives and to show them where they were. Since World War I, postcard manufacturing has evolved through several stages as printing technology has improved. In the 1920s and 1930s, multicolored postcards with white borders (in which a caption could be printed) dominated the market. By the late 1930s, these postcards were being supplanted by "linen" postcards, so-called because the card stock on which they were printed had a textured surface resembling linen cloth. In the early 1950s, further advances in color photographic processing allowed the manufacture of "chrome" postcards, with a photolike image on glossy stock that had a shiny finish like the chrome on automobiles of that era. Around 1970, the common size of postcards was increased from 3.5 by 5.5 inches to 4 by 6 inches, although the "chrome" appearance of the image remained the same. For collectors, each generation of postcards has special interests, and for the investor, values generally decline with each newer type of card.

As with stamp and coin collecting, postcard collecting demands specialization, and early on, virtually every collector decides that he or she is interested only in certain kinds of postcards. In the most general sense, postcards are divided into two categories—"greetings" and "scenes"—with hundreds of subcategories within each.

Greeting postcards, particularly popular in the pre–World War I era before they were replaced by greeting cards sent in envelopes, were used to wish relatives or friends a Merry Christmas, Happy Birthday, or for any other special day or were simply reminders of friendship or love in sentimental or humorous ways. Many greeting postcards were designed (and signed) by prominent artists and illustrators of the day and command a special premium on the market, while others are coveted for their embossing, use of anthropomorphic animals, or clever designs and use of color.

Postcards portraying scenes attract the collector who is interested in what his or her hometown looked like in earlier times or who is fascinated by certain topics that show up on postcards, such as skyscrapers, trains, nudes, or prisons, for example. Postcards, both then and now, have been closely associated with the tourist industry, and cards showing views of world's fairs, beaches and golf courses, ocean liners, and national parks are all popular with collectors.

For the more serious collector, postcards of scenes can be a visual lesson in political and social history. Robert Rydell has written an article showing how certain postcards produced for early world's fairs reinforced the notion of Anglo-Saxon racial superiority that was commonly held at the time. In a similar vein, many early-twentieth-century postcards portrayed African Americans in stereotypical ways, such as eating watermelon or being terrorized by alligators. Postcards of pre-1920 cityscapes give insight into commercial architecture and urban development, while many postcards produced during both world wars have an overtly patriotic flair. One need not be a postcard collector to take advantage of the historical value of postcards.

Compared with stamps and coins, postcards have a much less defined and more fluid market. While there are many published pricing guides, there are no large national postcard organizations to lend an air of authority to any of them. The value of any particular postcard may vary greatly from one part of the country to another, at least partly because of the interest in collecting postcards from one's own area, which drives up the price of local cards in that area. As a consequence, the buying and selling of relatively common postcards often have much more of a flea market ambience, with the give-and-take of bargaining often a central element in the transaction. For truly scarce postcards, however, there are auction houses specializing in their sale, and past realizations often prove a good guide to present market values.

REFERENCE WORKS

As already stated, the principal concerns of this chapter are the collecting of stamps, coins, and postcards as both aesthetic objects and social icons and the collecting of these objects as a phenomenon in and of itself. A remarkably large body of philatelic and numismatic literature exists, but little of it deals with these issues. Most published material addresses specialized audiences for the purposes of identifying, cataloging, and pricing collector's items. Although brief histories of collecting can be found in beginner's guides, and some good aesthetic and social interpretations have been published, primarily in philatelic and numismatic periodicals, much remains for the cultural historian to pull together and assess. The following is a selection of the general and more specialized reference works used by philatelists, numismatists, and deltiologists in their own fields that are likely to be useful for the student of popular culture or cultural history.

Stamps

At the moment no complete bibliography of American philatelic literature exists, and, despite valiant efforts among philatelic librarians and bibliographers, no thorough compilation is likely to be published soon. Specialized or incomplete bibliographies do exist; however, they are hard to find. William R. Ricketts, *The Philatelic Literature Bibliography Index* (1912) is typical: a privately mimeographed author-and-subject index of international material from 1863 to 1912, complete only up to the letter K. A more useful resource is Richard H. Rosichan, *Stamps and Coins* (1974), which includes detailed annotations for many of its 500 philatelic entries. While Rosichan seems to be an astute bibliographer, his selection is limited to works published primarily since 1959. Important early scholastic works are included only if they are still in print. Although international in scope, American works are emphasized, but there are glaring omissions (nothing, for instance, by Max Johl or August Dietz). Lists of current periodicals and libraries are incomplete. Rosichan's book is geared toward the hobbyist, but the scholar beginning to study philately should consult this resource.

One attempt to give some sense of order to bibliographic problems in philately is John B. Kaiser, "Bibliography: The Basis of Philatelic Research" (1953), which lists bibliographies, catalogs, and periodical indexes and is a good starting place for the researcher. Kaiser's "conspectus" of cumulative periodical indexes, for instance, is a simple, but useful, tool arranging a dozen periodical guides chronologically by coverage dates so that researchers can more readily locate indexes to journals of a particular era.

Published catalogs of philatelic libraries are the best substitutes for bibliographies, but they, too, are hard to find. John K. Tiffany, *The Philatelical Library: A Catalogue of Stamp Publications* (1874) is an excellent reference to nineteenth-century material by one of America's first collectors. The catalog lists 569 books and periodicals, nearly as many price lists and stamp catalogs, and 272 items on collecting and postal history. Catalogs of significant American collections of philatelic literature include *The Catalogue of the Philatelic Library of the Collectors Club* (1917) and *Postage Stamps: A Selective Checklist of Books on Philately in the Library of Congress* (1940). The latter volume includes a prose paean to philately by poet-librarian Archibald MacLeish as well as a fine list of nineteenth-century handbooks, guides, and scholastic works. Lamentably, the Library of Congress has not updated this catalog, even though its collection (now located in the National Postal Museum) has grown since 1940 to be the best in the nation. On par with the Collectors Club and Smithsonian collections is the American Philatelic Research Library (APRL), with its collection of nearly 18,000 books and periodicals.

Over the past two decades, significant bibliographic research has been carried on in the pages of the *Philatelic Literature Review*. As the journal for the American Philatelic Research Library, this quarterly supplements Kaiser's work by publishing indexes to philatelic periodicals. The *Philatelic Literature Review* also notes about fifty new philatelic publications per issue. The definitive list of nineteenth- and twentieth-century stamp journals with title, publisher, and dates of publication is Chester Smith, *American Philatelic Periodicals* (1978). A remarkable analysis of philatelic periodical literature in the United States is George T. Turner, "Trends in United States Philatelic Literature" (1974). Turner (whose massive philatelic library is now a part of the Smithsonian's collection) provides extensive quantitative analysis of periodical output from 1860 to 1945. The study, of course, needs significant updating, but it should provide a model for similar studies of trends in other forms of philatelic literature such as beginner's guides to the hobby.

A sign of the growing importance of philatelic literature to collectors is that many guides to the hobby include selected bibliographies, some of which can be useful to the researcher if the more complete bibliographies are not available. An exhaustive and convenient guide to the present state of the hobby is *Linn's World Stamp Almanac*, put out periodically (but not since 1990) by the publishers of America's principal philatelic trade weekly, *Linn's Stamp News*. This fact book includes an extensive (though poorly constructed) philatelic bibliography and a useful list of over 200 current periodicals. Also in the almanac are histories of the U.S. Postal Service and the Bureau of Engraving and Printing, descriptions of important research collections, and sections on how to get a stamp design accepted by the Citizen's Stamp Advisory Committee and how to start a collection or a stamp club. Linn's also publishes on an annual basis its *U.S. Stamp Yearbook*. This book includes a very detailed account of the U.S. stamps issued in the past year, with their design history, printing and plate details, and information about any varieties that may have surfaced in the market. It is indispensable for any collector wanting to know about the recent issues of the U.S. Postal Service.

Other reference works take the form of dictionaries or encyclopedias. Prominent philatelist Henry M. Konwiser, for instance, provides sometimes quirky, but always reliable, entries on stamp vocabulary and U.S. postal history in *The American Stamp Collector's Dictionary* (1949). Less ambitious but still useful is R. J. Sutton and K. W. Anthony, *The Stamp Collector's Encyclopedia* (1973). Another excellent philatelic dictionary is Douglas Patrick and Mary Patrick, *The Musson Stamp Dictionary* (1972), which includes not only philatelic terms but also short biographies of prominent collectors of the past and geographical identifications of obscure stamp-issuing places.

The student of stamps and collecting necessarily requires some acquaintance with postal history. Alvin Harlow, *Old Post Bags: The Story of the Sending of a Letter in Ancient and Modern Times* (1928) is dated but reliable. More recent is Wayne E. Fuller, *The American Mail: Enlarger of the Common Life* (1972), an excellent history of the people's conception of the post office, with an extensive bibliographical essay. For those interested in the Civil War era, August Dietz, *The Postal Service of the Confederate States of America* (1929) is the definitive work. Carl H. Scheele, A *Short History of the Mail Service* (1970) is a readable introduction to U.S. postal history in the context of Old World systems.

Given the limited circulation of philatelic literature, most publications are as rare as the stamps that they describe. Yet most libraries have at least one of the stamp catalogs put out each year by the publishing firm of Scott. *Scott's Specialized Catalogue of United States Stamps* is the most extensive. Its numbering systems for stamp types and individual stamps are almost universally accepted. Front matter includes information for collectors (explaining printing process and postal history) and an "Identifier of Definitive Issues." A black-and-white photo enlargement of each stamp is complemented by details concerning design source, designer, engraver, printer, and date of issue. Useful in gauging the relative scarcity of a stamp is the chart of quantities of the commemorative stamps issued. Also included are enlargements of revenue, local, and Confederate stamps. Although "unofficial," these stamps may in fact provide icons more suggestive of American life than official issues.

Several government publications are helpful. The U.S. Postal Service, *Stamps and Stories*, formerly known as *The Postal Service Guide to U.S. Stamps* and updated annually, does not deal with anomalies or variants but does provide good color photographs of each stamp type and a verbal description of its dimensions and printing history. End matter includes lists of souvenir pages, commemorative panels, and souvenir cards, all of which are collateral products of the Postal Service. *The United States Official Postal Guide*, also issued annually, is an important storehouse of stamp issues, lists of post offices, and postal regulations.

The general collector can benefit from any of a number of books and periodicals dealing with philately. Perhaps the most thorough introduction to the hobby is the authoritative *Fundamentals of Philately* (1971), by L. N. and M. Williams, a publication of the American Philatelic Society. This long and detailed book contains chapters on all the technical aspects of stamp production, including paper, watermarks, printing processes, gum, inks and color, and perforations. For those who are not quite ready to dive that deeply into philatelic research, a number of shorter introductions to the hobby are available. Ernest A. Kehr, *The Romance of Stamp Collecting* (1947) is an older work that presents information about sensible investment strategy and chatty information about Franklin D. Roosevelt's collection. Kehr also includes a section on "philatelettes," or prominent women in the hobby. More to the point is Herman Herst Jr., *Fun and Profit in Stamp Collecting* (1975). Herst, a longtime dealer and raconteur in the hobby, has also written autobiographical accounts: *Nassau Street* (1988) and *More Stories to Collect Stamps By* (1982).

Book-length and monographic studies by philatelists fall into four categories: general histories of the U.S. issues; specialized studies of stamp essays, types, and variants; topical studies; and works on nonstamp philately. Perhaps the most useful general histories are Lester G. Brookman, *Nineteenth Century Postage Stamps of the United States*, 2 vols. (1947) and the five-volume *United States Stamps of the Twentieth Century* (1938) by Max Johl and Beverly S. King. Supplementing the latter is Sol Glass, *United States Postage Stamps, 1945–52* (1954). Each work contains illustrations and data on the printing histories of each stamp. Superb design and printing histories of commemoratives alone are Johl's two-volume *United States Commemoratives of the Twentieth Century* (1947) and G. C. Hahn's treatment of an important set of stamps in *United States Famous American Series of 1940* (1950). For those who want to go back to the beginning of stamps, consult Eleanor C. Smyth, *Sir Rowland Hill: The Story of a Great Reform* (1907) and A. D. Smith, *The Development of Rates of Postage* (1918).

To understand the utility of the following specialized studies, the reader may require an explanation of stamp production. The final stamp design of a particular issue is chosen from various engraved trial entries submitted by individual engravers. The rejected samples are called "essays," and in many cases they are completely different in design from the final chosen entry. Thus, fascinating evidence of what officials could have chosen as our postal icons appears in such works as Clarence Brazer, *Essays for United States Adhesive Postage Stamps* (1941) and George T. Turner, *Essays and Proofs of United States Internal Revenue Stamps* (1974). The National Postal Museum also possesses in its vault a fine collection of stamp essays. Once a stamp goes to press, various plates, inks, and papers may be used before the run is complete. "Traditional" philatelic research has delineated the types and variants of many definitive U.S. issues. The specificity of this research will not likely aid the cultural historian. However, the art historian may find value in such landmark texts as Stanley B. Ashbrook, *The Types and Plates of the United States One-cent Stamp of 1851–57* (1938) and *The United States Ten-cent Stamp of 1855–57* (1936).

Works on "topicals" dating as far back as 1910 may be most useful to the cultural historian. The American Topical Association's bimonthly *Topical Times* is a good introduction to the various facets of this "subhobby." Social, cultural, or popular historians interested in such topics as women, minorities, Americana, art, and artists or such less "traditional" topics as games, toys, and sports might consult the appropriate topic handbooks published each year. ATA study units also publish their own journals ranging from *Biblical Philately* and *Biophilately* to everyone's favorite, *Let's Talk Parachutes*. (Do not assume that your specialized field has not been made a stamp topic.) Relevant to the nineteenth-century specialists is the *1869 Times*, focusing entirely on the important "pictorial" series of 1869. Journals dealing with airmails may provide insights into various conceptions of the history of flight; two such periodicals are the bimonthly *Aero Philatelist Annals* and the monthly *Airpost Journal*, both edited by the American Airmail Society.

Nonstamp philatelic material such as illustrated covers, postcards, postmarks, slogan cancellations, and forged or counterfeit stamps may serve as useful evidence for the student of popular culture. Covers come in various forms, official and unofficial, and sometimes decorated with elaborate vignettes (called cachets). There are many guides and catalogs for "first-day" covers, canceled on the first day a stamp was issued, but the multivolume works by Planty and Mellone are the most thorough for the issues of the 1930s through the 1950s. *Thorp-Bartel's Catalogue of the Stamped Envelopes and Wrappers of the United States* (1954), edited by Prescott H. Thorp, is a thorough analysis and pricing of postal stationery. The important illustrated catalogs of Civil War postal covers are Robert Laurence, *The George Walcott Collection of Used Civil War Patriotic Covers* (1934) and Robert W. Grant's continually updated, loose-leaf *Handbook of Civil War Patriotic Envelopes and Postal History*. An important early study of U.S. postmarks is Delf Norona's recently reprinted *Cyclopedia of United States Postmarks and Postal History* (1975). The subcategory of "fancy" cancellations, or a postmaster's individualized post-marks, is treated by Michel Zareski and Herman Herst Jr., in *Fancy Cancellations on 19th Century United States Postage Stamps* (1963). For expositon-related cancellations, see William J. Bomar, *Postal Markings of United States Expositions* (1986). Lists of postal clichés can be found in Moe Luff, *United States Postal Slogan Cancel Catalogue* (1975) and in the Smithsonian's Philatelic Collection.

From shortly after the first stamp was issued in 1840, clever forgers and counterfeiters have been active plying their skills on stamps, and prudent collectors must be aware that many faked stamps may be found in the marketplace. A classic work designed to help collectors identify forged stamps is R. D. Earee, *Album Weeds: How to Detect Forged Stamps* (1906). Collectors who want to make certain that their stamps are genuine may submit them to "expertizing" services offered by the American Philatelic Society or the Philatelic Foundation; a book explaining how that process is carried out is Elizabeth C. Pope, *Opinions IV: Philatelic Expertizing* (1987).

Coins

In recent decades, philatelic scholarship has expanded both in size and scope, but given the age and scholastic roots of numismatics, it is no surprise that the body of numismatic literature is still larger, better indexed, and broader in intellectual range than philatelic literature, as the excellent state of numismatic bibliography indicates. The chief work in the field is Elvira E. Clain-Stefanelli's impressive volume *Select Numismatic Bibliography* (1965). Although not "exhaustive," it is by far the researcher's best starting point. It places special emphasis on standard references and other important publications since 1885, as well as "the still used classical works of the past 200 years." Giving particular attention throughout to American references, the author's compilation lists guides, collection and exhibition catalogs, biographies of numismatists, and periodicals. Special sections such as "Art on Coinage" are also useful. Richard H. Rosichan's focus on post-1959 material in *Stamps and Coins* (1974) makes his annotated bibliography (discussed earlier in this section) of nearly 1,100 items a good supplement to Clain-Stefanelli. For an important nineteenth-century American bibliography, see Emmanuel J. Attinelli, *Numisgraphics, or a List of Catalogues, Price Lists and Various Publications of More or Less Interest to Numismatologists* (1876).

Since 1947, the American Numismatic Society has published *Numismatic Literature*, an excellent annotated listing of numismatic periodical literature appearing in nearly all scholarly journals and many non-numismatic publications. *The Numismatist*, published by the American Numismatic Association, is a felicitous blend of scholarship and trade news. Its author-subject indexes (1939 and 1959) will lead the researcher to important material on iconography, portraiture, coin design, medals, tokens, and the growth of the hobby.

As with philatelic literature, catalogs of numismatic literature are of vital importance. The American Numismatic Society's seven-volume *Dictionary Catalogue of the Library of the American Numismatic Society* reprints the card catalog for that society's excellent library. Included here are books, all periodicals since 1930, price list, unpublished manuscripts, and auction catalogs. Also available is the *Library Catalogue of the American Numismatic Association*. Of interest to nineteenth-century researchers is the *Catalogue of the Numismatic Books in the Library of the American Numismatic and Archaeological Society*.

A convenient introduction to the hobby and its present state is *Coin World Almanac*. Put out by the people who publish *Linn's World Stamp Almanac*, this publication includes articles on the year's numismatic news, numismatic law, and histories of gold, silver, and U.S. coins. Also found here are lists of designers, engravers, and portraits on coins and paper money. (Did you know that Martha Washington graced our one-dollar bill from 1886 to 1891?) Nearly half the book provides facts and analysis of market trends in gold and silver trading. *Cowles' Complete Encyclopedia of United States Coins* (1969), written and illustrated by *Coin World* columnist Mort Reed, is an enjoyable and well-researched introduction to American coins, their iconography, and minting process. Also useful is Richard G. Duty's *The Macmillan Encyclopedic Dictionary of Numismatics* (1982). Two fairly learned, adult-level guidebooks to the hobby and science are Philip Grierson, *Numismatics* (1975) and Norman M. Davis, *The Complete Book of United States Coin Collecting* (1976). Finally, two numismatic word books are Albert Frey, *Dictionary of Numismatic Names* (1975) and Mark Salton, *Glossary of Numismatic Terms* (1947). For a survey of monetary history that may be necessary before embarking upon any numismatic study, one can turn to Arthur Nussbaum, *A History of the Dollar* (1957), an authoritative study with a bibliography.

Standard pricing catalogs are generally the most convenient means that a researcher has to view coins. The most widely used is Richard S. Yeoman, *Guidebook of United States Coins*. Referred to as the "Red Book," this annual price list offers a brief introduction to American coinage and color photographs of colonial and official U.S. coin types. Don Taxay, *Comprehensive Catalogue and Encyclopedia of United States Coins* (1971), lists proofs and variants as well as their locations in various collections. Abe Kosoff, *An Illustrated History of United States Coins* (1962) gives glimpses of proposed coin designs as well as illustrations of definitive issues. Robert Friedberg, *Paper Money of the United States* (1972) is a good collector's guide illustrating all U.S. issues. Grover Criswell and Clarence Criswell, *Confederate and Southern States Currency* (1961) is the definitive, illustrated catalog in the field of southern numismatics. Studies acquainting the researcher with the facts of America's official and unofficial currency are found in general histories of our coinage and works on such specialized topics as commemoratives, essays, paper money, fractional currency, medals, and tokens. A well-researched assessment of the U.S. Mint and America's definitive issues is Don Taxay, *The United States Mint and Coinage: An Illustrated History from 1776 to the Present* (1966). J. Earl Massey, *America's Money: The Story of Coins and Currency* (1968) relates coinage to American history in general. Brief histories by established numismatists can be found in Theodore V. Buttrey Jr., editor, *Coinage of the Americas* (1973), which includes articles on "Colonial Coinages" by Eric P. Newman and "Coinage of the US" by Walter Breen. An excellent history (with bibliography) is Don Taxay, *Money of the American Indian and Other Primitive Currencies of the Americas* (1970). Other histories with a narrower focus are Neil Carothers, *Fractional Money: A History of the Small Coins and Fractional Paper Currency of the United States* (1967), William H. Griffiths, *The Story of the American Bank Note Company* (1959), and the U.S. Government Printing Office, *History of the Bureau of Engraving and Printing (1862–1962)* (1962).

General studies of America's commemorative coinage are of particular interest to cultural historians. Don Taxay, *An Illustrated History of United States Commemorative Coins* (1967) is the definitive work. Focusing more on topics depicted on coins is Warren A. Ruby, *Commemorative Coins of the United States* (1961). Not to be discounted is Arlie Slaubaugh, *United States Commemorative Coins: The Drama of America as Told by Our Coins* (1975). Despite the didactic subtitle, this study of America's 157 commemorative varieties provides important historical background as well as design and engraving information on each coin.

The numismatic counterpart of the stamp "essay" is the "pattern." Specialized studies of coins in this state are crucial in understanding the evolution of American coin iconography. They are Edgar H. Adams and William H. Woodin, *United States Patterns, Trial and Experimental Pieces* (1913), and J. Hewitt Judd and Walter Breen, *United States Patterns, Experimental, and Trial Pieces* (1962), both of which are fully illustrated.

A number of works designed to meet the needs of specialized collectors may also interest the historian of popular art. These include Roger S. Cohen and others, *American Half Cents, the "Little Half Sisters": A Reference Book on the United States Half Cent Coined from 1793 to 1857* (1971); William H. Sheldon and others, *Penny Whimsey* (1958); Martin Luther Beistle, *A Register of Half Dollar Varieties and Sub-Varieties* (1964); and Leroy C. Van Allen and A. George Mallis, *Guide to Morgan and Peace Dollars: A Complete Guide and Reference Book on United States Silver Dollars* (1971).

Also of interest to the cultural historian and aesthetician are the icons and designs found on America's "unofficial" currency: banknotes, fractional currency, and scrip. Monographic studies on banknotes by John A. Muscalus provide a wealth of material: *Index of State Bank Notes That Illustrate Characters and Events* (1938), *Index of State Bank Notes That Illustrate Washington and Franklin* (1939), *Index of State Bank Notes That Illustrate Presidents* (1939), *Famous Paintings Reproduced on Paper Money of State Banks, 1800–1866* (1938), and *The Views of Towns, Cities, Falls, and Buildings Illustrated on 1800–1866 Bank Paper Money* (1939). Matt Rothert, *A Guidebook of United States Fractional Currency* (1963) is well illustrated and has a good bibliography. For views of what happens to currency when times get tough, see Lyman H. Low, *Hard Times Tokens* (1955) and Charles V. Kappen and Ralph A. Mitchell, *Depression Scrip of the United States* (1961).

Just as philately has expanded to include the collection of nonstamp material, numismatics has, for over a century, embraced the medallic arts. Indeed, the design, iconography, and striking of American medals are as important to the scholar as coins themselves. General surveys of the field include Charles W. Betts, *American Colonial History Illustrated by Contemporary Medals* (1972); Joseph F. Loubat, *The Medallic History of the United States of America, 1776–1876* (1967); Clifford Mishler, *United States and Canadian Commemorative Medals and Tokens* (1959); and Georgia S. Chamberlain, *American Medals and Medalists* (1963). An indispensable resource is Leonard Forrer, *Biographical Dictionary of Medalists* (1971). See also Richard D. Kenney, *Early American Medalists and Die-Sinkers* (1954). Studies of special types of medals include Gilbert Grosvenor and others, *Insignia and Decorations of the United States Armed Forces* (1944), Evans E. Kerrigan, *American War Medals and Decorations* (1964), and Jennings Hood and Charles J. Young, *American Orders and Societies and Their Decorations* (1917). An important branch of American numismatics and one of special interest to American scholars in general is the Indian peace medals. A study of Britain's medals is Melvill Allan Jamieson, *Medals Awarded to North American Indian Chiefs, 1714–1922* (1961). U.S. government medals given to Indians are described and illustrated in a well-researched volume, Bauman L. Belden, *Indian Peace Medals Issued in the United States, 1789–1889* (1966). Studies of medals struck in honor of individuals or groups include the following: Elston G. Bradfield, "Benjamin Franklin: A Numismatic Summary" (1956), William S. Baker, *Medallic Portraits of Washington* (1965), and Edward C. Rochette, *The Medallic Portraits of John F. Kennedy: A Study of Kennediana* (1966).

Postcards

A revealing area of study for the cultural historian is the illustrated postcard, which dates back to the latter half of the nineteenth century. The best general history of early postcards and postcard collecting is Dorothy B. Ryan, *Picture Postcards in the United States, 1893–1918* (1982). A shorter history of postcards is found in Bernard Stadtmiller, *Postcard Collecting: A Fun Investment* (1973). A thorough and wonderfully illustrated book that focuses on British postcards is Martin Willoughby, *A History of Postcards* (1992) For pioneer cards (those printed before 1898), see Jefferson R. Burdick, *Pioneer Post Cards: The Story of Mailing Cards to 1898* (1964). The history of commercial trade cards, one of the forerunners of picture postcards, is detailed in Robert Jay, *The Trade Card in Nineteenth-Century America* (1987), and "real photo" postcards are discussed at length in Hal Morgan and Andreas Brown, *Prairie Fires and Paper Moons: The American Photographic Postcard, 1900–1920* (1981). Richard Carline, *Pictures in the Post* (1971), attempts to place this phenomenon in "the history of popular art" with engaging essays on various colorful, but generally European, examples. Frank Staff, *The Picture Postcard and Its Origins* (1966) and Marian Klamkin, *Picture Postcards* (1974) are similar offerings, although Klamkin has sections on American cards. John M. Kaduck's illustrated price list of over 1,000 patriotic American postcards, *Patriotic Postcards* (1974), provides the student of popular culture with solid evidence of the way that Americans have viewed their heroes and accomplishments from the Gilded Age on. Klamkin's book discusses both British and American patriotic postcards as well as the history of postcard collecting. Another specialized postcard reference work is Frederic Megson and Mary Megson, *American Exposition Postcards, 1870–1920*

(1992), describing postcards produced by and for world's fairs during the golden age of that cultural phenomenon.

RESEARCH COLLECTIONS

Generally speaking, it is unlikely that even the best university libraries will have extensive holdings in philatelic or numismatic literature. (In fact, major public libraries generally have better collections.) Even rarer are institutions that can make specimens available to the scholar. Researchers who desire more contact than either Scott's stamp catalogs or the Red Book of U.S. coins can provide will seek out the libraries and specimens of strong philatelic or numismatic collections. Although the best are located in the East, useful collections can be found in the Midwest and West.

Stamps

The three best research collections are the National Philatelic Collection, located in the Smithsonian's National Postal Museum in Washington, D.C.; the Collectors Club of New York; and the American Philatelic Research Library in State College, Pennsylvania. Once a part of the Library of Congress, the National Philatelic Collection is both library and archives. It maintains an extensive, but uncataloged, collection of philatelic literature and a massive stamp collection that includes all but one of the American issues and numerous essays. Its photographic collection of over 6,000 prints and slides is indispensable. The collection also maintains a postal history clipping file, statistics, paraphernalia, postmaster correspondence on all commemoratives, and a tape and film library.

The Collectors Club of New York maintains a limited membership of about 1,100 people, but its excellent library is open by appointment to scholars. Its John N. Luff Reference Collection is extensive, and the J. Bruce Chittenden Memorial Library, with 140,000 items, is particularly strong in pre-twentieth-century material, including postmasters' reports. The American Philatelic Research Library is the research wing of the American Philatelic Society. Its holdings include 18,000 books and monographs, 400 periodicals, and 150 catalogs but no stamp specimens.

Other major collections can be found in the B. K. Miller Collection of the New York Library; the Philatelic Foundation, New York; the George Linn Memorial Research Library, Sidney, Ohio, which holds 3,000 volumes and 100 periodicals; and the Western Philatelic Library of the Sunnyvale (California) Public Library, which maintains a collection of 2,500 books. Furthermore, the public libraries of Chicago, Cleveland, Los Angeles, Milwaukee, Newark (New Jersey), and Pomona (California) and the free libraries of Philadelphia and Baltimore have considerable holdings.

Specialized collections holding philatelic literature and stamps are also attractive to scholars. The Lincoln Shrine in Redlands, California, has philatelic materials relating to Old Abe. Eisenhower's collection can be found in the Cardinal Spellman Philatelic Museum along with the cardinal's personal collection of stamps and 8,000 volumes of philatelic literature. While most of Franklin D. Roosevelt's collection was sold after his death, philatelic material that was given to him and related materials were placed in the Roosevelt Library and Museum in Hyde Park,

New York. Finally, the Wiltsee Memorial Collection of Western Stamps in the Wells Fargo Bank History Room, San Francisco, houses stamps of 235 different companies, including the Pony Express.

Coins

The two major numismatic organizations maintain fine libraries. The American Numismatic Society (ANS), located near Broadway and West 155 Street in New York, has the smaller membership but a larger output of scholastic publication. Its library of 300,000 items, described earlier, is the nation's best. The American Numismatic Association (ANA), located in Colorado Springs, Colorado, has a much smaller library of 35,000 volumes, but it is likely to meet the needs of most researchers. Both institutions are open to scholars and lend books through inter-library loan.

While both ANS and ANA maintain superb numismatic museums, the best specimen collection continues to be the National Numismatic Collection housed in the Smithsonian's Museum of History and Technology, Washington, D.C. The collection began when the U.S. Mint transferred its collection to the Smithsonian in 1923. Since then and with the help of the ANA and ANS, the collection has grown from about 40,000 to over 150,000 pieces. The Smithsonian, like the ANA and ANS, displays many of its specimens, and visitors to all three collections may view vaulted material upon request. An excellent history and description of the National Collection is Vladimir Clain-Stefanelli's monograph *History of the National Numismatic Collections* (1968). The author's appendixes also provide interesting information for those researching the early growth of American numismatics.

Postcards

Unlike stamps and coins, no national postcard collection exists, nor does any postcard organization maintain a significant research or reference collection. Many university and public libraries and archives do, however, have accumulations of postcards that have been donated to them over the years. The Smithsonian Institution archives, for example, has postcard holdings in a number of different topics, including world's fairs and expositions, as does the Henry Madden Library at California State University at Fresno. Most major urban libraries will have some postcards related to their own location, and these are generally available to the serious researcher.

HISTORY AND CRITICISM

To our knowledge, no book-length work of scholarship on the history of stamp collecting or the cultural significance of American stamps exists. Some scholarly articles have appeared in the past three decades, but, generally speaking, the ideas and controversies related to philately have been limited to popular magazines and journals. Coins present a slightly different picture. Since numismatics is rooted in traditional scholarship, studies of ancient and some modern coins as cultural artifacts can be found. American coins, however, have only recently received proper attention. To a certain extent, then, what can be said for stamps may apply to coins: much study remains to be done.

Stamps

Critical works pertaining to philately may be broken down into three groups: those treating the growth of philately as a hobby or business, those exploring the artistic merit of stamps themselves, and those concerning stamps as social icons. It is with the latter issue that we will discuss what we consider to be this chapter's major problem: whether the postage stamp can serve as a reliable cultural indicator.

The scores of philatelic guides and memoirs of prominent collectors constitute a major resource of primary material for the student hoping to trace the development of collecting. Frederick Booty, *Stamp Collector's Guide* (1862) is probably the first philatelic handbook. Like Bellars, *Standard Guide* (1864), already mentioned, it is nothing more than an introduction to the hobby and a price list. Today, the beginner's guide has dispensed with the price list and become a form of "companion literature" that speculates on why people collect; explains modes of collecting, hobby technique, investment, and clubs; relates hobby lore; and lists philatelic literature and terminology. Philatelic glossaries, which include such locutions as "aerophilately" and "stampic," seem designed to pique the interest of sociolinguists on the trail of the deep structure of hobby language.

Themes in stamp guides often reflect the anxieties of a predominantly male leisure class. Early artifacts, for instance, adopt an apologetic tone that strongly argues that the hobby is not idle play but that it engenders care, method, and neatness. As late as the 1930s noted philatelist Ellis P. Butler in *The Young Stamp Collector's Own Book* (1933) felt compelled to remind his young, obviously male readership that collecting is a "form of play" that encompasses adventure, exploration, and hunting and that it is emphatically not a "sissy" pastime. The fear that philately is childish or sissified is frequently countered in such guides as Henry M. Ellis, *Stamps for Fun and Profit* (1953), and Joseph E. Granville, *Everybody's Guide to Stamp Investment* (1952), by the notion that stamps stimulate the manly endeavor of finance. Why philately still seems to be a predominantly male mode of collecting is a problem that may lead the feminist critic to fruitful speculations.

Popular magazines in nearly every decade have promoted the ideas that stamps are both educational and lucrative. Philately has been seen as an aid to teachers of geography, history, language, and literature. *Parents Magazine* argued that a child's "early collecting instinct should be encouraged." *School Life* stated that postage stamps can "stimulate patriotism." The *Journal of Educational Method* instructed us on how to make a "stamp map." Since the 1920s, articles gauging philately's investment potential have appeared in such periodicals as *Business Week*, the *Economist*, *Nation's Business*, *Newsweek*, *Popular Mechanics*, and *Time*. Other nonphilatelic periodicals that have published articles measuring the pulse of the hobby are *Hobbies*, *Popular Science*, *Profitable Hobbies*, *St. Nicholas*, and *Scientific American*.

Of course, the best resource for recent hobby developments is the trade weekly. *Linn's Stamp News* is the largest. *The Stamp Collector*, *Global Stamp News*, and *Mekeel's Weekly Stamp News* are also newspapers of considerable interest, while *The Stamp Wholesaler* focuses on the dealer's side of the counter. Deeper speculations and more arcane scholarship can be found in the hobby journals. Widely distributed is the *American Philatelist*, the monthly journal of the American Philatelic Society. Indexed every December, it is an attractive amalgam of trade notes, book reviews, committee reports, news of current stamp issues, specialized departments on taxes and other collecting problems, and a good deal of scholarship on U.S. and foreign stamp variants and the cultural history of stamps. Among other specialized journals are the *United States Specialist*, put out by the Bureau Issues Association, which focuses on issues produced by the Bureau of Engraving and Printing; the *American Revenuer*, published by the American Revenue Association; and *La Posta*, a journal devoted to postal history. These and the *Essay Proof Journal* are likely to offer the cultural historian important material on U.S. postal history and iconography.

A recurring issue in many hobby publications is why people collect in the first place. Do we collect in order to touch the past and thereby escape the present, thus making collecting a form of nostalgia? Do we collect in order to classify, to take a slice of a proliferating world, organize it, and create on our own a silent moment of order? Do we collect because we want to know the world, or because we enjoy pretty things? Do we collect, quite simply, because the things, pretty or not, are there in sufficient variety and quantity and are begging to be collected?

What have the psychologists to say of the collecting mania? One philatelist speculates that Freud might categorize the impulse to collect as "repressed imperialism." Lamentably, we have not been able to find any writings by Freud or his immediate brethren substantiating this speculation. However, a recent work by psychiatrist Werner Muensterberger, *Collecting: An Unruly Passion* (1994), sheds some light on the psychology of collecting in general. Muensterberger asks why people collect and why some collectors become obsessed with collecting. In his study, he interviewed many collectors (principally of art or antiques; his book does not deal specifically with stamp, coin, or postcard collecting) and learned that the inital impulse to collect was often a response to a frustration, and the acquisition of a collectible object works as both a palliative and a stimulant. To acquire a desired object provides a sense of self-worth to the collector and reduces his or her sense of self-doubt. In many cases, the collector's experience dates back to a frightening or painful childhood experience that was eased by the acquisition of a doll or some other comforting object. This established a pattern that continued into adulthood, when the acquisition of objects continues to provide a sense of self-assertion and personal triumph. In 1975, a group of psychologists led by R. T. Walls took a less psychoanalytic approach. They studied children's collection preferences and found that, when given a choice of collecting a prescribed set of objects or collecting several copies of one member of that set, children of ages four and ten overwhelmingly prefer to fill out a set. At best, this evidence may explain the popularity of topical over traditional stamp collecting. It may also prove the infantilism of collecting.

Clearly, the psychological aspects of collecting require more systematic study. For the time being the student of the phenomenon must be satisfied with the thin speculations of magazine writers. According to *Literary Digest*, for instance, the parameters of the impulse to collect range "from relaxation to big business." Trimming those limits neatly are F. Neilson, who calls for a "cultural avocation" in the nation, and A. Repplier, who discusses the "pleasure of possession."

Deeper speculations came from a group of magazine writers in the 1930s who explored what might be called the myth of nostalgia in collecting. For Y. Y. of *The New Statesman and Nation* (1924), philately signaled a return to childhood. In one Wordsworthian recollection, "Grand Passion," he discusses his childhood stamp collection and the loss of innocence inherent in the recent development of philately into a science. Even more sentimental is Guy Boas' belletristic piece, "The Mysterious Hobby of Stamp Collecting" (1939), which argues that stamps, "like poetry, are a link with salvation."

For every escapist there is a cynic, and for every enthusiast a naysayer. Dissenting opinions on the psychic needs and relevance of collecting come from Thomas H. Uzzell, whose "Postage Stamp Psychosis" (1935) lightly satirizes philatelists. Far from being an escape, stamp collecting, he says, is only a metaphor for the complexity of modern living. Indeed, "the real trouble with this country is its stamp collectors," because, for lack of anything else to do, they have over-examined stamps and found a maddening number of microscopic varieties to collect. Philately does not release us from such modern trends as overspecialization: it adds to them. Perhaps philately's biggest naysayer was the British writer/diplomat Harold Nicolson, who in his "Marginal Comments" (1946) for *Spectator* issues a scathing denunciation of the hobby. To be a philatelist is "to become excited by objects which are totally unworthy of man's unconquerable mind." Nicolson wants a hobby that will make contributions "to useful knowledge."

Presumably, art is the tacit object most worthy of a person's unconquerable mind, and some classify the postage stamp as art and worthy of study for its own sake. Cornelius Vermeule, *Philatelic Art in America: The Aesthetics of United States Postage and Revenue Stamps* (1987) is the most thorough discussion of the topic, while Barbara Moore, *The Art of Postage Stamps* (1979), and Sam Iker, "World's Richest Art Competition" (1978), also remind us that stamps more than ever are an important arena in the field of art and design.

Pursuing the aesthetic potentials of postage stamps, the artist Donald Evans, in *The World of Donald Evans* (1980), has used stamp design motifs to express his comic, somewhat odd vision. Here, it may be said, the stamp becomes art in and of itself. Art historian A. Hyatt Mayor devotes barely a paragraph to the postage stamp in his *Print and People: A Social History of Printed Pictures* (1971), but his characterization of the engraved, mass-produced "miniature print," or stamp, is significant. It "is published in the largest of all editions and exposes a country's taste to global criticism." Notions of taste aside, Mayor clearly sees stamps as a reflection of a nation's culture, and his observation provides us with a simple transition from the problems of the art of collecting and the art of the stamp to a third and yet perhaps most important focus: the problem of the stamp as icon and reliable cultural indicator.

The postage stamp is not only an obvious engine of propaganda but a potential symbol maker. It can sell an idea, and by placing a portrait or object in a perforated frame it can transform that portrait or object into an icon that presumably reflects the sentiments and acceptance of the people. David Scott pursues this idea for European stamps in *European Stamp Design: A Semiotic Approach to Designing Messages* (1995). Scott points out that stamps function mainly as "indexical signs," indicating the nation of origin, but are also important as "iconic" and "symbolic" signs. A stamp's design often shows a particular icon relevant to the country of origin and usually connected with its geography or history. The stamp also invokes symbols in the form of letters, numbers, names, or acronyms into its design. Sometimes, these kinds of symbols also serve as icons, depending on their use within the design. Scott makes the point that a stamp's design is of critical importance because the stamp needs to be instantly recognizable and because the stamp (and its design) is produced by the millions and used over a considerable period of time. To stamp collectors (and probably also to postal employees as well), European countries in particular have been consistent enough in their stamp designs over the years that their stamps have become, in most cases, instantly recognizable. No similar study exists for U.S. stamps, but the casual observer would likely conclude that design consistency has never rated as highly among U.S. stamp designers as it has for designers in many European countries. This is not to say that U.S. stamp designs are without merit. The Postal Service, especially in recent years, has worked hard to make stamps appealing to the public, even going so far as to allow public balloting on stamp designs or subjects. But the critical dilemma is whether these images are forced by the few upon the many or whether the few who issue the stamps are responding genuinely to the pulse of the many. Furthermore, any of a number of extraneous factors may enter into the selection of a stamp design. George Washington provides a good example. It is safe to say that the more than fifty stamps that bear the first president's likeness confirm Washington as an American icon, but in fact not every stamp derives from the man's popularity. Four of five essays submitted for one early Washington stamp bore likenesses of Indians; the fifth, accepted essay was simply better executed than the others. Also, the ninety-cent Washington stamp of 1861 was issued simply because the postmaster general wanted the likeness of the president on a stamp of high value. To be sure, these two examples do not undercut the general acceptance of Washington as an icon, but it is clear that with respect to other less-revered figures the cultural historian must not depend too heavily upon the assumption that whatever appears on a stamp is necessarily an icon. At times, U.S. postal authorities have issued stamps for political or propagandistic purposes. In 1948, a large number of commemorative stamps were issued in the months before the presidential election that year in the hopes that they would generate votes for the incumbent Truman adminsitration from the special interest groups so honored. In 1933, the Franklin Roosevelt administration issued a stamp celebrating the National Recovery Administration (NRA) simply to propagandize that important New Deal agency. The only systematic cultural history of stamps in the academic arena is David C. Skaggs' essay, "The Postage Stamp as Icon," published in Ray B. Browne and Marshall Fishwick, *Icons of America* (1978), and this essay deals only with stamps commemorating the Bicentennial of the American Revolution.

Scholars can and should turn more frequently to the postage stamp as a useful investigative tool. Handled properly, philatelic material can yield new insights into the myths, symbols, and icons that shape and reflect our lives. Comparative philatelic studies of Washington, Franklin, Jefferson, Jackson, and Lincoln seem to be the most obvious scholastic endeavors. The role of women and minorities in stamps is an equally significant problem. A study of philatelic landscapes might add a chapter to the "pastoral myth." But before we proceed with these projects, it is clear that the cultural historian must examine the work of philatelic researchers, learn the fundamentals of how a stamp is produced, determine the relevance of distribution figures, and distinguish between stamp icons and propaganda.

Coins

Numismatic literature, when it is not overly embroiled in gold and silver market trends, generally achieves a higher degree of scholastic merit than its philatelic counterpart. Numismatists have given us many monographic studies that approach coins aesthetically and socially, but to our knowledge academic aestheticians and social historians have not examined the topic. Those embarking upon the field of numismatics would do well to seek models in the works of Walter Breen, Elvira and Vladimir Clain-Stefanelli, Don Taxay, and Cornelius Vermeule.

Important material on the nascent age of the coin-collecting hobby can be found in the *Proceedings* of the Numismatic and Antiquarian Society of Philadelphia (1865–1867, 1877–1936), the American Numismatic and Archaeological Society (1878–1914), and the American Numismatic Society (1908–   ). Other important early periodicals are the *American Journal of Numismatics* (1866–1924) and J. W. Scott's *American Journal of Philately and Coin Advertisers* (1879–1886). An interesting nineteenth-century monograph that sheds light on the hobby's early days is Elizabeth B. Johnston's *A Visit to the Cabinet of the United States Mint at Philadelphia* (1876). These publications are not very accessible, however, and the hobby awaits the researcher who will incorporate them into a modern history of American numismatics.

Since numismatics did not become fully "democratized" until the 1930s, early guidebooks did not, generally speaking, address themselves to juveniles. Since World War II, however, numismatists have learned a great deal from philatelists on how to "push" their hobby, and the more recent guidebooks may be worth analyzing. Rosichan's section on juvenile literature in *Stamps and Coins* (1974) is a suitable starting point in this field. Various popular magazines have, of course, kept abreast of recent events in hobby development. The weekly column on numismatics in the *New York Times* provides excellent and readable analyses of the hobby's current state. Hobby magazines and newsweeklies are a major resource for hobby trends. *Coin World*, a weekly, and *Coins*, a monthly, are both market-oriented publications. *Calcoin News Quarterly Magazine*, the organ for the California State Numismatic Association, includes articles on coin history and biography. Articles on numismatics as a collecting phenomenon as well as trade news may also be found in the *Numismatist*.

Turning to the cultural analysis of numismatics, the best treatments focus on coins as art objects rather than social icons. Traditional numismatic studies of ancient specimens have used coins to clarify or even rectify notions of ancient architecture and portraiture. Aesthetic studies of modern coinage are Carol H. Sutherland, *Art in Coinage: The Aesthetics of Money from Greece to the Present Day* (1956), and Thomas W. Becker, *The Coin Makers* (1969). For decades U.S. coins have been derided for their comparative artlessness. Cornelius C. Vermeule's excellent study, *Numismatic Art in America: Aesthetics of the United States Coinage* (1971), sets out to overcome that prejudice by examining coins in the context of American sculpture. Also of interest is Lynn Glaser's series of articles on "Art in American Coinage" (1962) in the *Numismatic Scrapbook Magazine*.

There is something holy about money that makes coins and paper money better candidates for social icons than stamps. Coins are tokens of social confidence and political power; they last longer and circulate more than stamps. Apparently, their influence goes even deeper. According to William H. Desmonde in *Magic, Myth, and Money* (1962), an anthropological study of coins and coin iconography, money is a part of religious ritual. Also of interest here is Giovanni Gorini's article "Coin as Blazon or Talisman: Paramonetary Function of Money" (1978). As with stamps, though, the iconic power of coins is necessarily lessened when we realize the propagandistic uses of money designs. F. C. Ross in "Numismatic Thoughts" (1941) argues, for instance, that "currencies, from almost the beginning, have been propagandists." Finally, journals that generally publish scholarly works relating to the aesthetic and iconographic aspects of both coins and paper money are the *Numismatist*, *Paper Money* (quarterly for the Society of Paper Money Collectors), and for stamps the *Essay-Proof Journal*.

BIBLIOGRAPHY

Books and Articles

Stamps

Adams, R. M. "Making a Stamp Map." *Journal of Educational Method* 4 (October 1924), 63–69.

Ashbrook, Stanley B. *The Types and Plates of the United States One-cent Stamp of 1851–57.* New York: Lindquist, 1938.

———. *The United States Ten-cent Stamp of 1855–57.* New York: Lindquist, 1936.

Bellars, Henry John. *The Standard Guide to Postage Stamp Collecting.* London: John Camden Hotter, 1864.

Boas, Guy. "The Mysterious Hobby of Stamp Collecting. *Cornhill* 160 (July 1939), 46–64.

Bomar, William J. *Postal Markings of United States Expositions.* North Miami, Fla.: David Phillips, 1986.

Booty, Frederick. *Stamp Collector's Guide.* London: Hamilton, Adams, 1862.

Brazer, Clarence. *Essays for United States Adhesive Postage Stamps.* New York: American Philatelic Society, 1941.

Brookman, Lester G. *Nineteenth Century Postage Stamps of the United States.* 2 vols. New York: Lindquist, 1947.

Butler, Ellis P. *The Young Stamp Collector's Own Book.* Indianapolis: Bobbs-Merrill, 1933.

Catalogue of the Philatelic Library of the Collectors Club. New York: Collectors Club, 1917.

"Collecting: Impulse Ranges from Relaxation to Big Business." *Literary Digest* 123 (February 27, 1937), 30–32.

Collecting: United States. Cambridge, Mass.: Stamps Information, 1972.

Dietz, August. *The Postal Service of the Confederate States of America.* Richmond, Va.: Dietz Press, 1929.

Earee, R. B. *Album Weeds: How to Detect Forged Stamps.* 2 vols. London: Stanley Gibbons, 1906.

Ellis, Henry M. *Stamps for Fun and Profit*. New York: Funk and Wagnalls, 1953.

Evans, Donald. *The World of Donald Evans*. New York: Delacorte Press, 1980.

Fuller, R. T. "Collector's Luck: Early Collecting Instinct Should Be Encouraged." *Parents Magazine* 10 (June 1935), 19.

Fuller, Wayne E. *The American Mail: Enlarger of the Common Life*. Chicago: University of Chicago Press, 1972.

Glass, Sol. *United States Postage Stamps, 1945–52*. West Somerville, Mass.: Bureau Issue Association, 1954.

Grant, Robert W. *The Handbook of Civil War Patriotic Envelopes and Postal History*. Hanover, Mass.: Grant, 1977.

Granville, Joseph E. *Everybody's Guide to Stamp Investment*. New York: Heritage, 1952.

Green, P. D. "Postage Stamp Stampede." *Nation's Business* 32 (July 1944), 40.

Hahn, G. C. *United States Famous American Series of 1940*. State College, Pa.: American Philatelic Research Library, 1950.

Hallgreen, Mauritze. *All about Stamps: Their History and the Art of Collecting Them*. New York: Alfred A. Knopf, 1940.

Harlow, Alvin. *Old Post Bags: The Story of the Sending of a Letter in Ancient and Modern Times*. New York: Holt, 1928.

Herst, Herman. *Fun and Profit in Stamp Collecting*. New York: Duell, Sloan and Pearce, 1962.

———. "The Mistake of Approaching Your Hobby as Speculative Economic Investments." *Hobbies* 71 (August 1966), 99.

———. *More Stories to Collect Stamps By*. Florham Park, N.J.: Washington Press, 1982.

———. *Nassau Street*. Sidney, Ohio: Amos Press, 1988.

Hetisley, W. E. "Increasing Response Rate by Choice of Postage Stamp." *Public Opinion Quarterly*, 38 (Summer 1974), 280–83.

Iker, Sam. "World's Richest Art Competition." *National Wildlife* 17 (December 1978), 40–43.

Johl, Max. *United States Commemoratives of the Twentieth Century*. 2 vols. New York: Lindquist, 1947.

Johl, Max, and Beverly S. King. *United States Stamps of the Twentieth Century*. 5 vols. New York: Lindquist, 1938.

Kaiser, John B. "Bibliography: The Basis of Philatelic Research." In *The Congress Book*. Newark, N.J.: American Philatelic Congress, 1953, 37–54.

Kehr, Ernest A. *The Romance of Stamp Collecting*. New York: Crowell, 1947.

Konwiser, Henry M. *The American Stamp Collector's Dictionary*. New York: Minkus, 1949.

Laurence, Robert. *The George Walcott Collection of Used Civil War Patriotic Covers*. New York: N.Y.R. Laurence, 1934.

Linn's U.S. Stamp Yearbook. Sidney, Ohio: Amos Press, 1999.

Linn's World Stamp Almanac. Sidney, Ohio: Amos Press, 1987.

Luff, Moe. *United States Postal Slogan Cancel Catalogue*. Spring Valley, N.Y.: M. Luff, 1975.

Mayor, A. Hyatt. *Print and People: A Social History of Printed Pictures*. New York: Metropolitan Museum, 1971.

Mellone, Michael. *Mellone's Specialized Cachet Catalog of First Day Covers of the 1940s*. 2 vols. Stewartsville, N.J.: FDC, 1984.

———. *Mellone's Specialized Cachet Catalog of First Day Covers of the 1950s*. 2 vols. Stewartsville, N.J.: FDC, 1983.

Moore, Barbara. *The Art of Postage Stamps*. New York: Walker, 1979.

Muensterberger, Werner. *Collecting: An Unruly Passion*. New York: Harcourt, Brace, 1994.

Neilson, F. "Need for a Cultural Avocation." *American Journal of Economics* 16 (January 1957), 145–49.

New, H. S. "Postage Stamp Promotes Popular Education and Stimulates Patriotism." *School Life* 11 (September 1925), 1–4.

Newgold, Wilbert D. "Hobbies." *Encyclopedia Britannica: Macropaedia*. 15th ed. Chicago: Encyclopedia Britannica, 1978, vol. 8, 937–81.

Nicolson, Harold. "Marginal Comments." *Spectator* 176 (June 21, 1946), 634.

Norona, Delf. *Cyclopedia of United States Postmarks and Postal History*. Lawrence, Mass.: Quarterman, 1975.

Patrick, Douglas, and Mary Patrick, *The Musson Stamp Dictionary*. Toronto: Musson Book Co., 1972.

"Personal Business: Stamp Collecting." *Business Week* (March 3, 1962), 101–2.

"Philatelic Boom." *Newsweek* 22 (November 8, 1943), 64.

Philately of Tomorrow. New York: Philatelic Research Laboratory, 1940.

Planty, Earl. *Planty's Photo Encyclopedia of Cacheted FDCs: The Classic Period, 1923–29*. Stewartsville, N.J.: FDC, 1977.

Pope, Elizabeth C., ed. *Opinions IV: Philatelic Expertizing—An Inside View*. New York Philatelic Foundation, 1987.

Postage Stamps: A Selective Checklist of Books on Philately in the Library of Congress. Washington, D.C.: Library of Congress, 1940.

Postage Stamps of the United States. Washington D.C.: Government Printing Office, 1973.

Repplier, A. "Pleasures of Possession." *Commonweal* 13 (December 17, 1930), 181–88.

Ricketts, William R. *The Philatelic Literature Bibliography Index*. Forty-Fort, Pa.: N.p., 1912.

Rosichan, Richard H. *Stamps and Coins*. Littleton, Colo.: Libraries Unlimited, 1974.

Scheele, Carl H. *A Short History of the Mail Service*. Washington, D.C.: Smithsonian Insitution Press, 1970.

Schnitzel, Paul. "Note on the Philatelic Demand for Postage Stamps." *Southern Economics Journal* 45 (April 1979), 1261–65.

Scott, David. *European Stamp Design: A Semiotic Approach to Designing Messages*. London: Academy Editions, 1995.

Scott's Specialized Catalogue of United States Stamps. Sidney, Ohio: Scott, 1999.

Skaggs, David C. "The Postage Stamp as Icon." In *Icons of America*, ed. Ray B. Browne and Marshall Fishwick. Bowling Green, Ohio: Popular Culture Press, 1978.

Smith, A. D. *The Development of Rates of Postage*. New York: Macmillan, 1918.

Smith, Chester. *American Philatelic Periodicals*. State College, Pa.: American Philatelic Research Library, 1978.

Smyth, Eleanor C. *Sir Rowland Hill: The Story of a Great Reform*. London: T. Fisher Unwin, 1907.

Stoetzer, O. Carlos. *Postage Stamps as Propaganda*. Washington, D.C.: Public Affairs Press, 1953.

Sutton, R. J., and K. W. Anthony. *The Stamp Collector's Encyclopedia*. New York: Arco, 1973.

Thorp, Prescott H., ed. *Thorp-Bartel's Catalogue of the Stamped Envelopes and Wrappers of the United States*. Netcong, N.J.: Thorp, 1954.

Tiffany, John K. *The Philatelical Library: A Catalogue of Stamp Publications*. St. Louis, Mo.: John K. Tiffany, 1874.

Turner, George T. *Essays and Proofs of United States Internal Revenue Stamps*. Arlington, Mass.: Bureau Issues Association, 1974.

Turner, George T. "Trends in United States Philatelic Literature." In *The Congress Book 1945*. Cleveland, Ohio: American Philatelic Congress, 1945, pp. 145–52.

U.S. Postal Service. *Stamps and Stories*. Washington, D.C.: United States Postal Service, 1981– .

U.S. Postal Service. *The United States Official Postal Guide*. Washington, D.C.: U.S. Government Printing Office, 1905– .

Uzzell, Thomas H. "Postage Stamp Psychosis." *Scribners Magazine* 97 (June 1935), 368–70.

Vermeule, Cornelius. *Philatelic Art in America: The Aesthetics of United States Postage and Revenue Stamps*. Weston, Mass.: Cardinal Spellman Philatelic Museum, 1987.

Walls, R. T., et al. "Collection Preferences of Children." *Child Development* 46 (September 1975), 783–85.

Williams, L. N., and Maurice Williams. *Fundamentals of Philately*. State College, Penn.: American Philatelic Society, 1990.

Y. Y. "Grand Passion." *The New Statesman and Nation*, n.s. 24 (September 26, 1942), 204.

Zareski, Michel, and Herman Herst Jr. *Fancy Cancellations on 19th Century United States Postage Stamps*. Shrub Oak, N.Y.: Herst, 1963.

Coins

Adams, Edgar H., and William H. Woodin. *United States Patterns, Trial and Experimental Pieces*. New York: American Numismatic Society, 1913.

American Numismatic Society. *Dictionary Catalogue of the Library of the American Numismatic Society*. New York: Hall, 1972.

Attinelli, Emmanuel J. *Numisgraphics, or a List of Catalogues, Price Lists and Various Publications of More or Less Interest to Numismatologists*. New York: Attinelli, 1876.

Baker, William S. *Medallic Portraits of Washington*. Iola, Wis.: Krause, 1965.

Becker, Thomas W. *The Coin Makers*. Garden City, N.Y.: Doubleday, 1969.

Beistle, Martin Luther. *A Register of Half Dollar Varieties and Sub-Varieties*. Omaha: Beebe's, 1964.

Belden, Bauman L. *Indian Peace Medals Issued in the United States, 1789–1889*. New Milford, Conn.: N. Flayderman, 1966.

Betts, Charles W. *American Colonial History Illustrated by Contemporary Medals.* Lawrence, Mass.: Quarterman, 1972.

Bradfield, Elston G. "Benjamin Franklin: A Numismatic Summary." *Numismatist* 69 (1956), 1347–53.

Buttrey, Theodore V., Jr., ed. *Coinage of the Americas.* New York: American Numismatic Society, 1973.

Carothers, Neil. *Fractional Money: A History of the Small Coins and Fractional Paper Currency of the United States.* New York: Kelley, 1967.

Catalogue of thie Numismatic Books in the Library of the American Numismatic and Archaeological Society. Boston: American Numismatic and Archaeological Society, 1883.

Chamberlain, Georgia S. *American Medals and Medalists.* Annandale, Va.: Turnpike, 1963.

Clain-Stefanelli, Elvira E. *Numismatics—An Ancient Science: A Survey of Its History.* Washington, D.C.: Government Printing Office, 1965.

———. *Select Numismatic Bibliography.* New York: Stacks, 1965.

Clain-Stefanelli, Vladimir. *History of the National Numismatic Collections.* Washington, D.C.: Government Printing Office, 1968.

Cohen, Roger S., et al. *American Half Cents, the "Little Half Sisters": A Reference Book on the United States Half Cent Coined from 1793 to 1857.* Bethesda, Md.: N.p., 1971.

Coin World Almanac. Sidney, Ohio: Amos Press, 1979.

Criswell, Grover, and Clarence Criswell. *Confederate and Southern States Currency.* New York: House of Collectibles, 1961.

Davis, Norman M. *The Complete Book of United States Coin Collecting.* New York: Macmillan, 1976.

Desmonde, William H. *Magic, Myth, and Money.* New York: Free Press, 1962.

Doty, Richard G. *The Macmillan Encyclopedic Dictionary of Numismatics.* New York: Macmillan, 1982

Forrer, Leonard. *Biographical Dictionary of Medalists.* New York: Franklin, 1971.

Franklin and Numismatics. Colorado Springs, Colo.: American Numismatic Association, n.d.

French, Charles. "Changes in Coin Collecting." *Hobbies* 67 (February 1963), 102.

Frey, Albert. *Dictionary of Numismatic Names.* New York: Barnes and Noble, 1947.

Friedberg, Robert. *Paper Money of the United States.* New York: Coin and Currency Institute, 1972.

Glaser, Lynn. "Art in American Coinage." *Numismatic Scrapbook Magazine* (1962), 2462–79, 2792–2800, 3092–3101.

Gorini, Giovanni. "Coin as Blazon or Talisman: Paramonetary Function of Money." *Diogenes* (Spring-Summer 1978), 77–88.

Grierson, Philip. *Numismatics.* New York: Oxford University Press, 1975.

Griffiths, William H. *The Story of the American Bank Note Company.* New York: N.p., 1959.

Grosvenor, Gilbert, et al. *Insignia and Decorations of the United States Armed Forces.* Washington, D.C.: National Geographic Society, 1944.

History of the Bureau of Engraving and Printing (1862–1962). Washington, D.C.: Government Printing Office, 1962.

Hood, Jennings, and Charles J. Young. *American Orders and Societies and Their Decorations*. Philadelphia: Bailey, Banks, and Biddle, 1917.

Jamieson, Melvill Allan. *Medals Awarded to North American Indian Chiefs, 1714–1922*. London: Spitik, 1961.

Johnston, Elizabeth B. *A Visit to the Cabinet of the United States Mint at Philadelphia*. Philadelphia: J. B. Lippincott, 1876.

Judd, J. Hewitt, and Walter Breen. *United States Patterns, Experimental and Trial Pieces*. Racine, Wis.: Whitman, 1962.

Kappen, Charles V., and Ralph A. Mitchell. *Depression Scrip of the United States*. San Jose, Calif.: Globe, 1961.

Kenney, Richard D. *Early American Medalists and Die-Sinkers*. New York: W. Raymond, 1954.

Kerrigan, Evans E. *American War Medals and Decorations*. New York: Viking, 1964.

King, Robert P. "Lincoln in Numismatics: A Descriptive List." *Numismatist*, 37 (1924), 55–74; 40 (1927), 193–204; 46 (1933), 481–97.

Kosoff, Abe. *An Illustrated History of United States Coins: Proposed Designs as Well as the Standard Types*. Encino, Calif.: N.p., 1962.

Library Catalogue of the American Numismatic Association. Colorado Springs, Colo.: American Numismatic Association, 1972.

Loubat, Joseph F. *The Medallic History of the United States of America, 1776–1876*. New Milford, Conn.: N. Flayderman, 1967.

Low, Lyman H. *Hard Times Tokens*. San Jose, Calif.: Globe, 1955.

Massey, J. Earl. *America's Money: The Story of Coins and Currency*. New York: Crowell, 1968.

Mishler, Clifford. *United States and Canadian Commemorative Medals and Tokens*. Vandalia, Mich.: Mishler, 1959.

Muscalus, John A. *Famous Paintings Reproduced on Paper Money of State Banks, 1800–1866*. Bridgeport, Conn.: Muscalus, 1938.

———. *Index of State Bank Notes That Illustrate Characters and Events*. Bridgeport, Conn.: Muscalus, 1938.

———. *Index of State Bank Notes That Illustrate Presidents*. Bridgeport, Conn.: Muscalus, 1939.

———. *Index of State Bank Notes That Illustrate Washington and Franklin*. Bridgeport, Conn.: Muscalus, 1939.

———. *The Views of Towns, Cities, Falls, and Buildings Illustrated on 1800–1866 Bank Paper Money*. Bridgeport, Conn.: Muscalus, 1939.

Nussbaum, Arthur. *A History of the Dollar*. New York: Columbia University Press, 1957.

Rayner, G. "History of the Coin Investment Market." *Hobbies* 82 (October 1977), 131.

Reed, Mort. *Cowles' Complete Encyclopedia of United States Coins*. New York: Cowles, 1969.

Reiter, Ed. "Numismatics: College Level Training." *New York Times*, December 23, 1979; December 30, 1979.

Rochette, Edward C. *The Medallic Portraits of John F. Kennedy: A Study of Kennediana*. Iola, Wis.: Krause, 1966.

Roosevelt and Numismatics. Colorado Springs, Colo.: American Numismatic Association, n.d.

Ross, F. C. "Numismatic Thoughts." *Hobbies*, 46 (June 1941), 90–92.

Rothert, Matt. *A Guidebook of United States Fractional Currency*. Racine, Wis.: Whitman, 1963.

Ruby, Warren A. *Commemorative Coins of the United States*. Lake Mills, Iowa: Graphic, 1961.

Salton, Mark. *Glossary of Numismatic Terms*. New York: Barnes and Noble, 1947.

Sheldon, William H., et al. *Penny Whimsey*. New York: Harper, 1958.

Slaubaugh, Arlie R. *United States Commemorative Coins: The Drama of America as Told by Our Coins*. Racine, Wis.: Western, 1975.

Snowden, James Ross. *A Description of Ancient and Modern Coins in the Cabinet Collection at the United States Mint*. Philadelphia: J. B. Lippincott, 1860.

Sutherland, Carol H. *Art in Coinage: The Aesthetics of Money from Greece to the Present Day*. New York: Philosophical Library, 1956.

Taxay, Don. *Comprehensive Catalogue and Encyclopedia of United States Coins*. New York: Scott, 1971.

———. *An Illustrated History of United States Commemorative Coins*. New York: Arco, 1967.

———. *Money of the American Indian and Other Primitive Currencies of the Americas*. New York: Nummis, 1970.

———. *The United States Mint and Coinage: An Illustrated History from 1776 to the Present*. New York: Arco, 1966.

Todd, Richard Cecil. *Confederate Finance*. Athens: University of Georgia Press, 1954.

Van Allen, Leroy C., and A. George Mallis. *Guide to Morgan and Peace Dollars: A Complete Guide and Reference Book on United States Silver Dollars*. Silver Springs, Md.: Katen, 1971.

Vermeule, Cornelius C. *Numismatic Art in America: Aesthetics of the United States Coinage*. Cambridge: Harvard University Press, 1971.

Yeoman, Richard S. *Guidebook of United States Coins*. Racine, Wis.: Western, 1999.

———. *Handbook of United States Coins*. Racine, Wis.: Western, 1998.

Postcards

Burdick, Jefferson R. *Pioneer Post Cards: The Story of Mailing Cards to 1898*. New York: Nostalgia Press, 1957.

Carline, Richard. *Pictures in the Post: The Story of the Picture Postcard and Its Place in the History of Popular Art*. London: Gordon Fraser Gallery, 1971.

Jay, Robert. *The Trade Card in Nineteenth-Century America*. Columbia: University of Missouri Press, 1987.

Kaduck, John M. *Patriotic Postcards*. Des Moines, Iowa: Wallace-Homestead, 1974.

Klamkin, Marian. *Picture Postcards*. New York: Dodd, Mead, 1974.

Megson, Frederic, and Mary Megson. *American Exposition Postcards, 1870–1920*. Martinsville, N.J.: The Postcard Lovers, 1992.

Morgan, Hal, and Andreas Brown. *Prairie Fires and Paper Moons: The American Photographic Postcard, 1900–1920*. Boston: David R. Godine, 1981.

Ryan, Dorothy R. *Picture Postcards in the United States, 1893–1918*. New York: Clarkson N. Potter, 1982.

Rydell, Robert W. "Souvenirs of Imperialism." In *Delivering Views: Distant Cul-*

tures in Early Postcards, ed. Christraud M. Geary and Virginia-Lee Webb. Washington, D.C.: Smithsonian Institution Press, 1998.

Stadtmiller, Bernard. *Postcard Collecting: A Fun Investment*. Palm Bay, Fla.: Bernard Stadtmiller, 1973.

Staff, Frank. *The Picture Postcard and Its Origins*. New York: Praeger, 1966.

Willoughby, Martin. *A History of Postcards*. London: Bracken Books, 1992.

Periodicals

Stamps

Aero Philatelist Annals. New York, 1953– .
Airpost Journal. Albion, Pa., 1929– .
American Philatelist. State College, Pa., 1909– .
American Revenuer. New York, 1954– .
1869 Times. Memphis, Tenn., 1975– .
Essay-Proof Journal. Jefferson, Wis., 1944– .
Global Stamp News. Sidney, Ohio, 1990– .
La Posta, Lake Oswego, Oreg., 1969– .
Linn's Stamp News. Sidney, Ohio, 1928– .
Mekeel's Weekly Stamp News. Portland, Maine, 1905– .
Philatelic Literature Review. Canajoharie, N.Y., 1942– .
Scott Stamp Monthly. Sidney, Ohio, 1982– .
Stamp Collector. Iola, Wis., 1926– .
Stamp Wholesaler. Iola, Wis., 1937– .
Topical Times. Milwaukee, 1949– .
United States Specialist. West Somerville, Mass., 1930– .

Coins

Calcoin News Quarterly Magazine. San Jose, Calif., 1947– .
Coin World. Sidney, Ohio, 1960– .
Coins. Iola, Wis., 1962– .
Numismatic Literature. New York, 1947– .
Numismatic Scrapbook Magazine. Chicago, 1935– .
The Numismatist. Monroe, Mich., 1888– .
Paper Money. Jefferson, Wis., 1962– .

Postcards

Picture Postcard News. Syracuse, N.Y., 1980– .
Postcard Classics. Norwood, Pa., 1988– .
Postcard Collector. Iola, Wis., 1983– .
Postcard Dealer and Collector. Manassas, Va., 1977– .

TELEVISION

Rhonda Wilcox

As we enter the twenty-first century, virtually everyone in America is a child of television—or is living with those children. Viewers can choose from dozens of channels, buy videotapes of many series, or view reruns of popular shows from decades gone by. Though few understand the corporate structure behind television, more and more are sophisticated in their understanding of programs' construction and content. The nineteenth century, the great age of the novel, produced thousands more forgettable works than ones that have survived to gain the name of art; and surely it is also true of television that most of it is forgettable. But the few memorable works are well worth attention. As David Marc says in *Demographic Vistas*, "The self-proclaimed champions of 'high art' who dismiss TV shows as barren imitations of the real article simply do not know how to watch. They are like freshmen thrust into survey courses and forced to read Fielding and Sterne; they lack both the background and the tough-skinned skepticism that can make TV meaningful experience" (8). With an exponential increase of publications in the last decade of the twentieth century, scholars of both social sciences and the humanities (of various schools) have studied television, though they often do not follow each other's work. But social forces inform the art of television; and to evaluate the social impact of television, scholars need to understand how it operates—which involves understanding its art. Therefore, while this chapter emphasizes the humanities, it also includes works on television from a social science perspective. After the historic outline and sections on reference and history, the succeeding sections reflect the topics about which most scholars write: Theory and General Commentary, Audience Studies, Race and Ethnicity, Gender and Sexual Orientation, Religion, Children, Violence, News and Politics, Individual Series, Individuals, and Genre Studies.

HISTORICAL OUTLINE

Television is a quintessentially modern invention in that it is a system, not a single device. It required success not only with physics but also with sociopolitical structures. The two most important names in the creation of electronic television are Philo Farnsworth and Vladimir Zworykin. Utah farm-raised Philo Farnsworth succeeded in producing all-electric television on September 7, 1927. The story of television is also a story of big business, preeminently represented by General David Sarnoff, a visionary who foresaw first the importance of radio and then the importance of television. In 1926 the National Broadcasting Company (NBC) was formed as an RCA radio network company under the control of Sarnoff. By 1927 it had two national radio networks, the Red (premium) and the Blue. In 1928 Zworykin convinced Sarnoff to support him in his television research. The result was, among other things, a legal fight later between giant RCA and independent inventor Philo Farnsworth—which Farnsworth, to RCA's astonishment, actually won. But the result was also a race to progress. RCA demonstrated television at the 1939 New York World's Fair. Wartime research by RCA engineers improved on this work to create the more sensitive Image Orthicon tube in 1944. Sarnoff's NBC was forced by government antitrust lawyers to sell off one of its two networks in 1943, and thus the Red network became the American Broadcasting System (ABC). Back in 1927 the other major radio network, Columbia Phonograph Broadcasting System, had been created under William S. Paley. Companies that had preestablished networks of radio station affiliates around the country found it much easier to establish television networks. NBC, CBS, and ABC all came from radio roots. The Federal Communications Commission (FCC) had decided before World War II to allot only VHF, not UHF, frequencies for broadcasting and therefore significantly limited the number of available slots. In a 1952 ruling most cities were allowed a maximum of two or three stations. This meant that the FCC—in effect, the government—had, intentionally or not, set a course for there to be three major networks, a fact of significant sociological and aesthetic impact in the coming years. In 1955 the fourth network, the Dumont network, died.

Television as a whole had a near-death experience in 1947. At the National Association of Broadcasters meeting in Atlantic City, many members considered quitting. Early television suffered from many difficulties in technology, programming, and economics. Television broadcasts were of poor quality, often interrupted; before AT&T connected many cities with coaxial cable, there had to be line-of-sight connections, which were easily broken. Before the wartime invention of the Image Orthicon camera, experimental television station performers endured makeup–melting heat from hand-blistering cameras because of the extraordinary lighting requirements. Viewers endured programming such as a Junior League sewing show (Kisselhoff 151). Even after advertising was authorized in 1941, sales were poor because there were few viewers; most felt unwilling to spend $200–600 on a set that received weak programs, and so the stations had little money for programming, which perpetuated the problem. The available type of programming probably best suited to early television was sports, especially boxing and wrestling, which occupied a limited space and therefore provided fewer technical problems for camera work. Television came in through the barroom door; local taverns were persuaded to spend the money for sets to attract customers. Meanwhile, General Sarnoff had persuaded the 1947 National Association of Broadcasters convention to hold on for that time of golden profit.

In 1948, Mr. Television arrived: Milton Berle, former vaudevillian and now host of the Texaco Star Theater. Uncle Miltie's pie-in-the-face, cross-dressing slapstick was something that could not come through a radio, and American families were entranced. Other performers and producers were beginning to learn to exploit television's special nature in different ways. The Chicago school of production, under the direction of Captain Bill Eddy of WBKB, was a brief, but lively, creative sidestream in the history of television that produced in 1949 Dave Garroway's relaxed intimacy of conversation with guests (later transferred to NBC's *Today Show*) and the brilliant whimsy under the guise of a children's show that was *Kukla, Fran, and Ollie*. The Dumont network astonished everyone when it managed in 1952 to draw audiences away from Mr. Television on Tuesdays by broadcasting the charming moral homilies of Catholic Bishop Fulton J. Sheen, who proved the drawing power of a likable, understated presence.

Television was beginning to define itself as it moved into what is generally termed its golden age. The early 1950s brought the great situation comedies (as opposed to skits) *I Love Lucy* (1951–1961), *George Burns and Gracie Allen* (1950–1958), and *The Jack Benny Show* (1950–1965), with self-contained episodes involving regular characters (often transplanted from radio). In the pre-rerun age, when television seemed even more ephemeral than it does to many now, stars Lucille Ball and Desi Arnaz, with provident foresight, reserved the rights to film and re-air their series. In the same period, Irna Phillips and Agnes Nixon proved that daytime serials—soap operas—could make the transition from radio. *As the World Turns*, started in 1952, is still running. The two genres that were probably most characteristic of the golden age, however, are the variety shows and, above all, the live dramas—both attempts to reproduce live entertainment on-screen and perhaps therefore fated for eventual replacement. Variety performers such as Red Skelton (whose show lasted twenty years), Arthur Godfrey, and Jimmy Durante pleased the viewers. *The Ed Sullivan Show* (1948–1971) combined culture, comedy, and current hot performers (Elvis in the 1950s, the Beatles in the 1960s). Jackie Gleason introduced the classic humor of *The Honeymooners*—bus driver Ralph Kramden, his sewer-worker friend Norton, and the wives who managed their unlovely lower-class homes, Alice and Trixie—as skits in 1951 within Dumont's *Cavalcade of Stars*. But the pinnacle of golden age variety shows was undoubtedly Sid Caesar and Imogene Coca's *Your Show of Shows* (1950–1954), ninety minutes of live comedy skits, songs, dances, and stars. Carl Reiner, Howie Morris, and others supported Caesar and Coca; Mel Brooks, Neil Simon, Woody Allen, and Lucille Kallen, among others, served as writers.

The writers of live drama for television in the 1950s also indicate the quality of the work; Paddy Chayefsky, Horton Foote, Rod Serling, Reginald Rose, and J. P. Miller, among others, created works such as *Marty*, *A Trip to Bountiful*, *Requiem for a Heavyweight*, *Twelve Angry Men*, and *The Days of Wine and Roses*, respectively. Working for anthology series such as *Kraft Television Theatre*, *The Philco/Goodyear Playhouse*, *Ford Theatre*, and, pre-eminently, *Playhouse 90* (ninety minutes), these writers gave opportunities for such young actors as Paul Newman, Rod Steiger, Julie Harris, Jack Lemmon, Richard Kiley, Nancy Marchand, and

James Dean. *Studio One* presented mostly adaptations of classic literature, but the hallmark of the golden age was the original live drama, produced with stressful technical limitations of time, space, and money. These limitations may have contributed, however, to the small-screen, human-sized intimacy of such slice-of-life dramas as *Marty*, the story of a lonely butcher. Under directors such as Fred Coe, John Frankenheimer, and Sidney Lumet, live anthologies presented stories of character and conscience. With the introduction of videotape in 1956, much of the stress of creation disappeared, but so did much of the intensity.

The 1950s cannot, however, be seen as a time of prelapsarian purity. This was the era in which a single advertiser would sponsor an entire series and therefore exert some surprising control over content, ranging from the elemental—exclusion of social controversy—to the ridiculous, for example, avoidance of the word "lucky" because it named a rival cigarette. It is also the time period during which NBC could not find a permanent sponsor for popular African American singer Nat King Cole, though for months the network ran his 1956–1957 series anyway. The latter half of the 1950s also brought the wildly popular live quiz shows and their scandals because of rigged winnings. Such series as *The $64,000 Question* and *Twenty-One* were supposedly unscripted live drama, with contestants competing on the basis of their knowledge, but contestants with strong audience appeal were revealed to have been given answers. It might be argued that the golden age was already past at the time of these events, but the blacklist operated throughout the golden years. The 1950 publication of a list of supposed communists and communist sympathizers resulted in the exclusion from employment of Kim Hunter, Lee Grant, Jack Gilford, and many others. On the other hand, the golden age included one of television's finest hours when CBS news' Edward R. Murrow reported on the communist witch-hunter Senator Joseph McCarthy. The courage of Murrow (backed by Fred Friendly) was supplemented by the power of television: the camera exposed McCarthy.

In the latter 1950s and early 1960s, television moved from live presentations to widespread use of telefilms. Hollywood studios began producing series to sell to the networks. By far the largest trend was the adult western; instead of Davy Crockett with the coonskin cap, which kids throughout the country purchased in facsimile, adults were given first *Cheyenne*, then such others as *Wyatt Earp*, the two-decade run of *Gunsmoke*, *Bonanza* (the first color western), and the western-mocking western *Maverick*. In 1959 there were thirty-one westerns on prime-time televison. They are the roots of much of modern television drama, with their regular characters moving through a series of contained episodes. They are also, along with the action-adventure/detective series such as *77 Sunset Strip* (1958–1964), *Hawaiian Eye*, and *The Untouchables* (1959–1963) the roots of the violence that has concerned so many. More lasting drama was created by Rod Serling, an alumnus of the live drama anthologies, with his 1959–1966 science fiction/fantasy anthology *The Twilight Zone*, bizarre parables that exposed human nature.

Along with the shift to externally produced telefilms, another economic factor with implications for the creative process was the magazine-style advertising system, which replaced single-sponsor control. Nonetheless, television series in the conservative social atmosphere of the 1950s controlled themselves. The idealized homes of the family-based situation comedies such as *The Adventures of Ozzie and Harriet* (1952–1966), *Father Knows Best* (1954–1963), *Leave It to Beaver* (1957–

1963), and *The Donna Reed Show* (1958–1966) in some ways followed in the footsteps of *I Love Lucy*, with a step up in social class. But while former radio star Lucy had insisted, against network wishes, that her Cuban husband be allowed to portray her on-screen spouse, the dominant 1950s domestic comedies embodied conservative stances on class, gender, and race/ethnicity. Perhaps multiple sponsors meant that there were more groups to avoid offending. In 1961 the young Kennedy-appointed chair of the FCC, Newton Minow, made the famous speech to the broadcasters in which he declared television to be "a vast wasteland."

While Minow had urged change, many series of the 1960s would not seem to have carried it out. Gimmicky sitcoms riddled the airwaves, with *Mister Ed*, 1961–1965 (a talking horse), *My Favorite Martian*, 1963–1966 (an alien "uncle"), *Bewitched*, 1964–1972 (a magic wife), *Hogan's Heroes*, 1965–1971 (with humorous Nazis), and *The Munsters*, 1964–1966 (with Frankenstein as the Father Who Knew Best). *Gilligan's Island*, 1964–1967, was unabashedly a collection of stereotypes: the millionaire and his wife, the movie star, the professor. *The Beverly Hillbillies*, 1962–1971, did use Oliver Goldsmith's eighteenth-century device of the "different world" observer to successful effect for many seasons, with suddenly rich mountaineers questioning the ways of city folk. By comparison, the small-town North Carolina characters of *The Andy Griffith Show*, 1960–1968, seemed like real human beings. The cartoon-quality silliness of much television was exploited by the campy series *Batman*, 1966–1968, which featured fight scenes intercut with cartoon "ZAPS," and "POWS." *The Dick Van Dyke Show*, 1961–1966, successfully mocked television in a more realistic context through the character of television writer Rob Petrie (and his lovely wife Laura—Mary Tyler Moore), created by Carl Reiner of *Your Show of Shows*.

The inheritors of the westerns and detective series were a group of spy/detective series inspired by the James Bond movies. *The Wild, Wild West*, 1965–1970, crossed secret agents with westerns; the British-produced *Secret Agent*, 1965–1966, provided intense character and story lines; *The Man from U.N.C.L.E.*, 1964–1968, drolly exaggerated the genre; *I Spy* presented two buddies, one of whom was Bill Cosby, the first black regular in prime-time drama; *Mission: Impossible*, 1966–1973, had a signature opening and another black regular, an electronics expert; another British import, *The Avengers*, 1966–1969, brought subtly satirical whimsy and, with her partner John Steed, the dashing, intelligent Mrs. Emma Peel; and detective *Honey West*, 1965–1966, was her own boss. More realistic were the famed medical dramas—*Dr. Kildare* and *Ben Casey*, both running 1961–1966, and *The Nurses*, 1962–1965; and *Perry Mason* held court from 1957 to 1966. The 1960s also explored serious social issues in a few series such as *The Defenders*, 1961–1965, the short-lived George C. Scott vehicle *East Side/West Side*, 1963–1964, and—though many did not realize it at the time—in symbolic guise in the science fiction of *Star Trek*, 1966–1969, with its mixture of races and ethnicities on the bridge of the starship *Enterprise*. The fans' passion for the combined quest for mythic adventure and social justice would lead to a letter-writing campaign to revive the series after the second season, a string of movies, four later *Trek* television series, and a worldwide popular culture phenomenon.

Social impact could clearly be seen in the news coverage of the decade, which began with the Nixon-Kennedy debates, which helped propel Kennedy to the presidency. Television was there again to bring the shocked nation together at

Television station control room. © Painet

the time of his assassination, and to show the on-screen murder of his alleged killer, and to report the assassinations of Dr. Martin Luther King Jr. and Senator Robert Kennedy. In 1969 most viewers watched the moon landing with "Uncle Walter" Cronkite. Television almost certainly made a difference by its coverage of the civil rights movement and the Vietnam War. The controversies of the decade sometimes found vent in topical humor—*That Was the Week That Was*, 1964–1965, the censor-fighting *Smothers Brothers Comedy Hour*, 1967–1970, and even *Rowan and Martin's Laugh-In*, 1968–1973.

In the 1970s, also, serious issues appeared in comedic format. In situation comedies, Norman Lear's *All in the Family*, 1971–1983, led the way. Based on the British series *Till Death Us Do Part*, *All in the Family*, like *The Honeymooners*, focused on a working-class home. The central character, Archie Bunker, was a bigoted, but loving, family man who constantly argued with his liberal college student son-in-law. *All in the Family* was followed by a stable of Lear comedies that continued to explore social issues. *M*A*S*H*, 1972–1983, set in the Korean War, clearly spoke to the Vietnam conflict. The series brought home the reality of war by the unheard-of choice to kill off a regular (1975). The continuing story *Soap*, too, dealt with some social issues (for instance, introducing the first regular homosexual character). Skit comedy and live television were revived in NBC's late-night production *Saturday Night Live* (1975–), which presented satire to such effect that in 1977–1978 its ratings beat the king of late night, talk-show host Johnny Carson of *The Tonight Show* (1962–1993). Jim Henson's *Muppet Show*, 1976–1981, parodied the entertainment business and expanded the success of PBS'

Sesame Street (1969-) stars. The 1970s also brought *The Mary Tyler Moore Show*, 1970–1977, produced by the star and her husband, Grant Tinker (later head of NBC). Its underlying premise—with an unmarried woman who enjoyed her career and was not desperate for a husband—made a statement. Like Lear series, MTM series spread, producing more of what Feuer, Tise, and Vahimagi identify as "quality television."

Other series of this period were less memorable for content than for casting or characters. The continued dominance of the three major networks meant a commonality of viewing experience (the options were few), which supported a message of diversity being absorbed into the mainstream. *Julia*, 1968–1971, was a nurse played by Diahann Carroll, the first African American woman to be a central middle-class series character. *Barney Miller*, 1975–1982, set in a New York police precinct office, had more diversity among regulars than the crew of the starship *Enterprise*. Some of the same pattern of inclusiveness can be seen in the dramas. *Ironside*'s main character was a wheelchair-bound detective. Women detectives were in evidence as well; *Charlie's Angels*—three women who reported to the disembodied voice of their male superior—inaugurated what was called "jiggle" television, in reference to their omission of brassieres. More double messages: in daytime drama, viewers were enthralled by *General Hospital*'s Luke and Laura's relationship (1978-), which the network termed "rape" but which Martha Nochimson in *No End to Her* identifies as mutual choice, ambiguously feminist. Police work was also being done by "hippie" youth—a white male, a black male, and a white woman—in *The Mod Squad*, 1968–1973. These characters, despite their difficulties, found themselves ultimately able to serve justice and be accepted in the world of the largely white male establishment.

The establishment was questioned by the MTM drama *Lou Grant*, 1977–1982. Its cancellation after controversial social stances by star Ed Asner has often been questioned. In general it seemed that drama was well served in the 1970s when the characters were not in a continuing episodic series. The revolving *NBC Sunday Mystery Movies* introduced the rumpled police detective *Columbo*, 1971–1977, who provided the socially cathartic pleasure of capturing smart-aleck rich folk. More realistic were the telefilms of the anthology series *Police Story*, 1973–1977, created by former policeman Joseph Wambaugh. This decade was the age of the miniseries, most notably, *Roots*, 1977, the story of Alex Haley's search for his African American family history. The last of the eight episodes, telecast on succeeding nights, was the highest rated program to date.

Perhaps the most compelling drama, however, was unfolding on the news in 1973. The Watergate Hearings, chaired with folksy wisdom by North Carolina Senator Sam Ervin, beat out soap opera and game show competition, again proving the significance of television news coverage. The decade closed with the CBS newsmagazine *60 Minutes*, 1968- , the highest ranked series of the year (1979–1980).

The 1980s was the age of the nighttime television serial. The granddaddy of them all was *Dallas*, a feuding-families saga of oil barons led by villainous J. R. Ewing. The excited wait for the cliff-hanger answer to the 1980 question, "Who shot J. R.?" was a multinational popular culture event. *Dallas* was followed by *Dynasty*, *Falcon Crest*, *Knots Landing*, and others. In the age of Reaganomics, these series allowed viewers to fantasize about wealth while feeling the moral satisfaction that riches could not buy happiness. Alternatively, viewers might approach them as camp; large numbers of the gay community adopted *Dynasty* as a viewing pleasure.

Nonetheless, serious drama came into its own again in the 1980s, the period that begins (to use Robert Thompson's term) the second golden age of television. Fortunately, it was also in this period that videocassette recorders became widespread. Shows could be "time-shifted" by viewers; and viewers began, legally or not, to make collections of favorite episodes. Steven Bochco's *Hill Street Blues*, 1981–1987—an MTM production—is the seminal series for the new brand of more realistic, ensemble company, one-hour dramas with elements of continuing narration balanced by some episodic closure. "Make it messy" was the watchword of initial director Robert Butler in his attempt to carry out Bochco's vision (Gitlin 293). Bit players walked through the scenes, and confused ambient sound replaced much of the background music typical of filmed drama. *St. Elsewhere*, 1982–1988, set in an urban hospital, and *L.A. Law*, 1986–1994, followed *Hill Street*. The police drama *Cagney and Lacey*, 1982–1988, did not have the texture of Bochco productions but dealt seriously with the issues facing the two women protagonists. No longer did a happy episodic ending assert that the established social order would be rightly upheld. Sometimes the story had no real resolution. This narrative dissolution was matched by the beginning of the breakup of the three-network hegemony. Not only was there a fourth network on the rise—Fox, born from the remnants of the Dumont system—but also satellite distribution meant that such stations as the WTBS Atlanta "superstation" could be as widely received as networks, and then there were the cable stations such as MTV (music videos), ESPN (sports), the Weather Channel, and on and on. Neither stories nor stations were unified or simple anymore.

Other shows were more notable for formal elements than for social content. The romantic comedy/detective hybrids *Remington Steele*, 1982–1987 and *Moonlighting*, 1985–1989, played with the 1980s audience's consciousness of aesthetic construction. *Remington Steele*'s hero had been invented as a male figurehead to lure business for the real detective, a woman (commenting on gender relations); the unreal detective repeatedly discovered parallels to screen crimes. In *Moonlighting*, the consciousness of unreality went so far as to include the main characters' breaking the fourth wall by literally disassembling the sets. *Max Headroom*, 1987, with a computer-dwelling title character in a world where it was illegal to turn off the television, was another highly self-conscious examination of its own medium. The syndicated *Star Trek: The Next Generation*, 1987–1994, while generally focusing on time-displaced social problems, also occasionally explored questions of reality by having the crew interact with holographic characters. Another sort of consciousness of construction powered the detective series *Miami Vice*, 1984–1989; though it had elements of realism, the style of its pastel-clothed heroes, art deco settings, and MTV music video score was what made it distinctive.

In 1980s comedy, ensemble work (as in drama) produced some significant success. In *Cheers*, 1982–1993, a bar's various characters formed, in effect, a family. The king of family comedy was Bill Cosby, who was credited with reviving the sitcom. His 1984–1992 half hour was television-traditional except for the fact that it showcased an upper-middle-class black family. In general, 1980s comedy recalled 1970s drama in its implied resolution of social problems through the social absorption of seeming diversity. However, *It's Garry Shandling's Show*, 1986–1990, echoed *Moonlighting*'s school of construct-consciousness.

News in the 1980s began with the continued coverage of the fourteen-month Iran hostage crisis. Americans also witnessed not the funeral but the attempted assassination of a U.S president, Ronald Reagan, in 1981—through which the aging president became a television hero. But the most significant structural development of 1980s news was the introduction in 1980 by Ted Turner of CNN, the twenty-four-hour Cable News Network.

The advent of CNN is just one of many examples of the multiplication of avenues of broadcast information that continued ever faster in the 1990s. ABC, CBS, and NBC were now joined by not only Fox but also UPN (United Paramount) and the WB (Warner Brothers), not to mention the numerous satellite and cable networks. Certainly, viewers with a desire to be informed had more options in the 1990s. For instance, in the 1960s there were only a few hard-to-receive public television stations; there was no Discovery Channel. On the other hand, there was also no Home Shopping Network.

Production sources, however, did not undergo the same degree of diversification. Thus, though there has been some interesting evolution, there has been no revolution in television forms. The most widespread pattern is for existing genres to be demographically slanted by a particular network: in "niche marketing" or "narrowcasting," for example, the USA cable network is directed at women and the WB aims for a young audience. In general, advertisers—and therefore production—favor the youth market because of the belief that they are more malleable consumers.

Not surprisingly, then, *Dallas* and the like spawned the more youth-oriented 1990s nighttime soaps *Beverly Hills 90210*, 1990–2000, and *Melrose Place*, 1992–1999. Much of the quality drama also followed a set path—the grittier path of *Hill Street*. Such series include the police dramas *Homicide: Life on the Street*, 1993– , and *NYPD Blue*, 1993– , the medical drama *ER*, 1994– (which in 1998 essayed a live episode), and *Law and Order*, 1990– (half police, half lawyers). Social issues were also explored in David E. Kelley's quirky *Picket Fences*, 1992–1996, and a linguistically realistic drama about high school that almost validated the youth trend, *My So-Called Life*, 1994–1995.

Equally interesting, however, is a group of 1990s dramas that branch off from traditional realism, starting with the serial mystery *Twin Peaks*, 1990–1991. Filmmaker and artist David Lynch joined with Mark Frost to create one of the most visually striking television series ever, filmed on location in the Pacific Northwest. Watching *Twin Peaks* was like dreaming in color—with equal opportunity for horror and beauty. When *Northern Exposure*, 1990–1995, came to television many noted the similarities to *Twin Peaks*. *Northern Exposure*, however, along with the symbolic techniques that it shared with *Twin Peaks*, included more discursive presentation of ideas, philosophically argued among the townsfolk, and was therefore more accessible. It, too, however, had its quirky characters and occasional forays into the unreal. The central focus of *The X-Files*, 1993– , is the paranormal. Federal Bureau of Investigation (FBI) agents Mulder and Scully exchange traditional gender roles, with the female Scully as the skeptic and the male Mulder as the believer. *The X-Files* fans—x-philes—were notable in the trend to estabish Internet television discussion groups. The series appeals to television-raised skeptics with the possibility of a government conspiracy. The WB's (later UPN's) *Buffy the Vampire Slayer*, 1996– , suggests symbolically that parents don't know the real monsters that teens have to face. *Lois and Clark: The New Adventures of Superman*, 1993–1997, charmingly domesticated the unreal (and explored gender relations), but none of the others of this group of fin-de-siècle series assured viewers of a simple happy ending (and *Lois and Clark* died when it did). They questioned perceptions of reality in a way that the more televisually sophisticated 1990s viewers could appreciate.

In 1990s comedy, too, there were both widespread use of traditional formats and a trend of significant variation. A descendant of *Cheers*, *Friends*, 1994– , followed the market-driven youth trend. *Roseanne*, 1988–1999, starring a woman stand-up comic, tackled problems of lower-class women and families. *Seinfeld*, 1990–1998, a show billed as being about "nothing"—the trivial irritations of life— was also built around a stand-up comic. There were large numbers of traditional comedies whose only notable difference from past series was that they starred black actors, such as Will Smith—like Roseanne and Seinfeld, already a star (in rap music)—in *The Fresh Prince of Bel Air*, 1990–1995.

A new trend in 1990s comedy was the adult cartoon. Matt Groening's *The Simpsons*, 1989– , uses the family sitcom format for satire. The parody is sharp (e.g., the musical version, complete with happy ending, of *A Streetcar Named Desire*); the satire stings; and visual, verbal, and musical intertextual references abound. It takes full-fledged cultural literacy—including television literacy—to get all the jokes in *The Simpsons*. Less rich but equally trenchant was the mockery of Mike Judge's *Beavis and Butthead*, 1993– . *The Simpsons* starts every episode with the family ensconced on the couch before the television; in *Beavis and Butthead*, the characters rarely leave the couch. This MTV series incorporated intercut MTV music videos, which the cartoon characters watched and judged to be even stupider than they were. MTV's *Daria*, 1997– , Groening's *Futurama*, 1998– (which Groening says is designed to be taped and reviewed for details), and Judge's *King of the Hill*, 1997– , continue the trend.

The adult cartoon trend may, in part, be supported by the various networks' attempts to cut their budgets in the 1990s as the commercial pie is cut into more and more pieces and as corporate broadcasting becomes more interested in the "corporate" and less in the broadcasting. Certainly, the rise of talk shows is supported by the money-saving interests. The 1990s was the age of *The Oprah Winfrey Show*, on which the host-heroine tackled social and psychological issues through her guests and her own life. Many other talk shows, notably *The Jerry Springer Show*, appealed to prurient interest and even involved onstage fistfights among participants.

News coverage, too, in the 1990s was affected by budget cutbacks. Walter Cronkite was named the most trusted man in the United States, but the audience trusted television news less and less. The rise of newsmagazine series can be attributed in part to their relative cheapness to produce. Most of these spice news with sensationalism. *Dateline NBC*, 1992– , echoed the quiz show scandals of the 1950s when it rigged a demonstration of truck crashworthiness (1992). Nonetheless, modern technology combined with old-fashioned reporting sometimes rivets viewers to public events, as when in 1991 CNN reporters spoke live by satellite from behind enemy lines during the Gulf War. On the other hand, audiences were equally fascinated by the televised reports, from 1997 on, of President Clinton's dalliance with White House intern Monica Lewinski. Where news left off and sleaze began seemed harder and harder to define in the 1990s. The O. J. Simpson murder case was, painfully, a peculiarly resonant television event, with its sports/television/movie star in a slow, bizarrely distorted live variation on a television chase scene followed by courtroom drama with vivid characters and themes of race and gender. Questions of reality are as vexing here as in 1990s drama.

Despite the advent of fiber optics, HDTV, or Internet soap operas, it seems likely that many traditional formats and genres will remain. But within the forms (or in new forms), some makers will always find ways to be creative. It will also continue to be true that, as John Fiske says in *Television Studies*, a collection of essays edited by Burns and Thompson, "[t]he people make their own popular culture out of the offerings of the industry" (25).

REFERENCE WORKS

The two most important research tools are Tim Brooks and Earle Marsh's *The Complete Directory to Prime Time Network and Cable TV Shows: 1946–Present* and Horace Newcomb's Museum of Broadcasting Communications-sponsored *Encyclopedia of Television*. Brooks and Marsh provide a remarkably complete listing, including in the 1995 6th edition series from ABC, CBS, Dumont, NBC, Fox, WB, and UPN, major syndicated and cable series. They supply the dates of first and last telecast, time and day of broadcast, cast, and detailed synopsis. They also include a short history of television and a variety of appendixes, example, "Prime Time Spinoffs." Newcomb's three-volume encyclopedia (1997) provides articles not only on series but also on individual producers, performers, and topics (e.g., "Anthology Drama"). Articles, accompanied by some photos, are written by such luminaries as David Thorburn and Sue Brower and followed by brief bibliographies. While not as fully inclusive as Brooks and Marsh (e.g., the 1997 Newcomb has no entry on *The X-Files*, while the 1995 Brooks and Marsh has one), Newcomb is much more in-depth. Alex McNeil's *Total Television* more briefly follows the Brooks and Marsh model and also lists specials; however, specials are given their own full treatment in Vincent Terrace's *Television Specials: 3,201 Entertainment Spectaculars, 1939–1993*. Terrace has also published *Television Character and Story Facts* and *The Complete Encyclopedia of Television Programs*, with briefer entries than Brooks and Marsh. *Les Brown's Encyclopedia of Television* (3rd ed., 1992) and David Bianculli's *Dictionary of Teleliteracy* (1996) provide briefer overviews; and as Bianculli notes in justifying his selections, "memorable doesn't necessarily mean good" (16). Larry Gianakos offers a 1992 version of his *Television Drama Series Programming*. Roberta Pearson and Philip Simpson have edited *A Critical Dictionary of Film and Television Theory* (2001). There are also more specialized offerings. Harris M. Lentz's *Television Westerns Episode Guide* gives synopses of individual episodes of 180 westerns from 1949 to 1996, including titles, air dates, and actors' names. Three such episode guide sources for science fiction series are Mark Phillips and Frank Garcia's *Science Fiction Television Series* (1996), Roger Fulton and John Betancourt's *The Sci-Fi Channel Encyclopedia of TV Science Fiction* (1998), and the more narrowly focused *American Science Fiction Television Series of the 1950s*, by Patrick

Luciano and Gary Colville (1998). Children's television is covered by Jeffrey Davis' *Children's Television 1947–1990* and George W. Woolery's *Children's Television: The First Thirty-Five Years, 1946–1981*, which separates the material into a volume on cartoons and another on live series. More comprehensive is Hal Erickson's *Television Cartoon Shows: An Illustrated Encyclopedia, 1949 through 1993*, which includes detailed synopses enlivened by critical commentary. Erickson also provides a guide to *Syndicated Television: The First Forty Years, 1947–1987*, which divides material by decades and subdivides it into genre categories. Prime-time serials—including such series as *Twin Peaks*, *L.A. Law*, and *Soap*—get episode guides in Bruce B. Morris' *Prime Time Network Serials* (1997). Special news reports and documentaries are covered by Daniel Einstein's *Special Edition* (1997), with synopses of the broadcasts. Richard Lynch (1996) and Marill (1998) work on music, and Parish and the ever-active Terrace provide the two-volume *Complete Actors' Television Credits, 1948–1988*. An intriguing volume is Lance's *Written out of Television: The Encyclopedia of Cast Changes and Character Replacements, 1945–1994*, which evaluates the significance of the changes for each series.

One reason for the lack of unified conversation among television scholars—aside from television's inherent multiplicity—is the lack of a central, annual bibliography. Cassata in 1985 provided a onetime guide to the literature, usefully arranged by topic. *Film Literature Index* annually provides a large, useful section on television, but it is not complete. The bibliographical information provided after entries in Newcomb's *Encyclopedia of Television* is useful, as is the bibliography in Creeber's *The Television Genie Book*. Individual periodicals can be helpful; for example, the 1998 twentieth-anniversary issue of *Studies in Popular Culture* lists all its articles by subject, including a large group on television. The *MLA International Bibliography* annual subject volume lists many books and articles on television, though few series (such as *Star Trek*) get their own subject heading.

Finding primary sources has always been a challenge in this field. In recent years series such as *Seinfeld*, *Buffy the Vampire Slayer*, *thirtysomething*, *Monty Python* (Chapman et al.), and *Star Trek* have had books of scripts published. Any television series, however, is much more than the written word. Access to copies of the shows has been greatly aided by the Museum of Television and Radio Broadcasting, which has sites in New York and Los Angeles and a Web site. The Library of Congress provides a catalog of its holdings through 1979. Vanderbilt University provides a Television News Archive, with the index now on-line. Kaid and Haynes have published a catalog of the University of Oklahoma Political Commercial Archives (1991). The *Film Researcher's Handbook* (1996) gives advice (by country and subject) on places to access primary material. For those who wish to build their own libraries, Gale's *Video Source Book*, in its 22nd edition in 1999, will tell which episodes of *Buffy the Vampire Slayer* (among other things) are available for purchase.

HISTORY

The preeminent historian of television is Erik Barnouw. The history that he covers in his three-volume set *A Tower in Babel*, *The Golden Web*, and *The Image Empire* is condensed in the one-volume standard *Tube of Plenty*. Fascinating in the complexity and sometimes the contradictions of the reported memories of its many "witnesses" is Jeff Kisselhoff's excellent oral history *The Box*, covering 1920–1961 (1995). One of the witnesses is admired NBC executive Pat Weaver, who provides his own view of television's golden age in *The Best Seat in the House* (1994). A corrective external view can be found in the many chapters on American television in *Television: An International History* (1995), which provides a detailed presentation of the many contributions to the invention of television and a lucid chapter on the networks by Les Brown. Many histories focus on the golden age, such as *The Days of Live* (1998), with remembrances of directors; Anderson's *Hollywood TV: The Studio System in the Fifties* (1994); Harvey's *Those Wonderful, Terrible Years* (1996), on the American Federation of Television and Radio Artists; and see Foley on that period's *Political Blacklist in the Broadcast Industry*. There is an even narrower focus by R. D. Heldenfels on *Television's Greatest Year–1954* (1994). Jeff Greenfield's *Television: The First Fifty Years* is also still useful. In her *Defining Visions: Television and the American Experience since 1945* (1998), Mary Ann Watson interweaves history with sociological themes, making some intriguing, if not always fully persuasive, connections (e.g., in her concern about the violence of the Hawaiian Punch commercial). Watson provides a much more in-depth treatment of a shorter period, the 1960s, in *The Expanding Vista* (1990). Quality television of the 1980s and 1990s is discussed in Robert Thompson's *Television's Second Golden Age* (1996), which is both analysis and history and makes a persuasive case for the value of these series. Rob Owen considers lesser series in the context of the same general time period. The important role of the MTM company in the second golden age can be seen in Feuer, Kerr, and Vahimagi's *MTM: Quality Television*—again, both history and analysis, with reference information including brief episode synopses for many of the finest series. Grant Tinker, head of MTM and NBC, provides with Bud Rukeyser a more recent insider's view comparable to Pat Weaver's.

THEORY AND GENERAL COMMENTARY

A student of television would do well to begin with the excellent anthology *Television: The Critical View*, edited by Horace Newcomb. Though credit should be given to the early critical work of Gilbert Seldes, who soon became one of television's pioneer producers, and the general theory of McLuhan's 1964 *Understanding Media*, most of the modern stream of American critical thought on television can be traced to Newcomb. His 1974 *TV: The Most Popular Art* and, with Robert Alley, *The Producer's Medium* (1983) are essential. Across the Atlantic, also in 1974, Raymond Williams' *Television: Technology and Cultural Form* inaugurated serious consideration of form by British scholars with his theory of "flow"—the sequence that a viewer encounters, including, for example, the commercials. Another key work is John Fiske and John Hartley's 1978 *Reading Television*, emphasizing semiotic analysis in contrast, for example, to Newcomb and Alley's analysis of origination through *The Producers' Medium* or Newcomb's discussion of larger patterns of genres reflecting social currents in *TV: The Most Popular Art*. Like Newcomb, Fiske and Hartley are continuing their work. Fiske's *Television Culture* (1987), for example, emphasizes television's seeming naturalness as an ideological construct and provides sensible elements of analysis; Hartley's *Uses of Television*

Child watching *Sesame Street*. © Skjold Photographs

(1999) argues that television is now reintegrating government, education, and media. In their different ways, all these scholars value the television text.

In broad terms, television studies tend to be sociological or cultural: they focus on television as a symptom or cause of social patterns (usually problems), or they focus on television as humanistic expression—whether through analysis of text or audience. Many of the best are beginning to acknowledge both avenues to insight (see, e.g., the "Point-Counterpoint" that opens Burns and Thompson's collection *Television Studies*). Unfortunately, many of the best *known* are those that propound sociological problems. From quiz-show scandal survivor Marie Winn's *The Plug-In Drug* (1977), to Neal Postman's *Amusing Ourselves to Death* (1985), to Michael Medved's *Hollywood vs. America* (1992), critics have focused on television's baleful influence. From a very different context, famed French critic Pierre Bourdieu argues more or less the same view as many of the sociological studies—that television is a danger to democracy (1998). George Comstock in *Television in America* (rev. 1991) presents, along with some careful history of the medium, the unhappy view that watching television often means not thinking. In terms of causes rather than effects, Todd Gitlin's oft-cited *Inside Prime Time* (rev. 1994) depicts in detail the creation-by-committee process that makes doing good television so difficult— though he does acknowledge the rare success in *Hill Street Blues* (cf. Halberstam, 1979; Turow, 1984; and on PBS, Day, 1995; Engelman, 1996; Jarvik, 1999). Baker and Dessart's *Down the Tube* (1998) analyzes the same profit-influenced internecine wars of creation with emphasis on government misregulation. David Marc's *Bonfire of the Humanities* (1995) is an angry query about the damage done by television, in part, sadly, because we have failed to grapple with it as art, with all art's power. Lichter, Lichter, and Rothman in *Prime Time* (1994) fear that television's portrayal of social categories of gender, class, work, and so on puts viewers in "a dream from which we never fully awaken" (vii).

A very different view is provided by Michael Dunne, who celebrates the undreaming consciousness required for the flowering of self-reflexive television that he describes in *Metapop* (1992). John Thornton Caldwell's *Televisuality* (1995) similarly recognizes the "highly publicized ritual of aesthetic facility" (vii) of many series (he discusses *Northern Exposure* and, like Dunne and J. P. Williams, among others, *Moonlighting*). In fact, many critics seem to see analysis of the text (sometimes identified very broadly to include associated products, advertisements, etc.) as worthy not only for its own sake but also as antidote to sociological ills. Jane Feuer, in *Seeing through the Eighties: Television and Reaganism* (1995), notes the attempt to qualify some series (e.g., *thirtysomething*) as art by foregrounding the writers, and the oppositional readings of non-"art" series such as *Dynasty*. Jostein Gripsrud, in *The Dynasty Years* (1995), also argues in favor of textual interpretation leading to social analysis and uses secondary texts such as newspapers as well as tertiary texts such as viewers' letters. David Buxton discusses the ideology inherent in form in *From The Avengers to Miami Vice* (1990). *TV Drama in Transition: Forms, Values, and Cultural Change* (1997) praises what author Robin Nelson calls the "flexinarrative" of *Hill Street Blues* and the reality-framing of both *Middlemarch* and *The X-Files*. Anthologies such as E. Ann Kaplan's *Regarding Television* (1983), Gitlin's *Watching Television* (1987), Robert C. Allen's *Channels of Discourse, Reassembled* (1992), Nick Browne's *American Television* (1994), and editors Gary R. Edgerton, Michael T. Marsden, and Jack Nachbar's *In the Eye of the Beholder* (1997) all confront the interweaving of formal and social issues; and see Newcomb's Bakhtinian discussion of the subject (1984). Very specific analyses of form can be found in Metallinos' *Television Aesthetics* (1996), which covers such topics as defining the visual field, auditory focus, and motion. From the left field of Heidegger studies, Tony Fry's *RUA/TV* (1993) reminds us that television's form also includes the context of the content's arrival and, like Feuer and others, argues for the insubordination of authority possible in talking back to the television. Larger formal patterns are outlined in Brian Rose's 1985 *TV Genres*, which is also a bibliographical tool. Stuart M. Kaminsky's *American Television Genres*, from the same year, covers fewer categories, giving theoretical background such as a Jungian approach to science fiction and a Freudian approach to detective series. David Bianculli has done yeoman work in trying to popularize the valorization of quality television in *Teleliteracy: Taking Television Seriously* (1992). That television scholarship has come of age is suggested by the confidence required for the playful self-criticism of *Teleparody*, a collection of mock-scholarship edited by Angela Hague and the prolific David Lavery (2002).

AUDIENCE STUDIES

A whole area of studies has grown up around the debated issue of audience studies. Social scientists George Comstock and Erica Scharrer represent a view held by many outside television studies (as well as in) when they warn that television socializes audiences (especially young ones) toward antisocial behavior and a preference for "undemanding content" (262). But Camille Bacon-Smith, in her 1992 ethnographic study of *Star Trek* fandom, *Enterprising Women*, emphasizes the independent community created by an unusually active audience. Ien Ang explicates the polysemic nature of the text in the response of a more varied, generally noncommunal audience in *Watching Dallas* (1985). Both these studies deal mainly with women, as indeed do a great many qualitative adult audience studies—which are often also gender studies. In Ang's *Desperately Seeking the Audience* (1991), she points out that what is termed the audience is sometimes simply a marketing construct. Hay, Grossberg, and Wartella in the collection *The Audience and Its Landscape* (1996) reiterate Ang's argument for the necessity of contextualizing, as do John Tulloch and Henry Jenkins in *Science Fiction Audiences* (1995) and Jenkins' earlier *Textual Poachers: Television Fans and Participatory Culture* (1992). David Morley's *Television, Audiences, and Cultural Studies* (1992) argues against a simple transplantation of British cultural studies (e.g., Fiske and Hartley) but also against the mainstream pessimism of the Frankfurt school reduction of popular culture to commodification. Seiter's et al.'s *Remote Control* (1991), Lisa A. Lewis' collection *The Adoring Audience* (1992), and Jennifer Hayward's *Consuming Pleasures* (1997) also deal with the issue of the active audience.

RACE AND ETHNICITY

Earlier studies of race and ethnicity quite rightly recognize both the lack of imaging and the negative imaging of many minorities. J. Fred MacDonald, for instance, speaks of the "new minstrelsy" (149) in his 1983 *Blacks and White TV*; and see Anthony Jackson (1982) and Randall Miller (1978). Robin R. Means Coleman, in her audience reception study *African American Viewers and the Black Situation Comedy* (1998) uses the term "buffoonery" for the images in many sitcoms pre- and post-*Cosby*, though she excepts *The Fresh Prince of Bel Air* and the short-lived *Frank's Place* and *Roc*. Herman Gray in *Watching Race: Television and the Struggle for "Blackness"* (1995) agrees that much television representation of blackness feeds dominant culture but uses cultural studies and rhetorical analysis to argue that some series—such as *Frank's Place* and *In Living Color*—expose the hierarchy. Marie Gillespie (1995), Darnell M. Hunt (1997), Christopher P. Campbell (1995), Kristal Brent Zook (1999), Camille O. Cosby (1994) and Donald Bogle (2001) also offer significant work in the field. Sasha Torres' collection *Living Color* (1998) includes discussions of Middle Eastern, Asian, and Latino as well as black representations, while Darrell Y. Hamamoto (1994) focuses on Asian, Jack Shaheen (1984) on Middle Eastern, Jonathan and Judith Pearl (1999) on Jewish, and Luis Reyes and Peter Rubie (1994) on Hispanic images. Numerous studies of individual series—such as Bernardi, Pounds, and several of the essays in the collection *Enterprise Zones*—also study these issues.

GENDER AND SEXUAL ORIENTATION

There have always been women in television. There have never been many. From Pem Farnsworth's helping her husband Philo, to Madelyn Pugh Davis' writing for *I Love Lucy* (not to mention Lucy), to Ethel Winant's working as vice president of casting for CBS, to Marcy Carsey's production of *Roseanne* (not to mention Roseanne), to Barbara Corday's presiding over the television division of a major studio, to Lucie Salhary's heading a network (Fox), women have been involved. But, as Linda Seger says in her 1996 study, "behind the scenes, there are still few women" (261). Various other social views are covered by Donald (1995), Press and Cole (1999), and Carter, Branston, and Allan's collection *News, Gender, and Power* (1998). Gender studies often takes another angle, however, analyzing text and/or reception. Many audience studies focus on female spectators. Text and context analyses are also numerous. Many (whether they agree or demur) assume a knowledge of the foundational Freudian work on the male gaze by film scholar Laura Mulvey. Tania Modleski's *Loving with a Vengeance: Mass-Produced Fantasies for Women* (1982) has also been influential. Mary Ellen Brown's collection *Television and Women's Culture* (1990) provides a useful summary of feminist studies in television/film followed by readings that use both structural and social elements. Frances Gray's 1994 *Women and Laughter* provides insights such as the paradox of Lucy Ricardo's incompetence versus Lucille Ball's starring brilliance in representing that incompetence; Lynne Joyrich (1996) discusses the reproductive politics and Hilary Radner (1995) the cover girl imaging of *Moonlighting*; Bonnie J. Dow points out the postfeminist integration of professional and family roles in the fantasy of *Dr. Quinn, Medicine Woman*. Nochimson (1992), Brown (1994), Mumford (1995), Blumenthal (1997), and Brunsdon (2000), all working with soap opera; Meehan (1983), D'Acci (1994), Rapping (1994), Rowe (1995), Daddario (1998), Green (1998), Sochen (1999), Isaacs (1999), Inness (1999), Roberts (1999), Projansky (2001), Alley and Brown (2001), and Helford's collection (2000, *Fantasy Girls*) are among others studying gender issues.

Constance Penley's discussion of *Pee Wee's Playhouse* in *The Future of an Illusion* includes not only gender issues but also sexual orientation, specifically, homosexuality. Doty's *Making Things Perfectly Queer* (1993), Mayne's *Framed* (2000), Walker's *All the Rage* (2001), and the collections *Queer Words, Queer Images* (1994) and *Because I Tell a Joke or Two* (1998) also address the topic of the problems with television's images of gays and lesbians—or the lack thereof.

RELIGION

The lack of images of religion concerns the writers in Michael Suman's collection *Religion and Prime Time Television* (1997), ranging from the conservative Rev. Donald E. Wildmon, to pop critic Medved, to Buddhist Havanpola Ratanasara. These writers, however, generally overlook the embedded religious and spiritual content of many series such as *Northern Exposure* (Wilcox 1993), *Star Trek: Deep Space 9* (Wagner and Lundeen 1998), and even *The Simpsons* (Pinsky 2001) and *Mister Rogers' Neighborhood* (see the collection by Collins and Kimmel, 1996). Other writers concerned with religious issues include Hadden and Swann (1981), Horsfield (1984), Alexander (1994), Goethals (1990), Christopher Owen Lynch (1998), and Elizabeth Hirschman (2000).

CHILDREN

Another subject long of concern to television scholars is children and television. Comstock, in *Television and the American Child* (1991), argues for government regulation to enforce improvement of television programming. Social scientists' concerns are also explored in the collections *Media, Children, and the Family* (1994) and *Tuning in to Young Viewers* (1996), and Newton Minow (and Craig La May) returns to the concern that he expressed in 1961 with *Abandoned in the Wasteland* (1995). Children's Television Workshop crusader Peggy Charren and Martin Sandler have provided *Changing Channels* (1983). Clifford, Gunter, and McAleer examine the developmental changes in children's responses (1995), while Seiter attempts a non-elitist evaluation of children's television-influenced use of consumption to define self (1993). Particular concerns about advertising and children are investigated by Fox (1996), Kline (1993), Young (1990), who compares American and British advertising, Unnikrishnan and Bajpai (1996), who examine American product advertising in India, and Ann De Vaney (1994) in the collection *Watching Channel One*. Heather Hendershot (1998), who discusses product-based cartoons, also, however, notes that the now generally admired *Sesame Street* was initially attacked. Burke and Burke (1999) question the experimental models on which many social scientists' concerns about children and violence are based; Buckingham (1996), using qualitative research to suggest that kids' responses are not deadened by television violence (cf. Himmelweit, Oppenheim, and Vince, 1958), Palmer (1986), and Davies (1997) provide variant views of children as audience, with Davies calling television "a body of literature to which children are regularly exposed" (7); and Bazalguette and Buckingham's 1995 collection *In Front of the Children* includes analysis of some of the subtexts of that literature, such as good and bad father images and fantasies of transformation in *Teenage Mutant Ninja Turtles*.

VIOLENCE

Closely associated with the preceding studies (and sometimes overlapping) are a number of books on violence and television. UCLA has published *The UCLA Television Violence Report* (1996), and Sage has published the *National Television Violence Study* (1997). Cynthia A. Cooper surveys the history of reaction to violence on television, from Betty Boop, to the Kennedy assassinations, to Janet Reno versus *Beavis and Butthead*. Monroe E. Price's collection covers *The V-Chip Debate* (1998), and Geoffrey Cowan the behind-scenes network discussions of violence. James Hamilton (1998) recommends using the FCC's licensing powers to force a reduction in violence and gives a detailed statistical analysis without a comparably detailed definition of the factors constituting violence. The *Television Violence and Public Policy* collection (1998) explores more specific defining factors (e.g., intent to harm). John Leonard, on the other hand, mocks the idea that "guns don't kill people; television does" and argues that "except for hospital shows, there is less violence on television than there used to be" (3), supplementing his view with content analysis of such series as *Homicide* and *Alien Nation*. Martin Shaw (1996) discusses the propaganda choices to show or avoid violence in reporting on Iraq, Rwanda, and Bosnia.

NEWS AND POLITICS

News reporting in general has drawn much response. Daniel Dayan and Elihu Katz (1992) discuss the narratizing of events reporting. Liebes and Curran's collection *Media, Ritual, and Identity* (1998) follows in the same path. Jane Shattuc (1995) covers tabloid news, and John Langer (1998) analyzes it as cultural discourse with connections to the horror film. One should see also Matthew Kerbel (2000). Darnell M. Hunt (1999) narrows his sights to the O. J. Simpson coverage. William C. Spragens (1995) gives content analysis of "soft news programs" (e.g., *60 Minutes*) as distinguished from tabloids. Susan D. Moeller assesses news as entertainment and ascribes failings in foreign coverage to that fact (1999). Samuel P. Winch (1997) explicates several case studies (e.g. Gennifer Flowers and Bill Clinton) to show the difficulty of distinguishing news from entertainment. Philip Seib addresses the implications of online information (2001). Penn Kimball discusses the recent cutbacks in news services (1994), and a group of journalists discuss the changing role of the correspondent in *Live from the Trenches* (1998). Michael D. Murray (1994) covers CBS, long the premier news network; CBS executive Sig Mickelson (1998) discusses the shift from a fifteen-person staff in 1950 to 400 in 1960. Fred Friendly explains his break with CBS (1968). Richard S. Salant's memoirs also give a history of CBS, and Marc Gunther (1994) covers ABC by focusing on Roone Arledge. *See It Now* (Rosteck, 1994), *Meet the Press* (Ball, 1998), *Nightline* (Koppel and Gibson, 1996), the Monitor Channel (Bridge, 1998), and C-Span (Frantzrich and Sullivan, 1996) each gets its own volume. There are studies and reminiscences of luminaries such as Edward R. Murrow (Bliss, 1967; Kendrick, 1969), Eric Sevareid (Schroth 1995), Walter Cronkite (James, 1991; Cronkite, 1996), David Brinkley (1995), Dan Rather (1994, 1999), Lesley Stahl (1999), and local anchor Stan Chambers (1994). The construction of local news through market and other pressures is analyzed in depth, with case studies, by John H. McManus (1994). Brown, Firestone, and Mickiewicz (1994) discuss news and minorities; Hilt (1997), the news and the elderly (cf. Riggs 1998 on the elderly). In *Views on the News* (1994), television professionals such as Fred W. Friendly argue for hour-long news in spite of financial questions. They would probably be supported by Peter Phillips (1997, 1998) and Carl Jensen (1996), who report in *Censored* on significant print stories that never make it to television news, with the imprimatur of a Cronkite introduction for their twentieth annual volume. Slotnick and Segal (1998) cover interactions with the Supreme Court. Broad news subjects such as drug coverage (Reeves and Campbell, 1994), 1960s social conflict (Spigel and Curtin, 1997), nuclear power (*Television and Nuclear Power*, 1992), diplomacy (Strobel, 1997), and defense (Aubin, 1998) are discussed with their implications for public policy.

Books on news and books on politics, of course, overlap. The Suez Crisis (Shaw, 1996), the Cold War (Curtin, 1995), Vietnam, AIDS (Sturken, 1997), and Iran-Contra (Thelen, 1996) are among other general subjects that are both news and politics. But by far, the most political/news studies are written on presidential elections. A notable early study is Joe McGinniss' *The Selling of the President, 1968* (1970). More recently, Karen S. Johnson-Cartee and Gary A. Copeland (1997) use specific analysis of many ads to convey the use of storytelling and political mythologies. *Let America Decide* (1995) gives a brief history of the presidential debates, discussing scheduling, format, sponsorship, and control. Benoit and Wells (1996) give transcripts of debates as well as rhetorical analyses. Benoit, Blaney, and Pier (1998) expand beyond the debates to give a more general analysis of campaign discourse. Lichter and Noyes (1995) cover the rise of "character cops," and Hart (1999) discusses personality politics as opposed to civic affairs coverage. Liz Cunningham (1995) interviews a series of public figures from Robert MacNeil, to Larry King, to Geraldine Ferraro about the relationship between broadcasters and presidential candidates. CBS News' Martin Plissner (1999) discusses primary and convention coverage and notes that television overtook newspapers as the main source of public information in the same year that the news went from fifteen minutes to a half hour. Dover (1994, 1998), Morreale (1993), West (1997), Kerbel (1998) and the collections *Under the Watchful Eye* (1992) and *Political Advertising in Western Democracies* (1995) all cover television campaigning.

INDIVIDUAL SERIES

Not only news programs such as *See It Now* but many other series have books devoted to them. By far the most frequent object of study is *Star Trek* (in any of its five incarnations). A collection of serious scholarly essays is *Enterprise Zones* (1996), which has a useful bibliography. An often overlooked, but thoughtful, early study on archetypes is Karin Blair's *Meaning in Star Trek* (1977). There are studies on the biology of *Star Trek* (Andreadis, 1998), the physics (Krauss, 1995), and the metaphysics (Hanley, 1997). Harlan Ellison provides an indignant account of the changes forced on a script that he wrote for a famous episode. Two books concentrate on race and ethnicity in *Star Trek* (Bernardi, 1998; Pounds, 1999; and see *Enterprise Zones*). Penley (1997) also has a study, as do Richards (1997), Greenwald (1998), and, on *Deep Space 9*, Wagner and Lundeen (1998). Judith and Garfield Reeves-Stevens' *The Making of Star Trek, Deep Space Nine* (1994) joins Whitfield and Roddenberry's 1968 *The Making of Star Trek*. On the *Star Trek* audience, see Bacon-Smith (1992), Jenkins (1992), and Tulloch and Jenkins (1995), also on *Doctor Who*. *Doctor Who* is the subject of Haining (1983) and Tulloch and Alvarado (1983), as well. There has been a proliferation of work on *Buffy the Vampire Slayer*. See, for example, Tracy (1998) and the edited collections by Kaveney, *Reading the Vampire Slayer* (2001), Wilcox and Lavery, *Fighting the Forces* (2002), and James B. South, *Buffy the Vampire Slayer and Philosophy* (2002). David Lavery has also edited collections on *Twin Peaks* (*Full of Secrets*, 1995), *The Sopranos* (*This Thing of Ours*, 2002), and, with Hague and Cartwright, *The X-Files* ("*Deny All Knowledge*," 1996). Also see Delasara (2000) on *The X-files*. Other series with volumes on them include *M*A*S*H* (Wittebols, 1998; Gelbart, 1998), *All in the Family* (McCrohan, 1987; the Adler collection *All in the Family*, 1979), *The Andy Griffith Show* (Robinson and Fernandes, 1996; Brower, 1998; Kelly, 1981), *I Love Lucy* (Andrews, 1976; Arnaz, 1976); *The Honeymooners* (McCrohan, 1978; Meadows, 1994), *The Twilight Zone* (Presnell and McGee, 1998; Wolfe, 1997), Dick Clark's *American Bandstand* (Jackson, 1997; Clark, 1997), *The Dick Van Dyke Show* (Waldron, 1994; Weissman and Sanders, 1983), *The Avengers* (Buxton, 1990; Miller, 1997), *thirtysomething* (Heide, 1995), *Alfred Hitchcock Presents* (McCarthy and Kelleher, 1985), *The Today Show* (Metz, 1977), *Your Show of Shows* (Sennett, 1977), *Dick Cavett* (Cavett and Porterfield, 1975), *The Goldbergs* (Berg, 1961), *Beverly Hills 90210* (McKinley, 1997), *Lou Grant* (Daniel, 1996), *Buffy the Vampire Slayer* (Tracy, 1998), *Days of Our Lives* (Russell, 1995), *Saturday Night Live* (Hill and Weingrad, 1986), *The Civil War* (the Toplin collection *Ken Burns's The Civil War*, 1996), *The Rocky and Bullwinkle Show* (Chunovic, 1996); *The Saint* (Barer, 1993);

on *Dynasty*, see Feuer (1995) and Gripsrud (1995) earlier; and on *Dallas*, see Ang (1985).

INDIVIDUALS

Individuals have also been the subjects of books. These include Nochimson's study *The Passion of David Lynch* (1997), Thompson's *Adventures* about Stephen J. Cannell, Erickson on Sid and Marty Krofft (1998), and Fern's book-length interview with Roddenberry (1994). There are also mainly biographical works on Fred Coe (Krampner, 1997), David Sarnoff (Lyon, 1966), Laurence Tisch (Winans, 1995), Zworykin (Abramson, 1995), Johnny Carson (De Cordova, 1988; Leamer, 1989), Oprah Winfrey (Bly, 1993), Dick Van Dyke (Kearton, 1992), Rod Serling (Engel, 1989), and Rosie O'Donnell (Goodman, 1998). Autobiographies, self-examinations, and reminiscences include those of David Lynch (1997), George Takei (1994), Montel Williams (1996), Roseanne (then) Arnold (1989), Tom Baker (1997), sitcom director Alan Rafkin (1998), William S. Paley (1979), and Aaron Spelling (1996). On similar studies of reporters, see the section on News/Politics.

GENRES

Definitions of genres are provided by Rose and by Kaminsky. Studies of specific genres can also be found. Studies of soap operas are mentioned above under both Gender and Audience Studies; and see Brunsdon's 1997 *Screen Tastes*, Harrington and Bielby (1995), Cantor and Pingree (1983), Cassata and Skill (1983), and the 1995 Robert C. Allen collection *To Be Continued*, which discusses some American soap operas. Many writers discuss talk shows, including Heaton and Wilson (1995), Abt and Mustazza (1997), and Shattuc, whose 1997 *The Talking Cure* notes that this utilitarian therapy seems formed for consumerism and that greater civility might lead to less genuine confrontation of society's zones of discomfort. Alba et al. has a collection on *Interactive Home Shopping* (1997). On drama, see Robin Nelson (mentioned earlier). Turow discusses medical drama from *Kildare* to *Elsewhere* (1989); Sumser (1996) and Sparks (1992) write on crime drama; the Jarvis and Joseph collection *Prime Time Law* (1998) investigates implicit legal attitudes; and Delamater and Prigozy have a collection on *The Detective* (1998), a genre also discussed by Larka (1979). Family series are covered by Taylor (1989) and Marling (1994); and Leibman (1995) argues that so-called 1950s sitcoms are actually family melodrama. Marc's *Demographic Vistas* (1984) and *Comic Visions* (1997) both deal with comedy with many specific insights, noting, for example, the shift in point of view from the father in the 1950s to the son in the 1970s *Happy Days*. Individual westerns are analyzed in a lengthy work by Yoggy (1995); westerns are also discussed in Brauer (1975), *American Indian Studies* (1997), and *Back in the Saddle Again* (1998) and individual western actors in *Back in the Saddle* (1998) and Fagen's *White Hats* (1996). Forrest J. Ackerman describes science fiction (and see the studies of numerous individual SF series). Hammond deals with documentaries (1981), and Derek Paget (1998) writes on the "trauma drama" of docudrama. The Fishman and Cavender collection, *Entertaining Crime*, covers "reality programs" of both the United Kingdom and United States. There are even studies of infomercials (Evans, 1994) and ads (Savan, 1994; Rutherford, 1994). Kaplan responds to MTV in *Rocking around the Clock* (1987), classifying music videos (e.g., the romantic, the socially conscious, the postmodern) and discussing successes such as Tina Turner's "Private Dancer"; and see the collection on music videos titled *Sound and Vision* (1993).

Whatever will come in terms of genre, content, or forms of interaction with television in this century, it is worth, as Bianculli says, taking seriously. The following scholars enable us to do so, and some of them even help us to justify our enjoyment of the good work that television does.

BIBLIOGRAPHY

Books and Articles

Abramson, Albert. *Zworykin, Pioneer of Television*. Urbana: University of Illinois Press, 1995.

Abt, Vicki, and Leonard Mustazza. *Coming After Oprah: Cultural Fallout in the Age of the TV Talk Show*. Bowling Green: Bowling Green State University Popular Press, 1997.

Ackerman, Forrest J. *Forrest J. Ackerman's World of Science Fiction*. Foreword by John Landis; preface by A. E. Van Vogt. Los Angeles: General Publication Group, 1997.

The Adoring Audience: Fan Culture and Popular Media. Ed. Lisa A. Lewis. London: Routledge, 1992.

Alba, Joseph, et al. *Interactive Home Shopping and the Retail Industry*. Cambridge, MA: Marketing Science Institute, 1997.

Alexander, Bobby C. *Televangelism Reconsidered: Ritual in the Search for Human Community*. Atlanta: Scholars, 1994.

All in the Family: A Critical Appraisal. Ed. Richard P. Adler. New York: Praeger, 1979.

Alley, Robert S., and Irby B. Brown. *Women Television Producers: Transformation of the Male Medium*. Rochester, N.Y.: University of Rochester Press, 2001.

Alley, Robert, and Horace Newcomb. *The Producer's Medium: Conversations with the Creators of American TV*. New York: Oxford University Press, 1983.

American Indian Studies: An Interdisciplinary Approach to Contemporary Issues. Ed. Dane Morrison. New York: Peter Lang, 1997.

American Television: New Directions in History and Theory. Ed. Nick Browne. Studies in Film and Video. Langhorne, Pa.: Harvard Academic, 1994.

Andersen, Robin. *Consumer Culture and TV Programming*. Critical Studies in Communication and the Cultural Industries. Boulder, Colo.: Westview, 1995.

Anderson, Christopher. *Hollywood TV: The Studio System in the Fifties*. Texas Film Studies. Austin: University of Texas Press, 1994.

Andreadis, Athena. *To Seek out New Life: The Biology of Star Trek*. New York: Crown, 1998.

Andrews, Bart. *Lucy & Ricky & Fred & Ethel: The Story of "I Love Lucy."* New York: E. P. Dutton, 1976.

Ang, Ien. *Desperately Seeking the Audience*. London: Routledge, 1991.

———. *Watching Dallas: Soap Opera and the Melodramatic Imagination*. Trans. Della Couling. London: Routledge, 1985.

Arnaz, Desi. *A Book*. New York: Warner Books, 1976.

Arnold, Roseanne. *Roseanne: My Life as a Woman*. New York: Harper and Row, 1989.

Aubin, Stephen P. *Distorting Defense: Network News and National Security*. Westport, CN: Praeger, 1998.

The Audience and Its Landscape. Ed. James Hay, Lawrence Grossberg, Ellen Wartella. Cultural Studies. Boulder, Colo.: Westview, 1996.

Back in the Saddle: Essays on Western Film and Television Actors. Ed. Gary A. Yoggy. Jefferson, NC: McFarland, 1998.

Back in the Saddle Again: New Essays on the Western. Ed. Edward Buscombe and Roberta Pearson. London: BFI, 1998.

Bacon-Smith, Camille. *Enterprising Women: Television Fandom and the Creation of Popular Myth*. Series in Contemporary Ethnography. Philadelphia: University of Pennsylvania Press, 1992.

Baker, Tom. *Who on Earth Is Tom Baker?* London: HarperCollins, 1997.

Baker, William F., and George Dessart. *Down the Tube: An Inside Account of the Failure of American Television*. New York: Basic Books, 1998.

Ball, Rick, and NBC News. *Meet the Press: Fifty Years of History in the Making*. New York: McGraw-Hill, 1998.

Barer, Burl. *The Saint: A Complete History in Print, Radio, Film, and Television of Leslie Charteris' Robin Hood of Modern Crime, Simon Templar, 1928–1992*. Jefferson, NC: McFarland, 1993.

Barnouw, Erik. *The Golden Web: A History of Broadcasting in the United States*. Vol. 2, 1933 to 1953. New York: Oxford Press, 1968.

———. *The Image Empire: A History of Broadcasting in the United States*. Vol, 3, from 1953. New York: Oxford Press, 1970.

———. *A Tower in Babel: A History of Broadcasting in the United States*. Vol. 1, to 1933. New York: Oxford University Press, 1966.

———. *Tube of Plenty: The Evolution of American Television*. 2nd rev. ed. New York: Oxford University Press, 1990.

Because I Tell a Joke or Two: Comedy, Politics, and Social Difference. Ed. Stephen Wagg. London: Routledge, 1998.

Bellamy, Robert V., and James R. Walker. *Television and the Remote Control: Grazing on a Vast Wasteland*. New York: Guilford, 1996.

Benoit, William L., Joseph R. Blaney, and P. M. Pier. *Campaign '96: A Functional Analysis of Acclaiming, Attacking, and Defending*. Westport, Conn.: Praeger, 1998.

Benoit, William L., and William T. Wells. *Candidates in Conflict: Persuasive Attack and Defense in the 1992 Presidential Debates*. Studies in Rhetoric and Communication. Tuscaloosa: University of Alabama Press, 1996.

Berg, Gertrude. *Molly and Me*. New York: McGraw-Hill, 1961.

Bernardi, Daniel Leonard. *Star Trek and History: Race-ing Toward a White Future*. New Brunswick, N.J.: Rutgers University Press, 1998.

Bianculli, David. *Dictionary of Teleliteracy: Television's 500 Biggest Hits, Misses, and Events*. New York: Continuum, 1996.

———. *Teleliteracy: Taking Television Seriously*. New York: Continuum, 1992.

Billips, Connie, and Arthur Pierce. *Lux Presents Hollywood: A Show-by-Show History of the Lux Radio Theatre and the Lux Video Theatre, 1934–1957*. Jefferson, N.C.: McFarland, 1995.

Blair, Karin. *Meaning in Star Trek*. New York: Warner Books, 1977.

Bliss, Edward, Jr. *In Search of Light: The Broadcasts of Edward R. Murrow, 1938–1961*. New York: Knopf, 1967.

Blumenthal, Dannielle. *Women and Soap Opera: A Cultural Feminist Perspective*. Westport, Conn.: Praeger, 1997.

Bly, Nellie. *Oprah! Up Close and Down Home*. New York: Kensington, 1993.

Bogle, Donald. *Prime Time Blues: African Americans on Network Television*. New York: Farrar, Strauss, and Giroux, 2001.

Bourdieu, Pierre. *On Television*. Trans. Priscilla Parkhurst Ferguson. New York: New Press, dist. W. W. Norton, 1998.

Boyle, Dierdre. *Subject to Change: Guerilla Television Revisited*. New York: Oxford University Press, 1997.

Brauer, Ralph. *The Horse, the Gun, and a Piece of Property: Changing Images of the TV Western*. Bowling Green, OH: Bowling Green State University Popular Press, 1975.

Bridge, Susan. *Monitoring the News: The Brilliant Launch and Sudden Collapse of the Monitor Channel*. Armonk, N.Y.: M. E. Sharpe, 1998.

Brinkley, David. *David Brinkley: 11 Presidents, 4 Wars, 22 Political Conventions, 1 Moon Landing, 3 Assassinations, 2000 Weeks of News and Other Stuff on Television and 18 Years of Growing up in North Carolina*. New York: A. A. Knopf, 1995.

Brinkley, Joel. *Defining Vision: The Battle for the Future of Television*. New York: Harcourt, 1997.

Brooks, Tim, and Earle Marsh. *The Complete Directory to Prime Time Network and Cable TV Shows: 1946-Present*. 6th ed. New York: Ballantine, 1995.

Brower, Neal. *Mayberry 101: Behind the Scenes of a TV Classic*. Winston-Salem, N.C.: John F. Blair, 1998.

Brown, Les. *Les Brown's Encyclopedia of Television*. 3rd ed. Detroit: Gale Research, 1992.

Brown, Mary Ellen. *Soap Opera and Women's Talk: The Pleasure of Resistance*. Thousand Oaks, CA: Sage, 1994.

Browne, Donald R., Charles M. Firestone, and Ellen Mickiewicz. *Television/Radio News and Minorities*. Queenstown, Md.: Aspen Institute; Atlanta: Carter Center of Emory University, 1994.

Brunsdon, Charlotte. *The Feminist, the Housewife, and the Soap Opera*. Oxford: Clarendon Press; New York: Oxford University Press, 2000.

———. *Screen Tastes: Soap Opera to Satellite Dishes*. London: Routledge, 1997.

Buckingham, David. *Moving Images: Understanding Children's Emotional Responses to Television*. Manchester: Manchester University Press, 1996.

Budd, Mike, Steve Craig, and Clay Steinman. *Consuming Environments: Television and Commercial Culture*. Communications, Media, Culture. New Brunswick, N.J.: Rutgers University Press, 1999.

Buffy the Vampire Slayer and Philosophy. Ed. James B. South. Chicago, Ill.: Open Court, forthcoming.

Buffy the Vampire Slayer: The Script Book: Season One. New York: Simon and Schuster, 2000.

Burke, Timothy, and Kevin Burke. *Saturday Morning Fever*. New York: St. Martin's Press, 1999.

Buxton, David. *From The Avengers to Miami Vice: Form and Ideology in Television Series*. Cultural Politics. Manchester: Manchester University Press, 1990.

Caldwell, John Thornton. *Televisuality: Style, Crisis, and Authority in American Television*. Communications, Media, and Culture. New Brunswick, N.J.: Rutgers University Press, 1995.

Campbell, Christopher P. *Race, Myth, and the News*. Thousand Oaks, Calif.: Sage, 1995.

Carbaugh, Donal. *Talking American: Cultural Discourses on Donahue*. Norwood, N.J.: Ablex, 1988.

Carroll, Noel. *Theorizing the Moving Image*. Cambridge Studies in Film. Cambridge: Cambridge University Press, 1996.

Cassata, Mary. *Television: A Guide to the Literature*. Phoenix: Oryx Press, 1985.

Cassata, Mary, and Thomas Skill. *Life on Daytime Television: Tuning-In American Serial Drama*. Norwood, N.J.: Ablex, 1983.

Cavett, Dick, and Christopher Porterfield. *Dick Cavett*. New York: Harcourt, Brace, Jovanovich, 1974.

Chambers, Stan. *News at Ten: Fifty Years with Stan Chambers*. Santa Barbara: Capra, 1994.

Channels of Discourse, Reassembled: Television and Contemporary Criticism. Ed. Robert C. Allen. 2nd ed. Chapel Hill: University of North Carolina Press, 1992.

Chapman, Graham, et al. *The Complete Monty Python's Flying Circus: All the Words*. 2 vols. New York: Pantheon, 1989.

Charren, Peggy, and Martin Sandler. *Changing Channels*. Reading, MA: Addison-Wesley, 1983.

Chunovic, Louis. *The Rocky and Bullwinkle Book*. New York: Bantam, 1996.

Clark, Dick. *Dick Clark's American Bandstand*. New York: Collins, 1997.

Clifford, Brian R., Barrie Gunter, and Jill McAleer. *Television and Children: Program Evaluation, Comprehension, and Impact*. Hillsdale, N.J.: L. Erlbaum, 1995.

Cohn, Marjorie, and David Dow. *Cameras in the Courtroom: Television and the Pursuit of Justice*. Jefferson, N.C.: McFarland, 1998.

Comstock, George A. *Television and the American Child*. San Diego: Academic Press, 1991.

———. *Television in America*. 2nd ed. Newbury Park, Calif.: Sage, 1991.

Comstock, George, and Erica Scharrer. *Television: What's on, Who's Watching, and What It Means*. San Diego: Academic Press, 1999.

Cooper, Cynthia A. *Violence on Television: Congressional Inquiry, Public Criticism, and Industry Response: A Policy Analysis*. Lanham, MD: University Press of America, 1996.

Cosby, Camille O. *Television's Imageable Influences: The Self-Perceptions of Young African-Americans*. Lanham, MD: University Press of America, 1994.

Cowan, Geoffrey. *See No Evil: The Backstage Battle over Sex and Violence in Television*. New York: Simon & Schuster, 1979.

Creeber, Glen. *The Television Genre Book*. London: British Film Institute, 2001.

Critical Dictionary of Film and Television Theory. Ed. Roberta E. Pearson and Philip Simpson. New York: Routledge, 2001.

Cronkite, Walter. *A Reporter's Life*. New York: Knopf, 1996.

Cunningham, Liz. *Talking Politics: Choosing the President in the Television Age*. Westport, Conn.: Praeger, 1995.

Curtin, Michael. *Redeeming the Wasteland: Television Documentary and Cold War Politics*. Communications, Media, and Culture. New Brunswick, N.J.: Rutgers University Press, 1995.

D'Acci, Julie. *Defining Women: Television and the Case of Cagney and Lacey*. Chapel Hill: University of North Carolina Press, 1994.

Daddario, Gina. *Women's Sport and Spectacle: Gendered Television Coverage and the Olympic Games*. Westport, Conn.: Praeger, 1998.

Daniel, Douglas K. *Lou Grant: The Making of TV's Top Newspaper Drama, The Television Series*. Syracuse, N.Y.: Syracuse University Press, 1996.

Davies, Maire Messenger. *Fake, Fact, and Fancy: Children's Interpretations of Television Reality*. Mahwah, N.J.: L. Erlbaum, 1997.

Davis, Jeffrey. *Children's Television, 1947–1990: Over 200 Series, Game and Variety Shows, Cartoons, Educational Programs, and Specials*. Jefferson, N.C.: McFarland, 1995.

Day, James. *The Vanishing Vision: The Inside Story of Public Television*. Berkeley: University of California Press, 1995.

Dayan, Daniel, and Elihu Katz. *Media Events: The Live Broadcasting of History*. Cambridge, Mass.: Harvard University Press, 1992.

Day-Lewis, Sean. *Talk of Drama: Views of the Television Dramatist Now and Then*. Luton, Bedfordshire: University of Luton Press, 1998.

The Days of Live: Television's Golden Age as Seen by 21 Directors' Guild of America Members. Ed. Ira Skutch. Directors' Guild of America Oral History Series 16. Lanham, Md.: Scarecrow; Los Angeles: Directors' Guild of America, 1998.

De Cordova, Fred. *Johnny Come Lately: An Autobiography*. New York: Simon and Schuster, 1988.

Delasara, Jan. *PopLit, PopCult, and The X-Files: A Critical Exploration*. Jefferson, N.C.: McFarland, 2000.

De Moragas Spa, Michael, Nancy K. Rivenburgh, and James F. Larson. *Television in the Olympics*. Academic Research Monographs 13. London: J. Libbey, 1995.

"Deny All Knowledge": Reading the X-Files. Ed. David Lavery, Angela Hague, and Marla Cartwright. The Television Series. Syracuse, N.Y.: Syracuse University Press, 1996.

The Detective in American Fiction, Film, and Television. Ed. Jerome H. Delamater and Ruth Prigozy. Contributions to the Study of Popular Culture. Westport, Conn.: Greenwood, 1998.

Dienst, Richard. *Still Life in Real Time: Theory After Television*. Post-Contemporary Interventions. Durham, N.C.: Duke University Press, 1994.

Donald, Anabel. *The Glass Ceiling*. New York: St. Martin's, 1995.

Doty, Alexander. *Making Things Perfectly Queer: Interpreting Mass Culture*. Minneapolis: University of Minnesota Press, 1993.

Dover, E. D. *The Presidential Election of 1996: Clinton's Incumbency and Television.* Westport, Conn.: Praeger, 1998.

———. *Presidential Elections in the Television Age: 1960–1992.* Westport, Conn.: Praeger, 1994.

Dow, Bonnie J. *Prime-Time Feminism: Television, Media Culture, and the Women's Movement Since 1970.* Feminist Cultural Studies, The Media, and Political Culture. Philadelphia: University of Pennsylvania Press, 1996.

Dunne, Michael. *Metapop: Self-Referentiality in Contemporary American Popular Culture.* Jackson: University Press of Mississippi, 1992.

Einstein, Daniel. *Special Edition: A Guide to Network Television Documentary Series and Special News Reports, 1980–1989.* Lanham, Md.: Scarecrow, 1997.

Ellison, Harlan. *Harlan Ellison's The City on the Edge of Forever: The Original Teleplay That Became the Classic Star Trek Episode, with an Expanded Introductory Essay by Harlan Ellison.* Clarkson, Ga.: White Wolf, 1995.

Encyclopedia of Television. Ed. Horace Newcomb. Cary O'Dell, photographic ed. 3 vols. Chicago: Fitzroy Dearborn, 1997.

Encyclopedia of Television News. Ed. Michael D. Murray. Phoenix: Oryx, 1999.

Engel, Joel. *Rod Serling: The Dreams and Nightmares of Life in the Twilight Zone: A Biography.* Chicago: Contemporary Books, 1989.

Engelman, Ralph. *Public Radio and Television in America: A Political History.* Thousand Oaks, CA: Sage, 1996.

Enterprise Zones: Critical Positions on Star Trek. Ed. Taylor Harrison et al. Film Studies. Boulder, Colo.: Westview, 1996.

Entertaining Crime: Television Reality Programs. Ed. Mark Fishman and Gray Cavender. Social Problems and Social Issues. New York: Aldine de Gruyter, 1998.

Erickson, Hal. *Sid and Marty Krofft: A Critical Study of Saturday Morning Children's Television, 1969–93.* Jefferson, N.C.: McFarland, 1998.

———. *Syndicated Television: The First Forty Years, 1947–1987.* Jefferson, N.C.: McFarland, 1989.

———. *Television Cartoon Shows: An Illustrated Encyclopedia, 1949 through 1993.* Jefferson, N.C.: McFarland, 1995.

Ethnic Images in American Film and Television. Ed. Randall M. Miller. Philadelphia: Balch Institute, 1978.

Evans, Craig Robert. *Marketing Channels: Infomercials and the Future of Televised Marketing.* Englewood Cliffs, N.J.: Prentice-Hall, 1994.

Fagen, Herb. *White Hats and Silver Spurs: Interviews with 24 Stars of Film and Television Westerns of the Thirties Through the Sixties.* Jefferson, N.C.: McFarland, 1996.

Fantasy Girls: Gender in the New Universe of Science Fiction and Fantasy. Ed. Elyce Rae Helford. Lanham, Md.: Rowman & Littlefield, 2000.

Fern, Yvonne. *Gene Roddenberry: The Last Conversation.* Berkeley: University of California Press, 1994.

Feuer, Jane. *Seeing Through the Eighties: Television and Reaganism.* Console-ing Passions. Durham, N.C.: Duke University Press, 1995.

Feuer, Jane, Paul Kerr, and Tise Vahimagi. *MTM: Quality Television.* London: BFI Books, 1984.

Fighting the Forces: What's at Stake in Buffy the Vampire Slayer. Ed. Rhonda V. Wilcox and David Lavery. Lanham, Md.: Rowman & Littlefield, 2002.

Film Literature Index. Albany, N.Y. Filmdex, 1973– .

Film Researcher's Handbook: A Guide to Sources in North America, South America, Asia, Australasia, and Africa. Comp. Jenny Morgan. London: Routledge, 1996.

Fiske, John. *Television Culture*. London: Methuen, 1987.

Fiske, John, and John Hartley. *Reading Television*. London: Methuen, 1978.

Foley, Karen Sue. *The Political Blacklist in the Broadcast Industry: The Decade of the 1950's*. New York: Arno, 1979.

Fox, Roy F. *Harvesting Minds: How TV Commercials Control Kids*. Westport, Conn.: Praeger, 1996.

Frantzrich, Stephen, and John Sullivan. *The C-Span Revolution*. Norman: University of Oklahoma Press, 1996.

Friendly, Fred. W. *Due to Circumstances Beyond Our Control. . . .* New York: Random, 1968.

Full of Secrets: Critical Approaches to Twin Peaks. Ed. David Lavery. Contemporary Film and Television Series. Detroit: Wayne State University Press, 1995.

Fulton, Roger, and John Betancourt. *The Sci-Fi Channel Encyclopedia of TV Science Fiction*. New York: Warner Books, 1998.

Gabler, Neal. *Life the Movie: How Entertainment Conquered Reality*. New York: Knopf, 1998.

Gamson, Joshua. *Freaks Talk Back: Tabloid Talk Shows and Sexual Nonconformity*. Chicago: University of Chicago Press, 1998.

Gelbart, Larry. *Laughing Matters: On Writing M-A-S-H, Tootsie, Oh, God!, and a Few Other Funny Things*. New York: Random, 1998.

Gianokos, Larry James. *Television Drama Series Programming: A Comprehensive Chronicle, 1984–1986*. Metuchen, N.J.: Scarecrow, 1992.

Gillespie, Marie. *Television Ethnicity and Cultural Change*. London: Routledge, 1995.

Gitlin, Todd. *Inside Prime Time*. Rev. ed. Communication and Society Series. London: Routledge, 1994.

Goethals, Gregor T. *The Electronic Golden Calf: Images, Religion, and the Making of Meaning*. Cambridge, MA: Cowley, 1990.

Goodman, Gloria. *The Life and Humor of Rosie O'Donnell: A Biography*. New York: William Morrow, 1998.

Gray, Frances. *Women and Laughter*. Feminist Issues. Charlottesville: University Press of Virginia, 1994.

Gray, Herman. *Watching Race: Television and the Struggle for "Blackness."* Minneapolis: University of Minnesota Press, 1995.

Green, Philip. *Cracks in the Pedestal: Ideology and Gender in Hollywood*. Amherst: University of Massachusetts Press, 1998.

Greenberg, Gerald S. *Tabloid Journalism: An Annotated Bibliography of English-Language Sources*. Bibliographies and Indexes in Mass Media and Communications 10. Westport, Conn.: Greenwood, 1996.

Greene, Eric. *Planet of the Apes as American Myth: Race and Politics in the Films and Television Series*. Jefferson, N.C.: McFarland, 1996.

Greenfield, Jeff. *Television: The First Fifty Years*. New York: Harry N. Abrams, 1977.

Greenwald, Jeff. *Future Perfect: How Star Trek Conquered Planet Earth*. New York: Viking, 1998.

Gripsrud, Jostein. *The Dynasty Years: Hollywood Television and Critical Media Studies*. London: Routledge, 1995.

Gunther, Marc. *The House That Roone Built: The Inside Story of ABC News*. Boston: Little, Brown, 1994.

Hadden, Jeffrey, and Charles E. Swann. *Prime Time Preachers: The Rising Power of Televangelism*. Reading, MA: Addison-Wesley, 1981.

Haining, Peter. *Doctor Who, A Celebration: Two Decades Through Time and Space*. London: W. H. Allen, 1983.

Halberstam, David. *The Powers That Be*. New York: Knopf, 1979.

Hamamoto, Darrell Y. *Monitored Peril: Asian Americans and the Politics of TV Representation*. Minneapolis: University of Minnesota Press, 1994.

Hamilton, James. *Channeling Violence: The Economic Market for Violent Television Programming*. Princeton, N.J.: Princeton University Press, 1998.

Hammond, Charles M. *The Image Decade: Television Documentary 1965–1975*. New York: Hastings House, 1981.

Hanley, Richard. *The Metaphysics of Star Trek*. New York: Basic Books, 1997.

Harrington, C. Lee, and Denise D. Bielby. *Soap Fans: Pursuing Pleasure and Making Meaning in Everyday Life*. Philadelphia: Temple University Press, 1995.

Hart, Roderick P. *Seducing America: How Television Charms the Modern Voter*. Rev. ed. Thousand Oaks, Calif.: Sage, 1999.

Hartley, John. *Uses of Television*. London: Routledge, 1999.

Harvey, Rita Morley. *Those Wonderful, Terrible Years: George Heller and the American Federation of Television and Radio Artists*. Carbondale: Southern Illinois University Press, 1996.

Hasko, Janet. *Hollywood in the Information Age: Beyond the Silver Screen*. Texas Film Studies Series. Austin: University of Texas Press, 1995.

Hayward, Jennifer. *Consuming Pleasures: Active Audiences and Serial Fictions from Dickens to Soap Opera*. Lexington: University Press of Kentucky, 1997.

Heaton, Jeanne Albronda, and Nona Leigh Wilson. *Tuning in Trouble: Talk TV's Destructive Impact on Mental Health*. San Francisco: Jossey-Bass, 1995.

Heide, Margaret J. *Television Culture and Women's Lives: thirtysomething and the Contradictions of Gender*. Feminist Cultural Studies, the Media, and Political Culture. Philadelphia: University of Pennsylvania Press, 1995.

Heldenfels, R. D. *Television's Greatest Year—1954*. New York: Continuum, 1994.

Hendershot, Heather. *Saturday Morning Censors: Television Regulation Before the V-Chip*. Console-ing Passions. Durham, N.C.: Duke University Press, 1998.

Heroines of Popular Culture. Ed. Pat Browne. Bowling Green, OH: Bowling Green State University Popular Press, 1987.

Hill, Doug, and Jeff Weingrad. *Saturday Night: A Backstage History of Saturday Night Live*. New York: Beech Tree/Morrow, 1986.

Hilt, Michael L. *Television News and the Elderly: Broadcast Managers' Attitudes Towards Older Adults*. New York: Garland, 1997.

Himmelstein, Hal. *Television Myth and the American Mind*. 2nd ed. Westport, Conn.: Praeger, 1994.

Himmelweit, Hilde T., A. N. Oppenheim, and Pamela Vince. *Television and the Child: An Empirical Study of the Effect of Television on the Young*. London: Oxford University Press, 1958.

Hirschman, Elizabeth. *Heroes, Monsters, and Messiahs: Movies and Television Shows as the Mythology of American Culture*. Kansas City, Mo.: Andrews McNeel, 2000.

Hood, Stuart, and Thalia Tabary-Peterssen. *On Television*. 4th rev. ed. London: Pluto, 1997.

Horsfield, Peter. *Religious Television: The Experience in America*. New York: Longman, 1984.

Hunt, Darnell M. *O. J. Simpson Facts and Fictions: News Rituals in the Construction of Reality*. Cambridge, UK: Cambridge University Press, 1999.

———. *Screening the Los Angeles 'Riots': Race, Seeing, and Resistance*. Cambridge Cultural Social Studies. Cambridge, UK: Cambridge University Press, 1997.

In Front of the Children: Screen Entertainment and Young Audiences. Ed. Cary Bazalguette and David Buckingham. London: BFI, 1995.

In the Eye of the Beholder: Critical Perspectives in Popular Film and Television. Ed. Gary R. Edgerton, Michael T. Marsden, and Jack Nachbar. Bowling Green, Ohio: Bowling Green State University Press, 1997.

Inness, Sherrie A. *Tough Girls: Women Warriors and Wonder Women in Popular Culture*. Philadelphia: University of Pennsylvania Press, 1999.

Isaacs, Susan. *Brave Dames and Wimpettes: What Women Are Really Doing on Page and Screen*. New York: Ballantine, 1999.

Jackson, Anthony W. *Black Families and the Medium of Television*. Ann Arbor: Bush Program in Child Development, University of Michigan Press, 1982.

Jackson, John A. *American Bandstand: Dick Clark and the Making of a Rock'n'Roll Empire*. New York: Oxford University Press, 1997.

James, Doug. *Walter Cronkite: His Life and Times*. Brentwood, TN: J. M. Press, 1991.

Jankowski, Gene F., and David C. Fuchs. *Television Today and Tomorrow: It Won't Be What You Think*. New York: Oxford University Press, 1995.

Jarvik, Laurence A. *Masterpiece Theatre and the Politics of Quality*. Lanham, Md.: Scarecrow, 1999.

Jenkins, Henry. *Textual Poachers: Television Fans and Participatory Culture*. New York: Routledge, 1992.

Jensen, Carl. *Censored: The News That Didn't Make the News—And Why: The 1996 Project Censored Yearbook*. Introd. Walter Cronkite. 20th anniv. ed. New York: Seven Stories, 1996.

Johnson-Cartee, Karen S., and Gary A. Copeland. *Manipulation of the American Voter: Political Campaign Commercials*. Westport, Conn.: Praeger, 1997.

Joyrich, Lynne. *Re-Viewing Reception: Television, Gender, and Postmodern Culture*. Theories of Contemporary Culture 18. Bloomington: Indiana University Press, 1996.

Kaid, Lynda Lee, and Kathleen J. M. Haynes. *Political Commercial Archive: A Cat-

alog and Guide to the Collection. Norman: Political Communication Center, University of Oklahoma, 1991.

Kaminsky, Stuart M. *American Television Genres.* Chicago: Nelson-Hall, 1985.

Kaplan, E. Ann. *Rocking Around the Clock: Music Television, Postmodernism, and Consumer Culture.* New York: Methuen, 1987.

Kearton, Frances Adams. *Waiting for the Banana Peel.* Saratoga, Calif.: R & E Publishers, 1992.

Kelly, Richard. *The Andy Griffith Show.* Winston-Salem, NC: John F. Blair, 1981.

Ken Burns's The Civil War: Historians Respond. Ed. Robert Brent Toplin. New York: Oxford University Press, 1996.

Kendrick, Alexander. *Prime Time: The Life of Edward R. Murrow.* Boston: Little, Brown, 1969.

Kerbel, Matthew Robert. *Edited for Television: CNN, ABC, and American Presidential Elections.* 2nd ed. Boulder, Colo.: Westview, 1998.

———. *If It Bleeds, It Leads: An Anatomy of Television News.* Boulder, Colo.: Westview, 2000.

Kimball, Penn. *Downsizing the News: Network Cutbacks in the Nation's Capital.* Washington, D.C.: Woodrow Wilson Center, 1994.

Kisselhoff, Jeff. *The Box: An Oral History of Television, 1920–1961.* New York: Viking, 1995.

Kline, Stephen. *Out of the Garden: Toys, TV, and Children's Culture in the Age of Marketing.* London: Verso, 1993.

Koppel, Ted, and Kyle Gibson. *Nightline: History in the Making and the Making of Television.* New York: Times Books, 1996.

Krampner, Jon. *The Man in the Shadows: Fred Coe and the Golden Age of Television.* New Brunswick, N.J.: Rutgers University Press, 1997.

Krauss, Lawrence M. *The Physics of Star Trek.* Foreword by Stephen J. Hawking. New York: Basic Books, 1995.

Lance, Steven. *Written out of Television: The Encyclopedia of Cast Changes and Character Replacements, 1945–1994.* Lanham, Md.: Scarecrow, 1996.

Langer, John. *Tabloid Television: Popular Journalism and the "Other News."* Communication and Society. London: Routledge, 1998.

Langman, Larry, and Joseph A. Molinari. *The New Video Encyclopedia.* New York: Garland, 1990.

Larka, Robert. *Television's Private Eye: An Examination of Twenty Years of Programming of a Particular Genre, 1945–1969.* New York: Arno, 1979.

Larson, James F., and Heung-Soo Park. *Global Television and the Politics of the Seoul Olympics.* Politics in Asia and the Pacific. Boulder, Colo.: Westview, 1993.

Larson, Randall D. *Films into Books: An Analytical Bibliography of Film Novelizations, Movie, and TV Tie-Ins.* Metuchen, N.J.: Scarecrow, 1995.

Leamer, Laurence. *King of the Night: The Life of Johnny Carson.* New York: William Morrow, 1989.

Leibman, Nina C. *Living Room Lectures: The Fifties Family in Film and Television.* Texas Film Studies Series. Austin: University of Texas Press, 1995.

Lentz, Harry M. *Television Westerns Episode Guide: All United States Series, 1949–1996.* Jefferson, N.C.: McFarland, 1997.

Leonard, John. *Smoke and Mirrors: Violence, Television, and Other American Cultures.* New York: New Press; dist. Norton, 1997.

Let America Decide: The Report of the Twentieth Century Fund Task Force on Presidential Debates. New York: The Twentieth Century Fund, 1995.

Library of Congress. Motion Picture, Broadcasting, and Recorded Sound Division. *3 Decades of Television: A Catalog of Television Programs Acquired by the Library of Congress, 1949–1979.* Comp. Sarah Rouse and Katharine Loughney. Washington, D.C.: Library of Congress, GPO, 1989.

Lichter, S. Robert, Linda S. Lichter, and Stanley Rothman. *Prime Time: How TV Portrays American Culture.* Washington, D.C.: Regnery, 1994.

Lichter, S. Robert, and Richard E. Noyes. *Good Intentions Make Bad News: Why Americans Hate Campaign Journalism.* Lanham, Md.: Rowman and Littlefield, 1995.

Live from the Trenches: The Changing Role of the Television News Correspondent. Ed. Joe S. Foote. Foreword Ted Koppel. Carbondale: Southern Illinois University Press, 1998.

The Live Television Generation of Hollywood Film Directors: Interviews with Seven Directors. By Gorham Kindem. Jefferson, NC: McFarland, 1994.

Living Color: Race and Television in the United States. Ed. Sasha Torres. Consoling Passions. Durham, N.C.: Duke University Press, 1998.

Logics of Television: Essays in Cultural Criticism. Ed. Patricia Mellencamp. Bloomington: Indiana University Press, 1990.

Luciano, Patrick, and Gary Colville. *American Science Fiction Television Series of the 1950s: Episode Guides and Casts and Credits for 20 Shows.* Jefferson, N.C.: McFarland, 1998.

Lynch, Christopher Owen. *Selling Catholicism: Bishop Sheen and the Power of Television.* Lexington: University Press of Kentucky, 1998.

Lynch, David. *Lynch on Lynch.* Ed. Chris Rodley. London: Faber and Faber, 1997.

Lynch, Richard Chigley. *Broadway, Movie, TV, and Studio Cast Musicals on Record: A Discography of Recordings, 1985–1995.* Westport, Conn.: Greenwood, 1996.

Lyon, Eugene. *David Sarnoff.* New York: Harper and Row, 1966.

MacDonald, J. Fred. *Blacks and White TV: African Americans in Television Since 1948.* Chicago: Nelson-Hall, 1983.

Marc, David. *Bonfire of the Humanities: Television, Subliteracy, and Long-Term Memory Loss.* The Television Series. Syracuse, N.Y.: Syracuse University Press, 1995.

———. *Comic Visions: Television Comedy and American Culture.* 2nd ed. Malden, Mass.: Blackwell, 1997.

Marill, Alvin H. *Keeping Score: Film and Television Music, 1988–1997.* Lanham, Md.: Scarecrow, 1998.

Marling, Karal Ann. *As Seen on TV: The Visual Culture of Everyday Life in the 1950s.* Cambridge, Mass.: Harvard University Press, 1994.

Mattelart, Michelle. *Women, Media, and Crisis: Femininity and Disorder.* London: Comedia, 1986.

Mayne, Judith. *Framed: Lesbians, Feminists, and Media Culture.* Minneapolis: University of Minnesota Press, 2000.

McCarthy, John, and Brian Kelleher. *Alfred Hitchcock Presents.* New York: St. Martin's Press, 1985.

McCrohan, Donna. *Archie and Edith, Mike and Gloria: The Tumultuous History of All in the Family*. New York: Workman, 1987.

———. *The Honeymooners' Companion: The Kramdens and the Nortons Revisited*. New York: Workman, 1978.

McGinniss, Joe. *The Selling of the President, 1968*. New York: Pocket, 1970.

McKinley, E. Graham. *Beverly Hills 90210: Television, Gender, and Identity*. Feminist Cultural Studies, The Media, and Political Culture. Philadelphia: University of Pennsylvania Press, 1997.

McLuhan, Marshall. *Understanding Media: The Extensions of Man*. New York: McGraw-Hill, 1964.

McManus, John H. *Market-Driven Journalism: Let the Citizen Beware?* Thousand Oaks, Calif.: Sage, 1994.

McNeil, Alex. *Total Television: A Comprehensive Guide to Programming from 1948 to the Present*. 3rd ed. New York: Penguin, 1991.

Meadows, Audrey. *Love, Alice: My Life as a Honeymooner*. New York: Crown, 1994.

Means Coleman, Robin R. *African American Viewers and the Black Situation Comedy: Situating Racial Humor*. Studies in African American History and Culture. New York: Garland, 1998.

Media, Children, and the Family: Social Scientific, Psychodynamic, and Clinical Perspectives. Ed. Dolf Zillmann, Jennings Bryant, Aletha C. Huston. Hillsdale, N.J.: Lawrence Erlbaum, 1994.

Media, Ritual, and Identity. Ed. Tamar Liebes and James Curran. London: Routledge, 1998.

Mediated Women: Representations in Popular Culture. Ed. Marian Meyers. Cresskill, N.J.: Hampton Press, 1999.

Medved, Michael. *Hollywood vs. America*. New York: Harper Perennial, 1992.

Meehan, Diana M. *Ladies of the Evening: Women Characters of Prime Time Television*. New York: Scarecrow, 1983.

Metallinos, Nikos. *Television Aesthetics: Perceptual, Cognitive, and Compositional Bases*. Mahwah, N.J.: L. Erlbaum, 1996.

Metz, Robert. *The Today Show*. Chicago: Playboy, 1977.

Mickelson, Sig. *The Decade That Shaped Television News: CBS in the 1950s*. Westport, Conn.: Praeger, 1998.

Miller, Randall. *Ethnic Images in American Film and Television*. Philadelphia: Balch Institute, 1978.

Miller, Toby. *The Avengers*. London: British Film Institute, 1997.

Minow, Newton N., and Craig L. La May. *Abandoned in the Wasteland: Children, Television, and the First Amendment*. New York: Hill and Wang, 1995.

Mister Rogers' Neighborhood: Children, Television, and Fred Rogers. Ed. Mark Collins and Margaret Mary Kinnmel. Pittsburgh: University of Pittsburgh Press, 1996.

Modleski, Tania. *Loving with a Vengeance: Mass-Produced Fantasies for Women*. New York: Methuen, 1982.

Moeller, Susan D. *Compassion Fatigue: How the Media Sell Disease, Famine, War, and Death*. New York: Routledge, 1999.

Monaco, Paul. *Understanding Society, Culture, and Television*. Westport, Conn.: Praeger, 1998.

Morley, David. *Television, Audiences, and Cultural Studies*. London: Routledge, 1992.

Morreale, Joanne. *The Presidential Campaign Film: A Critical History*. Westport, Conn.: Praeger, 1993.

Morris, Bruce B. *Prime Time Network Serials: Episode Guides, Casts, and Credits for 37 Continuing Television Dramas, 1964–1993*. Jefferson, N.C.: McFarland, 1997.

Morse, Margaret. *Virtualities: Television, Media Art, and Cyberculture*. Theories of Contemporary Culture vol. 21. Bloomington: Indiana University Press, 1998.

Mullan, Bob. *Consuming Television: Television and Its Audience*. Oxford: Blackwell, 1997.

Mulvey, Laura. *Visual and Other Pleasures*. Bloomington: Indiana University Press, 1989.

Mumford, Laura Stempel. *Love and Ideology in the Afternoon: Soap Opera, Women, and Television Genre*. Arts and Politics of the Everyday. Bloomington: Indiana University Press, 1995.

Murray, Michael D. *The Political Performers: CBS Broadcasts in the Public Interest*. Westport, Conn: Praeger, 1994.

Murray, Scott. *Australia on the Small Screen, 1970–1995: The Complete Guide to Tele-Features and Mini-Series*. Melbourne: Oxford University Press, 1996.

National Television Violence Study. Thousand Oaks, Calif.: Sage, 1997.

Nelson, Robin. *TV Drama in Transition: Forms, Values, and Cultural Change*. New York: St. Martin's, 1997.

Neumann, Johanna. *Lights, Camera, War: Is Media Technology Driving International Politics?* New York: St. Martin's, 1996.

Newcomb, Horace. "On the Dialogic Aspects of Mass Communications." *Critical Studies in Mass Communications* 1 (1984): 34–50.

———. *TV: The Most Popular Art*. New York: Doubleday, 1974.

News, Gender, and Power. Ed. Cynthia Carter, Gill Branston, and Stuart Allan. London: Routledge: 1998.

News of the World: World Cultures Look at Television News. Ed. Klaus Bruhn Jensen. London: Routledge, 1998.

Nichols, Bill. *Blurred Boundaries: Questions of Meaning in Contemporary Culture*. Bloomington: Indiana University Press, 1994.

Nochimson, Martha. *No End to Her: Soap Opera and the Female Subject*. Berkeley: University of California Press, 1992.

———. *The Passion of David Lynch: Wild at Heart in Hollywood*. Austin: University of Texas Press, 1997.

Owen, Rob. *Gen X TV: The Brady Bunch to Melrose Place*. The Television Series. Syracuse, N.Y.: Syracuse University Press, 1997.

Passilinna, Reino. *Glasnost and Soviet Television: A Study of the Soviet Mass Media and Its Role in Society from 1985–1991*. Finland: YLE, Finnish Broadcasting Co., 1995.

Paget, Derek. *No Other Way to Tell It: Dramadoc/Docudrama on Television*. Manchester, UK: Manchester University Press, 1998.

Paley, William S. *As It Happened: A Memoir*. Garden City, N.J.: Doubleday, 1979.

Palmer, Patricia. *The Lively Audience: A Study of Children Around the TV Set*. Sydney: Allen & Unwin, 1986.

Papazian, Ed. *Medium Rare: The Evolution, Workings, and Impact of Commercial Television*. Rev ed. New York: dist. Media Dynamics, 1991.

Parish, James Robert, and Vincent Terrace. *The Complete Actors' Television Credits, 1948–1988*. 2nd ed. 2 vols. Metuchen, N.J.: Scarecrow, 1990.

Pearl, Jonathan, and Judith Pearl. *The Chosen Image: Television's Portrayal of Jewish Themes and Characters*. Jefferson, N.C.: McFarland, 1999.

Penley, Constance. *The Future of an Illusion: Film, Feminism, and Psychoanalysis*. Minneapolis: University of Minnesota Press, 1989.

———. *NASA/Trek: Popular Science and Sex in America*. London: Verso, 1997.

The Persistence of History: Cinema, Television, and the Modern Event. Ed. Vivian Sobchack. AFI Film Readers. New York: Routledge, 1996.

Phillips, Mark, and Frank Garcia. *Science Fiction Television Series: Episode Guides, Histories, and Casts and Credits for 62 Prime Time Shows, 1959 Through 1989*. Jefferson, N.C.: McFarland, 1996.

Phillips, Peter. *Censored, 1997: The News That Didn't Make the News—The Year's Top 25 Censored News Stories*. New York: Seven Stories, 1997.

———. *Censored, 1998: The News That Didn't Make the News—The Year's Top 25 Censored Stories*. New York: Seven Stories, 1998.

Pinsky, Mark I. *The Gospel According to the Simpsons: The Spiritual Life of the World's Most Animated Family*. Louisville, Ky.: Westminster John Knox Press, 2001.

Plissner, Martin. *The Control Room: How Television Calls the Shots in Presidential Elections*. New York: Free Press, 1999.

Political Advertising in Western Democracies: Parties and Candidates on Television. Ed. Lynda Lee Kaid, Christina Holtz-Bacha. Thousand Oaks, Calif.: Sage, 1995.

Postman, Neal. *Amusing Ourselves to Death*. New York: Elisabeth Sifton Books, 1985.

Postmodern After-Images: A Reader in Film, Television, and Video. Ed. Peter Brooker and Will Brooker. London: Arnold, 1997.

Pounds, Micheal C. *Race in Space: The Representation of Ethnicity in Star Trek: and Star Trek: The Next Generation*. Lanham, Md.: Scarecrow, 1999.

Presnell, Don, and Marty McGee. *A Critical History of Television's The Twilight Zone, 1959–1964*. Jefferson, N.C.: McFarland, 1998.

Press, Andrea Lee, and Elizabeth R. Cole. *Speaking of Abortion: Television and Authority in the Lives of Women*. Morality and Society Series. Chicago: University of Chicago Press, 1999.

Priest, Patricia Joyner. *Public Intimacies: Talk Show Participants and Tell-All TV*. Cresskill, N.J.: Hampton, 1995.

Prime Time Law: Fictional Television as Legal Narrative. Ed. Robert M. Jarvis and Paul R. Joseph. Durham, N.C.: Carolina Academic, 1998.

Projansky, Sarah. *Watching Rape: Film and Television in Postfeminist Culture*. New York: New York University Press, 2001.

Putterman, Barry. *On Television and Comedy: Essays on Style, Theme, Performer, and Writer*. Jefferson, N.C.: McFarland, 1995.

Queer Words, Queer Images: Communication and the Construction of Homosexuality. Ed. R. Jeffrey Ringer. New York: New York University Press, 1994.

Radner, Hilary, *Shopping Around: Feminine Culture and the Pursuit of Pleasure*. New York: Routledge, 1995.

Rafkin, Alan. *Cue the Bunny on the Rainbow: Tales from TV's Most Prolific Sitcom Director*. The Television Series. Syracuse, N.Y.: Syracuse University Press, 1998.

Rapping, Elayne. *Media-tions: Forays into the Culture and Gender Wars*. Boston: South End Press, 1994.

Rather, Dan. *The Camera Never Blinks Twice: The Further Adventures of a Television Journalist*. New York: Morrow, 1994.

———. *Deadlines and Datelines*. New York: Morrow, 1999.

Reading the Vampire Slayer. Ed. Roz Kaveney. London: I.B. Tauris, 2001; New York: St. Martin's Press, 2002.

Reed, Robert M., and Maxine K. Reed. *The Facts on File Dictionary of Television, Cable, and Video*. New York: Facts on File, 1994.

Reeves, Jimmie L., and Richard Campbell. *Cracked Coverage: Television News, the Anti-Cocaine Crusade, and the Reagan Legacy*. Durham, N.C.: Duke University Press, 1994.

Reeves-Stevens, Judith, and Garfield Reeves-Stevens. *The Making of Star Trek, Deep Space Nine*. New York: Pocket, 1994.

Regarding Television: Critical Approaches—An Anthology. Ed. E. Ann Kaplan. American Film Institute Monographs Series 2. Frederick, Md.: University Publications of America, 1983.

Religion and Prime Time Television. Ed. Michael Suman. Westport, Conn.: Praeger, 1997.

Remote Control: Television, Audiences, and Cultural Power. Ed. Ellen Seiter et al. London: Routledge, 1991.

The Remote Control in the New Age of Television. Ed. James R. Walker and Robert V. Bellamy, Jr. Westport, Conn.: Praeger, 1993.

Research Paradigms, Television, and Social Behavior. Ed. Joy Keiko Asamen, Gordon L. Berry. Thousand Oaks, Calif.: Sage, 1998.

Reyes, Luis, and Peter Rubie. *Hispanics in Hollywood: An Encyclopedia of Film and Television*. New York: Garland, 1994.

Richards, Thomas. *The Meaning of Star Trek*. New York: Doubleday, 1997.

Richardson, Kay, and Ulrike H. Meinhof. *Worlds in Common?: Television Discourse in a Changing Europe*. London: Routledge, 1999.

Riggs, Karen E. *Mature Audiences: Television in the Lives of Elders*. Communication, Media, Culture. New Brunswick, N.J.: Rutgers University Press, 1998.

Ritchie, Michael. *Please Stand by: A Prehistory of Television*. Woodstock, N.Y.: Overlook, 1994.

Roberts, Robin. *Sexual Generations: "Star Trek, the Next Generation" and Gender*. Urbana: University of Illinois Press, 1999.

Robinson, Dale, and David Fernandes. *The Definitive Andy Griffth Show Reference: Episode by Episode, with Cast and Production Biographies and a Guide to Collectibles*. Jefferson, N.C.: McFarland, 1996.

Rose, Brian G. *Directing for Television: Conversations with American TV Directors*. Lanham, Md.: Scarecrow, 1999.

Rosteck, Thomas. *See It Now Confronts McCarthyism: Television Documentary and the Politics of Representation.* Studies in Rhetoric and Communication. Tuscaloosa: University of Alabama Press, 1994.

Rowe, Kathleen. *The Unruly Woman: Gender and the Genres of Laughter.* Texas Film Studies Series. Austin: University of Texas Press, 1995.

Russell, Maureen. *Days of Our Lives: A Complete History of the Long-Running Soap Opera.* Jefferson, N.C.: McFarland, 1995.

RUA/TV?: Heidegger and the Televisual. Ed. Tony Fry. Sydney: Power, 1993.

Rutherford, Paul. *The New Icons: The Art of Television Advertising.* Toronto: University of Toronto Press, 1994.

Salant, Richard S. *Salant, CBS, and the Battle for the Soul of Broadcast Journalism: The Memoirs of Richard S. Salant.* Ed. Susan and Bill Buzenberg. Boulder, Colo.: Westview, 1999.

Savan, Leslie. *The Sponsored Life: Ads, TV and American Culture.* Culture and the Moving Image. Philadelphia: Temple University Press, 1994.

Schroth, Raymond A. *The American Journey of Eric Sevareid.* South Royalton, Vt.: Steerforth, 1995.

Schwartzman, David. *The Japanese Television Cartel: A Study Based on Matsushita v. Zenith.* Ann Arbor: University of Michigan Press, 1993.

Scott, Gini Graham. *Can We Talk? The Power and Influence of Talk Shows.* New York: Insight Books, 1996.

Seger, Linda. *When Women Call the Shots: The Developing Power and Influence of Women in Television and Film.* New York: Henry Holt, 1996.

Seib, Philip M. *Going Live: Getting the News Right in a Real-Time Online World.* Lanham, Md.: Rowman & Littlefield, 2001.

Seinfeld and Philosophy: A Book about Everything and Nothing. Ed. William Irwin. Chicago, Ill.: Open Court, 1999.

The Seinfeld Scripts: The First and Second Seasons. New York: HarperCollins, 1998.

Seiter, Ellen. *Sold Separately: Children and Parents in Consumer Culture.* Communication, Media, and Culture Series. New Brunswick, N.J.: Rutgers University Press, 1993.

———. *Television and New Media Audiences.* Oxford Television Studies. Oxford: Clarendon, 1999.

Selby, Keith, and Ron Cowdery. *How to Study Television.* Houndsmills, UK: MacMillan, 1995.

Seldes, Gilbert. *The Great Audience.* New York: Viking, 1950.

Sennett, Ted. *Your Show of Shows.* New York: MacMillan, 1977.

Shaheen, Jack G. *The TV Arab.* Bowling Green, OH: Bowling Green State University Popular Press, 1984.

Shattuc, Jane. *The Talking Cure: TV Talk Shows and Women.* New York: Routledge, 1997.

———. *Television, Tabloids, and Tears: Fassbinder and Popular Culture.* Minneapolis: University of Minnesota Press, 1995.

Shaw, Martin. *Civil Society and Media in Global Crises: Representing Distant Violence.* London: Pinter, 1996.

Shaw, Tony. *Eden, Suez, and the Mass Media: Propaganda and Persuasion During the Suez Crisis.* London: I. B. Tauris, 1996.

Silvia, Tony, and Nancy F. Kaplan. *Student Television in America: Channels of Change*. Ames: Iowa State University Press, 1998.

The Simpsons and Philosophy: The D'Oh! of Homer. Ed. William Irwin, Mark T. Conrad, and Aeon J. Skoble. Chicago, Ill.: Open Court, 2001.

Slotnick, Elliot E., and Jennifer A. Segal. *Television News and the Supreme Court: All the News That's Fit to Air?* Cambridge, UK: Cambridge University Press, 1998.

Sochen, June. *From Mae to Madonna: Women Entertainers in Twentieth-Century America*. Lexington: University Press of Kentucky, 1999.

Sound and Vision: The Music Video Reader. Ed. Simon Firth, Andrew Goodwin, Lawrence Grossberg. London: Routledge, 1993.

Sparks, Richard. *Television and the Drama of Crime: Moral Tales and the Place of Crime in Public Life*. New Directions in Criminology. Buckingham: Open University Press, 1992.

Spelling, Aaron. *Aaron Spelling: A Prime-Time Life*. New York: St. Martin's, 1996.

Spigel, Lynn, and Michael Curtin. *The Revolution Wasn't Televised: Sixties Television and Social Conflict*. New York: Routledge, 1997.

Spragens, William C. *Electronic Magazines: Soft News Programs on Network Television*. Westport, Conn.: Praeger, 1995.

Stahl, Lesley. *Reporting Live*. New York: Simon and Schuster, 1999.

Stark, Steven D. *Glued to the Set: The 60 Television Shows and Events That Made Us Who We Are Today*. New York: Free Press, 1997.

Star Trek and Sacred Ground: Explorations of Star Trek, Religion, and American Culture. Ed. Jennifer E. Porter and Darcee L. McLaren. Albany, N.Y.: State University of New York Press, 1999.

Stephens, Michael. *The Rise of the Image, the Fall of the Word*. New York: Oxford University Press, 1998.

Straczynski, J. Michael. *The Complete Book of Scriptwriting*. Rev. ed. Cincinnati, Ohio: Writer's Digest Books, 1996.

Strobel, Warren P. *Late-Breaking Foreign Policy: The News Media's Influence on Peace Operations*. Washington, D.C.: Institute of Peace, 1997.

Sturken, Marita. *Tangled Memories: The Vietnam War, the AIDS Epidemic, and the Politics of Remembering*. Berkeley: University of California Press, 1997.

Sumser, John. *Morality and Social Order in Television Crime Drama*. Jefferson, N.C.: McFarland, 1996.

Takei, George. *To the Stars: An Autobiography of George Takei, Star Trek's Mr. Sulu*. New York: Pocket, 1994.

Taylor, Ella. *Prime Time Families: Television Culture in Postwar America*. Berkeley: University of California Press, 1989.

Teleparody: Predicting/Preventing the TV Discourse of Tomorrow. Ed. Angela Hague and David Lavery. London: Wallflower Books, forthcoming.

Television: An International History. Ed. Anthony Smith. New York: Oxford University Press, 1995.

Television: The Critical View. Ed. Horace Newcomb. 5th ed. New York: Oxford University Press, 1994.

Television and Nuclear Power: Making the Public Mind. Ed. J. Mallory Wober. Communication and Information Science Series. Norwood, N.J.: Ablex, 1992.

Television and Women's Culture: The Politics of the Popular. Ed. Mary Ellen Brown. Communication and Human Values Series. London: Sage, 1990.

Television Histories: Shaping Collective Memory in the Media Age. Ed. Gary R. Edgerton and Peter C. Rollins. Lexington: University Press of Kentucky, 2001.

Television in America: Local Station History from Across the Nation. Ed. Michael D. Murray and Donald G. Godfrey. Ames: Iowa State University Press, 1997.

Television News Index and Abstracts. Nashville, Tenn.: Vanderbilt Television News Archive 1972–1995. Continued online to date.

Television Studies: Textual Analysis. Ed. Gary Burns and Robert J. Thompson. Westport, Conn.: Praeger, 1989.

Television Violence and Public Policy. Ed. James T. Hamilton. Ann Arbor: University of Michigan Press, 1998.

Terrace, Vincent. *The Complete Encyclopedia of Television Programs, 1947–1979*. 2nd ed. rev. South Brunswick, N.J.: A. S. Barnes, 1979.

———. *Television Character and Story Facts: Over 110,000 Details from 1,008 Shows, 1945–1992*. Jefferson, N.C.: McFarland, 1993.

———. *Television Specials: 3,201 Entertainment Spectaculars, 1939–1993*. Jefferson, N.C.: McFarland, 1995.

Thelen, David. *Becoming Citizens in the Age of Television: How Americans Challenged the Media and Seized Political Initiative During the Iran-Contra Debate*. Chicago: University of Chicago Press, 1996.

Thirtysomething writers. *Thirtysomething stories*. New York: Pocket, 1991.

This Thing of Ours: Investigating the Sopranos. Ed. David Lavery. New York: Columbia University Press, forthcoming.

Thompson, Robert J. *Adventures in Prime Time: The Television Programs of Stephen J. Cannell*. Westport, Conn.: Praeger, 1990.

———. *Television's Second Golden Age: From Hill Street Blues to ER: Hill Street Blues, St. Elsewhere, Cagney and Lacey, Moonlighting, L.A. Law, Thirty-something, China Beach, Twin Peaks, Northern Exposure, Picket Fences, with Brief Reflections on Homicide, NYPD Blue, Chicago Hope, and Other Quality Drama*. New York: Continuum, 1996.

Tinker, Grant, and Bud Rukeyser. *Tinker in Television: From General Sarnoff to General Electric*. New York: Simon and Schuster, 1994.

To Be Continued: Soap Opera Around the World. Ed. Robert C. Allen. London: Routledge, 1995.

Tracy, Kathleen. *The Girl's Got Bite: The Unofficial Guide to Buffy's World*. Los Angeles: Renaissance Books, 1998.

Transmission: Toward a Post-Television Culture. Ed. Peter d'Agostino, David Tafler. 2nd ed. Communication and Human Values Series. Thousand Oaks, Calif.: Sage, 1995.

Tulloch, John, and Manuel Alvarado. *Doctor Who: The Unfolding Text*. London: MacMillan, 1983.

Tulloch, John, and Henry Jenkins. *Science Fiction Audiences: Watching Dr. Who and Star Trek*. Popular Fiction Series. London: Routledge, 1995.

Tuning in to Young Viewers: Social Science Perspectives on Television. Ed. Tannis M. MacBeth. Thousand Oaks, Calif.: Sage, 1996.

Tunstall, Jeremy. *Television Producers*. Communication and Society Series. London: Routledge, 1993.

Turow, Joseph. *Media Industries: The Production of News and Entertainment*. New York: Longman, 1984.

———. *Playing Doctor: Television Storytelling and Medical Power*. New York: Oxford University Press, 1989.

TV Genres: A Handbook and Reference Guide. Brian Rose, ed. Westport, Conn.: Greenwood, 1985.

The UCLA Television Violence Report 1996. Los Angeles: UCLA Center for Communication Policy, 1996.

Under the Watchful Eye: Managing Presidential Campaigns in the Television Era. Ed. Mathew D. McCubbins. Washington, D.C.: Congressional Quarterly P, 1992.

Unnikrishnan, Namita, and Shailaja Bajpai. *The Impact of Television Advertising on Children*. New Delhi: Sage, 1996.

Variety and Daily Variety Television Reviews. New York: Garland, 1992.

The V-Chip Debate: Content Filtering from Television to the Internet. Ed. Monroe E. Price. Mahwah, N.J.: L. Erlbaum, 1998.

The Video Source Book: A Guide to Programs Currently Available on Video in the Areas of: Movies/Entertainment, General Interest/Education, Sports/Recreation, Fine Arts, Health/Science, Business/Industry, Children/Juvenile, How-to/Instruction. Ed. James M. Craddock. 22nd ed. Detroit: Gale, 1999.

Views on the News: The Media and Public Opinion. Ed. Michael P. Beabien and John S. Wyeth, Jr. Chet Huntley Memorial Lectures. New York: New York University Press, 1994.

Wagner, Jon G., and Jan Lundeen. *Deep Space and Sacred Time: Star Trek in the American Mythos*. Westport, Conn.: Praeger, 1998.

Waldron, Vince. *The Official Dick Van Dyke Show Book: The Definitive History and Ultimate Viewer's Guide to Television's Most Enduring Comedy*. New York: Hyperion, 1994.

Walker, James R., and Douglas A. Ferguson. *The Broadcast Television Industry*. Boston: Allyn and Bacon, 1998.

Walters, Susanna Danuta. *All the Rage: The Story of Gay Visibility in America*. Chicago: University of Chicago Press, 2001.

Watching Channel One: The Convergence of Students, Technology, and Private Business. Ed. Ann De Vaney. SUNY Series, Education and Culture. Albany: State University of New York Press, 1994.

Watching Television. Ed. Todd Gitlin. New York: Pantheon, 1987.

Watson, Mary Ann. *Defining Visions: Television and the American Experience Since 1945*. General Ed. Gerald D. Nash and Richard W. Etulain. Fort Worth: Harcourt Brace College, 1998.

———. *The Expanding Vista: American Television in the Kennedy Years*. New York: Oxford University Press, 1990.

Weaver, Pat. *The Best Seat in the House: The Golden Years in Radio and Television*. New York: Knopf, 1994.

Weissman, Ginny, and Coyne Steven Sanders. *The Dick Van Dyke Show: Anatomy of a Classic*. New York: St. Martin's, 1983.

West, Darrell M. *Air Wars: Television Advertising in Election Campaigns, 1952–1996.* 2nd ed. Washington, D.C.: Congressional Quarterly Press, 1997.

Whitfield, Stephen, and Gene Roddenberry. *The Making of Star Trek.* New York: Ballantine, 1968.

Wilcox, Rhonda V. " 'In Your Dreams, Fleischman': Dr. Flesh and the Dream of the Spirit in *Northern Exposure.*" *Studies in Popular Culture* 15.2 (1993): 1–13.

Williams, J. P. "The Mystique of Moonlighting: When You Care Enough to Watch the Very Best." *Journal of Popular Film and Television* 16.3 (1988): 90–99.

Williams, Montel. *Mountain, Get out of My Way: Life Lessons and Learned Truths.* New York: Warner Books, 1996.

Williams, Raymond. *Television: Technology and Cultural Form.* 2nd ed. London: Routledge, 1990.

Winans, Christopher. *The King of the Cast: The Inside Story of Laurence Tisch.* New York: J. Wiley, 1995.

Winch, Samuel P. *Mapping the Cultural Space of Journalism: How Journalists Distinguish News from Entertainment.* Westport, Conn.: Praeger, 1997.

Winn, Marie. *The Plug-In Drug.* New York: Penguin, 1985.

Wittebols, James H. *Watching M*A*S*H, Watching America: A Social History of the 1972–1983 Television Series.* Jefferson, N.C.: McFarland, 1998.

Wolfe, Peter. *In the Zone: The Twilight World of Rod Serling.* Bowling Green, Ohio: Bowling Green State University Popular Press, 1997.

Woolery, George W. *Children's Television: The First Thirty-five Years, 1946–1981.* 2 vols. Metuchen, N.J.: Scarecrow, 1983.

Yoggy, Gary A. *Riding the Video Range: The Rise and Fall of the Western in Television.* Jefferson, N.C.: McFarland, 1995.

Young, Brian M. *Television Advertising and Children.* Oxford: Clarendon, 1990.

Zook, Kristal Brent. *Color by Fox: The Fox Network and the Revolution in Black Television.* W.E.B. DuBois Institute Series. New York: Oxford University Press, 1999.

Periodicals

Access. Washington, D.C., 1969– .

American Film: Journal of the Film and Television Arts. Washington, D.C., 1975– .

American Journal of Semiotics. Cambridge, MA, 1981– .

Arts in Context. New York, 1974– .

Broadcasting & Cable: The Businessweekly of Television and Radio. Washington, D.C., 1931– .

Camera Observa. Durham, N.C., 1976– .

The Caucus Quarterly. Los Angeles: Caucus for Producers, Writers, and Directors, 1983– .

Channels: The Business of Communications. New York, 1980– .

Cinéaste. New York, 1967– .

Cinéfantastique. Oak Park, IL, 1990– .

Columbia Journalism Review. New York, 1962– .

Critical Studies in Mass Communications. Annandale, VA: National Communication Association, 1984– .

EMMY. Los Angeles: Academy of Television Arts and Sciences, 1978– .

Film History. New York, 1987– .

The Hollywood Reporter. Los Angeles, 1930– .

Journal of Broadcasting and Electronic Media. Philadelphia, 1956– .

Journal of Popular Culture. Bowling Green, Ohio, 1967– .

Journalism and Mass Communication Quarterly. Columbia, S.C., 1924– .

JPFT, The Journal of Popular Film and Television. Washington, D.C., 1924– .

Literature, Film, and Television Quarterly. Salisbury, Md., 1973– .

The Mid-Atlantic Almanack. Martin, Tenn., 1992– .

Popular Culture Review. Las Vegas, 1989– .

Quarterly Review of Film and Video. Lincoln, Neb., 1989– .

Spectrum. Arlington, Tex., 1994– .

Studies in American Culture. Murfreesboro, Tenn., 1996– .

Studies in Popular Culture. Murfreesboro, Tenn., 1977– .

Television and New Media. Thousand Oaks, Calif., 2000– .

Television Quarterly: The Journal of the National Academy of Television Arts and Sciences. Beverly Hills, Calif., 1963–78, and sporadically thereafter.

TV Guide. Radnor, Pa., 1953– .

Variety. New York, 1905– .

Variety and Daily Variety Television Reviews. New York, 1992– .

Women's Studies in Communication. Bozeman, Mont., 1982– .

Wrapped in Plastic. Arlington, Tex., 1992– .

I Love Lucy. © The Del Valle Archive

Dick Van Dyke. © The Del Valle Archive

I Dream of Jeannie. © The Del Valle Archive

The Honeymooners. © The Del Valle Archive

The Munsters. © The Del Valle Archive

Gilligan's Island. © The Del Valle Archive

The Monkees. © The Del Valle Archive

The Simpsons with creator Matt Groening. ©
Douglas Kirkland/CORBIS

Friends. Kobal Collection

TRAINS AND RAILROADING

Arthur H. Miller, Jr.

For the eminent historian and former librarian of Congress Daniel Boorstin, the "Age of the Railroad is perhaps the most romantic" in the history of American life.[1] This romance is best found in Lucius Beebe's books, which appeared from the 1930s to the 1960s. In introducing his first rail book, *High Iron*, in 1938, Beebe sounded his clarion call: "The most heroic of American legends is the chronicle of Railroading."[2] Its epic scale and its relation to the national destiny is further recognized by B. A. Botkin in his introduction to *A Treasury of Railroad Folklore*: "The impact of the railroad on the American imagination has been greater than that of any other industry."[3] In the 1950s Barton K. Davis observed that model railroading alone was the "absorbing interest of more than 100,000 Americans."[4] In the 1980s railroad enthusiasts provided the focus for their own microindustry: publishers of magazines and books, museums and preserved short lines, memorabilia, modeling, and associations and clubs across the country. Trains and railroading have a long history and a vital present and future in American popular culture.

A first step in understanding railroading in the context of popular culture comes in attempting to describe the range of interest of rail fans, dedicated railroad hobbyists, in the words of Paul B. Cors, whose 1975 *Railroads* is the standard reference bibliography on the topic. According to Cors, rail fans (mostly male) resemble one another little except in their "fascination with and devotion to railroading."[5] Two common characteristics seem to be rail fans' tendency to be both photographers and book collectors. Beyond these traits, rail fan interests tend to be specialized and partisan. A railroad buff may concentrate on steam or diesel locomotives, on traction (electric railroad and rapid transit) or narrow-gauge railroads, on short lines, on a particular railroad company, on railroad general history and literature, on cars, on stations, on models, on live steam (except scale engines run by real steam and large enough to ride upon), or on collecting toy trains, railroad art, and railroad memorabilia. A list based on recent memorabilia advertisements gives a sense of the range of collectibles: timetables, cap and hat badges, stocks and bonds, passes and tickets, engine plates, calendars, dining car china and silverware, lanterns and lamps, posters and signs, brass whistles, annual and trip passes, engine builder's plates, telegraph instruments, depot phones, keys and locks, and pocket watches. In addition, Paul Cors' reference guide lists six pages of publishers that specialize in books for rail fans or else cater to them significantly. Pictures, too, are collected, most often of locomotives and in all formats—from postcards and slides to glass negatives, stereopticon views, and steel engravings. Ephemeral material, preferably illustrated, is highly sought: manufacturer's catalogs, travel brochures, name-train folders, and the like. The rail fan's most valued pictures or ephemera will record personal experiences, such as snapshots of out-of-the-way and/or endangered lines or handouts from rail museums visited. Enthusiasts endeavor to visit and then ride (or, if too late, walk over) new railroads. These may range from mainline railroads to the most obscure interurban line. In sum, rail fan interest is specialized, passionate, cumulative, and oriented toward travel and printed material.

But the rail fan phenomenon is only the central core of popular interest in trains and railroading. As Daniel Boorstin has observed and as the very popular Beebe demonstrated, the romance of railroading appeals to a much wider audience—the general public—which is drawn by nostalgia. An example here is a magnificent coffee-table book called *Decade of the Trains: The 1940s*, by Don Ball Jr. and Rogers E. M. Whitaker ("E. M. Frimbo"). In the preface Ball draws a clear connection between life in the late 1970s and that three decades earlier:

> I hope this book captures the spirit of railroading in the forties and also the unique character . . . of America during the war and the rest of the decade. During the 1940s, America "worked." It seemed to be an era of good times and almost innocent merriment—even with the dark and terrible war.[6]

According to the jacket, here "the reader becomes an eyewitness. This trip *is* necessary—for everyone who remembers the war years and [of course] for every railroad fan." This nostalgia for a simpler era and for the values of the era—innocence, for example—provides the bridge from rail fans' special passions to more general currents of popular interest.

There has been considerable academic and professional interest in the literature of railroading. For the rail fan this is delightfully specialized and detailed. Historical material (primary and secondary), company literature, government reports and surveys, technical manuals, and investment information all reach the hobbyist or popular perception at some point.

Important background, too, for viewing America's romance with railroading is the awareness that this is part of an international phenomenon. Particularly in Britain the literature on the subject is well developed, and the level of interest is intense. Railroads (or railways) began there, first captured the popular imagination there, and first experienced significant abandonment, nostalgia, and comprehensive rail fan activity. Thus, British popular interest in railroading has provided a context for the development and continuation of Americans' preoccupation with their rail heritage.

HISTORIC OUTLINE

"Historically," according to Archie Robertson, "the railfan is at least as old as railroads." In his *Slow Train to Yesterday* Robertson provides a charming look at the rail fan phenomenon:

> The Charleston & Hamburg, . . . earliest American railroad, ran its first trains for enthusiasts who just couldn't wait for the public opening. Before the Civil War the B&O ran excursions for camera fans from Washington to Harper's Ferry. . . . Fan trips were commonplace throughout the nineteenth century although no one called them that.[7]

The history of American railroading cannot, indeed, be separated from the public enthusiasm for rail travel or for the advancement and progress of the railroad industry. In the 1820s the railroad had taken hold in England, and by Christmas 1830 the first scheduled steam-railroad train run in America took place on the Charleston & Hamburg, carrying 141 passengers. The engine, the "Best Friend of Charleston," was the first commercially built U.S. locomotive. The expansion westward from the coast in the early nineteenth century led to rapid deployment of the railroad, at first in what might seem like unusual locations. The new technology captured the imagination and backing first of southerners, whose seaports were suffering as the water routes farther north—particularly the Erie Canal—drew trade to New York and the Northeast. Laying track to the interior offered a new chance for ports such as Charleston and Baltimore to compete. Boston, too, coveted New York's success and in the early 1830s wisely decided to build not more canals but railroads. The nation's first Railway Exhibit was in Boston in 1827, to which enthusiastic crowds paid admission to view the display of English locomotives.

By the 1850s the rail system reached to the Mississippi, as the various coastal establishments tied themselves to western settlements. Already the call for Manifest Destiny was to be heard, to build a railroad to the Pacific. Sectional rivalry, at first, was a stimulus to discussion: should the transcontinental line go across from a more northerly or southerly route, building from slave states or free? In the end the struggle's intensity was so great that it served to delay the transcontinental route until after the Civil War. The North's by then superior rail system contributed significantly to the preservation of the Union, and railroading today forms a key subgrouping of Civil War buff interest. As a result, in the 1950s the "Great Locomotive Chase" was a popular story and film topic. But before this climactic encounter western cities had hosted railroad conventions to crystallize interest in a line—west from Memphis, St. Louis, or Chicago. As with the earlier Boston exhibition, these special events reflected and served to stimulate popular interest and support. Throughout the century the opening of new lines, anniversaries, and the great fairs of 1876 and 1893 were occasions for celebrating the progress, both geographical and technical, of the railroads.

After the Civil War, forces were mobilized quickly, thanks to government incentives, creative management and engineering, and no little corruption, to forge the link to the Pacific. In 1869 the Union Pacific and the Central Pacific met at Promontory Point, Utah, ending the "Great Race." This epic feat was followed

Streamlined diesel and steam trains. Courtesy of the Library of Congress

in rapid order by the completion of other lines to the north and south. By the end of the century the West was covered by a complete (often redundant) rail network, the Indians had been subdued, and the frontier (according to Frederick Jackson Turner) was closed.

From the end of the war to the closing of the frontier popular interest in the railroads was at a peak. The mighty task of crossing the continent was great by every measure: the profits, the speed at which track could be laid, the iniquity of life on the work gangs ("Hell on Wheels" and boomtowns), the tall tales, the personalities (General Dodge, Jack Casement, and Charles Crocker), and the celebrations. In the years that immediately followed, easterners and travelers from abroad made the trip across the plains and the mountains to San Francisco from Council Bluffs, Iowa, through prairie dog villages, mountain gorges, Indian lands, and deserts. Their accounts and the pictures by the illustrators and photographers who went along were printed and widely distributed, testifying to the railroad's popular appeal.

By the end of this period the railroads had begun to reach beyond opening new possibilities for Americans and immigrants. By the close of the century railroad domination had become a major issue, particularly in the trans-Mississippi West. Popular support waned as reports of scandals such as the Credit Mobilier matter, which concerned Union Pacific corruption, reached the public. Land prices, freight rates, and the continuing stock manipulations of what popularly became known as the "robber baron" period turned first the western farmers and later a majority of the public against railroad excesses. The Grange movement reflected the farmers' attempt to organize against the power of the railroads. Train robbers appeared as Robin Hoods in the popular imagination, dime novels, and the mass press. The spectacular exploits of Christopher Evans and John Sontag in the San Joaquin Valley of California are reflected in Frank Norris' ambitious novel of 1901, *The Octopus*. In general, *The Octopus* best characterizes the popular perception of the western railroads at the end of the nineteenth century: greed, corruption, impersonality, manipulation, and oppression.

Interestingly, "the best scholarship of late suggests" that the notion of a " 'robber baron' period" is "dead wrong," according to railroad historian H. Roger Grant.[8] An example of the kind of detailed research on which this new perspective is based is Maury Klein's 1986 *The Life and Legend of Jay Gould*. Klein's book is as much a study of the popular image of "the most hated man in America" as it is a story of one man's life.[9] As industrialization swept across the land, "Gould was not only part of this revolution, but one of its prime movers."[10] Not only successful but bluntly honest in an era still rooted in earlier conventions, Gould offended many. In a time of transition this mighty, visible harbinger of a new order was reviled by a public mind still rooted in a simpler age and susceptible to the influence of a hostile press.

The rail fan disappeared after the first blush of transcontinental travel. Archie Robertson reports that his return is first noted some half century later, by the *Railway Age* in 1927.[11] By the late 1920s automobiles were no longer a novelty, and trains had gained the dignity of age and tradition and, says Robertson, "the sympathy which belongs to the underdog." This respected position has prevailed through much of the last half century. Cors observes that "in the thirties . . . the rail hobbyist came into his own," with 1938 being a watershed year: the "first real railfan book," *Along the Iron Trail* by Frederick Richardson and F. Nelson Blount, appeared, along with Lucius Beebe's first rail book, *High Iron*. *Railroad Magazine* now served the railroad enthusiast as much as the working railroaders. In 1940 Kambach Publishing Company introduced *Trains*, the first "unequivocally" hobbyist periodical.[12] The war brought new reliance on the rail system, but this was short-lived. In the late 1940s further growth in automobile and air travel gave rail travel for passengers permanent underdog status and provided challenges for freight service as well. A new wave of nostalgia boosted modeling and other rail fan occupations to record levels in the mid-1950s. The 1960s—with the space program, war, and social change—once again eclipsed railroading in the popular mind. But by the end of the 1970s the railfan had been "born again," as one hobby dealer reported.[13] The reason echoed the heyday of the 1940s: gasoline shortages and a much-heralded return to the rails, nostalgia for a simpler and more personalized era of travel, and a sense of national tradition and destiny. In the 1980s, a century and a half of popular fascination with railroading continued.

According to John Shedd Reed, retired chair of Santa Fe Industries, rail fans of the 1920s and 1930s were slightly different from those of today.[14] Then they "were strong supporters of progressive railroading . . . always looking at new developments." These contrast with more recent rail fans, who seem to be more inclined to be sentimentalists, seeking a return to the past. With the demise of both the steam locomotive and the passenger train, by the 1970s the railroad industry "found itself attacked by the great body of fans who in earlier days had been their supporters." In an era of change and competition, the survival of traditional rail travel, which was championed by fans, was in conflict with the survival of the railroad industry itself.

Both the late nineteenth century and the late twentieth century were periods of major change for railroads. These times particularly saw a complex relationship between rail fans and the rail industry. In times like the 1860s and the 1940s, the glamour of rail travel cast a glow over these ties. But perhaps more often fans have been critical of, and hostile toward, railroad leadership.

REFERENCE WORKS

A number of reference and bibliographic tools exist on trains and railroading. For an overview of American railroading—reading beyond the quite useful articles in such encyclopedias as the *Britannica* or the *Americana*—the general reader should turn to two now somewhat venerable titles: Stewart H. Holbrook, *The Story of American Railroads*, and John F. Stover, *American Railroads*. Holbrook provides more business and engineering coverage, while Stover gives more emphasis to social history. A more popular approach is found in Lamont Buchanan's 1955 *Steel Trains and Iron Horses: A Pageant of American Railroads*.

The relation of railroading to culture is explored in *Railroad: Trains and Train People in American Culture*, edited by James Alan McPherson and Miller Williams. This collection of excerpts and illustrations opens with an essay by McPherson entitled "Some Observations on the Railroad and American Culture." The excerpts range from scholarly essays and poetry (Emily Dickinson, Karl Shapiro, William Stafford) to early pamphlet material and advertisements for escaped slaves. This attractive, illustrated trade publication missed being reviewed in the academic press, but the hint of regret in the *Library Journal* review is worth noting: "The compilers are, in sum, more successful in raising important questions about political matters, working conditions, and the like than in capturing the romance of steam locomotives, faraway places, and lonely whistles in the night.[15] *Railroad* provides a direct, rich visual and literary experience of the same material covered more formally by Holbrook, Stover, and Buchanan.

Narrower in coverage but providing a firm foundation for academic study are two classic American studies texts: Henry Nash Smith, *The Virgin Land*, and Leo Marx, *The Machine and the Garden*. Smith reviews the popular pressure to build the rail link to the Pacific and the Orient and the subsequent problems of the railroad's domination. The campaigning for a transcontinental route by Thomas Hart Benton, Eli Whitney, and others plays a prominent role, and the sense of the original documents comes through clearly. Marx extends this view of the railroad, relating it more to the literary culture and art.

A landmark railroad book is John R. Stigloe's 1983 *Metropolitan Corridor: Railroads and the American Scene*. Stigloe, associate professor of landscape architecture and visual and environmental studies at Harvard, follows Smith and Nash, relating railroads in the era of their dominance in America (about 1880–1930) to the development of the physical world of that time: terminals, viaducts, crossings, and industrial zones. For his sources he turned often to the material of popular culture:

fiction (often illustrated), Lionel catalogs, photographs, postcards, and advertisements. Grant suggests that "this may be one of the most important railroad books ever published."[16]

The literature of railroading is, to repeat, vast; fortunately, two very useful guides are available. Most important for the study of trains and railroading in America is *Railroads* by Paul B. Cors, published by Libraries Unlimited in their series Spare Time Guides: Information Sources for Hobbies and Recreation. As a guide to rail fan literature, Cors' volume begins with an introduction that relates briefly the history and definition of the genre and describes the rail fan as well. The rail fan has been treated earlier, but Cors' "identifying characteristics common to most railfan literature" are necessary at this point. Books often are published by small or specialist firms, in small editions that quickly become scarce and highly sought. There is great attention to "precise, technical detail" based on patient research. Emphasis is on equipment operations rather than corporate and financial matters. Books written for rail fans are heavily illustrated: photographs, maps, ephemera, and so forth. More highly priced items contain one or more specially commissioned paintings by one of a group of well-regarded railroad artists.[17] In his guide, Cors goes beyond this body of literature to cover more technical professional material as well as work by scholars. As a handbook to serious popular interest in trains, this guide is indispensable.

Beyond the scope of Cors' interest lies non-North American literature of railroading as well as writing on modeling. These topics—along with a good selection on U.S. railroads—are covered by the English librarian E. T. Bryant in his *Railways: A Readers' Guide*. Introducing his brief American coverage, Bryant points out that "the number of books on American railways probably rivals that on British companies."[18] The publication of books and periodicals outside the United States does center in England, and the resulting body of materials has been made easily accessible in this country. A number of U.S. and Canadian book dealers regularly channel British titles to railfan collectors, and their catalogs include nearly as many British and foreign titles as American. This literature, then, has provided a foundation for American interest in locomotive and station preservation, short lines, unusual railroads (or railways, in British parlance), and modeling. Thus, Bryant's guide is essential to gaining an overall sense of railroad literature.

A very useful survey for the researcher is Carl Condit's "The Literature of the Railroad Buff: A Historian's View," which appeared in the spring 1980 issue of *Railroad History*. Condit's aim is to open the specialized vernacular literature accessible to historians of technology, and he focuses on seventy representative titles: pictorial albums, railroad histories, and motive power catalogs. Noteworthy, too, for the student of popular culture is the suggestive introductory section.

The World of Model Trains, by Guy R. Williams, a 1970 British publication distributed in the United States by Putnam, provides an international perspective on making models, constructing layouts, garden railroads, and so on. American examples are included. The classic work in this country is Louis H. Hertz, *The Complete Book of Model Railroading*. An extensive chapter on the model railroad hobby provides a useful and relatively early survey of this aspect of railroad popularity.

These overviews and guides provide, then, a basic reference perspective on the subject. In addition, there are a number of more specialized reference and bibliographic tools on railroading that are useful to the study of railroading in popular culture and give a clue of the range of popular railroad interest. Both Cors and Bryant provide coverage here, but with an emphasis on more recent material. This sketch, therefore, is highly selective.

The *Railway Directory and Yearbook*, published in London, is a classic reference tool, which can be traced back to 1898 and which provides current international information on rail routes, companies, and personnel. Recent volumes devote forty pages to the United States. Even more basic is *Jane's World Railways*, according to Cors "the single most complete source of data.[19] More specialized but a delight to the railfan is the *Car and Locomotive Cyclopedia*. The 1970 edition bears a resemblance to earlier volumes dating back to 1879. An extensive "dictionary of car and locomotive terms" is included, along with an exhaustive catalog of current rolling stock.

More specifically designed for the railfan is John Marshall's *Rail Facts and Feats*. Though undocumented and probably requiring verification in more standard or specialized sources, it gives a good sense of the range of superlatives of most interest to railroad enthusiasts. Also, one cannot go far in railroading literature without recourse to a specialized glossary. The language of romantic railroading is made accessible by two guides: *The Language of the Railroader*, by Ramon F. Adams, and *Rail Talk: A Lexicon of Railroad Language*, collected and edited by James H. Beck in 1978. Reaching back to the heritage of Casey Jones and Steel Drivin' Men, the language of railroad builders and workers was and is "imaginative, emotional, sensitive, humorous, earthy, literal." Much of it is a permanent, colorful part of our modern speech: "double-header," "highball," "called on the carpet," "side-tracked," and many more such terms.[20]

A number of guides exist to serve the traveling needs of railfans. An annual (including even discount coupons) is the *Steam Passenger Service Directory Including Electric Lines and Museums*, published since 1966. For the person more interested in "high iron" (a main line), there is *Travel by Train*, by Edward J. Wojtas. Here the emphasis is on major Amtrak routes, but shorter routes—including non-Amtrak lines—earn coverage. Brief mention is made of Canada, Mexico, "auto train," and tourist railroads. The discussion of "America's Trains Today" provides a recent overview designed for a broader general public. For a more specialized group is *Right-of-Way: A Guide to Abandoned Railroads in the United States*, by Waldo Nielsen. Requiring perhaps less hiking are local train watchers' guides. A fine example is *The New Train Watcher's Guide to Chicago*, by John Szwajkart, which is accompanied by a large map. Indicated are what is to be found at a location, the best times to see it, and how to get there. This listing is preceded by capsule descriptions of each line and a discussion of passenger operations in Chicago.

Very briefly, two useful charts deserve mention for the non-specialist librarian or student of the railfan subculture. The first and most readily available is the table of "Railway Systems of Selected Countries" found under "Railroads and Locomotives" in the *New Encyclopedia Britannica*, 15th edition. Given here is a listing of the gauges for each country, standard or otherwise. At a glance, one can see whether or not a book on the rails of Taiwan would appeal to a narrow-gauge enthusiast. The second aims to aid the reader of literature on locomotives who encounters a series of numbers like the following: 2–4–0 or 2–8–4. These numbers represent the three groupings of locomotive wheels by diameters: the front-end, drivers, and truck wheels. The Whyte Classification is illustrated on a chart by Frederic Shaw in his 1959 *Casey Jones' Locker* (174), along with a brief discussion of the locomotive's evolution.

In addition to the guides by Cors and Bryant, a number of bibliographies are available. To support these guides, reference can be made to the *Railbook Bibliography, 1948–1972: A Comprehensive Guide to the Most Important Railbooks, Publications and Reports*, compiled by F. K. Hudson, which, though unannotated, attempts to list all U.S. and Canadian railroad books and government documents.

For more current information, searches should be made of standard bibliographical and index sources. A good selected list, "Railroads, Interurbans and Highways," appears in *The Frontier and the American West*, compiled by Rodman W. Paul and Richard W. Etulain. In the same series Robert H. Bremner's *American Social History since 1860* includes a list of works on "Mining, Transportation, and Lumbering" that treats railroading. But more comprehensive is the "Railroads" listings in the *Harvard Guide to American History*, edited by Frank Freidel. *America: History and Life*, a periodical index, provides good ongoing coverage of scholarship. More popular material is available in the *Readers' Guide* (*Poole's Index* for the last century) and the *New York Times Index*.

Some specialized bibliographies are available. By far the most important here is Frank P. Donovan Jr.'s landmark work, *The Railroad in Literature: Brief Survey of Railroad Fiction, Poetry, Songs, Bibliography, Essays, Travel and Drama in the English Language and Particularly Emphasizing Its Place in American Literature*. Donovan's survey puts a structure on a very substantial body of material and is a high point in the bibliographic control of American popular culture. Another listing of importance for earlier material is *A List of References to Literature Relating to the Union Pacific System* from the library of the Bureau of Railway Economics. The coverage is broad, encompassing the debates from the 1830s and 1840s, later travel literature, and government documents; it is a sweeping overview of a central element of the American rail phenomenon. Finally, the rail historian, the railfan, and the student of popular culture all can use *Railroads of the Trans-Mississippi West: A Selected Bibliography*, compiled by Donovan L. Hofsommer. Thorough but selective, three chapters indicate the level of usefulness for social and cultural study: "Regulation and Reaction to Railroad Excesses," "The Captains of Industry/The Robber Barons," and "Railroad Labor/Employees."

Finally, periodicals represent an important part of railfan literature. Two periodicals provide regular surveys of railroad historical literature, the *Lexington Newsletter* and *Railroad History*. Also, available from the National Model Railroad Association is an annual index to model railroad magazines. This last item is reported in an article on model making (with a section on railroads and live steam) by Frederick A. Schlipf in *Magazines for Libraries*, edited by Bill and Linda Sternberg Katz.[21] Much more than just a list of periodical titles, Schlipf's article describes the problem areas of model periodicals—thin coverage by libraries, lack of indexing, damage to precise drawings by library binding, and lack of microform availablity. These problems plague researchers in many areas of popular culture study, of course. In addition, Schlipf describes for his librarian audience the activities and needs of modelers and relates these to the structure of the literature. Schlipf's observations are directly relevant to understanding a key aspect of the railfan phenomenon.

RESEARCH COLLECTIONS

In this century libraries and archives provide much leadership in the serious study of all aspects of railroading. Even more significant than the Bureau of Railway Economics' Union Pacific list of 1922 was its 1912 *Railway Economics: A Collective Catalogue of Books in Fourteen American Libraries*. Because few comprehensive studies existed, the bureau's list sought to bring together from several collections the materials needed by the "student of railway transportation."[22] Included are materials from periodicals, collections of miscellaneous essays, and general works, as well as technical information of "historical or economic significance." Most documents and laws, guides, maps and atlases, and timetables are excluded. Still, the listing is massive: a specialized catalog for the bureau plus the Interstate Commerce Commission, the Library of Congress, the New York Public Library, the Crerar, and collections at Columbia, Stanford, Harvard, Chicago, Illinois, Michigan, Pennsylvania, Wisconsin, and Yale universities. Although the coverage may be more selective in some areas, guides, informal narratives, and maps are presented for many categories.

The best overview of library research collections today is found in Lee Ash's *Subject Collections*, which shows that the great library collectors of the turn of the twentieth century were joined by a number of others. Southern Methodist University's DeGolyer Library reports having one of the world's largest collections of railroad photographs, about 230,000 prints. In addition, there is a 12,000-volume collection of railroadiana. Northwestern University's Transportation Library also is a major resource, for the railfan phenomenon as well as for the specialist technical literature. Many local and regional libraries have comprehensive collections now, relating to more local developments, for example, Bowdoin College, the Maryland and Minnesota historical societies, and the Denver Public Library. Specialized collections can be found at the Connecticut Electric Railway Association, the Baltimore Streetcar Museum, Harvard's Baker Library, and—to savor the very earliest—the American Antiquarian Society. For some of the collections there are special catalogs or guides. In 1935 Columbia University Library published *The William Barclay Parsons Railroad Prints: An Appreciation and Check List*. A popular and important collection is chronicled in the Smithsonian's *The First Quarter Century of Steam Locomotives in North America: Remaining Relics and Operable Replicas with a Catalog of Locomotive Models in the U.S. National Museum*, by Smith Hempstone Oliver. A 1978 Smithsonian publication, *Guide to Manuscript Collections in the National Museum of History and Technology*, records vast holdings of material on railroad companies, individuals, and railroad preservation. Railroad maps have been drawn since the first U.S. tracks were laid in response to Americans' intense interest in routes. The motivating force of popular interest opens the preface to Andrew M. Modelski's *Railroad Maps of the United States: A Selective Annotated Bibliography of Original 19th Century Maps in the Library of Congress*. The thorough scholarly introduction provides a context that is a useful guide to other, smaller map collections. A list of railroads covered in their extensive files of reports and so on is available from the Center for Research Libraries in Chicago (researchers should inquire through their home libraries).

Like the Columbia railroad prints checklist, exhibit catalogs can call attention to promising material. A good example is *From Train to Plane: Travelers in the*

Railroad yard and depot in Nashville, Tennessee, 1864. Courtesy of the Library of Congress

American West, 1866–1936, the catalog for a 1979 exhibit at Yale's Beinecke Library. In their preface, Archibald Hanna Jr. and William S. Reese sound the call:

> The travel literature of the American West in the pre-Civil War era has been more closely examined than any other group of material on the Trans-Mississippi region. The opposite is true of the post-1865 era, when travel opened to the multitude rather than the hardy few. An extensive body of material on later travellers and tourists exists, but it remains largely untapped by researchers.[23]

A particular vision and desire to reach a range of publics are found at the Newberry Library. There, for the serious researcher, are housed the Illinois Central, Burlington, and Pullman archives and a printed *Guide to the Illinois Central Archives in the Newberry Library, 1851–1906* by Carolyn Curtis Mohr. But popular interest in railroad history was stimulated by the publication in 1949 of Lloyd Lewis and Stanley Pargellis' *Granger Country: A Pictorial Social History of the Burlington Railroad*. In a format attractive to general and railfan readers, the book calls attention to the collection and makes some of its riches widely accessible. Newberry "marketing" also resulted in serious, but accessible, scholarship, such as works by historian Richard Overton. Since Pargellis, Newberry librarian Lawrence Towner has added both the Pullman archives (rich in material on the porters) and also collections of railroad lithographs that testify to nineteenth-century popular enthusiasm for the locomotive particularly.

Some libraries have stimulated research and popular appreciation of railroading because their partners and backers have been private collectors. The Newberry, again, provides an example with its Everett D. Graff Collection of Western Americana. Colton Storm's catalog of this originally private library includes a substantial number of materials that either affected or reflected early popular interest in trains: guides to railroad land sales, travel accounts, reminiscences, and other ephemeral material. Similarly, the Thomas Streeter Collection is an important foundation for the American Antiquarian Society's railroad holdings.

Many collections of more recent railroad materials remain in private hands. Some of these are now coming into institutional collections. In the last few years the Saint Louis Mercantile Library Association has received the collection on American railroads (1913–1976) of John W. Barriger III. The Donnelley Library, Lake Forest College, provides a good example of this process. In the 1970s the family of the late Elliott Donnelley—an important figure in railway preservation and in live steam—gave to Lake Forest his collection. Built between 1940 and 1975, this collection reflects the era of the railfan; it encompasses steam, modeling, live steam, short lines, western railroads, narrow gauge, railroadiana, and international topics—including many British imprints, especially. Through family generosity the collection has continued to grow and includes over twenty periodical subscriptions. In the 1980s gifts by Professor James Sloss of MIT's Transportation Department have complemented the Elliott Donnelley material. In addition to enriching the coverage, timetables, rule books, maps, and travel literature have been added, often with an East Coast emphasis that complements Donnelley's collecting. These examples point to the general problem facing the researcher, the difficulty of locating broad, consistently built holdings of more modern material.

HISTORY AND CRITICISM

Much of the history of trains and railroading in the United States is a blend of hope and enthusiasm with frustration and criticism. Albro Martin's *Enterprise Denied: Origins of the Decline of American Railroads, 1897–1917* exemplifies this situation. In the preface the author speaks of his awareness as a child in the 1930s of the "American Railroad Problem." Martin finds the roots in early twentieth-century government regulation, and, in the words of the jacket blurb, the book "chronicles a tragedy for the American people whose hopes for a superb . . . system . . . were permanently blighted." The literature on American railroads centers either on epic moments or on blighted hopes and thus reflects a nostalgic tone reminiscent of the ambience of classic southern fiction. This special character can be traced from academic to more popular historical writings.

The history and study of railroads began in the nineteenth century. The Bureau of Library Economics' catalog and list on the Union Pacific both testify to this. Early writing reflected the epic quality of railroading. An example is *Memoir of Henry Farnum* by Henry W. Farnum. This key figure in the early trans-Mississippi railway construction and partner of Thomas C. Durant is celebrated here by his son. Nevertheless, the material is still useful: Dee Brown drew on it for *Hear That Lonesome Whistle Blow*, an account of the celebration in 1854 at the linking of the Atlantic to the Mississippi at Rock Island, Illinois. Brown drew on many such contemporary and firsthand accounts for his very useful study.

A unique study from 1906 is *North American Railroads: Their Administration and Economic Policy*, by W. Hoff and F. Schwabach. The report of a comprehensive, official German survey of the U.S. rail system, it provides a remarkable view of life behind the railroads' operations. For example: "The principle prevails in general with American business life that the payment of wages for services rendered constitutes the complete settlement between employee and employer."[24] Elsewhere the Germans marvel at companies that deal through ticket "scalpers."[25] Overall, the report gives a view of Americans' railroad expectations through European eyes.

By the 1920s academic studies were more common. One such study is Orville Thrasher Gooden's doctoral dissertation, "The Missouri and North Arkansas Railroad Strike." Gooden deals with the relation of public opinion to one moment of crisis between a railroad and its workers.

Railroad historical scholarship came of age in Richard C. Overton's *Burlington West: A Colonization History of the Burlington Railroad*. In its scope and accomplishment it opened a new era of study and, through its bibliography, pointed to new sources and approaches. An example is the late-nineteenth-century popular local history. Overton has continued to set a high standard in *Gulf to Rockies: The Heritage of the Fort Worth and Denver-Colorado and Southern Railways, 1861–1898*; *Burlington Route: A History of the Burlington Lines*; and many other works. As consulting editor of Macmillan's Railroads of America series, he has overseen the production of works covering the B & O, the Canadian Pacific and National, the Santa Fe, the Illinois Central, and others.

Personalities have been critical in the popular perception of railroads. Thomas C. Cochran, at the beginning of his *Railroad Leaders, 1845–1890*, notes that "our popular heroes have normally been politicians and businessmen."[26] He continues by observing that historians have been too ignorant of the psychology of these figures.

Thus, a number of recent biographies have looked anew at how the great railroad moguls were successful. This revision appears graphically in Stanley P. Hirshson's *Grenville M. Dodge: Soldier, Politician, Railroad Pioneer*. Hirshson finds Jacob R. Perkins' 1929 biography of Dodge inadequate because it sought to make his subject a "demi-god" and failed to capture his spirit or his energy, which was the source of his magnetism. Like Richard Overton, Albro Martin went directly to archival material for his *James J. Hill and the Opening of the Northwest*. Among available published material Martin had found relatively little, and what he did find closely fitted the robber baron stereotype.

In addition to studies of companies and individuals, modern scholarship has turned its interest to other subgroupings of railroad history. A classic of American sociology is W. Fred Cottrell's *The Railroader*, which gives the railroader's world in a well-defined hierarchy. At higher levels Cottrell found skills to be monopolized, by which he meant that trainmen maintained their superiority over the company, fellow railroaders, and the public. Even by 1940 the demise of this monopoly and, with it, the railroaders' proud community could be seen. The study provides a classic view of "romantic heroes" caught in change and obsolescence.

The field of urban history has also looked in detail at the railroad. Carl W. Condit sees the railroad as center to one development phase of the city, prior to the automobile. His *The Railroad and the City* focuses on Cincinnati and shows how fundamental the railroad was to the social organization of urban culture. George W. Hilton and John F. Due describe the important, but brief, role the interurban railway played in the development of intercity transport in *The Electric Interurban Railways in America*. In spite of the coincident appearance of the automobile, this peculiarly American institution was responsible for greatly increased passenger mobility. One recent dissertation points the way to a link between urban and popular cultural history in this area: David Lynn Snowden's "Rail Passenger Service in the United States since the Nineteen Thirties: Its Decline, Nostalgia and Esthetics (with Emphasis on Greater St. Louis)."

The notion of taking a more conscious look at rail nostalgia has begun to interest serious students. Rail literature is a primary source for George H. Douglas' article, "Lucius Beebe: Popular Railroad History as Social Nostalgia." Douglas finds that Beebe's books, such as *When Beauty Rode the Rails* or *Hear the Train Blow*, recall that "the railroad in its best days offered the American public an unbeatable combination of eccentric individuality, snob appeal, and high style." The railroad era, as found in Beebe's scores of books and articles, "still evokes fond memories . . . of an America that once was and doubtless still lies buried just underneath the surface of our consciousness."[27]

As mentioned earlier, special paintings have accompanied many railfan books. The wide appeal of this specialized kind of art is considered in the introduction to *Great Railroad Paintings*, edited by Robert Goldsborough. Growing out of the pioneer efforts of urban realists such as Reginald Marsh and Edward Hopper, a group of illustrators accepted commissions from railroads for calendars in the 1920s. Out of this development, based in advertising, have come this particular nostalgia and the preservation of a genre, one which was in eclipse in the two decades after 1950. More recently, the Santa Fe commissioned Howard Fogg to paint current scenes, and Amtrak brought back calendar paintings. Goldsborough's collection reproduces a selection demonstrating the range, from 1923 to the 1970s.

In rounding out this survey of literature relating to railroading in popular culture, a return to the railfan is inevitable. Cors' and Bryant's guides provide a good view, as does Archie Robertson's chapter on the movement in *Slow Train to Yesterday*. This "indefinable affection"[28] which affects so many, is discussed, too, by Frederic Shaw in a chapter entitled "Genus Railroadiac" in *Casey Jones' Locker*. Shaw, Robertson, and Cors all examine in detail the various railfan organizations, the vernacular, and the pioneers of the history of trains and railroading. The Railway and Locomotive Historical Society, based at Harvard's Baker Library, is the most scholarly of these organizations, publishing *Railroad History* (Carl Condit is among the contributors), which preserves, documents, and focuses on the industry. Largest is the National Railway Historical Society, which, in conjunction with local chapters, sponsors "fantrips." The oldest group is the Railroad Enthusiasts. Other specialized groups include the Central Electric Railfans' Association, the National Association of Timetable Collectors, the Rail-roadiana Collectors' Association, and the Railroad Station Historical Society. Perhaps most arcane is the American Vecturists' Association, many of whose members specialize in collecting railroad or streetcar tokens. The variety is endless. In Archie Robertson's words: "The fan deserves a closer scrutiny than I have given him. He shares many of the surface characteristics of all hobbyists, with one basic difference: he is essentially selfless. He just wants to be around trains and, if possible, to help them out when they get in trouble."[29]

NOTES

1. Daniel J. Boorstin, "Editor's Preface," in *American Railroads*, by John F. Stover (Chicago: University of Chicago Press, 1961), v.

2. Lucius Beebe, *High Iron: A Book of Trains* (New York: Appleton-Century, 1938), 3.

3. B. A. Botkin, "Introduction," in *A Treasury of Railroad Folklore: The Stories, Tall Tales, Traditions, Ballads and Songs of the American Railroad Man*, ed. B. A. Botkin and Alvin F. Harlow (New York: Bonanza Books, 1953), xi.

4. Barton K. Davis, *How to Build Model Railroads and Equipment* (New York: Crown, 1956), 4.

5. Paul B. Cors, *Railroads, Spare Time Guides: Information Sources for Hobbies and Recreation*, no. 8 (Littleton, Colo.: Libraries Unlimited, 1975), 12.

6. Don Ball Jr., "Preface," in *Decade of the Trains: The 1940s*, by Don Ball Jr. and Rogers E. M. Whitaker ("E. M. Frimbo") (Boston: New York Graphics Society, 1977), 11.

7. Archie Robertson, *Slow Train to Yesterday: A Last Glance at the Local* (Boston: Houghton Mifflin, 1945), 151–52.

8. H. Roger Grant to the author, January 16, 1987. Grant, professor of history at the University of Akron, is the author of *The Corn Belt Route: A History of the Chicago Great Western Railroad Company* (Northern Illinois Press, 1984) and (with Charles Bohi) *The Country Railroad Station in America* (Pruett, 1978).

9. Maury Klein, *The Life and Legend of Jay Gould* (Baltimore: Johns Hopkins University Press, 1986), 3.

10. Ibid., 492.

11. Robertson, 152.

12. Cors, 11–12.

13. Charles R. Day Jr., "All Aboard for a Lifelong Hobby," *Industry Week* 203 (December 10, 1979), 98.

14. John Shedd Reed to the author, January 17, 1987.

15. W. C. Robinson, review of *Railroad: Trains and Train People in American Culture*, ed. James Alan McPherson and Miller Williams, in *Library Journal* 101 (December 15, 1976), 2573.

16. Grant to author, January 16, 1987.

17. Cors, 13.

18. E. T. Bryant, *Railways: A Readers' Guide* (Hamden, Conn.: Archon, 1968), 116.

19. Cors, 15.

20. See Preface in James H. Beck, ed., *Rail Talk: A Lexicon of Railroad Language* (Gretna, Nebr.: James, 1978).

21. Frederick A. Schlipf, "Model Making," in *Magazines for Libraries*, ed. Bill Katz and Linda Sternberg Katz, 5th ed. (New York: R. R. Bowker, 1986), 715–27.

22. Bureau of Railway Economics, *Railway Economics: A Collective Catalogue of Books in Fourteen American Libraries* (Chicago: University of Chicago Press, 1912), v.

23. See Preface in *From Train to Plane: Travelers in the American West, 1866–1936* (New Haven, Conn.: Yale University Library, 1979).

24. W. Hoff and F. Schwabach, *North American Railroads: Their Administration and Economic Policy* (New York: Germania Press, 1906), 213.

25. Ibid., 245–50.

26. Thomas C. Cochran, *Railroad Leaders, 1845–1890: The Business Mind in Action* (New York: Russell and Russell, 1965), 1.

27. George H. Douglas, "Lucius Beebe: Popular Railroad History as Social Nostalgia," *Journal of Popular Culture*, 4 (Spring 1971), 907.

28. Frederic Shaw, *Casey Jones' Locker: Railroad Historiana* (San Francisco: Hesperian House, 1959), 165.

29. Robertson, 162–63.

BIBLIOGRAPHY

Books and Articles

Adams, Ramon F. *The Language of the Railroader*. Norman: University of Oklahoma Press, 1977.

Ash, Lee, ed. *Subject Collections: A Guide to Special Book Collections and Subject Emphases as Reported by University, College, Public and Special Libraries, and Museums in the United States and Canada*. 6th ed. New York: R. R. Bowker, 1985.

Ball, Don, Jr., and Rogers E. M. Whitaker. *Decade of the Trains: The 1940s*. Boston: New York Graphics Society, 1977.

Beck, James H., ed. *Rail Talk: A Lexicon of Railroad Language*. Gretna, Nebr.: James, 1978.

Beebe, Lucius. *Hear the Train Blow: A Pictorial Epic of America in the Railroad Age*. New York: E. P. Dutton, 1952.

———. *High Iron: A Book of Trains*. New York: Appleton-Century, 1938.

———. *When Beauty Rode the Rails*. Garden City, N.Y.: Doubleday, 1962.

Botkin, B. A., and Alvin F. Harlow, eds. *A Treasury of Railroad Folklore: The Stories, Tall Tales, Traditions, Ballads and Songs of the American Railroad Man*. New York: Bonanza Books, 1953.

Bremner, Robert H. *American Social History since 1860*. New York: Appleton-Century-Crofts, 1971.

Brown, Dee. *Hear That Lonesome Whistle Blow: Railroads in the West*. New York: Holt, Rinehart, and Winston, 1977.

Bryant, E. T. *Railways: A Readers' Guide*. Hamden, Conn.: Archon Books, 1968.

Buchanan, Lamont. *Steel Trains and Iron Horses: A Pageant of American Railroads*. New York: Putnam's, 1955.

Bureau of Railway Economics. *A List of References to Literature Relating to the Union Pack System*. Newton, Mass.: Crofton, n.d. (reprint of 1922 edition).

———. *Railway Economics: A Collective Catalogue of Books in Fourteen American Libraries*. Chicago: University of Chicago Press, 1912.

Car and Locomotive Cyclopedia. New York: Car and Locomotive Cyclopedia, 1879– . Quadrennial.

Cochran, Thomas C. *Railroad Leaders, 1845–1890: The Business Mind in Action*. New York: Russell and Russell, 1965.

Condit, Carl W. "The Literature of the Railroad Buff. A Historian's View." *Railroad History*, 142 (Spring 1980), 7–26.

———. *The Railroad and the City: A Technological and Urbanistic History of Cincinnati*. Columbus: Ohio State University Press, 1977.

Cors, Paul B. *Railroads.* Spare Times Guides: Information Sources for Hobbies and Recreation, no. 8. Littleton. Colo.: Libraries Unlimited, 1975.

Cottrell, W. Fred. *The Railroader.* Stanford, Calif.: Stanford University Press, 1940. Reprint. With an introduction by Scott Greer. Dubuque, Iowa: Brown Reprints, 1971.

Davis, Barton K. *How to Build Model Railroads and Equipment.* New York: Crown, 1956.

Day, Charles R., Jr. "All Aboard for a Lifelong Hobby." *Industry Week* 203 (December 10, 1979), 98–100.

Donovan, Frank P., Jr. *The Railroad in Literature: Brief Survey of Railroad Fiction, Poetry, Songs, Biography, Essays, Travel and Drama in the English Language and Particularly Emphasizing Its Place in American Literature.* Boston: Railway and Locomotive Historical Society, 1940.

Douglas, George H. "Lucius Beebe: Popular Railroad History as Social Nostalgia." *Journal of Popular Culture,* 4 (Spring 1971), 893–910.

Farnum, Henry W. *Memoir of Henry Farnum.* New Haven, Conn.: N.p., 1889.

Freidel, Frank, ed. *Harvard Guide to American History.* Rev. ed. 2 vols. Cambridge: Harvard University Press, 1974.

From Train to Plane: Travelers in the American West, 1866–1936. New Haven, Conn.: Yale University Library, 1979.

Goldsborough, Robert, ed. *Great Railroad Paintings.* New York: Peacock Press/Bantam, 1976.

Gooden, Orville Thrasher. "The Missouri and North Arkansas Railroad Strike." Ph.D. dissertation, Columbia University, 1926.

Grant, H. Roger. *The Corn Belt Route: A History of the Chicago Great Western Railroad Company.* Dekalb: Northern Illinois University Press, 1984.

Grant, H. Roger, and Charles Bohi. *The Country Railroad Station in America.* Boulder, Colo.: Pruett, 1978.

Guide to Manuscript Collections in the National Museum of History and Technology. Washington, D.C.: Smithsonian Institution Press, 1978.

Hertz, Louis H. *The Complete Book of Model Railroading.* New York: Simmons-Boardman, 1951.

Hilton, George W., and John F. Due. *The Electric Interurban Railways in America.* Stanford, Calif.: Stanford University Press, 1960.

Hirshson, Stanley P. *Grenville M. Dodge: Soldier, Politician, Railroad Pioneer.* Bloomington: Indiana University Press, 1967.

Hoff, W., and F. Schwabach. *North American Railroads: Their Administration and Economic Policy.* New York: Germania Press, 1906.

Hofsommer, Donovan L. *Railroads of the Trans-Mississippi West: A Selected Bibliography.* Plainview, Tex.: Wayland College, 1974.

Holbrook, Stewart H. *The Story of American Railroads.* New York: Crown, 1947.

Hudson, F. K., comp. *Railbook Bibliography, 1948–1972: A Comprehensive Guide to the Most Important Railbooks, Publications and Reports.* Ocean, N.J.: Specialty Press, 1972.

Jane's World Railways. London: Macdonald and Jane's, 1966– . Annual.

Klein, Maury. *The Life and Legend of Jay Gould.* Baltimore: Johns Hopkins University Press, 1986.

Lewis, Lloyd, and Stanley Pargellis, eds. *Granger Country: A Pictorial Social History of the Burlington Railroad.* Boston: Little, Brown, 1949.

Marshall, John. *Rail Facts and Feats.* New York: Two Continents, 1974.

Martin, Albro. *Enterprise Denied: Origins of the Decline of American: Railroads 1897–1917.* New York: Columbia University Press, 1971.

———. *James J. Hill and the Opening of the Northwest.* New York: Oxford University Press, 1976.

Marx, Leo. *The Machine in the Garden.* New York: Oxford University Press, 1964.

McPherson, James Alan, and Miller Williams, eds. *Railroad: Trains and Train People in American Culture.* New York: Random House, 1976.

Modelski, Andrew M., comp. *Railroad Maps of the United States: A Selective Annotated Bibliography of Original 19th Century Maps in the Library of Congress.* Washington, D.C.: Library of Congress, 1975.

Mohr, Carolyn Curtis. *Guide to the Illinois Central Archives in the Newberry Library, 1851–1906.* Chicago: Newberry Library, 1951.

New York Times Index. New York: New York Times, 1856– .

Nielsen, Waldo. *Right-of-Way: A Guide to Abandoned Railroads in the United States.* Bend, Oreg.: Old Bottle Magazine, 1972.

Norris, Frank. *The Octopus.* Cambridge, Mass.: Robert Bently, 1971.

Oliver, Smith Hempstone. *The First Quarter Century of Steam Locomotives in North America: Remaining Relics and Operable Replicas with a Catalog of Locomotive Models in the U.S. National Museum.* Washington, D.C.: Smithsonian Institution, 1956.

Overton, Richard C. *Burlington Route: A History of the Burlington Lines.* New York: Alfred A. Knopf, 1965.

———. *Burlington West: A Colonization History of the Burlington Railroad.* Cambridge: Harvard University Press, 1941.

———. *Gulf to Rockies: The Heritage of the Fort Worth and Denver-Colorado and Southern Railways, 1861–1898.* Austin: University of Texas Press, 1953.

Paul, Rodman W., and Richard W. Etulain, comps. *The Frontier and the American West.* Arlington Heights, Ill.: AHM, 1977.

Perkins, Jacob R. *Trails, Rails and War: The Life of General G. M. Dodge.* Indianapolis: Bobbs-Merrill, 1929.

"Railroads." In *Encyclopedia Americana.* International ed. Vol. 23. Danbury, Conn.: Americana, 1979, 152–69.

"Railroads and Locomotives." In *New Encyclopaedia Britannica.* 15th ed. Vol. 15. Chicago: Encyclopaedia Britannica, 1974, 477–91.

Railway Directory and Yearbook. London, Transport Press, 1898– . Annual.

Readers' Guide to Periodical Literature. New York: H. W. Wilson, 1900– . Annual.

Richardson, Frederick H., and F. Nelson Blount. *Along the Iron Trail.* 2nd ed. Rutland, Vt.: Sharp Offset, 1966.

Robertson, Archie. *Slow Train to Yesterday: A Last Glance at the Local.* Boston: Houghton Mifflin, 1945.

Robinson, W. C. Review of *Railroad: Trains and Train People in American Culture,* ed. James Alan McPherson and Miller Williams. *Library Journal* 101 (December 15, 1976), 2573.

Schlipf, Frederick A. "Model Making." In *Magazines for Libraries,* ed. Bill Katz and Linda Sternberg Katz, 5th ed. New York: R. R. Bowker, 1986, 715–27.

Shaw, Frederic. *Casey Jones' Locker: Railroad Historiana*. San Francisco: Hesperian House, 1959.

Smith, Henry Nash. *The Virgin Land*. Cambridge: Harvard University Press, 1950.

Snowden, David Lynn. "Rail Passenger Service in the United States since the Nineteen Thirties: Its Decline, Nostalgia and Esthetics (with Emphasis on Greater St. Louis)." Ph.D. dissertation, St. Louis University, 1975.

Steam Passenger Service Directory Including Electric Lines and Museums. New York: Empire State Railway Museum, 1966– . Annual.

Stigloe, John R. *Metropolitan Corridor: Railroads and the American Scene*. New Haven, Conn.: Yale University Press, 1983.

Storm, Colton, comp. *A Catalogue of the Everett D. Graff Collection of Western Americana*. Chicago: University of Chicago Press, 1968.

Stover, John F. *American Railroads*. Chicago: University of Chicago Press, 1961.

Szwajkart, John. *The New Train Watcher's Guide to Chicago*. Brookfield, Ill.: John Szwajkart, 1976.

The William Barclay Parsons Railroad Prints: An Appreciation and a Check List. New York: Columbia University Library, 1935.

Williams, Guy R. *The World of Model Trains*. New York: Putnam's, 1970.

Wojtas, Edward J. *Travel by Train*. New York: Rand McNally, 1974.

Periodicals

America: History and Life. Santa Barbara, Calif., 1964– .

Lexington Newsletter. Plainview, Tex., 1942– .

Railroad History. Westford, Mass., 1921– . (Formerly *Railway and Locomotive Historical Society Bulletin*.)

Railroad Magazine. New York, 1906– .

Railway Age. Bristol, Conn., 1856– .

Trains: The Magazine of Railroading. Milwaukee, 1940– .

VERSE AND POPULAR POETRY

Perry Frank and Janice Radway

While virtually every field in popular culture studies is plagued by the problems inherent in defining and identifying a proper object for analysis, these difficulties become particularly acute, in fact almost prohibitive, when the subject under scrutiny is popular poetry and verse. Several individual poets have become extraordinarily "popular" figures during the course of American cultural development, in the sense that they were, or are now, personally familiar to a large portion of the population. However, very few single volumes of actual poetry have ever achieved best-seller status at the time of their publication.

Frank Luther Mott, who conservatively defines the best seller as a work purchased in the decade of publication by 1 percent of the total population of the continental United States, lists only seven individual volumes of poetry by American poets as best sellers in the years from 1662 to 1945. Included in this list, however, is Walt Whitman's *Leaves of Grass* (1855), of which only a few hundred copies were actually sold in the year of publication itself. Mott is able to retain the work on his list only because, through cheap reprints, the requisite number of copies was eventually sold in the course of the entire decade. But there is a significant difference between Whitman's status as a popular poet and that of Henry Wadsworth Longfellow, whose *Hiawatha* (1855) sold 2,500 copies during the week of publication alone and nearly 18,000 more during the next three months.

Even if one could decide on an appropriate measure for the popularity of this genre, which has never approached the novel in sales, such publication figures for volumes of poetry are not readily available. Literary historians of the eighteenth and nineteenth centuries do include poets now unfamiliar to us in their dictionaries and encyclopedias, but there is almost no way of determining whether such figures were truly popular or only minor poets who produced elitist verse of secondary quality. At one time nearly every newspaper and popular magazine published in the United States included poetry that cannot be termed "elite" or "artistic." Many of these same versifiers never produced an entire volume of poetry nor reached a national audience. For eighteenth- and nineteenth-century poets, it is necessary to rely heavily on Rufus Wilmot Griswold's *The Poets and Poetry of America*, a best-selling literary encyclopedia which itself went through more than sixteen editions, to identify figures who made a lasting impact.

Sales figures and estimates of dissemination are also difficult to obtain for popular poets of the twentieth century and today. *Publishers Weekly*, the compiler of record for best-sellers since 1912, does not publish a separate best-selling poetry list, nor does the *New York Times*. The occasional volume of verse or poetry anthology that does attain best-seller status is included on the nonfiction lists. An electronic search turned up a few lists distributed by obscure groups, but all were stale and it was unclear how they were compiled. Perhaps the sales figures for popular poets are less important to the cultural historian, however, than determining the vein or style of verse that was popular with a broad cross-section of the population during a particular period, since this information sheds light on literary tastes, audience values, and the function that poetry fulfilled in people's lives.

With these caveats in mind, the poets mentioned in the following survey are representative of major trends in popular verse as expressed in periodical publications of wide circulation, anthologies that have gone through numerous printings, and, in the case of more recent genres, dissemination through readings, performance art, and media such as film and television. Individual figures that have gained a wide following have been singled out and remain important for study, but the evolution of popular genres and the relation of popular to elite poetry are also important areas for consideration. Significant primary source research involving the identification of relevant works found in large-circulation magazines, as well as examination of popular music and performance genres, will be required to explore these broader issues.

HISTORICAL OUTLINE

In the years immediately following the settlement of the American colonies, two distinct forms of verse emerged as the basis of a popular poetic tradition. While religious and practical considerations tended to diminish interest in the high art of poesy as it was then practiced in England, the early colonist found definite merit in religious poetry of a didactic nature and in informational verse designed for the circulation of news. Accordingly, it is not surprising to discover that the first truly popular American poems were those of the *Bay Psalm Book* (1640) and the numerous "broadsides" hawked by street peddlers.

While the two kinds of verse appeared vastly different on the surface, they exhibited a common interest in content as well as a very obvious disinterest in matters of aesthetic form. Indeed, the editors of the *Bay Psalm Book* apologized for the rustic quality of their verse with the observation that "if therefore the verses are not always so smooth and elegant as some may desire or expect, let them consider that God's Altar needs no polishing."

Like the broadside verse that told of specific crimes, births, deaths, and holidays, early American religious poetry was thus designed to refer explicitly to the world inhabited by its reader. Language was not something to be manipulated for its own sake, but rather a tool to be used for instruction and information. It is this exclusive emphasis on the referential aspect of language that has continued to differentiate America's popular verse from her more self-conscious, deliberately aesthetic poetry of the elite tradition.

Throughout the late seventeenth and early eighteenth centuries, most of the poetry read by the majority of the populace was amateur verse published outside the three major literary centers of Philadelphia, New York, and Boston. Such verse was highly topical and therefore largely ephemeral. It was published by a local printer in pamphlet form and financed by the author himself. Much of the verse, like the "Massachusetts Liberty Song," took the Revolutionary War as its subject, although religious teaching continued to be the primary subject of American amateur verse for the next 150 years. A vast quantity of this sort of verse was included in the almanacs that began to appear as early as 1639 and that quickly became an indispensable guide for every colonial home.

Two professional poets, however, did reach a relatively large audience even before growing industrialization began to revolutionize the printing industry. As far as can be determined, Michael Wigglesworth's *Day of Doom* (1662) was the most popular poem in America for well over one hundred years. The first edition of 1,800 copies was exhausted in the year of publication, a remarkable achievement considering the sparse population of the colonies at the time. While Wigglesworth's verse was certainly more accomplished than that of his amateur contemporaries, the poem probably achieved popular status because its theological content was remarkably expressive of the people's beliefs.

That this was the case with John Trumbull's "McFingal" (1775) is obvious since none of the poetry he later produced ever excited the interest of readers as did this patently political, Hudribrastic attack on the manners and men of Tory America. The poem went through thirty editions during the next century and, according to one literary historian, furnished many popular proverbs that were quoted long after the war that had sparked it had ended. "McFingal's" patriotic sentiments were quoted by innumerable political orators, and the poem itself was a standard entry in both poetic anthologies and school textbooks for the next hundred years.

Until Lydia Huntley Sigourney's poetry began to dominate the scene, most eighteenth-century Americans read little more verse than that appearing in the almanacs. Occasionally, a poem by a professional poet would strike the popular imagination and it would then be widely circulated and much discussed. It is, however, difficult to determine exactly how well-known such figures as William Treat Paine, John Pierpont, or James Gates Percival ever became. Paine's publication of *Adams and Liberty* earned him $750, a very large sum for any book in 1797. Pierpont's "The Airs of Palestine" (1816) seems to have attracted a great deal of attention, as did Percival's sentimental Byronic epic, "The Suicide," which occupied twelve long magazine pages. While it is fairly certain that these men were widely known and read outside the small literary community of the period, none ever achieved the general popularity enjoyed by Sigourney, the "Sweet Singer of Hartford."

Lydia Huntley Sigourney began writing poetry in 1798, published forty-six volumes of poetry in her lifetime, and, until the appearance of Longfellow, was America's most popular poet. Her first verse collection, *Moral Pieces in Prose and Verse* (1816), made it abundantly clear that for her, poetry was not a mere ornament to life, but rather a direct vehicle for moral instruction. Although her poems dealt with nearly every subject imaginable, each was designed to instruct the reader in the inestimable value of the chaste and moral Christian life. *Her Letters to Young Ladies* (1833) was especially popular—it eventually went through twenty American editions—and was followed by the equally popular *Letters to Mothers* (1838).

Sigourney was one of the first American poets to compose lines upon request for the commemoration of special events. Her "occasional" poems memorialized many of her dedicated readers, whose relatives sought solace for their loss in her highly "poetical" sentiments and "uplifting language." It is important to note that although Sigourney's poetry always referred directly to the world, it did so in language that clearly set itself off from the mundane discourse of everyday life. She was extraordinarily adept at striking a balance between the events of this world and the meaning they were thought to have in the more important ethereal realm of the spirit. While it is not completely accurate to think of American popular poetry as a "formula," Sigourney's combination of the sublime with the small seems to have set a pattern followed fruitfully thereafter by nearly every popular American bard.

Lydia Sigourney's extraordinary popularity was challenged for a time in the 1830s by that of another occasional poet, Charles Sprague. He first attracted attention in 1829 when he delivered the Phi Beta Kappa poem at Harvard University's commencement. Although the poem was a highly conventional treatment of the forms "Curiosity" could take, it seems to have struck a popular chord, for it was widely circulated during the next ten years. Sprague thereafter wrote many odes for public and private occasions, including one "written on the accidental meeting of all the surviving members of a family."

Although William Cullen Bryant never became as popular a figure as Longfellow, he was able to earn a substantial living on the basis of his poetry publication. By 1842, he could command a $50 fee for a single magazine poem, while his individual volumes sold at the respectable rate of 1,700 copies per year. His work seems not to have excited as much general interest as that of some of his contemporaries, for he is included less often in anthologies and textbooks than either Sigourney, Sprague, or the remarkable Longfellow. Still, he appears to have been generally known and popularly appreciated.

It was, however, Henry Wadsworth Longfellow who established himself most successfully in the minds of his fellow Americans as the country's unofficial poet laureate. At a time when the poetic vocation was still scorned as a generally ornamental, effeminate occupation, he was able to command respect as a spokesman for the American spirit. His first volume of poetry, *Voices of the Night* (1839), sold 900 copies in thirty days, and 4,300 in a single year. This seems to have set a precedent, for Longfellow earned more than $7,000 in royalties on *Hiawatha* alone in the next ten years. In fact, every volume he produced after the first was subject to advance sale. *Evangeline* (1847) sold 6,050 copies in the first two years after publication; 20,000 copies of *Hiawatha* (1855) were purchased in the first three months alone; and in London, 10,000 copies of *The Courtship of Miles Standish* (1858) sold in a single day.

No doubt many factors contributed to Longfellow's unprecedented popularity, not the least of which was the skill with which he played the part demanded of him by his readers. However, it is also certain that his ability to combine European

Henry Wadsworth Longfellow. Courtesy of the Library of Congress

erudition and a sense of the past with a characteristically American enthusiasm and optimism was also widely appreciated. This variation of Sigourney's method, characterized by the combination of the elevated with the ordinary, served Longfellow well. He produced innumerable very learned poems, complete with classical allusions, on ordinary topics familiar to his mass of readers. He was generally extolled for his high moral sentiment, for the depth of his feeling, and for the breadth of his knowledge. It did not matter to most of his readers that his versification was conservative or that his poetic treatment occasionally bordered on the sentimental or the melodramatic. What was of primary importance to them was his ability to comment on the higher meaning of their daily lives in an easily comprehensible style. As Russel B. Nye has suggested in *The Unembarrassed Muse* (1970), it was Longfellow's clarity and ability to unravel apparent complexities that most endeared him to his huge audience.

Longfellow was aided in his task of satisfying the young country's need for poetic interpretation and edification by men such as James Russell Lowell, Oliver Wendell Holmes, Josiah Gilbert Holland, and John Greenleaf Whittier. Although none ever came close to Longfellow's popularity, each was called on again and again to comment publicly on the "meaning" of the American experience.

Holmes was a well-known occasional poet who produced lines on commencements, feasts, town meetings, births, deaths, and special holidays. Lowell also produced topical poetry, but he was best known for his satirical verse in *The Biglow*

Papers as well as for his extravagant historical epic, *The Vision of Sir Launfal* (1848), which sold nearly 175,000 copies during the decade after publication. Holland began his career as a poet in the magazines but graduated soon thereafter to complete volumes of verse. His 200-page epic, *Bittersweet* (1858), setting forth the thesis that evil is part of the Divine Plan, first made his reputation as a poet of the people. When he composed *The Life of Abraham Lincoln* in 1865, 80,000 readers snatched up his eulogy. Like his poetic forefathers, Holland's goal was didactic, and his message emphasized the need for religion in American life.

But even though Holmes, Lowell, and Holland were thus well known, their poetry did not touch the hearts of their fellow Americans in the exact way that the verses of John Greenleaf Whittier did. Indeed, Whittier's preoccupation with the pastoral values of rural existence seems to have endeared him all the more to America because at that precise moment industry and urbanization were becoming a serious threat to a disappearing way of life. Although his first volume, *Lays of My Home* (1843), was well received, it was "Snowbound" (1866) which solidified Whittier's reputation with the masses. The poem's homely but sincere language, its nostalgic sentimentality, and detailed evocation of the hardship of country life made it especially attractive to a swiftly urbanizing people who were anything but sure that they wished to put the past behind them. Twenty-eight thousand copies of "Snowbound" were sold during the first year, and Whittier eventually realized more than $100,000 in royalties from its sale alone. As Van Wyck Brooks has pointed out, "Snowbound" was the safeguard of America's memory and the touchstone of its past. Whittier, like Longfellow and Sigourney before him, was remarkably good at couching America's highest sentiments about God, country, and the family in language slightly but definitely removed from the vernacular of the people. As a result, he was quoted and deferred to unceasingly throughout the nineteenth century as one of America's most honored sages.

Although Alice and Phoebe Cary never achieved the status of American sages, they did produce more than fifteen volumes between them that reached a specific segment of the American population. Born in Cincinnati, Ohio, the sisters composed verses on motherhood, family, and farm life that were especially well known among women and in the midwestern United States. While their verse was neither so refined nor so polished as that of their better-known contemporaries, the sentiments they expressed were almost identical to those of Holmes, Holland, or Whittier.

Several other popular poets were less well known. John Godfrey Saxe, "the witty poet," was read for his satirical comments on the follies of social life, but he actually made his reputation by traveling throughout the country giving oral presentations. Nathaniel Parker Willis published nine volumes of verse throughout his lifetime, but he was better known as an editor, literary fop, and travel writer. In addition, many versifiers developed a following during the Civil War, when poetic sentiments were in particular demand. But as the war ended, and the broadsides in which they were published disappeared, so too did the poets.

This situation did not alter drastically in the last half of the century. Thomas Bailey Aldrich achieved a measure of popularity with his "Ballad of Babie Bell" (1858) and thereafter published numerous poems on love, God, and the ubiquitous family. Still, he was most widely celebrated for his fiction and criticism, which he produced while he was editor of the *Atlantic Monthly*. Bayard Taylor, also an editor, wrote a great deal of poetry that sold fairly well. However, his reputation was not strong enough to guarantee the success of any of his verse, for several of his epic poems, including "Lars, a Pastoral of Norway" (1873) and "The Prophet" (1874), were definite failures.

Perhaps the one poet of the late nineteenth century who came closest to rivaling the popular reputations of Longfellow and Whittier was James Whitcomb Riley, whose rustic Hoosier dialect and homespun philosophy struck a responsive chord in the now almost-wholly urban America. His idealizations of farm and country life were enormously popular throughout the country, despite the fact that the peculiar language he employed was nearly incomprehensible to some. Riley produced fourteen volumes of cheerful poetic sentiment, all of which were characterized by regular rhythms and easily memorized rhymes. Like nearly all of America's popular poets, he was obsessed with the family, childhood, and days gone by. His poetry, like Whittier's and Longfellow's, embodied the vision of America in which his fellow Americans most wanted to believe. The fact that the vision existed only in the poetry troubled almost no one, least of all Riley.

During the final decades of the century, three poets developed national reputations similar to Riley's in that they were identified with a unique section of the country. Will Carleton, a Michigan newspaperman, began his poetic career with "Betsy and I Are Out," a ballad about lost love, first published in the *Toledo Blade* in 1871. When newspapers across the country reprinted the poem, it was an immediate success. Three years later, Carleton published *Farm Ballads* (1873), a collection full of lavish sentiment and careful descriptions of the farming Midwest. The combination was perfectly suitable for the popular demand, and by his death in 1912, more than 600,000 copies of the book had been sold.

Madison Cawein of Louisville, Kentucky, with thirty-six volumes of verse, was the most prolific Southern writer of the decade. Although most of his lyrics were as sentimental, patriotic, and religious as those of nearly every other poet of the period, his realistic description of the southern landscape tended to set his work apart. Joaquin Miller was not, like Cawein, known for the precision of his imagery. Indeed, he was extravagantly praised as the one American poet capable of capturing the grandeur of the magnificent West. Something of a showman, Miller exploited his frontier roots, traveling about the country dressed in buckskins to give poetry readings. Except for his evocative portrayal of the desert and the life of the American Indian, Miller's poetry is indistinguishable from the "heartfelt lyrics" of Carleton or Cawein.

This characteristic emphasis on sentimentality continued throughout the first years of the twentieth century. Most of the American popular verse published in 1900 expressed the same themes of home, God, and family, as poets a century earlier. Although the kind of subject that could be treated in a poem had been extended and realistic description tended to appear more often, rhyme was still a necessary component, as was a lightly lilting rhythm. No doubt this was, in part, due to the continuing use of poetry for recitations in the schools and for orations at official occasions.

During the latter years of the nineteenth century more and more poets found their major audience in periodicals and newspapers of the period—there was hardly a major daily that did not publish verse after 1890, and many poets of the period were known primarily through these channels. The public and rhetorical function of verse began to disappear, and the advent of modernism marked the beginning of a deepening schism between elite and popular poetry. While major poets of the nineteenth century found expression in forms that were enjoyed by elite and popular audiences alike, when elite verse struck out for the avant-garde and an allusiveness unknown to nineteenth-century bards, most of the reading public was left behind, as remains the case today. Popular verse in the first half of the twentieth century took a number of different forms. Some poets adopted the subjective tone of elite poetry while retaining referential imagery and pronounced rhyme schemes. Others specialized in witty, clever poetry that pricked the foibles of society, while still another brand of popular poet produced homilies of the type that had also been a staple of nineteenth-century verse.

The shift to new genres was noticeable at the end of the century in newspaper poets such as Eugene Field and Ella Wheeler Wilcox. Field, who was associated with the city of Chicago, was particularly good at producing poetry about the innocence and beauty of childhood and was perhaps best known for "Little Boy Blue" (1887) and "Dutch Lullaby: Wynken, Blynken, and Nod" (1895). Wilcox, like Field, was adept at describing their earlier life in studied but sentimental terms and once remarked that her purpose was "to raise the unhappy and guide those who need it."

The new tone was also apparent in the response to World War I in popular verse. Poetry enjoyed something of a renaissance after 1915, when large numbers of people were willing to purchase single volumes of verse in addition to the traditional anthologies that had continued in popularity throughout the early years of the century. This increase in the "demand" for verse that spoke to the people is also evident in both the local newspapers and national magazines of the period. While many of the poems were written by the "mothers," "fathers," and "sisters" of the American soldier, by far the largest segment of verse was produced by the young infantrymen who had gone to Europe, in Woodrow Wilson's words, to "make the world safe for democracy." Among the most well known were John McCrae ("In Flanders Field," 1919), Alan Seeger ("I Have a Rendezvous with Death," 1917), and Joyce Kilmer ("Trees," 1913), all of whom were killed on the battlefields of France.

None of the soldier poets, however, could match the popularity of the Michigan newspaper poet, Edgar A. Guest, who extended his early regional reputation by publishing large quantities of verse about the war. Although Guest did not participate in the conflict, it was the implicit subject behind most of his poetry. Indeed, his primary concern during the years 1914–1917 was the war experience on the home front. Then, throughout the 1920s, he consolidated his national reputation by continuing to write about home, work, and God. He rightly conceived of his verse as a "mirror" of the values adhered to by his audience, and that audience ratified his conception by purchasing his volumes in increasingly large numbers.

While Guest and most of the popular war poets did not aim for a sophisticated or literary audience, many of the early twentieth-century popular poets did. Ogden Nash, who epitomized the genre, was a master of light wit and was widely read in periodicals of the 1920s and 1930s. Known for his outrageous rhymes and trenchant comments on the modern world, he also published thirteen books of verse between 1931 and 1953.

Berton Braley, another light poet, was widely read in newspapers during the 1920s. Braley had a narrative gift somewhat reminiscent of Edwin Arlington Robinson and a knack for capitalizing on current issues. His collection *Suffragette*, for example, includes the first-person narrative of the debutante who joins the suffrage movement mostly out of curiosity, focuses on the impression made by her clothes, and finds a boyfriend in the cause. Although the poem would hardly find favor today, it was widely admired and is still amusing as an example of human foibles.

Morris Bishop published light verse in the *Saturday Evening Post* and the *New Yorker*, combining the avocation with a post in romance languages at Cornell. His rhymed couplets poked fun at solemn occasions and technology. A fellow New Yorker, Arthur Guiterman, produced humorous verse and ballads dealing with American history and legend. Guiterman was deeply influenced by Longfellow and spun tales about early New York; his poems were published in popular magazines such as the *Woman's Home Companion*.

Samuel Hoffenstein, who wrote mock-heroic verse in rhymed couplets, was a master of parody, turning out poems on slight subjects studded with literary and historical allusions. While not all of his readers may have understood the literary apparatus embedded in his verse, they did understand that he was making fun of pedantry and of the difficult modernist poetry that was supplanting more accessible verse among elite audiences. Hoffenstein, a native Pennsylvanian, made his living as a New York journalist and published in the leading periodicals of his day. He also brought out five volumes of verse between 1916 and 1946.

Another periodical poet who captured the public imagination, especially that of women, was Margaret Fishback. She published light verse focusing on matters of the heart and family in such magazines as the *Ladies' Home Journal*, the *Saturday Evening Post*, and *Redbook*. Three books of her verse were published during the 1930s.

A far more sophisticated woman poet who achieved wide readership in the 1930s was Dorothy Parker. Parker's gift was a humorous but morbid one, and she often wrote about death. Born in New Jersey and raised a Catholic, she shucked the social constraints of her class and period and traveled widely. While her early periodical verse drew many fans, her first book, *Enough Rope*, was a phenomenal success when it was published in 1927.

Beginning in the early 1950s with the proliferation of television, popular culture in America underwent a marked change that affected verse and other literary forms as well. Prior to the 1950s, much fun and family entertainment derived from the serialized fiction and light verse that appeared in popular periodicals, as well as on radio and in film. Television influenced not only the radio serials that mesmerized children and adults of the 1930s and 1940s, but also the content, and ultimately the circulation, of the newspapers and magazines that had been the most important outlet for light verse for fifty years. Popular poetry rarely appeared in major dailies after 1955, and magazines that had been the staple of the genre, such as *Collier's* and the *Saturday Evening Post*, folded or sharply curtailed their offerings in the 1960s. At the beginning of the twenty-first century popular verse has disappeared from mass-marketed periodicals, although general circulation magazines aimed at more sophisticated audiences continue to publish elite modernist poetry, often by acclaimed national and international figures.

A few popular poets span the quite distinct periods of the first and second halves of the twentieth century. One of these is Don Blanding, who was born in Oklahoma and ran away from home at the age of fifteen. Becoming the quintessential American vagabond, he lived in Hawaii, Florida, the northwest, and California, and wrote about all his habitats. His first book, *Leaves from a Grass House*, based on his experiences in Hawaii, was self-published and sold 2,000 copies overnight. The book went through twelve printings in four years, making him a literary lion of sorts. Over the years Blanding produced fifteen volumes of thumping, vivid verse that shows the influence of Kipling, or, perhaps, Vachel Lindsay. He was able to evoke a sense of place, and no doubt owed his popularity partly to his Bohemian mystique, which he promoted in his collection *Vagabond's House*. The public bought the romantic image of a hobo who was conveniently never out of money (thanks to the steady sales of his books throughout his life), and who celebrated the still-exotic parts of America while not questioning too deeply or explicitly mainstream American values or experience.

Another popular poet of the 1930s through the 1960s was Phyllis McGinley, one of the most prolific and gifted light versifiers of the century. Born in Ontario, Oregon, McGinley grew up in Utah and began writing verse after marrying and moving to New Rochelle, New York, in 1929. McGinley's wit and pointed aphorisms caught the exact spirit of her corner of society, summing up for many the experience of suburbia, marriage, family, travel, and ordinary life at mid-twentieth century. Although she won a Pulitzer Prize in 1960, her poetry found a broad audience and is very different from the modernist and postmodernist verse of the same period.

A final figure who attained popularity in the 1930s and enjoys a cult status today is Kahlil Gibran. Gibran first developed a large audience in the 1920s, when his Oriental mysticism satisfied the American public's interest in the exotic and the Bohemian. He wrote eleven volumes before he died in 1931, all of which included a curious mix of parables, aphorisms, verses, and short narratives. His best-known book, however, is *The Prophet* (1923), which was resurrected in the 1960s as a kind of handbook for the counterculture. To date, *The Prophet* has sold more than three million copies.

The number of popular poets who began writing after 1940 and achieved wide success in the twentieth century is considerably smaller than that of the preceding period. The genre of extremely clever and sophisticated verse exemplified by Nash, Parker, and McGinley has virtually passed away, while the inward, sentimental strain of Eugene Field and Edgar Guest is sustained in popular verse and songs of varying quality. At the same time, the increasing primacy and rigidity of the modernist canon created a deepening schism between popular and elite verse in the second half of the twentieth century.

A prolific and widely read poet of the mid-twentieth-century sentimental type is Rod McKuen. His first book, *Stanyan Street and Other Sorrows*, appeared in 1954 to an indifferent reception. But when *Listen to the Warm* was published in 1963, it immediately made the best-seller list, and McKuen became an instant celebrity. His verse differs somewhat from traditional popular poetry in that it is explicitly erotic, written in a free-verse style, and lacks any kind of end-rhyming. However, the language is as referential and familiar as that of Longfellow, Riley, or Guest. Although his themes—loneliness, lost love, and the need for human communication—resemble in many respects the poetry of his modernist contemporaries, the generally hopeful note sounded by his sentimental conclusions invokes the spirit of his forebears. In that sense, it is possible to see a direct line of development in American poetry extending from Lydia Huntley Sigourney through Henry Wadsworth Longfellow, Riley, Guest, and McKuen.

In somewhat the same mode but for a slightly more mature audience, Walter Benton created a one-book sensation in the 1950s with his long narrative *This Is My Beloved*, a poem that was first published in 1943. Benton's free-verse soft-core pornographic chronicle of a love affair went through several printings and was a favored gift of would-be lovers before its appeal waned in the wake of more explicitly erotic material in the 1960s.

Beginning in the 1950s, however, popular verse began to take new directions leading to wider audiences and a greater connection with social issues. One expression of the public impetus of poetry was found in the works of the "beat generation." The group of alienated writers who prefigured the counterculture of the 1960s initiated public readings, and open-mike events proliferated in coffee houses throughout the United States. The best known of the beat poets is Allen Ginsberg, whose most famous book, *Howl* (1956), lamented the sterility of modern life.

Ginsberg and his circle, which included such poets as Lawrence Ferlinghetti and Diana DiPrima, wrote in the allusive free verse style of the modernists and produced some powerful and complex works. However, the poetry of the beats differs from the modernists in a number of key respects. First, the writing is more concrete and includes more references to popular culture than contemporaries of the elite tradition such as Wallace Stevens, Theodore Roethke, and Robert Lowell. Additionally, the beat poetry is overtly political in subject, thereby entering the public sphere by definition. Ginsberg's self-promotion and the celebrity status that he achieved also mark him as a popular culture figure. Examples of beat poetry with an historical and critical framework can be found in Ann Charters's *The Portable Beat Reader* (1992), while *Repression and Recovery: Modern American Poetry and the Poetry and the Politics of Cultural Memory* (1989) by Cary Nelson places the poetry of the beats within a tradition of political discourse that includes Walt Whitman, Vachel Lindsay, Carl Sandburg, and Langston Hughes. Beat motifs have evolved in a number of ways, one of which is toward self-conscious incorporation of the iconography of popular culture into verse. A recent anthology exemplifying this trend is Jim Elledge and Susan Swartwout's *Real Things* (1999).

Another form of popular poetry is arguably expressed in various musical genres of the twentieth century. A number of cultural critics have written about the literary tropes contained in jazz and popular lyrics of the 1940s, 1950s, and 1960s. These connections have deep roots: aside from the obvious relationship of poetry to music, the modernist poets of the Harlem Renaissance, including Langston Hughes and Sterling Brown, incorporated jazz into both the rhythm and the content of their poems. Their protegés in the Black Arts Movement of the 1960s, including poets such as Amiri Baraka and Sonia Sanchez, adapted and elaborated the tropes and rhythms of jazz. An excellent collection on this topic is *African American Jazz and Rap: Social and Philosophical Examinations of Black Expressive Behavior* (2001), edited by James L. Conyers, Jr.

This motif was also picked up by the beats in the 1950s, who often combined poetry with jazz in public readings. The incorporation of music into popular po-

Dorothy Parker. Courtesy of the Library of Congress

etry—or the expression of popular verse as music—continues today in the vernacular forms of rap and hip hop. These poetic/musical genres span the period from the 1930s to the present; they include the subjective, sometimes sentimental, but often wryly humorous commentary on modern life found in the songs of Oscar Hammerstein, Irving Berlin, Lorenz Hart, and Harold Arlen, as well as the edgy works of Bob Dylan, the Beatles, Joni Mitchell, and Leonard Cohen. Much background on this topic is found in *The Poets of Tin Pan Alley: A History of America's Great Lyricists* (1990) by Philip Furia, and Jim Elledge's *Sweet Nothings: An Anthology of Rock and Roll in American Poetry* (1994) is an outstanding resource.

Current manifestations of popular verse as music are found in the work of rap and hip hop artists such as Jessica Care Moore and Saul Stacey Williams. Some of the best of this genre is now available in Zoë Anglesey's collection, *Listen Up! Spoken Word Poetry*. Two recent studies explore the roots and cultural implications of rap: *Hip Hop America* (1998) by Nelson George, and *The Hip Hop Years* (2001) by Alex Ogg.

Finally, verse in the traditional sense of limericks, solemn didactic poetry, and naive verse on topics of family, nature, and God continued to appear throughout the final decades of the twentieth century and into the first years of the twenty-first century. A small amount was found until recently in women's magazines and special interest publications, but the major outlet is in anthologies that are still published in considerable profusion. One of the most important, and certainly a model for the others, is Hazel Felleman's *The Best Loved Poems of the American People*. First published in 1936, the book has gone through numerous printings and is still selling steadily. It includes poems by the earlier figures cited above and many others. Russell Baker's 1996 collection, *Light Verse*, is an entertaining volume whose organization scheme includes "Bile," and "Money, Money, Money." The book contains many old favorites along with fresh offerings. Other anthologies select old and new popular poems with a particular slant: for example, John Hollander's *Committed to Memory: 100 Best Poems to Memorize* (1996), and Hollander's *Ten Poems to Change Your Life* (2001), collected and discussed as self-help texts by Roger Housden.

New poets of the conventionally popular type still occasionally capture the attention of American readers and wind up on the best-seller lists: an example is teen poet Mattie J. T. Steponek, whose *Journey through the Heartstrings* and *Heartstrings* were both published in 2001. Steponek, who has muscular dystrophy, has written sentimental verse focusing on love, faith, and nature. His appeal to readers may be intensified by his unfortunate illness and frequent appearances on the television talk circuit. Another book whose strong sales probably benefits from association with celebrity is *Best-Loved Poems of Jacqueline Kennedy Onassis* (2001), edited by Caroline Kennedy. Most of Onassis's alleged favorites turn out to be canonical rather than popular works, with a few patriotic classics such as "Paul Revere's Ride" thrown in. The popularity of the Kennedy and the Steponek books underscores the importance of media and celebrity in current popular culture, as well as the need of American publics to identify personally with cultural icons.

The increased interest of public culture in broadening understanding and appreciation of poetry has also played a role in exposure to popular verse. The National Endowment for the Arts has funded poetry programs for public schools since the 1960s, and local cultural institutions have followed suit. The incorporation of poetry readings into public occasions such as presidential inaugurations is also significant; the publication in 1996 of Donald W. Whisenhunt's *Poetry of the People: Poems to the President, 1925–1945* reflects a renewed interest in poetry as an expression of public civility and national pride.

Beginning with the appointment of Joseph Brodsky as Poet Laureate in 1991, the Library of Congress has made public poetry projects a special focus. Robert Pinsky, who held the office from 1997–2000, launched an unprecedented initiative to identify the favorite poems of the American people. The project, which included readings and discussions throughout the country, resulted in publication of *Americans' Favorite Poems* in 2000. Most of the poems contained in the book are part of the accepted canon—poems by Shakespeare, Emerson, and Eliot. A few, however, such as "Casey at the Bat" by Ernest Lawrence Thayer are certainly popular verse. Additional research would be required to discover to what extent the poems chosen for this volume were representative of those submitted for consideration. In any case, the enormous public response to the project and brisk sales of the book, which has been on some best-seller lists, suggests that Americans are looking to poetry for recreation and inspiration, and perhaps not making as sharp a distinction between elite and popular verse as previously. At the beginning of the twenty-first century elite and popular poetry may be moving closer together.

REFERENCE WORKS

Since the divergence of American popular and elite traditions in the early decades of the twentieth century, American popular poetry has, until recently, excited very little serious critical attention. As a consequence of this state of neglect, there is no full-length reference work available that is devoted solely to the "poets of the people." However, a good introduction to the field can be found in Russel B. Nye's comprehensive history of the popular arts, *The Unembarrassed Muse*. Nye's chapter on "Rhymes for Everybody" is a historical survey that is both more detailed and complete than the one provided here. While Nye does not list all the volumes published by the authors he cites, the essay is a good starting point in any attempt to identify those poets who did achieve a measure of popularity in the United States.

Frank Luther Mott's *Golden Multitudes* (1947) and *Eighty Years of Best Sellers* (1977) by Alice Payne Hackett and James Henry Burke are both useful in that they provide specific figures for some of the most popular poets. However, neither volume goes much beyond the two or three poets who could compete with American novelists in overall sales. James Hart's *The Popular Book* includes a few names and details missing from these other general studies, and as a result, it is a useful supplement. His *Oxford Companion to American Literature* also includes short paragraphs on a small number of popular versifiers, but once again his comments are generally limited to the most obvious and best-documented among them.

Biographical sketches and bibliographical listings are scattered throughout a number of sources. Perhaps the most useful volume for the earliest poets is Rufus Wilmot Griswold's *The Poets and Poetry of America*, initially published in 1842 and revised through 1872. Although Griswold only occasionally identifies his poets as popular, he includes many minor figures whose renown can usually be verified elsewhere. This volume is particularly noteworthy because it includes selections from poets whose work might otherwise be hard to locate.

The *Cyclopaedia of American Literature* by Evert Duyckinck and George Duyckinck is another good guide to America's early popular poets. The Duyckincks include biographical and critical sketches on many minor figures although, unfortunately, they usually make no reference to the popularity of the poetry. If this volume is supplemented by Frank McAlpine's *Our Album of Authors* and Oscar F. Adam's *A Dictionary of American Authors*, a fairly good picture can be developed of the major popular poets through the early years of the twentieth century. Additional biographies can be found in Stanley J. Kunitz and Howard Haycraft's *American Authors, 1600–1900*, which is particularly useful because it includes bibliographical material on works by and about the authors it includes.

Jacob Blanck's *Bibliography of American Literature* includes complete citations for many important popular poets. In addition, full-length studies have been produced on a number of the figures discussed above. Royce Howes's biography, *Edgar Guest*, is sound, as is *Kahlil Gibran: Wings of Thought, the People's Philosopher*, by Joseph P. Ghougassin. Several books have also been written about Dorothy Parker (*You Might as Well Live: The Life and Times of Dorothy Parker*, by John Keats, *Dorothy Parker*, by Arthur F. Kinney, *Dorothy Parker*, by Marian Meade, and *The*

Late Mrs. Dorothy Parker, by Leslie Ronald Frewin). Both Ogden Nash and Phyllis McGinley have been the subject of biographies (*Ogden Nash*, by David Stuart and *Phyllis McGinley*, by Linda Welshimer Wagner). For others, introductions to posthumous collections of poems provide the best information: one example would be *The Best of Bishop*, edited with an introduction by Charlotte Putnam Reppert and containing a foreword by David McCord.

Besides these sources, there are several volumes available devoted exclusively to poetry produced in colonial America. While much of the verse that is documented is elite, anonymous, or folk, the listings are complete and thus include those works that achieved a national reputation. The single best source here is Oscar Wegelin's *Early American Poetry*, which has been supplemented by Roger Stoddard's *A Catalogue of Books and Pamphlets Unrecorded in Oscar Wegelin's "Early American Poetry."* Leo Lemay's *A Calendar of American Poetry in the Colonial Newspapers and Magazines* extends the list supplied by Wegelin and Stoddard, while William J. Scheick and Jo Ella Doggett's *Seventeenth-Century American Poetry: A Reference Guide* provides a comprehensive survey of the criticism devoted to the period.

Attempts to provide comparable guides to popular verse in the twentieth century have been sporadic. Granger Books published an *Index to Poetry in Periodicals* during the 1910s and 1920s (*Index to Poetry in Periodicals: American Poetic Renaissance, 1915–1919*; *Index to Poetry in Periodicals, 1920–1924*; and *Index to Poetry in Periodicals, 1925–1929*). The number of periodicals covered expanded from 122 in the first volume to over 300 in the third, and over 20,000 poems are cited in all. Since periodicals were rich in popular verse during the years covered, these volumes are undoubtedly an important bibliographic contribution. Poets are listed alphabetically, and each citation includes a biographical sketch, an example of verse, and a critical assessment.

An *Anthology of Magazine Verse for . . . and Yearbook of American Poetry* was published under varying imprints and slightly different titles from 1913 into the 1950s. Occasional reprints seem to have consolidated several annual volumes. Based on bibliographical information, this source relied on the Granger indexes, at least for the earlier years. Then, after a lapse of over twenty years, Alan Frederick Pater, one of the previous editors, resumed publication in 1980. The volumes examined include a great variety of popular and elite verse from virtually every periodical publishing poetry for the years covered.

In 1971 Scarecrow Press began to publish an *Index to American Periodical Verse*. However, the resource covers primarily poetry journals and little magazines. Greenwood Press apparently tried to fill the growing need to index and preserve popular verse with two volumes covering the mid-twentieth century, *Index to Poetry in Popular Periodicals, 1955–1959* and *Index to Poetry in Popular Periodicals, 1960–1965*. Both books were published in the 1980s.

For those interested in pursuing the connection between jazz and popular poetry, Greenwood has published *A Bibliographic Guide to Jazz Poetry* (1998). One final source is the *Chicorel Index to Poetry in Collections, on Discs and Tapes*, published in 1970 by the Chicorel Library Publications Corp. This reference source undoubtedly provides access to some materials unavailable elsewhere.

All of these sources draw upon a broad array of publications for their information, and none are organized by periodical. Therefore, it is necessary to know the name of the poet prior to consulting the index to locate work, or, alternatively scan the indexes for references to periodicals known to have published popular verse. This limitation holds true, also, for research conducted through electronic data bases available through affiliation with research libraries. Consequently, despite the dramatic advances in research capabilities, location of popular verse aside from that produced by established figures remains labor intensive.

RESEARCH COLLECTIONS

American popular verse is well represented in several major research collections devoted more generally to American poetry at large. The most comprehensive among these is the Harris Collection of American Poetry housed at Brown University. This extraordinary collection includes more than 100,000 volumes of poems and plays, many of which were written by poets forgotten long ago. A complete, twelve-volume catalog to the collection was issued in 1972 by G. K. Hall.

The New York Public Library also possesses a major collection of American poetry, although its holdings are confined largely to the years 1610 to 1820. A catalog to this grouping was compiled and published by J. G. Frank in 1917. The Van Pelt Library at the University of Pennsylvania also houses a large collection relating to American poetry, including many first editions and hard-to-locate volumes of the popular poets. Two catalogs cover earlier works contained in the collections. *The Checklist of Poetry by American Authors Published in the English Colonies* lists works printed before 1865. *Literary Writings in American: A Bibliography* is a photo-offset of the card catalog representing volumes of poetry at Van Pelt Library, prepared as a WPA project.

In his *Subject Collections* (fourth edition, 1974), Lee Ash lists several other concentrations of books of major interest to any researcher concerned with popular American poetry. The New York State Library in Albany holds a 10,000-volume collection of American poetry, strong in both the minor poets and early broadside ballads. The Florida State University at Tallahassee has two important poetry archives. The Childhood in Poetry Collection includes the works of "hundreds of minor poets" relating specifically to childhood. A five-volume catalog, *Childhood in Poetry*, was compiled by John Mackay Shaw and published in 1967. A collection of newspaper poets of the 1920s and 1930s has been inventoried in *The Newspaper Poets: An Inventory of Holdings in the John M. Shaw Collection* (1983), compiled by John Mackay Shaw and Frederick Korn. In addition, the Poetry Society of America at the Van Voorhis Library in New York maintains a 4,000-volume collection of poetry, while the Beloit College Library in Wisconsin holds 3,000 volumes of contemporary American poetry published by vanity presses.

The manuscripts and papers of America's popular poets, like those of most of her authors, are scattered throughout the country. The Houghton Library at Harvard University, however, possesses at least one or two manuscripts or letters by every important popular poet. Its most significant holdings are the papers of Longfellow, Lowell, and Whittier, although it also has substantial portions of the papers of Thomas B. Aldrich, Eugene Field, Joyce Kilmer, Charles Sprague, Alan Seeger, and Bayard Taylor.

The Huntington Library in San Marino, California, also holds large numbers of manuscripts and letters by America's popular poets. Among its large collections are papers relating to Alice and Phoebe Cary, Eugene Field, Joaquin Miller, James Whitcomb Riley, Lydia Huntley Sigourney, Bayard Taylor, Nathaniel Parker Willis, and Ella Wheeler Wilcox. The Alderman Library at the University of Virginia also holds significant portions of the papers of the Cary sisters, Joyce Kilmer, James Russell Lowell, Joaquin Miller, John Godfrey Saxe, Charles Sprague, and Nathaniel Parker Willis.

The New York Public Library holds most of the papers of William Cullen Bryant and Josiah Gilbert Holland, while those of Oliver Wendell Holmes are located at the Library of Congress. All of Will Carleton's papers are held by the Hillsdale College Library in Hillsdale, Michigan, while most of Madison Cawein's papers are split between the Bentley Historical Library at the University of Michigan and Yale University. Yale also possesses most of the papers of James Gates Percival, John Pierpont, and Lydia Huntley Sigourney, as well as some by Holland, Saxe, Miller, Taylor, and Willis. The Rutgers University Library holds four scrapbooks relating to Joyce Kilmer, while the Indiana University Library holds a 6,200-piece collection pertaining to James Whitcomb Riley. The few extant papers of Michael Wigglesworth can be found at the Massachusetts Historical Society and the Indiana University Library.

Poetry anthologies are also a good source for anyone interested in American popular verse. In addition to the volumes mentioned above, a number of anthologies have attempted to collect the best of popular verse published during this and previous centuries. The best known of these are probably Burton Stevenson's *The Home Book of Verse* and Hazel Felleman's *The Best Loved Poems of the American People*. Both of these have gone through several printings. Other older volumes that provide good coverage and balance are Slason Thompson's *The Humbler Poets* (1886); George Cheever's *The American Commonplace Book of Poetry* (1831); Henry M. Coates's *The Fireside Encyclopedia of Poetry* (1879), Brander Matthews's *American Familiar Verse* (1904), and Roy J. Cook's *One Hundred and One Famous Poems* (1929). William Harmon's *The Oxford Book of American Light Verse* (1979) provides a good selection through the first half of the twentieth century.

As noted above, popular verse continued to be written and collected throughout the twentieth, and new anthologies are constantly published. The *Clover Collection of Verse* (1969), for example, contains 300 examples of popular verse. *From Sea to Sea in Song*, a collection published in 1972 by the American Poetry League to commemorate the group's founding in 1922, contains sentimental, nature-oriented poetry. The Pennsylvania Poetry Society published *Prize Poems*, an anniversary volume containing a mix of popular and elite verse, in 1969. *The Golden Anniversary Anthology*, published by the Poetry Society of Virginia in 1974, includes both elite and better-known popular poets, such as Rod McKuen and Phyllis McGinley. *Best Loved Poems*, published in 1983, contains popular religious and spiritual verse from the nineteenth century to the present. Another spiritually oriented anthology, *Virginia Originals*, published by the United Methodist Women in 1982, contains topical verse, prayers, and occasional pieces. Specialty collections of popular verse published at the beginning of the twenty-first century include Elizabeth Bonner Kea's *Poems for Grandmother: A Tapestry of Love* (2001), and Martin Gardner's *Favorite Poetic Parodies* (2001).

HISTORY AND CRITICISM

Russel B. Nye's chapter in *The Unembarrassed Muse* remains the only analysis that focuses on the entire history of American popular poetry; however, several other general volumes on American literature treat the poets in question in more than a cursory manner. Most notable among these is perhaps Van Wyck Brooks's four-volume study, *Makers and Finders: A History of the Writer in America, 1800–1915*. Although Brooks's subject is all of American literature, he mentions many of the country's popular writers and is generally sensitive to the qualities in their work that appealed to a large portion of the population.

Equally, if not more, valuable to the student of popular poetry is James Lawrence Onderdonk's *History of American Verse, 1610–1897*. Onderdonk also covers "all" of American poetry, but his definition of the canon is much broader than that of modern literary historians. As a result, he includes most of the country's nationally popular poets and attempts to discern the peculiar "excellence" he believed they must have had in order to warrant such popularity. His opinions are an excellent guide to the sort of middle-of-the-road taste in the nineteenth century that understood the significance of Whitman and Dickinson but actually preferred the work of Bryant, Longfellow, and Whittier.

Alfred Kreymborg also treats several of America's popular poets in *A History of American Poetry: Our Singing Strength*, but his critical evaluations are all affected by the typical twentieth-century bias toward the avant-garde. As a result, he tends to dismiss as insignificant any poetry that was formally conservative. This sort of bias is not so evident in Fred Lewis Pattee's *A History of American Literature since 1870*, which includes sympathetic treatments of Will Carlton, Madison Cawein, James Whitcomb Riley, and Eugene Field, among others. Pattee's long discussion of Joaquin Miller is especially interesting. His evaluation often seems to accord with that of the populace at large—a fact that confers a sort of "guide" status on the volume.

Another more specific historical study of use to the student of popular verse is Carlin Kindilien's *American Poetry of the 1890's*. Based on the Harris Collection at Brown University, Kindilien's study covers "the general state of poetry during the decade," including, as a consequence, both anthology and newspaper verse, the work of the most familiar popular poets, and that of several "lost" elite poets as well. His initial chapter on "The Literary Scene" treats poetry publication in the decade as part of an overall state of affairs or tradition, and his analysis of the "average" poetry anthology produced from within that tradition is most interesting. Kindilien treats both Joaquin Miller and Madison Cawein at some length as representative figures of the dominant romantic tendency in the poetry of the period. He is also quite sympathetic to the work of Carleton and Riley since he is willing to accord validity and legitimacy to the tradition of rural humor within which they worked. His discussions, while not uncritical, are judicious and careful in their attempt to discover those elements that made this poetry appealing to so many.

Harold S. Jantz's *The First Century of New England Verse* includes a historical and critical discussion of many unknown early poets and poems; it also contains selections and an extensive bibliography. While the poetry Jantz treats were not "popular" in the sense that they were read by large numbers of people, most of the poets he includes were amateur verifiers writing for their own personal reasons and thus cannot be considered in the "high-art" tradition. Scholarship continues on the popular (which were also the elite) poets of the nineteenth century, as exemplified by James Justus's "The Fireside Poets: Hearthside Values and the Language of Care," in Robert A. Lee's *Nineteenth-Century American Poetry* (1985). Howard Cook's *Our Poets of Today* (1919) covers most of the elite poets of the early twentieth century, but also discusses popular figures such as John McCrae, Joyce Kilmer, Alan Seeger, Edgar Guest, and Ella Wheeler Wilcox. His format provides a biographical sketch, a selection of verse, and a critical assessment, which once again attempts to determine the reasons for the people's verdict.

Two last historical studies, while not devoted exclusively to popular poetry, can be of some use to the student of the subject. These are William Charvat's *Literary Publishing in America, 1790–1850*, and *The Profession of Authorship in America, 1800–1870*. The first volume provides some interesting background material on the rise of an American publishing industry that was always concerned with the desires of its audience. Charvat extends his interest in the relationship between publisher and public in the second volume, where he specifically considers "The Popularization of Poetry" in the early nineteenth century and then attempts to measure the extent and reasons for Longfellow's popularity. Charvat here includes a discussion of Longfellow's earnings as a poet as well as sales figures for nearly all the poetry he produced in his lifetime.

Important recent work on the formation of canons sheds light on the direction of popular verse in the twentieth century. *American Poetry and Culture*, by Robert von Hallberg, makes the point that the media are probably responsible for the decline of the popularity of poetry, if not of popular poetry itself. He goes on to argue that the avant-garde poets who wrote in the 1950s and were read in the 1960s—most notably Allen Ginsberg—should be accorded "popular" status, especially in view of their large sales. Alan Golding's "History of American Poetry Anthologies," which is included in Robert von Hallberg's *Canons* (1984), sheds light on the formation of literary taste through the selection of poets, popular and otherwise, for inclusion in major collections. Golding's 1996 book, *From Outlaw to Classic*, traces the history of American literary anthologies and the role of the academy in their development. *American Poetry between Community and Institution* (1999) by Christopher Beach is an exceedingly valuable study of institutional influences on popular verse and new forms represented in various musical and performance art genres.

The subject of popular verse lacks bibliographic sources for articles, reviews, and dissertations. Some of the relevant pieces are listed in Lewis Leary's separate volumes, *Articles on American Literature, 1900–1950* and *Articles on American Literature, 1950–1967*. However, scholarly articles and doctoral dissertations can now be searched electronically through data bases maintained by research libraries. Some of the best sources for these materials are *Arts and Humanities Index*, *Book Review Index*, *Humanities Abstracts*, *Humanities Index*, the *MLA International Bibliography*, and *Dissertation Abstracts*.

A number of articles published early in the century treat popular verse seriously, and many of these can still be of use to the student interested in the American popular poetic tradition. Two of the most interesting are A. C. Henderson's "The Folk Poetry of These States" and R. Z. Deats's "Poetry for the Populace," both of which attempt some sort of definition of the aims and purposes of "poetry for the people." Henderson tends to collapse the distinctions between folk and popular poetry and thus considers James Whitcomb Riley, Bret Harte, and James Russell Lowell as indigenous American folk poets. Nevertheless, his article is of use because of its willingness to consider verse appreciated by large audiences as a literary tradition related to, but distinct from, classical "art" poetry.

Deats's essay is an examination of the poetry printed in America's popular magazines in an attempt to determine the nature of America's "thought patterns" in 1942. As a result, he focuses on the themes and moods of the poetry rather than on its verse patterns or language. His perspective on the poetry is thus much closer to that of the people who enjoy it, and he is accordingly quite sympathetic to the popular poet's attempt to keep the "spirit and flame of poetry" alive in a "prosy age."

A large number of recent articles and dissertations treat topics raised in this chapter. Issues of canon formation are represented by Marjorie Perloff's "Whose New American Poetry? Anthologizing in the Nineties," which appeared in *Diacritics* (1996). "Understanding Rap as Rhetorical Folk-Poetry" by Brent Wood (*Mosaic*, 1999) explores the meaning and definition of new vernacular poetry forms. R. S. Gwynn's "Vices and Versions: Public Television Presents Modern American Poetry" (*Sewanee Review*, 1989) takes up the impact of dissemination of verse through electronic media. The *Journal of Popular Culture*, which is not indexed by MLA, is notable for its lack of treatment of popular poetry—in an issue devoted to popular literature published in 1982, poetry was not even touched upon. Two issues contained articles on Bob Dylan ("Dylan as Auteur," by Leland Poague, 1974, and "Bob Dylan and the Pastoral Apocalypse," by Gregg M. Campbell, 1975), and one article suggests that Chicano poetry can be seen as a popular statement ("A Popular Manifesto," by Frank Pino, 1973).

Some relatively early dissertations are relevant to issues presented here. Wilma J. Clark's "The Levels of Poetry: An Exploration of the Dichotomy between Nineteenth-Century American Popular Poetry and Elitist Poetry" (1972) discusses general theoretical issues and the work of Lydia Huntley Sigourney, Ella Wheeler Wilcox, Bayard Taylor, Will Carleton, and Henry Wadsworth Longfellow. Delwyn L. Sneller's "Popular and Prophetic Traditions in the Poetry of John Greenleaf Whittier" (1972) is also of note, because, like Clark's article, the piece directly confronts the problem of a popular poetic tradition and the nature of its relationship to the more widely known and studied elite tradition.

More recent dissertations on aspects of popular verse include Angela Sorby's "Learning by Heart: Poetry, Pedagogy, and Daily Life in America, 1855–1915" (1996); Andrew John Rathmann's "The Social Imagination of American Poetry" (2000); and Thomas J. Anderson's "Notes to Make the Sound Come Right: Towards a Definition of Jazz Poetry" (1999).

All in all, it appears that modernism on the one hand and diminishing outlets on the other have contributed to a decline in the production of popular verse as it was known during most of the twentieth century. However, new and vigorous forms of popular poetry have evolved over the last seventy-five years. The exploration of popular verse and its connection with elite traditions, public life, and individual experience is long overdue.

BIBLIOGRAPHY

Anthologies and Collections

Anglesey, Zoë, ed. *Listen Up! Spoken Word Poetry*. New York: One World, 1999.

Baker, Russell, ed. *Light Verse*. New York: W. W. Norton, 1986.

Best Loved Poems. New Rochelle, N.Y.: Salesian Missions, 1983.

Bishop, Morris. *The Best of Bishop*. Charlotte Putnam Reppert, ed. Ithaca, N.Y.: Cornell University Press, 1980.

Campbell, John, ed. *Today's Greatest Poems*. Sacramento, Calif.: World of Poetry Press, 1983.

Charters, Ann, ed. *The Portable Beat Reader*. New York: Praeger, 1992.

Cheever, George B. *The American Commonplace Book of Poetry*. Boston: Carter, Hendee, 1831.

Cook, Roy J. *One Hundred and One Famous Poems*. Rev. ed. Chicago: Cable, 1929.

Elledge, Jim, ed. *Sweet Nothings: An Anthology of Rock and Roll in American Poetry*. Bloomington: Indiana University Press, 1994.

Elledge, Jim, and Susan Swartwout. *Real Things: An Anthology of Popular Culture in American Poetry*. Bloomington: Indiana University Press, 1999.

Felleman, Hazel. *The Best Loved Poems of the American People*. New York: Garden City Publishing, 1936.

Gardner Martin, ed. *Martin Gardner's Favorite Poetic Parodies*. Amherst, N.Y.: Prometheus Books, 2001.

The Golden Anniversary Anthology of Poets by Member Poets. Williamsburg: Poetry Society of Virginia, 1974.

Hansel, Alfareta, and Maybelle A. Lyon, eds. *From Sea to Sea in Song, 1975: A Compilation of Verse by Members of the American Poetry League, a National Organization Founded in 1922*. Charleston, Ill.: League, 1975.

Harmon, William, ed. *The Oxford Book of American Light Verse*. New York: Oxford University Press, 1979.

Hollander, John, ed. *Committed to Memory: 100 Best Poems to Memorize*. New York: Berkley Publishers, 1996.

Housden, Roger. *Ten Poems to Change Your Life*. New York: Harmony Books, 2001.

Kea, Elizabeth Bonner, ed. *Poems for Grandmother: A Tapestry of Love*. Nashville, Tenn.: Ideals Publications, 2001.

Kennedy, Caroline, ed. *The Best-Loved Poems of Jacqueline Kennedy Onassis*. New York: Hyperion, 2001.

Matthews, Brander. *American Familiar Verse*. New York: Longmans, Green, 1904.

Pennsylvania Poetry Society. *Prize Poems*. Harrisburg, Pa.: Keystone Press, 1969.

Petry, Evelyn. *The Clover Collection of Verse*. Washington, D.C.: Clover, 1968.

Pinsky, Robert, and Maggie Dietz, eds. *Americans' Favorite Poems: The Favorite Poem Project Anthology*. New York: W. W. Norton and Co., 2000.

Steponek, Mattie J. T. *Heartstrings*. New York: Hyperion Books, 2001.

———. *Journey through the Heartstrings*. New York: Hyperion, 2001.

Stevenson, Burton. *The Home Book of Verse, American and English, 1850–1920*. 6th ed. New York: Henry Holt, 1930.

Thompson, Slason. *The Humbler Poets: A Collection of Newspaper Poets and Periodical Verse*. Chicago: Jansen, McClurg, 1886.

Whisenhunt, Donald W. *Poetry of the People: Poems to the President, 1929–1945*. Bowling Green, Ohio: Bowling Green State University Popular Press, 1996.

Reference Sources

Adams, Oscar F. *A Dictionary of American Authors*. 5th ed. Boston: Houghton Mifflin, 1905.

Anthology of Magazine Verse and Yearbook of American Poetry. Alan Frederick Pater, ed. Beverly Hills, Calif.: Monitor Book Co., 1980–1997.

Anthology of Magazine Verse for 1913–29 and Yearbook of American Poetry. William Staley Braithwaite, ed. New York: G. Scully, n.d. (Reprint.)

Anthology of Magazine Verse for 1936 and Yearbook of American Poetry. Alan Frederick Pater, ed. New York: The Poetry Digest Association, 1936.

Anthology of Magazine Verse for 1937 and Yearbook of American Poetry. Frederick Pater, ed. New York: Paebar Co., 1938.

Ash, Lee. *Subject Collections: A Guide to Special Book Collections and Subject Emphases as Reported by University, College, Public, and Special Libraries and Museums in the United States and Canada*. 4th ed. New York: R. R. Bowker, 1974.

Axford, Lavonne B. *An Index to the Poems of Ogden Nash*. Metuchen, N.J.: Scarecrow Press, 1972.

Blanck, Jacob. *Bibliography of American Literature*. New Haven, Conn.: Yale University Press, 1955– .

Brown University Library. *Dictionary Catalogue of the Harris Collection of American Poetry and Plays*. 12 vols. Boston: G. K. Hall, 1972.

Checklist of Poetry by American Authors Published in the English Colonies of North America and the United States through 1865 in the Possession of the Rare Book Collection at the University of Pennsylvania. Comp. Albert von Chorba, Jr. Philadelphia: University of Pennsylvania Press, 1951.

Chicorel Index to Poetry in Anthologies, Periodicals, Discs, and Tapes. New York: Chicorel Library Publishing Corp., 1970.

Coates, Henry M. *The Fireside Encyclopedia of Poetry*. Philadelphia: Porter and Coates, 1879.

Duyckinck, Evert, and George Duyckinck. *The Cyclopaedia of American Literature*. New York: Scribner's, 1856.

Early American Poetry, 1610–1820, a List of Works in the New York Public Library. Comp. J. G. Frank. New York. New York Public Library, 1917.

Feinstein, Sascha. *A Bibliographic Guide to Jazz Poetry*. Westport, Conn.: Greenwood Press, 1998.

Hackett, Alice Payne, and James Henry Burke. *Eighty Years of Best Sellers, 1900–1975*. New York: R. R. Bowker, 1977.

Index of American Periodical Verse. Sander W. Zulauf and I. H. Weiser, comps. Metuchen, N.J.: Scarecrow Press, 1971– .

Index to Poetry in Periodicals: American Poetic Renaissance, 1915–1919. 1919. Great Neck, N.Y.: Granger, 1981.

Index to Poetry in Periodicals, 1920–1924. 1924. Great Neck, N.Y.: The Company, 1983.

Index to Poetry in Periodicals, 1925–1929. 1929. Great Neck, N.Y.: The Company, 1984.

Index to Poetry in Popular Periodicals, 1955–1959. Jefferson D. Caskey, comp. Westport, Conn.: Greenwood Press, 1984.

Index to Poetry in Popular Periodicals, 1960–1964. Jefferson D. Caskey, comp. Westport, Conn.: Greenwood Press, 1988.

Griswold, Rufus Wilmot. *The Poets and Poetry of America.* New York: James Miller, 1872.

Hart, James. *The Oxford Companion to American Literature.* 4th ed. New York: Oxford University Press, 1965.

Kunitz, Stanley J., and Howard Haycraft. *American Authors, 1600–1900.* New York: H. W. Wilson, 1938.

Leary, Lewis. *Articles on American Literature, 1900–1950.* Durham, N.C.: Duke University Press, 1954.

———. *Articles on American Literature, 1950–1967.* Durham, N.C.: Duke University Press, 1970.

Lemay, Leo. *A Calendar of American Poetry in the Colonial Newspaper and Magazines.* Worcester, Mass.: American Antiquarian Society, 1972.

Literary Writings in America: A Bibliography. WPA Project at the University of Pennsylvania. Millwood, N.Y.: Kto Press, 1977.

McAlpine, Frank. *Our Album of Authors: A Cyclopedia of Popular Literary People.* Philadelphia: Elliot and Beezley, 1886.

MLA International Bibliography of Books and Articles on the Modern Languages and Literatures. New York: Modern Language Association of America, 1922– .

Mott, Frank Luther. *Golden Multitudes.* New York: Macmillan, 1947.

Scheick, William J., and Jo Ella Doggett. *Seventh-Century American Poetry: A Reference Guide.* Boston: G. K. Hall, 1977.

Shaw, John Mackay. *Childhood in Poetry: A Catalogue of the Books of English and American Poets in the Library of the Florida State University.* Tallahassee: Robert M. Strozier Library, Florida State University, 1967.

Shaw, John Mackay, and Frederick Korn. *The Newspaper Poets: An Inventory of the Holdings in the John M. Shaw Collection.* Tallahassee: Robert Manning Strozier Library, Florida State University, 1983.

Stoddard, Roger. *A Catalogue of Books and Pamphlets Unrecorded in Oscar Wegelin's "Early American Poetry."* Providence, R.I.: Friends of the Library of Brown University, 1969.

Wegelin, Oscar. *Early American Poetry: A Compilation of the Titles and Volumes of Verse and Broadsides by Writers Born or Residing in North America.* New York: P. Smith, 1930.

History and Criticism

Anderson, Thomas J., III. "Notes to Make the Sound Come Right: Towards a Definition of Jazz Poetry." Ph.D. Dissertation. New York: State University at Binghamton, 1998.

Baxt, George. *The Dorothy Parker Murder Case*. New York: St. Martin's Press, 1984.

Beach, Christopher. *Poetry Culture: Contemporary American Poetry between Community and Institution*. Evanston, Ill.: Northwestern University Press, 1999.

Brooks, Van Wyck. *Makers and Finders: A History of the Writer in America, 1800–1915*. 4 vols. New York: E. P. Dutton, 1956.

Campbell, Gregg M. "Bob Dylan and the Pastoral Apocalypse." *Journal of Popular Culture*, 8 (Spring 1975), 696–707.

Charvat, William. *Literary Publishing in America, 1790–1850*. Philadelphia: University of Pennsylvania Press, 1959.

———. *The Profession of Authorship in America, 1800–1870*. Columbus: Ohio State University Press, 1968.

Clark, Wilma J. "The Levels of Poetry: An Exploration of the Dichotomy between Nineteenth-Century American Popular Poetry and Elitest Poetry." Ph.D. dissertation, Michigan State University, 1972.

Conyers, James L. Jr., ed. *African American Jazz and Rap: Social and Philosophical Examinations of Black Expressive Behavior*. Jefferson, N.C.: McFarland, 2001.

Cook, Howard. *Our Poets of Today*. New York: Moffat, 1919.

Deats, R. Z. "Poetry for the Populace." *Sewanee Review*, 50 (July 1942), 374–88.

Dissertation Abstracts International. Ann Arbor, Mich.: University Microfilms International, 1969– .

Feinstein, Sascha. *Jazz Poetry from the 1920s to the Present*. Westport, Conn.: Praeger, 1997.

Frewin, Leslie Ronald. *The Late Mrs. Dorothy Parker*. New York: Macmillan, 1986.

Furia, Philip. *The Poets of Tin Pan Alley: A History of America's Great Lyricists*. New York: Oxford University Press, 1990.

George, Nelson. *Hip Hop America*. New York: Viking, 1998.

Ghougassin, Joseph P. *Kahlil Gibran: Wings of Thought, the People's Philosopher*. New York: Philosophical Library, 1973.

Golding, Alan. "A History of American Poetry Anthologies." In *Canons*, ed. Robert Von Hallberg. Chicago: University of Chicago Press, 1984.

———. *From Outlaw to Classic: Canons in American Poetry*. Madison: University of Wisconsin Press, 1995.

Guilar, Mary Karen. "Allen Ginsberg and the Development of Popular Poetry." Ph.D. dissertation, Temple University, 1984.

Gwynn, R.S. "Vices and Versions: Public Television Presents Modern American Poetry." *Sewanee Review*, 97 (Winter 1989), 119–23.

Harmon, William, ed. *The Top 500 Poems*. New York: Columbia University Press.

Hart, James. *The Popular Book*. New York: Oxford University Press.

Henderson, A. C. "The Folk Poetry of These States." *Poetry*, 16 (August 1920), 264–73.

Howes, Royce. *Edgar Guest: A Biography*. Chicago: Reilly and Lee, 1953.

Jantz, Harold S. *The First Century of New England Verse*. Worcester, Mass.: American Antiquarian Society, 1962.

Justus, James H. "The Fireside Poets: Hearthside Values and the Language of Care." In *Nineteenth-Century American Poetry*, ed. Robert A. Lee. London: Vision, 1985.

Keats, John. *You Might as Well Live: The Life and Times of Dorothy Parker*. New York: Simon and Schuster, 1970.

Kindilien, Carlin T. *American Poetry in the 1890's*. Providence, R.I.: Brown University Press, 1956.

Kinney, Arthur F. *Dorothy Parker*. Boston: Twayne, 1978.

Kreymborg, Alfred. *A History of American Poetry: Our Singing Strength*. New York: Tudor, 1934.

Lyon, Mabelle A. *From Sea to Sea in Song*. Orange, Calif.: American Poetry League, 1972.

Meade, Marian. *Dorothy Parker*. New York: Villard Books, 1988.

Nelson, Cary. *Repression and Recovery: Modern American Poetry and the Politics of Cultural Memory, 1910–1945*. Madison: University of Wisconsin Press, 1989.

Nye, Russel B. *The Unembarrassed Muse: The Popular Arts in America*. New York: Dial Press, 1970.

Ogg, Alex, and David Upshal. *The Hip Hop Years: A History of Rap*. New York: Fromm International, 2001.

Onderdonk, James Lawrence. *History of American Verse, 1610–1897*. Chicago: A. C. McClurg, 1901.

Pattee, Fred Lewis. *A History of American Literature Since 1870*. New York: Century, 1921.

Perloff, Marjorie. "Whose New American Poetry? Anthologizing in the Nineties." *Diacritics*, 26: 3–4 (1996), 104–23.

Pino, Frank. "A Popular Manifesto." *Journal of Popular Culture*, 6 (Spring 1973), 718–30.

Poague, Leland. "Dylan as Auteur: Theoretical Notes, and an Analysis of 'Love Minus Zero/No Limit.' " *Journal of Popular Culture*, 8 (Summer 1974), 53–58.

Rathmann, Andrew John. "The Social Imagination in American Poetry, 1970–2000." Ph.D. dissertation. Chicago: University of Chicago, 2000.

Schmittroth, John. *New Poets, New Music*. Cambridge, Mass.: Winthrop, 1970.

Sneller, Delwyn L. "Popular and Prophetic Traditions in the Poetry of John Greenleaf Whittier." Ph.D. Dissertation, Michigan State University, 1972.

Sorby, Angela. "Learning by Heart: Poetry, Pedagogy, and Daily Life in America, 1855–1915." Ph.D. dissertation. Chicago: University of Chicago, 1996.

Stuart, David. *Ogden Nash*. New York: Stein and Day, 1987.

Von Hallberg, Robert. *American Poetry and Culture, 1945–1980*. Cambridge, Mass.: Harvard University Press, 1985.

———. *Canons*. Chicago: University of Chicago Press, 1983.

Wagner, Linda Welshimer. *Phyllis McGinley*. New York: Twayne, 1971.

Wood, Brent. "Understanding Rap as Rhetorical Folk-Poetry." *Mosaic: A Journal for the Interdisciplinary Study of Literature*, 32.4 (December 1999), 129–46.

WESTERNS

Richard W. Etulain

HISTORICAL OUTLINE

Before the 1950s little had been written about the Western. Like most types of American popular culture, the Western was not considered worthy of scholarly scrutiny. The rise of the American studies movement of the 1950s and the birth of the Popular Culture Association in the late 1960s, however, encouraged students and teachers to examine the form and content of popular literary genres such as the Western. During the 1970s, 1980s, and 1990s, interest in the Western as a form of popular culture continued to grow. It is now acceptable in many English, history, and American studies departments to undertake a study of the Western for a thesis or dissertation. Some of this new interest in the Western has emerged in a series of recently published books and essays. Still, even though systematic study of this genre is expanding, much remains to be done.

This chapter deals with the Western, the popular fiction of such authors as Owen Wister, Max Brand, Zane Grey, Ernest Haycox, Luke Short, and Louis L'Amour. Generally, these writers follow the familiar patterns of action, romance, and the clash of heroes and villains typical of Westerns. Their plots are predictable, confirming rather than challenging or satirizing American culture. Writers of Westerns do not produce the less stylized Western novels of Willa Cather, John Steinbeck, Wallace Stegner, and Larry McMurtry. To make these distinctions between the Western and the Western novel is not to denigrate the former and praise the latter but to make clear the subject of the following pages.

In discussions of the Western, two points of view about its historical development have surfaced. One group argues that the Western is strongly tied to several nineteenth-century sources: the *Leatherstocking Tales* of James Fenimore Cooper, dime novels, and Western local color writing. Another group asserts that though these early roots are significant for a large understanding of popular literature about the West, the Western is primarily the product of the dynamic climate of opinion surrounding 1900. The present account leans toward the second point of view while not overlooking the earlier influences upon the Western.

Many Americans did not take a positive view of the frontier until the last decades of the eighteenth century. Before that time, the earliest settlers and their descendants saw the frontier as a region for expansion but also as a forbidding and evil wilderness. As Richard Slotkin has pointed out in his book *Regeneration through Violence*, it was not until John Filson published his legend-making volume, *The Discovery, Settlement and Present State of Kentucky* (1784), that Americans were provided with a Western hero in the author's account of Daniel Boone.

In the fifty years following the publication of Filson's work, other information necessary for the creation of a Western literature became available. Even before Thomas Jefferson became president, he was encouraging exploration of the West. After Jefferson was elected, he sent Lewis and Clark to traverse the West and to provide written records of what they saw and experienced. The publication of their journals and the accounts of such travelers as Josiah Gregg, Jedediah Smith, and Stephen H. Long convinced many Americans that the empty spaces beyond the frontier were indeed a "passage to India" and part of the nation's "untransacted destiny."

The stage was set for an imaginative writer who could synthesize the information available about the West and the emotions that these facts and rumors had inspired. James Fenimore Cooper was that person. He was able to use these materials to create the earliest full-blown hero of western fiction in Natty Bumppo (or Leatherstocking, the Long Rifle, or the Deerslayer). Many interpreters argue that Cooper produced the first widely read novels about the West and hence deserves to be called the father of the Western novel.

Cooper utilized many ingredients in his fiction that became standard parts of the Western. In the first place, his hero, Leatherstocking, embodied several of the virtues of the Romantic hero. He was a man of nature who loved animals, forests, and good Indians (Cooper made sharp distinctions between what he considered good and bad Indians) and was at home in the wilderness. Although Natty was interested in the women whom his creator provided for him, when he had the opportunity to choose between these heroines and the forest, he selected the frontier rather than hearth, home, and domesticity. On numerous occasions Leatherstocking conflicted with white men or Indians who challenged his sense of territory or what he thought to be his rights. These conflicts foreshadowed the famous walkdowns that appeared later in such novels as *The Virginian*. Anyone acquainted with the modern Western will also recognize its indebtedness to the chase-and-pursuit plot that Cooper utilized in his Leatherstocking Tales.

Cooper's Western novels attracted hundreds of thousands of readers throughout the world, and thus it is not surprising that several American authors rushed to imitate his work. Such writers as James Hall, Charles Webber, Mayne Reid, and Emerson Bennett turned out dozens of adventure novels set in the West. By the Civil War, American readers were widely acquainted with the frontier West through the fiction of Cooper and other novelists. Then, over the next three decades, two developments changed the content and direction of western fiction and helped pave the way for the rise of the modern Western.

The first of these innovations was the appearance of the earliest dime novels shortly before the Civil War. Sales of the dime novel rose spectacularly until the

Scene from the film *Little Big Man*, 1970. Courtesy
of the Library of Congress

late 1880s. As one might expect, authors of this new popular fiction, in their search
for salable materials, made wide use of themes and formats contained in earlier
writing about the West. Some writers sensationalized the deeds of historical persons, such as Kit Carson and Buffalo Bill; others like Edward L. Wheeler and
Edward S. Ellis created the fictional characters Deadwood Dick and Seth Jones.
As demands for the dime novel increased, writers were less inclined to stick to
the Leatherstocking figure inherited from Cooper and instead fashioned heroes
more adventurous and less reflective. Gradually, the actions of these heroes—and
heroines—were melodramatized beyond belief. The potential power of the western setting was lost in the drive to turn out hundreds of dime novels in which
action and adventure were paramount. The dime novel popularized the West, but
its lurid sensationalism revealed a lack of serious intent in dealing with the Western materials introduced earlier in the nineteenth century.

The other development that influenced writing about the West was the rise of
the local color movement after the Civil War. In the first decades following Ap-
pomattox many American writers began to emphasize local dialect, customs, and
settings in their fiction. Bret Harte was a well-known participant in this movement; indeed, his stories about California mining camps and prostitutes and hard-
bitten miners with hearts of gold were pathbreaking developments in the local
color movement. Other writers like Joaquin Miller, Mary Hallock Foote, and
Alfred Henry Lewis wrote poems, stories, and novels about explorers, engineers,

and cowpunchers. These authors, whose works never sold as widely as those of the dime novelists, were more serious of purpose and proved that literary treatment of the West need not fall victim to sensationalism.

In addition to the rise of the dime novel and the local color movement, several other developments in late nineteenth-century America prepared the way for Owen Wister and the Western. Not the least of these was the realization of many Americans that the frontier was gone or rapidly disappearing. As the wide-open spaces vanished, cities, industrialism, and numbers of immigrants seemed to increase; and writers, sensing the public's desire to hold onto the frontier, began to write about the cowboy and other symbols of an older West. The same nostalgic mood helped popularize Buffalo Bill's Wild West show, which played to large audiences in the United States and abroad. The show included real Indians, cowboys, and sharpshooters, and it aided in keeping alive an era that was rapidly disappearing. Probably the most important of the cultural happenings leading to the birth of the Western novel was the discovery of the cowboy. A few dime novelists, journalists, and travelers mentioned the cowboy before 1890, but during the 1890s and early 1900s the fiction of Wister and the illustrations of Frederic Remington and Charles Russell helped to make the cowboy a new cultural hero worthy of a major literary treatment.

Owen Wister was the man worthy of the task. Philadelphia-born and Harvard-educated, Wister first saw the West in the 1880s during a series of trips designed to relieve his boredom and restore his health. At first, he was satisfied to wander throughout the West as a dilettantish sightseer, but at the suggestion of his friends he began to record in his journals what he saw and experienced. Wister was a keen observer and talented writer—he had already published on a variety of subjects—and his first Western stories published in magazines in the early 1890s attracted a good deal of attention. By the turn of the century, Wister was known as a prominent writer about Western subjects.

Wister's position in 1900 was similar to Cooper's in 1820: he had at his disposal the materials necessary for significant works of fiction, and his previous writings proved that he could produce work that attracted readers. His first Western books, *Red Men and White* (1896) and *Lin McLean* (1897), dealt with cowboys, although these heroes were most often picaresque protagonists who were not as adventurous and winsome as many Romantic heroes, but in *The Virginian*, published in 1902, Wister put his brand on the most popular Western ever written. After its publication, writing about the West was never the same.

The Virginian occupies the central position in the historical development of the Western. The novel not only contains the action, adventure, romance, and good-versus-bad characters that became standard parts of nineteenth-century western fiction but also reveals how much its creator participated in several cultural currents at the turn of the century. Wister's novel is shot through with nostalgia. From the prefatory note to the closing pages of the book, the tone is elegiac. The Virginian and other cowboys are dealt with as symbols of a vanishing frontier. Wister also treats the West as another (perhaps the final) arena in which Anglo-Saxons can prove their superiority through vigorous competition with other people and the environment. In *The Virginian*, the hero and setting are used to illustrate these ideas: the Virginian is the Anglo-Saxon protagonist who wins his competition with others and who proves his superiority through conflict.

Yet there is an ambivalent strain in the novel. Although Wister seems drawn to the openness, the challenge, the romance of the West, he also implies that life in Wyoming may turn men brutal and careless in their treatment of land, horses, and people. It is necessary for Molly Wood, the eastern schoolmarm, to bring civilization (as eastern women had often done in earlier western fiction) to the West in the form of literature and culture. Finally, the marriage of the East (Molly) and West (the Virginian) is a union of the best qualities of each region and a union that bodes well for the future of America.

If Wister provided in *The Virginian* a paradigm for the modern Western, B. M. Bower (Bertha Muzzy Sinclair Cowan), Zane Grey, Max Brand (Frederick Faust), and Clarence Mulford followed his lead and produced hundreds of novels that hardened the ingredients of Wister's novel into a durable formula. Although each of these writers turned out numerous works—most of which were notable for their predictable plots, stereotyped characters, and conventional morality—they exhibited individual talents and tendencies.

B. M. Bower, the only woman to produce a string of notable Westerns in the early twentieth century, is best known for her characters in *Chip of the Flying U.* She dealt authentically with the details of cattle ranching, and reviewers noted her use of humor and her varied plots. Like Wister, she used East-versus-West conflicts and tried to capture the complexities of a closing frontier. Overall, her heroines were more convincing than those of her contemporaries, but the organization of her novels was often chaotic, and conflicts between characters were too easily resolved. Even more damaging to her reputation, too often she seemed unable to deal with serious cultural or social issues and during her long career was reluctant to make changes in her plots and ideas.

Zane Grey was a much better known writer than Bower. In fact, between 1910 and 1930 he did more than any other writer to popularize the Western. Several of Grey's works topped best-seller lists, largely because he portrayed a West of picturesque and restorative power that appealed to Americans increasingly distraught with urban, industrial, and international problems. The public seemed convinced that Grey's West, pictured as able to redeem effete easterners, was a marvelous and wonderful place. His descriptive and narrative abilities were particularly apparent in novels such as *Riders of the Purple Sage* (1912), *The U.P. Trail* (1918), and *The Vanishing American* (1925). Grey's popularity has endured. Many readers, when asked to define the Western, still point to Grey's works as epitomizing the elements of the formula Western.

Max Brand (the most popular of Frederick Faust's numerous pen names) was much less interested than Grey in specific settings, natural or historical. Nor did Brand place a high value on his Westerns. Although Grey was convinced that his novels should place him among the leading writers of his time, Brand referred to his novels set in the West as "Western stuff" or "cowboy junk." He was interested, however, in showing human nature in conflict, and to enlarge the significance of these battles, he frequently made his heroes titanlike. Between World War I and his death in 1944, Brand turned out nearly 500 books, more than 100 of which were Westerns.

Another writer, Clarence Mulford, was more serious than Brand in his approach to writing Westerns. Mulford prided himself on his careful research into the historical backgrounds of his fiction. He gathered a large library and boasted of knowing intimately the West, even though most of his writing was carried out in Maine. Early in his career he introduced Hopalong Cassidy, a wise, humorous, and appealing cowboy who appeared later in many of Mulford's Westerns and became one of the well-known series characters in Western fiction. Hopalong was a working cowboy and rancher—much different from the image of Cassidy that William Boyd depicted in Western movies.

By the early 1930s these novelists, in addition to such writers as Stewart Edward White, Emerson Hough, W. C. Tuttle, and Eugene Manlove Rhodes, had helped to identify the Western as a separate fictional type. Reviewers and readers were now aware of what the term "Western" meant when it was applied to a novel. Unfortunately, for many negative critics the Western denoted a subliterary type that they considered beneath their scholarly interests.

Part of this negative reaction arose because the Western was associated with the pulp magazines of the 1920s and 1930s. Publishers found that after the demise of the dime novel and the popular story weeklies in the years surrounding 1900, there was still a large audience for adventure fiction about the West. Firms such as Munsey's, Doubleday, and Street and Smith capitalized on this huge market. *Love Story*, *Detective Story*, *Western Story*, and *Adventure* were four of the most widely read pulps, but Western stories and magazines were the most popular. By 1930, more than thirty Western magazines were on the market, and writers like Frank C. Robertson, Frank Richardson Pierce, W. C. Tuttle, and Max Brand especially dominated the pulp Western scene.

Then, a new group of writers began to write Westerns. From the mid-1930s until his death in 1950, Ernest Haycox was the premier figure in this emerging group of authors. Haycox served his apprenticeship in the pulps during the 1920s, and by the mid-1930s his stories and serials were appearing in *Collier's*, which, along with *Saturday Evening Post*, was considered the leading slick magazine. When Zane Grey lost his place in the major serial markets in slick magazines, Haycox quickly moved into his vacated slot and won the attention of editors and many readers. Several writers of Westerns who began their careers in the 1940s and 1950s were later to testify that they learned their craft by reading and studying Haycox serials in *Collier's*.

Haycox was interested in producing more believable Westerns. Not only did he try to create more persuasive characters, but he also tinkered with the stereotyped characterizations of the Western by using two or more heroes and heroines and thereby added a measure of complexity to an uncomplex genre. In addition, Haycox peopled his Westerns with what one interpreter calls "Hamlet heroes." These protagonists were reflective men who often wrestled with their consciences in deciding what was the right course of action. These heroes were far more serious and contemplative than the leading men in the Westerns of Grey and Brand.

Finally, Haycox added a historical dimension to several of his Westerns. He was convinced that by basing his fiction on historical events he could increase the realism of the Western. In such novels as *The Border Trumpet* (1939), *Alder Gulch* (1942), and particularly his novel on General George Custer, *Bugles in the Afternoon* (1944), he carefully gathered data on historical occurrences and organized his plots around recorded events. Because of his tinkerings with, and his additions to, the format of the Western, Ernest Haycox occupies a large niche in the development of the popular genre.

No single writer can be said to have inherited Haycox's mantle, but three authors of the last three decades have attracted more attention than other writers of Westerns. Henry Wilson Allen, who wrote under the pen names of Will Henry and Clay Fisher, adhered closely to the historical Western that Haycox popularized in the 1940s. Particularly in his Will Henry Westerns, Allen demonstrated an experienced hand in joining history and fiction to produce high-caliber Westerns. His Clay Fisher Westerns, on the other hand, emphasized action and adventure and rarely dealt with specific historical events. (Allen, by the way, argued that this division of his works into Will Henry and Clay Fisher Westerns was not tenable.) Among the best of the Will Henry novels are *From Where the Sun Now Stands* (1959), *The Gates of the Mountains* (1963), and *Chiricahua* (1972).

Frederick Glidden, better known by his nom de plume Luke Short, was probably the most popular writer of Westerns during the 1950s and 1960s. Short emphasized action, and he packed his Westerns with suspense. His novels were tightly written with carefully structured adventure. In several of his works, Short drew upon his knowledge of frontier and western occupations to make his characters more believable. Sometimes he set a Western in a twentieth-century mining town, but most of his settings were frontier communities of no specific location. Short frequently dealt with town life, although he seemed little interested in using historical characters or events in his novels. He was skillful in handling women characters and knew how to picture heroes as good men who had made a mistake in the past and were now bent on redeeming themselves. In the 1950s Short's Westerns began to appear as original paperbacks after markets for magazine serials had disappeared.

The third of the triumvirate of recent writers of Westerns was Louis L'Amour. During the early 1970s L'Amour became the most widely published writer of Westerns in the history of the genre. Readers of L'Amour's novels praise his abilities as a storyteller. His speedy narratives seem to contain fresh stories within the familiar format of the Western. One survey of nearly two dozen of L'Amour's Westerns (he wrote ninety books, more than 400 stories, and about 100 television scripts) noted a pattern in L'Amour's fiction: his emphasis on families, their origins and characteristics, and their historic roles in settling the West. Another critic stressed L'Amour's use of violence; in ten randomly selected Westerns, 156 persons were killed, not counting those destroyed in massacres and other mass killings. The same commentator observed that most of the heroes of L'Amour's Westerns are self-made men who espouse traditional and popular causes. It seems clear that L'Amour gained his audience primarily because he produced Westerns that contain predictable characters, plots, and endings. His narrative skills hold his readers while he relates stories strongly tied to the familiar structure of the Western.

If Allen, Short, and L'Amour have made, at the most, tinkering changes with the content and format of the Western, other writers and film producers have given the popular genre a total overhaul. These people appear convinced that the Western—like much of popular culture of the 1960s, 1970s, 1980s, and 1990s—has not been very relevant to an understanding of America. Yet they also seem convinced that because the nature of the Western is so well known, parodies of its tone, structure, and focus could be used to reveal dangerous tendencies in the formula Western and the popular genre's inadequacies as a moral and ethical base for American ideology.

In the 1960s such books and films as *The Rounders* (Max Evans, 1960), *Little Big Man* (Thomas Berger, 1964), *Cat Ballou* (1965), *North to Yesterday* (Robert Flynn, 1967), and *Soldier Blue* (1970) satirized the Western. Some of the treatments were gentle: *The Rounders* dealt with a pair of cowpokes cavorting about as drunken and lusting failures; *Cat Ballou* pictured a renowned Western gunslinger as a drunk (Lee Marvin) and utilized a pretty and naive schoolmarm (Jane Fonda) as protagonist; *North to Yesterday* described a cattle drive that arrived two decades late in a midwestern town. Other accounts were more biting: *Little Big Man* portrays General Custer as a vicious killer of Indians and suggests, on the other hand, that the Indians were the Western heroes (the film based on Berger's novel was even more harsh and pro-Indian than the book); *Soldier Blue* implied that the army on the frontier was little more than a pack of killers who slaughtered Indians.

In 1960, E. L. Doctorow prefigured this attack on the Western in his first novel, *Welcome to Hard Times*. Through his narrator-historian, Blue, Doctorow hinted that early western experiences were, at best, depressing and more often savage. Most of the residents of Hard Times are grotesques: ludicrous whores, grasping merchants, and violent killers—all of whom rip into one another and show little or no sense of community. Another author, John Seelye, is equally devastating in his attack on the Western in his brief novel *The Kid* (1972). Seelye, who dedicated his work to Leslie Fiedler and who was obviously indebted to the writing of Mark Twain and Herman Melville, pictured a frontier Wyoming town ripe with violence, racism, and perversion. In addition to parodying the usual makeup of the Western, Seelye hinted at the detrimental impact that violence, racism, and sexual prejudices had on America. Thus, *The Kid* undercuts the form and content of the Western while it also attacks what the author sees as the major weaknesses of American culture. Although parodies of the Western continued to be popular into the 1980s, interest in this approach to the popular genre has fallen off during the last decades. Perhaps satiric Westerns have now run their course; at least the predominant tone and plot types of fictional and cinematic Westerns produced since 1980 point toward this conclusion.

Finally, there are other small signs the Western is changing. Writers are dealing more explicitly with sex. For example, Playboy Press publishes its line of Jake Logan Westerns, which emphasize the hero's abundant sexual prowess. Other recent Westerns treat homosexuality. Women are playing a more conspicuous role; the protagonists in some Westerns are women (see Jack Bickham's novels dealing with a female character named Charity Ross and a paperback series by Stephen Overholser starring a female detective and marshal). More and more writers are avoiding picturing their heroines as merely pawns of their men; even several of L'Amour's Westerns feature strong leading women. Moreover, the treatment of Indians, blacks, and Mexican Americans is more balanced than in earlier Westerns. Indians, for example, are often described in these recent novels as embodying a culture different from white society. Obviously, these differences will lead to conflict, but the Indians who fight their white enemies are not portrayed as inferior people or as savages.

These innovations suggest that the Western is reflecting the changing ideas and customs of the United States during the last two decades of the twentieth century. If this surmise is true, the Western remains a valuable source for attempting to understand the American popular mind in the twenty-first century as well.

REFERENCE WORKS

Since the 1960s, the growing number of general reference guides on the Western and on individual writers is another indication of the expanding interest in the study of popular culture in the United States. Although no compilation of secondary sources dealing with the Western appeared until the 1960s, several works containing selective listings of Westerns and commentaries on the Western and individual authors have been published since that time. An extensive bibliography containing the titles of all works by the leading writers of the Western is still much needed. Meanwhile, the most extensive and best source of information on the American Western is the revised, thick volume edited by Geoff Sadler, *Twentieth-Century Western Writers*. This fact-filled reference book contains brief biobibliographical essays on more than 300 Western authors, including such well-known authors as Jack London, Willa Cather, John Steinbeck, and Wallace Stegner, as well as sections on a host of authors writing popular Westerns. Each entry includes nearly exhaustive bibliographies of a writer's published work, evaluations of his or her career, and lists of pertinent secondary materials for major writers. The essays were prepared by nearly eighty writers, many of whom are specialists in Western studies. This is now the reference source with which to begin serious study of the Western.

A similar volume, *Encyclopedia of Frontier and Western Fiction*, by Jon Tuska and Vicki Piekarski, even though not as extensive and valuable as Sadler's book, nonetheless includes helpful entries for most major writers of Westerns. The discussions include brief commentaries on the authors, listings of their most notable works, and sometimes names of films based on these Westerns. Except for the tendency of the editors to be too dogmatic in their evaluations and assertions, this volume is a handy guide to the Western and other pertinent, closely related topics.

Tuska and Piekarski, again with the aid of a few others, have prepared another useful reference volume, *The Frontier Experience: A Reader's Guide to the Life and Literature of the American West*. The extended section on "Western Fiction" (239–334) purports to be "a brief literary history," but when it deals with twentieth-century authors of Westerns, it is more a string of plot summaries and iconoclastic assertions and asides than a well-formed, sound literary history. This section also includes annotations on the major books treating the American literary West and concludes with a nine-page bibliography of Western fiction.

A book that parallels somewhat the format of these volumes is Fred Erisman and Richard W. Etulain's *Fifty Western Writers: A Bio-Bibliographical Guide*. Although most of the essays in this reference volume treat Western novelists, it also includes essays on Owen Wister (by Neal Lambert), Emerson Hough (Delbert E. Wylder), Zane Grey (Gary Topping), Max Brand (William Bloodworth), Ernest Haycox (Robert L. Gale), Luke Short (Richard W. Etulain), Louis L'Amour (Michael T. Marsden), and Jack Schaefer (Michael Cleary). Each of these essays includes biographical, thematic, and critical commentaries and concludes with selective listings of primary and secondary sources on each author.

Another useful source of information on the Western is Clarence Gohdes, *Literature and Theatre of the States and Regions of the U.S.A.: An Historical Bibliography*. This state-by-state listing also includes a special section on the Western. A few entries are annotated. Some overlapping occurs among the sections on Western states, regionalism, and the Western, and Gohdes' definition of the Western is fuzzy, but if one is acquainted with the names of writers of Westerns, this bibliography will be useful. For articles and books that have been published since Gohdes' volume, one should consult two listings in the winter issues of *Western American Literature*, the scholarly journal of the Western Literature Association. The "Annual Bibliography of Studies in Western American Literature" lists books and essays about specific topics and individual writers, and "Research in Western American Literature" notes theses and dissertations. These bibliographies are particularly helpful because most research and writing about the Western have been so recent.

Richard W. Etulain has provided other bibliographies. His "Western American Literature: A Selective Annotated Bibliography" emphasizes secondary works published since 1960. Divided into four sections (Bibliographies, Anthologies, History and Criticism—Books, and History and Criticism—Articles), this list contains brief annotations on more than sixty items, about fifteen of which deal with the popular Western. Much more extensive are the listings in Etulain and Howard's *A Bibliographical Guide to the Study of Western American Literature* (2nd ed.). This book-length compilation contains sections on bibliographies, anthologies, general books and essays, specific listings on fictional and cinematic Westerns, and lists of secondary materials on more than 350 writers. The part on dime novels and fictional Westerns lists about 130 items—books, essays, theses, dissertations, and book review essays. Notable among the bibliographies on specific writers are those on Wister, Haycox, Brand, and Grey. Etulain and Howard's bibliography includes works published through 1994. Although the bibliography is not annotated or exhaustive, it does attempt to bring "together in one volume . . . [citations to] the most important research on the literature of the American West." Two other regional bibliographies add beneficial information on the Western, numerous regional writers, and general backgrounds for two subregions of the West: John Q. Anderson et al., eds., *Southwestern American Literature: A Bibliography*, and Gerald Nemanic, ed., *A Bibliographical Guide to Midwestern Literature*.

In another reference guide, "The Western: A Selective Bibliography," Michael D. Gibson lists twenty-six books and dissertations and eighty-one essays. He includes general items on Western fiction and film as well as materials on specific authors. Some of the same items are listed in "Suggestions for Further Research," in *The Western Story: Fact, Fiction, and Myth*, edited by Philip Durham and Everett L. Jones. The most recent bibliography of interpretive treatments of Western literature is that in Richard W. Etulain et al., *The American West in the Twentieth Century: A Bibliography*. The sections on Western literature and popular culture contain nearly 600 unannotated items, many of which treat popular Western fiction and film.

Except for scattered listings on individual authors in the reference volumes noted in this chapter and in the Nation Union Catalogue (NUC), no comprehensive bibliography of Westerns is in print. The most extensive checklists—other than the brief listings in the NUC—are those of Sadler and of Jack VanDerhoff,

Poster for the film *Billy the Kid*, 1941. Courtesy of the Library of Congress

A Bibliography of Novels Related to American Frontier and Colonial History. Van-Derhoff deals with areas other than the trans-Mississippi frontier, and his definition of the Western includes such unlikely choices as Walter Van Tilburg Clark's *The City of Trembling Leaves.* Sometimes he lists but one or two novels to illustrate an author's works, but the major writers of Westerns are well represented: Zane Grey (fifty items), Ernest Haycox (twenty-seven), and Max Brand (seventy-nine). Another incomplete listing of Westerns is that by Philip Durham and Everett L. Jones. Published from 1969 to 1970 in the *Roundup*, the house organ of the Western Writers of America (WWA), their bibliography includes only the works of then-present members of WWA. Thus, Wister, Grey, Brand, and Haycox are not cited, but Nelson Nye and Luke Short are among those who are. Most of the items listed are novels, but nonfiction works are included for authors who have written little or no fiction.

Although there is no comprehensive bibliography of Westerns, checklists on individual writers are available. Dean Sherman provides the most useful published listing of Owen Wister's fiction, nonfiction, shorter pieces, and books in "Owen Wister: An Annotated Bibliography." Most of the annotations are summary in nature. Complementing Sherman's work is Sanford E. Marovitz's outstanding compilation "Owen Wister: An Annotated Bibliography of Secondary Material." Reliable and thoroughly annotated, Marovitz's listing is arranged chronologically from 1887 to 1973. This bibliography, which contains hundreds of items and a very useful author index, remains *the* bibliographical source of commentary on Wister's life and writings. Lists of Wister's writings and citations to many essays and books about him are contained in John L. Cobbs, *Owen Wister*, and Darwin Payne, *Owen Wister: Chronicler of the West, Gentleman of the East.*

On Frederick Faust (Max Brand), Darrell C. Richardson has provided an extensive bibliography in his *Max Brand: The Man and His Work.* Richardson's bibliography is an exhaustive listing of Faust's writings, including work that he published under several pen names. Noted are books, novelettes, short stories, and other magazine and newspaper work and several magazine articles about Faust. Meant to be complete through 1950, the checklist contains enormous amounts of information, but it is a bit disorganized and difficult to follow. Less extensive but easier to use is the bibliography contained in Robert Easton, *Max Brand: The Big "Westerner."* Organized chronologically, this list contains American original publications only and includes books and magazine and newspaper writings, as well as work published under the author's numerous pseudonyms. Helpful listings of essays and books about Faust and Faust's works used in film, radio, and television are included. The section on Faust in Sadler's *Twentieth-Century Western Writers* also includes a long list of Faust's novels and short stories. *The Max Brand Companion,* edited by Jon Tuska and Vicki Piekarski, also includes much helpful bibliography. The material by and about Brand in William Nolan's *Max Brand* is likewise extensive and useful.

The most significant works on Zane Grey also include bibliographies. In *Zane Grey*, Carlton Jackson lists novels, manuscripts, and articles in periodicals (the latter list contains only six items). In addition, he produces a helpful map indicating the settings of Grey's Westerns. Jackson lists but eleven secondary items on Grey. Another writer, Frank Gruber (*Zane Grey: A Biography*), includes a listing of Grey's numerous novels with an indication of prior appearances as magazine serials, and he provides a more extensive listing of magazine pieces (largely nonfiction and juveniles) than Jackson. An annotated bibliography of Grey's works appears in Jean Karr's *Zane Grey: Man of the West*. These annotations, which deal with novels, juveniles, and outdoor books, are not analytical but provide useful information on settings and plots. Karr does not list Grey's numerous short stories. A brief bibliography is also contained in Ann Ronald's pamphlet, *Zane Grey*, in the Boise State Western Writers Series. She lists the novels alphabetically and notes juveniles, outdoor books, and general and specific studies about Grey. But now supplanting all these reference works on Grey is Kenneth W. Scott, *Zane Grey: Born to the West*, an exhaustive and very useful guide to the Zane Grey industry. More recently, Arthur G. Kimball includes a very helpful annotated listing of Grey's novels in his book *Ace of Hearts*.

Selective bibliographies of the works of Luke Short, Henry Wilson Allen, and Louis L'Amour appear in the recent Twayne volumes on each of these writers by Robert L. Gale. Even more extensive are the listings in Sadler's volume and in some of the entries in Tuska and Piekarski's *Encyclopedia*. Bibliographies on Ernest Haycox also appear in the last source, and his writings are conveniently listed in Jill Haycox and John Chord, "Ernest Haycox Fiction—A Checklist." This excellent compilation contains information on novels, anthologies, paperback anthologies and reprints, and short stories in periodicals and includes a helpful index.

The authors provide dates for serial appearances and further information on each novel. Stephen L. Tanner's Twayne volume on Haycox also includes a brief listing of pertinent primary and secondary sources. Meanwhile, Hal W. Hall has completed a very useful annotated bibliography of works by and about Louis L'Amour.

RESEARCH COLLECTIONS

The three largest research collections pertaining to the Western are those at the university libraries of Oregon, Wyoming, and UCLA. For at least three decades these libraries have been collecting the manuscripts and correspondence of writers of Westerns. In addition, they have useful collections of Western novels.

The University of Oregon library houses several manuscript collections dealing with the Western. Not only does it have a growing assemblage of the papers of Ernest Haycox and Luke Short, but it also has numerous letters concerning the origin and development of the WWA. Some of these letters are contained in the correspondence of Charles Alexander, Brian Garfield, Dwight Newton, John and Ward Hawkins, Thomas Thompson, and Robert O. Case.

An even larger number of writers are represented at the University of Wyoming library. The American Heritage Center in the library at Laramie contains numerous small collections of letters and manuscripts. The Jack Schaefer Collection is particularly useful, as is the correspondence dealing with the WWA. The original Western journals of Owen Wister are on deposit at Wyoming.

The UCLA library houses a large collection of Westerns, and it, too, contains useful information about the WWA. The collections at this library and those at Bowling Green State University in Ohio, the New York Public Library, and the Library of Congress are the most notable gatherings of Westerns.

The papers of other leading writers of Westerns are scattered throughout the United States. The Max Brand collection is at the Bancroft Library in Berkeley, and the largest collection of Owen Wister correspondence is on file at the Library of Congress. The Huntington Library contains the papers of Eugene Manlove Rhodes and Eugene Cunningham. Most of Emerson Hough's letters are housed in the Iowa State Department of History and Archives in Des Moines. Nearly all of Zane Grey's manuscripts and correspondence are in the private collection of Zane Grey, Inc., in Pasadena, California.

Other useful materials are still in the hands of publishers. Little, Brown and Company holds a sizable collection of Haycox's letters, and some of Grey's correspondence is on file with Harper and Row. Dodd, Mead and Conde Nast Publications (successor to Street and Smith) have Brand letters, and Houghton Mifflin has some of the correspondence of Andy Adams and Jack Schaefer. Unfortunately, many of the papers of Street and Smith, *Collier's*, *Saturday Evening Post*, and Doubleday and Company are not available or easily accessible. These collections will be necessary sources for a full-scale history of the Western.

HISTORY AND CRITICISM

Although a few authors dealt with facets of the Western prior to the appearance of Henry Nash Smith's *Virgin Land* (1950), that book has stimulated more research and writing about popular Western literature than any other volume. First of all, Smith was one of the first scholars willing to study, as literature, several types of writing that previous scholars had relegated to the nonliterary categories of history, propaganda, and pulp novels. Through careful analysis of a wide variety of fiction and nonfiction about the West, Smith outlined what Americans came to believe about the Western frontier. Second, he described the symbols and myths about the West that fascinated Americans. He was able to show how the West as a "passage to India," as a stage for the "sons of Leatherstocking," and as a desert and a garden was a large part of Americans' mental images of the West in the nineteenth century. Third, Smith demonstrated one way that scholars could approach popular literature in his probing discussion of dime novel Westerns. No scholar who aims at completeness in his research on Western writing can afford to overlook Smith's brilliant book.

If Smith opened the door for early studies of Western writing, John G. Cawelti marked out another corridor that students could follow in pursuing the Western. First in *The Six-Gun Mystique* and then in *Adventure, Mystery, and Romance*, he encouraged systematic thinking about the nature of popular fiction about the West. He urged scholars to study the Western as a species of formula literature (he defined formulas as "structures of narrative conventions which carry out a variety of cultural functions in a unified way") to see how these patterns changed over time as they responded to the culture that produced them. Although Cawelti provided useful sketches of the historical development of the Western, he was more concerned with the social and cultural implications of the formulas that he found in Westerns. In Cawelti's volumes, the plots and characters of novels by Cooper, Wister, and Grey are scrutinized and used to illustrate what Cawelti believed to be the major themes of the authors' cultural environments. *Adventure, Mystery, and Romance*, which in addition to dealing with the Western treats crime novels, detective stories, and social melodramas, incorporates much information from Cawelti's earlier volume, but it also includes extensive treatments of nineteenth-century Western fiction and recent Western films. Unfortunately, Cawelti chose to break off discussion of the fictional Western after his treatment of Zane Grey. One wishes that he had also dealt with Haycox, Short, and L'Amour. Still, his books are necessary beginning points for all serious study of the Western.

The volume that comes nearest to being a brief history of the twentieth-century Western is *Selling the Wild West: Popular Western Fiction, 1860–1960*, by Christine Bold. Tracing the Western from Cooper and dime novelists in the nineteenth century, Bold devotes extensive discussion to Owen Wister, Frederic Remington, Zane Grey, Max Brand, and Ernest Haycox. She also treats Alan LeMay, Jack Schaefer, and Louis L'Amour. Professor Bold not only deals with the ingredients of the Western formula but also discusses the individuality of specific authors and attempts to discern readers' responses to Westerns. Her provocative volume is a beginning place for the study of the fictional Western. Also of use is *The Popular Western*, a collection of essays edited by Richard W. Etulain and Michael T. Marsden. Some of the essays deal with individual topics and writers, such as the dime novel Western, B. M. Bower, Zane Grey, Clay Fisher, Will Henry, Luke Short, and Jack Schaefer; another essay traces the historical development of the Western; and in a superb piece Don D. Walker argues for more rigorous application of standard methods of literary criticism to the Western.

In addition to these books on the Western, several other volumes offer useful background information on the popular genre. Three books by Richard Slotkin—*Regeneration through Violence*, *The Fatal Environment*, and *Gunfighter Nation*—do not focus on the Western but provide lengthy discussions of the frontier and American West in American imaginative literature and in movies up to the present. Slotkin's massive volumes—nearly 700, 650, and 850 pages, respectively—trace Americans' feelings about the frontier from the first settlers into the twentieth century. He is particularly interested in writers' attitudes toward land, Indians, and pioneers who moved west and in the important roles of such heroes as George Armstrong Custer. In addition, the third volume furnishes extensive plot summaries of numerous Western films.

In his book *The Western Hero in History and Legend*, Kent Ladd Steckmesser offers another perspective for students of the Western. He outlines how four historic characters—Kit Carson, Billy the Kid, Wild Bill Hickok, and George Armstrong Custer—became legendary figures. Working his way through large amounts of history, literature, and propaganda, Steckmesser points out what writers, ideas, and events shaped the legendary lives of these four men. Along the way, he discusses the role of a few Westerns in helping to make these reputations, but more importantly, his book outlines the manner in which historical figures can and have been used in popular literature. Joseph G. Rosa does the same for one Western type in his study, *The Gunfighter: Man or Myth!* Both of these authors—in research method and findings—owe a great deal to *Virgin Land*.

Two other studies comment upon the early historical and literary treatments of the cowboy. E. Douglas Branch's *The Cowboy and His Interpreters* was a pioneer work that has been largely superseded in Joe B. Frantz and Julian E. Choate Jr., *The American Cowboy: The Myth and the Reality*. Although these authors employ a narrow and misleading definition of myth—the opposite of historical fact—they do provide useful summaries of cowboy novels published from about 1890 to 1920. Even more useful is William W. Savage Jr.'s study of varying roles of the cowboy in American popular culture in his *The Cowboy Hero: His Image in American History and Culture*, which includes chapters on such topics as history, literature, music, athletics, and selling the cowboy. Another volume that collects eight essays about the images of cowboys in early movies, recent films, and music and their associations with Indians and dude ranching is the lively book edited by Charles W. Harris and Buck Rainey, *The Cowboy: Six-Shooters, Songs, and Sex*. Only the book by Savage, however, approaches the full-scale study we need of the cowboy in the Western and other kinds of American literature. For a recent and very useful reference volume on these subjects, see Richard Slatta, *The Cowboy Encyclopedia*.

Russel Nye's brief history of the Western in *The Unembarrassed Muse* and that of Tuska and Piekarski in *The Frontier Experience* are the best brief accounts of the origins and flowering of the popular genre. In fact, these two sections should be the starting points for students of the Western. Cooper's role in the rise of the Western is covered in *Virgin Land*, in Cawelti's two books, in James K. Folsom's *The American Western Novel*, and in a host of other essays and books. The classic study of the dime novel is Albert Johannsen's three-volume *House of Beadle and Adams and Its Dime and Nickel Novels*, but Daryl Jones' *The Dime Novel Western* is thorough, well written, and illuminating and is now the best concise study of the dime novel. A more recent study by Michael Denning, *Mechanic Accents*, emphasizes "working-class culture" and dime novels. A briefer introduction to Western dime novels appears in Bill Brown, editor, *Reading the West*. No complete study of the pulp Western has been published, but Quentin Reynolds offers a helpful volume on Street and Smith in *The Fiction Factory*. Also useful is John A. Dinan, *The Pulp Western*. Much narrower in scope and less analytical and also more personal in tone is Frank Gruber's *The Pulp Jungle*.

In the past two decades or so, as much scholarship on the film Western as on the fictional Western has appeared. Several of these more recent studies are useful for scholars undertaking research on writers. The most useful history of the film Western is George N. Fenin and William K. Everson, *The Western: From Silents to the Seventies*, which is comprehensive, detailed, and well illustrated but focuses primarily on pre-1950s Westerns. Also helpful is Jon Tuska's encyclopedic, chatty book *The Filming of the West*. Both of these volumes are stronger on the silent, B-Western, and classic Western films than on those produced after 1960. Two other indispensable reference guides to the Western are Brian Garfield, *Western Films*, and Phil Hardy, *The Western*. Garfield's volume is organized alphabetically and is more iconoclastic in tone, whereas Hardy arranges his coverage by date and includes less extensive commentaries on each film discussed. One should also consult Jon Tuska, *The American West in Film*, for a series of "critical approaches" to the Western. But the most indispensable source on film Westerns is now Edward Buscombe, editor, *The BFI Companion to the Western*. It is thorough, well written, and nearly exhaustive in its coverage.

Jenni Calder attempts to discuss the myths and reality of Western films in her book, *There Must Be a Lone Ranger*. Along with treatments of such filmmakers as John Ford, Sam Peckinpah, and Howard Hawks, she includes analyses of the Westerns of Brand, Grey, Haycox, and Short. A sociologist who employs the structural insights of Vladimir Propp and Claude Lévi-Strauss, Will Wright deals with such well-known films as *Stagecoach*, *Shane*, *High Noon*, *Rio Bravo*, *Butch Cassidy and the Sundance Kid*, and *True Grit* in his *Sixguns and Society*. His comments about narrative formats are illuminating for those interested in the formulas endemic to many Westerns. Another example of the most useful studies of Western films is *Horizons West* by Jim Kitses, who analyzes the films of Anthony Mann, Budd Boetticher, and Sam Peckinpah. In an adjacent field, Ralph and Donna Brauer provided the first book-length study of the television Western in their volume, *The Horse, the Gun and the Piece of Property*. But the best one-volume historical treatment of recent Westerns is John H. Lenihan's *Showdown: Confronting Modern America in the Western Film*, which persuasively views Westerns as cultural indexes of their times. Lenihan's study is particularly provocative for those dealing with racial, foreign relations, and sociocultural themes in the post–world war era. Essays treating the historical development of the Western film are gathered in Richard W. Etulain, *Western Films: A Brief History*, which also contains a bibliographical essay by the editor, "Recent Interpretations of the Western Film." For the most extensive listings of publications about Western films, however, one must consult John G. Nachbar, *Western Films: An Annotated Critical Bibliography*, and the companion volume by Nachbar, Jackie R. Donath; and Chris Foran, *Western Films 2: An Annotated Critical Bibliography from 1974 to 1987*.

The select number of scholars who have dealt with larger topics of Western American literature have not always devoted much attention to the fictional West-

John Wayne in *Stagecoach*, 1939. © The Del Valle Archive

ern. Among these overviews, James K. Folsom's *The American Western Novel* remains a good summary. His chapters are largely topical in nature with emphases on Indians, Western heroes, and agrarian novels. He treats major writers like Cooper, Garland, and Clark, and he discusses the Westerns of Wister, Grey, and Alan LeMay; but he does not reveal how the writings of the latter group differ from the works of major Western novelists like Cather and Steinbeck. His handy book would have been even more stimulating had he chosen to make some of these distinctions. Another study, John R. Milton's *The Novel of the American West*, contains an unenthusiastic chapter on the popular Western but illuminating chapters on several major Western writers. Richard W. Etulain discusses several other interpretations of Western literature and the Western in his essay "The American Literary West and Its Interpreters: The Rise of a New Historiography" and much more extensively in his book *Re-imagining the Modern American West: A Century of Fiction, History, and Art*.

Although we lack a full-scale study of the Western, several studies of individual writers have appeared. For example, Darwin Payne provided a smoothly written biography of Owen Wister; he treats his subject's literary career but fails to include much commentary on Wister's writings. Less successful is *Owen Wister* by John L. Cobbs, a book that overlooks the indispensable Wister collection in the Library of Congress and that clearly exhibits the author's idiosyncratic tastes. Ben M.

Vorpahl's *My Dear Wister* contains a lively account of Frederic Remington's friendship with, and influence upon, Wister. Even more useful as a model for understanding Wister as a man, a writer, and a cultural figure is G. Edward White's penetrating book, *The Eastern Establishment and the Western Experience*. White reveals how Wister became an integral part of a cultural consensus of the East and West in the decades surrounding 1900. A short summary of Wister's life and Western writings is presented in Richard W. Etulain, *Owen Wister*.

Judging solely on the numbers of studies published, Zane Grey has fared much better with scholars than Wister. Early on, Jean Karr, Frank Gruber, Carlton Jackson, Kenneth W. Scott, and Candace C. Kant wrote books about Grey. The first two are weak on interpretation, and the third lacks sufficient critical insights to be labeled the literary study of Grey. As noted, however, Scott's volume is a notable reference guide to Grey and his career. Meanwhile, Kant's book, *Zane Grey's Arizona*, while narrowly focused and a bit too accepting of Grey's view of his world, is nonetheless a thorough work on the influence of Arizona settings on Grey's writings. Another writer, Gary Topping, provides a more searching analysis of Grey's Westerns in his essays and dissertation. His articles should be gathered, expanded, and published as a book. Two other book-length studies of Grey have appeared recently. Kimball's *Ace of Hearts* and Stephen May's *Zane Grey: Romancing the West* are both useful literary studies of Grey and his Westerns.

On another writer, Frederick Faust, his son-in-law, Robert Easton, produced a fine biography in his *Max Brand: The Big "Westerner."* No one will need to cover that ground again, but, unfortunately, Easton does little with Faust as a writer of Westerns. He is reluctant to evaluate Faust's novels and is unaware of the scholarship available on Western writing. On the other hand, William Bloodworth's *Max Brand* provides the useful, brief introduction to the author's life and major works that one expects of a Twayne volume. Meanwhile, Eugene Manlove Rhodes is the subject of W. H. Hutchinson's lively book, *A Bar Cross Man*. Although Hutchinson is more interested in biography and in presenting long sections of Rhodes' valuable letters than in evaluating Rhodes as a writer, his book is nonetheless rewarding reading. Useful as a brief introduction to Rhodes' life and writings is Edwin W. Gaston Jr.'s pamphlet in the Boise State Series. Other writers, such as B. M. Bower, Clarence Mulford, and Stewart White, merit extended monographs, but no published book-length studies of their lives and works have appeared. In another area, two books have appeared recently that furnish helpful feminist interpretations of the Western. The more outspoken of the two is Jane Tompkins, *West of Everything*. Also useful is Norman Yates, *Gender and Genre: An Introduction to Women Writers and Formula Westerns, 1900–1950*.

More than three decades ago, Richard W. Etulain prepared the first literary study of a writer of Westerns in his unpublished dissertation on Ernest Haycox. Chapters of that dissertation have been published as essays. In addition, one should also utilize Robert Gale's essay on Haycox in Erisman and Etulain, *Fifty Western Writers*. Now, however, we have the book-length study of Haycox that his career merits. Stephen L. Tanner furnishes that introduction in his well-researched Twayne volume on Haycox. At the same time, no one has yet written the needed book on Jack Schaefer's notable career. Until that volume is completed, scholars should utilize Gerald Haslam's pamphlet, which reviews Schaefer's life and major works.

In the last two decades, Robert L. Gale has done more than any other scholar to examine and evaluate the careers of recent writers of Westerns. In addition to his essay on Haycox and his helpful pamphlet on Henry Wilson Allen, he prepared volumes on Allen, Luke Short, and Louis L'Amour for the Twayne United States Authors Series. Each of these volumes gives evidence of Gale's thorough reading, his thoughtful consideration of these writers' talents as novelists and historians, and their varied uses of plot, setting, and characterization. If the tone of the volume on Allen is the most sympathetic and personal and that on L'Amour the least friendly, his study of Short is perhaps the most balanced of these three important studies. Altogether, these books are models of clarity and reasoned readings. One hopes that they may become paradigms for similar volumes on such authors as B. M. Bower, Clarence Mulford, Zane Grey, and Alan LeMay.

ANTHOLOGIES AND REPRINTS

There are few collections of Western stories in print—largely because little demand seems to exist for such books among general readers and for use in classrooms. In addition, short story collections most often lose out in the stiff competition with reprints of older novels and the new paperback originals. If one wishes to make money writing Westerns, one must turn out novels; neither the skimpy remuneration available to short story writers nor the moderate interest of general readers in short fiction is enough to encourage the publication of many collections of short stories. There are, however, a few anthologies of stories worthy of mention.

The best anthology of Western fiction—*The Western Story: Fact, Fiction, and Myth*, edited by Philip Durham and Everett L. Jones—is currently out of print. This collection was designed as a text for college courses—for freshman composition courses and for classes concentrating on the Western. The book is divided into three sections: *fact*—five primary essays dealing with cowboys, cattlemen, and the cattle country dating from the time of Theodore Roosevelt to the present; *fiction*—sixteen stories from Bret Harte's "Tennessee's Partner" to Walter Van Tilburg Clark's "The Indian Well"; and *myth*—six interpretive essays on Western fiction and films. This is a useful anthology, even though the editors' reasons for selecting the stories are not clear. Included are the works of popular Western writers such as Mulford, Grey, Haycox, Short, and Thomas Thompson, but, strangely, the editors also have chosen stories by Jack London, Vardis Fisher, and Walter Van Tilburg Clark, not good examples of the Western. Conversely, a brief introduction and lists of discussion questions after each selection will help students and teachers to reflect on the nature of the Western. An insightful publisher should secure new editors, update the collection, and reprint it.

Another notable collection is J. Golden Taylor's *Great Stories of the West*, which appeared originally as a hardcover book, *Great Western Short Stories*. Taylor has organized his anthology into ten chronological divisions, from Indians to contemporary Westerners. Among the twenty-eight stories are works by Will Henry, Emerson Hough, Max Brand, Owen Wister, E. M. Rhodes, and Conrad Richter. Wallace Stegner's essay "History, Myth, and the Western Writer" serves as a first-rate introduction. Unfortunately, Taylor's book is also out of print.

Another fine collection currently not in print is Harry E. Maule's *Great Tales of the American West.* Maule, who edited pulp magazines in the 1920s and 1930s and later became an executive with Doubleday and Random House, appreciates the historical development of the Western (as his brief introduction demonstrates) and senses which authors have made the largest contributions to the popular genre. His book contains eighteen stories from Harte to Clark and includes works from Wister, Rhodes, Grey, Raine, Mulford, Short, Haycox, and Brand. Maule has selected the best stories from the most important writers of Westerns.

Two other anthologies reprint stories that appeared first in two periodicals. E. N. Brandt edited *The Saturday Evening Post Reader of Western Stories*, and Ned Collier collected short stories from the pulp magazine *West* in his book, *Great Stories of the West*. Brandt's volume, which contains eighteen stories and two novelettes from leading Western writers, demonstrates how well the *Post* did in securing the best Western fiction for its pages. Collier reprints fourteen pieces not as well written as those in Brandt's volume, but the *West* stories illustrate the kinds of fiction that appeared in a leading pulp periodical of the 1920s and 1930s.

Three other earlier anthologies should be mentioned because they reprint stories from the best Western writers of the first half of the twentieth century. They are William Targ's *Western Story Omnibus*, William MacLeod Raine's *Western Stories*, and Leo Margulies' *Popular Book of Western Stories*.

One should note, too, the anthologies of short Western fiction published by the WWA, which the WWA sponsored from the 1950s into the 1980s. The first books in the series used reprinted stories, but the more recent anthologies contain original pieces written by members of the WWA for specific collections. These volumes reflect changing trends in Western fiction of the last twenty-five years, but one cannot say that the anthologies always contain the best Western writing. A later collection that attempts to illustrate the accomplishments of the WWA is edited by August Lenninger, *Western Writers of America: Silver Anniversary Anthology*. The editor has chosen twelve novelettes and stories and two poems. Most of his selections appeared first in the 1940s and 1950s, but two stories are original publications. Among the authors included are Luke Short, S. Omar Barker (author of the two poems), Elmer Kelton, and Nelson Nye. The introduction contains a brief account of the WWA's dealings with outlets for the publications of Western fiction in the 1940s, 1950s, and 1960s.

Among the most recent anthologies, the best is Jon Tuska's *The American West in Fiction*. Collecting twenty stories from such authors as Twain, Harte, Cather, and Walter Van Tilburg Clark, the editor also includes works by Wister, Rhodes, Grey, Brand, Short, L'Amour, Will Henry, and Elmer Kelton. In addition to a useful, but very opinionated and spread-eagle, introduction, Tuska provides instructive introductions to each story and a brief appended section of "Suggested Further Reading." Although *The Arbor House Treasury of Great Western Stories*, edited by Bill Pronzini and Martin H. Greenberg, contains thirty-three stories, allowing them to illustrate the diversity and historical development of short Western fiction, the introductory comments by John Jakes and the comments prefacing each selection are neither insightful nor very useful. The same editors have compiled *The Western Hall of Fame: An Anthology of Classic Western Stories Selected by the Western Writers of America*. This collection contains even fewer editorial aids, but the balance of contents between the classics of Crane, Twain, Harte, and O. Henry with the works of the popular writers such as Haycox, Grey, Brand,

Clay Fisher, Lewis B. Patten, and Thomas Thompson makes this anthology useful for classroom use. For the most extensive listing of other collections and anthologies, readers should check the references in the Etulain and Howard bibliography. They should also consult the collections by Jon Tuska listed in the following bibliography.

The recent publication of these collections, the appearance of several books and numerous essays on the Western in the last two decades, and the ongoing interest in popular images of the West attest to the continuing fascination of Americans—as well as readers and audiences around the world—with things Western. New Western films are being produced, and reruns of classic Westerns on television and on videotape are everywhere available. Millions of readers are devouring the Westerns of Louis L'Amour, and Western music, art, dress, and lifestyles remain fashionable. Together, these recent trends reinforce one's conviction that the Western and popular images of the West will continue to be important icons of American popular culture for years to come.

BIBLIOGRAPHY

Books and Articles

Alter, Judy, and A. T. Row, eds. *Unbridled Spirits: Short Fiction about Women in the Old West*. Fort Worth: Texas Christian University Press, 1994.

Anderson, John Q. et al., eds. *Southwestern American Literature: A Bibliography*. Chicago: Swallow Press, 1980.

Bloodworth, William. "Literary Extensions of the Formula Western." *Western American Literature* 14 (Winter 1980), 287–96.

———. *Max Brand*. Boston: Twayne, 1993.

———. "Max Brand's West." *Western American Literature* 16 (Fall 1981), 177–91.

———. "Zane Grey's Western Eroticism." *South Dakota Review* 23 (Autumn 1985), 5–14.

Bold, Christine. *Selling the Wild West: Popular Western Fiction, 1860–1960*. Bloomington: Indiana University Press, 1987.

Branch, E. Douglas. *The Cowboy and His Interpreters*. New York: D. Appleton, 1926, 1961.

Brandt, E. N., ed. *The Saturday Evening Post Reader of Western Stories*. Garden City, N.Y.: Doubleday, 1960; New York: Popular Library, 1962.

Brauer, Ralph, with Donna Brauer. *The Horse, the Gun and the Piece of Property: Changing Images of the TV Western*. Bowling Green, Ohio: Bowling Green State University Popular Press, 1975.

Brown, Bill, ed. *Reading the West: An Anthology of Dime Westerns*. Boston: Bedford Books, 1997.

Buscombe, Edward, ed. *The BFI Companion to the Western*. New York: Atheneum, 1988.

Calder, Jenni. *There Must Be a Lone Ranger: The American West in Film and in Reality*. New York: Taplinger, 1975.

Cawelti, John G. *Adventure, Mystery, and Romance: Formula Stories as Art and Popular Culture*. Chicago: University of Chicago Press, 1976.

————. *The Six-Gun Mystique*. Bowling Green, Ohio: Bowling Green State University Popular Press, 1971; 2nd ed., 1984.

Cobbs, John L. *Owen Wister*. Boston: Twayne, 1984.

Collier, Ned, ed. *Great Stories of the West*. Garden City, N.Y.: Doubleday, 1971.

Denning, Michael. *Mechanic Accents: Dime Novels and Working-class Culture in America*. London: Verso, 1987.

Dinan, John A. *The Pulp Western*. San Bernardino, Calif.: Borgo Press, 1983.

Drew, Bernard. *Hopalong Cassidy: The Clarence E. Mulford Story*. Metuchen, N.J.: Scarecrow Press, 1991.

Durham, Philip, and Everett L. Jones, eds. *The Western Story: Fact, Fiction, and Myth*. New York: Harcourt Brace Jovanovich, 1975.

Easton, Jane Faust. *Memories of the '20s and '30s*. Santa Barbara, Calif.: N.p., 1979.

Easton, Robert. *Max Brand: The Big "Westerner."* Norman: University of Oklahoma Press, 1970.

Erisman, Fred, and Richard W. Etulain, eds. *Fifty Western Writers: A Bio-Bibliographical Guide*. Westport, Conn.: Greenwood Press, 1982.

Etulain, Richard W. *The American Literary West*. Manhattan, Kans.: Sunflower University Press, 1980.

————. "The American Literary West and Its Interpreters: The Rise of a New Historiography." *Pacific Historical Review* 45 (August 1976), 311–48.

————. "Changing Images: The Cowboy in Western Films." *Colorado Heritage* 1 (1981), 37–55.

————. *Ernest Haycox*. Western Writers Series, No. 86. Boise, Idaho: Boise State University, 1988.

————. *Owen Wister*. Western Writers Series, No. 7. Boise, Idaho: Boise State University, 1973.

————. *Re-imagining the Modern American West: A Century of Fiction, History, and Art*. Tucson: University of Arizona Press, 1996.

————. "Western American Literature: A Selective Annotated Bibliography." In *Interpretive Approaches to Western American Literature*, ed. Daniel Alkofer et al. Pocatello: Idaho State University Press, 1972.

————. *Western Films: A Brief History*. Manhattan, Kans.: Sunflower University Press, 1983.

Etulain, Richard W., and N. Jill Howard. *A Bibliographical Guide to the Study of Western American Literature*. 2nd ed. Albuquerque: University of New Mexico Press, 1995.

Etulain, Richard W., and Michael T. Marsden, eds. *The Popular Western: Essays toward a Definition*. Bowling Green, Ohio: Bowling Green State University Popular Press, 1974.

Etulain, Richard W., et al., eds. *The American West in the Twentieth Century: A Bibliography*. Norman: University of Oklahoma Press, 1994.

Fenin, George N., and William K. Everson. *The Western: From Silents to the Seventies*. New York: Grossman, 1973.

Folsom, James K. *The American Western Novel*. New Haven, Conn.: College and University Press, 1966.

Folsom, James K., ed. *The Western: A Collection of Critical Essays*. Englewood Cliffs, N.J.: Prentice-Hall, 1979.

Frantz, Joe B., and Julian E. Choate Jr. *The American Cowboy: The Myth and the Reality*. Norman: University of Oklahoma Press, 1955.

Fussell, Edwin. *Frontier: American Literature and the American West*. Princeton, N.J.: Princeton University Press, 1965.

Gale, Robert L. *Louis L'Amour*. Rev ed. New York: Twayne, 1992.

———. *Luke Short*. Boston: Twayne, 1981.

———. *Will Henry/Clay Fisher*. Western Writers Series, No. 52. Boise, Idaho: Boise State University, 1982.

———. *Will Henry/Clay Fisher (Henry W. Allen)*. Boston: Twayne, 1984.

Garfield, Brian. *Western Films: A Complete Guide*. New York: Rawson Associates, 1982.

Gaston, Edwin W., Jr. *Eugene Manlove Rhodes: Cowboy Chronicler*. Southwest Writers Series, No. 11. Austin, Tex.: Steck-Vaughn, 1967.

Gibson, Michael D. "The Western: A Selective Bibliography." In *The Popular Western*, ed. Richard W. Etulain and Michael T. Marsden. Bowling Green, Ohio: Bowling Green State University Popular Press, 1974.

Gohdes, Clarence. *Literature and Theatre of the States and Regions of the U.S.A.: An Historical Bibliography*. Durham, N.C.: Duke University Press, 1967.

Gruber, Frank. *The Pulp Jungle*. Los Angeles: Sherbourne Press, 1967.

———. *Zane Grey: A Biography*. Cleveland, Ohio: World, 1970.

Hall, Hal W. *The Works of Louis L'Amour: An Annotated Bibliographical Guide*. 2nd ed., rev. and enlarged. San Bernardino, Calif.: Borgo Press, 1995.

Hamilton, Cynthia. *Western and Hardboiled Detective Fiction in America*. London: Macmillan, 1987.

Hardy, Phil. *The Western: The Complete Film Sourcebook*. New York: William Morrow, 1983.

Harris, Charles W., and Buck Rainey, eds. *The Cowboy: Six-Shooters, Songs, and Sex*. Norman: University of Oklahoma Press, 1976.

Haslam, Gerald. *Jack Schaefer*. Western Writers Series, No. 20. Boise, Idaho: Boise State University, 1975.

Haycox, Jill, and John Chord. "Ernest Haycox Fiction—A Checklist." *Call Number* (University of Oregon) 25 (Fall 1963/1964), 5–27.

Hutchinson, W. H. *A Bar Cross Man: The Life and Personal Writings of Eugene Manlove Rhodes*. Norman: University of Oklahoma Press, 1956.

Jackson, Carlton. *Zane Grey*. Rev ed. Boston: Twayne, 1989.

Johannsen, Albert. *The House of Beadle and Adams and Its Dime and Nickel Novels*. 3 vols. Norman: University of Oklahoma Press, 1950, 1962.

Jones, Daryl. *The Dime Novel Western*. Bowling Green, Ohio: Bowling Green State University Popular Press, 1978.

Kant, Candace C. *Zane Grey's Arizona*. Flagstaff, Ariz.: Northland Press, 1984.

Karr, Jean. *Zane Grey: Man of the West*. New York: Greenberg, 1949.

Kimball, Arthur G. *Ace of Hearts: The Westerns of Zane Grey*. Fort Worth: Texas Christian University Press, 1993.

Kitses, Jim. *Horizons West: Anthony Mann, Budd Boetticher, Sam Peckinpah: Studies of Authorship within the Western*. Bloomington: Indiana University Press, 1969.

Klaschus, Candace. "Louis L'Amour: The Writer as Teacher." Ph.D. dissertation, University of New Mexico, 1983.

Lenihan, John H. *Showdown: Confronting Modern America in the Western Film*. Urbana: University of Illinois Press, 1980.

Lenninger, August, ed. *Western Writers of America: Silver Anniversary Anthology*. New York: Ace Books, 1977.

Margulies, Leo, ed. *Popular Book of Western Stories*. New York: Popular Library, 1948.

Marovitz, Sanford E. "Owen Wister: An Annotated Bibliography of Secondary Material." *American Literary Realism 1870–1910* 7 (Winter 1974), 1–110.

Marsden, Michael T. "The Concept of Family in the Fiction of Louis L'Amour." *North Dakota Quarterly* 46 (Summer 1978), 12–21.

———. "The Modern Western." *Journal of the West* 19 (January 1980), 54–61.

Maule, Harry E., ed. *Great Tales of the American West*. New York: Random House, 1945.

May, Stephen. *Zane Grey: Romancing the West*. Athens: Ohio University Press, 1997.

McDonald, Archie P., ed. *Shooting Stars: Heroes and Heroines of Western Film*. Bloomington: Indiana University Press, 1987.

Milton, John R. *The Novel of the American West*. Lincoln: University of Nebraska Press, 1980.

Mitchell, Lee Clark. *Westerns: Making the Man in Fiction and Film*. Chicago: University of Chicago Press, 1996.

Nachbar, John G., ed. *Western Films: An Annotated Critical Bibliography*. New York: Garland, 1975.

Nachbar, John G., Jackie R. Donath, and Chris Foran. *Western Films 2: An Annotated Critical Bibliography from 1974 to 1987*. New York: Garland, 1988.

Nemanic, Gerald, ed. *A Bibliographical Guide to Midwestern Literature*. Iowa City: University of Iowa Press, 1981.

Nesbitt, John D. "Change of Purpose in the Novels of Louis L'Amour." *Western American Literature* 13 (Spring 1978), 65–81.

———. "A New Look at Two Popular Western Classics." *South Dakota Review* 18 (Spring 1980), 30–42. (Haycox and L'Amour.)

Nevins, Francis M. *Bar-20: The Life of Clarence Mulford, Creator of Hopalong Cassidy*. Jefferson, N.C.: McFarland, 1993.

Nolan, William F. *Max Brand: Western Giant*. Bowling Green, Ohio: Bowling Green State University Popular Press, 1985.

Nye, Russel. "Sixshooter Country." In *The Unembarrassed Muse: The Popular Arts in America*. New York: Dial Press, 1970.

Paul, Rodman W., and Richard W. Etulain. *The Frontier and American West*. Goldentree Bibliographies in American History. Arlington Heights, Ill.: AHM, 1977.

Payne, Darwin. *Owen Wister: Chronicler of the West, Gentlemen of the East*. Dallas, Tex.: Southern Methodist University Press, 1985.

Pronzini, Bill, and Martin H. Greenberg, eds. *The Arbor House Treasury of Great Western Stories*. New York: Arbor House, 1982.

———. *The Best Western Stories of Steve Frazee*. Carbondale: Southern Illinois University Press, 1984.

———. *The Best Western Stories of Wayne D. Overholser*. Carbondale: Southern Illinois University Press, 1984.

———. *The Western Hall of Fame: An Anthology of Classic Western Stories Selected by the Western Writers of America*. New York: William Morrow, 1984.

Raine, William MacLeod, ed. *Western Stories*. New York: Dell, 1949.

Reynolds, Quentin. *The Fiction Factory*. New York: Random House, 1955.

Richardson, Darrell C., ed. *Max Brand: The Man and His Work*. Los Angeles: Fantasy, 1952.

Ronald, Ann. *Zane Grey*. Western Writers Series, No. 17. Boise, Idaho: Boise State University, 1975.

Rosa, Joseph G. *The Gunfighter: Man or Myth!* Norman: University of Oklahoma Press, 1969.

Sadler, Geoff, ed. *Twentieth-Century Western Writers*. 2nd ed. Chicago and London: St. James Press, 1991.

Savage, William W., Jr. *The Cowboy Hero: His Image in American History and Culture*. Norman: University of Oklahoma Press, 1979.

Scott, Kenneth W. *Zane Grey: Born to the West*. Boston: G. K. Hall, 1979.

Sherman, Dean. "Owen Wister: An Annotated Bibliography." *Bulletin of Bibliography* 28 (January–March 1971), 7–16.

Slatta, Richard. *The Cowboy Encyclopedia*. New York: Norton, 1996.

Slotkin, Richard. *The Fatal Environment; The Myth of the Frontier in the Age of Industrialization, 1800–1890*. New York: Atheneum, 1985.

———. *Gunfighter Nation: The Myth of the Frontier in Twentieth-Century America*. New York: Atheneum, 1992.

———. *Regeneration through Violence: The Mythology of the American Frontier, 1600–1860*. Middletown, Conn.: Wesleyan University Press, 1973.

Smith, Henry Nash. *Virgin Land: The American West as Symbol and Myth*. Cambridge: Harvard University Press, 1950, 1970.

Sonnichsen, C. L. *From Hopalong to Hud: Thoughts on Western Fiction*. College Station: Texas A&M University Press, 1978.

Speck, Ernest B. *Benjamin Capps*. Western Writers Series, No. 49. Boise, Idaho: Boise State University, 1981.

Steckmesser, Kent Ladd. *The Western Hero in History and Legend*. Norman: University of Oklahoma Press, 1965.

Tanner, Stephen L. *Ernest Haycox*. New York: Twayne, 1996.

Targ, William, ed. *Western Story Omnibus*. Cleveland, Ohio: World, 1945. (An abridged edition appeared as *Great Western Stories*. New York: Penguin, 1947.)

Taylor, J. Golden, ed. *Great Stories of the West*. 2 vols. New York: Ballantine Books, 1971. (The American West Publishing Company printed the hardcover version as *Great Western Short Stories*, Palo Alto, Calif., 1967).

Taylor, J. Golden, Thomas J. Lyon, et al. *A Literary History of the American West*. Fort Worth: Texas Christian University Press, 1987.

Tompkins, Jane. *West of Everything: The Inner Life of Westerns*. New York: Oxford University Press, 1992.

Topping, Gary. "The Rise of the Western." *Journal of the West* 19 (January 1980), 29–35.

———. "Zane Grey: A Literary Reassessment." *Western American Literature* 13 (Spring 1978), 51–64.

———. "Zane Grey's West." In *The Popular Western*, ed. Richard W. Etulain and

Michael T. Marsden. Bowling Green, Ohio: Bowling Green State University Popular Press, 1974.

———. "Zane Grey's West: Essays in Intellectual History and Criticism." Ph.D. dissertation, University of Utah, 1977.

Tuska, Jon, ed. *The American West in Fiction.* 1982; Lincoln: University of Nebraska Press, 1988.

———. *The American West in Film: Critical Approaches to the Western.* Westport, Conn.: Greenwood Press, 1985.

———. *The Filming of the West.* Garden City, N.Y.: Doubleday, 1976.

———. *The Morrow Anthology of Great Western Stories.* New York: W. Morrow, 1997.

———. *Shadow of the Lariat: A Treasury of the Frontier.* New York: Promontory Press, 1995, 1997.

———. *The Western Story: A Chronological Treasury.* Lincoln: University of Nebraska Press, 1995.

Tuska, Jon, and Vicki Piekarski, eds. *Encyclopedia of Frontier and Western Fiction.* New York: McGraw-Hill, 1983.

———. *The Max Brand Companion.* Westport, Conn.: Greenwood Press, 1996.

———. *The Frontier Experience: A Reader's Guide to the Life and Literature of the American West.* Jefferson, N.C.: McFarland, 1984.

Updating the Literary West. Fort Worth: Texas Christian University Press, 1997. Includes several essays on fictional and movie Westerns.

VanDerhoff, Jack. *A Bibliography of Novels Related to American Frontier and Colonial History.* Troy, N.Y.: Whitston, 1971.

Vinson, James, with D. L. Kirkpatrick, eds. *Twentieth-Century Western Writers.* London: Macmillan, 1982.

Vorpahl, Ben M. *My Dear Wister.* Palo Alto, Calif.: American West, 1972.

Walker, Dale, ed. *Will Henry's West.* El Paso: Texas Western Press, 1984.

Weinberg, Robert, ed. *The Louis L'Amour Companion.* Kansas City, Mo.: Andrews and McNeel, 1992.

White, G. Edward. *The Eastern Establishment and the Western Experience: The West of Frederic Remington, Theodore Roosevelt, and Owen Wister.* New Haven, Conn.: Yale University Press, 1968.

Work, James. *Gunfight! Thirteen Western Stories.* Lincoln: University of Nebraska Press, 1996.

"The Works of Elmer Kelton." *Southwestern American Literature* 9 (Spring 1984), 5–52.

Wright, Will. *Sixguns and Society: A Structural Study of the Western.* Berkeley: University of California Press, 1975.

Yates, Norman. *Gender and Genre: An Introduction to Women Writers of Formula Westerns, 1900–1950.* Albuquerque: University of New Mexico Press, 1995.

Periodicals

Roundup Magazine. Encampment, Wyo., 1953– .
Western American Literature. Logan, Utah, 1966– .
Zane Grey Collector. Williamsport, Md., 1968–[1975?].
New Zane Grey Collector. Hagerstown, Md., 1984– .

YOUNG ADULT FICTION

Ken Donelson and Alleen Pace Nilsen

The definition of young adult fiction used in this chapter is either short stories or novels chosen by readers between the ages of twelve and eighteen. Much of this literature has been published in magazines designed for young readers or in books produced by juvenile divisions of publishing houses. Other terms that have been used to designate this type of literature include teenage books, adolescent literature, and juvenile fiction. Considerable disagreement exists among publishers, librarians, educators, and others who work with young people. For example, many psychologists refer to young adults as being between the ages of eighteen and twenty-five, while some publishers who are eager to expand the sales of their books have now begun putting such messages as "Fifth grade and up" on the covers of books whose authors intended them to be for young adults. Specialists in young adult literature worry that if the category is confused with children's books, then there will be inadequate editing and marketing support given to books for teenagers who are too old for children's books but whose interests are quite different from those explored in most books written for general adult audiences.

An alternative way of defining young adult literature is to look at its structure. In an October 1983 article in *School Library Journal*, English teachers Maia Pank Mertz and David K. England identified the following as characterizing modern adolescent literature:

1. Adolescent fiction involves a youthful protagonist.

2. It often employs a point of view that presents the adolescent's interpretation of the events of the story.

3. It is characterized by directness of exposition, dialogue, and confrontation between principal characters.

4. It is characterized by such structural conventions as being generally brief, taking place over a limited period of time and in a limited number of locales, having

few major characters, and resulting in a change or growth step for the young protagonist.

5. The main characters are highly independent in thought, action, and conflict resolution.

6. The protagonists reap the consequences of their actions and decisions.

7. The authors draw upon their sense of adolescent development and the concomitant attentions to the legitimate concerns of adolescents.

8. Adolescent fiction strives for relevance by attempting to mirror current societal attitudes and issues.

9. The stories most often include gradual, incremental, and ultimately incomplete "growth to awareness" on the part of the central character.

10. The books are hopeful.

If stories are judged by these criteria rather than by whether or not a specific label has been attached by a publisher, young adult literature is nothing new. It has been around as long as people have been telling stories.

For several reasons, teenagers make good protagonists in popular literature. They are physically attractive, and readers or listeners identify with them. They are at a psychological stage in their lives when their emotions are intense, and because they are faced with making major decisions about how they will live their lives apart from their parents, there is ample material for developing interesting plots. The result is a myriad of folktales and fairy tales, legends, and myths telling about young people setting out on adventures that lead to personal growth, for example, *Snow White*, Dorothy in *The Wizard of Oz*, and Joseph in the Old Testament.

This common story pattern resembles the formal initiation that some cultures have for making a young person's passage from childhood to adulthood. The young and innocent person is separated from the nurturing love of family and friends. During the separation he or she undergoes a test of courage and stamina that may be either physical, mental, or emotional. After passing the test, the person is reunited with family and friends but in a new role with increased respect.

In spite of the long-standing existence of stories fitting into the literary mold of adolescent or young adult literature, formal recognition of such stories as being particularly appropriate or being specifically prepared for teenage readers is relatively recent. It coincides with the development of adolescence itself as a unique period of one's life. Puberty is universal, but adolescence is not. This period between childhood and adulthood has been created by industrialization and the complexities of modern life. Before the Civil War in the United States and even today in some nontechnological societies, the change from childhood to adulthood occurred fairly rapidly. Children were considered adults as soon as they could begin contributing to the economic well-being of the family. But today the careers that many young people aspire to require such high-level skills that they are likely to be in training long past their teenage years. This lengthening of time before one is considered a full-fledged adult has brought many changes to society, but this discussion focuses on only one such change—the creation and marketing of books specifically for readers caught between being children and adults.

HISTORICAL OUTLINE

In the 1986 May Hill Arbuthnot lecture, English critic and novelist Aidan Chambers said,

> The family of literature for young readers has its own parentage to live out. It was born of a humble, well-intentioned mother named Simple Didactics, and sired by a cunning but aggressive father called Cheap Commerce. Many children of the family inherited the worst of the genes from both sides. Even now, they stick close to home and carry on the business of telling readers what to think in off-the-shelf stories more notable for the craft of their marketing than the skill of their crafting.[1]

Chambers' comment, unhappily but not surprisingly, applies to most adolescent literature, past and present, just as it applies to most popular literature.

Prior to 1800, literature read by adolescents consisted largely of religious novels like John Bunyan's *Pilgrim's Progress* and pietistic tracts like Hannah More's *Repository Tracts*, which warned of the brevity of life and the wrath of God to come. After 1800, adolescent reading remained somber and didactic, but more often it hinted at the possibility of a longer and more satisfying life here on earth. In part, the change came from the decreasing infant mortality. In part, it came from our national expansion and a society that was increasingly urban and less agrarian. Sermons on becoming a better person mixed with heavy doses of the Protestant ethic, and lessons on patriotism were common, particularly in the works of the prolific and didactic Samuel Goodrich—who wrote 170 books under the pen name of Peter Parley—and the even more prolific and equally sermonistic Jacob Abbott—who wrote more than 200 books, 28 of them about noble, but tiresome, Rollo. The title of the 1838 Rollo book, *Rollo at Work, or The Way for a Boy to Learn to Be Industrious*, sounds the tenor of the book, the series, and the time.

The favorite reading of young women in the 1850s through the 1880s was the domestic novel. Born out of the belief that humanity was redeemable, the domestic novel preached the glories of suffering, women's submission to men, and a religion of the heart and the Bible and made several women writers rich. Susan Warner's *The Wide, Wide World* (1850) was both the first domestic novel and the form's prototype. Ellen Montgomery's mother is dead and her father improvident, so off she goes to her aunt's home. There she finds a faithful friend, the daughter of the minister, who showers Ellen with pity, piety, and platitudes. Tears flow constantly as Ellen surmounts insurmountable problems, and during those rare moments when Ellen is not weeping, someone is cooking or talking about food. Later domestic novels, particularly the best-selling of them all, Augusta Jane Evans Wilson's *St. Elmo* (1867), added more melodramatic gothic devices like mysterious deaths, disappearing wills, evil men, frightened virgins, and trances, but they maintained the domestic novel's belief in morality, religion, suffering, and the possibility of redemption here on earth.

As girls avidly read domestic novels, boys were equally fascinated by dime novels. When Beadle and Adams published the first dime novel, Ann S. Stephen's *Malaeska: The Indian Wife of the White Hunter* (1860), and the even more successful eighth dime novel later that year, Edward S. Ellis' *Seth Jones*, it assumed the likely

Nancy Drew. Courtesy of the Library of Congress

audience was men. Sometime later, Beadle and Adams recognized the obvious, that the primary audience was boys, and the price was dropped to a nickel. Action-packed dime novels grabbed readers immediately. The lurid cover was followed by a first sentence that announced thrills and chills to come, and readers were rarely disappointed. If the plots were ridiculous and exaggerated, written by hacks who had no idea of the real West, countless boys were hooked on the adventures of Buffalo Bill, Deadwood Dick, or Young Wild West. Detective dime novels were no more sensible, but readers followed the wild exploits of Young Sleuth and Nick Carter novel after novel. Boys learned what real heroism on the baseball field was like as they read amazing stories featuring Frank Merriwell and Fred Fearnot. Boys learned through dime novels what adults learned through their reading of the time, that success awaited any person who was willing to fight to get ahead. Family and social position counted for little. Ambition and hard work counted for everything.

Two writers for adolescents stand out in the last half of the nineteenth century. Louisa May Alcott and Horatio Alger both wrote about youngsters moving from childhood to early maturity, but any similarities end there. Alcott wrote about happy families, while Alger wrote about broken or unhappy families. Alcott wrote honestly about the problems of growing up. Alger's books were romantic fantasies about life as he wished it might be, for himself and his heroes. Alcott's *Little*

Women (1868–1869) retains its vitality and joy and popularity today. Other books—*Little Men* (1871), *Eight Cousins* (1875), and *Jo's Boys* (1886)—are inferior to *Little Women*, but they remain in print and are still read. Alger's best book was also his first try at an adolescent novel, *Ragged Dick, or Street Life in New York* (1868). The plot, as in other Alger books, is a series of semiconnected episodes illustrating a boy's first step toward maturity, respectability, and affluence. Typically, Alger is not content to let Dick rise through pluck but adds a fortuitous bit of luck that allows Dick to speed along faster toward success. About 119 books followed, all much the same.

Of the many other writers for adolescents of the time, a few are still readable. Under the pen name of Susan Coolidge, Sarah Chauncey Woolsey wrote a series of books about tomboy Katy that once rivaled Alcott's books in popularity and sales—*What Katy Did* (1873), *What Katy Did at School* (1874), and *What Katy Did Next* (1886). Howard Pyle's *Otto of the Silver Hand* (1888) and *Men of Iron* (1892) are occasionally read. John Meade Falkner's *Moonfeet* (1898) once captivated readers with its tale of smuggling and a cursed diamond, and, of course, Robert Louis Stevenson's *Treasure Island* (1883) and *Kidnapped* (1886) and Mark Twain's *The Adventures of Tom Sawyer* (1876) and *Adventures of Huckleberry Finn* (1884) remain basic adventure reading for adolescents today.

Incredibly popular at the time, almost unbelievably so for most readers today, were several girls' books about terribly brave and noble young women. Martha Finley's *Elsie Dinsmore* (1867) was the first of a long series preaching love and obedience to adults, no matter how little Finley's grown-ups deserved either. Far worse and an adult best-seller for two consecutive years was Eleanor Porter's *Pollyanna* (1913), a tiresome tale of a child who delights in playing the "glad game" and saving unfortunates for miles around. Fortunately, two potentially sticky, but ultimately refreshing, novels were available as antidotes to the sugary Elsie and Pollyanna, Kate Douglas Wiggin's *Rebecca of Sunnybrook Farm* (1903) and L. M. Montgomery's *Anne of Green Gables* (1908).

By the early 1900s, Edward Stratemeyer's Literary Syndicate was both the major producer of adolescent novels and a perpetual irritation to librarians and teachers who wanted the young to read better, more honest, and less melodramatic books. After learning the publishing business by editing a Street and Smith children's magazine and working with Alger and other writers for adolescents, Stratemeyer wrote *Under Dewey at Manila, or, The War Fortunes of a Castaway* (1898), which reached bookstores in time to capitalize on Admiral Dewey's victory. The book, like those that followed, was melodramatic morality with a young boy (or boys) proving his manhood and his equality with—or superiority to—adults. After completing several series for boys, Stratemeyer decided that he was faster at creating plots than in finishing books, so he advertised for writers to develop his plots into books. He then edited the writing to ensure that the book dovetailed with earlier books in a series. His series under many pseudonyms about the wondrous exploits of Baseball Joe, the Rover Boys, the Moving Picture Boys, the Moving Picture Girls, Bomba the Jungle Boy, and more were extremely popular, but his greatest successes came with three series—Tom Swift, the Hardy Boys, and Nancy Drew, the latter two likely to go on forever.

The school/sports novels of Ralph Henry Barbour and William Heyliger were far more honest about real boys, but the success of the form created its own formulas and stereotypes. Beginning with *The Half-Back* (1899), Barbour wrote about boys entering eastern private schools and playing various sports. The books soon became repetitious, but early books like *The Crimson Sweater* (1906) advanced the cause of adolescent literature through honest portraits of real boys with real problems. William Heyliger followed Barbour's formula in his early books, but later novels like *High Benton* (1919) and *High Benton, Worker* (1921) brought school and sports together with the world of work. Girls' school stories were rarely as successful or popular, though Marjorie Hill Allee's *Jane's Island* (1931) and *The Great Tradition* (1937) intelligently mixed romance with college life. Even better was Mabel Louise Robinson's *Bright Island* (1937) for its warmth, charm, and delight in describing a loving family on a small island off the Maine coast.

The development of juvenile divisions in many publishing companies and the first use of "junior novels" came in the 1930s. Rose Wilder Lane's *Let the Hurricane Roar* (1933) had first been marketed for adults by Longmans, Green. Late that year, the publishers began to advertise the novel as the first in their series of Junior Books. Their reasoning was obvious. The novel tells of a young married couple and their hard, dangerous, but always loving, life on the North Dakota plains. In only a few pages, Lane made readers—old and young—care about two likable young people. By 1937 other publishers had followed suit, as John Tunis learned when he submitted a draft of *Iron Duke* (1938) to Harcourt. Tunis was invited to the publisher's office, met a somewhat evasive Harcourt, and soon was marched out and taken to the head of the juvenile division. Shortly to become *the* sports novelist for adolescents, the bewildered Tunis had no idea what a "juvenile" book was, though it was a term that he hated throughout his career.

By the 1940s adolescent literature appeared in almost every major publisher's catalog. More important than mere quantity, the quality rose steadily. The popularity of series books, save the ubiquitous Nancy Drew and the Hardy Boys, declined because of the increasing education and sophistication of adolescents. Much of the material continued to celebrate the wonders and problems of high school years, but other themes appeared. Esther Forbes' *Johnny Tremain* (1943) told of a cocky young silversmith who gets his comeuppance and learns about himself. Social issues, rarely noticed in earlier adolescent literature, were the center of books by two important novelists. Florence Crannell Means' earlier books, *Tangled Waters* (1936) and *Shuttered Windows* (1938), brought minority characters into a field that had almost entirely ignored them, save as servants or menials, but *The Moved Outers* (1945) was even more powerful. The story of a forced relocation of Japanese American families after Pearl Harbor shocked readers then and still has bite. John Tunis deeply believed in American democracy, and his tales of corruption in sports, presumably the bastion of fairness and equality, were moral lessons and at the same time exciting accounts of games and heroes. If his inclination toward preaching sometimes made him forget his story, as in *A City for Lincoln* (1945), readers stayed with Tunis because he knew what locker rooms smelled like and he knew the game and its players. *All-American* (1942) is a remarkable football story about racial prejudice, and *Yea! Wildcats!* (1944) and *Go, Team, Go!* (1954) are perceptive novels about the evil and corruption that can arise out of small town basketball mania.

Romance and love along with a small bit of discreet sex remained popular with girls, and few authors since have done better at portraying that first love of an innocent young girl than Maureen Daly's *Seventeenth Summer* (1942). Mary Stolz's books are even better, particularly *To Tell Your Love* (1950), her first novel and an introspective story of a girl waiting vainly for *that* phone call from *that* boy; *A Love, or a Season* (1964), a story of a love that nearly gets out of hand; and Stolz's most distinguished novel *Pray Love, Remember* (1954), the story of a popular girl who does not like herself.

Daring as these novels were by 1940s and 1950s standards, they continued the moral strain of earlier adolescent literature, though they were less blatantly didactic. Their excellence is surprising given the unwritten, but widely known, taboos for adolescent literature of the time. Many writers fought the taboos, others (supposedly teachers and librarians) supported the taboos, and publishers, happily or not, enforced the taboos on manuscripts aimed at adolescents. These taboos were simple, direct, and negative—no smoking, no drinking, no divorce, no profanity, no suicide, no violence, no pregnancy, no protests about anything significant, no comments on social or racial unrest, no scenes showing young people disagreeing with parents or other authority figures on serious matters, and on and on. In effect, adolescent literature allowed for little reality. Means, Tunis, Daly, Stolz, and a few others may have skirted the edges of the taboos. Others either went along with the taboos or believed in them.

Movies had broken through the sterility of the Hays Office Code, and American writers were writing about serious adult themes without apology. Since paperbacks of fine adult books like *The Catcher in the Rye, 1984, Brave New World, Of Mice and Men*, and *A Farewell to Arms* were easily available and much read by adolescents, it is surprising that the taboos endured into the 1960s. Then in 1967–1968, several groundbreaking adolescent novels took care of most of the taboos by ignoring them. Ann Head's *Mr. and Mrs. BoJo Jones* (1967), in which a young couple *do it* and *have* to get married, seems innocuous now, but it shocked many adults, one of whom announced at a gathering of parents that "this is an evil book because teenagers are too young to learn about pregnancy." Ridiculous as the comment is, it reflects a mental set that held back the growth and honesty of adolescent literature.

Three other novels from 1967–1968 are far better literature and still read. Robert Lipsyte's *The Contender* (1967) is a compassionate story of a black ghetto teenager who believes that boxing is his way to a better life. S. E. Hinton's *The Outsiders* (1967) tells of a sensitive young man living on the edge of gang warfare who endures while his friends do not. Paul Zindel's *The Pigman* (1968) portrays two lonely and alienated youngsters desperately trying to find a reason to hope in a selfish world. All three novels describe a world that adolescent readers recognized as real, not a perfect world or the world that many adults had described, but a real world. Protagonists in all three books used language that shocked some adults but rarely fazed adolescents. Protagonists sought what adolescents really wanted—acceptance, love, honesty—most of all, honesty. All three books caused problems in communities where adults fought to keep honesty out of adolescent literature.

As more freedom in themes and language was granted by publishers, often grudgingly, to writers for adolescents, the gap between the talented and the hack became wider and more apparent. Good writers produced better and more honest books, while poorer writers used the freedom to preach about social problems with a few characters and a bit of plot attached. Good adolescent literature today does not allow readers to feel comfortable or complacent. It engages readers and forces them to see themselves and other people and the state and nature of humanity a little more perceptively. Good adolescent literature respects its readers, neither condescending nor pandering to the lowest common denominator of taste or intelligence. It gives readers the ultimate satisfaction that things and people are not always right or good but that the book is about honesty and reality.

Four themes dominate adolescent literature today just as they dominate good adult literature. First is the need of young people to find who and what they are in books as good as Barbara Wersba's *Run Softly, Go Fast* (1970), Robert Newton Peck's *A Day No Pigs Would Die* (1972), Katherine Paterson's *Jacob Have I Loved* (1980), Michael Marsden's *Letters from the Inside* (1994), and Michael Cadnum's *Heat* (1998).

Second is the need of young people to find something or someone to love in books as good as Alice Childress' *A Hero Ain't Nothin but a Sandwich* (1973), Mildred Taylor's *Roll of Thunder, Hear My Cry* (1976), Cynthia Voigt's *When She Hollers* (1994), and Vivian Vande Velde's *A Coming Evil* (1998).

Third is the need of young people to search for the truth and fight for what they believe in, in books as good as Paula Fox's *The Slave Dancer* (1973), Robert Cormier's *The Chocolate War* (1974), Walter Wangerin Jr.'s *The Book of the Dun Cow* (1978), Lois Lowry's *The Giver* (1993), and Jerry Spinelli's *Wringer* (1997).

Fourth is the need of young people to laugh at themselves and recognize that the world is sometimes mad in books as amusing as Leon Garfield's *The Strange Affair of Adelaide Harris* (1971), Bruce Clements' *I Tell a Lie Every So Often* (1974), Judie Angell's *Suds* (1983), Robert Kaplow's *Alex Icicle: A Romance in Ten Torrid Chapters* (1984), and Gary Paulsen's *Harris and Me* (1993).

Robert Cormier is the premier writer for adolescents in the United States, though critics disagree on whether *The Chocolate War* (1974), his first book, is better than *I Am the Cheese* (1977) or *After the First Death* (1979). Other writers highly regarded in America include Sue Ellen Bridgers, Alice Childress, Paula Fox, Robin McKinley, Katherine Paterson, and Mildred Taylor.

In England, the four major writers are Leon Garfield, Alan Garner, Rosemary Sutcliff, and Robert Westall. Other highly respected writers include Aidan Chambers, Peter Dickinson, Jane Gardam, and Jill Paton Walsh.

REFERENCE WORKS

There is no standard bibliography of adolescent literature. Virginia Haviland's *Children's Literature: A Guide to Reference Sources* is helpful, as is Jane Bingham and Grayce Scholt's *Fifteen Centuries of Children's Literature: An Annotated Chronology of British and American Works in Historical Context*. Both works, however, mix children's books and adolescent literature, a problem common to most reference works in the field, and make scholarly work unnecessarily complicated and difficult. The recent and scholarly *Children's Fiction, 1876–1984* inevitably covers any one item so briefly that its usefulness is limited.

Two checklists provide excellent coverage for areas previously difficult to work with. Harry K. Hudson's *A Bibliography of Hard-Cover Boys' Books* is limited in scope, covering only boys' series largely of the first half of the present century, but it is a pioneer in the field. *Girls' Series Books: A Checklist of Hardcover Books Published 1900–1975* is more scholarly, the work of researchers and librarians at the University of Minnesota.

A recent dictionary attempts to cover the entire scope of adolescent and children's books. Alethea K. Helbig and Agnes Regan Perkins' two-volume *Dictionary of American Children's Fiction* contains entries for authors, book titles, and major characters in the most significant novels covering the period from 1859 to 1984 and provides useful details and contemporary criticism. The *Dictionary of British Children's Fiction* is equally helpful.

The major scholarly reference works in adolescent literature are historical. Two general histories of the field, again mixed with children's literature as well, are basic sources for the scholar. Cornelia Meigs, Anne Thaxter Eaton, Elizabeth Nesbit, and Ruth Hill Viguers' *A Critical History of Children's Literature* is long and occasionally ponderous. Far more readable, if sometimes slanted more toward British than American material, is John Rowe Townsend's *Written for Children: An Outline of English-Language Children's Literature*. Townsend's perceptive and succinct criticism and his ability as a novelist make his work both scholarly and entertaining. One chapter in Alleen Pace Nilsen and Kenneth L. Donelson's *Literature for Today's Young Adults* (1999) attempts to cover the history of adolescent literature, unmixed with children's books, from 1800 to today. Two brief booklets, neither likely to be easily found, are most satisfying British accounts of the history of adolescent/children's literature. Christine A. Kloet's *After Alice: A Hundred Years of Children's Reading in Britain* was prepared for an exhibition to celebrate the centenary of the British Library Association. Even better is John Rowe Townsend's *25 Years of British Children's Books*, a sixty-page alphabetized and annotated list of books by authors whom Townsend considered most important in the field.

Less significant histories are Elva S. Smith's *The History of Children's Literature*, though a groundbreaker when it appeared in 1937, and Mary F. Thwaite's *From Primer to Pleasure in Reading: An Introduction to the History of Children's Books in England from the Invention of Printing to 1914 with an Outline of Some Developments in Other Countries*.

Scholars seeking information about adolescent literature in America prior to 1900 have several fine books to consult. William Sloane's *Children's Books in England and America in the Seventeenth Century* is a standard source, scholarly and accurate. Bernard Wishy's *The Child and the Republic: The Dawning of Modern American Child Nurture* is obviously more concerned with children than adolescents, but it is a book that no scholar working in early adolescent literature can afford to ignore. A.S.W. Rosenbach's *Early American Children's Books* is precisely what the title suggests, children's books, but Rosenbach's pioneer work in a hitherto largely ignored field and his fascination with his material are contagious. Also scholarly and equally enthusiastic is Jacob Blanck's *Peter Parley to Penrod: A Bibliographical Description of the Best-Loved American Juvenile Books*.

Scholars working with nineteenth-century children's and adolescent books must consult three basic tools. Monica Kiefer's *American Children through Their Books, 1700–1835*, Anne Scott MacLeod's *A Moral Tale: Children's Fiction and American Culture, 1820–1860*, and Anne Scott MacLeod's *American Childhood*. Raymond L. Kilgour's *Lee and Shepard: Publishers for the People* is more limited in interest, but since this publisher produced much adolescent literature, scholars should know of

Kilgour's work. Richard L. Darling's *The Rise of Children's Book Reviewing in America, 1865–1881* is superb and illustrates the kind of historic research that remains to be done in the field. Esther Jane Carrier's *Fiction in Public Libraries, 1876–1900* is mainly devoted to adult literature, but the material on adolescent literature and the problems that it caused is worth consulting.

Almost any history of the American novel would touch on the domestic novel, but two histories are especially good, Herbert Ross Brown's *The Sentimental Novel in America, 1789–1860* and Fred Lewis Pattee's *The Feminist Fifties*. The most enjoyable source is Helen Waite Papashvily's *All the Happy Endings: A Study of the Domestic Novel in America, the Women Who Wrote It, the Women Who Read It, in the Nineteenth Century*.

The standard source on the dime novel is Albert Johannsen's three-volume *The House of Beadle and Adams and Its Dime and Nickel Novels: The Story of a Vanished Literature*. Daryl Jones' *The Dime Novel Western* is broader in scope and better written. Henry Nash Smith's *Virgin Land: The American West as Symbol and Myth* is basic for any study of the western novel or the dime novel. Chapter 8, "The Dime Novel Tradition," in Russel Nye's *The Unembarrassed Muse: The Popular Arts in America* is an excellent and brief introduction to the dime novel.

Of the many biographies of Louisa May Alcott, Madeleine Stern's *Louisa May Alcott* is both sensible and well written, though some critics have argued for Martha Saxton's *Louisa May: A Modern Biography of Louisa May Alcott*. While dated, Ednah D. Cheney's edition of *Louisa May Alcott: Her Life, Letters and Journals* is still helpful. Alma J. Payne's "Louisa May Alcott (1832–1888)" in *American Literary Realism, 1870–1910* is a model of bibliographical information.

Most of the material on Horatio Alger is dubious or worse. Gary Scharnhorst's *Horatio Alger, Jr.* for the Twayne United States Authors Series corrects a mass of historic misinformation. Scharnhorst and Jack Bales' *Horatio Alger, Jr.: An Annotated Bibliography of Comment and Criticism* is essential in an area that has been largely chaotic.

Of the writings on Edward Stratemeyer's Literary Syndicate, Deidre Johnson's *Stratemeyer Pseudonyms and Series Books: An Annotated Checklist of Stratemeyer and Stratemeyer Literary Syndicate Publications* serves as a sound introduction, suggesting some of the intricacies of working through problems in popular culture. Bobbie Ann Mason's *The Girl Sleuth: A Feminist Guide* is a delightful way of looking at Nancy Drew (and others) through a particular literary eyeglass. Leslie McFarlane's *Ghost of the Hardy Boys: An Autobiography of Leslie McFarlane* is a chatty history of his relationship with the syndicate.

Although their work mixes children's and adolescent literature, English historians and critics have provided us with a number of helpful books. E.J.H. Darton's *Children's Books in England: Five Centuries of Social Life* is standard if a bit stuffy. Alec Ellis' *A History of Children's Reading and Literature* and Roger L. Green's *Tellers of Tales: British Authors of Children's Books from 1800 to 1964* are standard if unexciting. More stimulating and psychologically perceptive about young people and their books are Frank Eyre's *British Children's Books in the Twentieth Century* and Marcus Crouch's *Treasure Seekers and Borrowers: Children's Books in Britain, 1900–1960* and *The Nesbit Tradition: The Children's Novel in England, 1945–1970*.

Two works deserve particular attention in an area that is sometimes stuffy if not downright boring. Gillian Avery's *Childhood's Pattern: A Study of the Heroes and*

Huckleberry Finn. Courtesy of the Library of Congress

Heroines of Children's Fiction 1700–1950 is wise and witty, and Mary Cadogan and Patricia Craig's *You're a Brick, Angela! A New Look at Girls' Fiction from 1839 to 1975* is as delightful and thoughtful as the title suggests.

Edward Salmon's *Juvenile Literature as It Is* was published in 1888, long before adolescent literature (or children's literature, for that matter) was considered a respectable or wholesome enterprise for a grown-up. Salmon's book is a delight no matter what the age of the book, and anyone curious about the field misses a necessary and fascinating book if Salmon is ignored.

Canadian adolescent literature is covered brilliantly in Sheila Egoff's *The Problem of Childhood: A Critical Guide to Canadian Children's Literature in English*. Scholars seeking the standard coverage of European adolescent literature will find much that is helpful in Bettina Hurlimann's *Three Centuries of Children's Books in Europe*.

Biographical information is readily accessible. Anne Commire's *Something about the Author*, a multivolume work, is standard and valuable, if sometimes little more than chatty. Far more detailed, although in its early multivolume stage, is Adele Sarkissian's *Something about the Author: Autobiography Series*, which devotes more pages to each author. D. L. Kirkpatrick's *Twentieth Century Children's Writers* is a model of the one-volume biographical tool, comprehensive yet allowing authors of individual entries to condense the biographies and include some brief, but often pointed, critcism. Sara and Tom Pendergast's *St. James Guide to Young Adult Lit-*

erature and Ted Hipple's four-volume *Writers for Young Adults* are worthy additions to the field.

Less valuable biographical data can be found in Brian Doyle's *The Who's Who of Children's Literature*, Stanley J. Kunitz and Howard Haycraft's *The Junior Book of Authors*, Muriel Fuller's *More Junior Authors*, and Doris DeMontreville and Donna Hill's *Third Book of Junior Authors*.

Of the several collections of interviews with authors of adolescent books, the best are Justin Winkle and Emma Fisher's *The Pied Pipers: Interviews with the Influential Creators of Children's Literature* and M. Jerry Weiss' *From Writers to Students: The Pleasures and Pains of Writing*.

Biographical data along with critical assessment of nineteenth-century writers for adolescents can be found in Glenn E. Estes' *American Writers for Children before 1900*. Later writers are treated in John Cech's *American Writers for Children, 1900–1960*. The multivolume *Children's Literature Review* is the standard source for criticism of adolescent literature.

Booklists are a commonplace in various journals concerned with adolescent books. Standard book-length lists include G. Robert Carlsen's *Books and the Teenage Reader*; *Books for You*, published by the National Council of Teachers of English approximately every three years for high school students and teachers; and *Your Reading*, from the same source and at approximately the same interval, for junior high students and teachers. Barbara Dodds Stanford and Karima Amin's *Black Literature for High School Students* and Anna Lee Stensland's *Literature by and about the American Indian, an Annotated Bibliography* are basic specialized lists.

RESEARCH COLLECTIONS

Irvin Kerlan, a Washington, D.C., doctor who had graduated from the University of Minnesota medical school, collected rare books, including Caldecott Medal winners. Eventually, his interest included the process of bookmaking, and he collected editorial correspondence as well as various stages of manuscripts and illustrations. In 1949, he began donating material to the University of Minnesota library. When he died in 1963, his collection went to the library to form the base of the Kerlan Collection, *the* leading research center for children's books in the United States. A catalog of holdings printed in 1985 is available for thirty dollars from the Children's Literature Research Collection, 109 Walter Library, University of Minnesota, Minneapolis, Minn. 55455.

Although Kerlan's initial interest was in children's books, the collection has since been expanded to include literature for teenagers. All material is available for use in the Kerlan Collection Reading Room. Among the manuscripts are Judy Blume's *Are You There God? It's Me Margaret* (1970), Lois Duncan's *Stranger with My Face* (1981), Bette Greene's *Summer of My German Soldier* (1973), Felice Holman's *Slake's Limbo* (1974), M. E. Kerr's *Dinky Hocker Shoots Smack* (1972), Robert Lipsyte's *The Contender* (1967), Robert C. O'Brien's *Z for Zachariah* (1975), and Katherine Paterson's *Jacob Have I Loved* (1980).

The second largest collection is the Lena Y. deGrummond Collection at the University of Southern Mississippi in Hattiesburg. Lena deGrummond was the supervisor of school libraries in Louisiana. Upon her retirement in 1965, she joined the faculty of the Library School at Hattiesburg and soon began asking authors for their manuscripts and correspondence. The response surprised even deGrummond, and, according to curator John Kelly, the collection now contains 27,000 items from over 1,000, authors, editors, and illustrators. Ninety percent of the collection is children's books, but in the other 10 percent are manuscripts from such young adult writers as Madeleine L'Engle, Isabelle Holland, Richard Peck, and Ouida Sebestyen. Researchers are welcome to work with the materials.

During the late 1960s and 1970s, the University of Oregon under the leadership of librarian Ed Kemp searched for books, manuscripts, correspondence, and illustrations. Most of the material concerns children's books, but there are six shelf-feet of papers from young adult author Hila Colman and fifteen from nonfiction writer Milton Meltzer. Maureen Daly's papers are in the collection, dating from 1938 to 1973.

A different kind of collection is one devoted to a few authors or to a single author, for example, the collection of Robert Cormier's published and unpublished manuscripts, correspondence, taped speeches, and newspaper columns at Fitchburg State College in Massachusetts. Wheaton College in Illinois has fifty-seven volumes of Madeleine L'Engle manuscripts dating from childhood through 1978. Boston University has eighty-eight manuscript boxes of material from John Tunis. The University of Louisville has over 6,000 items related to Edgar Rice Burroughs and the Tarzan series. Iowa writers Jeannette Eyerly and Henry Gregor Felsen donated their papers to the University of Iowa Library.

Authors whose work was published for a general audience but found a special place with teenage readers include Jack London, the focus of 395 volumes in the Oakland Public Library, and Harriet Beecher Stowe, whose papers are preserved at the Stowe-Day Foundation in Hartford, Connecticut. Mark Twain is featured in eleven different libraries, notably, the University of California at Berkeley for general information and the Buffalo and Erie County Public Library for items on *Huckleberry Finn*. Robert Louis Stevenson is the subject of collections at the University of California in Los Angeles, Yale University, and the University of Texas at Austin. The Silverado Museum in St. Helena, California, has 7,000 items related to Stevenson.

Many libraries have extensive historical collections of materials on authors who purposely set out to win young adults as readers in the 1800s. Seven libraries have collections of Louisa May Alcott papers, including Harvard University, the Library of Congress, and the Orchard House Museum in Concord, Massachusetts. Twelve libraries have Horatio Alger collections, the largest being the Library of Congress; the others include the Free Library of Philadelphia, Northern Illinois University of Dekalb, the University of Southern Mississippi in Hattiesburg, and Ohio University in Athens.

Other historical collections are organized by type of material rather than by individual authors. The largest such collections contain dime novels, and probably the largest of the dime novel collections is one named for collector George H. Hess Jr., who in 1954 donated 75,000 items to the University of Minnesota Library. Besides dime novels, the Hess collection contains story papers, pulps, periodicals, and boys' and girls' series books. More fragile items have recently been microfilmed, but most materials are available for researchers. Other libraries with extensive collections of dime novels include the University of Arkansas in Fayetteville, San Diego Public, Northern Illinois University in DeKalb, Brandeis University, and Michigan State Library.

Libraries with collections of serialized stories for young readers include Bowdoin College in Brunswick, Maine, with the Rollo books of Jacob Abbott, the New Hampshire State Library in Concord with the Tom Swift books, Dartmouth College with books by Horatio Alger, the Donnell Center of the New York Public Library with books by Abbott and Alger, Indiana University with Susan Coolidge's *Katy* books, and the Public Library of Cincinnati and Hamilton County with a complete 245-volume set of the Frank and Dick Merriwell sports stories. Northern Illinois University in DeKalb has complete runs of *Beadle's Monthly*, *Beadle's Weekly*, *Saturday Journal*, and the *Young New Yorker*, while the American Antiquarian Society in Worcester, Massachusetts, has an extensive collection of periodicals published between 1700 and 1876, including *Parley's Magazine* and *Youth's Companion*.

For scholars of young adult literature, working in research collections is often depressing because the books for teens are Johnny-come-latelies and sometimes treated like poor relations. As one curator reported, "Of course I keep track of [scholarship dealing with] children's literature first and foremost, but we do try to be watchful and in fact have a clipping folder of articles on YA lit."

The prime reason that young adult literature takes a backseat to children's books in most research collections is simply that it is relatively new. It does not have traditions such as the Newbery and Caldecott medals, nor are young adult books illustrated. Many research collections were originally based on someone's interest in gathering illustrations and then the accompanying manuscripts.

Ironically, just as manuscripts for young adult books are beginning to be sought by collectors, the word processor has changed the way that authors write. Ann Seymour, library assistant at the Kerlan Collection, said that changes are already evident. They have received a few "perfect" manuscripts fresh off a word processor. Other authors have sent in an early and a late word-processed copy so that a careful reader can compare changes made but not nearly as easily as with the old typed copies filled with authors' penciled changes.

HISTORY AND CRITICISM

The criticism of adolescent literature falls mainly into four types: historical, pedagogical or promotional, social, and literary. The critic who writes from a historical viewpoint analyzes books of a certain period or compares books from one period with books from another or shows how the books of a particular period reflect the culture of that period. Many of the outstanding books of this type are mentioned under Reference Works.

Pedagogical criticism is written from the viewpoint of educators, mainly librarians and teachers of reading or English who want to encourage young people to read. The Russian launching of Sputnik in 1957 jarred Americans into taking a new look at the way their children were educated. One result was the National Defense Education Act, which in the 1960s and 1970s provided financial support for school libraries. Publishers responded by printing large numbers of books designed to entice both children and teenagers into extensive leisure-time reading. The public was supportive, as shown by the popularity of two books written to help adults bring books and teenagers together. Daniel Fader's 1966 *Hooked on Books* recounted his successful experiment introducing large quantities of paperback books to boys in a training school in Michigan. G. Robert Carlsen's *Books and the Teenage Reader* went through seven Bantam printings between its publication in April 1967 and a revised edition in December 1971. Fader's and Carlsen's philosophies had a common belief, that if a knowledgeable adult will get the right book to the right student, something almost magical will happen as young people take steps toward becoming lifelong readers.

Many educators are less enthusiastic than Fader or Carlsen but nevertheless accept the idea that if students enjoy what they are reading, they will read more and consequently develop into better readers. Critics who serve as defenders of using adolescent literature in the schools say that when compared to what has been traditionally assigned for class reading, the best young adult literature is more appealing because of its contemporary settings, plots, and diction. Comfortable readers become emotionally involved with interesting characters of their own age. Of course, teachers and librarians do not intend to limit young people to adolescent novels but rather to use adolescent literature as a bridge to more complex, adult literature.

The first of several college textbooks introducing teachers to the genre was Dwight L. Burton's 1970 *Literature Study in the High Schools*. A collection of articles edited by Richard A. Meade and Robert C. Small Jr., *Literature for Adolescents: Selection and Use*, was published in 1973. Later textbooks for college classes of potential or in-service teachers included Sheila Schwartz's *Teaching Adolescent Literature: A Humanistic Approach*, published in 1972; the Nilsen and Donelson text mentioned earlier, first published in 1980 and in its sixth edition in 1999; Ruth Cline and William McBride's *A Guide to Literature for Young Adults: Background, Selection, and Use* in 1983; and Arthea J. S. Reed's *Reaching Adolescents: The Young Adult Book and the School* in 1985.

The interest of English teachers, who for the most part had snubbed the "junior novel," is reflected in the founding of ALAN (Assembly on Literature for Adolescents—National Council of Teachers of English) by a small group of teachers who in 1973 gathered as part of the NCTE annual conference. ALAN now has approximately 2,000 members, holds an annual November two-day workshop attended by 400 people, and three times a year publishes a journal. The *ALAN Review* has articles by and about young adult authors as well as reviews of dozens of recently published books. Another indication of the interest of English teachers in young adult books is the inclusion on a regular basis of reviews as well as frequent articles on them in the *English Journal*.

Several NCTE state affiliates have published special issues of their journals devoted to adolescent literature, including the *Arizona English Bulletin* in April 1972 and April 1976, the Southeastern Ohio Council's *Focus* in winter 1977, the *Iowa English Bulletin* in spring 1980, the *Connecticut English Journal* in fall 1980, and *English in Texas* in winter 1981.

Teachers of reading also began taking a more serious look at adolescent literature because with falling reading scores, many high schools created reading classes not just for remedial students but for everyone. Elective courses such as individualized reading, science fiction, and black (or women's or Hispanic or Indian, etc.) studies forced teachers to search for new books that students would like. The International Reading Association's *Journal of Reading* began a regular review column of young adult books.

During this same period, more libraries opened young adult rooms or sections, and membership climbed in the Young Adult Services Division of the American Library Association. Its annual list of Best Books increased in length, and as the quality of books coming from juvenile divisions of publishing houses increased, more titles were included on the annual list. *Booklist*, *Wilson Library Bulletin*, *Top of the News*, and *School Library Journal* gave more attention to young adult books. Margaret A. Edwards' 1969 classic, *The Fair Garden and the Swarm of Beasts*, a how-to for young adult librarians wanting to encourage reading, was reissued in an expanded 1974 version. In 1978 librarian Jana Varlejs edited *Young Adult Literature in the Seventies: A Selection of Readings*, and in 1980 the American Library Association published *Young Adult Literature: Background and Criticism*, edited by Millicent Lentz and Ramona M. Mahood. In the same year, the H. W. Wilson company published Joni Bodart's *Booktalk! Booktalking and School Visiting for Young Adult Audiences*.

The enthusiasm of librarians and teachers was shared by publishers and by producers of television and movies, who in a youth-oriented society were looking for relatively simple stories that could be dramatized within the time limitations of television. Many books written for teenagers became either films or television programs. Librarians, teachers, and publishers capitalized on the interest through media-related paperbacks, which could be used in promotional efforts.

Even though the primary goal of most of the people just described was to promote reading, evaluation was still a part of the matter as they tried to decide which books to promote. A popular form of research was to conduct reading preference surveys among young people to find which books they enjoyed the most. These could then be recommended for purchase by other schools and libraries.

A goal quite different from that of matching "the right book with the right reader" to increase pleasure and promote widespread reading is that of using books to influence readers to whatever social beliefs and behaviors the critic thinks are desirable. The social consciousness that rose out of the turmoil of the 1960s found its way into the criticism of young adult literature, as did the backward swing of the pendulum in the 1980s. The result has been tremendous variety both in the types of groups and individuals involved in social criticism and in the recommendations that they make.

During the 1980s, scholarly, religious, civic, and political organizations were all involved in criticizing particular young adult books. None admit to being censors, yet all have protested certain titles because of the social messages that the books carried. Critics have presented well-prepared cases against the stereotyping of parents in teenage books, the glorification of violence for young men, the demeaning portrayals of minorities, the absence of good books about handicapped people, and, most recently, the unrealistic expectations promoted by popular romance novels.

By far the most influential and well known of several groups criticizing from a social issues viewpoint was the Council on Interracial Books for Children (CIBC), founded in the mid-1960s and now apparently moribund. The CIBC believed that books should "become a tool for the conscious promotion of human values that

Reading during summer vacation. © Skjold Photographs

lead to greater human liberation." Its checklist for evaluation included such categories as racism, sexism, elitism, materialism, ageism, cultural authenticity, and positive versus negative images of females and minorities. Reviews and articles in its *Interracial Books for Children Bulletin* focused on such matters. As might be expected, their reviews were often controversial, for example, this sentence in a review of Lawrence Yep's *Dragonwings* (1975): "The book, though highly recommended, does have a weakness. While oppression and racism are well described, blame is not placed squarely on the economic system which then, as now, used non-whites for maximum profit."

Books by individuals writing from a social issues viewpoint include Dorothy Broderick's 1973 *Images of the Black in Children's Fiction*; Bob Dixon's 1977 *Catching Them Young: Political Ideas in Children's Fiction* and *Catching Them Young: Sex, Race and Class in Children's Fiction*; Donnarae McCann and Gloria Woodward's 1972 *The Black American in Books for Children: Readings on Racism*; and Masha Kabakow Rudman's 1976 *Children's Literature: An Issues Approach*. Most social issues critics take a positive approach by recommending books whose messages they like. For example, the American Council on Education and the National Council of Teachers of English have for decades jointly sponsored the publication of *Reading Ladders for Human Relations*, a 400-page book edited by Eileen Tway, now in its sixth edition. Its goal is "to advance the cause of better human relations." The method that it espouses is reading and discussing books—both children's and young adult—under such ladders as "Interacting in Groups," "Appreciating Different Cultures," and "Coping in a Changing World."

Voice of Youth Advocates (VOYA) was founded in 1978 by Dorothy M. Broderick and Mary K. Chelton to change the traditional linking of young adult services from children's to adult sections of libraries. As part of its anticensorship stand, *VOYA* reviews and promotes the use of books dealing with all kinds of previously taboo topics.

An extensive body of literature has grown up around the problem of censorship of books for young readers, for example, *Censors in the Classroom: The Mind Benders*, by Edward B. Jenkinson; *Limiting What Students Shall Read*, published jointly by the Association of American Publishers, the American Library Association, and the Association for Supervision and Curriculum Development; and the NCTE publications *The Students' Right to Read*; *The Students' Right to Know*, by Lee Burress and Edward B. Jenkinson; and *Dealing with Censorship*, edited by James E. Davis. The most recent source for information on young adult books is the remarkable four-volume set edited by Ken Wachsberger, *Banned Books*, with these subtitles for individual volumes: *Literature Suppressed on Political Grounds*, *Literature Suppressed on Social Grounds*, *Literature Suppressed on Sexual Grounds*, and *Literature Suppressed on Religious Grounds*.

A quite different approach to young adult books is that of literary criticism similar to that applied to the best adult books. This criticism is about the books themselves and the relationships between the authors and what they have written, patterns that appear, techniques that authors use, and themes and underlying issues. Two pioneer dissertations exemplifying this kind of criticism were A. Stephen Dunning's "A Definition of the Role of the Junior Novel Based on Analyses of Thirty Selected Novels," completed in 1959, and Dorothy J. Petitt's "A Study of the Qualities of Literary Excellence Which Characterize Selected Fiction for Younger Adolescents," completed in 1961.

In looking for books of literary criticism, one meets the same problem as in the research collections. Most critics have mixed children's and young adult books, so it takes a knowledge of the latter to pick out what is applicable. In 1975, Glenna Davis Sloan applied Northrop Frye's critical theories to children's and adolescent literature in *The Child as Critic*. A year later Rebecca Lukens wrote *A Critical Handbook of Children's Literature*. Most of her examples came from children's literature, but the literary principles that she discusses are equally applicable to young adult books.

Sheila Egoff's 1981 *Thursday's Child: Trends and Patterns in Contemporary Children's Literature* proves that an intelligent critic can find plenty of intellectual meat in contemporary books for young readers. Betsy Hearne and Marilyn Kaye's 1981 *Celebrating Children's Books: Essays on Children's Literature in Honor of Zena Sutherland* does the same with papers by young adult writers Lloyd Alexander, Robert Cormier, Virginia Hamilton, John Donovan, John Rowe Townsend, and David Macaulay. *The Arbuthnot Lectures*, edited by Zena Sutherland, is a similar collection featuring talks by John Rowe Townsend, Ivan Southall, Jean Fritz, and Sheila Egoff.

More such criticism of young adult literature is being done as authors write books serious enough to support it. For example, the Twayne literary criticism series published by G. K. Hall recently expanded to include young adult authors.

The first two volumes by Patricia J. Campbell and Alleen Pace Nilsen published in 1985 and 1986 proved that the books of Robert Cormier and M. E. Kerr are worthy of full-length analyses. Other good examples of literary criticism are David Rees' 1980 *The Marble in the Water: Essays on Contemporary Writers of Fiction for Children and Young Adults* and his 1984 *Painted Desert, Green Shade: Essays on Contemporary Writers of Fiction for Children and Young Adults*; John Rowe Townsend's 1975 *A Sounding of Storytellers: Essays on Contemporary Writers for Children*; Aidan Chambers' 1985 *Booktalk: Occasional Writing on Literature and Children*; and the 1976 collection of articles from *Children's Literature in Education* entitled *Writers, Critics, and Children*, edited by Geoff Fox et al. An excellent example of literary criticism and a good one on which to end this discussion is Robert E. Probst's 1984 *Adolescent Literature: Response and Analysis*. He uses teenage books as the focus for outstanding discussions of reader response and literary analysis.

COLLECTIONS AND REPRINTS

Most major libraries have current or nearly current adolescent books in their holdings, and many have a sprinkling of older adolescent books in their rare book or special collections. The best early adolescent literature—Alcott's *Little Women* (1868), Twain's *The Adventures of Tom Sawyer* (1876) and *Adventures of Huckleberry Finn* (1864), and Stevenson's *Treasure Island* (1883) and *Kidnapped* (1876)—have continuously been in print since publication. Wiggin's *Rebecca of Sunnybrook Farm* (1903) and Montgomery's *Anne of Green Gables* (1908) have frequently been reprinted and are currently available in inexpensive paperback, the first from Dell and the latter from Bantam. Alger's *Ragged Dick* has been reprinted in *Struggling Upward and Other Works* (1940).

Collections of dime novels are not difficult to find. The Hess Collection is unquestionably the standard source for scholars. Austin J. McLean's "The Hess Collection of Dime Novels" in the *American Book Collector* serves as a good introduction to the holdings.

Recently, two publishers have reprinted several dime novel libraries. Garland Publishing reprinted ten volumes (the complete run) of the Frank Reade Library. University Microfilms International has published a collection of 3,000 dime novels, mostly westerns.

For a number of years, Charles Bragin published reprints of dime novels. Many of these can still be found. The *Dime Novel Roundup* (Edward LeBlanc, 87 School St., Fall River, Mass. 02720), a chatty magazine for dime novel enthusiasts that often contains invaluable information, carries advertisements for dime novels in nearly every issue. The best of the several single-volume dime novel collections is *Eight Dime Novels*—with a Nick Carter, a Buffalo Bill, a Frank Merriwell, and an Alger—with an admirable introduction by E. F. Bleiler.

The sole attempt to reprint a large library of older books is Garland Publishing's Classics of Children's Literature, 1621–1932. Fine as the selection is by Alison Lurie and Justin G. Schiller, the 117 titles are mostly children's books. The few adolescent titles are, with the exception of Goodrich's *Tales of Peter Parley about America* and Helen Hunt Jackson's *Nelly's Silver Mine*, relatively easy to find in secondhand bookstores.

NOTE

1. "All of a Tremble to See His Danger," *Top of the News* 42 (Summer 1986), 415.

BIBLIOGRAPHY

Books and Articles

"Adolescent Literature." *English in Texas* 13 (Winter 1981), special issue.

"Adolescent Literature, Adolescent Reading and the English Class." *Arizona English Bulletin* 14 (April 1972), special issue.

"Adolescent Literature: Dimensions and Directions." *Iowa English Bulletin* 29 (Spring 1980), special issue.

"Adolescent Literature Revisited after Four Years." *Arizona English Bulletin* 18 (April 1976), special issue.

Avery, Gillian. *Childhood's Pattern: A Study of the Heroes and Heroines of Children's Fiction 1700–1950.* London: Hodder and Stoughton, 1975.

Bingham, Jane, and Grayce Scholt. *Fifteen Centuries of Children's Literature: An Annotated Chronology of British and American Works in Historical Context.* Westport, Conn.: Greenwood, 1980.

Blanck, Jacob. *Peter Parley to Penrod: A Bibliographical Description of the Best-Loved American Juvenile Books.* New York: R. R. Bowker, 1956.

Bleiler, E. F., ed. *Eight Dime Novels.* New York: Dover, 1974.

Bodart, Joni. *Booktalk! Booktalking and School Visiting for Young Adult Audiences.* New York: H. W. Wilson, 1980.

Broderick, Dorothy M. *Images of the Black in Children's Fiction.* New York: R. R. Bowker, 1973.

Brown, Herbert Ross. *The Sentimental Novel in America, 1789–1860.* Durham, N.C.: Duke University Press, 1940.

Burress, Lee, and Edward B. Jenkinson. *The Students' Right to Know.* Urbana, Ill.: National Council of Teachers of English, 1982.

Burton, Dwight L. *Literature Study in the High Schools.* New York: Holt, 1970.

Cadogan, Mary, and Patricia Craig. *You're a Brick, Angela! A New Look at Girls' Fiction from 1839 to 1975.* London: Victor Gollancz, 1976.

Campbell, Patricia J. *Presenting Robert Cormier.* Boston: Twayne, 1985.

Carlsen, G. Robert. *Books and the Teenage Reader.* 2nd rev. ed. New York: Harper and Row, 1980.

Carrier, Esther Jane. *Fiction in Public Libraries, 1876–1900.* Metuchen, N.J.: Scarecrow Press, 1965.

Cech, John, ed. *American Writers for Children, 1900–1960. Dictionary of Literary Biography.* Vol. 22. Detroit: Gale Research, 1983.

Chambers, Aidan. *Booktalk: Occasional Writing on Literature and Children.* New York: Harper and Row, 1985.

Cheney, Ednah D., ed. *Louisa May Alcott: Her Life, Letters and Journals.* Boston: Little, Brown, 1901.

Children's Fiction, 1876–1984. 2 vols. New York: R. R. Bowker, 1984.

Children's Literature Review. Detroit: Gale Research, 1976– .

Cline, Ruth, and William McBride. *A Guide to Literature for Young Adults: Background, Selection, and Use*. Glenview, Ill.: Scott, Foresman, 1983.

Commire, Anne, ed. *Something about the Author*. Detroit: Gale Research, 1971–   .

Council on Interracial Books for Children. *Human (and Anti-Human) Values in Children's Books*. New York: CIBC, 1976.

Crouch, Marcus. *The Nesbit Tradition: The Children's Novel in England, 1945–1970*. London: Ernest Benn, 1972.

———. *Treasure Seekers and Borrowers: Children's Books in Britain, 1900–1960*. London: Library Association, 1962.

Darling, Richard L. *The Rise of Children's Book Reviewing in America, 1865–1881*. New York: R. R. Bowker, 1968.

Darton, E.J.H. *Children's Books in England: Five Centuries of Social Life*. 2nd ed. Cambridge: Cambridge University Press, 1958.

Davis, James E., ed. *Dealing with Censorship*. Urbana, Ill.: National Council of Teachers of English, 1979.

DeMontreville, Doris, and Donna Hill, eds. *Third Book of Junior Authors*. New York: H. W. Wilson, 1963.

Dixon, Bob. *Catching Them Young: Political Ideas in Children's Fiction*. London: Pluto Press, 1977.

———. *Catching Them Young: Sex, Race and Class in Children's Fiction*. London: Pluto Press, 1977.

Doyle, Brian. *The Who's Who of Children's Literature*. New York: Schocken, 1968.

Dunning, A. Stephen. "A Definition of the Role of the Junior Novel Based on Analyses of Thirty Selected Novels." Ph.D. dissertation, Florida State University, 1959.

Edwards, Margaret A. *The Fair Garden and the Swarm of Beasts: The Library and the Young Adult*. Rev. ed. New York: Hawthorn, 1974.

Egoff, Sheila. *The Problem of Childhood: A Critical Guide to Canadian Children's Literature in English*. Toronto: Oxford University Press, 1967.

———. *Thursday's Child: Trends and Patterns in Contemporary Children's Literature*. Chicago: American Library Association, 1981.

Ellis, Alec. *A History of Children's Reading and Literature*. New York: Pergamon Press, 1968.

Estes, Glenn E., ed. *American Writers for Children before 1900. Dictionary of Literary Biography*. Vol. 42. Detroit: Gale Research, 1985.

Eyre, Frank. *British Children's Books in the Twentieth Century*. New York: E. P. Dutton, 1971.

Fader, Daniel. *Hooked on Books*. New York: Berkley, 1966.

"Fiction for Adolescents." *Focus* (Ohio) 3 (Winter 1977), special issue.

Fox, Geoff, Graham Hammond, Terry Jones, Frederic Smith, and Kenneth Sterck, eds. *Writers, Critics, and Children*. New York: Agathon Press, 1976.

Fuller, Muriel, ed. *More Junior Authors*. New York: H. W. Wilson, 1963.

Girls' Series Books: A Checklist of Hardcover Books Published 1900–1975. Minneapolis: Children's Literature Research Collection, University of Minnesota Library, 1978.

Green, Roger L. *Tellers of Tales: British Authors of Children's Books from 1800 to 1964*. Rev. ed. New York: Franklin Watts, 1965.

Haviland, Virginia, ed. *Children's Literature: A Guide to Reference Sources*. Washington, D.C.: Library of Congress, 1966.

Hearne, Betsy, and Marilyn Kaye, eds. *Celebrating Children's Books: Essays on Children's Literature in Honor of Zena Sutherland*. New York: Lothrop, Lee, and Shepard, 1981.

Helbig, Alethea K., and Agnes Regan Perkins. *Dictionary of American Children's Fiction, 1960–1984*. Westport, Conn.: Greenwood Press, 1986.

———. *Dictionary of American Children's Fiction, 1859–1959*. Westport, Conn.: Greenwood Press, 1985.

———. *Dictionary of British Children's Fiction*. Westport, Conn.: Greenwood, 1989.

Hipple, Ted. *Writers for Young Adults*. 3 vols. New York: Scribners, 1997; 1 vol. Supplement, 1999.

Hudson, Henry K. *A Bibliography of Hard-Cover Boys' Books*. Rev. ed. Tampa, Fla.: Data Print, 1977.

Hurlimann, Bettina. *Three Centuries of Children's Books in Europe*. Trans. and ed. Brian W. Alderson. Cleveland, Ohio: World, 1968.

Jenkinson, Edward B. *Censors in the Classroom: The Mind Benders*. Carbondale: Southern Illinois University Press, 1979.

Johannsen, Albert. *The House of Beadle and Adams and Its Dime and Nickel Novels: The Story of a Vanished Literature*. 3 vols. Norman: University of Oklahoma Press, 1950–1952.

Johnson, Deidre. *Stratemeyer Pseudonyms and Series Books: An Annotated Checklist of Stratemeyer and Stratemeyer Literary Syndicate Publications*. Westport, Conn.: Greenwood Press, 1981.

Jones, Daryl. *The Dime Novel Western*. Bowling Green, Ohio: Bowling Green State University Popular Press, 1978.

Kiefer, Monica. *American Children through Their Books, 1700–1835*. Philadelphia: University of Pennsylvania Press, 1948.

Kilgour, Raymond L. *Lee and Shepard: Publishers for the People*. Hamden, Conn.: Shoestring Press, 1965.

Kirkpatrick, D. L., ed. *Twentieth Century Children's Writers*. 2nd ed. New York: St. Martin's Press, 1983.

Kloet, Christine A. *After Alice: A Hundred Years of Children's Reading in Britain*. London: Library Association, 1977.

Kunitz, Stanley J., and Howard Haycraft, eds. *The Junior Book of Authors*. 2nd ed. New York: H. W. Wilson, 1951.

Lentz, Millicent, and Ramona M. Mahood, eds. *Young Adult Literature: Background and Criticism*. Chicago: American Library Association, 1980.

Limiting What Students Shall Read: Books and Other Learning Materials in Our Public Schools—How They Are Selected and How They Are Removed. Washington, D.C.: Association of American Publishers, American Library Association, and Association for Supervision and Curriculum Development, 1981.

"Living with Adolescent Literature." *Connecticut English Journal* 12 (Fall 1980), special issue.

Lukens, Rebecca J. *A Critical Handbook of Children's Literature*. Glenview, Ill.: Scott, Foresman, 1976.

MacLeod, Anne Scott. *American Childhood: Essays on Children's Literature of the*

Nineteenth and Twentieth Centuries. Athens: University of Georgia Press, 1994.

———. *A Moral Tale: Children's Fiction and American Culture, 1820–1860*. Hamden, Conn.: Shoestring Press, 1975.

Mason, Bobbie Ann. *The Girl Sleuth: A Feminist Guide*. Old Westbury, N.Y.: Feminist Press, 1975.

McCann, Donnarae, and Gloria Woodward, eds. *The Black American in Books for Children: Readings on Racism*. Metuchen, N.J.: Scarecrow Press, 1972.

McFarlane, Leslie. *Ghost of the Hardy Boys: An Autobiography of Leslie McFarlane*. New York: Two Continents, 1976.

McLean, Austin J. "The Hess Collection of Dime Novels." *American Book Collector*, 25 (January-February 1975), 25–29.

Meade, Richard A., and Robert C. Small Jr., eds. *Literature for Adolescents: Selection and Use*. Columbus, Ohio: Charles E. Merrill, 1973.

Meigs, Cornelia et al. *A Critical History of Children's Literature*. Rev. ed. New York: Macmillan, 1969.

Mertz, Maia Pank, and David K. England. "The Legitimacy of American Adolescent Fiction." *School Library Journal*, 30 (October 1983), 119–23.

National Council of Teachers of English. *Books for You*. Urbana, Ill.: National Council of Teachers of English, 1982– .

National Council of Teachers of English. *Your Reading*. Urbana, Ill.: National Council of Teachers of English, 1996– .

Nilsen, Alleen Pace. *Presenting M. E. Kerr*. Boston: Twayne, 1986.

Nilsen, Alleen Pace, and Kenneth L. Donelson. *Literature for Today's Young Adults*. 6th ed. New York: Longman, 1999.

Nye, Russel. *The Unembarrassed Muse: The Popular Arts in America*. New York: Dial Press, 1970.

Papashvily, Helen Waite. *All the Happy Endings*. New York: Harper and Brothers, 1956.

Pattee, Fred Lewis. *The Feminist Fifties*. New York: Appleton, 1940.

Payne, Alma J. "Louisa May Alcott (1832–1888)." *American Literary Realism, 1870–1910* 6 (Winter 1973), 23–43.

Pendergast, Sara, and Tom Pendergast. *St. James Guide to Young Adult Literature*. Detroit: St. James Press, 1999.

Petitt, Dorothy J. "A Study of the Qualities of Literary Excellence Which Characterize Selected Fiction for Younger Adolescents." Ph.D. dissertation, University of Minnesota, 1961.

Probst, Robert E. *Adolescent Literature: Response and Analysis*. Columbus, Ohio: Charles E. Merrill, 1984.

Reed, Arthea J. S. *Reaching Adolescents: The Young Adult Book and the School*. New York: Holt, Rinehart, and Winston, 1985.

Rees, David. *The Marble in the Water: Essays on Contemporary Writers of Fiction for Children and Young Adults*. Boston: Horn Book, 1980.

———. *Painted Desert, Green Shade: Essays on Contemporary Writers of Fiction for Children and Young Adults*. Boston: Horn Book, 1984.

Rosenbach, A.S.W. *Early American Children's Books*. 1933; New York: Kraus Reprint, 1966.

Rudman, Masha Kabakow. *Children's Literature: An Issues Approach*. Lexington, Mass.: D. C. Heath, 1976.

Salmon, Edward. *Juvenile Literature as It Is*. London: Henry J. Drane, 1888.

Samuels, Barbara, and G. Kylene Beers, eds. *Your Reading: An Annotated Booklist for Middle School and Junior High*, Urbana, Ill.: National Council of Teachers of English, 1996.

Sarkissian, Adele, ed. *Something about the Author: Autobiography Series*. Detroit: Gale Research, 1986– .

Saxton, Martha. *Louisa May: A Modern Biography of Louisa May Alcott*. Boston: Houghton Mifflin, 1977.

Scharnhorst, Gary. *Horatio Alger, Jr*. Boston: G. K. Hall, 1980.

Scharnhorst, Gary, and Jack Bales. *Horatio Alger, Jr.: An Annotated Bibliography of Comment and Criticism*. Metuchen, N.J.: Scarecrow Press, 1981.

Schwartz, Sheila. *Teaching Adolescent Literature: A Humanistic Approach*. Rochelle Park, N.J.: Hayden, 1972.

Sloan, Glenna Davis. *The Child as Critic*. New York: Teachers College Press, 1975.

Sloane, William. *Children's Books in England and America in the Seventeenth Century*. New York: King's Crown Press, 1955.

Smith, Elva S. *The History of Children's Literature*. Chicago: American Library Association, 1937.

Smith, Henry Nash. *Virgin Land: The American West as Symbol and Myth*. Cambridge: Harvard University Press, 1950.

Stanford, Barbara Dodds, and Karima Amin. *Black Literature for High School Students*. Urbana, Ill.: National Council of Teachers of English, 1978.

Stensland, Anna Lee. *Literature by and about the American Indian, an Annotated Bibliography*. 2nd ed. Urbana, Ill.: National Council of Teachers of English, 1979.

Stern, Madeleine. *Louisa May Alcott*. Norman: University of Oklahoma Press, 1950.

Stover, Lois T. and Stephanie F. Zenker, eds. *Books for You: An Annotated Booklist for Senior High*. Urbana, Ill.: National Council of Teachers of English, 1997.

The Students' Right to Read. Urbana, Ill.: National Council of Teachers of English, 1982.

Sutherland, Zena, ed. *The Arbuthnot Lectures, 1976–1979*. Chicago: American Library Association, 1980.

Thwaite, Mary F. *From Primer to Pleasure in Reading: An Introduction to the History of Children's Books in England from the Invention of Printing to 1914 with an Outline of Some Developments in Other Countries*. Boston: Horn Book, 1972.

Townsend, John Rowe. *A Sounding of Storytellers: Essays on Contemporary Writers for Children*. New York: J. B. Lippincott, 1975.

———. *25 Years of British Children's Books*. London: National Book League, 1977.

———. *Written for Children: An Outline of English-Language Children's Literature*. 2nd ed. New York: J. B. Lippincott, 1983.

Tway, Eileen, ed. *Reading Ladders for Human Relations*. Washington, D.C.: American Council on Education and National Council of Teachers of English, 1981.

Varlejs, Jana, ed. *Young Adult Literature in the Seventies: A Selection of Readings.* Metuchen, N.J.: Scarecrow Press, 1978.

Wachsberger, Ken, ed. *Banned Books.* 4 vols. New York: Facts on File, 1998.

Weiss, M. Jerry, ed. *From Writers to Students: The Pleasures and Pains of Writing.* Newark, Del.: International Reading Association, 1979.

Winkle, Justin, and Emma Fisher. *The Pied Pipers: Interviews with the Influential Creators of Children's Literature.* New York: Paddington Press, 1974.

Wishy, Bernard. *The Child and the Republic: The Dawning of Modern American Child Nurture.* Philadelphia: University of Pennsylvania Press, 1968.

Periodicals

ALAN Review. Urbana, Ill., 1974–   .

Booklist. Chicago, 1905–   .

English Journal. Urbana, Ill., 1912–   .

Journal of Reading. Newark, Del., 1957–   .

Journal of Youth Services (formerly *Top of the News*). Chicago, 1946–   .

New York Times Book Review. New York, 1896–   .

School Library Journal. New York, 1954–   .

Voice of Youth Advocates (VOYA). Virginia Beach, Va., 1978–   .

INDEX

"Alice Comedies," 28, 59, 70
Alice Doesn't Live Here Anymore, 657
"Alice in Plunderland," 496
Alice in Wonderland (Disney film), 80
Alice in Wonderland (Henry version), 148
Alice in Wonderland (novel), xxx, 886
Alice Lloyd College, Appalachian Oral History Project at, 1213
Alice's Restaurant, 657
Alien, 1642
Alien and Sedition Acts of 1798, 1166, 1378
Alinova, Francesca, 820
Alkon, Paul, 1648–49
All-American, 1874
Allan, Robin, 73
Allan, Stuart, 1771
Allan Quartermain, 1635
Allee, Marjorie Hill, 1874
Allen, Barbara, 1549
Allen, Brigid, 705
Allen, Douglas and Douglas, Jr., 891
Allen, E. C., 192, 203
Allen, Edison, 516
Allen, Edward, 831
Allen, Fred, 1479, 1481, 1491
Allen, Gerald, 825, 830
Allen, Gracie, 1475, 1757
Allen, Henry Wilson, 1849, 1854, 1856, 1861, 1862–63
Allen, Hervey, 1245
Allen, Ida Reade, 1561
Allen, John (author of *Aviation and Space Museums of America*), 940
Allen, John ("Racer"), 20
Allen, Marjorie, 731
Allen, Mea, 769
Allen, Mel, 1472
Allen, Nancy, 666
Allen, Neil, 1223, 1227
Allen, Paul, 344
Allen, Paula Gunn, 567–68
Allen, Ralph G., 1306
Allen, Raye Virginia, 614
Allen, Robert, 1300
Allen, Robert C., 1769, 1775
Allen, R. R., 447

Allen, Stan, 1046
Allen, Tim, 465, 478
Allen, William Charles, 1397
Allen, Woody, xxxviii, 580, 656–57, 1475, 1757
Allender, Nina, 498
"Allentown," 166
Allentown, Penn., Dorney Park in, 27
Alley, Robert S., 1081, 1767, 1771
Alley Oop, 148, 310
All in the Family, 1760, 1774
Allman, Greg, 1526
Allman Brothers Band, 1526
All Music Guide, 1124
Allport, Gordon A., 1493
Allred, Randal, 964, 980–81, 981, 984, 1102
All-Story, 1440–41, 1442, 1448, 1452, 1655 n. 2
All the President's Men, 1246
All Things Considered, 1481
All Thumbs Guide series, 478
Almanacs, 1–13, 1602, 1667, 1668, 1888; advertising in, 5; in Alabama, 8; *Art Almanack*, 8; *Balloon Almanac*, 5; Billings' almanacs, 5, 12, 13; calendars in, 1, 2, 5; in California, 12; *Christian Almanac*, 5; *Commodore Rollingpin's Almanac*, 5, 13; in Connecticut, 8; Davy Crockett almanacs, 5, 11; in Delaware, 8; in District of Columbia, 8; in Georgia, 8; history and criticism, 1–5, 11–13; humor in, 5, 12, 13; in Illinois, 8; importance of, 1; in Indiana, 8; in Kentucky, 8; in Louisiana, 8–9; in Maine, 9; in Maryland, 9; in Massachusetts, 8; in Michigan, 10; in Minnesota, 10; in Mississippi, 10; in Missouri, 10; in New Hampshire, 10; in New Jersey, 10; in New York State, 10; in North Carolina, 10; *Nurse's Almanac*, 5; in Ohio, 10; *Old Farmer's Almanac*, 4, 5, 12, 765, 769; *The (Old) Farmer's Almanack*, 4, 5, 9–10; in Oregon, 10; in Pennsylvania, 1, 2–3, 10, 13; *The People's Almanac*, 5; poetry in, 1819; *Poor Richard's Alman-*

American Public Address, 451
American Public Radio (APR), 1465, 1494
American Revenue Association, 1743
American Revenuer, 1743
Americans with Disabilities Act, 848
American Society of Composers, Authors, and Publishers (ASCAP), 1116, 1467
American Stereoscopic Co., 1213
American Studies Association, xxxvi, 578
American Sunday School Union, 216
American Topical Association (ATA), 1725, 1726, 1735
American Town Meeting of the Air, 433
American Tract Society, 216
An American Tragedy, 1282
American Turf Register, 1703
American Vecturists' Association, 1811
The American Way of Death, 402, 404
American West, 265
American Yachtsman, 933, 942
America First Committee, 1334, 1358
America Online, 507
America's Architectural Roots: Ethnic Groups that Built America, 93
"America's Castles," 87
America's Cup, 933, 941, 1466
America's Public Television Stations (APTS), 1480
Ames, Blanche Ames, 498
Ames, Kenneth, 623
Ames, Nathaniel, 2, 11
Amey, Lawrence, 1292
Amherst, Mass., Jones Library in, 1568
Amin, Karima, 1880
Amis, Kingsley, 1644, 1648
Amish, 756
Amistad (film), 660
Ammons, Elizabeth, 1552
Amon Carter Museum of Western Art, 511, 524, 525, 528, 1216
Among the Folks in History, 496
The Amorous Intrigues of Aaron Burr, 1279

Amory, Cleveland, 1006
Amory, Richard, 1295
Amos 'n' Andy (radio program), xxviii, 1467, 1473, 1475, 1481, 1490
Amsterdam, Sex Museum in, 1286
Amtrak, 1804, 1810
Amusement Business, 263
Amusement parks, 17–20, 22–29, 31–35, 243, 1643; architecture in, 96, 107; Astroworld, 32; Busch Gardens, 32; Canada's Wonderland, 32; carousels in, 19–20, 42, 43; Cedar Point, 20, 22, 27, 33, 42, 43; Cheltenham Beach, 23; the Chutes, 23; Coney Island (Cincinnati), 26, 43–44; Coney Island (New York City), 20, 22, 23–26, 34, 39; Crystal Beach, 27; Darien Lake, 32; Disneyland Park, 18, 23, 25, 27–28, 29, 32, 33, 42, 44; Dorney Park, 27; Dreamland, 25–26; Electric Park, 26, 28; Elitch Gardens, 20, 26, 32; EPCOT Center, 33, 34, 44, 71; Euclid Beach, 20, 23, 26, 43; Ferris wheels at, 22–23, 24, 42; Forest Park, 28; Forest Park Highlands, 23, 26; Freedomland USA, 31; Glen Echo, 26; Great Adventure park, 32; Great America parks, 32, 42; Great Escape, 32; Hershey Park, 27; history and criticism, 40–45; Kennywood Park, 23, 27, 43; Kings Dominion, 32; King's Island, 20; Kings Island, 32; Knott's Berry Farm, 33, 44; Louisiana Purchase Exposition, 23; Luna Park, 20, 25; Magic Mountain (Denver), 31; Magic Mountain (Los Angeles), 32; Manhattan Beach, 23; midways at, 22, 25; Old Country, 32; Olympic Park, 26, 43; Pacific Ocean Park, 27, 31; Palisades Park, 23, 26; Pan American Exposition of 1901, 24; Playland, 20, 27; Playland at the Beach, 26; and pleasure gardens, 19, 40; Pleasure Island, 31; Prater park, 19, 23; Ranelagh Gardens, 19, 40; reference works related to, 39–40;

Revere Beach, 23, 26; Riverview Park, 20, 26, 27, 43; Rockaway's Playland, 27; Rocky Glen Park, 27; roller coasters in, 19, 20, 22, 26–27, 33, 42, 43, 45; Sea Lion Park, 24; Sea World parks, 32, 35; Six Flags parks, 31, 32; Steeplechase Park, 24–25, 42, 43; and technology, 17, 19–20, 22–23, 29, 31, 34, 35; theme parks, 17, 18, 20, 27, 31–32, 33–34, 35, 42, 44, 66; Tivoli Gardens, 28; Tokyo Disneyland, 44, 71; trolley parks, 23; Universal Studios parks, 25, 33, 35; Vauxhaul Gardens, 19, 40; Venice Amusement Park, 27; Walt Disney World, 22, 28, 33–35, 42, 44; Willow Grove Park, 23; World's Columbian Exposition of 1893, 22–23, 24, 25, 26, 28, 34, 37, 38, 39, 41, 42, 253

Amusements of America, 38

Analog, 990, 1654, 1656 n. 5

Anatomy of Wonder 4, 1636

Anaya, Rudolfo A., 569

Andersen, Alice, 149

Andersen, Hans Christian, 218

Anderson, Alexander, 884

Anderson, B., 833

Anderson, Benedict, 564

Anderson, Charles E., 1262

Anderson, Christopher, 71, 1767

Anderson, Elizabeth L., 1180

Anderson, Elliott, 1004

Anderson, Gail, 513

Anderson, George McCullough, 518

Anderson, James, 838

Anderson, Jay, 958–59, 961, 966, 968, 969–71, 978, 1102

Anderson, John B., 421

Anderson, John Henry, Jr., 1026

Anderson, John Henry "Professor," 1024–25, 1038

Anderson, John Q., 1852

Anderson, John R., 827

Anderson, Judith, 449

Anderson, Ken, 73

Anderson, Laurie, 1306

Anderson, L. O., 831

Anderson, Magnus, 966–67

Anderson, Marian, 450

Anderson, Maxie, 946

Anderson, Patrick, 1303

Anderson, Poul, 582, 1639, 1654

Anderson, Rachel, 1570

Anderson, Robert, 1201

Anderson, Rudolph E., 123

Anderson, Scott, 133

Anderson, Sherwood, 1076

Anderson, Thomas J., 1836

Anderson, Vicki, 224

Anderson, Warren H., 128

"And I Awoke and Found Me . . . ," 1640

Andrae, Johann Valentin, 1634

Andrae, Tom, 294

Andreadis, Athena, 1774

Andresen, Julie Tetel, 1580

Andrew, J. Cutler, 1183

Andrew, J. Dudley, 674

Andrews, Bart, 1774

Andrews, Gregory, 833

Andrews, Howard F., 855

Andrews, James R., 438, 447

Andrews, J. J. C., 128

Andrews, Siri, 226

Andrews, Val, 1041

Andrews, Virginia, 1579

Andrews, W. L., 513–14

Andriola, Alfred, 310

Andy Burnett on Trial, 150

Andy Capp, 321, 322

The Andy Griffith Show, 1759, 1774

Andy Panda, 151

Ang, Ien, 1770, 1775

Angelcynn, 965

Angelesey, Zoë, 1828

Angell, Judie, 1876

Angell, Roger, xxxix, 1708

Angelou, Maya, 1475

Angels, 1151, 1152

Angels: God's Secret Agents, 1247

Anger, Kenneth, 76, 1285

Anglo, Michael, 1459

Angry Women, 1291

Anheuser-Busch, 32

Animal Comics, 277

Collectors Club of America, 154–55, 160; Blue Ribbon Pop-Up, 157; Chronicle Books, 153, 155, 157; comic strip adaptations in, 146, 148, 149, 150, 151, 152, 153, 154, 155, 157, 160, 161; crime and police in, 148, 149, 159; Dell Publishing Company, 152, 156; Fawcett Publishing Co., 152; film adaptations in, 148, 149, 151–52, 153, 155, 160, 161; Five Star Library, 145, 153, 156; Goldsmith Publishing Company, 152–53; historical outline, 146–55; history and criticism, 159–61; Lynn Publishing Company, 153, 156; Mighty Chronicles, 155, 157; Moby Books, 154; Ottenheimer Publishers, 153; and race, 149; reference works related to, 155–57; research collections related to, 157–59; Saalfield Publishing Co., 145, 151–52, 154, 155, 156, 158, 896; television adaptations in, 150; Waddle Books, 157; Waldman and Son, 153, 154; Web sites related to, 156, 160; Whitman Publishing Company, 145, 146, 147–51, 152, 155, 156, 157, 158–59; World Syndicate Publishing Company, 153, 156
The Biglow Papers, 1821–22
Big Night, 691
Bigsby, C. W. E., xviii–xix
The Big Sleep (film), 655
Big Star, 1523
The Big Time, 1640
The Big Wheel, 1005
Bilbrew, Gene, 1304
Bilby, Kenneth M., 1131
Billboard, 262, 265, 912, 920, 1127, 1264
Billboards, 104–5, 128, 1394
Bill Haley and the Comets, 374
Billings, Josh, 5, 12, 13
Billington, Ray, 263
Bill of Rights, 1166
Billy the Kid, 1857
Bilstein, Roger, 946
Bindas, Kenneth J., 1132

Binder, Paul, 249
Bingham, Clarence, 7
Bingham, Jane, 232, 1876
Bingham, Richard D., 827
Biological Sciences Curriculum Study, 1607
Biophilately, 1735
Bird, S. Elizabeth, 568, 1296
Birdsall, Esther K., 1547
Birkhead, Edith, 798
Birnbaum, Jeffrey H., 1372
Biro, Charles, 277
Birren, James E., 851
Birth control, 195, 1302
"The Birthmark," 787
The Birth of a Nation, 651, 678, 1284
Bishop, George, 261
Bishop, George F., 440–41
Bishop, Joseph Bucklin, 508
Bishop, Morris, 1825, 1831
Bishop, Robert L., 1343, 1361
Bishop, Rudine Sims, 224
Bishop, Washington Irving, 1040
Bissette, Stephen R., 293
Bissonette, Anne, 610
Bitter Creek Outlaws, 965
Bittersweet, 1822
Bittman, Ladislav, 1367–68
Bitton, Davis, 513, 524, 1686
Bitzer, Billy, 651
Bitzer, Lloyd F., 436, 437, 441
Bizarre, 1282, 1304, 1305
Black, Alexander, 1227
Black, Bob, 1304
Black, Edwin, 436, 437
Black, Gregory D., 1387
Black Aces, 1444
Black Arts Movement, 1827
Blackbeard, Bill, 315, 320, 321–22, 326, 1188
Black Beauty (novel), 151, 154
Blackboard Jungle, 1118
Blackburne-Maze, Peter, 743
Black Canary, 295
"The Black Cat," 786, 802
Black English Vernacular, 567
Blackhawk, 276
Blackhawks, the, 288

750, 994, 1168–69, 1670; literature during, 1255; photography during, 1169, 1183, 1201, 1206, 1212; poetry during, 1822; pornography during, 1279–80, 1294; press during, 1168–69, 1183; propaganda during, 1331–32, 1352–53, 1394, 1397–98, 1399; railroads in, 1799; reenactments, 959, 961–62, 963–65, 966, 968, 969, 975, 977, 978–84; stamps during, 1734. *See also* Slavery; *Uncle Tom's Cabin*

The Civil War, 1736, 1774

Civil War Centennial Commission (CWCC), 961–62, 984 n. 2

Claflin, Edward, 1036

Claiborne, Craig, 701

Clain-Stefanelli, Elvira E., 1727, 1736, 1746

Clain-Stefanelli, Vladimir, 1741, 1746

Clair, Colin, 262

Clambakes, 693

Clampett, Bob, 66

Clancy, Deirdre, 618

The Clansman, 1254

Clapham, H. L., 1039

Clapp, Jane, 1290

Clapp, William W., Jr., 257

Clardy, Andrea Fleck, 1289

Clarens, Carlos, 675

Clareson, Thomas D., 583, 1076, 1636, 1644, 1649

Clarissa, 1241

Clark, Anna, 1578

Clark, Arthur Hamilton, 940–41

Clark, Beverly Lyon, 232

Clark, Brian, 1070

Clark, Clifford E., 107, 830, 835

Clark, David G., 1186

Clark, Dick, 373, 1488, 1510, 1524, 1774

Clark, H. Nichols B., 231, 890

Clark, Jerome, 1151, 1153–54, 1156

Clark, Keith, 1047

Clark, Larry, 1305

Clark, Thomas D., 45

Clark, Trinkett, 231, 890

Clark, Walter Van Tilburg, 1853, 1859, 1861, 1862

Clark, Wilma J., 1836

Clarke, Arthur C., 341, 1639, 1640, 1651, 1653

Clarke, Donald, 919, 1127

Clarke, I. F., 1650

Clarke, Rene, 895

Clarke, Shirley, 677

Clarke, Sidney W., 1030, 1036, 1045

Clarke, VeVe A., 384

Clash, the, 1119

Class, socioeconomic, 945, 1608, 1637, 1707, 1711; and battle reenactments, 976, 980; and business, 166, 174; class conflict, xlvii, 174; and dime novels, 1858; emergence of middle class, 243, 467, 1167; and feminism, 1559, 1574; and housing, 825, 826–29; middle class values, 1678, 1680–81, 1682; and music, 1488; the poor, 149, 397, 448, 558, 559, 695, 828–29, 835, 944, 1225, 1243, 1608; and popular culture, xviii–xix, xxxi, xxxiii–xxxiv, xxxviii, xliv–xlv, xlvii, 34, 1101; and popular fiction, 1254, 1255; and pornography, 1293, 1297, 1300; and propaganda, 1332, 1336, 1384; and romance fiction, 1574, 1575, 1578, 1581; and stamp collecting, 1723–24; and television, 1757, 1760, 1769; and Walt Disney World, 34. *See also* Unions, labor

Classics Illustrated, 285, 1641

"Class Struggle," 717

Clausen, Meredith L., 106

Claven, Cliff, 193

Claxton, William, 920

Clay, Bertha M., 1561

Clay, Grady, 103, 843

Clay, Henry, 413–14

Clayton, Jo, 586

Clayton, W. M., 1444

Clayton Magazines, 1445

Cleary, James W., 425

Cleary, Johanna, 1189

Cleary, Michael, 1851

Cleaver, Eldridge, 420, 438, 442

281, 284, 288, 290, 293, 295–96; educational uses for, 282; *Eerie*, 281; and ethnicity, 321; *Famous Funnies*, 276; fan magazines, 285–86; *Fantastic Four*, 279, 285; Fawcett Publishing Co., 152, 277, 288; *The First Kingdom*, 281; *Frontline Combat*, 277; *Funnies on Parade*, 276, 325; *The Haunt of Fear*, 277; historical outline, 276–82, 316; history and criticism, 287–94; and homosexuality, 292; horror comic books, 277, 287, 295; *Jimmy Corrigan: The Smartest Kid on Earth*, 282; *Little Lulu*, 277, 295–96; *Looney Tunes and Merrie Melodies*, 277; *Mad*, 279; Marvel Comics, 279, 281, 282, 284–85, 288, 290, 295, 323; *Master Comics*, 152; *Maus*, 281–82, 292, 504, 525; *More Fun*, 276; *Planet Comics*, 1641; popularity of, 275–76; pornography in, 280–81, 289, 1290, 1297–98, 1303–4; Quality Comic Books, 288; and race, 292; reference works related to, 282–86; research collections related to, 286–87; science fiction comic books, 277, 288, 1641; *The Silver Surfer*, 281; superheroes in, 275, 276–77, 279, 284–85, 288, 290, 291, 292, 292–93, 294–95, 1636–37, 1641; *Superman*, xxix, 279, 284, 288, 290, 291, 292–93, 294, 295, 1636, 1641; *Tales from the Crypt*, 277; *Tantrum*, 504; and technology, 291, 314; Tijuana Bibles, 289, 1282, 1298, 1303–4; *Two-Fisted Tales*, 277; underground publication of, 283, 288–89, 513; *Vampirella*, 281; *The Vault of Horror*, 277; *Walt Disney's Comics and Stories*, 277; *Watchmen*, 282; Web sites related to, 285; *Weird Fantasy*, 277; *Weird Science*, 277; *Whiz Comics*, 152; ZAP comics, 814
Comic Cuties, 1289
Comic Relief, 534
Comic Research Library, 159

Comics Code Authority, 278–81, 287, 288
Comics Magazine Association of America, 287
Comic strips, xviii, xxiii, xxxix–xl, 307–8, 310–18, 321–27, 491, 513, 523, 894, 1188, 1448; *Abbie 'n' Slats*, 152; adaptations in Big Little Books, 146, 148, 149, 150, 151, 152, 153, 154, 155, 157, 160, 161; adaptations in film, 313; adventure strips, 310; *Alley Oop*, 148, 310; *Alphonse and Gaston*, 310; as American phenomenon, 308; *Andy Capp*, 321, 322; anthologies and reprints, 325–27; *Apartment 3-G*, 310; *Apple Mary*, 310; *Balderdash*, 504; *Barney Google*, 310, 321; *B.C.*, 311; *Beetle Bailey*, 311, 320, 321; *Blondie*, 149, 150, 153, 310; *Bloom County*, 311, 501; *Bobby Thatcher*, 310; *Boondocks*, 311; *Brick Bradford*, 151; *Bringing Up Father*, xxix, xxxii, 278, 310; *Broom Hilda*, 311; *Buck Rogers*, 148, 151, 310, 1641; *Buster Brown*, 276, 310, 325; *Buzz Sawyer*, 310; *Calvin and Hobbes*, 311, 324; "Cathartic Comics," 502; *Cathy*, 311, 352–53; *Charlie Chan*, 310; *Dan Dunn*, 1447; *Dennis the Menace*, 320; *Dick Tracy*, 146, 148, 151, 155, 161, 307, 310, 313, 321; *Dilbert*, 181, 324, 352–53; *Don Winslow of the Navy*, 149; *Doonesbury*, xxix, 199–200, 311, 314, 352–53, 522, 525; educational uses for, 314–15, 326; *Ernie*, 311; and ethnicity, 326–27; fan magazines, 324–25; *The Far Side*, 311, 324; *Flash Gordon*, xl, 149, 152, 160, 307, 310, 325, 1447, 1641; *For Better or for Worse*, 311; *Foxy Grandpa*, 325; *Garfield*, 311, 320, 321; *Gasoline Alley*, 149, 308; *The Gumps*, 148, 160, 308; *Hagar the Horrible*, 311; *Hairbreath Harry*, 310; *Happy Hooligan*, 310, 496; *The Heart of Juliet Jones*, 310; *Herman*, 311; historical outline, 308, 310–12; history and criticism, 315–

Macdonald, Dwight, xvi, xxxiii–xxxiv, xxxv, xxxvii

MacDonald, George, 577, 578, 588, 589, 590

Macdonald, Gina, 1257

MacDonald, John D., 1449, 1450, 1451

MacDonald, J. Fred, 918, 1473, 1483, 1770

Macdonald, Sharon, 1103

Mace, Gillian S., 401

Mace, Ronald L., 848

The Machine and the Garden, 1802

Machlis, Gary E., 972

Machor, James L., 1262

Machotka, Hana, 258

MacIsaac, Fred, 1449

Mack, Arien, 406

MacKay, Lamar, 1360–61

MacKaye, Steele, 252

Mackey, Douglas, 1651

Mackey, Nathaniel, 914

MacKinnon, Catharine A., 1283, 1294, 1296

Mackintosh, Elizabeth, 838

MacLaine, Shirley, 1156

MacLeish, Archibald, 1468, 1733

MacLeod, Anne Scott, 226, 228, 1877

Macmillan, Kirkpatrick, 934

MacMurray, Fred, 153, 277

MacNeil, Robert, 1774

MacNeil-Lehrer Newshour, 507

MacNelly, Jeff, 311, 501, 504, 505, 520

MacRae, Cathi Dunn, 590

Macy's, 202

Mad (comic book), 283, 290, 293

Madden, David, 1456

Madden, Samuel, 1634

Maddex, Diane, 833

Maddox, William S., 1370

Madeira, Karen, 704

Madeline, 60

Madison, Charles Allen, 1259

Madison, James, 413, 446, 1166, 1331, 1351

Madison, Wis., State Historical Soci-

ety in, 727, 1179, 1180–81, 1213, 1220, 1398, 1452, 1481

Madison Square Garden, 247, 252, 253, 1484

Mad Magazine, xxxv, 279, 290, 293, 323, 501, 502

Mad Max 2, 1642

Madonna, 1120, 1527

Maelzel, Johann Nepomuk, 1021

Magazine (novel), 1005

Magazine Advertising Bureau, 1005

Magazine of Fantasy & Science Fiction, 1639, 1654

Magazine Publishers Association, 1005

Maggie and Jiggs, 310

Magazines and journals, xxviii–xxix, xxxii, 989–1007, 1602; *A. B. C. of Magic Sets*, 1033; *Abracadabra*, 1042; *Accessories*, 613; *Adam Black Video Illustrated*, 1291; *Adult Film World*, 1291; *Adult Video News*, 1291; *Advances in Thanatology*, 405; *Advertising Age*, 613; advertising in, 989, 994–95, 1004, 1005, 1006, 1186; *Aero Philatelist Annals*, 1735; *Aethlon*, 1711; *Affair de Coeur*, 1566; *African American Review*, 567; *AIM Report*, 1187; *Air Progress*, 947; *Airwaves Radio Journal*, 1479; *Amerasia Journal*, 569; *America*, 1683; *American Architect and Building News*, 91; *American Artist*, 899; *American Aviation Historical Society*, 947; *American Bicyclist and Motorcyclist*, 942; *American Brewer*, 994; *American Builder*, 91; *American Cinematographer*, 666; *American Economic Review*, 181; *American Film*, 666; *American Historical Review*, 623; *American Home*, 468, 469, 473, 744, 1005; *American Indian Culture and Research Journal*, 568; *American Indian Quarterly*, 568; *American Journalism Review*, 1174–75, 1187, 1188; *American Journal of Numismatics*, 1727, 1746; *American Journal of Philately and Coin Advertiser*, 1746; *American Journal of Science*, 1605; *American*

Maskelyne, John Nevil, 1043, 1044, 1046, 1047
The Mask of Zorro, 155
Maslach, Christina, 1347
Mason, Alexandra, 158
Mason, Bobbie Ann, 232, 1878
Mason, Frank Early, 1398
Mason, Perry, 1261
Mason, Philip, 1292
"The Masque of Saint Louis," 973
The Masquerader or the Affairs of Sissie, 1282
Massa, Mark, 1688
Massachusetts, 503, 1348; almanacs published in, 1, 4, 5, 8, 9–10; Berkshire County Fairs in, 36; Gerrymandering in, 492; Historical Society, 11, 1394, 1833; Lenox School of Jazz in, 915; newspapers in, 1163–64, 1165, 1182; Old Sturbridge Village in, 87, 957, 959; sports in, 1700; Wayside Inn in, 960
Massachusetts Centinel, 492
Massachusetts Institute of Technology, 350; Television Archives of the News Study Group at, 1396
"Massachusetts Liberty Song," 1819
Massachusetts Spy, 1182
Mass Comm Review, 1188
"Masscult and Midcult," xxxiii–xxxiv, xxxv, xxxvii
Massè, Michelle, 801
Massee, May, 227, 230
Massengill, Pat, 963
The Masses, 497–98, 510, 522–23, 527
Massey, Douglas S., 828
Massey, J. Earl, 1738
Massey, Jessica (Alison Hart), 1589
Massie, Sonja, 1585
Mass media, xviii, xxxvii–xxxviii, xliii; academic courses on, xvi–xvii. *See also* Magazines and journals; Newspapers; Radio; Television
Mass transit, 131
Massy, Don, 259
Mast, Gerald, 669–70, 675
Masteller, Richard N., 1225
Master Comics, 152

Master of Orion II, 1643
Masters, William E., 1246
"The Master Showman of Coney Island," 43
Masthead, 533
Material culture, 606, 623, 1094, 1100, 1104–6
Mates, Julian, 382
Mather, Anne, 1584
Mather, Cotton, 381, 412, 580, 1164, 1666, 1669–70, 1701
Mather, Increase, 369, 370, 381, 412, 580, 1669
Mather, Kirtley F., 1394
Mather, Richard, 412
Mathew, Laura J., 853
Mathews, Richard, 586
Mathis, Johnny, 1118
Matlaw, Myron, 382
Matlon, Ronald J., 426
Mattel, 721, 730
Mattelart, Armand, 71, 293, 324
Mattern, K. B., Jr., 531–32
Mattfeld, Julius, 1124
Matthew, Brander, 1833
Matthews, Jack, 790
Matthews, J. Brander, 530
Matthews, Roy T., 512
Matthews, Walter, 351
Matthiessen, Peter, 947
Maturin, Charles Robert, 783, 787, 789, 798
Mauchly, John, 342
Maude the Mule, 310
Maugh, Thomas, 1616
Mauldin, Bill, 321, 498, 499, 500, 502, 516
Maule, Harry E., 1861–62
Maurice, Arthur Bartlett, 508, 518
Maus, 281–82, 292, 504, 525
Mauss, Armand L., 1686
Maverick (television series), 1758
Maverick, Augustus, 1182
Mavericks, 1447
Max Headroom, 1762
Maxim, Hiram P., 123
Maximo, the Amazing Superman, 150
Maxwell, Ann, 586

New York Life, 1437
New York Magazine, 914, 1441
New York Mirror, 993, 1296
New York Morning Journal, 1170
New York Newsday, 504
New York Post, 1171
New York Psychology Group, 1675
New York Public Library: aeronautics material in, 939; American History Division at, 1393–94; Bancroft Collection at, 1394; best seller collection at, 1251; Billy Rose Theater Collection at, 1132; Broadway musical materials at, 1132; Dance Collection, 377, 378, 384; Ellis Gray Loring Collection at, 1568; illustration collection at, 894, 895; Laura Jean Libby papers at, 1569; Library and Museum of the Performing Arts, 667; Macmillan Collection at, 1569; magic collection at, 1033, 1034; newspaper collection at, 1176, 1180; papers of Ann Sophia Stephen at, 1568; philatelic collection at, 1740; photography collection at, 1212; poetry collection at, 1832, 1833; propaganda collection at, 1393–94; Record Collection of the Donnell Library Center, 433; Rodgers and Hammerstein Archives of Recorded Sound, 433, 1131, 1518; romance fiction collection at, 1567; Schomberg Center for Research in Black Culture at, 1519; Science and Technology Research Center, 123; Western collection at, 1855; young adult fiction collection at, 1882
New York Review of Books, 1264
New York Society for the Suppression of Vice, 1280
New York State: almanacs published in, 10; anticartoon legislation in, 496; Board of Censors, 1395; Erie Canal, 1799; fairs in, 37, 45, 960; Somers, 245–46
New York State Historical Society, 1213, 1568; Westervelt Collection at, 255

New York State Library, 1395; poetry collection at, 1832
New York Sun, 1167, 1180, 1184
New York Telegram, 495
New York Times, 88, 164, 224, 282, 376, 397, 524, 533, 610, 703, 757, 812, 817, 1167, 1169, 1171, 1172, 1173, 1178, 1184, 1186, 1189, 1277, 1486, 1618, 1746, 1818; best-seller list, 582–83, 1249, 1250, 1487, 1676; *Book Review*, 1264–65; film reviews in, 679
New York Times Guide to Home Repairs with a Man, 478
New York Times News Service, 1172
New York Tribune, 394, 1167, 1169, 1184
New York University: food studies at, 689; Oral History of the American Left Project at, 1394; romance fiction collection at, 1567; Taminant Labor History Collection at, 1394
New York Weekly, 1436
New York Weekly Journal, 1164
New York World, 495, 498, 1170, 1183, 1354
New York Yacht Club, 932
Nicaragua, 1365–66
Nicholls, Peter, 1647, 1651
Nichols, Arthur and Ora, 1473
Nichols, Egbert Ray, 430
Nichols, Peter, 577
Nichols, Richard, 767
Nicholson, William, 886, 899
Nickell Magazine, 1280
Nickelodeon (cable network), 63
Nickelodeons, 651
Nicola, 1028
Nicolson, Harold, 1744
Niebuhr, Reinhold, 1675
Nielsen, Kay, 886
Nielsen, Waldo, 1804
Nieman Reports, 1187
Niessen, Sandra, 621, 622
"Nightfall," 1638
Nightingale, Frank "The Mystifier," 1040
Nightline, 1773

Planet Hollywood, 105
Planet Stories, 1641
Plank, Robert, 1077
Planned Parenthood, 1287
Planty, Earl, 1736
Plasketes, George, 1127, 1129
Plastic Man, 276, 288, 294, 295
Plate, Adrian, 1045
Plato, xxxv, 434, 435, 1330
Platoon, 658
Platt, Larry A., 401
Platters, the, 374
Playboy, 794, 995, 1283, 1290, 1297, 1304, 1305
Playboy Press, 1850
Play and Culture, 734
Playdough, 727
The Player, 657
Playford, John, 370
The Playground, 719
Playgrounds, 719–20, 731, 732, 733
Playhouse 90, 1757
Playland, 20, 27
Playland at the Beach, 26
Playskool, 730
Playthings, 723
A Plea for Polygamy, 1279
Please Touch Museum, 725
Pleasure gardens, 19, 40
Pleasure Island, 31
Pleck, J. H., 842
Plecket, H. W., 1711
PLENTY, 771–72
Plimoth Plantation, 957, 958, 967, 970, 972, 976, 978
Plissner, Martin, 1774
Plowden, Gene, 258, 259, 262
Plowright, Frank, 284
The Plow That Broke the Plains, 1334
Plumb, J. H., 227, 733
Plummer, Ken, 1295–96
Pluto (cartoon character), 814
PMLA, 583
Poague, Leland, 1836
Pocahontas, 67, 73
Pochna, Marie France, 615
The Pocket Idiot's Guide to Home Repair, 478

Podrazik, Walter, 1525
Poe, Edgar Allan, 278, 581, 585, 586, 779, 785, 786, 787, 788, 789, 794, 798, 800, 802, 993, 1021, 1635, 1638
Poetry. *See* Verse and popular poetry
Poetry Society of America, 1832
Pogany, Willy, 888
Poggio Bracciolini, Gian Francesco, 1281
Pogo (comic strip), xl, 277, 311, 313, 317, 501, 515–16
Pohl, Frederik, 1639, 1640, 1654
Poinier, Art, 526
Poison, 663
Pojar, Bretislav, 73
Poland, 1246
Polar Lander, 1608
Polaroid cameras, 1204
Polhemus, Ted, 619
Police, the, 1119
Police Gazette, 1296, 1303
Police Story, 1761
Policy Analysis, 1371
Policy Review, 1371
Polidori, John, 791
Polish Americans, 699
Political action committees (PACs), 1336–37, 1371, 1372
Political Communication and Persuasion, 1345
Political correctness (PC), 551
Political Pix, 534
Politics, 166, 173; advertising in, 1334, 1344, 1347, 1389, 1394, 1395–96, 1398, 1399, 1766, 1774; and children's literature, 231; and comic strips, 311; and games/toys, 716; and gothic fiction, 783; newspaper reporting, 1166, 1182, 1185, 1186; political action committees (PACs), 1336–37, 1371, 1372; political graffiti, 819; propaganda in, 1334, 1344, 1347, 1389, 1394, 1395–96, 1398, 1399; and religion, 1667; and television, 419–20, 421, 452 n. 14, 1759, 1772–74. *See also* Editorial cartoons
Polito, Ronald, 1211

Rebecca of Sunnybrook Farm, 218, 1244, 1873, 1887

Reber, Deborah, 79

Reboot, 64

Rebora, Carrie, 616

Reboredo, Aida, 734

Reck, Franklin M., 46

Reconstruction, 415, 651, 750, 1378

Record album covers, 1516–17

Recording industry, 1503–27; Ace Records, 1521; Aladdin/Imperial Records, 1515; A&M Records, 1513; Apple Records, 1525; Atlantic Records, 1508, 1510, 1515; Blue Note Records, 1515, 1516; Brunswick Records, 1507; Capitol Records, 1508, 1510–11; Chess Records, 1508; Clef-Verve Records, 1515; Columbia Records, 1506, 1507, 1508, 1509, 1513; cover records, 1509; Death Row Records, 1521; Decca Records, 1507, 1508, 1515; Elektra Records, 1510, 1521; foreign ownership in, 1513; historical outline, 1504–14; history and criticism, 1502–27; independent companies, 1508–9, 1521; and the Internet, 1513–14; King Records, 1515, 1521; MCA Records, 1513; Mercury Records, 1508, 1515; MGM Records, 1508, 1515; Motown Records, xliv, 374, 1119, 1513, 1524–25; and performer image, 1510–11; pirated recordings, 1514, 1521; RCA-Victor Records, 1506, 1507, 1508, 1509, 1513; record album covers, 1516–17; reference works related to, 1514–17; research collections related to, 1517–20; Riverside Records, 1521; SAR Records, 1524; Savoy Records, 1508; Star Records, 1521; Stax Records, 1522; Sun Records, 1521; and technology, 1503–4, 1506, 1507–8, 1512, 1513–14; trends in, 1512; Warner Records, 1510, 1513; Web sites related to, 1517, 1518, 1519; women in, 1523; during World War

II, 1507. *See also* Jazz; Music; Rock and roll

Recreational vehicles (RVs), 120, 122

Rector, Justine J., 1183

Red Book, 1441

"Red Book," the, 1728, 1737

Redbook, 887, 1825

Red Cloud, 253

Redding, Otis, 1521

Red Dwarf, 1643

The Redeemed Captive, 1240

Reder, Alan, 1125

Redfern, 608

Red Harvest, 1444

Red Jacket, 439

Redlands, Calif., Lincoln Shrine in, 1740

Redlich, Frederick, 1078

Red Mars, 1641

Red Men and White, 1846

Red Nightmare, 1387

Red Rainbow, 1388

Red Ryder (comic strip), 150, 310

Red Ryder (radio program), 1475

Reed, Barbara Straus, 1183

Reed, Evelyn, 616

Reed, Henry, 892

Reed, James W. Reed, 39

Reed, John Shedd, 1801–2

Reed, Mort, 1737

Reed, Rebecca, 1331

Reed, Walter, 892, 896

Reed, Dr. Walter, 1078

Reeder, Warren A., 258

Reems, Harry, 1300

Rees, C. Roger, 1713

Rees, Dafyyd, 1128

Rees, David, 1887

Reese, William S., 1807

Reeve, Clara, 781

Reeves, Jimmie L., 1773

Reeves, Martha, 1525

Reeves-Stevens, Judith and Garfield, 1774

Reflections in a Golden Eye, 788–89

Refugee Relief Act of 1953, 557

Regan, Colm, 523

Regency romances, 1563, 1564

ABOUT THE CONTRIBUTORS

JUDITH A. ADAMS-VOLPE is the Director of Lockwood Memorial Library, University at Buffalo, State University of New York, and was previously a librarian at Lehigh University, the Library of Congress, the Kennedy Institute of Ethics at Georgetown University, and Auburn University. She is the author of *The American Amusement Park Industry: A History of Technology and Thrills*; and co-author of *Technology and Values in American Civilization*, and *Jules Verne: A Primary and Secondary Bibliography*. Her main research and publication interests are the interaction of technology and society, the history of technology, and information science, with numerous journal articles on such topics as electricity at the World's Columbian Exposition, the on-line catalog as democratic or authoritarian technology, medical ethics, the bibliography of the history of technology, and faculty use of information technologies.

RANDAL ALLRED is Associate Professor in the Literature, Language, and Cultural Studies Division at Brigham Young University-Hawaii, where he also directs the Honors Program. He has recently published articles on battle reenacting and on Stephen Crane and is working on a book that examines the writing of the Civil War in American fiction.

ROBERT A. ARMOUR was a Professor of English at Virginia Commonwealth University and served as Assistant Secretary General of the Board of Higher Education of the United Methodist Church before his retirement. He is the author of *Film: A Reference Guide*.

RAY BARFIELD is Professor of English at Clemson University and author of *Listening to Radio, 1920–1950*.

EVELYN BECK teaches English at Piedmont Technical College in Greenwood, South Carolina. She was named Educator of the Year in 1996 by the South Carolina Technical Education Association.

ELIZABETH S. BELL received her Ph.D. from the University of Louisville, in Louisville, Kentucky, in Twentieth-Century American and British Literature, and is currently the Grew Palmetto Professor of American Studies at the University of South Carolina Aiken. She has published three books, *Words That Must Somehow Be Said*, *The Short Fiction of Kay Boyle*, and *Sisters of the Winds: Voices of Early American Women Aviators*. In addition, she has published numerous articles on composition and women writers. She is currently editor of *Studies in American Culture*, published by the Popular Culture/American Culture Association of the South.

MICHAEL L. BERGER is Vice President for Academic Affairs at Arcadia University in Glenside, Pennsylvania and Secretary of the Society of Automotive Historians. His research interests center on the impact of technology on society and human behavior, especially as it relates to automotive history. He is the author of *The Devil Wagon in God's County: The Automobile and Social Change in Rural America, 1893–1929* and *The Automobile: A Reference Guide*.

JAMES J. BEST is Associate Professor of Political Science, Kent State University. He developed his academic interest in American popular illustration from his collection of illustrated books and his desire to know more about the illustrators and the context in which they worked. He has published on this topic in the *Journal of Popular Culture* and has written *American Popular Illustration: A Bibliographic Reference Guide* and *A Bibliography and Price Guide for Scribner's Illustrated Classics*. When not in the classroom, he works as an antiquarian book dealer (The Bookman of Kent) specializing in, among others, illustrated books.

BILL BLACKBEARD is an independent writer, editor, and historian of popular culture, with a special interest in comics and pulps. He is director of the San Francisco Academy of Comic Art and coeditor of *The Smithsonian Collection of Newspaper Comics*.

DAVID A. BRAT teaches in the Department of Economics at Randolph-Macon College, Ashland, Virginia.

RUTH BRENT chairs the Department of Environmental Design at the University of Missouri at Columbia.

JOHN BRYANT is a Professor of English at Hofstra University, editor of *A Companion to Melville Studies*, co-editor of *Melville's Evermoving Dawn: Centennial Essays*, and author of *Melville and Repose: The Rhetoric of Humor in the American Renaissance*.

LORETTA CARRILLO is currently Senior Lecturer in Romance Studies and Latino Studies at Cornell University. Her teaching and research interests include Latino literature and popular culture, especially dance.

SARAH L. CROY, a graduate student and teaching assistant in the English Department, University of Louisville, where she pursued her primary interest in creative writing, provided essential editorial assistance in the development of this edition of the *The Greenwood Guide to American Popular Culture*.

PATRICIA A. CUNNINGHAM is an Associate Professor in the Department of Consumer and Textile Sciences, College of Human Ecology, at Ohio State University. Her scholarly interests are in the history of clothing and textiles and dress as a phenomenon in popular culture. She co-edited *Dress and Popular Culture* and *Dress in American Culture*.

ROBERT K. DODGE is Professor of English at the University of Nevada, Las Vegas, where he teaches American literature. He is co-editor of *Voices from Waht Kon-tah*, and of *New and Old Voices of Waht Kon-tah*, anthologies of poetry by contemporary native Americans. He is editor of *Early American Almanac Humor* and *A Topical Index of Early U.S. Almanacs*.

KEN DONELSON teaches in the English Department at Arizona State University. He is coauthor with Alleen Pace Nilsen of *Literature for Today's Young Adults*, which in 1999 came out in its sixth edition. It was the first comprehensive textbook prepared for teachers and librarians that focused on books for teenage readers. He has also published in *English Journal*, *School Library Journal*, *The ALAN Review*, and *Para*Doxa*, and other publications dealing with literature and young readers. He has a particular interest in censorship issues.

MAURICE DUKE is a retired Professor of English at Virginia Commonwealth University in Richmond and the author and editor of numerous books and articles on American literature. He was for twelve years the Book Page editor and a weekly book columnist for the *Richmond Times-Dispatch*.

MICHAEL DUNNE, Professor of English at Middle Tennessee State University, is the author of *Metapop: Self-referentiality in Contemporary American Popular Culture*, *Hawthorne's Narrative Strategies*, and numerous articles on literature, film, and popular culture.

SARA LEWIS DUNNE, Associate Professor of English at Middle Tennessee State University, has published articles on a wide variety of popular culture topics and teaches cultural studies as well as English courses.

RICHARD W. ETULAIN, Professor of History at the University of New Mexico, is the editor and author of numerous articles and books including *Western Films: A Brief History*, *The Saga of Billy the Kid*, *A Bibliographical Guide to the Study of Western American Literature*, *American West* (with Michael Malone), *Reimagining the Modern American West*, *By Grit and Grace*, *Myths and the American West*, *Portraits of Basques in the New World*, and *Hollywood West*, among others.

JOHN P. FERRÉ is a Professor of Communication at the University of Louisville, where he investigates ethical, religious, and historical dimensions of mass media in the United States. He has written numerous articles and reviews as well as several books, including *A Social Gospel for Millions: The Religious Bestsellers of Charles Sheldon, Charles Gordon, and Harold Bell Wright*.

DAVID FILLINGIM teaches in the Department of Religion and Ethics at Chowan College in Murfreesboro, North Carolina.

JOHN E. FINDLING teaches History at Indiana University Southeast in New Albany and is the series editor of The Greenwood Histories of Modern Nations;

he has published on a very wide variety of topics including baseball and other sports, fairs and expositions, as well as stamps.

PERRY FRANK is a freelance writer and editor working in Washington, D.C., and President of American Dreams and Associates, Inc.

MAUREEN FURNISS is the Founding Editor of *Animation Journal*, a scholarly journal devoted to animation history and theory, and author of *Art in Motion: Animation Aesthetics*. She teaches at the Savannah College of Art and Design in Georgia.

AGNES HOOPER GOTTLIEB teaches in the Department of Communications at Seton Hall University.

SUZANNE ELLERY GREENE is a professor of history at Morgan State University and author of *Books for Pleasure: Popular Fiction 1914–1945*.

THOMAS GREENFIELD is Dean of the College and Professor of English at the State University of New York at Geneseo. He is the author of *Radio: A Reference Guide* and *Work and the Work Ethic in American Drama, 1920–1970*. He also writes, produces and hosts "Folkal Point," a weekly program for WXXI Public Radio in Rochester, New York.

DALE ALLEN GYURE is a Ph.D. candidate in Architectural History at the University of Virginia, specializing in American art and architecture of the nineteenth and twentieth centuries. He has contributed articles on a wide variety of architectural and cultural subjects to *Icons of Architecture: The 20th Century*, *American National Biography*, and *The St. James Encyclopedia of Popular Culture*. He has also published "Modernism and Domesticity in Le Corbusier's Early Worker Housing Projects" in *Oculus: Journal for the History of Art*.

DENNIS HALL has published articles on a wide variety of popular culture topics, teaches English, and serves as a utility infielder at the University of Louisville.

PATSY HAMMONTREE teaches English at the University of Tennessee, Knoxville. She is the author of *Elvis Presley* and *Shirley Temple Black: A Bio-Bibliography*; her publications have appeared in the *Southern Quarterly*, the *Country Music Journal* and the *Association for Communication Administration Bulletin*, among others.

JOSEPH HANCOCK is a Ph.D. candidate in the Department of Consumer and Textile Sciences, College of Human Ecology, at Ohio State University.

RAY HELTON, formerly the Director of Computer Literacy for the University of Louisville Libraries, now works as a technology consultant.

ROBERT J. HIGGS is currently Emeritus Professor of English at East Tennessee State University where he taught Southern and Appalachian literature and the literature of sports. He is the author of *Laurel and Thorn: The Athlete in American Literature*, *Sports: A Reference Guide* and *God in the Stadium: Sports and Religion in America*.

ROBERT P. HOLTZCLAW is a Professor of English and Director of the Film Studies program at Middle Tennessee State University. He has published articles on the adaptation of fiction to film, gangster films, and the careers of such actors as Edward G. Robinson and Humphrey Bogart. Among his teaching interests are courses in film theory and criticism, film genres, and documentary film.

LISA N. HOWORTH teaches Art History at the University of Mississippi and is a research bibliographer at the Center for the Study of Southern Culture. With the Center and the United States Information Agency, she has written and produced a series of slide and videotape programs on American art, and she is co-editor of a bibliographic guide to the blues. She contributed articles on popular culture and architecture to the *Encyclopedia of Southern Culture*, is the editor of *The South: A Treasury of Art and Literature*, and is the author of *Yellow Dogs, Hushpuppies, and Bluetick Hounds: The Official "Encyclopedia of Southern Culture" Quiz Book*.

M. THOMAS INGE is Robert Emory Blackwell Professor of English and Humanities at Randolph-Macon College in Ashland, Virginia, where he teaches courses in American culture, film, humor, animation, and literature. He was the editor of the two editions of the *Handbook of American Popular Culture* and has served as series editor for reference guides in popular culture for Greenwood Press. His books on the comic arts include *Comics as Culture* and *Charles M. Schulz: Conversations*.

ROBERT H. JANKE was a Professor in the School of the Arts at Virginia Commonwealth University in Richmond, where he taught and served as Director of the school's program in speech communication. He was a president of the Virginia Communication Association.

ANNE HUDSON JONES is Associate Professor of Literature and Medicine at the Institute for the Medical Humanities of the University of Texas Medical Branch at Galveston. She is the editor of *Literature and Medicine: Images of Healers* and *Images of Nurses: Perspectives from History, Art, Literature*, and the author of numerous articles on various aspects of literature and medicine.

ELIZABETH BARNABY KEENEY served as Lecturer on the history of science at Harvard University. Her teaching and research interests include popular science and medicine in nineteenth-century America.

R. GORDON KELLY has directed the American Studies Program at the University of Maryland and is author of *Mother Was a Lady: Self and Society in Selected Children's Periodicals, 1865–1890* and *Mystery Fiction and Modern Life* and editor of *Children's Periodicals of the United States*.

WILLIAM KENNEY is Professor of History and Coordinator of the American Studies Program at Kent State University. His scholarly articles have appeared in *American Studies, American Music, American Studies International*, and the *Black Perspective in Music*, and he has contributed articles on Eddie Condon, Sidney DeParis, and Wilbur DeParis to the *New Grove Dictionary of Jazz*.

WILLIAM R. KLINK teaches language and literature at Charles County Community College, Maryland, and publishes on general topics in popular culture, with a special interest in detective fiction.

LESLIE LEWIS is a faculty member in the Department of English at the College of St. Rose in Albany, New York, where she teaches African American and twentieth-century American literature. Her research focuses on African American narrative literature, and race and gender issues in American studies.

RICHARD N. MASTELLER is Professor of English and American Studies at Whitman College. His teaching interests include the history, art, and cultural influence of photography, "little magazines" of the early twentieth century, twentieth-century American poetry, the 1930s, and the relation between art and literature. He has organized exhibitions of photography and of graphic art, including 'We, the People?' Satiric Prints of the 1930s, for which he wrote the catalog. He has published on western stereographs, on the reception of the sculptor Constantin Brancusi, on the satiric vision of Reginald Marsh and John Dos Passos, and on American poetry. His current research focuses on the relation of artists, photographers, writers, and their audiences in little magazines from 1910 to 1940.

BERNARD MERGEN is Professor of American Civilization at George Washington University and associate editor of the *American Quarterly*. His research interests include the history of children's play, material culture, and environmental history. He is the author of *Play and Playthings: A Reference Guide*, *Recreational Vehicles and Travel: A Resource Guide*, and *Snow in America*.

ARTHUR H. MILLER, JR., is College Librarian at Lake Forest College. He supervises the Elliott Donnelley Railroad Collection in the college's Donnelley Library and is a member of the American Studies Program committee. He has taught in the American Studies Program and has published articles on library topics.

KAY MUSSELL is a scholar working in the American studies Program at the American University who has published extensively on romance fiction including *Women's Gothic and Romantic Fiction: A Reference Guide*, and *Fantasy and Reconciliation: Contemporary Formulas of Women's Romance Fiction*, and edited with Johanna Tunon *North American Romance Writers*.

RICHARD ALAN NELSON is Professor and Public Relations Sequence Head in the A. Q. Miller School of Journalism and Mass Communications at Kansas State University, following a long academic association with the University of Houston. Accredited by the Public Relations Society of America, he regularly serves as a consultant to business and government. Nelson is on the editorial board of *American Journalists* and authored numerous refereed articles. In addition, Nelson is the author of *Florida and the American Motion Picture Industry, 1898–1980*, co-author of *Issues Management: Corporate Public Policymaking in an Information Society*, and author of *Propaganda: A Reference Guide* for Greenwood Press.

ALLEEN PACE NILSEN teaches in the English Department at Arizona State University. She is co-author with Ken Donelson of *Literature for Today's Young Adults*, which in 1999 came out in its sixth edition. It was the first comprehensive textbook prepared for teachers and librarians that focused on books for teenage readers. She has also published in *English Journal, School Library Journal, The ALAN Review*, and *Para*Doxa*, and other publications dealing with literature and young readers. She has a special interest in humor.

AMY KISTE NYBERG teaches in the Department of Communications at Seton Hall University and is author of *Seal of Approval: The History of the Comics Code*.

DONALD E. PALUMBO teaches English at East Carolina University at Greenville, North Carolina.

GEORGE PLASKETES teaches in the Department of Communications at Auburn University and is the author of numerous articles on all aspects of popular music, as well as (with R. Serge Denisoff) *True Disbelievers: The Elvis Contagion* and *Mystery Terrain: Images of Elvis Presley in American Culture, 1977–1995*.

JANICE RADWAY is Professor of literature at Duke University and author of *Reading the Romance: Women, Patriarchy, and Popular Literature* and *A Feeling for Books: The Book-of-the-Month Club, Literary Taste, and Middle-Class Desire*.

LUCY ROLLIN, Professor of English at Clemson University, is author of *The Uses of Enticement: Fantasy and Growth in English Nursery Rhymes*, co-author of *Psychoanalytic Responses to Children's Literature*, and editor of *Twentieth-Century Teen Culture by the Decade*, and has written numerous articles on popular culture and children's literature.

ANNE ROWE is a professor of English at Florida State University, where she has taught since 1972, serving as chair from 1994 to 1997, and as Associate Dean of the College of Arts and Sciences. Specializing in southern literature, she is the author of two books, *The Enchanted Country: Northern Writers in the South, 1865–1910* and *The Idea of Florida in the American Literary Imagination*. She is also the author of numerous articles on southern literature and was a contributor to *The History of Southern Literature*, the *Encyclopedia of Southern Culture*, *Fifty Southern Writers before 1900* and *Contemporary Fiction Writers of the South*.

JOEL D. RUDINGER teaches cultural studies at the Firelands College of Bowling Green State University in Huron, Ohio.

ERICA SCHARRER is Assistant Professor of Communication at the State University of New York at Geneseo and is Faculty Director of WGSU-FM campus radio station. Her interests include the social effects of media and portrayals of gender and aggression. She is coauthor with George Comstock of *What's on, Who's Watching and What It Means*.

ROGER SCHLOBIN is Professor of English at the North Central Campus of Purdue University. He has written six scholarly books and edited over fifty. His various other publications include over 100 essays, various poems, short stories, reviews, and bibliographies that range over such varied topics as fantasy literature, pedagogy, science fiction, medieval and Arthurian literature, feminism, shamanism, linguistics, and microcomputer hardware and software. He is one of the founders of the International Association for the Fantastic in the Arts and its conference and of the "Year's Scholarship in Science Fiction and Fantasy." Currently, he is the editor of *The Journal of the Fantastic in the Arts*.

DOROTHY S. SCHMIDT is Professor of English at Pan American University. Founder of Pan American University Press as well as the small presses riverSedge and Double SS Press, she is also an adviser for the prizewinning student literary magazine, *Gallery*.

BENYAMIN SCHWARZ teaches in the Department of Environmental Design at the University of Missouri at Columbia.

RICHARD SCHWARZLOSE is Professor of journalism at Northwestern University and author of *Newspapers: A Reference Guide*, a study of *The American Wire Services*, and *The Nation's Newsbrokers*.

THEODORE F. SHECKELS is a Professor of English at Randolph-Macon College and author of *The Lion on the Freeway: A Thematic Introduction to Contemporary South African Literature Written in English* and *When Congress Debates: A Bakhtinian Paradigm*.

JOSEPH W. SLADE teaches in the Department of Communications at Ohio University and is the author or editor of numerous books and articles, including *Beyond the Two Cultures: Essays on Science, Technology, & Literature*, *Thomas Pynchon*, and *Pornography & Sexual Representation: A Reference Guide*.

PAUL SOMERS was a Professor of American Thought and Language at Michigan State University and served as contributing editor of *The National Lampoon*. The author of *Johnson J. Hooper* and *Editorial Cartoons: A Reference Guide*, he also published short stories and numerous articles on American literature and humor.

GEORGE F. SPAGNA JR. teaches in the Department of Physics at Randolph-Macon College, Ashland, Virginia.

DOUGLASS H. THOMPSON is an Associate Professor of English at Georgia Southern University. He has published essays on such topics as English Romanticism, the gothic imagination, and critical theory in *Studies in Romanticism*, *The Wordsworth Circle*, *SEL: 1500–1900*, and *Romanticism on the Net*, among others. He, Fred Frank, and Jack Voller have written *Major Gothic Writers*, a critical and bibliographical study of 75 international gothic authors.

STEVEN S. TIGNER is Professor of Philosophy at the University of Toledo. His non-magical research interests and publications lie mainly in ancient Greek philosophy and philology and in moral education. He was founding editor of the *Journal of Magic History* and has lectured widely on magic and fraud in culture as well as on numerous other topics in the liberal arts.

RALPH LAMAR TURNER, a native of Petersburg, Virginia, studied English literature and education at Emory and Henry College. He has worked at a variety of jobs, ranging from an assistant chaplain in Canada, to rehabilitation therapist, college instructor, coach and lecturer. A freelance writer and researcher, he holds advanced degrees in exercise physiology/exercise science, education, and religion. He recently co-authored with Robert J. Higgs, *The Cowboy Way: The Western Leader in Film*.

JAMES A. VON SCHILLING is Assistant Professor in the Humanities Division of Northampton Community College in Bethlehem, Pennsylvania, where he teaches writing and journalism. He has written on contemporary music for the

Popular Culture Reader, *Creem*, and other publications, and has taught popular music at Bowling Green State University.

JEFFERY WASICK received his B.A. in History from Kent State University in 1998 and has been a writer for the Worldmark Chronology of the Nations and Year in Review.

RICHARD F. WELCH is Professor of Communication at Kennessaw State College in Georgia.

RHONDA WILCOX teaches humanities and cultural studies at Gordon College in Barnesville, Georgia; she has published articles on television programs and is a past president of the Popular Culture Association in the South.

RICHARD GUY WILSON is Professor of Architectural History at the University of Virginia. His specialty is American and European architecture of the nineteenth and twentieth centuries. He has been the curator of a number of museum exhibitions and author of books and articles, among them *The American Renaissance, 1876–1917*, *McKim, Mend and White Architects*, *The AIA Gold Medal*, and *The Machine Age in America*, and contributed to *"The Arts That Is Life": The Arts and Crafts Movement in America*.